270

P9-DFJ-394

DEMCO

ENCYCLOPEDIA OF MODERN U.S. MILITARY WEAPONS

The *Army Times*
Navy Times
Air Force Times

ENCYCLOPEDIA OF MODERN U.S. MILITARY WEAPONS

COLONEL TIMOTHY M. LAUR
AND STEVEN L. LLANSO

Edited by Walter J. Boyne

B
BERKLEY BOOKS, NEW YORK

Page i photo: MLRS Missile Launch (courtesy US Army).

ENCYCLOPEDIA OF MODERN U.S. MILITARY WEAPONS

A Berkley Book
Published by The Berkley Publishing Group
200 Madison Avenue, New York, New York 10016

Book design by Irving Perkins Associates

First edition: August 1995

Library of Congress Cataloging-in-Publication Data

Laur, Timothy M.
    Encyclopedia of modern U.S. military weapons / Timothy M. Laur and
Steven L. Llanso ; edited by Walter J. Boyne. — 1st ed.
        p.   cm.
    ISBN 0-425-14781-9
    1. Military weapons—United States—Encyclopedias.   2. Military weapons—
History—20th century—Encyclopedias.   I. Llanso, Steven L.
II. Boyne, Walter J., 1929–.   III. Title.
    U818.L38   1995
    355.8′2′0973—dc20   95-11912
                                                                                              CIP

Printed in the United States of America

10   9   8   7   6   5   4   3   2   1

ACKNOWLEDGMENTS

The authors are indebted to several people and organizations who have helped us during the progress of this work. Of particular value early in the discussions of the book were Norman Polmar and Walter Boyne, who suggested it and encouraged us to do it in the first place.

In the accumulation of data, photos, and other supporting documents, many people and agencies provided us with help. Most of the photographs are from the Department of Defense's Public Affairs slide and photographic library. Major Jim Bates of the Air Force Space Command and Staff Sergeant George Hayward of USSPACECOM provided key materials. Marge Holtz, Tricia Larsen, and Nancy Breen of the Military Sealift Command helped with sealift and underway-replenishment-ship information.

The cooperation and support of the United Communications Group, specifically Bruce Levenson, Ed Peskowitz, and Nancy Becker, are particularly appreciated, along with former Periscope Military Database editors Deborah Boyle Hoffman, Patricia Byars Ramirez, Doris Roth Carr, David Wilton, and Ladda Tammy Duckworth. Current database senior editor Greg Beaudoin also contributed by keeping us supplied with last-minute data changes.

Also helping us were Mary Anna Kaufer of the Air Mobility Command Historian Office, Rita Marcus of Air Weather Service's Historian Office, and Joe Wilson and Betty Dahl of the AMC Public Affairs Office. Master Sergeant Thomas E. Pennington of the 89th Military Airlift Wing provided presidential aircraft information. Guy Asito of the Air Force Association helped with his time and resources.

Several defense industry public affairs specialists helped us find and use graphics of their weapons systems, including Dick Sherman and Don Bernstein of Raytheon, Don Gilleland and Karl G. Oskoian of General Dynamics Land Systems, George Baldwin of Bath Iron Works, and Karen Hagar of Lockheed–Fort Worth.

Naturally, any errors are the sole responsibility of the authors.

CONTENTS

FOREWORD

For the first half of the twentieth century, most major weapons systems had relatively short life spans; the Spad XIIIs, which Captain Edward Rickenbacker flew over the Western Front, had a service life of only a few years. During World War II, it was unusual for an aircraft or a tank to have a service life of more than five or six years. Ships were by their size and expense somewhat longer lived, but almost inevitably their mission was downgraded over time. For supporting systems, like field telephones, artillery, radio sets, bomb sights, rockets, radar and electronic countermeasures, the life span was even shorter, sometimes measured in months, not years, as technology overtook it.

Today, however, the life span of weapon systems is often measured in decades; who would have imagined when the B-52 first flew in April 1952 that the Stratofortress would be scheduled for service well into the next century? Who would have thought that the great battleships *Iowa*, *New Jersey*, and *Missouri* would be hauled from their mothballs to be put into combat again? Times and technology have changed, and as costs have risen and the defense budget reduced, more effort is placed in extending the useful lives of the weapons already in existence.

This is but one of the reasons that the *Encyclopedia of Modern U.S. Military Weapons* is such a valuable contribution to the literature, for the weapons it describes will be relied upon by the American armed forces and their allies for the foreseeable future. The book is the most comprehensive and complete reference available on U.S. military equipment, and will satisfy the requirements of anyone from novice to expert.

Written in a brisk, accessible style, this encyclopedia provides a collective description of the principal weapons systems of the United States at the most definitive juncture of American defense policy, which is being redefined to an unprecedented degree by the end of the cold war. For the first time in two centuries, Europe is not threatened by a single great continental power. The U.S. defense policy is no longer predicated on mutually assured destruction, or on the defeat of massive Soviet land armies pouring through the Fulda Gap. Instead, attention now has to be focused on the proliferation of threats—it was not obvious to the West that during the cold war the Soviet Union was maintaining peace within its sphere of influence. Russia's sphere of influence is now much diminished, and the policies of many of the former states of the Soviet Union unpredictable, to say the least. With the inevitable proliferation of nuclear weapons, the United States faces new and imponderable threats which, because of continuing cuts in the U.S. military budget, will have to be addressed primarily with the weapons systems currently in existence.

The authors have provided listings for all U.S. weapons anywhere in the world, encompassing systems as old as the Douglas C-47 "Gooney Bird" and as new as its twenty-first-century successor, the McDonnell Douglas C-17 Globemaster III. Each individual listing provides information on the weapons system, its evolution, development, variants, combat experience, and specifications. The coverage of ships is particularly valuable, for it includes a listing of every ship within its class, by hull number, ship's name, builder, and with key dates. Similarly exhaustive detail is provided for armored fighting vehicles, missiles, and other weapons.

Tim Laur and Steve Llanso are experts in the field and their book is an important contribution to military literature, providing as it does an instant reference to the weapons systems of all the services of the United States.

—Walter J. Boyne

ENCYCLOPEDIA OF MODERN U.S. MILITARY WEAPONS

AIRCRAFT

ATTACK

Avenger (A-12)

The Avenger was to be a night/all-weather, high-performance strike aircraft. After several years of controversial secret development and several months of accelerating cost projections and schedule stretch-outs, the program was canceled in January 1991. The proposed A-12, also known as the Advanced Tactical Aircraft (ATA), was to provide an eventual replacement for the Navy and Marine Corps A-6 Intruder/EA-6B Prowler series.

The artist's conception showed a relatively high-aspect-ratio delta wing with approximately 2½ times the area of the A-6's wing. The leading-edge sweep was about 47°; the trailing edge was straight and continuous from tip to tip. The A-12's shape led to nicknames such as Manta Ray and Dorito (after the tortilla chip).

Roll control involved two sections of elevons on the trailing edge near the wingtip and spoilers ahead of the elevons; used differentially, the elevons provided yaw control. A control surface was centered on the trailing edge to control pitch. When the wings would be folded, the A-12's span was reduced to 34 ft (10.36 m). Movable surfaces on the outer half of the leading edge increased lift for takeoff and landing.

The two General Electric engines were derived from the F/A-18 Hornet's F404s; the fan diameter was increased for greater airflow. The delta wing planform combined with a deep center section provides a large internal volume for fuel while keeping the wing's thickness/chord ratio relatively low.

The ATA design featured "stealth" technology so that it would be difficult to detect on radar. The ATA's avionics were to be controlled by an IBM computer using Very High Speed Integrated Circuits (VHSIC) technology and Central Processing Units (CPU) with 1.4 million words of memory and capable of 3 million instructions per second.

Westinghouse, with Texas Instruments, was to develop the AN/APQ-183 electronically scanned, phased-array multimode radar. Harris Corp. developed the multifunction antennas, to have been located in the wing's leading edges. Magnavox was supplying the A-RPX-5 Global Positioning System (GPS) receiver while Westinghouse was developing the A-12's combined-functions Forward-Looking Infrared (FLIR) system.

Tandem seats for the pilot and weapons officer were enclosed by a bubble canopy. The instrumentation included Kaiser's Kroma liquid-crystal Multifunction Displays (MFD) and Bendix Tactical Situation Displays (TSD). The front-seat Head-Up Display (HUD) had a 30° × 23° field of view. An 8-in × 8-in (203-mm × 203-mm) TSD was flanked by two 6-in × 6-in (152-mm × 152-mm) MFD. In the rear cockpit were a TSD and three MFDs.

Defensive avionics were to be Litton's electronic surveillance measures system and General Electric's missile-warning system.

The maximum payload was 40% higher than that of the A-6, or 25,200 lb (11,431 kg) vs. 18,000 lb (8,165 kg), and its range would be 80% greater.

DEVELOPMENT • The Avenger was canceled on January 7, 1991. Its planned initial operational capability was scheduled for 1992 but was slipped to at least 1996 or 1997. First flight had been expected to occur in summer 1990 but was delayed several times.

The program cost was estimated to be $42 billion for 450 Navy and $31–$36 billion for 300–350 Air Force aircraft. Total Navy buy was to be 858 aircraft (to outfit both Navy and Marine Corps attack squadrons) and another 400 for the Air Force. These plans too were revised during the plane's planning.

SPECIFICATIONS •

MANUFACTURER McDonnell Douglas and General Dynamics

CREW 2 (pilot, navigator/weapons systems operator)

ENGINES 2 General Electric F412-GE-D5F2 turbofan

max power more than 16,000 lb (7,257 kg) each

WEIGHT

max takeoff approx 70,000 lb (31,751 kg)

DIMENSIONS (EST.)

wingspan 70 ft (21.34 m)
length 37 ft (11.28 m)
wing area 1,300 ft² (120.8 m²)

PERFORMANCE

max speed approx. Mach 1

RADAR Westinghouse AN/APQ-183 radar

Dragonfly (A-37)

The Dragonfly is adapted from the T-37 "Tweet" trainer, intended for use in counterinsurgency operations. The wing is mounted low on the fuselage, having a straight leading edge and slightly tapered trailing edge. Streamlined fuel tanks are permanently fixed to the wingtips. The fin and full-height rudder are nearly upright; the fin has a dorsal fillet. The double-taper tailplanes are fitted

approximately one-third of the way up the fin.

The two General Electric J85-17 turbojets are in thickened wing roots. The oval intakes are considerably larger than those of the T-37; the nozzles exhaust through the wing root at the trailing edge. A refueling probe is fitted to the nose of many A-37s, located on the centerline, and extends forward. The short, wide-stance main gear retracts inward into the wing root, while the nose gear retracts forward into the nose.

The bulbous forward section of the fuselage contains an oversize side-by-side cockpit with a single-piece clamshell canopy bubble hinged at the rear. The fuselage then tapers gently toward the tail.

The Dragonfly's 7.62-mm, 6-barrel minigun is mounted in the lower left nose, and four store pylons under each wing carry a variety of conventional and cluster bombs, rocket pods, gun pods, and drop tanks.

The A-37 is characterized by its simple operating characteristics, its efficient ordnance-carrying capability, and its relatively high operational ceiling. The forgiving flying qualities stem from its trainer origins.

DEVELOPMENT • The A-37's initial operational capability was in 1967; its first flight was on October 22, 1963. A total of 577 were produced from 1967 to 1978. In addition to its US Air Force service, the A-37 is operated in nine Latin American countries, South Korea, Thailand, and probably Vietnam.

VARIANTS • YA-37A (prototype), A-37A, A-37B, OA-37, T-37 Tweet.

COMBAT EXPERIENCE • In December 1989, 21 OA-37s from the Air Force's 24th Composite Wing flew 255 sorties over three days during the US military operation to remove Panamanian leader

General Noriega. The aircraft were not used for ground attack, but rather for radio relay, medical evacuation coordination, and flare dispensing.

SPECIFICATIONS •
MANUFACTURER   Cessna Aircraft
CREW   2
ENGINES   2 General Electric J85-GE-17A turbojet
  max power   2,850 lb (1,293 kg) static thrust each
  fuel capacity
      507 US gal (1,920 liters)
WEIGHTS
  empty   6,211 lb (2,817 kg)
  max payload
      5,680 lb (2,576 kg)
  max takeoff   14,000 lb (6,350 kg)
DIMENSIONS
  wingspan   35 ft 10½ in (10.93 m)
  length   29 ft 3 in (8.92 m)
  height   8 ft 10½ in (2.7 m)
  wing area   184 ft² (17.09 m²)
PERFORMANCE
  max speed   440 kts (507 mph; 816 km/h)
  max diving   455 kts (524 mph; 843 km/h)
  max cruise   425 kts (489 mph; 787 km/h)
  stall speed   max weight: 98 kts (113 mph; 182 km/h)
      normal weight: 75 kts (86 mph; 139 km/h)
  climb rate   6,990 ft/min (2,130 m/min)
  ceiling   both engines: 41,765 ft (12,730 m)
      1 engine: 25,000 ft (7,620 m)
  radius   with 4,700-lb (2,132-kg) weapons load: 74 nm (85 mi; 137 km)
      with 3,700-lb (1,678-kg) weapons load: 217 nm (250 mi; 402 km)
      with 1,300-lb (590-kg) weapons load: 478 nm (550 mi; 885 km)
  range   with 4,100-lb (1,860-kg) weapons load: 399 nm (460 mi; 740 km)
      with 4 100-US gal (379-liter) drop tanks: 877 nm (1,000 mi; 1,625 km)
  armament   1 GAU-2B/A 7.62-mm minigun with 1,500 rounds
      8 wing pylons for up to 5,600 lb (2,540 kg) of ordnance

Harrier (AV-8B)

The AV-8B Harrier is an advanced Vertical Short Takeoff and Landing (VSTOL) fighter/attack aircraft that is coproduced by McDonnell Douglas Aircraft and British Aerospace. It has the ability to take off vertically and hover. The AV-8B differs from previous Harriers by having a larger, more efficient wing shape, larger trailing-edge flaps and ventral air brake, strakes under the gun/ammunition pods, redesigned engine intakes and nozzles, strengthened landing gear, a ventral air dam, and a more powerful engine, providing twice the payload of the AV-8A.

The shoulder-mounted, low-aspect-ratio swept wings have supercritical airfoil sections and Leading-Edge Root Extensions (LERX) that increase instantaneous turn rate. In later aircraft, the LERX is enlarged for better handling and survivability. Single-slotted trailing-edge flaps are located inboard of the midwing landing-gear pods. Drooping ailerons are located outboard. The flaps are positioned automatically during flight to generate the best lift at a given angle of attack.

The tail unit features a swept, pointed fin and rudder with a ventral fin below the fuselage. The aircraft is also fitted with a Stability Augmentation and Attitude Hold System (SAAHS) and a short tailboom.

The Harrier's single engine provides both lift and thrust. It has large, semicircular engine air intakes with two vertical rows of auxiliary air doors on each side of the fuselage. The engine power has been upgraded several times during production. In place of a conventional exhaust nozzle, the Harrier uses swiveling exhausts that can be repositioned for hovering flight and for better combat maneuvering. A water injection system increases thrust by 2,500 lb (1,134 kg) for 1½ minutes to aid in hot-weather takeoffs and landings.

Retractable bicycle landing gear retracts into the fuselage; a single-wheel unit is forward, a twin-wheel unit aft. Rearward-folding outrigger landing gear retracts into pods extending aft from the midspan of each wing. The aircraft's net weight consists of 26% composite components. Compared to the original Harrier design, the cockpit has been raised 12 in (305 mm) and upgraded to include a Multipurpose Display (MPD) for attack and navigation as well as Hands on Throttle and Stick (HOTAS) technology.

The principal attack avionics system is the Hughes nose-mounted AN/ASB-19(V)2 or (V)3 Angle Rate Bombing Set (ARBS), which uses a TV/laser target seeker and tracker. Navigation is aided by the Litton AN/ASN-130A Carrier Aircraft Inertial Navigation System (CAINS). The ARBS feeds information to the Sperry AN/AYK-14(V) mission computer, the Lear-Siegler AN/AYQ-13 Stores Management Set (SMS), and Smiths Industries SU-128A dual combining, wide field-of-view Head-Up Display (HUD). Radar warning is provided by the Litton AN/ALR-67(V)2 radar-warning receiver; the Loral AN/ALE-39 chaff/flare dispenser is fitted in the lower rear fuselage.

The aircraft carries an external 25-mm gun pack faired into the underfuselage, with a 1,000-lb (454-kg) capacity fuselage hardpoint for bombs or an AN/ALQ-164 defensive ECM pod, four 2,000-lb (907-kg) capacity wing pylons, two 620-lb (281-kg) capacity outboard pylons available for bombs, rockets, air-to-air and air-to-ground missiles, and fuel tanks. Outrigger pylons were added to USMC AV-8Bs beginning with aircraft number 167.

DEVELOPMENT • The Harrier's initial operational capability for US Marine Corps service was in January 1985; the YAV-8B's first flight was on November 9, 1978, AV-8B on November 5, 1981, and EAV-8B in August 1987. Until the AV-8A/C's retirement, the AV-8B was known as the Harrier II.

The Marine Corps has been procuring 300 AV-8B and 28 TAV-8B aircraft. The first three aircraft of an order of 12 EAV-8B were delivered to the Spanish Navy in October 1987, with the last two delivered by the end of 1988. The production share for the US and Spanish aircraft is 60% for McDonnell Douglas and 40% for British Aerospace.

The Royal Air Force acquired GR Mk 5 aircraft, with the first delivered on July 1, 1987; production for the GR Mk 5 is shared equally between the two companies.

In October 1990, the United States, Italy, and Spain drafted a Memorandum of Understanding (MU) that guides development of the AV-8B Plus, a Harrier II variant fitted with a version of the AN/APG-65 radar used in the F/A-18 Hornet. Some of the Marines' AV-8Bs, including those ordered in FY1991, were upgraded to the Plus standard. The Spanish Navy plans to remanufacture its 11 EAV-8Bs and buy an additional seven.

In May 1990, following the MU negotiations, the Italian Parliament approved the purchase of 16 AV-8B Plus and two TAV-8B trainers; delivery of the $111-million order for the TAV-8Bs was made in August 1991. The AV-8B replaced the earlier British-built AV-8A/C Harrier and A-4M Skyhawk aircraft in US attack squadrons.

VARIANTS • YAV-8B, GR Mk 5, TAV-8B (trainer), EAV-8B Matador II (Spain), AV-8D Night Attack Harrier, Harrier GR Mk 7, Harrier T10 (trainer), and AV-8B Plus.

COMBAT EXPERIENCE • US Marine Corps AV-8Bs were deployed to Saudi Arabia in mid-August 1990 as part of Operation Desert Shield.

When Operation Desert Storm began, 86 AV-8Bs—60 operating from airstrips in Saudi Arabia and 26 flying from amphibious assault ships *Tarawa* (LHA 1) and *Nassau* (LHA 4) in the Persian Gulf—compiled 3,567 sorties against Iraqi targets in Kuwait and Iraq. Almost 3,000 tons of ordnance were delivered by the aircraft.

The Harriers used their ARBS to detect targets and dropped laser-guided bombs and launched laser-guided AGM-65 Mavericks. In one attack, four AV-8Bs were credited with the destruction of 25 Iraqi tanks. On almost every sortie, 25-mm cannon fire was directed against a variety of vehicles (armored and "soft") and was said to have been very effective.

Five AV-8Bs were lost during the war, four in combat and one noncombat. Postwar Marine Corps analysis revealed that the midfuselage location of the engine nozzles made the Harriers much more vulnerable to an infrared missile hit than other aircraft.

Many believe that the AV-8B, particularly the Night Attack and AV-8B Plus variants, represents the first truly effective VSTOL combat aircraft.

SPECIFICATIONS •
MANUFACTURER McDonnell Douglas and British Aerospace
CREW 1 (2 in TAV-8B)
ENGINES
1 Rolls-Royce F402-RR-406 Pegasus 11-21 turbofan
or 1 Rolls-Royce F402-RR-408 Pegasus 11-61 turbofan

max power -406: 21,450 lb (9,730 kg) static thrust
-408: 23,400 lb (10,614 kg) static thrust
internal fuel capacity
1,100 US gal (4,164 liters)
max internal and external fuel capacity
approx 2,300 US gal (8,705 liters)
WEIGHTS
empty -406: 13,086 lb (5,936 kg)
-408: 13,968 lb (6,336 kg)
max weapons load
-406: 9,200 lb (4,173 kg)
-408: 13,235 lb (6,003 kg)
design limit for 7 g operation
22,950 lb (10,410 kg)
max takeoff -406, sea level, vertical takeoff: ISA, 18,950 lb (8,595 kg); at 90°F (32°C), 17,950 lb (8,142 kg)
-408, tropical day: 20,595 lb (9,342 kg) with 1,640-ft (500-m) takeoff roll: 31,000 lb (14,061 kg)
DIMENSIONS
wingspan 30 ft 4 in (9.25 m)
length 46 ft 4 in (14.12 m)
height 11 ft 7 ¾ in (3.55 m)
wing area 230 ft² (21.37 m²)
PERFORMANCE
max speed sea level: 580 kts (668 mph; 1,075 km/h; Mach 0.88)
at altitude: Mach 0.91
climb rate more than 13,000 ft/min (3,962 m/min)
ceiling 50,000 ft (12,240 m)
radius with 1,200-ft (366-m) roll, 7 500-lb (227-kg) bombs, and 2 300-US gal (1,136-liter) drop tanks
-406: 471 nm (542 mi; 873 km)
-408: 594 nm (684 mi; 1,100 km)
ferry range with 300-US gal (1,136-liter) drop tanks

dropped
-406: 2,067 nm (2,380 mi;
3,850 km)
-408: 1,965 nm (2,263 mi;
3,639 km)
retained
-406: 1,720 nm (1,981 mi;
3,187 km)
-408: 1,638 nm (1,886 mi;
3,034 km)

range   2,560 nm (2,946 mi;
4,741 km) max fuel

armament   1 GAU-12/U multibarrel
25-mm cannon, 250
rounds
and 16 500-lb (227-kg)
bombs
or 10 Paveway laser-
guided bombs
or 12 cluster bombs
or 10 rocket pods
or 6 AIM-9 Sidewinder
AAM
or 2 Sidewinder + 4
AGM-65 Maverick ASM

Intruder (A-6)

The Intruder is the US Navy's carrier-based all-weather, night-attack aircraft. It can deliver a variety of conventional and nuclear ordnance. The Intruder was developed on the basis of night-attack requirements generated during the Korean War in the early 1950s.

The A-6 configuration is relatively conventional. The wing is mounted at mid-fuselage height and has a modest 25° sweep at the quarter-chord. Nearly the entire leading edge is occupied by slats; virtually all of the trailing edge has single-slotted flaps. Spoilers that run parallel to the flaps provide roll control when operated differentially, lift dumping when operated collectively. The rear half of each wingtip can be opened into upper and lower halves, thus acting as air brakes.

Almost 180 A-6Es are receiving composite wings to extend their service lives.

The fin leading edge has a slight sweep aft; the trailing edge, with its inset rudder, sweeps slightly forward. The all-moving tailplanes are slightly swept and are mounted on the fuselage ahead of the rudder hinge line.

The two J52 turbojet engines are contained in pods under the wing flanking the fuselage; the airflow is a straight line from intake to exhaust. Each intake, headed by a boundary-layer splitter plate, is mounted in a cheek position below the cockpit; the exhausts appear beyond the wing trailing edge on either side of the fuselage. Both wings house integral fuel tanks, and additional tankage is in the fuselage behind the cockpit and near the center of gravity. Intruders are fitted with an in-flight refueling probe mounted immediately ahead of the cockpit.

The fuselage, with its large nose radome, bulged side-by-side cockpit, and tapered after section, resembles to some a tadpole. The side-by-side cockpit imposes some drag penalty.

The remainder of the fuselage tapers aft and is filled with avionics equipment and fuel. The retractable main gear units fold forward and inward into the intake pod; the nose gear retracts to the rear. The arrestor hook for carrier landings swings down from a fuselage point midway between the wing trailing edge and the tail. Dual hydraulic systems power the control surfaces, flaps, speed brakes, and wheel brakes. The design load factor is +6.5 g.

The A-6 was one of the first attack aircraft with an integrated offensive avionics suite, known as DIANE (Digital Integrated Attack and Navigational Equipment). The later Navy and Marine Corps A-6Es had a major revision in its avionics package when the two-radar system was replaced by the Norden AN/APQ-148 multimode radar, which offers terrain avoidance as well as target acquisition and tracking; an improved version is designated APQ-156. The Litton ballistic computer was replaced by the IBM AN/ASQ-133 (later improved as the ASQ-155) digital, solid-state ballistic computer, which oversees some 60 displays and sensors.

The primary cockpit display is the Kaiser AVA-1 Vertical Display Indicator (VDI), which accepts information from the radar and navigational avionics, including the Litton AN/ASN-92 Carrier Aircraft Inertial Navigation System (CAINS). Defensive avionics include the Lockheed Sanders AN/ALQ-126B, AN/ALE-39 chaff dispenser, and Litton AN/ALR-67 Threat-Warning System.

The A-6E also has the Hughes AN/AAS-33 Target-Recognition Attack Multisensor (TRAM), which integrates a Forward-Looking Infrared (FLIR), a combination laser designator/rangefinder, and a laser designation receiver. Northrop's Infrared Video Automatic Tracking (IRVAT) automates the tracking portion of TRAM. The TRAM sensor is fitted in a small, spherical turret under the nose; the BN uses a separate viewing scope for the TRAM.

Some A-6s have been retrofitted with blue-green cockpit lighting that is compatible with Cats Eye Night Vision Goggles (NVG). These aircraft are able to reduce their minimum altitude during night flying (in good weather) from 500–800 ft (152–244 m) to 200 ft (61 m) and can maneuver more sharply because of the pilot's improved field of view.

Weapons and external fuel tanks are carried on the four wing pylons and an underfuselage attachment point; each weapons station has a capacity of 3,600 lb (1,633 kg) for a maximum payload of up to 18,000 lb (8,182 kg). The Intruder's bomb load makes it the most capable "bomber" in US naval service. A Harpoon antiship missile capability has been fitted to all aircraft, and the aircraft can carry Sidewinder air-to-air missiles for self-defense as well as Brunswick Tactical Air-Launched Decoys (TALD). The aircraft is "wired" for carrying nuclear bombs.

A KA-6D tanker variant—converted from earlier attack models—has avionics deleted to provide space for the reel and drogue; up to five 400-US gal (1,514-liter) drop tanks can be carried.

DEVELOPMENT • The A-6's initial operational capability was in 1963; its first flight was on April 9, 1960, and the KA-6D tanker prototype was on May 23, 1966. Over 700 A-6s have been built, with 240 converted to the A-6E configuration. Intruders suffered a series of wing fatigue problems, with hairline fractures occurring after approximately 2,200 flight hours. Over 180 A-6 aircraft were grounded for wing inspections in early 1987 after a series of crashes.

VARIANTS • A-6A, EA-6A Intruder (EW), A-6B, EA-6B Prowler (EW), A-6C, KA-6D, A-6E, A-6E Block 1 (A-6E Systems/Weapons Integration Program SWIP), A-6E Composite Rewing Program, A-6F, A-6G.

COMBAT EXPERIENCE • Intruders were used extensively in the Vietnam War. A total of 68 Navy and Marine Corps A-6 aircraft were lost in combat from 1965 to 1973.

In December 1983, Intruders from the USS *Independence* (CV 62) and *John F. Kennedy* (CV 67) participated in air strikes against Lebanon's Bekaa Valley; one Intruder and an A-7E Corsair were shot down by Syrian missile batteries.

In March 1986, an A-6 aircraft from the USS *Coral Sea* (CV 43) fired an AGM-84 Harpoon missile at a Libyan Nanuchka-class corvette, sinking it. In April 1986, Intruders from the *Coral Sea* and the USS *America* (CV 66) attacked five targets in northern Libya in retaliation for alleged Libyan involvement in a terrorist bombing in West Berlin.

In April 1988, A-6s from the USS *Enterprise* (CVN 65) attacked Iranian Boghammer patrol boats, sinking one and chasing away four others. Later that day, A-6s helped sink the Iranian frigate *Sahand* and damaged the *Sabalan* (*Sahand's* sister ship).

On January 17, 1991, 90 A-6Es from six aircraft carriers in the Persian Gulf and Red Sea, along with 20 US Marine Corps Intruders, attacked Iraqi targets at the initiation of Operation Desert Storm. For the entire conflict, the Navy's A-6E contingent flew 4,071 sorties and Marine Corps aircraft amassed 854. Four Navy A-6Es were lost in combat and one was a noncombat loss.

Two US Navy Intruders on separate missions from the USS *Abraham Lincoln* (CVN 72) fired single HARM missiles at Iraqi surface-to-air missile sites after being illuminated by the radar. The aircraft were monitoring the no-fly zone over southern Iraq in July 1993.

SPECIFICATIONS •

MANUFACTURER   Grumman Aerospace
CREW   2 (pilot, bombardier/navigator)
ENGINES   2 Pratt & Whitney J52-P-8B turbojet
  max power   9,300 lb (4,218 kg) static thrust each
  internal fuel capacity
    2,344 US gal (8,873 liters)
WEIGHTS
  empty   26,600 lb (12,065 kg)
  max weapons load
    18,000 lb (8,165 kg)
  max takeoff   catapult: 58,600 lb (26,580 kg)
    land-based: 60,400 lb (27,397 kg)
DIMENSIONS
  wingspan   53 ft (16.15 m)
  length   54 ft 9 in (16.69 m)
  height   16 ft 2 in (4.93 m)
  wing area   529 ft² (49.1 m²)
PERFORMANCE
  max speed (sea level)
    560 kts (644 mph; 1,036 km/h)

cruise speed
    412 kts (474 mph; 763 km/h)
stall speed   flaps up: 148 kts (164 mph; 264 km/h)
    flaps down: 98 kts (113 mph; 182 km/h)
climb rate   clean: 7,620 ft/min (2,323 m/min)
    1 engine: 2,120 ft/min (646 m/min)
ceiling   clean: 42,400 ft (12,924 m)
    1 engine: 21,000 ft (6,400 m)
range   combat: 880 nm (1,012 mi; 1,629 km)
    with tanks: 2,375 nm (2,733 mi; 4,399 km)
    without tanks: 2,818 nm (3,245 mi; 5,222 km)
g limits   +6.5
armament   4 3,600-lb (1,933-kg) capacity wing pylons and 1 fuselage hardpoint for external fuel and weapons
    30 Mk 82 500-lb bombs *or* 10 Mk 83 1,000-lb bombs *or* 3 Mk 84 2,000-lb bombs *or* 3 B43/B57/B61H nuclear bombs *or* up to 4 missiles:
      AGM-84A Harpoon
      AGM-88 HARM
      AGM-65 Maverick
      AGM-123A Skipper II
      AIM-9 Sidewinder
radar   AN/APQ-156 multimode

Skyhawk (A-4)

The Skyhawk is a small attack aircraft, originally developed for daylight-only nuclear strike missions from US aircraft carriers. It has subsequently been modified to serve as a highly versatile, light attack aircraft for conventional strike and close air support missions.

The A-4 has a nonfolding, low-aspect-ratio delta wing mounted low on the fuselage. The wing's quarter-chord sweep is 33.2° and the wing dihedral angle is 2.67°. The wing's three spars run from tip to tip; virtually all of the wing is an integral fuel tank. The leading edge has automatic slats and wing fences. The trailing edge has split flaps inboard of horn-balanced ailerons; ahead of the flaps are lift-dumping spoilers.

The A-4 has a "cropped delta" fin and ribbed rudder; the ribbing reduces flutter, although not by design.

The engine air intakes are located on the fuselage above the wing and behind the cockpit. Rectangular air brakes are fitted on either side of the fuselage behind the wings. The aircraft's long-stroke landing gear retracts forward into the wings and nose. The pilot sits well forward and has excellent visibility. The cockpit is enclosed by a single-piece, rear-hinged canopy.

The 20-mm or 30-mm cannon are located in the wing roots, and five attachment points are provided for weapons and external fuel tanks. The outboard wing pylons are rated at 570 lb (258 kg) each, the inboard wing pylons at 1,750 lb (794 kg) without roll restrictions and 2,240 lb (1,016 kg) with restrictions, and the centerline fuselage hardpoint at 3,575 lb (1,622 kg). These hardpoints carry antiradar and land-attack missiles as well as conventional bombs, rocket pods, and mines. Avionics include a Head-Up Display (HUD), Angle Rate Bombing Set (ARBS), a loft bomb computer system, and a tailfin-mounted ECM system.

DEVELOPMENT • The A-4's initial operational capability was in 1956; its first flight (the XA4D-1) was on June 22, 1954. The Skyhawk's production from 1956 to 1979 totaled 2,960, of which 555 were two-seat variants. Although the aircraft is no longer in service with active US Navy or Marine Corps units (last active USMC aircraft retired on July 6, 1990), New Zealand and Singapore are updating many of their A-4s, enabling them to serve to the end of the century.

When Iraq invaded Kuwait in August 1990, five single-seat A-4KUs and all six trainers were captured, but Kuwait's other 25 attack aircraft escaped to Saudi Arabia.

The aircraft has been replaced by the A-7 Corsair. It was replaced in the US Blue Angels flight demonstration team in 1987 by the F/A-18 Hornet. It is replaced in US Marine Corps service by the AV-8B Harrier. Both the Navy and Marine Corps fly large numbers of A-4s for training, target tow, and other special missions.

The A-4 is operated by seven foreign air forces. The Skyhawk has enjoyed a reputation for durability and possesses good handling characteristics. Recent Argentina, New Zealand, and Singapore update programs reflect the airplane's versatility.

VARIANTS • XA4D-1,   A-4A,   A-4B, TA-4B, A-4C, A4D-3, A-4E, A-4F, TA-4F, EA-4F (EW), A-4G/TA-4G, A-4H/TA-4H, TA-4J,   A-4K/KAHU,   A-4KU/TA-4KU, A-4L, A-4M Skyhawk II, A-4N, A-4P, A-4Q, A-4PTM/TA-4PTM ("Peculiar to Malaysia"), A-4S, A-4S-1 Super Skyhawk.

COMBAT   EXPERIENCE • Skyhawks were used extensively by the US Navy and Marine Corps in the Vietnam War and by Israel in the Middle East wars. During the 1973 Yom Kippur War, Israel lost 53 of its Skyhawks. Argentina flew the A-4 in the 1982 Falklands War against Britain.

Skyhawks were often used for simulating Soviet threat aircraft in US military pilot training during the cold war.

During the Iraqi invasion of Kuwait in August 1990, Kuwaiti Skyhawks bombed and strafed Iraqi forces until resistance ended on August 4. A total of 21 helicopters and four Iraqi patrol boats were destroyed. 25 A-4KUs from the 9th and 25th Squadrons flew to Saudi Arabia to regroup.

When Operation Desert Storm began on January 17, 1991, the Kuwaiti A-4s flew against targets in Kuwait. The squadron commander was shot down by ground fire in an early raid; no other A-4KUs were lost. Limited by the lack of radar or radar-warning systems, the relatively "low-tech," day-attack A-4s relied on E-3 Airborne Warning and Control System (AWACS) for defense against Iraqi fighters. Kuwaiti A-4 sorties continued until the cease-fire on February 28, 1991.

SPECIFICATIONS •
MANUFACTURER   McDonnell Douglas
CREW   1 (2 in TA-4 and OA-4 variants)
ENGINES   1 Pratt & Whitney J52-P-408 turbojet
  max power   11,200 lb (5,080 kg) static thrust
  internal fuel capacity
          800 US gal (3,208 liters)
WEIGHTS
  empty   10,456 lb (4,743 kg)
  max external load
          9,195 lb (4,139 kg)
  max takeoff   25,500 lb (13,113 kg)
DIMENSIONS
  wingspan   27 ft 6 in (8.38 m)
  length   40 ft 4¼ in (12.3 m)
               TA-4/OA-4: 42 ft 7¼ in
               (12.98 m)
  height   14 ft 11 in (4.55 m)
               TA-4/OA-4: 15 ft 3 in
               (4.66 m)
  wing area   260 ft² (24.16 m²)
PERFORMANCE
  max speed (sea level)
          clean: 582 kts (670 mph;
          1,078 km/h)
          with 4,000 lb (1,814 kg) of
          weapons: 560 kts (645
          mph; 1,038 km/h)
  climb rate   8,440 ft/min (2,573
               m/min)
  ceiling   42,250 ft (12,878 m)

  radius with 4,000 lb (1,814 kg) of weapons and external fuel
          335 nm (386 mi; 620 km)
  range with 4,000-lb (1,814-kg) of weapons and external fuel
          799 nm (920 mi; 1,480 km)
  ferry range   2,055 nm (2,366 mi; 3,808 km)
  armament   2 20-mm Mk 12 cannon with 200 rounds each
          or 2 30-mm DEFA cannon with 150 rounds each
          and 14 500-lb (227-kg) bombs
          or 3 1,000-lb (454-kg) bombs
          or 1 2,000-lb (907-kg) bomb
          or 1 4,500-lb (2,041-kg) bomb
          or 4 AGM-45 Shrike missiles
          or 3 AGM-62 Walleye missiles
          or 4 AGM-65 Maverick missiles
          or 1 Mk 43/57 nuclear store

Spectre (AC-130)

The Spectre gunship is derived from the C-130 Hercules, the most widely used military transport in the modern military era. AC-130s were first used in Vietnam and more recently to support Special Operations Forces (SOF) missions. (For a description of the basic C-130, see Cargo Aircraft.)

The weapons in the AC-130H consist of a 105-mm howitzer, two 20-mm Vulcan Gatling cannon, and a Bofors 40-mm/70-cal cannon, all mounted athwartships and firing to port. The howitzer is carried in a hydraulic mount just ahead of the rear cargo ramp. It has a shortened barrel and a 49-in (1.24-m) recoil and is fired by a three-man crew (gunner at the control

AC-130 Spectre
U.S. GOVERNMENT DEPARTMENT OF DEFENSE

AN/AAD-7 Forward-Looking Infrared (FLIR) ball is mounted on the nose of the port-landing-gear sponson. The AN/APQ-150 beacon tracking radar is fitted in between the 40-mm cannon and the 105-mm howitzer. The AN/AVQ-17 IR/ whitelight searchlight is mounted on the port rear fuselage.

The three sensor operators are housed in a single position in the cargo hold between the two sets of gun positions. Because the location of armament and the pilot's Head-Up Display (HUD) are both on the port side, all firings are in a port orbit.

A Litton AN/ALR-69 radar-warning receiver is fitted in the fuselage. Four chaff/flare launcher systems are fitted to each side of the aircraft, and two more are in the tail; a total of 300 cartridges are carried. Westinghouse AN/ALQ-119 noise/deception jamming and SUU-42 IR countermeasures pods can be carried on the Triple Ejection Racks (TER) that are fitted to the external fuel tanks.

panel, loader, and unloader). The howitzer's pointing angle is 20° in azimuth fore and aft and 40° elevation. 76 ready rounds are carried near the gun with another 24 stowed farther forward.

The Bofors cannon is ahead of the 105-mm howitzer in a hydraulic, trainable mount served by two crew members. It has a rate of fire of 100 rounds per minute and 69 4-round clips. The two Vulcan Gatling cannon are mounted in parallel between the forward door and the landing-gear sponson. Each fires at a rate of 2,500 rounds/min and has a magazine of 3,000 rounds.

Avionics are comprehensive and include several sensors. A General Electric AN/ASQ-145 Low-Light-Level Television (LLLTV) and an AN/AVQ-19 laser designator are mounted in a stabilized turret located in the forward door. Ahead of the door is a large radome for the AN/ASD-5 Black Crow ignition tracking system. The

DEVELOPMENT • Although the basic C-130 is flown throughout the world, the AC-130 is flown only by the US Air Force. The AC-130's initial operational capability was in 1967. Two AC-130 variants, the -A and -H, serve with Special Operations Squadrons, the former in an Air Force reserve unit and the latter in an active unit. The AC-130As are in service with a US Air Force Reserve Special Operations Squadron, while AC-130Hs are in active service with the 16th Special Operations Squadron.

The latest variant, the AC-130U program, suffered from delays and cost increases. Problems in design of the software and the Electronic Warfare (EW) suite and compressed development and production schedules were singled out as causes. It is air refuelable and includes a side-firing weapons system. The AC-130U variant's mission is to provide precision fire support for Special

Operations Forces, as well as conventional forces, plus performing escort, surveillance, search and rescue, and armed reconnaissance/interdiction missions.

VARIANTS • C-130 Hercules, AC-130, AC-130A, AC-130E, AC-130H, AC-130U.

COMBAT EXPERIENCE • In December 1989, seven AC-130 aircraft flew 74 sorties against Panamanian forces as part of the American military operation to oust General Noriega. Gunfire from an AC-130 destroyed or disabled nine vehicles from a Panamanian convoy appeared heading toward US forces at Tocumen/Torrijos International Airport.

In late January 1991, an AC-130 was shot down off the Kuwaiti coast during Operation Desert Storm against Iraqi forces in Kuwait. All 14 men on board were listed as missing; the wreckage was found in shallow water in early March. AC-130s supported Special Operations Command missions that placed small teams in Iraq and Kuwait to gather intelligence and conduct operations.

Spectres were deployed to Somalia in mid-1993 and used against the forces of warlords, marking the first military engagement under the Clinton administration.

SPECIFICATIONS •
MANUFACTURER   Lockheed-Georgia
CREW   14 (2 pilots, navigator, flight engineer, radio operator, 3 sensor operators, and gun crews)
ENGINES   4 Allison T56-A-15 turboprop
  max power   4,591 effective hp each
  internal fuel capacity
        9,679 US gal (36,636 liters)
WEIGHTS
  empty   76,469 lb (34,686 kg)
  max payload   42,673 lb (19,356 kg)
  takeoff   normal: 155,000 lb (70,310 kg)
        max: 175,000 lb (79,380 kg)

DIMENSIONS
  wingspan   132 ft 7 in (40.41 m)
  length   97 ft 9 in (29.79 m)
  height   38 ft 3 in (11.66 m)
  wing area   1,745 ft² (162.12 m²)
  ramp opening
        length: 9 ft 1 in (2.77 m)
        width: 10 ft (3.05 m)
PERFORMANCE
  cruise speed
        max: 325 kts (374 mph; 602 km/h)
        econ: 300 kts (345 mph; 556 km/h)
  stall speed   100 kts (115 mph; 185 km/h)
  climb rate   1,900 ft/min (579 m/min)
  ceiling at 130,000 lb (58,970 kg)
        4 engines: 33,000 ft (10,060 m)
        3 engines: 26,500 ft (8,075 m)
  range   max payload: 2,046 nm (2,356 mi; 3,791 km)
        max fuel with 15,611-lb (7,081-kg) payload: 4,250 nm (4,894 mi; 7,876 km)
        takeoff run: 3,580 ft (1,091 m)
  armament   1 × 105-mm howitzer (76 ready rounds, 24 stowed)
        1 × 40-mm Bofors cannon (276 rounds)
        2 × 20-mm Vulcan Gatling cannon (6,000 rounds)
  radar   APQ-150

Thunderbolt (A-10)

The Thunderbolt was designed specifically for Close Air Support (CAS) operations. It was especially designed and armed to engage tanks and other armored vehicles and to operate from austerely equipped forward bases, a mission

U.S. Air Force A-10 Thunderbolt II
U.S. GOVERNMENT DEPARTMENT OF DEFENSE

it carried out effectively during Operation Desert Storm. (The World War II–era Soviet Il-2 Sturmovik ground-attack aircraft and the more recent Su-25 Frogfoot were designed for a similar mission.) The A-10 originally had only a visual targeting capability but subsequently was upgraded with a laser spot seeker.

The design and construction of the A-10 was governed by the desire to deliver a heavy weapons load, require little maintenance, and remain survivable in an intensely antiaircraft environment; speed and ceiling were deemphasized. The low wing is a thick-sectioned airfoil with little taper. The center section has no dihedral or taper; the outer panels, which are attached just outboard of the leading-edge landing-gear "knees," have dihedral, some taper, and turned-down tips. High-lift devices include slats on the center-section leading edge and trailing-edge double-slotted flaps inboard of broad-chord ailerons.

The tail group has low-mounted, rect-angular horizontal tailplanes, each with an upright endplate fin and rudder. The fin and rudder have converging taper. All movable tail surfaces are left/right interchangeable; the aircraft can fly with an entire vertical tail missing. Hydraulic control systems for the control surfaces are duplicated, with each system taking a different path through the airframe; there is also a mechanical backup system. The A-10 is also fitted with a General Electric two-axis, two-channel Stability Augmentation System (SAS).

The two TF34 turbofans are housed in large nacelles mounted on short stubs on the fuselage flanks ahead of the tail group. The engine position reduces vulnerability to small-arms fire while the Infrared (IR) signature is blanketed by the wing and tailplane. Engine-out control asymmetry is reduced because the engine thrust lines are relatively close to the centerline. Internal fuel tankage consists of tear-resistant, self-sealing, foam-filled cells.

The fuselage is relatively slender, with

the cockpit placed well ahead of the wing leading edge. As part of the aircraft's ballistic protection, the pilot sits in a 700-lb (318-kg) titanium tub designed to resist 23-mm antiaircraft artillery fire. Further passive protection is provided by Electronic Support Measures (ESM), such as the Litton AN/ALR-46/69 radar-warning receiver, and 16 Tracor AN/ALE-40(V)10 chaff cartridge dispensers mounted in groups of four in each wingtip and wheel well; Westinghouse AN/ALQ-119, AN/ALQ-131, or Raytheon AN/ALQ-184 active jammer pods can also be carried on wing pylons.

The main landing struts retract forward into "knees" located at the dihedral break of the wing leading edges. The wheels are partially exposed when retracted. The nose gear is offset to port to provide clearance for the 30-mm cannon barrel; it retracts forward under the cockpit.

The cockpit is enclosed by a single-piece canopy that is hinged at the rear. Avionics include a Kaiser Head-Up Display (HUD) with a MIL-STD-1553 multiplex digital databus system, a Litton LN-39 Inertial Navigation System (INS), and the Martin Marietta AN/AAS-35(V) Pave Penny day/night laser tracker. The Pave Penny is mounted on a small pylon attached to the port side of the fuselage below the cockpit.

For the A-10's offensive ground-attack capability, a General Electric GAU-8/A Avenger 7-barrel 30-mm Gatling gun is mounted in the forward fuselage. The installation, including the 1,174-round ammunition drum, is 19 ft 10 in (6.05 m) long and weighs 4,029 lb (1,829 kg). The cannon has a maximum rate of fire of 70 1.5-lb (0.68-kg) rounds per second.

Fuselage weapons stations include three side-by-side ventral hardpoints. Either the outer two, each with a 3,500-lb (1,588-kg) capacity, or the centerline 5,000-lb (2,268-kg) capacity hardpoint can be used, but not all three simultaneously. The center-section wing pylons have a 3,500-lb (1,588-kg) capacity. Outboard of the landing gear on each wing are three pylons, the inner one capable of a 2,500-lb (1,134-kg) load, the middle one 1,200 lb (544 kg), and the outer pylon 1,000 lb (454 kg).

The maximum weapons load of 16,000 lb (7,258 kg) can include AGM-65 Maverick TV- or IR-guided air-to-ground missiles, conventional and laser-guided bombs, rocket pods, gun pods, submunitions dispensers, AIM-9 Sidewinder Air-to-Air Missiles (AAM), and fuel tanks.

DEVELOPMENT • The A-10's official name was originally Thunderbolt II in honor of Republic's P-47 fighter-bomber of World War II; the "II" was later dropped. Pilots and ground crew more commonly refer to the A-10 as the Warthog or Hog; the latter nickname has been applied to most Republic Aviation aircraft since World War II. The Warthog's initial operational capability was in 1977, and its first flight was on May 10, 1972. Production ended in 1984 after 707 aircraft, and six preproduction aircraft, were delivered. The A-10 has served for the Air National Guard in addition to the active US Air Force. Thailand announced plans to purchase 25 A-10s in the early 1990s.

The FY1991 Defense Authorization bill required that A-10s replace US Army OV-1 Mohawks and US Marine Corps OV-10 Broncos over a five-year period.

VARIANTS • A-10A, A-10 NAW (Night/Adverse Weather), A-10 upgrades: Low Altitude Safety and Target Enhancement (LASTE) program, Close-Air Support/Battlefield Air Interdiction (CAS/BAI) program, OA-10.

COMBAT EXPERIENCE • The A-10 participated with distinction in Operation Desert Storm, attacking tactical and theater targets in Iraq and Kuwait. Before the ground war began on February 24, Warthogs attacked a variety of targets including Scud mobile ballistic missile launchers, radar sites, and surface-to-air missile positions. When preparation for the ground war began, most A-10 sorties were directed against Iraqi armored and unarmored vehicles. In all, A-10s flew approximately 8,100 sorties.

Limitations imposed by the lack of a radar or FLIR were overcome by using the AGM-65D Maverick's IR seeker to search for targets. The 30-mm cannon proved effective against a variety of targets, including two helicopters shot down over Kuwait. Accounts credited pairs of A-10s with destroying 20 or more tanks in a single day. Altogether, Warthogs were credited with over 1,000 tanks, 2,000 military vehicles, and 1,200 artillery pieces destroyed.

Five A-10s were shot down during the seven-week war.

SPECIFICATIONS •
MANUFACTURER   Fairchild-Republic
CREW   1
ENGINES   2 General Electric TF34-GE-100 turbofan
max power   9,065 lb (4,112 kg) static thrust each
WEIGHTS
empty   21,519 lb (9,761 kg)

forward airstrip weight, armed and fueled
33,412 lb (15,155 kg)
max takeoff   50,000 lb (22,680 kg)
DIMENSIONS
wingspan   57 ft 6 in (17.53 m)
length   53 ft 4 in (16.26 m)
height   14 ft 8 in (4.47 m)
wing area   506 ft² (47 m²)
PERFORMANCE
max speed   367 kts (423 mph; 681 km/h)
cruise   300 kts (345 mph; 555 km/h)
climb rate   6,000 ft/min (1,829 m/min)
radius   with 9,000-lb (4,309-kg) weapons load, 1.8-hr loiter: 250 nm (288 mi; 463 km)
single-store deep strike penetration: 540 nm (622 mi; 1,000 km)
FERRY RANGE   2,209 nm (2,542 mi; 4,091 km)
ARMAMENT
1 GAU-8/A 30-mm multibarrel gun in fuselage w/1,174 rounds
18 Mk 82 500-lb (227-kg) *or* 6 Mk 84 2,000-lb (907-kg) bombs
or 6 AGM-65 Maverick air-to-surface missiles
or 18 Rockeye II cluster bombs
or 6 500-lb (227-kg) *or* 4 2,000-lb (907-kg) laser-guided bombs

BOMBERS

F-111/FB-111

The FB-111 was the strategic/theater bomber version of the US F-111 multipurpose aircraft. Both are described here. The FB-111 design differs from the tactical strike aircraft variants by having different engines, a 3½-ft (1.07-m) extension on each wingtip, strengthened landing gear and fuselage, greater fuel capacity, and improved avionics.

In the basic F-111 design, the pivot points for the variable-sweep, shoulder-mounted wings are located relatively close to the fuselage inside fixed wing "gloves"; the gloves extend forward to the rear of the cockpit and give the plane a "hooded cobra" look. Although the close-set pivots complicated design and required a titanium wing carry-through structure, they also result in a low minimum sweep angle of 16° and a high maximum sweep angle of 72½°; such a wide range results in an aircraft with relatively low takeoff, landing, and stall speeds as well as supersonic, low-altitude penetration flight.

High lift surfaces line the full span of the leading and trailing edges of the wing; the trailing-edge flaps are double-slotted. Roll control is achieved through spoilers and large, all-moving swept tail-planes that move differentially for roll, collectively for pitch. The broad-chord, swept fin has a full-height rudder.

The two TF-30-P-7 twin-spool turbofan engines are buried in the aft fuselage and fed by variable-area intakes that are fitted with boundary-layer splitter plates and located on the fuselage flanks under the leading edge of the fixed wing gloves. The engines are fitted with variable-area noz-zles with blow-in door ejector. Fuel tanks occupy much of the fuselage ahead and behind the wing carry-through structure as well as most of each wing. All F/FB-111s have in-flight refueling capability.

The fuselage is broad enough to accommodate a side-by-side cockpit for the pilot and navigator. The aircraft's maximum design load factor at design weight is 3 g.

The cockpit is protected by individual canopies over each seat; these are hinged on a common centerline rail and, when open at the same time, have a gull-wing appearance. The cockpit and glazing are combined in an escape pod that is ejected by a single rocket; the crew remains with the pod while it parachutes to earth.

The F/FB-111's high wing-loading and low aspect ratio at full aft sweep makes the aircraft relatively insensitive to low-level turbulence, which extends its low-altitude, terrain-following flight endurance. In low-level flight, the primary avionics unit is the Texas Instruments AN/APQ-117 Terrain-Following Radar

F-111
U.S. GOVERNMENT DEPARTMENT OF DEFENSE

(TFR) fitted in the nose radome. Other avionics include the General Electric AN/APQ-117 attack radar (upgraded to the AN/APQ-169), General Dynamics AN/AYK-6 digital computer, AN/AYN-3 Horizontal Situation Display, AN/ASG-25 optical display sight, AN/AJN-16 inertial bomb navigation system, AN/APN-167 radar altimeter, and AN/APN-185 Doppler radar.

The comprehensive Electronic Support Measures/Electronic Countermeasures (ESM/ECM) suite includes a Cincinnati Electric AN/AAR-34 Infrared (IR) warning receiver, Loral AN/ALR-41 homing receiver, Dalmo Victor AN/APS-109B Radar Homing and Warning System (RHAWS), Sanders AN/ALQ-94 or AN/ALQ-137 internal noise/deception jammer, and an AN/ALE-28 countermeasures dispenser.

The internal weapons bay is located between the nose and main gear bays and has a volume of 126 ft³ (3.57 m³). The bay carries either two nuclear bombs or two AGM-69 nuclear Short-Range Attack Missiles (SRAM). Of the six external weapons pylons, the center and inboard pylons under each wing swivel with the wing sweep. The outermost pylon on each wing is fixed so that it creates the least drag at a 26° sweep angle; these pylons are used for fuel tanks and are jettisoned with the tanks when the latter are empty. The other four pylons carry SRAMs, nuclear bombs, conventional 750-lb (340-kg) bombs, cluster bombs, or 600-US gal (2,271-liter) drop tanks.

DEVELOPMENT •
The FB-111's initial operational capability was in October 1969, and its first flight was in July 1967. While in production from 1968 to 1971, 76 were built. The last was retired on July 10, 1991. 22 FB-111s, designated FB-111Gs, were converted to trainers beginning in June 1990 and would be retired by early 1994 at the latest.

An unofficial US Air Force nickname for the F/FB-111 is the Aardvark, refer-ring to the long nose. The FB-111 saw service only with the USAF and is no longer in operation; the F-111 is in service with Australia.

VARIANTS •
FB-111A, FB-111G, FB-111H (upgraded engines, stretched fuselage), F-111G.

COMBAT EXPERIENCE •
First combat use of the US Air Force F-111 aircraft came in 1972–1973 with limited results and relatively heavy losses during raids into North Vietnam.

Twelve England-based F-111Fs aircraft attacked Libyan targets at night on April 15, 1986. (Five more developed problems that forced them to turn back.) One was lost with its two-man crew. Each F-111 required three in-flight refuellings enroute to the target and two more on the return flight.

On January 17, 1991, the 38 F-111Fs deployed in the region attacked Iraqi targets as part of the air assault that began Operation Desert Storm. Together with the F-117 Stealth "Fighter" and the F-15E Eagle, the F-111Fs were responsible for many of the precision-bombing strikes using laser-guided bombs that dislocated the Iraqi air-defense system. F-111Fs also attacked Scud fixed and mobile ballistic missile sites, as well as delivering LGBs against 1,500 armored vehicles (known as "tank plinking"). No F-111s were lost in the seven-week campaign.

SPECIFICATIONS (FB-111) •
MANUFACTURER General Dynamics
CREW 2 (pilot, navigator)
ENGINES 2 Pratt & Whitney TF30-P-7 turbofan
  max power with afterburner: 20,350 lb (9,231 kg) st (static thrust) each
    intermediate without afterburner: 12,350 lb (5,602 kg) st each
    max fuel capacity: 5,623 US gal (19,088 liters)

WEIGHTS

empty	47,481 lb (21,537 kg)
combat	70,380 lb (31,924 kg)
design	110,646 lb (50,188 kg)
max takeoff	119,243 lb (54,088 kg)

DIMENSIONS

wingspan 70 ft (21.34 m) extended,
33 ft 11 in (10.34 m)
swept

length 75 ft 6½ in (23.03 m)

height 17 ft 1 in (5.22 m)

wing area 550 ft² (51.11 m²)

PERFORMANCE

max speed at high altitude
1,262 kts (1,453 mph;
2,338 km/h) or Mach
2.2

basic speed at 35,000 ft (10,668 m)
1,188 kts (1,368 mph;
2,201 km/h) or Mach
2.05

max combat speed at sea level
728 kts (838 mph; 1,349
km/h) or Mach 1.1

max dash speed, high altitude
1,147 kts (1,321 mph;
2,125 km/h) or
Mach 2

max dash speed, low-level
562 kts (647 mph; 1,041
km/h) or Mach 0.85

range cruise
444 kts (511 mph; 823
km/h)

max rate of climb, with external weapons
stores
22,870 ft/min (6,971
m/min)

ceiling at combat weight
50,263 ft (15,320 m)

armament internal weapons bay with
2 B43/B61/B83
nuclear bombs
and 6 wing pylons for up
to 31,500 lb (14,288
kg) weapons load
including:
4 SRAMs
or 24 750-lb (340-kg)
M117 bombs

radar AN/APQ-134 or -171
TFR
AN/APQ-114 or -169
attack

SPECIFICATIONS (F-111) •

MANUFACTURER General Dynamics

CREW 2 (pilot, navigator)

ENGINES

F-111A: 2 Pratt & Whitney TF30-P-3
turbofan
F-111F: 2 Pratt & Whitney TF30-P-100
turbofan

max power with afterburner
F-111A 18,500 lb (8,391
kg) st each
F-111F 25,100 lb (11,385
kg) st each

max fuel capacity
5,043 US gal (19,088 liters)

WEIGHTS

empty F-111A: 46,172 lb (20,943
kg)
F-111F: 47,481 lb (21,537
kg)

combat weight
F-111A: 64,728 lb (29,360 kg)
F-111F: 63,048 lb (28,598 kg)

typical takeoff
F-111A: 82,819 lb (37,566 kg)
F-111F: 85,589 lb (38,823 kg)

max takeoff F-111A: 98,850 lb (44,838
kg)
F-111F: 100,000 lb
(45,360 kg)

DIMENSIONS

wingspan 63 ft (19.2 m) extended,
31 ft 11 in (9.74 m)
swept

length 73 ft 6 in (22.4 m)

height 17 ft 1 in (5.22 m)

wing area 525 ft² (48.77 m²)

PERFORMANCE

max speed at high altitude
F-111A: 1,262 kts (1,453
mph; 2,338 km/h) or
Mach 2.2
F-111F: 1,436 kts (1,653
mph; 2,660 km/h) or
Mach 2.5

basic speed at 35,000 ft (10,668 m)
        1,196 kts (1,377 mph;
        2,216 km/h) or Mach
        2.1
max combat speed at sea level
        794 kts (914 mph; 1,471
        km/h) or Mach 1.2
range cruise
        444 kts (511 mph; 823
        km/h)
max rate of climb with external weapons stores
        F-111A: 26,600 ft/min
        (8,108 m/min)
        F-111F: 43,050 ft/min
        (13,122 m/min)
ceiling at combat weight
        F-111A: 55,300 ft (16,855
        m)
        F-111F: 57,100 ft (17,404
        m)
radius   F-111A, hi-lo-lo-lo-hi at
        combat weight with 12
        750-lb (340-kg) bombs:
        681 nm (784 mi; 1,262
        km)
        F-111F, hi-lo-hi at com-
        bat weight with 24
        750-lb (340-kg) bombs:
        440 nm (507 mi; 815
        km)
range with 4 600-US gal (2,271-liter) drop tanks
        F-111A: 3,156 nm (3,634
        mi; 5,848 km)
        F-111F: 2,934 nm (3,379
        mi; 5,437 km)
armament   internal weapons bay for
        1 M61A1 20-mm gun
        (2,050 rounds)
        and 1 B43 nuclear bomb
        or 2 B43/61/83 nuclear
        bombs
        and 4 wing pylons for
        31,500-lb (14,288-kg)
        weapons load
        or 4 AIM-9 Sidewinder
        AAM
        or 4 600-US gal (2,271-
        liter) drop tanks

Lancer (B-1)

The B-1 is the long-range strategic bomber designed originally for low-altitude penetration missions against mobile ICBMs or standoff Air-Launched Cruise Missile (ALCM) attacks. 100 were procured in the early 1980s as a "bridge" in capability between the aging B-52 Stratofortress and the planned B-2 Advanced Technology Bomber (ATB or "Stealth").

The B-1B features variable-geometry wings mounted at midfuselage. The wing pivot is located relatively close to the fuselage, which yields a large change in wing aspect ratio from its minimum sweep angle of 15° to the maximum sweep angle of 67½°. As with several other "swing-wing" aircraft designs, the pivots and wing carry-through structure are titanium. The outer panels are of more conventional aluminum-alloy construction.

In addition to the low-sweep angle, takeoff and landing performance is aided by leading- and trailing-edge lift devices. Each leading edge has full-span slats in seven sections that droop 20° for takeoff. Each trailing edge is fitted with six single-slotted flap sections with a maximum down flap setting of 40°. Roll control is provided by four sections of spoilers on each wing; there are no ailerons.

The vertical tail is a relatively upright surface made of titanium and aluminum alloy. The three-section rudder is inset into the trailing edge with the lowest section set below the tailplane. Large, swept tailplanes are mounted on a common spindle that passes through the fin at a reinforced station approximately one-third up the fin. The tailplanes can be used differentially to aid roll control as well as collectively for pitch control.

Four independent 4,000-psi (276-bar) hydraulic systems power the flight controls, flaps, landing-gear actuation, landing-gear doors, and weapons-bay doors. A quadruplex Automatic Flight Control System (AFCS) is fitted. Ride control at low altitudes is provided by the Structural Mode Control Subsystem (SMCS) that uses accelerometers to dampen the rough ride at low altitude. Two small, swept vanes are fitted at 30° anhedral in the lower fuselage just ahead of the cockpit; these work in conjunction with the lowest rudder section under command of the SMCS.

The B-1B initially had little inherent stall warning, and its terrain-following performance had deteriorated due to the substantially higher gross weights compared to the B-1A. A Stall Inhibitor System (SIS-1) was fitted to the first 18 aircraft to force the pilot to "fail-safe" by limiting his control system power near the B-1B's Angle of Attack (AoA) limits.

A later SIS-2 is a backup to the triple-redundant Stability Enhancement Function (SEF), which is designed to expand the AoA limits and permit Mach 0.95 speeds at max gross weight from sea level to about 6,000 ft (1,829 m) while retaining an adequate margin of controllability. In addition to reducing the necessary stall warning margin from 20% to 5% above aerodynamic stall, the SEF system has permitted successful automatic terrain-following flights at 200 ft (61 m) in a "hard-ride," hands-off mode. All B-1Bs were retrofitted with the SIS-2/SEF system, with fully equipped B-1Bs entering squadron service between January and April 1990.

Four General Electric turbofans are housed in pairs in nacelles under the wings. They are fed through fixed-geometry intakes that limit maximum speed to approximately Mach 1.25. Problems with the engine's first-stage compressor fan led to the Air Force's cessation of all B-1 routine training flights in December 1990 until the source of the failures could be found.

Internal fuel tankage is located in the fuselage midbody and in the outer wings.

The in-flight refueling receptacle is fitted ahead of the cockpit.

The fuselage has a blended wing-body union similar to that of the F-16 Fighting Falcon. The B-1B's Radar Cross Section (RCS) that gives the plane its "stealthiness" is approximately ½ that of the FB-111A, ⅒ of the B-1A, and ¹⁄₁₀₀ of the B-52. The small RCS is achieved through shaping and Radar-Absorbent Materials (RAM) used at many points on the airframe.

Although much of the structure is aluminum alloy, titanium is used where high heat is generated (firewalls, engine bays) or high stress is expected (tail, rear fuselage skinning). The main landing gear was strengthened to accept the B-1B's higher gross weights; the two four-wheel bogies retract into the fuselage between the engine nacelles. The nose gear retracts forward.

The pressurized flight deck provides for two pilots and two weapons systems officers, each seated in his own Weber ACES II ejection seat. The pilots use control sticks rather than wheels and have the engine throttles on consoles to the left of each seat, which is said to enhance the aircraft's fighterlike feel. Instrument displays include vertical tape displays and Sperry Multifunction Displays (MFD).

Avionics are grouped under two main systems: the Boeing Offensive Avionics System (OAS) and Eaton-AIL AN/ALQ-161 Electronic Countermeasures (ECM) suite; together the two suites account for over 197 Line Replaceable Units (LRU) weighing more than 10,000 lb (4,536 kg). The main systems computers are linked through a MIL-STD-1553 databus.

The Westinghouse AN/APQ-164 dual-channel, multimode Offensive Radar System (ORS) is based on the F-16's APG-66 and is located in the nose. Additional OAS avionics include dual Honeywell AN/APN-224 radar altimeter systems, the Teledyne Ryan AN/APN-218 Doppler velocity sensor, and three Sperry

MFDs, two for the offensive-weapons officer and one for the defensive-weapons officer. The Air Force plans to fit a Forward-Looking Infrared (FLIR) sensor.

The AN/ALQ-161 detects, classifies, and analyzes enemy emitters and develops passive and active responses to them. Three sets of phased-array antennas are fitted in the wing leading edges and the tail for high-frequency coverage while other antennas are distributed at several points of the fuselage. The ALQ-161 has suffered significant problems and has frequency gaps in its passive coverage. In January 1989, the Loral AN/ALR-56M radar-warning system was selected to fill in those gaps.

Internal weapons are carried in weapons bays ahead and behind the wing carry-through structure. The 31-ft 3-in (9.53-m), two-section forward bay has a movable bulkhead that allows stowage of eight extended-range AGM-86B Air-Launched Cruise Missiles (ALCM) on a Common Strategic Rotary Launcher (CSRL). The bays can also hold nuclear gravity bombs.

When converted to the conventional role, a special bomb-handling module is inserted into each bay. As a result, up to 84 Mk 82 500-pound conventional bombs can be carried. The Air Force would also like to carry CBU-87, CBU-89, and CBU-97 cluster munitions dispensers as well as Mk 56, Mk 62, and Mk 65 unguided weapons. Eight external-stores stations under the fuselage can hold additional weapons such as the Paveway Laser-Guided Bomb (LGB) series, the AGM-137 Tri-Service Standoff Missile (TSSAM), and possibly the AIM-120 AM-RAAM air-to-air missile. Up to 24 GBU-10 2,000-lb (907-kg) LGBs can be carried at once.

DEVELOPMENT • The B-1B's initial operational capability was on October 1, 1986. The aircraft's first flight was a B-1A on December 23, 1974; the B-1B first flew on March 23, 1983. Four B-1A prototypes were built in the mid-1970s and used for test and evaluation.

The Air Force had originally proposed a force of 244 B-1s to replace the entire B-52 force. Production was approved on December 2, 1976, but the Carter administration entered office a month later, and in June 1977, the entire program was canceled in favor of the development of the Air-Launched Cruise Missile (ALCM) and modernization of the B-52 force as an alternative.

The manned bomber became an issue in the 1980 presidential campaign. In August 1980, to help justify the decision to cancel the B-1, then Secretary of Defense Harold Brown announced that the US was in fact developing a new bomber in secret, the "Stealth" aircraft (later called the B-2 Advanced Technology Bomber or ATB). The Reagan administration, which took office in January 1981, gave immediate support to the B-1 program (reportedly based on successful test flights that demonstrated the upgraded bomber's stealthier qualities), and gained congressional funding.

100 B-1Bs were acquired by the US Air Force, funded as follows:

FISCAL YEAR	AIRCRAFT
1982	1
1983	7
1984	10
1985	34
1986	48

A crash in September 1987 and two crashes in November 1988 reduced the number in service to 97. The last aircraft was delivered on April 30, 1988.

The name Lancer was officially adopted in 1990 after permission had been granted from Fairchild Republic to use the nickname, which in 1941 was assigned to the P-43 fighter, an underpowered predecessor of the Republic P-47 Thunderbolt. Air Force personnel reportedly never refer to the B-1 as the

Lancer, choosing instead to call it the Bone ("B-One").

As part of the overall reduction in active US nuclear weapons, President George Bush announced that all US strategic bombers were taken off 24-hour strip alert and their nuclear weapons put in storage.

A B-1B unofficially set several flight records in early July 1987. While carrying 33 tons of water as ballast, the aircraft averaged 676.48 mph on a 620-mile (1,000-km) course, and 669.52 mph on a 1,240-mile (2,000-km) circuit. The previous records for that weight/speed/distance were set, respectively, in 1959 by a Soviet bomber and in 1962 by a US Air Force C-135 transport. The B-1 set 12 time-to-climb records in three weight classes on February 29, 1992

VARIANTS • B-1A, B-1B.

COMBAT EXPERIENCE • During the deployment of US weapons for Operation Desert Storm in February 1991, the potential role of the B-1 was debated, but the aircraft was held out of the conflict. The Air Force gave two official reasons for the B-1 not being used: because there were not enough available to significantly contribute to the effort without degrading strategic deterrence and because the B-1 simply wasn't operationally prepared to deploy with conventional arms.

SPECIFICATIONS •
MANUFACTURER   Rockwell International
CREW   4 (2 pilots, 2 systems operators)
ENGINES   4 General Electric F101-GE-F102 turbofan
max power   30,000 lb (13,620 kg) static thrust each
fuel capacity   196,600 lb (89,176 kg)
with bay tank   214,000 lb (97,069 kg)
WEIGHTS
empty   192,000 lb (87,090 kg)

max internal weapons load   75,000 lb (34,019 kg)
max external weapons load   59,000 lb (26,762 kg)
max takeoff   477,000 lb (216,365 kg)
DIMENSIONS
wingspan   extended: 136 ft 8½ in (41.67 m) (15° sweep) 67.5° sweep: 78 ft 2½ in (23.84 m)
length   147 ft (44.81 m)
height   34 ft (10.36 m)
wing area   1,950 ft² (181.2 m²)
PERFORMANCE
max speed   at altitude: 717 kts (826 mph; 1,329 km/h) or Mach 1.25
at 500 ft (152 m): 660 kts (760 mph; 1,223 km/h) or Mach 0.99
cruise speed   at low altitude: 550 kts (633 mph; 1,019 km/h) or Mach 0.83
ceiling   60,000 ft (18,300 m)
combat radius   1,100 nm (1,267 mi; 2,037 km)
range   max at high altitude: 5,600 nm (6,449 mi; 10,377 km)
low altitude with 8 SRAM and 8 B-61 bombs: 1,500 nm (1,727 mi; 2,780 km)
armament   2 internal weapons bays for up to 42,000 lb of ordnance, such as:
84 Mk 82 500-lb bombs
or 24 Mk 84 2,000-lb bombs
or 12 B28 free-fall nuclear bombs
or 24 B61/B83 free-fall nuclear bombs
or 24 Short-Range Attack Missiles (SRAM)
or 8 Air-Launched Cruise Missiles (ALCM) *and* 8 hardpoints under

fuselage for 14 ALCM or SRAM *or* 8 B28 *or* 14 B43/B61/B83 nuclear or Mk 84 conventional bombs *or* 44 Mk 82

radar   AN/APQ-164 forward-looking

Stealth (B-2)

The Advanced Technology Bomber (ATB) is popularly called the Stealth bomber but its official name is "Spirit." Although not operational, this controversial batlike aircraft has flown test missions. The combination of its performance problems, the end of the cold war with the collapse of the Soviet Union, and the high cost of the plane may preclude the B-2 from joining the active US Air Force.

The B-2 was designed to complement the B-1B. It is designed to present the lowest possible visual, radar, acoustic, and infrared signatures. Its original mission was to attack mobile ICBMs and hardened command-and-control installations. After the loss of a structured nuclear threat, the aircraft's mission was redefined to emphasize long-range conventional strike missions.

The B-2 achieves "invisibility" to radar and infrared sensors for as long as possible by reducing the aircraft's Radar Cross Section (RCS) and decreasing engine exhaust gas temperatures; it also is claimed to be 50% more aerodynamically efficient than the B-1.

The B-2's general design resembles earlier Northrop flying wings (the YB-35 and YB-49 of the 1940s), a configuration that has the smallest head-on and side-view RCS. A further reduction in RCS is attained by using surface skins made of a composite, ferrite-based carbon-fiber honeycomb Radar Absorbent Structure

(RAS) over titanium main structural members.

The wing carry-through section was modified in 1984 from single front and rear spars to narrow torque boxes to enable the aircraft to better withstand low-level flight and to reduce the wing's weight. The wing is quite rigid, showing only 1/12th the deflection that the B-52 shows at high load.

The wing's leading edges are swept at approximately 40° to tips that are raked back toward the centerline to decrease the flying wing's tendency to yaw while rolling. The wing's sawtooth trailing edge is unique, designed to cope with a flying wing's natural instability even as it helps to reduce RCS and exhaust heat signature.

At approximately midspan (moving toward the fuselage), the trailing edges turn and head aft to a point just outboard of the engine installations on each side. The two control surfaces are elevons that can also be used as flaps. At this point, the trailing edges again turn almost 90°, heading forward to a point directly aft of the center of the unusual engine exhausts. Finally, the two halves of the flying wing's trailing edge turn aft and meet in a movable fuselage "beavertail," which operates with the elevons for gust alleviation. The hydraulic actuators are the fast-action type and are supported by a 4,000-psi (281.2-kg/cm²) system.

When seen from ahead, the fuselage is thickest through the center, with the cross section tapering out to the outer panels. Over the center section are two low engine intakes, one on each side of a shallow, rounded cockpit section that has large window panels. The windshield is designed to be a load-bearing structure and has an integral metal mesh designed to prevent strong returns from the glazing or emission leakage from flight deck instruments or systems.

The two four-wheel, main-landing-gear bogies retract inward while the wheels are stowed close to the centerline. The two-wheel nose gear retracts to the rear. The aircraft is able to use any runway that will support a Boeing 727 jet transport.

Each engine intake feeds two of the four GE nonafterburning turbofan engines that are in the wing. Each engine intake has two rear-hinged auxiliary inlet doors that face forward and are angled off the centerline. These doors are open at low speeds to provide sufficient airflow to the engines.

In October 1990, Northrop was contracted to convert the B-2's fuel system from JP-4 fuel, which requires pressurization, to JP-8, which has a higher flash point.

The two-man cockpit has control sticks linked to a computer-controlled, quadruple-redundant Stability Augmentation System (SAS) produced by General Electric. Honeywell is developing the Radar Altimeter Set (RAS) and GEC Avionics (formerly Kearfott) is responsible for the advanced Inertial Navigation System (INS). The aircraft has two flat-plate antennas for the Hughes AN/APQ-181 multimode phased-array radar. Multifunction Displays (MFD) provide instrumentation, navigation, and attack information.

Nuclear weapons such as gravity bombs and Short-Range Attack Missiles (SRAM) are carried in side-by-side internal weapons bays. Up to 16 B83 gravity bombs, AGM-69A SRAM or AGM-131 SRAM II cruise missiles, or 20 smaller nuclear weapons could be stowed; alternative loads include up to 80 conventional 500-lb (227-kg) bombs or sea mines.

DEVELOPMENT • The B-2 is under development. First flight had originally been planned for late 1987, but a $1-billion design modification to permit low-level flight delayed the program. After high- and low-speed taxi tests, the first flight took place on July 17, 1989, at Edwards AFB, California. First flight of the second aircraft came on October 19, 1990; this aircraft (AV-2) is the only one of the six test aircraft not to be refitted as an operational bomber.

The planned total number of aircraft has been reduced first from 132 to 75 aircraft and then to 20. The initial operational capability is currently planned for the mid-1990s. When the 20 B-2 bombers are properly equipped near the turn of the century, they could drop 160 tons of bombs a day in a war area, compared to the 146 tons/day dropped by 20 B-52 bombers in Operations Desert Shield/Desert Storm.

SPECIFICATIONS •
MANUFACTURER
Northrop Grumman
Vought (former LTV) (subcontractor)
Boeing Advanced Systems (subcontractor)
CREW 2 (pilot, weapons systems officer)
ENGINES 4 General Electric F118-GE-100 turbofan
max power 19,000 lb (8,618 kg) static thrust each
WEIGHTS
empty weight approx 158,000 lb (71,668 kg)
max takeoff 240,000–376,000 lb (108,862–170,551 kg)
max payload 50,000 lb (22,680 kg) internal
DIMENSIONS
wingspan 172 ft (52.42 m)
length 69 ft (21.03 m)
height 17 ft (5.18 m)
wing area more than 5,000 ft² (464.5 m²)
PERFORMANCE
speed Mach 0.85
operational ceiling
approx 50,000 ft (15,240 m) with weapons load
range (w/weapons)
high altitude: 6,600 nm (7,600 mi; 12,230 km)
hi-lo-hi: 4,500 nm (5,182 mi; 8,339 km)

hi-lo-hi (optimized):
5,400 nm (6,218 mi;
10,006 km)

armament   2 internal weapons bays
for up to:
16 B83 gravity bombs,
AGM-69A SRAM or
AGM-131 SRAM II
cruise missiles
or 20 smaller nuclear
weapons (e.g., B61
gravity bombs)
or up to 80 500-lb (227-
kg) bombs or sea
mines

radar   Hughes APQ-181
multimode

Stratofortress (B-52)

The B-52 strategic bomber celebrated its 40th anniversary in 1992 and is still operational. Its mission has been altered several times since its inception, to adjust to US military operational requirements. B-52s were used in the conventional bombing role in the Vietnam War and some are now dedicated to conventional strike missions.

The B-52 is a multiengine, long-range aircraft capable of both conventional free-fall bomb delivery and air-to-ground missile launch missions. The B-52 carried the largest nuclear payload of any US strategic platform.

The B-52 has long shoulder wings swept at 36° and has a relatively high aspect ratio of 8.5; the wings flex considerably during flight. Each wing has two engine pods spaced equidistantly along its leading edge; each pod carries two engines (all have turbojets but the B-52H, which has turbofans). Retractable outrigger wheels and fuel tank pods are outboard of the engines.

Contemporary B-52s have a 40-ft (12.20-m) tall fin and full-height rudder with squared-off tops; earlier B-52s had a taller, pointed fin. The relatively large, low-aspect-ratio horizontal stabilizers are

mounted midfuselage, directly below the tailfin.

In addition to the extensive internal fuel tankage, two 700-US gal (2,650-liter) drop tanks are usually carried on dedicated pylons outboard of the outer pair of engines.

The fuselage is long, slab-sided, and capacious. The flight deck is well forward, behind a stepped windshield and blunt nose. The two main gear legs are arranged side by side, ahead and behind the weapons bay. The wheels can be "crabbed" into a crosswind, which is a compensation for the aircraft's inability to drop a wing during a crosswind landing due to its great span. Operational aircraft have undergone extensive offensive avionics and electronic warfare updates as well as improvements to basic systems. In 1969, the G and H models were fitted with a Stability Augmentation System (SAS) to improve low-altitude ride and extend airframe life.

264 B-52G and B-52H aircraft were refitted with the digital, solid-state Offensive Avionics System (OAS) from 1980 to 1986. Two IBM navigational/attack computers coordinate the IBM/ Raytheon AN/ASQ-38 analog bombing and navigational equipment, Teledyne Ryan AN/APN-218 Common Strategic Doppler navigation system, Honeywell AN/ASN-131 precision inertial navigation system and AN/APN-224 radar altimeter, and Lear-Siegler Model 6000 series attitude/heading reference system.

As part of the OAS program, the strategic radar has been reworked by Norden, incorporating solid-state, digital components to greatly improve reliability and to enhance the radar's ground-mapping and terrain-avoidance capability. The B-52G and B-52H are also fitted with a chin-mounted Electro-Optical Viewing System (EVS), which consists of a Westinghouse AN/AVQ-22 Low-Light-Level TV (LLLTV) and a Hughes AN/AAQ-6 Forward-Looking

B-52
U.S. GOVERNMENT DEPARTMENT OF DEFENSE

Infrared (FLIR) system. B-52Gs were being fitted with a Global Positioning System (GPS) to improve accuracy in long-range strike missions.

Defensive avionics currently include the Northrop AN/ALQ-155 EW power management system, Motorola AN/ALQ-122 Smart Noise Operation Equipment (SNOE) false target generator, Dalmo Victor ALR-46 digital radar-warning receiver, Westinghouse AN/ALQ-153 tail-warning system, and ITT AN/ALQ-117 tail-mounted deception jammer for use against radar-guided missiles. B-52Hs are fitted with ALQ-172(V)2 with phased-array antennas.

The weapons payload can be carried in internal weapons bays and on wing pylons located between the inboard pair of engines and the fuselage. 98 B-52Gs carry 12 Air-Launched Cruise Missiles (ALCM) on pylons. 69 non-ALCM B-52Gs are being fitted with the Integrated Conventional Stores Management System (ICSMS), a software upgrade that permits weapons computers to target and launch both nuclear and conventional weapons.

The B-52H has been fitted with the Common Strategic Rotary Launcher (CSRL) in the weapons bay that will carry free-fall nuclear weapons, Short-Range Attack Missiles (SRAM), and ALCMs.

Operational models have an in-flight refueling capability. A remote-control tail turret is fitted, controlled by the AN/ASG-15 radar gunsight, and is the only gun armament the B-52 has ever carried.

DEVELOPMENT • Initial operational capability was in June 1955, and the first flight (the YB-52) was on April 15, 1952. 744 aircraft were produced through October 1962. On September 28, 1991, as part of an overall reduction in active US nuclear weapons announced by President Bush, all US strategic bombers were removed from 24-hour strip alert and their nuclear weapons were put in storage. Airframe aging is a problem with some B-52s, since some airframes have been in service for over 30 years. Modernization programs have helped keep the B-52 in operation well into the 1990s. The US Air Force has been the only operator of the B-52.

VARIANTS • XB-52 (prototype), YB-52, B-52A, NB-52A (NASA), B-52B, B-52C/D (production versions, first flight in 1956), B-52E, B-52F, B-52G, B-52H.

COMBAT EXPERIENCE • B-52 aircraft were used for conventional high-altitude bombing operations in the Vietnam War.

The first aircraft to take off on missions supporting Operation Desert Storm's air assaults on January 17, 1991, were seven B-52s from Barksdale AFB, Louisiana, that departed at 6:35 A.M. CST (1135 Greenwich), almost 12 hours before the first bombs fell. These aircraft carried AGM-86C ALCMs that had been secretly modified to carry conventional warheads and a guidance system based on the GPS.

Approximately 1½ hours after the attacks began, 35 ACLMs were launched against eight "high-priority" targets. What the Air Force later called the longest combat mission in aviation history took 35 hours, covered 14,000 nm (16,121 mi; 25,928 km), and required four refuelings and an augmented crew to complete. No other ALCMs were used during Desert Storm, and damage assessment was difficult to separate from other bomb damage. The mission was termed "successful."

Despite the bombers' age, few missions had to be aborted, and the mission-capable rate was over 81%, a 2% increase over peacetime operations.

Over 72,000 weapons were dropped, totaling more than 25,700 tons. This total was 29% of all US bomb tonnage delivered. A total of 60–70 B-52Gs were used against Iraq.

SPECIFICATIONS •
MANUFACTURER Boeing Military Airplane

CREW 6 (2 pilots, navigator, radar navigator, electronic warfare operator, gunner)
ENGINES
B-52G: 8 Pratt & Whitney J57-P-43W turbojet
B-52H: 8 Pratt & Whitney TF33-P-3/P-103 turbofan
max power J57: 13,750 lb (6,237 kg) static thrust each
TF33: 17,000 lb (7,718 kg) static thrust each
internal fuel capacity 46,000 US gal (174,130 liters)
WEIGHTS
empty 195,000 lb (88,450 kg)
max bomb load 60,000 lb (27,216 kg)
max long-range weapons load 43,500 lb (19,731 kg)
max takeoff 488,000 lb (221,350 kg)
max with in-flight refueling 566,000 lb (256,783 kg)
DIMENSIONS
wingspan 185 ft (56.39 m)
length 157 ft 7 in (48.03 m)
height 40 ft 8 in (12.4 m)
wing area 4,000 ft² (372 m²)
PERFORMANCE
max speed at altitude 516 kts (595 mph; 957 km/h) or Mach 0.90
cruise speed at altitude 442 kts (509 mph; 819 km/h) or Mach 0.77
penetration speed at low altitude 352–365 kts (405–420 mph; 652–676 km/h) or Mach 0.53–0.55
takeoff run 9,500 ft (2,895 m)
ceiling 55,000 ft (16,775 m)
range B-52G with 30,000-lb (13,608-kg) internal payload, no loiter: no refueling, approx 6,200 nm (7,139 mi; 11,482 km); 1 refueling, approx 7,800 nm (8,982 mi; 14,446 km)

armament

B-52H: 8,800 nm (10,133 mi; 16,306 km)
1 20-mm Vulcan M61A1 gun with 1,242 rounds in tail turret

max internal conventional bomb load consists of:
27 250/500/750-lb (113/227/340-kg)
or 8 2,000-lb (907-kg) bombs

external payloads:
24 250/500/750-lb (113/227/340-kg) bombs
or 10 2,000-lb (907-kg) bombs

nuclear weapons payload consists of:
up to 20 AGM-69A SRAM
or 12 AGM-86B ALCM
or 12 AGM-129 ACM
or 4 gravity nuclear bombs in weapons bay
and 12 SRAM or ALCM on wing pylons
(approx 70 B-52G are fitted with AGM-84 Harpoon antiship missiles)

radar

AN/ASQ-38 bombing/ navigation
AN/ASG-15 turret control system
AN/ALQ-172 Pave Mint ESM
AN/ALQ-153 pulse-Doppler tail-warning
AN/ALQ-155(V) ECM suite
AN/ALT-16 jammer
AN/ALE-29 chaff dispensers

CARGO

Galaxy (C-5)

The C-5 Galaxy is a strategic airlift transport and one of the largest aircraft in the world. It has a slightly longer fuselage than the Soviet An-124 Condor but has a 10% lower maximum payload compared to the Soviet aircraft.

The Galaxy was designed to operate from rough fields and has the requisite low stalling speed and extensive landing gear. However, size and weight limitations usually restrict the aircraft to improved airfields. The Galaxy has held several world records for payload and weight.

The C-5 has a shoulder-mounted wing. Corrosion and fatigue in the original C-5A wings considerably shortened their lifetimes and led to a rebuilding project in the mid-1980s.

The tall T-tail has a slightly swept fin ahead of a two-section, full-height rudder. The fin has a cross section thick enough to enclose a ladder used by aircrew to inspect and maintain the flying tail.

The immense fuselage has a pear-shaped cross section for most of its length. The nose comes to a blunt point and is hinged below and behind the flight deck, allowing it to swing up and over the flight deck like a visor and affording unobstructed access to the main cargo deck. The appearance of the "mouth" profile led to the C-5's informal nickname Jaws, after the cinematic great white shark. The upper deck has space forward for a relief crew.

C-5
U.S. GOVERNMENT DEPARTMENT OF DEFENSE

The 19-ft (5.79-m) wide rear ramp forms the bottom of the rear fuselage, which tapers up to meet the tail. The hinged side panels swing out for ground access but are not required to be open during airdrops. The four General Electric turbofans are mounted in nacelles that extend on pylons below and ahead of the leading edges of the wings.

The unusual landing gear has a total of 28 wheels. Four wheels are mounted side by side on the single nose-gear strut, which retracts to the rear. The other 24 wheels are carried on four six-wheel bogies in tandem sets left and right that retract into bulged fairings on the lower fuselage sides under the wing. The gear can "kneel" to lower the aircraft to put the cargo deck floor at truck-bed height.

DEVELOPMENT • The Galaxy's initial operational capability was in 1969; the first flight of the C-5A was on June 30, 1968, and the C-5B on September 10, 1985. The C-5A has been transferred to Air Force Reserve and Air National Guard units. By early 1990, the C-5 fleet had accumulated 1 million flight hours.

During its initial development, the C-5 experienced intense disputes over its costs. The original C-5A wings eventually were all replaced on operational aircraft.

In June 1989, a C-5B set an airdrop record at the International Airlift Rodeo 1989 by dropping four M551 Sheridan Armored Reconnaissance Vehicles and 73 paratroopers for a total delivery weight of 190,346 lb (86,340 kg).

VARIANTS • C-5A, C-5B, Pacer Snow, C-5A (Space Cargo Modification/SCM; capable of holding a Shuttle Container Transport System/SCTS and its tractor).

COMBAT EXPERIENCE • The C-5 first gained combat experience during the

Vietnam conflict. A Galaxy was the lead military aircraft in Operation Babylift, the 1975 airlift of orphans from Vietnam, when it crashed after takeoff, killing 138 people, including 78 orphans.

C-5s supported many other crises in which the US was tasked to transport personnel and cargo. In support of Operation Desert Shield, C-5s began moving equipment to Saudi Arabia in August 1990. A C-5A from the 60th Military Airlift Wing crashed on takeoff from Ramstein AFB in Germany on August 28, 1990. Of the crew of 17, 13 were killed and four injured.

From August 7, 1990, to April 2, 1991, C-5s flew more than 3,800 missions carrying 87,850 passengers and 230,600 tons of cargo to the theater of operations. Each C-5 carried on the average three times as much cargo per mission as the C-141. Their pilots were flying between 80 and 100 hours a month, more than twice the peacetime rate for active-duty airlift pilots and more than six times a reservist's average monthly total.

SPECIFICATIONS •
MANUFACTURER   Lockheed
CREW   5 (pilot, copilot, flight engineer, 2 loadmasters) + 75 troops on upper flight deck + 275 in main cargo bay
WEIGHTS
empty   374,000 lb (169,643 kg)
max payload 291,000 lb (131,995 kg)
max fuel   332,500 lb (150,815 kg)
max takeoff 837,000 lb (379,657 kg)
DIMENSIONS
wingspan   222 ft 8 in (67.88 m)
length   247 ft 10 in (75.54 m)
height   65 ft 2 in (19.85 m)
wing area   6,200 ft² (576 m²)
cargo hold length, lower deck
                   without ramp: 121 ft 1 in (36.91 m)
                   width: 19 ft (5.79 m)
                   height: 13 ft 6 in (4.11 m)
volume   upper deck, forward: 2,010 ft³ (56.91 m³)

upper deck, aft: 6,020 ft³ (170.46 m³)
lower deck: 34,795 ft³ (985.29 m³)
ENGINES   4 General Electric TF39-GE-1C turbofan
max power   43,000 lb (19,505 kg) static thrust
FUEL
internal capacity
                   51,150 US gal (193,624 liters)
SPEED
max speed   496 kts (571 mph; 919 km/h)
cruise speed
                   max: 480-490 kts (552-564 mph; 888-908 km/h)
                   econ: 450 kts (518 mph; 833 km/h)
                   flap: 104 kts (120 mph; 193 km/h)
climb rate   1,725 ft/min (525 m/min)
RANGE
max payload 2,982 nm (3,434 mi; 5,526 km)
CEILING   35,750 ft (10,895 m)

Nightingale (C-9)

The C-9A/C and C-9B are militarized versions of the DC-9 civil air transport. In the US Air Force, the C-9 is employed as a medical (C-9A/C) and as a VIP (C-9B) transport. The aircraft is also used by the US Navy and Marine Corps as a medium-range transport. Other than markings and a large cargo door, there are no observable external differences between the commercial and military versions. They differ mainly in avionics and in accommodations for cargo and passengers.

The C-9 design features a swept, low wing located well aft on the fuselage. The planform is a simple triangle with the leading edge swept at a greater angle than the trailing edge. The two turbofan

C-9

engines are mounted on short stubs near the rear of the fuselage.

During the aircraft's long production history, fuselage "stretches" became commonplace. Consequently, what began as a stubby, 90-passenger aircraft has been expanded to 139 seats. All of the aircraft have a distinctive sloping nose and small "eyebrow" windows above the windshield.

The cabin is fitted with 22 standard electrical outlets, 11 vacuum and therapeutic oxygen outlets, ceiling receptacles for intravenous bottles, separate special-care area, hydraulically operated folding ramp, medical refrigerator, medical supply work area, medical crew director's station, galleys, and lavatories.

DEVELOPMENT • The military C-9 achieved initial operational capability in 1973. Its first flight was in 1968. It is no longer in production. Italy, Kuwait, and Venezuela have used the civil version of the aircraft in their military as VIP transports.

VARIANTS • C-9A (medical evacuation), C-9B (Skytrain II; USN/USMC passenger/cargo), C-9C (USAF VIP).

COMBAT EXPERIENCE • The C-9 has supported aeromedical airlift requirements during several US and allied conflicts.

SPECIFICATIONS •

MANUFACTURER   McDonnell Douglas
CREW   5 (2 pilots, crew chief, 2 attendants/crew) + 5 medical attendants + 40 patients (C-9A)
WEIGHTS
  empty   59,706 lb (27,082 kg)
  max payload 32,444 lb (14,716 kg)
  max takeoff 110,000 lb (49,895 kg)
DIMENSIONS
  wingspan   93 ft 5 in (28.47 m)
  length   119 ft 4 in (36.37 m)
  height   27 ft 6 in (8.38 m)
  wing area 1,000 ft² (92.97 m²)
ENGINES   2 Pratt & Whitney JT8D-9 turbofan
  max power   14,500 lb (6,577 kg) static thrust each

SPEED

max   500 kts (576 mph; 927 km/h)

cruise   437 kts (504 mph; 811 km/h)

RANGE

max payload 1,670 nm (1,923 mi; 3,095 km)

CEILING 37,000 ft (11,278 m)

Huron (C-12)

The C-12 Huron is a military version of the popular Beechcraft Super King Air B200C. It is used in the liaison, VIP transport, special-operations, and support roles in its military service.

The C-12 wing is mounted low on the fuselage. The center section is rectangular. The outer sections have a small leading-edge extension alongside the nacelles.

The slightly swept vertical tail is broad and has a constant chord and a dorsal fillet. The full-height rudder has a deep chord and a trim tab. The slightly swept horizontal surfaces are carried at the top of the fin and have full-span, balanced elevators with trim tabs.

The fuselage has a sloping nose leading to a raked windshield. The cabin has a series of portholes along each side and a door in the rear on the left side.

The twin-wheel main-landing-gear legs retract forward into bays in the nacelles. The nose gear retracts to the rear.

DEVELOPMENT • The initial operational capability of the basic aircraft was in 1975. Delivery of the C-12F to the Military Airlift Command was accomplished between May and December 1984. More than 250 C-12s have been delivered to the US military, with production continuing into the 1990s. About 20 other countries operate approximately 60 of the aircraft in liaison or VIP transport roles.

VARIANTS • C-12A (US Army and USAF), UC-12B (USN and USMC),

C-12C, C-12D (electronic warfare), C-12E, C-12F, UC-12F, UC-12M, C-12J, C-12L, B200T (maritime patrol; more than 20 of this variant are in service in Algeria, Chile, Japan, Peru, and Uruguay), King Air 90 (C-6B, U-21A).

SPECIFICATIONS •
MANUFACTURER Beechcraft
CREW 2 (pilot, copilot) + 8 passengers or 2 litters and attendants
WEIGHTS

empty   7,538 lb (3,419 kg)

max cargo 2,300 lb (1,043 kg)

max takeoff 12,500 lb (5,670 kg)

DIMENSIONS

wingspan 54 ft 6 in (16.61 m)

length   43 ft 9 in (13.34 m)

height   15 ft (4.57 m)

cabin   length: 22 ft (6.71 m)
            width: 4 ft 6 in (1.37 m)
            height: 4 ft 9 in (1.45 m)

volume   392 ft^3 (11.1 m^3)

cargo volume
            253 ft^3 (7.16 m^3)

wing area   303 ft^2 (28.15 m^2)

ENGINES 2 Pratt & Whitney PW-PT6A-42 turboprop

max power 850 hp each

FUEL

internal capacity
            544 US gal (2,059 liters)

SPEED

max   294 kts (339 mph; 545 km/h)

cruise at 25,000 ft (7,620 m)
            max: 289 kts (333 mph; 536 km/h)
            econ: 282 kts (325 mph; 523 km/h)

RANGE

at 25,000 ft (7,620 m)
            max cruise: 1,461 nm (1,682 mi; 2,707 km)
            econ cruise: 1,802 nm (2,075 mi; 3,339 km)

at 35,000 ft (10,670 m)
            2,027 nm (2,334 mi; 3,756 km)

CEILING 35,000 ft (10,670 m)

C-17
MCDONNELL DOUGLAS

Globemaster III (C-17)

The C-17 is a long-range, heavy-lift cargo/transport aircraft under construction and intended to combine great intertheater cargo lift capacity with ease of operation from semi-improved airfields. Although similar in size to the C-141 Starlifter, the C-17 has the ability to land equipment usually volume-limited to the mammoth C-5 Galaxy at airfields usually open only to much smaller C-130 Hercules transports.

The C-17's wing offers part of the solution to the severe design constraints. The wing is swept at 25°, to fulfill the requirement for short-field operation, and has full-span leading-edge slats and externally blown, double-slotted flaps that span two-thirds of the trailing edge. Small, swept vertical surfaces ("winglets") are mounted on the wingtips; McDonnell Douglas estimates that the use of winglets permits a wingspan reduction of 20 ft (6.10 m).

The T-tail is tapered so that the top is slightly wider than the bottom; an inset rudder is divided into upper and lower sections. Above the rudder, the tail has a thicker cross section that supports the horizontal tailplanes.

The four turbofans are fitted in pods that extend below and forward of the wing; their exhaust passes through the slotted flaps to increase lift during takeoff and landing. Unlike other jet transports, the engines' thrust reversers in the C-17 divert the exhaust upward, allowing use of the engines for backing the plane along the ground or up a 2° slope. The backing ability permits six C-17s to be parked in a space normally holding four C-141s. Eight C-17s can park in the same space as three C-5s, theoretically increasing the cargo delivery per day by almost three times. The landing-field length of a C-17 with max payload is estimated at 2,700 ft (823 m), far less than the C-141 or the C-5.

The fuselage has a stubby nose, high flight deck, and a height and width that is only slightly smaller than the C-5's lower deck. It has an 83% increase in volume over the C-141B. The floor can handle tied-down cargo or pallets and is designed to be reconfigured quickly in flight.

Possible vehicle loads include one M1 Abrams tank or three M2/M3 Bradley armored fighting vehicles; smaller vehicles can be loaded side by side. Also, up to three AH-64 Apache attack or four UH-60 Blackhawk utility helicopters can be carried. 54 fiberglass seats are permanently fixed to the sides of the cabin. A typical transatlantic configuration could include an M2, an M3, two five-ton trucks, and two jeeps with trailers.

The lower fourth of the cargo hold has bulletproof composite armor to protect seated troops. Most of the airframe and wings are aluminum alloy, and composites will be used in the winglets, control surfaces, landing-gear sponsons, and landing-gear doors. The aircraft can be refueled in flight and can also refuel other aircraft on the ground.

The retractable landing gear reduces the aircraft's turning radius. Main gear sponsons extend from the fuselage sides at the bottom and under the wing; each sponson contains two three-wheel units arranged in tandem, with the inside wheel offset. The two-wheel nose gear retracts forward. In the cockpit, the pilots use stick controls rather than wheels.

DEVELOPMENT • The C-17's first flight was scheduled for February 1990, but delays slipped the date at least three times. The first flight finally took place on September 16, 1991. During its first 100 hours of flight testing, pilots described the plane's handling as "like a fighter" aircraft. Its initial operational capability was originally planned for September 1992 but also has been slipped.

The Full-Scale Development (FSD) of the aircraft was approved in February 1985, and in December 1985, a $3.4-billion contract was awarded.

In April 1990, the Secretary of Defense cut the total procurement from 210 aircraft to 120. Only two C-17s were sought in FY1991 funding, and a full production rate of 24 (down from a planned 29) was planned for funding in FY1994, a year later than originally scheduled. An August 1993 study sponsored by DoD concluded that the USAF may exercise an option to buy half the 120 aircraft.

The C-17 is the third aircraft to be called the Globemaster. The inaugural flight of the first Globemaster was in 1945; it was followed by the C-124 Globemaster II, which first flew in 1949.

The first C-17, #91192, entered operational service with the Air Mobility Command's first operational C-17 wing, the 437th Airlift Wing, at Charleston AFB, South Carolina, on June 14, 1993. The lead aircraft was christened the *Spirit of Charleston*.

SPECIFICATIONS •
MANUFACTURER　McDonnell Douglas
CREW　3 (pilot, copilot, loadmaster) + 102 paratroops
WEIGHTS
　empty　　　　269,363 lb (122,181 kg)
　max payload 167,000 lb (75,750 kg)
　gross takeoff
　　　　　　　　580,000 lb (263,084 kg)
DIMENSIONS
　wingspan　165 ft (50.29 m)
　length　　175 ft 2 in (53.39 m)
　height　　55 ft 1 in (16.79 m)
　wing area　3,800 ft² (353 m²)
　cargo hold　length: 88 ft (26.82 m)
　　　　　　　　width: 18 ft (5.49 m)
　　　　　　　　height: 13 ft 6 in
　　　　　　　　(4.11 m)
　　　　　　　　volume: 20,900 ft³ (592 m³)
ENGINES　4 Pratt & Whitney F117-PW-100 turbofan
　max power　37,000 lb (16,783 kg) static thrust

SPEED
normal cruise
    high level: 450 kts (518 mph; 834 km/h)
    low level: 350 kts (403 mph; 648 km/h)
radius short-field takeoff/ landing, 86,100-lb payload: 500 nm (575 mi; 925 km)
    short-field takeoff/ landing, zero payload: 1,900 nm (2,190 mi; 3,520 km)
    landing-field length 3,000 ft, 140,800-lb payload: 1,900 nm (2,190 mi; 3,520 km)

RANGE
2,900-ft landing field, 158,500-lb payload: 2,700 nm (2,765 mi; 4,445 km)
3,000-ft landing field, max payload: 2,400 nm (2,765 mi; 4,445 km)
ferry: 4,700 nm (5,412 mi; 8,709 km)

Gulfstream (C-20)

The C-20 is the military version of the Gulfstream III commercial executive transport. In its military configuration, it is used as a VIP transport, reconnaissance aircraft, and special-missions aircraft. The C-20 differs from the commercial versions only with its communications equipment, interior layout, and markings. The Gulfstream IV is a larger variant with very similar commercial missions.

The C-20 has a broad, tall vertical tail with a full-height rudder. Swept horizontal stabilizers top the vertical "T" and have inset elevators. Flight controls, flaps, spoilers, landing gear, and brakes are powered by two independent hydraulic systems.

The Gulfstream is powered by Rolls-Royce Spey engines. Fuel is carried in two integral wing tanks.

The pointed nose is nearly stepless as it leads back to the windshield subdivided by three thin mullions. The fuselage cross section is circular.

DEVELOPMENT • The C-20's initial operational capability was 1983; its first flight as the Gulfstream III was on December 24, 1979. The US Army, Navy, and Air Force operate the Gulfstream, along with the air forces of about eight other nations.

The Air Force originally employed the C-20 to replace the C-140 Jetstar as a primary VIP transport.

VARIANTS • C-20A, C-20B, C-20C, C-20D (Navy), C-20E (Army).

SPECIFICATIONS •
MANUFACTURER Gulfstream Aerospace
CREW 5 + 14 passengers
WEIGHTS
empty 38,000 lb (17,236 kg)
max payload 4,000 lb (1,814 kg)
max takeoff 69,700 lb (31,615 kg)
max landing 58,500 lb (26,535 kg)
DIMENSIONS
length 83 ft 1 in (25.32 m)
height 24 ft 4½ in (7.43 m)
wing area 935 ft^2 (86.86 m^2)
cabin length: 41 ft 4 in (12.60 m)
    width: 7 ft 4 in (2.24 m)
    height: 6 ft 1 in (1.85 m)
    volume: 1,502 ft^3 (42.53 cu m^3)
ENGINES 2 Rolls-Royce Spey Mk 511-8 turbofan
max power 11,400 lb (5,171 kg) static thrust
SPEED
max 488 kts (561 mph; 903 km/h); Mach 0.85
long-range 442 kts (508 mph; 818 km/h); Mach 0.77
climb rate, both engines
    4,270 ft/min (1,300 m/min)
RANGE 3,650 nm (4,200 mi; 6,760 km)
CEILING 46,000 ft (13,940 m)

C-20 Gulfstream
U.S. GOVERNMENT DEPARTMENT OF DEFENSE

C-21A

The C-21A is an adaptation of the Learjet business jet. Several models of the Learjet have been adapted by various nations as VIP transports, or as utility, reconnaissance, and special-purpose aircraft.

The classic Learjet shape is preserved in all of the Learjet variants, although some are adorned with winglets and delta ventral fins and the fuselage is stretched to varying lengths. Most Learjets, including the Military Airlift Command's C-21As, are fitted with long wingtip tanks carried on short stubs extending out from the wings.

Contributing to the aircraft's low profile is the slightly swept vertical tail, which is relatively short and has a broad chord and a full-height rudder. Swept, variable-incidence horizontal tailplanes are mounted at the top of the fin. A small ventral fin is fitted below the tail.

A large engine nacelle is mounted on a short stub on either side of the aft fuselage in line with the wing's trailing edge.

Most of the passenger cabin is ahead of the wing, which accounts for the trademark fuselage taper that begins at the wing leading edge. The long, pointed nose slopes up to a two-piece windshield that has a central mullion and curved transparencies. The flight deck holds two pilots, and the cabin seats six passengers. A boarding door is located on the forward left side. The main gear legs retract inward, the wheels nestling in fuselage bays; the nose gear retracts forward.

DEVELOPMENT • The C-21A's initial operational capability was in 1984. The Air Force initially leased 80 C-21As from Gates Learjet on September 19, 1983, for $175.4 million to replace CT-39 Sabreliners in the Operational Support Aircraft (OSA) program that transports cargo and personnel on time-sensitive missions. The lease was converted to a purchase in September 1986. Deliveries were made from March 1984 to October 1985.

The first flight of the initial Learjet was on October 7, 1963. Over 20 nations operate the Learjet in a military/VIP role.

VARIANTS • C-21A, Learjet 24D (VIP), Learjet 25/25B (stretched), U-36A, EC-35A (EW training), PC-35A (maritime patrol), RC-35 (reconnaissance), UC-35A.

SPECIFICATIONS •
MANUFACTURER   Learjet
CREW   2 + 6 passengers
WEIGHTS
   empty   9,571 lb (4,342 kg)
   max payload 3,153 lb (1,430 kg)
   max takeoff 18,300 lb (8,301 kg)
DIMENSIONS
   length   48 ft 8 in (14.83 m)
   height   12 ft 3 in (3.73 m)
   cabin   length: 21 ft 9 in
                  (6.63 m)
                  width: 4 ft 11 in (1.50 m)
                  height: 4 ft 4 in (1.32 m)
                  volume: 322 ft³ (9.12 m³)
   wing area   253 ft² (23.5 m²)
   wingspan   39 ft 6 in (12.04 m)
ENGINES   2 Garrett TFE731-2-2B turbofan
   max power   3,500 lb (1,588 kg) static
                  thrust
SPEED
   max speed   471 kts (542 mph; 872
                  km/h)
   cruise speed
                  max: 460 kts (530 mph;
                  852 km/h)
                  long-range: 420 kts (484
                  mph; 778 km/h)
                  stall speed: 96 kts (111
                  mph; 178 km/h)
RANGE   2,289 nm (2,634 mi; 4,239 km), with 4 pax
CEILING   45,000 ft (13,715 m)

C-22

The C-22 is an adaptation of commercial Boeing 727 aircraft for staff transport and operational support airlift missions.

The C-22 has swept wings set low at the fuselage midpoint, a long, tubular fuselage ending in an exhaust nozzle for its topmost engine, three turbofan engines, with two set in nacelles on each side of the rear fuselage and one set on top of the fuselage at the base of the single tailfin, swept tailfin and tailplane, with the tailplane set atop the tailfin, and retractable tricycle landing gear.

Modifications for military service are primarily in the avionics suite and interior layout.

DEVELOPMENT • The initial operational capability of the Boeing 727 was in 1963; its first flight was in February 1963. C-22A aircraft are currently in service.

VARIANTS • C-22A (staff transport), C-22B (operational support).

SPECIFICATIONS •
MANUFACTURER   Boeing
CREW   3
WEIGHTS
   empty   89,537 lb (40,613 kg)
   max payload 38,000 lb (17,236 kg)
   max takeoff 169,000 lb (76,655 kg)
DIMENSIONS
   wingspan   108 ft (32.92 m)
   length   133 ft 2 in (40.59 m)
   height   34 ft (10.36 m)
   wing area   1,700 ft² (158 m²)
ENGINES   3 Pratt & Whitney JT8D-7 turbofan
   max power   14,000 lb static thrust
                  each
SPEED
   max   548 kts (630 mph; 1,014
                  km/h)
RANGE   2,303 nm (2,650 mi; 4,265 km)
CEILING   37,400 ft (11,400 m)

Sherpa (C-23)

The C-23 Sherpa is an adaptation of the Shorts 330 civil Short Takeoff and Landing (STOL) utility transport, used by the

Air Force for the US Air Force European Distribution Aircraft System. In its more powerful C-23B variant, the Sherpa has also been adopted by the US Army National Guard to replace aging C-7 Caribou STOL transports.

The C-23 has a straight, high-aspect-ratio wing set high on the boxy fuselage. Three sections of single-slotted flaps are inboard of the single-slotted aileron on each wing. Wing struts extend from the landing-gear main wheel pods to the middle of the outer sections. The later C-23B wing is strengthened to permit flight at 25,000 lb (11,340 kg), which permits slightly higher payload weights and a higher zero-fuel weight for greater range.

The tail unit consists of two rectangular vertical surfaces mounted as endplates to the stubby horizontal tailplanes. The horn-balanced rudders are fitted into the upper two-thirds of the fin trailing edges. The elevator extends the full span between the rudder. The flight controls are moved by rods; a hydraulic system powers the flaps, landing gear, wheel brakes, and nosewheel steering.

The cabin is nearly square in cross section. The nose is pointed and slopes up to a stepped windshield. The top line of the fuselage continues up and back in a gentle curve to the wing, where it begins a gentle slope to the tail. The lower fuselage line is mostly straight, eventually sloping up to the tail. The sloped floor has a hydraulically operated, full-width rear ramp.

The two turboprop engines are fitted in wing nacelles. The main-landing-gear pods are mounted on short stubs that extend from the lower fuselage under the wing. The single-wheel main wheels retract into the pods, leaving some of the tire showing. The nose gear retracts to the rear.

DEVELOPMENT • The C-23's initial operational capability was in 1984, and its first flight was in December 1982.

The Military Airlift Command had 18 Sherpas, obtained between November 1984 and December 1985. With the anticipated closing of Zweibrücken AB, Germany, in the early 1990s, the aircraft were redistributed among the Air Force System Command (AFSC), the US Army, and the US Forest Service. Militarized variants (Shorts 330/UTT) have been sold to Thailand's army and police and the United Arab Emirates.

VARIANTS • C-23A, C-23B (Super Sherpa), Shorts 330/UTT, Shorts 330.

SPECIFICATIONS •
MANUFACTURER   Shorts Brothers (Northern Ireland)
CREW   2 + 30 passengers, or 30 paratroopers + 1 jumpmaster, or 15 litters + 1 attendant
WEIGHTS
empty   14,000 lb (6,350 kg)
max payload 7,000 lb (3,175 kg)
max takeoff 22,900 lb (10,387 kg)
DIMENSIONS
wingspan   74 ft 8 in (22.76 m)
length   58 ft 0½ in (17.69 m)
height   16 ft 3 in (4.95 m)
cabin   length: 29 ft 10 in (9.09 m)
    width: 6 ft 5½ in (1.97 m)
    height: 6 ft 2⅔ in (1.89 m)
    volume: 1,246 ft^3 (35.28 m^3)
wing area   453 ft^2 (42.10 m^2)
ENGINES   2 Pratt & Whitney PT6A-45R turboprop
max power   1,198 hp each
FUEL
internal   673 US gal (2,546 liters)
SPEED
max cruise   190 kts (218 mph; 352 km/h)
econ cruise   157 kts (181 mph; 291 km/h)
climb rate   1,180 ft/min (360 m/min)

RANGE
max payload 195 nm (225 mi; 362 km)
5,000 lb   669 nm (770 mi; 1,239 km)
CEILING   20,013 ft (6,100 m)

Air Force One (VC-25A)

The VC-25A is the newest in the series of Air Force One aircraft, the official transport for the President of the United States. It is adapted from the Boeing 747 civil airliner. The only observable differences between the VC-25A and the standard Boeing 747 are the insignia, markings, and antennas. The airframe and engines are identical.

The low wing has 37½° sweep at the quarter-chord and 7° dihedral from the root. Each wing has a profusion of high-lift devices on the leading and trailing edges. The tall, swept fin has an inset, two-section rudder. The horizontal stabilizers are mounted on the fuselage below the fin and have two-section elevators. Flight controls, flaps, brakes, and landing gear are driven by four independent hydraulic systems.

The fuselage has a sharply sloped nose leading up to a raised flight deck with a nearly stepless windshield. The flight-deck level extends aft, the top line sloping down to the main fuselage at a point in line with the wing's leading edge. The fuselage has a constant cross section to well aft of the wing trailing edge, at which point the lower fuselage line tapers up to meet the tail. The VC-25 is equipped for air refueling.

The interior layout and communications suite of the VC-25 have been modified considerably from that of the basic 747 to permit the aircraft to operate as an airborne presidential office and residence. The 4,000 ft² (371.6 m²) of floor space are subdivided into the President's suite, work, and rest areas for 70 passengers (including up to 14 news reporters) and 23 crew (including accommodations for a complete traveling ground crew). Each of the two galleys is capable of preparing meals for 50 people and has a 10-ft³ (0.28-m³) oven, two 5-qt (4.73-liter) coffeemakers, a microwave oven, and a four-burner stove. Each refrigerator holds 1,000 entrees, and each freezer stores 1,000 lb (454 kg) of frozen provisions. The aircraft has seven lavatories and a medical aid station.

The two engines are carried on pylons under each wing. The inboard, four-wheel main-landing-gear bogies retract forward into fuselage bays that are in line with the wing. When extended, the two outboard bogies are farther forward than the inboard pair; they retract inward, being stowed in wing root bays. The two-wheel nose gear retracts forward under the flight deck.

The communications gear includes 85 telephones, some secured, a facsimile machine that can transmit secret documents securely, a jamming system offering protection from antiaircraft missiles, and 55 different antennas.

The aircraft is hardened against Electromagnetic Pulses (EMP) resulting from a nuclear blast. It is also fitted with an automatic collision-avoidance system. A Canadian Marconi landing system permits automatic landings in zero-visibility conditions. Additionally, two Auxiliary Power Units (APU) are installed in the tail.

DEVELOPMENT • The VC-25A's initial operational capability was in September 1990 following its delivery to the 89th Military Airlift Wing (MAW) at Andrews AFB, Maryland, on August 23. The VC-25's first flight was on January 26, 1990. Its first flight with then President Bush onboard was September 6, 1990.

The VC-25A is replacing the two VC-137 holdovers from the Kennedy and Nixon administrations as Air Force One. Only two aircraft were built, with the air-

VC-25A
U.S. GOVERNMENT DEPARTMENT OF DEFENSE

craft rotated as primary and backup. The second VC-25A was scheduled to enter service on June 30, 1991, but was delivered to the 89th MAW on December 20, 1990. The aircraft have the tail numbers 28,000 and 29,000.

The plane was built at a fixed-price cost to the government of $266 million; Boeing absorbed $360 million in costs, making the planes the most expensive transport aircraft ever produced.

The basic Boeing 747 commercial airliner is in limited military service in four other nations. Two are used as VIP transports for the Japanese Air Self-Defense Force (JASDF), and eight are serving as cargo aircraft in Iran, Oman, and Saudi Arabia.

VARIANTS • Boeing 747, VC-25A Air Force One, E-4 (the National Emergency Airborne Command Post/NEACP).

SPECIFICATIONS •
MANUFACTURER   Boeing

CREW   23 crew (3 flight, 20 ground) + 70 passengers
WEIGHTS
empty   526,500 lb (238,816 kg)
mission   803,700 lb (364,552 kg)
               long-range
DIMENSIONS
wingspan   195 ft 8 in (59.64 m)
length   231 ft 10 in (70.66 m)
height   63 ft 5 in (19.33 m)
wing area   5,500 ft² (511 m²)
ENGINES   4 General Electric CF6-802B1 turbofan
max power   56,750 lb (25,741 kg)
FUEL
internal capacity
               53,611 US gal (202,940 liters)
SPEED
max speed   530 kts (610 mph; 981 km/h)
cruise   482 kts (555 mph; 893 km/h)
RANGE   6,200 nm (7,410 mi; 11,491 km)
CEILING   45,000 ft (13,715 m)

C-29A

The C-29A is a variant of the British Aerospace BAe125-800, itself a development of the earlier HS125 light executive transport. The basic design has been progressively improved; several of the 800 series are in use as VIP transports. Six were ordered by the United States as the C-29A flight inspection aircraft after undergoing modification by Sierra Research of Buffalo, New York.

The low, two-spar wing is mounted in a prominent fairing below the fuselage. The trailing edge has four-position, double-slotted flaps inboard of cable-operated, mass-balanced ailerons. Lift-dumping air brake/spoilers are located ahead of the flaps.

The relatively tall fin and rudder have a moderately swept tailplane mounted well up on the fin and above the rudder. A low dorsal fin extends forward. The full-span elevators are cable-operated and mass-balanced.

Two turbofan engines are carried in nacelles on either side of the rear fuselage. The fuel tanks are located in the wings, and a ventral tank is behind the passenger cabin. The main gear legs have twin wheels and retract into the wings; the nose gear retracts forward. A single hydraulic system operates the flaps, spoilers, landing gear, main-wheel doors and brakes, nosewheel steering, and the antiskid braking system.

A passenger door is located on the left side of the fuselage, forward of the wing. The bulged cockpit roof of the earlier series has been replaced by a straight top line, and the nose has been lengthened. There are six windows along each side of the roomy cabin.

DEVELOPMENT • The initial operational capability of the C-29A was in 1984, and its first flight was on May 26, 1983.

Six C-29As were built for the US Air Force under a $70-million contract awarded in March 1988. The final unit was delivered to the Military Airlift Command on January 11, 1991.

Three other nations have used the aircraft, the most recent being the Japanese Air Self-Defense Force (JASDF), which ordered three BAe125-800 aircraft in August 1989.

The mission of the C-29A Combat Flight Inspection (C-FIN) is to verify the accuracy of airport navigational and landing aids.

VARIANTS • Dominie TMk1 (British trainer), BAe125, C-29A.

SPECIFICATIONS •

MANUFACTURER   British Aerospace
CREW   2 + 6 passengers
WEIGHTS
  empty   14,720 lb (6,676 kg)
  max payload 2,400 lb (1,088 kg)
  max takeoff 27,400 lb (12,430 kg)
DIMENSIONS
  wingspan   51 ft 4 in (15.66 m)
  length   51 ft 2 in (15.60 m)
  height   17 ft 7 in (5.36 m)
  cabin   length: 21 ft 4 in (6.5 m)
               width: 6 ft (1.83 m)
               height: 5 ft 9 in (1.75 m)
               volume: 604 ft^3 (17.1 m^3)
  wing area 374 ft^2 (34.75 m^2)
ENGINES   2 Garrett TFE731-5R-1H turbofan
  max power 4,300 lb (1,950 kg) static thrust
FUEL
  internal   1,499 US gal (5,674 liters)
SPEED
  max cruise   456 kts (525 mph; 845 km/h)
  econ cruise 400 kts (461 mph; 741 km/h)
RANGE
  max payload 2,870 nm (3,305 mi; 5,318 km)
  max fuel   3,000 nm (3,454 mi; 5,560 km)
CEILING   43,000 ft (13,100 m)

Commando (C-46)

The C-46 Commando first became famous when it flew over the "hump" of the Himalayan Mountains between India and China during World War II. The aircraft, also known as the Dumbo, had almost double the payload and cabin volume of the C-47 Dakota (but not the reliability) and represented the first military transport to be built in significant numbers.

The Commando's low wing had a rectangular center section and tapered outer panels. It had a broad vertical tail and a curved, full-height rudder.

The Commando's "double-bubble" fuselage was originally designed to have a pressurized upper half for the comfort of commercial passengers. As a military transport, the C-46 was unpressurized. The main cabin had a large cargo double door on the port side with an inset personnel door.

The two radial piston engines were in nacelles faired into the leading edges of the wings. The landing gear consisted of one-wheel main gear legs that retracted forward into each engine nacelle and a fixed, castoring tailwheel under the fuselage ahead of the tail group.

DEVELOPMENT • The C-46's first flight was on March 26, 1940, and its initial operational capability was in 1941. A total of 3,180 aircraft were built between 1941 and 1945. Of the original military production version, 1,039 C-46A-CUs were built in Buffalo, 438 C-46A-CKs in Louisville, 12 C-46A-CSs in St. Louis, and two C-46A-HIs by Higgins in New Orleans. The last C-46E retired from active US service in 1953. Reserve units continued to fly C-46A/D/F aircraft until 1960. Remarkably, some foreign airlines and air forces have continued to fly the C-46 into the 1990s.

VARIANTS • CW-20/C-55, C-46A, XC-46B, C-46D, C-46E, C-46F, C-46G, XC-46L (test bed), R5C-1/2/3/4/5 (US Marine Corps).

SPECIFICATIONS (C-46D) •
MANUFACTURER   Curtis-Wright
CREW   4 + 50 passengers, or 33 litters and 4 attendants
WEIGHTS
  empty   32,400 lb (14,696 kg)
  max payload 16,000–17,600 lb (7,257–7,983 kg)
  max takeoff normal: 45,000 lb (20,410 kg)
            overload: 48,000 lb (21,772 kg)
DIMENSIONS
  wingspan   108 ft 1 in (32.92 m)
  length   76 ft 4 in (23.27 m)
  height   21 ft 9 in (6.63 m)
  cabin   length: 48 ft (14.63 m)
            width: 9 ft 10 in (3.0 m)
            height: 6 ft 8 in (2.03 m)
            volume: 2,300 ft³ (12.88 m³)
  wing area   1,360 ft² (126.8 m²)
ENGINES   2 2,000-hp Pratt & Whitney R-2800-51 2-row, 18-cylinder radial piston
SPEED
  max   233 kts (269 mph; 433 km/h)
  max cruise 197 kts (227 mph; 365 km/h)
  econ cruise 162 kts (187 mph; 301 km/h)
  landing   62 kts (71 mph; 114 km/h)
  climb rate 1,300 ft/min (396 m/min)
RANGE   27,600 ft (8,410 m)
CEILING   955 nm (1,100 mi; 1,770 km) (with 11,500 lb); 2,562 nm (2,950 mi; 4,748 km) (with 2,000 lb)

Dakota (C-47)

The C-47 is the military version of the Douglas DC-3 commercial airliner. Throughout aviation history, it has been one of the most widely used aircraft. The official names of the C-47 have been the

Dakota and the Skytrain, but the most widely used nickname of the airplane was the affectionate Gooney Bird.

The popularity of the C-47 stems from its low cost of operation and maintenance, ruggedness, ease of pilot training, and versatility. It has served primarily in the cargo and transport roles but has been adapted to a wide variety of other missions, including reconnaissance, extreme weather conditions, gunship, special operations, trainer, and electronic countermeasures.

The plane's basic configuration includes a low-set wing with a rectangular center section and long, tapered outer panels. The trailing edge has plain split flaps inboard and a narrow, long aileron outboard.

The two radial engines are mounted in nacelles that extend forward from the leading edge of the center section. The main wheels are carried on struts that retract into the rear of the nacelle; the main wheel remains partially exposed and reduces the damage from belly land-ings. The nonretractable, castoring tail-wheel is fitted below the fin.

The fuselage has a pointed nose, stepped windshield, large cockpit side windows, and a two-section cargo door aft of the trailing edge on the left side.

The aircraft has been extensively modified during its life and has flown with a number of different engines and minor airframe modifications.

DEVELOPMENT • The C-47's initial operational capability was in 1941. The first flight of the DC-3 was on December 17, 1935. 10,368 were built in the United States, and approximately 2,000 were built under license by the Soviet Union as the Lisunov Li-2 (still in service in China and Vietnam). It remained active with the USAF's Military Airlift Command until the late 1960s.

The C-47 is no longer in US service. More than 400 C-47s remain in service in more than 40 countries into the mid-1990s. The C-47 has served in almost

C-47
TIMOTHY M. LAUR

every Western and Third World air force and several communist air forces.

In the 1990s, a few Latin American countries have had some of their C-47s converted by Basler Turbo Conversions Inc. into a turboprop version of the Gooney Bird (Turbo-67), but faster and with a higher payload.

VARIANTS • C-47, AC-47 (USAF Spooky gunship), EC-47 (USN Electronic Warfare/EW; formerly R4D-5Q/6Q), HC-47 (USAF rescue; formerly SC-47), LC-47 (USN ski-equipped; formerly R4D-5L/6L), RC-47A (USAF reconnaissance), TC-47 (trainer), VC-47 (VIP), C-53, C-117 (USN TC-117 trainer; formerly R4D-8T), VC-117 (VIP), C-117D, Li-2 (Soviet-built), Turbo-67.

COMBAT EXPERIENCE • The Gooney Bird distinguished itself as a US cargo aircraft in World War II, the Berlin Airlift, and in Korea. The gunship variant was flown in the Vietnam War by US and South Vietnamese air forces. The Royal Laotian Air Force also flew C-47 gunships. El Salvador has used its AC-47s to attack guerrilla positions.

SPECIFICATIONS •
MANUFACTURER Douglas
CREW   4 + 26 troops or 24 litters
WEIGHTS
empty   16,970 lb (7,697 kg)
normal payload
              6,000 lb (2,721 kg)
max payload 7,500 lb (3,402 kg)
max takeoff 26,000 lb (11,793 kg)
max overload
              30,600 lb (13,880 kg)
DIMENSIONS
length   64 ft 6 in (19.65 m)
height   16 ft 9 in (5.16 m)
wing area   987 ft² (91.69 m²)
cargo volume
              1,245 ft³ (35.25 m³)
ENGINES   2 Pratt & Whitney R-1830-92 radial piston
max power   1,200 shp each

SPEED
cruise speed
              160 kts (185 mph; 296 km/h)
max speed   199 kts (229 mph; 368 km/h)
stall, wheels and flaps down
              58 kts (67 mph; 108 km/h)
RANGE
normal   1,296 nm (1,500 mi; 2,400 km)
max range   2,346 nm (2,700 mi; 4,345 km)
CEILING   24,100 ft (7,345 m)

Hercules (C-130)

The C-130 Hercules airlifter has had a long and distinguished career in several wars throughout the world. It is the most versatile and widely flown military transport in the post–World War II era. The four-engine, medium turboprop transport has been used for passenger and cargo, paratroop, aerial refueling, passenger, Search and Rescue (SAR), Electronic Warfare (EW), combat command and control, communications relay, and as a gunship. The US Navy has flown C-130 aircraft from an aircraft carrier without the use of arresting wires or catapult. The Hercules is a utilitarian combination of a graceful, high-aspect-ratio wing on a hulking fuselage followed by a large, triangular tail. The high wing has a rectangular center section and outer panels with tapered trailing edges.

The tail is carried high as a result of the sloped, rear cargo ramp that forms the aft end of the fuselage. The fin has a small dorsal fillet and full-height rudder. The large, double-taper tailplanes are mounted just below the fin, in line with the wings.

The four Allison turboprops are carried in thin nacelles along the leading edge of the wing. The plane has six integral wing tanks. Additionally, external

Hercules
U.S. GOVERNMENT DEPARTMENT OF DEFENSE

fuel tanks are semipermanently fixed to pylons between the engines under each wing.

The squat, constant-section fuselage has a short nose; the nearly flat, "Roman" nose of the early versions received a bulbous "thimble" radome that is now characteristic of virtually all C-130s still in service. The flight deck has two levels of glazing and "eyebrow" windows on each side.

The pressurized main cabin has a nearly square cross section and has an unobstructed run from aft of the flight deck to the rear ramp. Cargo can include five pallets, a 155-mm howitzer and towing vehicle, plus troops or litters. The ramp can be lowered in flight for parachute drops or Low-Altitude Parachute Extraction System (LAPES) operations. The aircraft has cargo doors at the front and rear of the cabin on both sides. Large sponsons run along the lower sides of the fuselage; each carries two one-wheel main gear legs in tandem.

DEVELOPMENT • The initial operational capability of the C-130 was in 1956, and its first flight was on August 23, 1954. C-130H variants are still in production; about 2,000 had been built by the early 1990s. The US Air Force, Navy, Marines, and Coast Guard operate the C-130 along with about 24 other nations. There are numerous variants of the basic C-130 that have been designed to meet the various requirements of the many operators. Latest in the line is the C-130J, ordered by Britain in 1994. It has new engines, electronic flight instrumentation, and several other upgrades.

VARIANTS • YC-130, C-130B, C-130D (Arctic/Antarctic operations), C-130E,

C-130H (main production version), C-130J (High-Technology Test Bed/HTTB), C-130K (RAF), C-130 AEW (proposed Airborne Early Warning/AEW), AC-130 (gunship), HC-130H (search and rescue/aerial recovery), HC-130N, HC-130P (rescue), LC-130H, MC-130H Combat Talon II (Special Operations Command/SOC), WC-130E/H (weather reconnaissance).

SPECIFICATIONS (C-130H) •

MANUFACTURER   Lockheed

CREW   5 (2 pilots, navigator, flight engineer, radio operator/loadmaster) and 92 troops or 64 paratroops or 74 litters and 2 attendants

WEIGHTS

empty   76,469 lb (34,686 kg)

max payload 42,673 lb (19,356 kg)

takeoff   normal: 155,000 lb (70,310 kg)

max: 175,000 lb (79,380 kg)

DIMENSIONS

wingspan   132 ft 7 in (40.41 m)

length   97 ft 9 in (29.79 m)

height   38 ft 3 in (11.66 m)

wing area   1,745 ft^2 (162.12 m^2)

ramp opening

length: 9 ft 1 in (2.77 m)

width: 10 ft (3.05 m)

cargo hold   length: 40 ft 1 in (12.22 m)

width: 10 ft 3 in (3.30 m)

height: 9 ft 3 in (2.81 m)

volume: 4,500 ft^3 (127.4 m^3)

ENGINES   4 Allison T56-A-15 turboprop

max power   4,591 effective hp each

FUEL

internal capacity

9,679 US gal (36,636 liters)

SPEED

cruise speed

max: 325 kts (374 mph; 602 km/h)

econ: 300 kts (345 mph; 556 km/h)

stall speed   100 kts (115 mph; 185 km/h)

EC130M
U.S. GOVERNMENT DEPARTMENT OF DEFENSE

climb rate   1,900 ft/min (579 m/min)
RANGE
   max payload 2,046 nm (2,356 mi;
               3,791 km)
   max fuel   4,250 nm (4,894 mi;
               7,876 km)
CEILING *at 130,000 lb (58,970 kg)*
   4 engines: 33,000 ft (10,060 m)
   3 engines: 26,500 ft (8,075 m)

Starlifter (C-141)

The C-141 Starlifter is a strategic airlift aircraft used primarily for cargo, but also used for medical evacuation, paratroop drops, and troop transport.

The C-141's high wing has a low quarter-chord sweep that reduces the maximum cruising speed when compared to other jet transports, but improves handling near stall speed and reduces the required takeoff and landing-field lengths. Four sections of spoilers, two ahead of each flap section, act as airbrakes and ground lift dumpers. The tail group forms a "T." The verti-cal tail consists of a slightly swept fin with low dorsal fillet and a full-height rudder. Flight controls, flaps, landing gear, and brakes are operated by two redundant hydraulic systems.

The current operational version, the C-141B, was "stretched" to increase its capabilities. Most of the modifications to the basic design involved the fuselage. The original design adopted the cross section of the earlier C-130 Hercules; this was not changed in the C-141B. Neither was the nose section, which consists of a stubby radome and low-stepped flight deck. An air-refueling capability was added.

Side and cargo doors are used as paratroop drop exits. A C-141A set a world record for airdropping a 70,195-lb (31,840-kg) mass. Large clamshell doors swing out to expose a ramp that drops down to create an 11° slope for loading. The modifications improved the cargo capacity of the aircraft, increasing the load from 10 to 13 standard cargo pallets. Total volume increased by 55%, and max payload capacity grew to 94,508 lb

C-141 Starlifter

(42,869 kg). Passenger and medical evacuee capacity was not changed.

The four turbofan engines are mounted on pylons that extend below and ahead of the wing's leading edges. The main, four-wheel landing gear retracts into streamlined pods mounted on the lower fuselage below the wings. These pods also contain the single-point refueling point hookups. The two-wheel nose gear retracts forward.

The C-141B program was a success on several grounds, including meeting all milestones ahead of schedule.

DEVELOPMENT • The Starlifter's initial operational capability was on April 23, 1965; its first flight was on December 17, 1963. 285 were built before production ceased in 1968.

The stretch program began in 1979 with the 270 operational C-141As. The initial operating capability of the C-141B was April 1980. The final converted unit was delivered on June 29, 1982. The USAF is the only operator of the C-141.

VARIANTS • C-141A, ARTB (Advanced Radar Test Bed), YC-141B (stretched prototype), C-141B, SOF C-141 (special ops).

COMBAT EXPERIENCE • The Starlifter distinguished itself in all conflicts since it started operations. It flew virtually daily missions during the Vietnam War. It was a primary resource for the resupply effort to Israel during the Yom Kippur War of October 1973. On December 20, 1989, C-141s made 77 flights to Panama in support of the US ouster of Panamanian General Noriega, dropping paratroopers airlifting cargo and troops.

The aircraft again distinguished itself during the 1990–91 deployment of troops and cargo in support of the Desert Shield/Desert Storm operations in the Middle East.

SPECIFICATIONS •
MANUFACTURER Lockheed
CREW 5 + 155 paratroops or 200 troops or 103 patient litters with attendants

WEIGHTS
empty   144,492 lb (65,542 kg)
max payload 94,508 lb (42,869 kg)
max takeoff 343,000 lb (155,585 kg)

DIMENSIONS
wingspan   159 ft 11 in (48.74 m)
length   168 ft 3 in (51.29 m)
height   39 ft 3 in (11.96 m)
wing area   3,228 ft² (299.9 m²)
cargo hold length without ramp
            (C-141B): 93 ft 4 in
            (28.45 m)
            width: 10 ft 3 in (3.12 m)
            height: 9 ft 1 in (2.77 m)
            volume with ramp: 11,399
            ft³ (322.7 m³)

ENGINES   4 Pratt & Whitney TF33-P-7
turbofan
    max power   21,000 lb (9,525 kg)

FUEL
    internal capacity
            23,592 US gal (89,296
            liters)

SPEED
    max cruise   492 kts (566 mph; 911
                 km/h)
    long-range   430 kts (495 mph; 797
                 km/h)
    climb rate   2,600 ft/min (792
                 m/min)

RANGE
    with payload of 90,880 lb (41,223 kg)
                 2,549 nm (2,935 mi;
                 4,723 km)
    max fuel   5,330 nm (6,140 mi;
                 9,880 km)

CEILING   41,600 ft (12,680 m)

Trader (C-1A)

The C-1A Trader is a derivative of the S-2 Tracker aircraft, using the same airframe and engines minus the Tracker's mission avionics. The Trader is used as a US Navy Carrier Onboard Delivery (COD) cargo/passenger aircraft.

The Trader has a fairly distinctive appearance, featuring a short, stubby fuselage, long, slightly tapered wings set high just forward of the midfuselage, two very large engine nacelles for its radial piston engines, and a large tailfin and rudder with slightly dihedral tailplanes set at the base. Landing gear is retractable tricycle, with the main wheels retracting into the engine nacelles.

The cargo capacity of the Trader is restricted by its limited payload and side door loading system.

DEVELOPMENT • The Trader's initial operational capability (C-1A) was in 1955; the first flight (as the S-2) was in December 1952. Few Trader aircraft remained operational by the US Navy by the early 1990s, being gradually phased into retirement, replaced by the C-2 Greyhound.

VARIANTS • TF-1, C-1A, EC-1A (Electronic Countermeasures/ECM).

SPECIFICATIONS •

MANUFACTURER   Grumman
CREW   2 (pilot, copilot) + 7 passengers
ENGINES   2 Wright R-1820-82WA 9-cylinder radial piston
   max power   1,525 hp each
WEIGHTS
   empty   19,033 lb (8,561 kg)
   max payload 3,500 lb (1,587 kg)
   max takeoff 27,000 lb (12,272 kg)
DIMENSIONS
   wingspan   69 ft 8 in (21.23 m)
   length   42 ft (12.8 m)
   height   16 ft 4 in (4.98 m)
   wing area   485 ft² (45.07 m²)
PERFORMANCE
   max speed   290 kts (334 mph; 538 km/h)
   ceiling   22,000 ft (6,706 m)
   range   1,200 nm (1,381 mi; 2,222 km)

Greyhound (C-2A)

The C-2A Greyhound is derived from the E-2C Hawkeye Airborne Early Warning (AEW) aircraft and is the primary US Navy Carrier Onboard Delivery (COD) aircraft, providing transport for high-priority cargo and passengers between shore bases and aircraft carriers. The Greyhound shares the E-2 wings, powerplant, and four-fin tail configuration but has a larger fuselage and a rear-fuselage loading ramp.

The high-aspect-ratio wing is mounted on top of the fuselage. The tapered leading edge is detachable for access to hydraulic systems. The trailing edge has inboard Fowler-type flaps and long ailerons; the ailerons are drooped by a flap-aileron interconnection for low-speed handling. The wings fold outboard of the engines, ending up perpendicular to the center section and parallel to the aft fuselage; the folded wings are secured by jury strut locks fitted on the leading edge of the outer fins.

The tail-group design reflects the need for a low profile on US carrier hangar decks. Unlike the E-2, which has considerable dihedral on the horizontal tailplanes, the C-2's tail has none; an elevator is inset in the trailing edge. Large endplate fins are joined at right angles to the stabilizer; each has a double-section rudder above and below the stabilizer plane.

The aircraft is fitted with a Sperry AN/AWS-15 Automatic Flight Control System (AFCS) and two independent hydraulic systems. The wing and tail-group leading edges are fitted with deicing boots.

The two Allison turboprop engines are housed in deep nacelles on the wing leading edges and drive four-blade Hamilton Standard propellers. The two large fuel tanks are in the wing center section.

The main gear struts retract forward into the nacelles, pivoting 90° to lie flat. The two-wheel nose gear (derived from the Grumman A-6 Intruder) retracts to the rear under the flight deck.

DEVELOPMENT • The initial operational capability was in December 1966; its first flight was on November 18, 1964. 19 were originally procured. A $687-million, multiyear contract signed in 1983 provided for 39 uprated aircraft, the last being delivered in 1989. The original C-2A aircraft retired from USN service by 1987. The second series of 39 aircraft were also called C-2A by the Navy to preclude the necessary government documentation required for a "new" aircraft.

VARIANTS • C-2A.

COMBAT EXPERIENCE • During the Operations Desert Shield/Desert Storm deployments, C-2s were embarked on nearly every carrier and proved invaluable for shuttling personnel, high-value cargo, and mail from the carriers to bases in Saudi Arabia.

SPECIFICATIONS •
MANUFACTURER   Grumman
CREW   3 (2 pilots, flight engineer) + 39 troops or 28 passengers or 12 litters
ENGINES   2 Allison T56-A-425 turboprop
   max power   4,910 equivalent shp each
   internal fuel capacity
      1,824 US gal (6,904 liters)
WEIGHTS
   empty   36,346 lb (16,486 kg)
   max payload land-based: 15,000 lb (6,804 kg)
      carrier ops: 10,000 lb (4,536 kg)
   max takeoff   54,354 lb (24,655 kg)
DIMENSIONS
   wingspan   80 ft 7 in (24.57 m)
   length   56 ft 10 in (17.32 m)
   height   15 ft 11 in (4.85 m)
   wing area   700 ft² (65.03 m²)
   cargo hold   length: 27 ft 6 in (8.38 m)
      width: 7 ft 4 in (2.24 m)
      height: 5 ft 5 in (1.65 m)
      volume: 1,920 ft³ (54.37 m³)

PERFORMANCE
   max speed   310 kts (357 mph; 574 km/h)
   cruise speed   260 kts (299 mph; 482 km/h)
   climb rate   2,610 ft/min (796 m/min)
   ceiling   33,500 ft (10,211 m)
   range with 10,000-lb (4,536-kg) payload
      more than 1,042 nm (1,200 mi; 1,931 km)
   max ferry range
      1,560 nm (1,796 mi; 2,889 km)

Academe (C-4)

The C-4 Academe is a "flying classroom" used for training A-6E Intruder navigators and bombardiers. It is based on the Grumman Gulfstream I twin-turboprop executive transport.

The basic Gulfstream I has a double-taper, high-aspect-ratio wing mounted low on the fuselage. Large nacelles are mounted on each wing, with the thin turboprops extending well forward, driving four-blade propellers. The rest of the nacelle houses the jet pipe, which extends to the trailing edge over the wing, and the main landing gear, which is housed in a bulged section below the wing. The fin and balanced rudder are swept; a small dorsal fillet extends forward. The tailplane is double-tapered.

The fuselage has five oval windows. There is little step in the windshield, which tapers to a pointed nose in the US Coast Guard's single VC-4A executive transport. The TC-4C Academe has a large, bulbous nose grafted onto the original nose; a Forward-Looking Infrared (FLIR) turret was fitted under the false nose sometime after the original deliveries. The aircraft is fitted with an A-6 Intruder cockpit and four navigator/bombardier training consoles ahead of the A-6 cockpit installation.

DEVELOPMENT • The initial operational capability (VC-4A) was in March 1963. The Academe's first flight was on June 14, 1967. Only 11 military Gulfstream Is were built (nine USN TC-4C and two USCG VC-4A) and used by the Navy and Coast Guard.

VARIANTS • VC-4A, TC-4C.

SPECIFICATIONS •

MANUFACTURER Grumman Aerospace
CREW 2 (pilot, copilot) + 2 instructors and 5 students
ENGINES 2 Rolls-Royce Dart Mk 529-8X turboprop
  max power 2,210 shp each
WEIGHTS
  empty 24,575 lb (11,147 kg)
  max takeoff 36,000 lb (16,329 kg)
DIMENSIONS
  wingspan 78 ft 4 in (23.87 m)
  length 67 ft 10¾ in (20.69 m)
  height 23 ft 4 in (7.1 m)
  wing area 610 ft² (186 m²)
PERFORMANCE
  max speed 317 kts (365 mph; 587 km/h)
  cruise speed
    217 kts (250 mph; 402 km/h)
  ceiling 30,000 ft (9,144 m)
  range at 5,000 ft (1,524 m): 996 nm (1,147 mi; 1,846 km)
    at 30,000 ft (9,144 m): 1,741 nm (2,005 mi; 3,226 km)

King Air 90 (U-21A, C-6B)

The King Air was originally designed as a general aviation aircraft but has been adapted for use in many nations as a light utility/liaison/VIP transport aircraft.

Its configuration is fairly conventional for an aircraft of its type, featuring a low-set, slightly dihedral wing, two turboprop engines in wing nacelles, a single, swept tailfin, slightly dihedral tailplanes set on the tailboom, retractable tricycle landing gear, and a passenger/cargo door on the left side of the fuselage, behind the wing.

DEVELOPMENT • The King Air's initial operational capability was in 1965; its first flight was in January 1964. Over 250 are in military service worldwide. It is operated by almost 20 nations, including the US, mostly as VIP transport or liaison aircraft.

VARIANTS • C-6B (USAF), U-21A (US Army), King Air 90, King Air 100 (stretched), King Air 200 (USAF C-12).

COMBAT EXPERIENCE • None directly; used to support local flights of key personnel during conflicts in developing areas.

SPECIFICATIONS •

MANUFACTURER Beechcraft
CREW 2 (pilot, copilot) + 8 passengers
ENGINES 2 Pratt & Whitney PT6A-20 turboprop
  max power 550 shp each
WEIGHTS
  empty 5,680 lb (2,576 kg)
  max takeoff 9,300 lb (4,218 kg)
DIMENSIONS
  wingspan 45 ft 10½ in (13.98 m)
  length 35 ft 6 in (10.82 m)
  height 14 ft 8 in (4.47 m)
  wing area 280 ft² (26 m²)
PERFORMANCE
  max speed 241 kts (278 mph; 447 km/h)
  ceiling 31,600 ft (9,632 m)
  range 1,372 nm (1,580 mi; 2,543 km)

Gulfstream II (VC-11)

The Gulfstream II is a large executive jet that is used as a VIP aircraft by several air forces. A single US Coast Guard Gulfstream II is designated VC-11.

The low wing has 25° of leading-edge sweep, 3° of dihedral from the roots, and low wing fences at midspan. The trailing edge has one-piece, single-slotted, Fowler-type flaps inboard of inset ailerons. Ahead of the ailerons is a span-wise line of vortex generators. Farther inboard, two sections of spoilers are located ahead of the flaps. These can be used for roll-control assist, air brakes, and lift dumpers.

The T-tail has a broad, slightly swept vertical fin with a small dorsal fillet and full-height rudder. At the top of the tail are swept, horizontal stabilizers with full-span elevators. All controls are powered by dual independent, 1,500-psi hydraulic systems with mechanical reversion.

The two Rolls-Royce turbofan engines with Rohr thrust reversers are mounted on short stubs that are located high on the rear fuselage; the inlets overlap the trailing edges of the wings. Fuel is carried in wing tanks. The long, semimonocoque fuselage extends well ahead of the wings. An entry door is located on the forward left side between the flight deck and the passenger cabin. The cabin has five oval, "porthole" windows on each side.

The main gear legs retract inward, the two-wheel assemblies being stowed in fuselage bays. The two-wheel nose gear retracts forward.

DEVELOPMENT • The aircraft's initial operational capability was in 1969; its first flight was on October 2, 1966. Production ended in the 1980s after 258 were completed. The US Coast Guard VC-11 is normally stationed at National Airport in Washington, DC. The plane is operated by six other countries.

VARIANTS • Gulfstream II-B, Gulfstream III/IV.

SPECIFICATIONS •
MANUFACTURER   Grumman Aircraft (later Gulfstream Aerospace)
CREW   2–3 + 19 passengers
ENGINES   2 Rolls-Royce RB163-25 Spey Mk 511-8 turbofan
    max power   11,400 lb (5,171 kg) static thrust

internal fuel capacity
    23,300 lb (10,569 kg) or 3,452 US gal (13,065 liters)
WEIGHTS
operating weight empty
    36,900 lb (16,737 kg)
cargo   2,000 lb (907 kg)
max takeoff   65,500 lb (29,711 kg)
DIMENSIONS
wingspan   68 ft 10 in (20.98 m)
length   79 ft 11 in (25.36 m)
height   24 ft 6 in (7.47 m)
cabin   length 34 ft (10.36 m)
    width 7 ft 4 in (2.24 m)
    height 6 ft 1 in (1.85 m)
    volume 1,270 ft³ (36.0 m³)
wing area   809.6 ft² (75.21 m²)
PERFORMANCE
max cruise speed at 25,000 ft (7,620 m)
    505 kts (581 mph; 936 km/h)
econ cruise at 40,000 ft (12,192 m)
    431 kts (496 mph; 798 km/h)
stall speed   flaps and gear up: 130 kts (150 mph; 241 km/h)
    flaps and gear down: 108 kts (124 mph; 200 km/h)
minimum control speed (Vmc)
    102 kts (117 mph; 189 km/h)
climb rate   2 engines: 4,350 ft/min (1,325 m/min)
    1 engine: 1,525 ft/min (465 m/min)
ceiling, 2 engines
    43,000 ft (13,106 m)
max fuel range
    3,712 nm (4,275 mi; 6,880 km)

Spartan (C-27A)

The C-27A Spartan is the Italian G222 in service with the United States. The aircraft is a low-cost, short-haul cargo aircraft developed for Italian service but subsequently exported to a number of other nations including the United States. It is a versatile two-engine turboprop used for transport and special-purpose missions such as fire fighting, communications calibration, and Electronic Warfare (EW). The G222 is similar to, but smaller than, the US C-130 Hercules and the French-German C160 Transall.

The G222's high wing is mounted forward of midfuselage. The high-aspect-ratio airfoil has a rectangular center section and double-taper outer panels with 2½° dihedral. Two sections of double-slotted flaps line the trailing edge inboard of the ailerons; two sections of spoilers fitted ahead of the outer flap sections assist in roll control and are used as lift dumpers.

The large tail has a tall fin and full-height, powered rudder. The stubby, variable-incidence horizontal tailplanes have a slightly swept leading edge and full-span elevators and are "shoulder-mounted" at the base of the fin. The two independent hydraulic systems power the rudder, flaps, spoilers, landing gear, and brakes.

The two General Electric turboprops are mounted in thin nacelles set in the wing's leading edge and drive three-blade Hamilton Standard propellers. Internal fuel storage is two center-section tanks and an additional tank in each outer section.

The fuselage has a nearly stepless nose with extensive glazing. The pressurized main cabin has a nearly constant section aft to the trailing edge of the wing, where it tapers up to the high-flown tail. The rear loading ramp forms the floor of the aft fuselage when stowed. Typical loads include 53 fully equipped troops, 40 paratroopers, 36 litters and four attendants, two light trucks or small armored vehicles, small artillery pieces, or five A-22-size standard freight containers; up to 19,840 lb (9,000 kg) can be carried. Long narrow sponsons along the lower fuselage hold the main landing gear, which consists of tandem, single-wheel units; the nose gear folds forward.

DEVELOPMENT • The aircraft's initial operational capability was in 1976; its first flight was July 18, 1970.

In August 1990, the Air Force ordered five G222s as the C-27A under an $80-million contract, with options for 15 more. An option for five more C-27s was exercised in February 1991. Aeritalia teamed with Chrysler Airborne Technology Systems to build the aircraft, the latter providing navigation and other avionics equipment.

The Air Force accepted the first C-27 on September 27, 1991, when the nickname Spartan was adopted.

VARIANTS • G-222.

SPECIFICATIONS •
MANUFACTURER   Aeritalia (Naples, Italy)
CREW   3 (2 pilots, flight engineer/radio operator)
ENGINES   General Electric T64-GE-P4D turboprop
  max power   3,400 shp each
  internal fuel capacity
       3,170 US gal (12,000 liters)
WEIGHTS
  empty   32,165 lb (14,590 kg)
  max payload 19,840 lb (9,000 kg)
  max takeoff 61,730 lb (28,000 kg)
DIMENSIONS
  wingspan   94 ft 2 in (28.7 m)
  length   74 ft 5½ in (22.7 m)
  height   32 ft 1¾ in (9.8 m)
  cabin   length: 28 ft 1¾ in (8.58 m)
               width: 8 ft ½ in (2.45 m)
               height: 7 ft 4½ in (2.25 m)
               volume: 2,048 ft³ (58 m³)
  wing area 883 ft² (82.00 m²)
PERFORMANCE
  max speed at 15,000 ft (4,575 m)
       291 kts (336 mph; 540 km/h)

cruise speed at 19,680 ft (6,000 m)
    237 kts (273 mph; 439 km/h)
stall speed, flaps and gear down
    84 kts (97 mph; 155 km/h)
climb rate   1,705 ft/min (520 m/min)

single-engine climb rate
    410 ft/min (125 m/min)
time to height (to 14,760 ft/4,500 m)
    8 min 35 sec
ceiling   25,000 ft (7,620 m)
range with 19,840-lb (9,000-kg) payload
    740 nm (852 mi; 1,371 km)

ELECTRONIC/RECONNAISSANCE/OBSERVATION

Hawkeye (E-2C)

The E-2C Hawkeye is a US Navy carrier-based, all-weather Airborne Early Warning (AEW) aircraft developed specifically for carrier operation. It is used for long-range early warning and threat assessment as well as fighter direction. A four- or five-plane E-2C squadron is provided to each US aircraft carrier.

The Hawkeye's most distinctive feature is the 24-foot-diameter, saucerlike rotodome for the AN/APS-120, -125, -138, -139, or -145 UHF radar. The Randtron AN/APA-171 antenna system includes UHF and Identification Friend or Foe (IFF) endfire Yagi arrays. The rotodome revolves freely in the airstream at the rate of 6 rpm. It provides sufficient lift to offset its own weight in flight and can be lowered to facilitate handling the aircraft aboard ship.

The AN/APS-138 in the E-2C has an effective aircraft-detection range of approximately 260 nm (300 mi; 482 km) with an improved over-land/water capability through a Total Radiation Aperture Control Antenna (TRAC-A) that features low sidelobes.

Using a Loral array track processor, the aircraft can simultaneously track more than 600 air targets and control up to 40 interceptions. The APS-139, which was fitted to E-2Cs delivered after 1987, has an upgraded processor that allows tracking of more than 2,000 targets. The follow-on APS-145 features "environmental processing" to screen out ground clutter as well as a lower pulse repetition frequency and rotodome rotation rate. To make the most effective use of the radar, the E-2 cruises with a 10° flap setting, which gives the rotodome the desired 3° of incidence for scanning.

The E-2 has a high-aspect-ratio wing mounted on top of the fuselage. The tapered leading edge is detachable for access to hydraulic systems. The trailing edge has inboard Fowler-type flaps and long ailerons; the ailerons are drooped by a flap-aileron interconnection for low-speed handling. The wings fold outboard of the engines, ending up perpendicular to the center section and parallel to the aft fuselage; the folded wings are secured by jury strut locks fitted on the leading edge of the outer fins.

The tail group design reflects the need for a low profile on US carrier hangar decks and the control-blanketing effects of the larger rotodome. The horizontal tailplanes are joined on the centerline, each having 11° of dihedral relative to the fuselage and an elevator inset in the trailing edge. Large endplate fins are joined at right angles to the stabilizer; each has a double-section rudder above and below the stabilizer plane. Inboard of the endplates are fins with

E-2C
U.S. GOVERNMENT DEPARTMENT OF DEFENSE

single-section rudders. The aircraft is fitted with a Sperry AN/AWS-15 Automatic Flight Control System (AFCS). The wing and tail-group leading edges and the rim of the rotodome are fitted with deicing boots. The two Allison turboprop engines are housed in deep nacelles on the wing leading edges and drive four-blade propellers originally manufactured by Aero Products (with square tips) and later by Hamilton Standard (foam-filled with rounded tips). Beginning in 1988, E-2Cs were fitted with the uprated T56-A-427 engine of greater power and 13% lower fuel consumption. The main gear struts retract forward into the nacelles; the two-wheel nose gear retracts to the rear under the flight deck. Fuel tankage is confined to integral tanks in each inboard wing section; an extended-range version with outer-panel tanks has not entered production.

The fuselage is conventional semi-monocoque construction. The E-2C nose is longer than earlier variants to accommodate forward-looking Litton AN/ALR-73 Passive Detection System (PDS) antennas. The other three antenna sets are located in the aft fuselage belly and on the outer face of the endplate fins. The flight deck is raised above the fuselage top line and has bulged side windows.

Behind the flight deck are racks of electronic equipment flanking a passageway leading to the Air Tactical Data System (ATDS) compartment. Three stations are lined up along the port wall for the radar operator, combat information officer, and air controller; each operator has a display. The extensive electronics fit requires its own vapor cycle cooling system, which has a large radiator housed in a pod mounted on the fuselage behind the flight deck.

The ALR-73 PDS is claimed to have twice the detection range of the APS-125/138 radar. The Litton AN/ASN-92 Carrier Airborne Inertial Navigation System (CAINS) is used with the

AN/APN-153 Doppler navigation radar; other navigation information is supplied by the Lear-Siegler AN/ASN-50 Heading and Attitude Reference System (HARS).

The E-2 transmits its data to a carrier combat information center through two-way Collins AN/ARC-34 HF and ARC-158 UHF data links. The first E-2C fitted with the Joint Tactical Information Distribution System (JTIDS) flew in February 1990, with the first delivery scheduled in December 1990. Existing E-2Cs are scheduled for JTIDS installations beginning in 1993.

DEVELOPMENT • The E-2C series was designated W2F until 1962. The aircraft's initial operational capability (US Navy) was in 1965; its first flight (W2F-1) on October 21, 1960; the later E-2C first flew on January 20, 1971. More than 100 E-2 aircraft have been built for the Navy.

In February 1987, the Navy announced the grounding of seven of its 91 aircraft and ordered flight restrictions for 10 more because of potential wing cracks. The problem was later determined to be confined to the first 80 aircraft built, and in December 1987, a $200-million contract was awarded to Grumman to strengthen the wings at the rate of 16 aircraft per year.

Four E-2Cs were loaned to the US Coast Guard from the US Navy for anti-drug-smuggling patrols from 1986 to October 1991. In FY1991, the four E-2Cs were deployed for a total of 293 days.

After an original plan for a $300-million contract to supply four E-2Cs to the Royal Thai Air Force, the plan was temporarily abandoned because of the high cost, but was revived in January 1992 with a $382-million letter of offer for three E-2Cs. Also operated by Egypt, Israel, Japan, Singapore, and Taiwan.

On December 17, 1991, an E-2C Plus set new class records in closed-course speed and time to altitudes. Over a 54-nm (62-mi; 100-km) closed course, the E-2 averaged 324 kts (373 mph; 600 km/h),

which was 51 kts (59 mph; 95 km/h) faster than the old record. The aircraft reached 9,842 ft (3,000 m) in 2 min 48 sec, 19,685 ft (6,000 m) in 5 min 37 sec, and 29,527 ft (9,000 m) in 10 min 1 sec.

VARIANTS • E-2A, E-2B, TE-2C, E-2C, E-2C Plus, E-2T (Taiwan).

COMBAT EXPERIENCE • Early E-2 aircraft were used extensively in Vietnam.

The E-2C was first used in combat by Israel when it controlled Israeli fighters during a dogfight with Syrian MiG-21s in June 1979, in which six MiGs were downed.

A Hawkeye from the US carrier *Saratoga* (CV 60) in November 1985 helped track the terrorists from the *Achille Lauro* who were attempting to escape on an Egyptian civilian airliner; the E-2C vectored Navy F-14s that forced the airliner down.

In January 1989, an E-2C from the *John F. Kennedy* (CV 67) detected two Libyan MiG-23 Flogger fighter aircraft taking off from Al-Bunbah airfield near Tobruk. The E-2 directed two F-14 Tomcat fighters toward the MiG-23s; the F-14s downed the MiGs after a series of evasive maneuvers.

A total of 27 E-2Cs were deployed on the aircraft carriers that launched strikes against Iraqi targets during Operation Desert Storm. The Hawkeyes flew 1,196 sorties, during which they vectored strike aircraft onto Iraqi naval units as well as forming part of the integrated airborne warning and control network over Iraq, Kuwait, Saudi Arabia, and the Persian Gulf. None was lost during the seven-week war.

SPECIFICATIONS •
MANUFACTURER   Grumman Aerospace
CREW   5 (2 pilots, combat information center officer, air controller, and radar operator or technician)
ENGINES   2 Allison T56-A-425 or -427 turboprop

power	-425: 4,910 equivalent shp each (flat-rated to 4,508 eshp each) -427: 5,250 eshp each
internal fuel capacity	1,824 US gal (6,904 liters)
WEIGHTS	
empty	37,678 lbs (17,090 kg)
max takeoff	51,569 lbs (23,391 kg)
DIMENSIONS	
wingspan	extended: 80 ft 7 in (24.58 m) folded: 29 ft 4 in (8.94 m)
length	57 ft 7 in (17.56 m)
height	rotodome raised: 18 ft 3 ¾ in (5.58 m) rotodome lowered: 16 ft 5½ in (5.02 m)
wing area	700 ft² (65.05 m²)
PERFORMANCE	
max speed	326 kts (375 mph; 604 km/h)
cruise speed	max: 311 kts (358 mph; 576 km/h) econ: 269 kts (310 mph; 499 km/h)
stall, power off	at takeoff weight: 97 kts (112 mph; 180 km/h) at landing weight and approach power: 71 kts (82 mph; 132 km/h)
climb rate	2,515 ft/min (767 m/min)
time to 20,000 ft (6,096 m)	13 min
time to ceiling	33 min 30 seconds
ceiling	30,800 ft (9,388 m)
radius	175 nm (200 mi; 320 km) with 3–4 hr on station
ferry range	1,394 nm (1,605 mi; 2,583 km)
radar	AN/APS-139 (APS-120/125/138 in early E-2C aircraft)

Sentry/AWACS (E-3)

The E-3 Sentry is the primary Airborne Early Warning (AEW) aircraft of the NATO alliance and is popularly known by the acronym AWACS (for Airborne Warning and Control System). It is a Boeing 707 aircraft modified to carry an extensive mission avionics package to provide long-range target acquisition and identification, and control/communications for directing other combat aircraft to the targets.

The E-3 has a conventional planform with low wings swept 35° at the quarter-chord; they are mounted at a +7° dihedral. Along the crescent-shaped trailing edge are two sections of double-slotted flaps that flank the midspan flight aileron. The larger, low-speed aileron is outboard of the outer set of flaps. The tall, slightly swept fin has an antenna extending forward from the tip, and a large, powered rudder. The low, swept tailplanes have full-span elevators.

The four TF33 turbofan engines are mounted on pylons that extend ahead of the wing leading edge. The E-3 has an in-flight refueling receptacle over the flight deck. The aircraft's profile is dominated by the 30-ft (9.14-m) diameter rotodome mounted on two struts that rest on a reinforcement ring buried in the rear fuselage. The oval rotodome weighs 11,800 lb (5,352 kg), is 6 ft (1.83 m) thick, and is mounted on a 7-ft 2-in (2.34-m) turntable at the top of the struts.

The rotodome's central rectangular structure holds ancillary equipment; this structure is flanked by a Westinghouse AN/APY-2 slotted, phased-array antenna on one side and combined Eaton AN/APX-103 Identification Friend or Foe (IFF) interrogator and Tactical Digital Information Link (TADIL-C) data link array for the Joint Tactical Information Distribution System (JTIDS) on the other. While in flight, but not in operation, the rotodome is hydraulically rotated at ¼ rpm to lubricate the bearings.

E-3 Sentry
U.S. GOVERNMENT DEPARTMENT OF DEFENSE

When the radar is operating, the rotation speed is 6 rpm.

All aircraft in the series are similar in appearance, varying only in the avionics package and engines. AWACS sold to Saudi Arabia and France have CFM56 engines. Some have been fitted with upgraded Electronic Counter-Countermeasures (ECCM) equipment.

DEVELOPMENT • The aircraft's initial operational capability was in 1976; its first flight with full mission capability was in October 1975. 35 were built for the US Air Force, 18 for NATO, and five for Saudi Arabia. The Reagan administration's 1985 sale of E-3 and KE-3 aircraft to Saudi Arabia was strongly opposed by many pro-Israeli congressmen, who believed the aircraft could be used against Israel in a future Arab-Israeli conflict. In December 1986, Great Britain ordered six E-3D AWACS aircraft with CFM-56 engines; an option for one additional aircraft was exercised later. Britain passed over its domestically produced Nimrod AEW in favor of the E-3D AWACS, leading to criticism that the Thatcher government was undercutting Britain's own aircraft industry.

Negotiations with Pakistan over a potential transfer of the aircraft through sale or lease in 1987 did not occur because of congressional displeasure with Pakistan's alleged nuclear weapons development program.

France ordered three E-3F AWACS in February 1987, later exercising an option for one more.

AWACS assigned to NATO service are registered in Luxembourg; these are the only aircraft operated directly by NATO.

VARIANTS • E-3A, E-3A NATO Standard, Peace Sentinel (Saudi), E-3B, E-3C, E-3D Sentry AEW Mk 1 (British), E-3F (French).

COMBAT EXPERIENCE • On May 17, 1987, a Saudi AWACS detected the Iraqi Mirage jet that subsequently attacked the USS *Stark* (FFG 31). A US liaison officer on board the AWACS requested the Saudis to vector interceptors against the Mirage, but the interception was not accomplished because command clearance was not obtained in time. Although the Reagan administration did not accuse the Saudis of foot-dragging in the incident, the noninterception was cited by some congressmen as grounds for opposition to sales of AGM-65 Maverick missiles to the Saudis. The proposal for the sale of Mavericks was withdrawn because of the likelihood that Congress would not approve it.

Four US Air Force AWACS aircraft were based in Saudi Arabia from 1987 to 1989 in support of US Navy convoys of reflagged Kuwaiti oil tankers. They were withdrawn in April 1989.

In February 1990, at least five E-3s were deployed from Tinker AFB, Oklahoma, to Roosevelt Roads, Puerto Rico, to provide improved surveillance of drug-smuggling aircraft ships. The Air Force also stated that 40% of worldwide AWACS' flying hours were being devoted to anti-drug-smuggling surveillance.

US E-3s returned to the Persian Gulf in August 1990 as part of Operations Desert Shield/Desert Storm. Before Desert Storm began on January 17, 1991, Saudi and US E-3s coordinated air patrols flown by Saudi, US, and British fighter aircraft. By the end of hostilities, 15 of the 33 US Air Force E-3s were supporting Desert Storm.

SPECIFICATIONS •

MANUFACTURER Boeing Aerospace
CREW   17 (4 in flight crew, 13 in mission crew)
ENGINES   4 Pratt & Whitney TF33-PW-100A turbofan
  max power   21,000 lb (9,525 kg) static thrust each
  internal fuel capacity
       23,855 US gal (90,292 liters)
WEIGHTS
  empty   170,277 lb (77,236 kg)
  max takeoff 325,000 lb (147,417 kg)
DIMENSIONS
  wingspan   145 ft 9 in (44.42 m)

length   152 ft 11 in (46.61 m)
height   42 ft 2 in (12.73 m)
wing area 2,892 ft² (269.02 m²)
PERFORMANCE
  max speed   473 kts (545 mph; 876 km/h)
  cruise speed
       416 kts (479 mph; 771 km/h)
  on-station speed
       327 kts (377 mph; 606 km/h)
  stall speed, power off
       129 kts (149 mph; 239 km/h)
  climb rate   2,640 ft/min (805 m/min)
  on-station altitude
       29,000 ft (8,839 m)
  ceiling   41,900 ft (12,771 m)
  time on station at radius of 1,000 nm
  (1,151 mi; 1,852 km)
       unrefueled: 6 hr
       1 refueling: 14.4 hr

NEACP (E-4)

The NEACP (pronounced "kneecap"), the National Emergency Airborne Command Post, is a Boeing 747 fitted with communications equipment and antennas to act as the National Command Authority (NCA) operations center in the event of nuclear war. At the height of its operations, the alert staff consists of a Joint Chiefs of Staff (JCS) joint service operations team, a Defense Intelligence Agency (DIA) element, a flight crew from the former Strategic Air Command (SAC), a communications team from the former Air Force Communications Command, a maintenance crew, and security forces.

Aside from the markings, the only observable difference between the NEACP and a commercial 747 aircraft is the NEACP's array of antennas and a small radome bulge on the rear of the upper flight deck. Like the 747, the NEACP features a fuselage with a distinctive upper-deck bulge, wings mounted low at mid-fuselage, a high single tailfin, and four engines mounted on wing pylons. Internal modifications, however, are much more extensive. The interior of the NEACP has 4,350 ft² (404.3 m²) of floor space and has been divided into six working compartments fore to aft that carry a total of 149,000 lb (67,585 kg) of command-and-control and communications equipment. The NCA working area is located under the flight deck. Farther aft is a secure conference room and a briefing room. The operations team area has 31 console work areas. The communications control area is subdivided into a voice area and a data area. The rearmost compartment contains a technical control area on the left side forward and a mission crew rest area in the rear. The upper deck houses the flight deck and flight crew rest area.

The communications capability spans the frequency spectrum from Very Low Frequency (VLF) to Super High Frequency (SHF) systems, permitting the NEACP staff to contact almost all nuclear delivery systems directly. The systems have been hardened against Electromagnetic Pulse (EMP) effects. In February 1990, Rockwell Collins was awarded a contract to install an automatic data processing system in all four E-4Bs that is controlled by a Rolm Mil-Spec Hawk 32 computer system possessing a 1.2-gigabit memory and 32-bit processor. All NEACP aircraft are fitted with in-flight refueling capability to permit an endurance aloft of over 72 hours.

DEVELOPMENT • The NEACP's initial operational capability was in 1975; its first flight was on October 10, 1974. Three were completed as E-4A and later converted to E-4B, and a fourth E-4B was built subsequently, entering service in January 1980.

VARIANTS • E-4A, E-4B.

SPECIFICATIONS •

MANUFACTURER Boeing
CREW 4 (pilot, copilot, navigator, flight engineer) + 31 battle staff + command and technical support personnel (numbers vary)
ENGINES 4 General Electric F103-GE-100 turbofan
max power 52,500 lb (23,814 kg) static thrust each
internal fuel capacity
      332,976 lb (151,036 kg)
WEIGHTS
max takeoff 803,000 lb (364,232 kg)
DIMENSIONS
wingspan 195 ft 8 in (59.64 m)
length 225 ft 2 in (68.63 m)
height 63 ft 5 in (19.33 m)
wing area 5,500 ft² (511.0 m²)
PERFORMANCE
max speed 527 kts (607 mph; 977 km/h)
ceiling 45,000 ft (13,715 m)

range 7,100 nm (8,176 mi; 13,158 km) unrefueled

Hermes (E-6A)

The Hermes replaces the EC-130 in the TACAMO (Take Charge and Move Out) role of providing Very Low Frequency (VLF) radio relay to strategic missile submarines at sea.

The E-6A is a military version of the Boeing 707-320B aircraft, which also serves as the airframe for the E-3A AWACS (Airborne Warning and Control System); the two aircraft share approximately 75% of their airframe components. The aircraft will provide an on-station/all-ocean link between the US National Command Authority and the US Navy Trident submarine fleet.

The E-6 has a conventional planform with low wings swept 35° at the leading edge. Along the crescent-shaped trailing edge are two sections of double-slotted flaps that flank the midspan flight aileron. The larger, low-speed aileron is outboard of the outer set of flaps.

The tall, slightly swept fin has an antenna extending forward from the tip, and a large, powered rudder. The low, swept tailplanes have full-span elevators.

The four CFM turbofan engines are mounted on pylons that extend ahead of the wing leading edge. The E-6 can be refueled in flight; the large oil tanks on each engine permit a maximum refueled endurance of 72 hours.

In the TACAMO role, the E-6A has essentially the same VLF communications equipment as the EC-130Q, with two Trailing-Wire Antennas (TWA). The shorter wire is 4,000 ft (1,220 m) long and streams horizontally from a reel in the aft fuselage. The other wire is 26,000 ft (7,925 m) long and extends below the E-6; it is stabilized by a 95-lb (43.6-kg) drogue. Only the shorter wire is electrically charged, with energy reradiating from the longer wire.

To communicate with submarines, the wires are let out and the E-6 flies a low-speed, high-angle (30°–50°) bank; the object is to achieve 70% "verticality" for the main lower wire by having it stall into a near-vertical line. Wingtip pods on the E-6A contain satellite receiving antennas; the starboard pod also holds a General Instruments ALR-66 threat-warning receiver.

The Hermes is said to be more resistant to the electromagnetic pulses, gamma and neutron radiation, and blast and thermal effects of nuclear war than any other aircraft in service.

DEVELOPMENT • The E-6A's initial operational capability was in October 1990. 16 E-6A aircraft were funded, including a research-and-development aircraft. The prototype was rolled out on December 18, 1986, and its first flight was February 19, 1987.

In September 1990, Boeing announced a Navy order for 10 more E-6s, bringing the total to 16. An $85.5-million modification to a contract for seven E-6A "TACAMO aircraft weapons systems" was awarded to Boeing in July 1991.

In May 1991, the Navy announced the end of a 30-year policy of having a TACAMO aircraft continuously airborne, moving instead to a ground-based "strip alert" posture.

SPECIFICATIONS •

MANUFACTURER Boeing
CREW 4 flight, 6 mission, 8 relief crew seats
ENGINES 4 General Electric/SNECMA CFM-56-2A2 (F108-CF-100) turbofan
  max power 22,000 lb (9,979 kg) static thrust each
  internal fuel capacity
    23,855 US gal (90,299 liters)
WEIGHTS
  empty 172,795 lb (78,379 kg)
  max takeoff 342,000 lb (155,129 kg)
DIMENSIONS
  wingspan 148 ft 2 in (45.17 m)
  length 152 ft 11 in (46.62 m)
  height 42 ft 5 in (12.93 m)
  wing area 3,050 ft² (283.4 m²)

PERFORMANCE
  speed cruise: 454 kts (523 mph; 842 km/h)
    max: 530 kts (610 mph; 982 km/h)
    orbit: 127–183 kts (146–211 mph; 235–339 km/h)
  ceiling 40,000+ ft (12,192 m)
  range 6,350 nm (7,312 mi; 11,767 km)
  endurance 1,000 nm (1,152 mi; 1,853 km) radius with 10.5 hr of loiter
    normal mission duration will be about 15 hr with in-flight refueling extending it to 29 hr
  radar AQS-133 Bendix weather radar

Joint-Stars (E-8A)

The E-8A aircraft carries the airborne elements of the Air Force and Army Joint Surveillance Target Attack Radar System (Joint-STARS). Joint-STARS (sometimes referred to as JSTARS) combines technologies developed in the Air Force's Pave Mover and Army's Standoff Target Acquisition System (SOTAS) programs.

The E-8A's principal mission components are a Norden AN/APY-3 multimode Side-Looking Airborne Radar (SLAR); extensive on-board computer processing capability; and Command, Control, Communications, and Intelligence (C3I) links with ground-based commanders. The only noticeable indication of the aircraft's particular role is the 30-ft (9.14-m) "canoe" ventral fairing for the APY-3 SLAR antenna, located just aft of the nose gear.

The APY-3 has four Traveling Wave Tube (TWT) transmitters and 456 phase shifters; beams are scanned mechanically in elevation and electronically in azimuth. It can be operated as a Synthetic Aperture Radar (SAR), which has a wide, high-resolution field of view of +/-60°. Smearing of the SAR image is countered through precision interferometry calibration and a Litton LR-85A Inertial Measurement System (IMS). Doppler Moving- or Fixed-Target Indicator (MTI/FTI) processing is used to detect slow-moving targets amid the ground clutter.

At least 10 operator consoles are fitted in the aircraft; space and power are reserved for a total of 17 consoles. 23 different radio sets are provided, 16 of which are Magnavox Have Quick Electronic Countermeasures (ECM)-resistant, UHF radios; two of the five VHF radios are SINCGARS and two more radios operate in HFband. Targeting information for Air Force use will be processed on board the aircraft and transmitted to other aircraft or missiles through a Joint Tactical Information Distribution System (JTIDS) data link.

DEVELOPMENT • JSTARS' development contract was awarded to Grumman Corp. in September 1985. Original planning called for 10 conversions, later revised to 22 newly built aircraft. First flight of E-8A (modified ex-commercial 707) was on April 1, 1988; first radar test flight was on December 22, 1988. First flight of second test aircraft was on August 31, 1989. The first two prototypes were deployed to Saudi Arabia in January 1991 as part of Operations Desert Shield/Desert Storm.

Production E-8s were to be based on the Navy's E-6 Hermes TACAMO aircraft (a 707-320 airframe with more powerful CFM turbofans). This plan was derailed in October 1989 when Boeing announced that it would end production of that airframe upon completion of British and French Airborne Warning and Control System (AWACS) aircraft in 1991. Therefore, refitted used 707s are used; they are designated E-8Cs.

Other customers could include NATO, which operates E-3 AWACS aircraft.

VARIANTS • Pave Mover, SOTAS (Standoff Target Acquisition System), E-8B.

COMBAT EXPERIENCE • Joint-STARS aircraft were deployed to Saudi Arabia but were limited to 20-hour flights because of cavitation problems in their engines. Despite this limitation and their untested systems, the Joint-STARS aircraft flew 12-hour missions beginning on January 14, 1991. The two aircraft flew 54 missions totaling more than 600 flight hours; no mission was canceled because of system problems.

SPECIFICATIONS •
MANUFACTURER Grumman
airframe Boeing Military Airplane
CREW 3 (pilot, copilot, navigator) +
10–15 surveillance technicians and

airborne operators (24 total during Operation Desert Storm)

ENGINES   4 Pratt & Whitney JT3D turbofan

max power   18,000 lb (8,165 kg) static thrust each

WEIGHTS

empty   172,795 lb (78,378 kg)

mission payload
57,000 lb (25,855 kg)

max takeoff   342,000 lb (155,129 kg)

DIMENSIONS

wingspan   148 ft 2 in (45.16 m)

length   152 ft 11 in (46.61 m)

height   42 ft 5 in (12.93 m)

wing area   3,050 ft² (283.4 m²)

PERFORMANCE

max speed   530 kts (610 mph; 981 km/h)

cruise speed
455 kts (523 mph; 842 km/h)

ceiling   42,000 ft (12,800 m)

unrefueled range
6,700 nm (7,715 mi; 12,415 km)

endurance   unrefueled: 11 hr
refueled: 21 hr

radar   Norden Systems APY-3

Prowler (EA-6B)

The EA-6B is a modified Intruder design with significantly more Electronic Warfare (EW)/Electronic Countermeasures (ECM) capability than the earlier EA-6A variant of the A-6 Intruder.

The EA-6B layout resembles that of the A-6 but has a 4-ft 6-in (1.37-m) longer fuselage to accommodate two more crew members. The wing is mounted at mid-fuselage height and has a modest 25° sweep at the quarter-chord. Nearly the entire leading edge is occupied by slats; virtually all of the trailing edge has single-slotted, semi-Fowler-type flaps. Spoilers that run parallel to the flaps provide roll control when operated differentially, lift dumping when operated collectively. The rear half of each wingtip can be opened

into upper and lower halves, thus acting as air brakes.

The fin leading edge has a slight sweep aft; the trailing edge, with its inset rudder, sweeps slightly forward. The all-moving tailplanes are slightly swept and are mounted on the fuselage ahead of the rudder hinge line.

The two J52 turbojet engines are contained in pods under the wing, flanking the fuselage; the airflow is a straight line from intake to exhaust. Each intake, headed by a boundary-layer splitter plate, is mounted in a cheek position below the rear cockpit; the exhausts appear beyond the wing trailing edge on either side of the fuselage. Each of the two J52s used in the EA-6B develops 1,900 lb (822 kg) more thrust than those installed in the A-6.

Both wings have integral fuel tanks, and there is additional tankage in the fuselage behind the cockpit and near the center of gravity. Prowlers are fitted with an in-flight refueling probe mounted immediately forward of the cockpit.

The fuselage has a bulged cockpit with a short radome well forward. The pilot and an Electronic Countermeasures Officer (ECMO) fly side by side in the front cockpit while two more ECMOs are seated in the rear, side-by-side cockpit. The canopy enclosing the forward cockpit is essentially unchanged from the Intruder, while the rear canopy provides side and top visibility only; both canopies are hinged at the rear.

The retractable main gear units fold forward and inward into the intake pod; the nose gear retracts to the rear. The arrester hook swings down from a fuselage point midway between the wing trailing edge and the tail.

The Prowler's extensive ECM capability derives from successive generations of the Raytheon AN/ALQ-99 Tactical Jamming System (TJS) known as the Basic, EXCAP, and ICAP-1 phases. Some earlier EA-6Bs have been upgraded to ICAP-2.

All EA-6B variants have the distinctive pod mounted atop the tailfin that holds the receivers and antennas for Bands 4–9 (known as the System Integrated Receiver/SIR group); antennas for Bands 1 and 2 are mounted on the fin below the pod. Overall coverage ranges from A through I bands.

Information on specific enemy emitters likely to be encountered is fed into the ALQ-99 system by the Tactical EA-6B Mission Planning System (TEAMS) before launch.

Up to five jamming pods can be carried on four wing pylons and a centerline fuselage hardpoint; each external-stores station has a capacity of 3,600 lb (1,633 kg). In ICAP-2 aircraft, each pod has a universal exciter capable of generating signals in any of seven frequency bands; a colocated transmitter can jam in two bands simultaneously.

The weight of internal avionics/EW equipment totals 8,000 lb (3,629 kg) in addition to 950 lb (431 kg) for each pod. Wing pylons can also be used for fuel tanks or AGM-88 HARM antiradar missiles; the latter were introduced in 1986.

The front seat ECMO is responsible for navigation using information supplied by the Norden AN/APS-130 radar mounted in the nose, and self-defense countermeasures dispensing with the Lundy AN/ALE-29 chaff/infrared decoy dispenser. The Prowler is also fitted with the Litton AN/ASN-130 Carrier Aircraft Inertial Navigation System (CAINS).

DEVELOPMENT • The EA-6B has undergone a number of EW system upgrades since the original configuration, with these modifications being given the designations EXCAP (Expanded Capability), first delivered in 1973, ICAP-1 (Improved Capability), first delivered in 1976, and ICAP-2, first delivered in 1984.

These upgrades respond to changing foreign radar/SAM threats. By 1979 all earlier aircraft were updated to ICAP-1 configuration; the ICAP-2 became operational in 1984.

ADVCAP (Advanced Capability) was planned for an initial operational capability of 1993–94. Funding plans for remanufactured EA-6Bs consist of one in FY1991, three in FY1993, eight in FY1994, and 12 in FY1995–2002.

The aircraft's first flight was on May 25, 1968, and its initial operational capability was in July 1971. The EA-6B continues in production. The EA-6B name was changed from Intruder to Prowler in February 1972.

VARIANTS • EA-6B, Extended Capability EA-6B (EXCAP), Improved Capability EA-6B (ICAP-1), ICAP-2, Advanced Capability EA-6B (ADVCAP).

COMBAT EXPERIENCE • Prowlers from two squadrons saw service in the Vietnam War beginning in June 1972. They flew 720 sorties, conducting EW missions for USAF B-52 Stratofortress bombers as well as for US Navy attack aircraft.

In October 1983, four Prowlers from the USS *Independence* (CV 62) operated in support of the US landings in Grenada.

On October 10, 1985, EA-6Bs provided Electronic Support Measures (ESM) protection for four F-14s from the aircraft carrier USS *Saratoga* (CV 60) that forced an EgyptAir Boeing 737 to land at Sigonella AB in Sicily. The airliner was carrying the four terrorists who hijacked the cruise ship *Achille Lauro* and killed American Leon Klinghoffer.

In April 1986, Prowlers jammed Libyan radars while aircraft from the *Coral Sea* and the USS *America* (CV 66) struck at five targets in Libya in retaliation for alleged Libyan involvement in a terrorist bombing in West Berlin.

On April 18, 1988, EA-6Bs from the USS *Enterprise* (CVN 65) were used to jam Iranian Ground Control Intercept (GCI) radars, surface-to-air missile guidance radars, and communications systems during daylong action against Iranian frigates and missile boats.

The combination of the ALQ-99 now fitted in the Prowlers and the ability to fire HARMs made these aircraft the most effective EW aircraft used during the Operation Desert Storm conflict. 39 Prowlers—27 operating from six aircraft carriers and 12 flying from Marine Corps shore bases—jammed Iraqi air defenses during the air campaign that began on January 17, 1991. EA-6Bs also fired more than 150 HARM missiles. In more than 4,600 flying hours, Navy Prowlers flew 1,132 sorties, and Marine Corps aircraft amassed 516. None was lost during the seven-week war.

SPECIFICATIONS •

MANUFACTURER   Grumman Aircraft
CREW   4 (pilot, navigator, 2 electronic systems operators)
ENGINES   2 Pratt & Whitney J52-P-408 turbojet
max power   11,200 lb (5,080 kg) static thrust each

WEIGHTS
empty   32,162 lb (14,588 kg)
takeoff   with 5 pods: 54,461 lb (24,703 kg)
   max: 65,000 lb (29,484 kg)
DIMENSIONS
wingspan   53 ft (16.15 m)
length   59 ft 10 in (18.24 m)
height   16 ft 3 in (4.95 m)
wing area   528.9 ft² (49.1 m²)
PERFORMANCE
max speed   clean: 566 kts (651 mph; 1,048 km/h)
   with 5 pods: 532 kts (613 mph; 987 km/h) at sea level
cruise speed
   419 kts (483 mph; 777 km/h)
stall speed, clean, power on
   flaps up: 124 kts (143 mph; 230 km/h)

   flaps down: 84 kts (97 mph; 156 km/h)
climb rate   clean: 12,900 ft/min (3,932 m/min)
   with 5 pods: 10,030 ft/min (3,057 m/min)
ceiling   clean: 41,200 ft (12,550 m)
   with 5 pods: 38,000 ft (11,580 m)
range   with max external load, 20 min at sea level: 955 nm (1,099mi; 1,769 km)
   ferry, max fuel: 1,756 nm (2,022 mi; 3,254 km) (tanks retained); 2,085 nm (2,400 mi; 3,861 km) (tanks dropped)
armament   2 HARM AGM-88A antiradar missiles
radar   AN/APS-130

Looking Glass (EC-135/RC-135)

The EC-135/RC-135 series of research and special-purpose electronics aircraft are conversions of the basic C-135/KC-135 family of aircraft. The C-135 design is related to the Boeing 707 commercial airliner series, which evolved from the same design program.

The EC-135 has a conventional planform with low, swept wings, swept 35° at the leading edge. Along the straight trailing edge are two sections of double-slotted flaps that flank the midspan flight aileron. The larger, low-speed aileron is outboard of the outer set of flaps. The tall, slightly swept fin has an antenna extending forward from the tip, and a large, powered rudder. The swept tailplanes have inset elevators.

The four turbojet or turbofan engines are mounted on wing pylons. Many of the EC-135 variants retain tanker equipment, which includes the long refueling boom mounted under the rear fuselage.

The EC-135/RC-135 aircraft are used for Electronic Warfare (EW), Electronic Intelligence (ELINT), and Airborne Command Post (ACP) missions and have a number of blisters, antennas, and radomes, depending on the specific mission.

DEVELOPMENT • The aircraft's initial operational capability was in 1957, and its first flight was on August 31, 1956. Production ended in 1965.

From February 3, 1961, to July 24, 1990, at least one Looking Glass aircraft (EC-135C) was airborne at all times. The procedure was changed to maintaining a Looking Glass air ground alert and flying random sorties.

Operated by the US Air Force and Navy.

VARIANTS • KC-135A, C-135A, EC-135, EC-135A/G/H/P (command posts), EC-135C/J, EC-135E, EC-135K, EC-135L, EC-135Y, NC-135A (nuclear research), NKC-135, NKC-135A, RC-135 (EW/ELINT), RC-135B/C/D, RC-135E, RC-135M, RC-135S (Cobra Ball), RC-135T, RC-135U (Combat Scent), RC-135V, RC-135W (Rivet Joint), RC-135X (Cobra Eye, Advanced Range Instrumented Aircraft [ARIA]), EC-135B/N, EC-18, EC-18B, EC-18C, EC-18D (Pacer Link/Pacer Power), Big Crow.

COMBAT EXPERIENCE • In August 1990, RC-135s were sent to the Persian Gulf as part of Operation Desert Shield. ELINT/COMINT RC-135U Combat Scent, RC-135V, and RC-135W Rivet Joint aircraft conducted surveillance along the Iraqi border in the months before Desert Storm. They were also part of the integrated airborne surveillance, warning, and control network that dislocated the Iraqi air defense network during the seven-week war.

SPECIFICATIONS •
MANUFACTURER   Boeing Military Airplane
CREW   3 (pilot, copilot, navigator) + 15 crew
ENGINES
4 Pratt & Whitney J57-59W or -43W turbojet
or 4 Pratt & Whitney TF33 or JT3D turbofan
max power   J57: 13,750 lb (6,237 kg) static thrust each
TF-33/JT3D: 18,000 lb (8,165 kg) static thrust each
WEIGHTS
empty   98,466 lb (44,664 kg)
max payload 89,000 lb (40,370 kg)
max takeoff   322,500 lb (146,285 kg)
DIMENSIONS
wingspan   130 ft 10 in (39.88 m)
length   134 ft 6 in (40.99 m)
height   38 ft 4 in (11.68 m)
wing area   2,433 ft² (226.0 m²)
PERFORMANCE
cruise speed
461 kts (530 mph; 853 km/h)
max speed   508 kts (585 mph; 941 km/h)
climb rate at sea level
max: 1,290 ft/min (393 m/min)
1 engine out: 580 ft/min (177 m/min)
time to 30,500 ft (9,300 m)
27 min
ceiling   36,000 ft (10,900 m)
radius   2,998 nm (3,450 mi; 5,552 km)

Raven (EF-111A)

The General Dynamics/Grumman EF-111A Tactical Jamming System (TJS) is based on the F-111A variable-geometry strike aircraft. 42 aircraft were extensively modified to carry a comprehensive Electronic Warfare (EW) suite that detects, locates, classifies, and counteracts hostile radars. The Raven is designed to perform three missions: barrier standoff, in which the aircraft remains on the "friendly" side of the battle line while it jams enemy emitters; deep penetration, in which the Raven flies with the strike aircraft well into hostile airspace; and close support, in which the aircraft loiters in a target area, detecting and jamming emitters.

The EF-111 retains many of the advantages of the basic F-111 design. Its high wing loading and low-aspect ratio at full aft sweep makes the aircraft relatively insensitive to low-level turbulence, which extends its low-altitude, terrain-following flight endurance. Mach 2 speed permits it to accompany strike aircraft flying their optimum penetration profiles. Finally, the EF-111's large fuel capacity and variable sweep allow it to remain on station for hours.

In low-level flight, the primary avionics unit is the Texas Instruments radar suite fitted in the nose radome; this fit consists of an AN/APQ-160 attack radar and two AN/APQ-110 Terrain-Following Radar (TFR) scanners. Other avionics include an AN/AJQ-20A Inertial Navigation System (INS), Honeywell AN/APN-167 radar altimeter, AN/APX-64 Identification Friend or Foe (IFF) transponder, and Collins AN/ARN-118 TACAN. Coordination of avionics and EW equipment is managed by three IBM 4 Pi general-purpose digital computers.

The TFR has been upgraded and designated the AN/APQ-171; the GE attack radar was modified as the AN/APQ-169 with pulse compression and narrow pulse widths. In addition, the aircraft has been refitted with the Honeywell H-423 ring laser gyro INS, Global Positioning System (GPS) receiver, and two digital computers with dual-redundant multiplex buses.

The pilot and the Electronic Warfare Officer (EWO) sit side by side in a pressurized escape pod under a gull-wing canopy. The EWO commands the 6,500 lb (2,950 kg) of full-spectrum jamming equipment. A 16-ft (4.88-m) long pallet fitted into the weapons bay holds the 10 transmitters and five multiband exciters of the Raytheon ALQ-99E tactical jamming system; the pallet can be lowered for servicing. The bottom of the pallet is covered by a "canoe" radome that creates a shallow bulge in the aircraft's profile.

A 600-lb (273-kg) System Integrated Receiver (SIR) pod constructed by Canadair is mounted on top of the fin. The SIR pod (known as the football) holds the ALQ-99 receivers and forward, lateral, and aft-facing ALQ-99 antennas. ALQ-99 Band 1 and Band 2 antennas are fitted in fairings on the sides of the fin. The football also contains lateral antennas for the Dalmo Victor AN/ALR-62(V) series Terminal Threat Warning System (TTWS), and the aft-facing Cincinnati Electronics AN/ALR-23 infrared tail-warning receiver.

Other ALR-62 antennas are mounted in "bullets" on the trailing edges of the tailplanes and in small side-by-side bullets fitted on the fuselage behind the cockpit. The fuselage bullets also house antennas for the Sanders AN/ALQ-137 internal noise/deception jammer; other ALQ-137 antennas are fitted in the forward fuselage sides and at the aft ends of the tailplane root fairings, outboard of the engines. General Dynamics AN/ALE-28 chaff dispensers are fitted in the tailplane root fairings, ahead of the ALQ-137 antenna.

Unlike the F-111 series, the EF-111A has no attack or self-defense armament. The two stores pylons under each wing swivel with the wing sweep. The inboard pylons usually carry 600-US gal (2,271-liter) external fuel tanks; the outboard pylons carry data link pods.

DEVELOPMENT • The EF-111's initial operational capability was in 1982, and its first flight was on March 10, 1977. 42 were converted from the F-111A.

In February 1991, the US Air Force announced that all EF-111s would be assigned to the Nebraska Air National Guard as part of a general paring down of F-111 numbers.

VARIANTS • F-111, FB-111, EF-111 ECM upgrade, EF-111 ECM Upgrade II.

COMBAT EXPERIENCE • Three EF-111As of the 42nd and 66th Electronic Combat Squadrons took part in the April 15, 1986, raid against Libya, jamming all surveillance radars in and around Tripoli.

EF-111s from the 390th Electronic Combat Squadron jammed Panamanian radars during the first hours of Operation Just Cause, the December 1989 military ouster of General Noriega.

EF-111s from the same squadron were based in Saudi Arabia as part of Operations Desert Shield/Desert Storm. On January 17, 1991, these aircraft (and EA-6B Prowlers) led Operation Desert Storm air assault formations against Iraqi targets, effectively jamming Iraq's air defense system. Iraqi interceptors that took off to look for the Ravens were detected by E-3 AWACS airborne warning aircraft radar operators, who warned allied aircraft. EF-111s used their terrain-following ability to elude Iraqi aircraft, air-to-air, and surface-to-air missiles. One EF-111 was lost to noncombat causes during the seven-week war.

SPECIFICATIONS •
MANUFACTURER Grumman
CREW 2 (pilot, navigator)
ENGINES 2 Pratt & Whitney TF30-P-3 turbofan
max power dry: 10,750 lb (4,876 kg) static thrust each with afterburner: 18,500 lb (8,391 kg) static thrust each
max fuel capacity 4,998 US gal (18,919 liters)

WEIGHTS
empty 55,275 lb (25,072 kg)
combat weight 70,000 lb (31,751 kg)
max takeoff 88,948 lb (40,346 kg)
DIMENSIONS
wingspan 63 ft (19.2 m) (extended); 31 ft 11 in (9.74 m) (swept)
length 76 ft (23.16 m)
height 20 ft (6.1 m)
wing area 525 ft^2 (48.77 m^2)
PERFORMANCE
max speed at 35,000 ft (10,668 m) 1,227 kts (1,412 mph; 2,274 km/h) or Mach 2.15
basic speed at 35,000 ft (10,668 m) 1,196 kts (1,377 mph; 2,216 km/h) or Mach 2.1
max combat speed at sea level 794 kts (914 mph; 1,471 km/h) or Mach 1.2
average speed over combat area barrier standoff: 321 kts (370 mph; 595 km/h) deep penetration: 507 kts (584 mph; 940 km/h) close support: 462 kts (532 mph; 856 km/h)
stall speed, power off 143 kts (164 mph; 264 km/h)
max rate of climb at combat weight 11,000 ft/min (3,353 m/min)
ceiling at combat weight 45,000 ft (13,715 m)
radius barrier standoff, 4-hr loiter: 200 nm (230 mi; 371 km) close support, 1-hr loiter: 623 nm (717 mi; 1,155 km) deep penetration: 807 nm (929 mi; 1,495 km)
radar AN/APQ-169 attack AN/APQ-171 terrain-following

Viking (ES-3A)

The ES-3A Viking is an adaptation of the carrier-based S-3 Viking maritime patrol aircraft to the Electronic Intelligence (ELINT) intercept mission. They replaced the aging EA-3 Skywarriors that entered service in 1960. The ES-3A is the platform for the airborne part of the Battle Group Passive Horizon Extension System (BGPHES).

The basic S-3 design reflects the need to cruise at patrol speeds for long periods of time, to carry a comprehensive set of sensors, to take off and land on a carrier deck, and to occupy as little deck and hangar space as possible. The aircraft has a shoulder wing with a modest 15° sweep and 3° 50-min incidence at the root washing out to −3° 50 min at the tip. The wings have asymmetrical wing fold points outboard of the engines such that the left wing is behind the right wing when both outer wings are folded over the center section. The folding section has leading-edge flaps extending to the tip; the trailing edge has two sections of single-slotted, Fowler-type flaps inboard of the ailerons. Spoilers fitted above and below the middle third of the wing help roll control and are used for lift dumping; the Direct Lift Control (DLC) uses the upper surface spoilers for flight path refinement without pitch change during carrier approaches. Each wingtip has a pod containing antennas relating to the aircraft's AN/ALR-76 Electronic Support Measures (ESM) suite.

All tail surfaces are mildly swept. The aerodynamic surfaces are close-coupled, which necessitates a tall, broad-chord fin and rudder that have a fold joint that angles down from a point one-third of the way up the leading edge of the fin; the folding section includes the balanced rudder. The large tailplanes have horn-balanced elevators. All control surfaces are hydraulically powered and are harmonized by the dual-channel Automatic Flight Control System (AFCS) autopilot and yaw damper.

The two high-bypass turbofan engines are mounted on pylons below the wing center section. The turbofans are based on the T64 turboshaft fitted in several US helicopter designs and have low fuel consumption and high reliability. An internal fuel tank is in each wing; drop tanks can be mounted on each wing stores pylon. A retractable, midair refueling probe is housed over the cockpit windshield.

The boxy, semimonocoque fuselage has a sturdy keel on the centerline that divides the weapons bay in half. The four crew members fly in individual McDonnell Douglas Escapac ejection seats forward of the wing. An arrester hook swings down from a two-point anchorage under the tail. The modified F-8 Crusader main gear legs fold in and back into fuselage wells; the two-wheel nose gear retracts to the rear behind the radome.

Approximately 6,000 lb (2,722 kg) of EW equipment is installed, replacing approximately 3,000 lb (1,361 kg) of ASW equipment. The avionics and electronics come from several sources. The Texas Instruments AN/APS-137 Inverse Synthetic Aperture Radar (SAR), the IBM AN/ALR-76 Radar-Warning Receiver (RWR) with eight wingtip antennas, and the TI OR-263 Forward-Looking Infrared (FLIR) ball were developed for the S-3B upgrade.

For ELINT operations, the ES-3A is fitted with 63 antennas. The weapons bay doors are being removed and replaced by bulged fairings, and a dorsal hump will hold an omnidirectional receiver aerial. Other ELINT conical antennas protrude from the sides of the aircraft ahead of the tail. Many of the avionics systems are being carried over from the Lockheed EP-3E Aries upgrade program, including the entire mission avionics suite, the AN/AYK-14 digital computers, displays, and recording equipment. The BGPHES wideband common data link will be supplemented with UHF voice and UHF and HF data links using Link 11.

DEVELOPMENT • The aircraft's initial operational capability was in 1992, a year later than originally scheduled; its first flight of the aerodynamic prototype was in May 1989; first flight with full avionics in March 1990. Conversion of 16 aircraft began in March 1988, scheduled to complete mid-1992.

Flight test of the first conversion began in January 1992 after delivery six months behind schedule. The gap would close over the next four aircraft, with the sixth being delivered according to the original schedule.

VARIANTS • S-3A, ES-3A.

SPECIFICATIONS •
MANUFACTURER   Lockheed Aeronautical Systems
CREW   4 (2 pilots, tactical coordinator, systems operator)
ENGINES   2 General Electric TF34-GE-400 turbofan
  max power   9,275 lb (4,207 kg) static thrust each
WEIGHTS
  empty   approx 29,000 lb (13,154 kg)
  max takeoff   52,539 lb (23,831 kg)
DIMENSIONS
  wingspan   68 ft 8 in (20.93 m)
  length   53 ft 4 in (16.26 m)
  height   22 ft 9 in (6.94 m)
  wing area   598 ft² (55.96 m²)
PERFORMANCE
  cruise speed
    348 kts (400 mph; 644 km/h)
  max speed   440 kts (506 mph; 814 km/h)
  ceiling   40,000 ft (12,192 m)
  range   3,000 nm (3,452 mi; 5,556 km)
  armament   not armed
  avionics   ELINT equipment

Guardrail (RC-12/RU-21)

The Guardrail and Improved Guardrail aircraft are based on the Beechcraft King Air and Super King Air series of turboprop executive transports. The basic design has been modified to carry several variants of the Electromagnetic Systems Laboratories (ESL) AN/USD-9 Guardrail Electronic Intelligence (ELINT) and Signals Intelligence (SIGINT) system. The RU-21H flies the Guardrail V while the RC-12D carries the Improved Guardrail V (IGRV). The Army introduced the Guardrail Common Sensor (GRCS) in the RC-12K in FY1991.

The RU-21 is derived from the King Air 90 and 100 series, while the later RC-12 was developed from the Super King Air 200. (Three Super King Airs were procured as RU-21J but were later redesignated.) Both series have a low wing, but the RC-12 series has a higher aspect ratio (9.8 versus 7.6). Most of the difference is realized in a change in the planform of the center section from a swept leading edge to a rectangular layout and slimmer outer panels. Both series have two sections of trailing-edge flaps inboard of ailerons.

The tail group on the RU-21s consists of a swept vertical tail with full-height, balanced rudder. The large, slightly swept horizontal tailplanes are mounted low on the fuselage and have full-span, balanced elevators. On the RC-12s, the vertical tail is broader with a broad, full-height rudder and a larger dorsal fillet. The horizontal surfaces are carried at the top of the fin and have similar planform to those of the RU-21s.

RU-21s have a relatively stubby fuselage, while the RC-12s are longer. All Beech King Airs and Super King Airs have the characteristic sloping nose leading to a raked windshield. All have two Pratt & Whitney Canada PT6 series free-turbine turboprop engines in long nacelles that also contain the main-landing-gear bays. The nose gear retracts to the rear.

The SIGINT equipment varies greatly among models, as does the avionics fit. The RC-12D has the Improved Guardrail V system—USD-9(V)2—that operates in the 20–75, 100–150, and 350–450 MHz frequency bands. Ground support equipment includes the AN/TSQ-105(V)4 threat processing facility, AN/TSC-87 tactical commander's terminal, and the AN/ARM-63(V)4 flightline van.

An Aircraft Survivability Equipment (ASE) suite includes the ITT AN/ALQ-136 Electronic Countermeasures (ECM), a Sanders AN/ALQ-156 Missile-Warning Set (MWS), and the Northrop AN/ALQ-162 ECM set. The Inertial Navigation System (INS) is the Delco AN/ASN-119 Carousel IV-E. Wingtip pods carry part of the ASE antenna system as well as the AN/ARW-83 airborne data relay antennas. Vertical dipole Guardrail antennas are on each wing and behind the tail.

None of the Guardrail variants is armed.

DEVELOPMENT • The RU-21 initial operational capability was in the late 1960s and the RC-12D's was in 1983; the first flight of the RU-21A was in March 1967. Production of the RC-12K continues, as do update programs for the RU-21H and the RC-12D.

King Airs are in US Army, Navy, and Air Force service as C-12 Hurons and U-21 Utes, operating as light utility/liaison aircraft.

VARIANTS • RU-21A, RU-21B, RU-21C, RU-21D, RU-21E, RU-21H, RU-21J, RC-12D (Improved Guardrail V), RC-12F (Navy), RC-12G (Army), RC-12H, RC-12K (GuardRail Common Sensor/GRCS or Guardlock, for ELINT and COMINT), RC-12M.

COMBAT EXPERIENCE • Guardrail aircraft were deployed to Saudi Arabia during Operation Desert Storm in 1991, but the number of aircraft and missions conducted was not made public.

SPECIFICATIONS •
MANUFACTURER Beech Aircraft
CREW 2
ENGINES
  RC-12D: 2 Pratt & Whitney PT6A-42 turboprop
  RC-12K: 2 Pratt & Whitney PT6A-67 turboprop
  max power RC-12D: 850 shp each
         RC-12K: 1,100 shp each
WEIGHTS
  mission payload
         RC-12D: 2,027 lb (919 kg)
         RC-12K: 1,413 lb (640 kg)
  max takeoff RC-12D: 14,200 lb (6,441 kg)
         RC-12K: 16,000 lb (7,257 kg)
DIMENSIONS
  wingspan 54 ft 6 in (16.61 m); with pods, 57 ft 10 in (17.31 m)
  length 43 ft 9 in (13.34 m)
  height 15 ft (4.57 m)
  wing area 303 ft² (28.15 m²)
PERFORMANCE
  cruise speed
         RC-12D: 200 kts (230 mph; 371 km/h)
         RC-12K: 250 kts (288 mph; 463 km/h)
  ceiling more than 27,000 ft (8,230 m)
  range 1,200 nm (1,382 mi; 2,224 km)
  endurance 5.8 hr

Blackbird (SR-71)

The SR-71, a high-speed, high-altitude strategic reconnaissance aircraft, was one of the world's fastest airplanes, holding several speed and altitude records before its retirement.

The SR-71 was popularly known as the Blackbird because of its black heat-

Lockheed SR-71 Blackbird
LOCKHEED CORPORATION

emissive surface, but this nickname was unofficial. The SR-71 was the successor to the Lockheed U-2, which was also a product of the famed Lockheed "Skunk Works."

The SR-71 was an unconventional design with a long, tapering fuselage of very small cross section blending into a delta wing with rounded wingtips. The forward part of the fuselage is flattened and has sharp chines along each side. An engine nacelle is blended into the middle of each wing, and each supports a low tailfin, canted slightly inward. Skin temperatures on the fuselage rise considerably during high-altitude, high-speed flight, and the fuselage stretches 11 in (280 mm) as a result.

The engines are continuous-bleed afterburning turbojets with large centerbody cones; they require special JP-7 fuel.

The immense amount of fuel needed fills most of the fuselage and acts as a heat sink. The aircraft can be refueled in flight.

The Blackbird has no horizontal stabilizers but has a relatively deep underfuselage, retracting ventral fin and two shallow underengine fins. Construction is mainly of titanium, to resist the stresses of upper atmospheric flight, and composites are used in the remainder of the surface components.

Reconnaissance instrumentation is normally contained internally, with a minimum of bulges or blisters that add drag in flight. It is believed to include Side-Looking Airborne Radars (SLAR) and infrared linescanning equipment that can be interchanged. The two-seat tandem cockpit also presents a minimal profile, with the systems officer position having side windows only. Sensors provide coverage of up to 100,000 mi² (259,000 km²) in one hour.

DEVELOPMENT • The SR-71's initial operational capability was in 1966; first flight as the YF-12A was on April 26, 1962. Although actual numbers are not available, best estimates suggest about 32 SR-71s were produced, including variants. Approximately 20 were in the inventory when the type was retired, of which eight or nine were operational at any one time.

Because of its flight profile and exotic design, the SR-71 was a maintenance-intensive aircraft, with a relatively long turnaround time between missions. Early efforts to develop the Blackbird into a high-performance interceptor foundered because of this, as well as its long-runway requirement and relatively low weapons payload.

In January 1989, the Air Force announced that it would retire all SR-71s effective October 1989. The final operational flight was on January 18, 1990, at Kadena AB, Okinawa. One aircraft was offered to a British museum, another to a museum in Japan. The rest returned to California. Later congressional action led to 3 SR-71s being restored to U.S. Air Force service in 1995.

VARIANTS • YF-12A, YF-12C, SR-71A, SR-71B (two-seat trainer), SR-71C (two-seat trainer).

SPECIFICATIONS •
MANUFACTURER Lockheed-California
CREW 2 (pilot, reconnaissance systems officer)
ENGINES 2 Pratt & Whitney JT11D-20B continuous-bleed turbojet
max power 23,000 lb (10,440 kg) each dry
32,500 lb (14,755 kg) each with afterburner

WEIGHTS
empty 60,000 lb (27,240 kg)
max takeoff 170,000 lb (77,180 kg)
DIMENSIONS
wingspan 55 ft 7 in (16.95 m)
length 107 ft 5 in (32.74 m)
height 18 ft 6 in (5.64 m)
wing area 1,800 ft² (167.4 m²)
PERFORMANCE
speed max: Mach 3+
approach: 180 kts (207 mph; 384 km/h)
touchdown: 150 kts (173 mph; 278 km/h)
ceiling 80,000 ft (24,400 m)
turn radius at Mach 3
78–104 nm (90–120 mi; 145–193 km)
typical operating radius
1,043 nm (1,200 mi; 1,931 km)
range 2,607 nm (3,000 mi; 4,828 km)
max fuel consumption per hr
8,000 US gal (30,280 liters)

TR-1/U-2

The U-2R is a long-range, high-altitude strategic reconnaissance aircraft that is a primary component of the US national technical means of strategic intelligence collection, including Communications Intelligence (COMINT) and Electronic Intelligence (ELINT). US Air Force TR-1s were originally designed for high-altitude standoff ELINT, COMINT, and surveillance missions in Europe, providing the capability for day/night, all-weather surveillance without having to overfly the target. The two aircraft missions and designators were merged as U-2R in late 1991.

The design features midmounted, double-tapered, high-aspect-ratio wings designed to function like sailplane wings; the aircraft can soar without power to extend its range. 70% of the wing trailing

TR-1
U.S. GOVERNMENT DEPARTMENT OF DEFENSE

edges are fitted with slotted flaps inboard of long ailerons; the U-2R has spoilers fitted ahead of the flaps that assist roll and also act as lift dumpers. The lift/drag ratio of the later U-2R is reportedly as high as 27:1. The U-2R has a significantly larger wing than the earlier U-2 with integral fuel tanks and slender, permanently fitted "superpods" spliced into the wing structure at midspan. The pods carry sensor equipment and up to 105 US gal (398 liters) of fuel.

The tall fin has a slightly swept leading edge and inset rudder. The double-tapered horizontal tailplanes are mounted at the base of the fin and have balanced, full-span elevators. The U-2R has a taller fin than the earlier U-2 and a revised tailplane attachment structure. Air brakes are fitted on the lower fuselage sides ahead of the tailplanes. At the U-2's service ceiling, the difference between the never-exceed (Vne) and the stall speeds is 5 kts (6 mph; 8 km/h); the U-2R reportedly has a greater margin.

The fuselage has a sloping nose up to a small cockpit. The rest of the fuselage has a circular section and is flanked by D-section engine air intakes. These feed the single turbojet engine that is installed in the aft fuselage. In May 1990, the Air Force decided to retrofit approximately 40 U-2R/TR-1s with the 19,000-lb (8,618-kg) F101-GE-F29 engine under a $160-million program that had deliveries beginning in 1992. The retrofit improved the aircraft's thrust-to-weight ratio, reduced specific fuel consumption, raised the operating ceiling to more than 100,000 ft (30,480 m), and increased maximum range to more than 3,474 nm (4,000 mi; 6,437 km).

Most surveillance U-2s were fitted with a "sugar scoop" lip to the exhaust nozzle to reduce the aircraft's infrared signature from below. The U-2R enjoyed a 100% increase in fuselage volume over its predecessors.

The U-2 gained notoriety as one of the most difficult aircraft to land because of the narrow speed range between recommended approach speed and its stall speed. Its main landing gear is tandem-bicycle type with the larger, forward unit and a much smaller assembly near the tail; the landing gear in the U-2R is more closely spaced. Downturned winglets at each wingtip also serve as skids during the U-2's landing roll-out. Because of the great span of the wings, the U-2 landing gear also includes two balancing wheels (one under each wing) that are jettisoned on takeoff. The U-2 was designed from the outset to take off from aircraft carriers, although it was not so used operationally.

The sensors fit on the U-2 series varied with the variant and the operational context. The original aircraft used large, long-focus cameras and ELINT equipment. The U-2R has wingtip Radar Homing and Warning System (RHAWS) pods and ELINT antennas. The 1,200-lb (544-kg) superpods may carry the Senior Spear COMINT/ELINT system that is thought to have a 350-nm (403-mi; 649-km) line-of-sight range at 70,000 ft (21,336 m). U-2Rs may also carry the Senior Stretch near-real-time COMINT system.

The nose section is detachable, permitting rapid reconfiguration.

DEVELOPMENT • Initial operational capability was in 1957, and first flight was on August 1, 1955. Taiwan received six U-2 aircraft in the early 1960s, but all were subsequently lost (at least three in operations over mainland China). Approximately 60 of the U-2 series were built in the late 1950s and early 1960s, more than 40 of which were lost on missions or in operational accidents. A later batch of 12 larger U-2Rs were manufactured in the late 1960s.

First flight of TR-1 was in August 1981. Production of the TR-1 variant ended in October 1989 with a total of 25 TR-1As, two TR-1Bs, and two ER-1s built. Redesignated U-2R in late 1991.

All pre-U-2R U-2s were retired by April 1989, the last being flown as NASA research aircraft.

VARIANTS • U-2A, WU-2A (weather reconnaissance), U-2B, U-2C (ELINT), U-2CT (two-seat trainer), U-2D (two-seat, special mission), WU-2D (weather reconnaissance), U-2EPX (Navy ocean surveillance), U-2R, U-2R (COMINT), U-2R/TR-1, TR-1B (two-seat trainer), ER-2 (NASA).

COMBAT EXPERIENCE • U-2 aircraft regularly overflew the Soviet Union on reconnaissance missions until 1960. A mission flown by Francis Gary Powers led to the shooting down of a U-2 over Sverdlovsk on May 1, 1960, by an SA-2 surface-to-air missile. The U-2 had a major role in intelligence during the Cuban missile crisis of 1962.

The U-2 was succeeded in service in the late 1960s by the SR-71 Blackbird.

U-2Rs from the 9th Strategic Reconnaissance Wing based at Beale AFB, California, flew surveillance missions during Operations Desert Shield/Desert Storm. As many as 12 U-2R/TR-1 aircraft and 28 pilots are said to have been used. After the cease-fire, concern that Iraq was continuing to hide installations producing nuclear or biological weapons led to flights in August 1991 of a U-2R over Iraq under United Nations auspices.

SPECIFICATIONS •
MANUFACTURER Lockheed Aeronautical Systems
CREW 1
ENGINES 1 Pratt & Whitney J75-P-13 turbojet
  max power 17,000 lb (7,718 kg) static thrust
WEIGHTS
  empty U-2C: 11,700 lb (5,350 kg)
     U-2R: 14,990 lb (6,800 kg)

takeoff	U-2C, clean: 16,000 lb (7,285 kg)	
	U-2C, with 2 89-US gal (337-liter) wing tanks: 17,270 lb (7,833 kg)	
	U-2R: 41,000 lb (18,598 kg)	
DIMENSIONS		
wingspan	U-2C: 80 ft (24.4 m)	
	U-2R: 103 ft (31.89 m)	
length	U-2C: 49 ft 7 in (15.13 m)	
	U-2R: 62 ft 9 in (19.13 m)	
height	U-2C: 13 ft (3.97 m)	
	U-2R: 16 ft 1 in (4.9 m)	
wing area	U-2C: 565 ft² (52.5 m²)	
	U-2R: 1,000 ft² (92.9 m²)	
PERFORMANCE		
max speed	U-2C: 459 kts (528 mph; 850 km/h)	
	U-2R: 443 kts (510 mph; 821 km/h)	
cruise speed	400 kts (460 mph; 740 km/h)	
ceiling	U-2C: 85,000 ft (25,908 m)	
	U-2R: 90,000 ft (27,432 m)	
range	U-2C: 2,605 nm (3,000 mi; 4,827 km)	
	U-2R: 3,039 nm (3,500 mi; 5,633 km)	

Orion (P-3)

The P-3 Orion is the US Navy's long-range maritime patrol and Antisubmarine Warfare (ASW) aircraft, and also serves in the navies and air forces of several other countries. Some have been adapted to Electronic Intelligence (ELINT) collection and special reconnaissance roles.

The basic airframe is adapted from the L-188 Electra commercial airliner. The Orion has wings with straight leading edges, 6° dihedral from the roots, tapered tailing edges, and squared wing-

tips. The trailing edge has two sections of Fowler-type flaps inboard of ailerons.

The single, rounded fin has a dorsal fillet and full-height rudder. The relatively long horizontal stabilizers are mounted at the base of the fin at a dihedral angle, well up on the fuselage. A tail "stinger" houses the Magnetic Anomaly Detector (MAD).

The semimonocoque fuselage has a circular cross section. Compared to the Electra, the Orion has a more pointed nose. The cockpit glazing includes small "eyebrow" windows over the side windows. The constant cross section continues well aft, at which point the bottom line tapers up to the tail.

The four turboprop engines are fitted in nacelles on the wing, each driving four-blade Hamilton Standard propellers. Because the propeller slipstreams cover a large percentage of the wing, Electra transports and lightly loaded Orions are known for their impressive takeoff performance and maneuverability.

The ASW variants have a comprehensive suite of communications, navigation, acoustic and nonacoustic sensors, and data processing equipment. Capability has greatly increased during the Orion's operational life, with most P-3s now having HF/VHF/UHF radios, a data link, Identification Friend or Foe (IFF) interrogator, Litton LTN-72 Inertial Navigation System (INS), Doppler navigation radar, 360° search radar, MAD and magnetic compensator, Magnavox AN/AQA-7 Direction Low-Frequency Analyzer and Ranging (DIFAR) system, chin-mounted Texas Instruments Forward-Looking Infrared (FLIR) system, bathythermograph, and general-purpose digital computer.

The Orion has an internal weapons bay and 10 external stations for carrying a mix of ASW torpedoes, depth bombs, and AGM-84 Harpoon antiship missiles. Six of the 10 wing pylons are grouped in threes outboard of the engines; the outermost one on each wing has a 500-lb (227-

kg) capacity while the middle pylons can carry 1,000 lb (454 kg) of stores. Each of the other six pylons—the inner pylon of each outboard group and the four pylons grouped under the wing's center section—has a 2,000-lb (907-kg) capacity. The internal weapons bay can accommodate a variety of depth bombs and mines or up to eight lightweight ASW torpedoes. Sonobuoys can be launched from external pods or from a set of tubes located internally aft of the weapons bay. AIM-9 Sidewinder air-to-air and AGM-65F Maverick antiship missiles have been test-launched from the P-3.

DEVELOPMENT • The P-3's initial operational capability was in 1962; its first flight as the YP3V-1 was on November 25, 1959. 641 had been delivered by mid-1991; the November 1990 order of eight P-3D Update IIIs for South Korea brought a last-minute reprieve from the shutdown of production. All P-3 production before 1991 rolled out of Burbank, California; after 1990, all Lockheed production and modification was moved to Marietta, Georgia, actual metal-cutting beginning in August 1991.

The latest ASW variant in service is the P-3C Update III; originally planned for 138 P-3Cs, later plans suggested 109 Update IV candidates would also get Update III.

Boeing Aerospace was the prime contractor on the Update IV mission avionics package that had been scheduled to enter production in 1991; it was canceled by the US Navy in October 1992.

More than 50 P-3s have been produced under license by Kawasaki Heavy Industries in Japan with more planned. The original Memorandum of Understanding (MU) covering production of 75 aircraft was revised in April 1989 to manufacture 100; production of an additional 30 (20 P-3 and 10 EP-3J Electronic Intelligence/ELINT aircraft) began in 1991.

The transfer of five ex–US Naval Reserve P-3As to Thailand over a two-year period was announced in April 1990; the total cost of the program is $100 million.

In July 1990, the US agreed to seek the free transfer of six P-3As to Greece in a letter accompanying the newly signed eight-year renewal of US basing rights.

In December 1990, South Korea announced that it would buy eight P-3Ds for a unit cost of $82.49 million. The first delivery is planned for 1995.

In addition to the US Navy and Navy Reserve, and the above countries, the P-3 has also operated in Australia, Iran, Norway, Pakistan, Portugal, Netherlands, New Zealand, and Spain.

VARIANTS • Electra test bed, P3V-1/P-3A, P-3B, P-3C, P-3C Update I, P-3C Update II, P-3C Update II.5, P-3C Update III, P-3C Update IV (Long-Range Air ASW Capable Aircraft/LRAACA begun in July 1987 and canceled in October 1992), ASUTAA (ASW), IPADS, P-3D, P-3F, P-3G, P-3H, EP-3E Aries/EP-3B Batrack, EP-3E Aries II, EP-3C (ELINT, Kawasaki-built), EP-3J (Japanese), RP-3A (oceanographic reconnaissance), RP-3D, TP-3A (training), VP-3A (Navy VIP transport), UP-3A/UP-3B (utility), UP-3C, WP-3D (weather research), Outlaw Hunter (Tomahawk Antiship Missile/TASM), P-3W (Australia), P-3K/Rigel I/II/III (New Zealand), P-3N (Norway), Spanish P-3 modernization, Trap Shot, P-3 Sentinel (Airborne Early Warning and Control/AEW&C; US Customs Service), CP-140 Aurora (Canadian maritime patrol).

COMBAT EXPERIENCE • During Operation Desert Storm, P-3s searched for Iraqi naval units and directed strike aircraft to them. According to the Navy, of the 105 Iraqi Navy units destroyed, more than half were initially detected by P-3s. The P-3's APS-137 in the ISAR mode and the aircraft's AAS-36 IRDS were both described as "ideally suited for antisurface warfare operations and made the difference in coalition efforts to destroy the Iraqi Navy." P-3s flew 369 combat sorties totaling 3,787 flight hours during Desert Storm.

SPECIFICATIONS (P-3C) •

MANUFACTURER   Lockheed Aeronautical Systems
CREW   10 (command pilot, 2 pilots, flight engineer, navigator, radio operator, tactical coordinator, 3 systems operators)
ENGINES   4 Allison T56-A-14 turboprop
  max power   4,910 equivalent hp each
  internal fuel capacity
    9,200 US gal (34,826 liters)
WEIGHTS
  empty   61,491 lb (27,892 kg)
  max weapons load
    19,252 lb (8,733 kg)
  max takeoff   142,000 lb (64,410 kg)
DIMENSIONS
  wingspan   99 ft 8 in (30.37 m)
  length   116 ft 10 in (35.61 m)
  height   33 ft 8 in (10.29 m)
  wing area   1,300 ft² (120.77 m²)
PERFORMANCE
  max speed   at 105,000 lb (47,625 kg) at 15,000 ft (4,575 m): 411 kts (473 mph; 761 km/h) at max takeoff, same altitude: 380 kts (438 mph; 704 km/h)
  cruise speed
    max speed at same altitude: 350 kts (403 mph; 649 km/h) econ at 110,000 lb (48,895 kg) at 25,000 ft (7,620 m): 328 kts (378 mph; 608 km/h)
  patrol speed at 1,500 ft (457 m) altitude
    203 kts (234 mph; 376 km/h)
  stall speed   flaps up: 133 kts (154 mph; 248 km/h)

flaps down: 112 kts (129 mph; 208 km/h)
  climb rate   at 135,000 lb (61,235 kg): 1,950 ft/min (594 m/min) at 101,440 lb (46,012 kg): 3,140 ft/min (957 m/min)
  ceiling   4 engines: 28,300 ft (8,626 m) 3 engines: 19,000 ft (5,790 m)
  radius   3 hours on station at 1,500 ft/min (457 m/min): 1,346 nm (1,550 mi; 2,494 km) no time on station at 135,000 lb (61,235 kg): 2,070 nm (2,383 mi; 3,835 km)
  ferry range   4,830 nm (5,562 mi; 8,950 km)
  armament   internal weapons bay and 10 external weapons stations for such weapons mixes as: 12 Mk 46 torpedoes *or* 2 2,000-lb (907-kg) mines + 4 Mk 46 torpedoes *or* 4 1,000-lb (454-kg) mines + 4 Mk 46 torpedoes *or* 8 Mk 46 torpedoes + 16 5-in rockets *or* B57 nuclear depth charges *or* Mk 82 500-lb (227-kg) bombs *or* Mk 20 Rockeye cluster bombs *or* AGM-84 Harpoon antiship missiles
  radar   AN/APS-115 I-band search AN/APN-187 Doppler navigation

FIGHTERS

Stealth Fighter (F-117)

The F-117 is a production fighter aircraft designed under the "Stealth" low-observability technology program. It is intended to provide the lowest possible Radar Cross Section (RCS) as well as Infrared (IR), noise, and visual signatures, thus enhancing its survivability and ability to penetrate enemy air defenses. The aircraft is subsonic and has a relatively high radius of action. Its mission is to attack high-value targets in raids that depend on low-altitude flight and stealth characteristics for its defense.

The F-117 is an angular aircraft that resembles a flat arrowhead with a narrow V-tail (or "butterfly" tail). Its shape is intended to focus incoming radar beams into a few narrow beams, greatly reduc-ing a radar's ability to detect the reflections. As a result, the F-117's shape is subdivided into triangular and trapezoidal facets. The low-aspect-ratio wing is swept at approximately 67°–68° and has a sawtooth trailing edge. A low beak continues the wing's continuous and severe leading-edge sweep from wingtip to nose.

The five-piece cockpit glazing is fronted by a narrow glazed triangle below which is the opening for the electro-optical navigation/targeting system. A downward-looking IR head is located on the right-hand side of the nosewheel bay. The nose window is trimmed with serrated appliqués to align its edges with other major components, as are other ex-

F-117 Stealth Fighter
U.S. GOVERNMENT DEPARTMENT OF DEFENSE

crescences, including the landing-gear doors. Behind the cockpit's peak, the top line slopes continuously to the tail. Viewed from above, the flat top of the fuselage and the intake openings parallel the wing's leading-edge angle; the exhausts parallel the opposite outer trailing edge.

The wing's trailing edge returns to the fuselage at a lesser angle, creating high-aspect-ratio outer sections; each wing has inboard and outboard elevons. The tail surfaces have short fixed stubs with all-moving "ruddervators" pivoting for pitch and yaw control. All tail airfoils are prismatic in cross section, again to focus radar returns into a few narrow beams. The original metal-alloy tails are being replaced by graphite thermoplastic surfaces developed after an F-117 lost a tail during flight tests.

The overall configuration requires continuous, active control by a Lear-Siegler digital on-board computer in a flight control system derived from that used in the F-16 Fighting Falcon.

Much of the fuselage structure (95%) is reported to be aluminum, although some elements may be made of a Dow Chemical pre-preg (fibers and resin combined) boron fiber/polymer material called Fibaloy. The surface is said to be sheathed with tiles made of a Radar-Absorbing Material (RAM), and the leading edges and nose section are heat-absorbing and nonreflective. Component door mountings were designed to reduce the change in RCS due to lateral motion. Cockpit transparencies have a special coating to distort and diffuse incoming radar pulses and outgoing avionics emissions, and the sensor turret window has a copper-wire screen that reduces its signature.

Engine intake placement is on the upper wing surface aft of the cockpit. The bulky, faceted intakes have a radar-blanking composite mesh covering the openings; the mesh size makes the inlet appear solid to most search radars. The

engines are nonafterburning derivatives of the General Electric F404 series engines that are modified to raise the by-pass ratio, which contributes to reducing the IR signature and stretching the range. A dorsal refueling receptacle extends the F-117's range.

The exhausts are narrow slots along the inboard trailing edge and use small vanes to diffuse the exhaust and cool-air blending to reduce exhaust temperature. The bottom lip of the exhaust is extended aft so that no part of the exhaust can be seen from below; the lip is covered with thermal tiles. The tailpipes are nickel-alloy 718 honeycomb sandwich to withstand acoustic, heat, and pressure stress. The engine exhaust ends are circular.

Modifications to the exhaust system are aimed at reducing maintenance costs due to heat stress and include new airflow paths, improved thermal "bricks," better seals, and better heat shields. Although this area glows in certain conditions, neither Lockheed nor the Air Force believes this compromises the aircraft's stealth characteristics.

The tricycle landing gear retracts forward. Modifications in this area include the fitting of carbon/carbon brakes in place of the original steel brakes. An arresting hook is located between the engines, and the aircraft streams a brake parachute from the tail upon landing.

The single-seat cockpit is heavily framed and bordered by serrated appliqués along some of the edges; it is hinged at the rear.

Avionics include the Texas Instruments Infrared Acquisition and Designation System (IRADS), which includes FLIR, a laser designator, and Downward-Looking IR (DLIR) systems. Both the FLIR and the DLIR are mounted in turrets that are controlled by joystick-mounted buttons. During a typical attack, the pilot closes on the target using the FLIR, then switches to the DLIR view in the final phase. The IRADS can be used in an air-to-air role as well as for ground attack.

The Kaiser Electronics Head-Up Display (HUD) is adapted from the F/A-18. The two Cathode-Ray Tube (CRT) Multifunction Displays (MFD) are being modified to Honeywell Digital Tactical Displays (DTD) with color CRTs that incorporate a Harris digital moving map display. Although space and cooling were reserved for a radar, none has been fitted.

The mechanical SPN/GEANS Inertial Navigation System (INS) used in the B-52 Stratofortress is fitted. A "four-dimensional" (4D) navigational system was added that ensures extreme accuracy in time as well as position; autothrottles have been fitted to the engines to assist 4D navigation.

Armament is usually the Paveway II and Paveway III laser-guided bombs fitted with a BLU-109/B warhead. AGM-65 Maverick TV- or laser-guided air-to-ground missiles and the AGM-88 HARM antiradar missile can also be delivered as well as Sidewinder Air-to-Air Missiles (AAM). The side-by-side internal weapons bays are each 15 ft 5 in (1.75 m) long; each is fitted with a trapeze to launch weapons that are normally carried on external pylons.

DEVELOPMENT • The F-117's initial operational capability was in October 1983. Its first flight was in June 1981. The final F-117 was transferred to the Air Force on July 12, 1990; a total of 59 were delivered.

Prior to November 1988, the aircraft designator for the stealth fighter was believed to be F-19.

Three F-117s crashed during the aircraft's "black years." The first went down while under Lockheed testing. Two other fatal crashes occurred during Air Force operations; the first went down in July 1986, the second in October 1987. The F-117 reportedly has operated in Great Britain, being transported to forward bases by the C-5 Galaxy.

VARIANTS • Have Blue (prototypes), F-117.

COMBAT EXPERIENCE • The F-117 was first used in combat on December 20, 1989, during Operation Just Cause, the US military action that removed Panamanian leader General Noriega. In the predawn attack, two F-117s flying nonstop from a US base dropped 2,000-lb (907-kg) bombs in a field near a Panamanian Defense Force barracks to "confuse, stun, and disrupt" the troops; the mission was judged a success. It was later revealed that one of the two aircraft missed its target.

The US dispatched 19 or 20 F-117s, refueled in flight, to Saudi Arabia in the middle of August 1990 as part of its buildup in the region. Another 20–22 aircraft were dispatched in late November.

When Operation Desert Storm's air assaults on Iraqi targets began on January 17, 1991, F-117s hit 31% of the precision targets in Baghdad. Overall, the aircraft flew approximately 1,300 sorties and dropped more than 2,000 tons of bombs, including most of the aircraft missions against military targets in Baghdad as well as attacks against hardened aircraft shelters. Released videos suggested that the laser-guided bombs had been very accurate; the official success rate was reportedly 60%.

No F-117s were lost during the seven-week conflict; the Air Force claimed that none was even damaged. The F-117's apparent invulnerability was attributed to its low radar, IR, and noise signatures. Reports suggested that in most instances the first indication of an F-117 attack was the explosion of the bomb on the target.

SPECIFICATIONS •
MANUFACTURER   Lockheed Aeronautical Systems
CREW   1
ENGINES   2 General Electric F404-GE-F1D2 nonafterburning turbofan

max power   11,000 lb (4,990 kg) static thrust each

WEIGHTS

max payload 5,000 lb (2,268 kg)
max takeoff 52,500 lb (23,813 kg)

DIMENSIONS

wingspan   43 ft 7 in (13.7 m)
length   65 ft 11 in (20.09 m)
height   12 ft 5 in (3.78 m)

PERFORMANCE

max speed   560 kts (645 mph; 1,038 km/h)

takeoff speed at combat weight
             165 kts (190 mph; 306 km/h)

landing speed
             approx 150 kts (173 mph; 278 km/h)

radius with 5,000-lb (2,268-kg) weapons load
             unrefueled: 600 nm (691 mi; 1,111 km)
             2 refuelings: 1,800 nm (2,073 mi; 3,334 km)

armament   2 internal stations for 2,000-lb (907-kg) GBU-10/B Paveway II or GBU-24 Paveway III laser-guided bombs AGM-65B TV or -65E laser-guided Maverick air-to-surface missiles AGM-88 HARM antiradar missiles

Tomcat (F-14)

The F-14 Tomcat is the US Navy's standard carrier-based fighter. Its missions include Combat Air Patrol (CAP), Deck-Launched Intercept (DLI), and air superiority. It is a large, fast, heavy aircraft designed around the long-range AIM-54 Phoenix Air-to-Air Missile (AAM) and the powerful Hughes AWG-9 weapons control system, which weighs 1,300 lb (590 kg) and occupies a volume of 25 ft³ (0.71 m³).

The Tomcat is a two-seat, twin-engine fighter with twin tails and variable-geometry wings. Its general arrangement consists of a long nacelle containing the large nose radar and crew positions extending well forward and above the widely spaced engines. The engines are parallel to a central structure that flattens toward the tail; butterfly-shaped air brakes are located between the fins on the upper and lower surfaces. Altogether, the fuselage forms more than half of the total aerodynamic lifting surface. The original-design airframe life for the F-14 was 6,000 hours but was later extended to 7,200 hours.

The wings are shoulder-mounted and programmed for automatic sweep during flight, with a manual override provided. The twin, swept fin-and-rudder vertical surfaces are mounted on the engine housings and canted outward. The wing pivot carry-through structure crosses the central structure; the carry-through is 22 ft (6.7 m) long and constructed from 33 electron-welded parts machined from titanium; the pivots are located outboard of the engines. Normal sweep range is 20° to 68° with a 75° "oversweep" position provided for shipboard hangar stowage; sweep speed is 7.5°/sec.

For roll control below 57°, the F-14 uses spoilers located along the upper wing near the trailing edge in conjunction with its all-moving, swept tailplanes, which are operated differentially; above 57° sweep, the tailplanes operate alone. For unswept, low-speed combat maneuvering, the outer two sections of trailing-edge flaps can be deployed at 10°, and the nearly full-span leading-edge slats are drooped to 8.5°. At speeds above Mach 1.0, glove vanes in the leading edge of the fixed portion of the wing extend to move the aerodynamic center forward and reduce loads on the tailplane.

The sharply raked, two-dimensional four-shock engine intakes have two variable-angle ramps, a bypass door in the intake roof, and a fixed ramp forward;

F-14 Tomcat
U.S. GOVERNMENT DEPARTMENT OF DEFENSE

exhaust nozzles are mechanically vari-able. Viewed from ahead, the top of the intakes are tilted toward the air-craft centerline; from above, the en-gines are canted outward slightly to re-duce interference between intake airflow and the fuselage boundary layer. The engines exhaust through mechan-ically variable, convergent-divergent nozzles.

The F-14's AWG-9 pulse-Doppler, mul-timode radar has a designed capability to track 24 targets at the same time while simultaneously devising and executing fire control solutions for six targets. The cockpit is fitted with a Kaiser AN/AVG-12 Head-Up Display (HUD) colo-cated with an AN/AVA-12 vertical situa-tion display and a horizontal situation display. A chin-mounted Northrop AN/AXX-1 Television Camera Set (TCS) is used for visual target identification at long ranges.

Electronic Support Measures (ESM) equipment include the Litton AN/

ALR-45 radar warning and control sys-tem, the Magnavox AN/ALR-50 radar-warning receiver, Tracor AN/ALE-29/-39 chaff/flare dispensers (fitted in the rear fuselage between the fins), and Sanders AN/ALQ-100 deception jam-ming pod.

The Tomcat has an internal 20-mm Vulcan Gatling-type gun fitted on the left side, and can carry Phoenix, Sparrow, and Sidewinder AAMs. Up to six Phoenix missiles can be carried on four fuselage stations between the engines and on two pylons fitted on the fixed portion of the wing; two Sidewinder AAMs can be car-ried on the wing pylons above the Phoe-nix mount.

Since the early 1980s, F-14s have had provision for the attachment of the Tacti-cal Air Reconnaissance Pod System (TARPS), carrying optical and infrared cameras and permitting the aircraft to perform the photo reconnaissance role without degrading its performance in other roles. The only modifications required are wiring changes and cockpit readouts.

DEVELOPMENT • The F-14's initial operational capability was in 1973; its first flight was December 21, 1970. 79 Tomcats were delivered to Iran before the 1979 revolution. They are normally grounded for lack of parts. The US Navy had almost 700 in service or on order in the early 1990s; deliveries were continuing.

A complete F-14D fleet was planned for 1998, with 127 new-production F-14Ds and modification of 400 F-14A and F-14A+ to D configurations.

VARIANTS • F-14A, F-14A+ (later F-14B) Super Tomcat, F-14C, F-14D, Quickstrike, Tomcat 21 (Grumman private-venture long-range, air-to-ground variant), Attack Super Tomcat 21 (proposed attack variant).

COMBAT EXPERIENCE • F-14 Tomcats from the carrier USS *Nimitz* (CVN 68) shot down two Libyan Su-22 Fitter aircraft in an encounter over the Gulf of Sidra in August 1981.

On October 10, 1985, four F-14s from the aircraft carrier USS *Saratoga* (CV 60) forced an EgyptAir Boeing 737 to land at Sigonella AB in Sicily. The airliner was carrying four terrorists who hijacked the cruise ship *Achille Lauro* and killed an American.

On January 4, 1989, two F-14s from the carrier USS *John F. Kennedy* (CV 67) intercepted and downed two Libyan MiG-23 Flogger-E aircraft, one with a radar-guided Sparrow AAM and the other with an IR-seeking Sidewinder. The US pilots claimed to have seen two parachutes.

99 F-14s flew 3,401 sorties as Combat Air Patrol (CAP) aircraft from five carriers during the air assault on Iraqi targets that began Operation Desert Storm; another 781 sorties were devoted to TARPS reconnaissance missions. The F-14 compiled the most flight hours (14,248) of any Navy fixed-wing aircraft.

Mission-capable rate overall was 77%; of TARPS aircraft 88%.

An F-14 downed an Iraqi Mi-8 Hip helicopter in early February 1991. One F-14 was lost during the war.

SPECIFICATIONS •
MANUFACTURER   Grumman
CREW   2 (pilot, radar intercept officer)
ENGINES   2 Pratt & Whitney TF30-P-412A turbofan
max power with afterburner
    20,900 lb (9,480 kg) static thrust each
internal fuel capacity
    2,385 US gal (9,029 liters)
WEIGHTS
empty   39,762 lb (18,036 kg)
fighter escort, 4 AIM-7 Sparrow missiles
    58,904 lb (26,718 kg)
fleet air defense with 4 AIM-54 Phoenix and 2 267-US gal (1,010-liter) drop tanks
    68,649 lb (31,139 kg)
max takeoff   74,348 lb (33,724 kg)
DIMENSIONS
wingspan   64 ft 1½ in (19.54 m) (extended)
    38 ft 2½ in (11.65 m) (swept)
length   62 ft 8 in (19.1 m)
height   16 ft (4.88 m)
wing area   565 ft² (52.49 m²)
PERFORMANCE
max possible speed at 49,000 ft (14,395 m)
    1,342 kts (1,544 mph; 2,485 km/h) or Mach 2.34
F-14A operational limit speed
    1,079 kts (1,242 mph; 1,998 km/h) or Mach 1.88
sea level   793 kts (913 mph; 1,469 km/h) or Mach 1.2
F-14D max cruise without afterburner
    631 kts (727 mph; 1,169 km/h) or Mach 1.1
range cruise
    407 kts (469 mph; 754 km/h)

acceleration from 245 kts (282 mph; 456 km/h), military power
F-14A: 46 sec to 400 kts (461 mph; 741 km/h)
F-14D: 30 sec to 420 kts (484 mph; 778 km/h); 46 sec to 500 kts (576 mph; 926 km/h)

acceleration from 250 kts (288 mph; 463 km/h), with afterburner
F-14A: 21 sec to 400 kts (461 mph; 741 km/h)
F-14D: 10 sec to 350 kts (403 mph; 648 km/h); 19 sec to 450 kts (518 mph; 833 km/h); 21 sec to 500 kts (576 mph; 926 km/h)

stall speed, power off, at 52,357 lb (23,749 kg)
110 kts (127 mph; 204 km/h)

time to 60,000 ft (18,288 m) at 55,000 lb (24,948 kg)
2 min 6 sec

ceiling   more than 56,000 ft (17,070 m)

combat radius
500 nm (576 mi; 927 km)

ferry range 1,735 nm (2,000 mi; 3,220 km)

armament   M61A1 20-mm Vulcan multibarrel cannon with 675 rounds plus AAM:
6 AIM-54 Phoenix + 2 AIM-9 Sidewinder
or 6 AIM-7 Sparrow + 2 Sidewinder
or 2 Phoenix + 3 Sparrow + 2 Sidewinder
or 4 Phoenix + 2 Sparrow + 2 Sidewinder

radar   F-14A: AWG-9 long-range search/weapons control
F-14D: APG-71 digital monopulse multimode

Eagle (F-15)

The F-15 is an air superiority and strike fighter for the US Air Force and a few foreign air forces. Along with the F-16 Fighting Falcon, the F-15 will be the principal USAF fighter aircraft into the 21st century.

The Eagle's broad wings have a relatively low leading-edge sweep, a 1° anhedral, and raked tips. The trailing edge is fitted with plain flaps and ailerons; the wings do not have leading-edge lift devices, spoilers, or trim tabs.

The two vertical surfaces have no cant; their rudders are inset in the lower trailing edges. All-moving tailplanes are mounted on the fuselage outboard of the engines; the outer leading edge of each tailplane extends forward in a dogtooth. Roll control at low speeds is by aileron; above Mach 1, the tailplanes are operated differentially.

The fuselage layout consists of a central structure flanked by engine bays; this large volume holds more than 2,000 US gal (7,570 liters) of fuel. Aluminum/light alloy/titanium material is used for the majority of airframe components. The sharply raked, two-dimensional, external-compression engine air intakes feed two afterburning turbofans fitted side by side between the tails. The intakes vary their inlet angle depending on speed and aircraft attitude; variable-area nozzles exhaust the afterburners. The engine thrust lines converge as they move toward the tail.

Beginning with F-15Cs that became operational in mid-1986, F-15s are powered by the F100-PW-220 engine with Hamilton Standard Digital Electronic Engine Control (DEEC) and 4,000-cycle core life. DEEC reduces acceleration time from flight idle to maximum power by 30% and eliminates restrictions on engine throttling throughout flight regime.

1,500 US gal (5,678 liters) of additional fuel can be carried in Conformal Fuel Tanks (CFT) that flank the engine nacelles. CFTs reduce subsonic drag and add less supersonic drag than do conventional drop tanks. The F-15 also has inflight refueling.

Located on the centerline and in line with the wing root's leading edge is a large single-piece air brake hinged on its forward edge; it is made of composite materials. The Eagle has retractable tricycle landing gear, the main gear wheels retracting into fuselage bays outboard of the intakes and the nose gear folding forward under the cockpit.

The cockpit and nose extend well forward from a point between the large intakes. The nose holds a Hughes Aircraft multimode, pulse-Doppler radar, which has a look-down, shoot-down capability; the original APG-63 was replaced in production by the APG-70 in 1984. The APG-70 is faster and has a higher resolution and a larger memory.

Other avionics include a Litton AN/ASN-109 Inertial Navigation System (INS), AN/AWG-20 fire control system, and a central digital computer. The cockpit is fitted with a McDonnell Douglas Electronics Head-Up Display (HUD) and a Sperry vertical situation display. The radar and HUD symbology are controlled by Hands-On Throttle and Stick (HOTAS) switches.

The F-15's Tactical Electronic Warning System (TEWS) includes Electronic Support Measures/Electronic Countermeasures (ESM/ECM) equipment such as the Loral AN/ALR-56C radar-warning receiver (with aerials in the fin tips, wingtips, and under the fuselage), the Magnavox AN/ALQ-128 threat-warning receiver, Tracor AN/ALE-45 countermeasures dispenser, and Northrop AN/ALQ-135 jamming system.

A wide variety of armament may be carried on external weapons stations, which vary in number depending on whether the aircraft is fitted with CFT. Two Sparrow Air-to-Air Missile (AAM) points are located on the lower outer edges of each intake. Two Sidewinder AAMs can be fitted to a weapons station under each wing. The single fuselage hardpoint and the two wing pylons can carry a total of 16,000 lb (7,258 kg); each CFT has additional stub pylons, raising the warload capacity to 23,600 lb (10,705 kg).

DEVELOPMENT • The aircraft's initial operational capability was in 1975, and its first flight was on July 27, 1972. Over 1,100 have been delivered to US Air Force squadrons. More than 280 additional aircraft have been delivered to or ordered by three other air forces.

Israeli Peace Fox F-15As began delivery in the late 1970s (25 aircraft). 15 Peace Fox 2 F-15C/D aircraft arrived in 1981, followed by 11 Peace Fox 3s. Deliveries in 1991–92 included five new-build F-15C/Ds and 25 surplus F-15A/Bs.

The first US-built Japanese F-15s were delivered in May 1981 (Squadron initial operational capability in 1982). License production in Japan by Mitsubishi began in 1982; 171 are planned, with more than 120 delivered.

Saudi Arabia took delivery of its 60 Peace Sun F-15C/Ds from January 1982 to May 1983; two more were purchased as attrition aircraft. October 1987 order of 12 more (nine C, three D) under Peace Sun VI, with delivery ending February 1992. 24 more were transferred from US Air Force units in Europe in September 1990 in a $682-million deal.

On September 15, 1992, the Bush administration notified Congress of plans to sell 72 F-15XP aircraft to Saudi Arabia.

VARIANTS • F-15A, F-15B, F-15C, F-15D/DJ (Japanese), F-15 Multistage Improvement Program (MSIP), F-15E Dual-Role Fighter, F-15J (Japan-built), F-15F, F-15XP (Saudi Arabia), NF-15 S/MTD Agile Eagle/STOL Eagle.

COMBAT EXPERIENCE • On June 7, 1981, the Israeli Air Force conducted an air raid against the Iraqi Osirak nuclear reactor facility with eight F-15 Eagles flying cover for the F-16 Fighting Falcons that bombed the facility. The strike destroyed the target without the loss of any aircraft.

During the protracted Israeli campaign in the Middle East from the late 1970s, approximately 60 Syrian MiG-21, MiG-23, and MiG-25 fighters were downed. Another 45 of this type of aircraft were claimed during the 1982 invasion of Lebanon; the Israelis reported no losses.

In August 1990, the United States dispatched two squadrons of F-15C/Ds and a squadron of F-15Es to Saudi Arabia as part of Operations Desert Shield/Desert Storm. F-15Es flew more than 2,200 sorties against targets in Iraq and Kuwait as part of the air assaults. The two F-15E squadrons flew 40–60 sorties per night with a mission-capable rate of 95.9% (8% higher than peacetime).

US and Saudi F-15Cs flew escort missions that resulted in several Iraqi fighters being downed. Two F-15Es were shot down during the seven-week war; one was the first US Air Force aircraft lost in the conflict.

SPECIFICATIONS •

MANUFACTURERS
McDonnell Douglas
Mitsubishi Heavy Industries, Tokyo, Japan (F-15J/DJ)
CREW   1 (2 in F-15B/D/E/DJ)
ENGINES   2 Pratt & Whitney F100-PW-100 or -220 afterburning turbofan
max power (each engine)
  dry
    -100: 14,670 lb (6,654 kg) static thrust
    -220: 14,370 lb (6,518 kg) static thrust
  with afterburning
    -100: 23,830 lb (10,809 kg) static thrust
    -220: 23,450 lb (10,637 kg) static thrust

fuel capacity
  F-15C, internal: 2,070 US gal (7,836 liters)
  F-15E, internal: 2,019 US gal (7,637 liters)
  F-15C, max internal and external capacity: 5,400 US gal (20,441 liters)
  F-15E, 2 CFT and 3 610-US gal (2,304-liter) tanks: 5,349 US gal (20,246 liters)
WEIGHTS
  empty   F-15C: 28,600 lb (12,973 kg)
    F-15E: 31,700 lb (14,379 kg)
    F-15C interceptor with 4 Sparrow AAMs: 44,630 lb (20,244 kg)
  max takeoff   F-15C with 3 610-US gal (2,309-liter) drop tanks: 58,470 lb (26,521 kg)
    F-15C with 4 Sparrow, 4 Sidewinder, and full CFT: 59,500 lb (26,989 kg)
    F-15C with CFT and external tanks: 68,000 lb (30,845 kg)
    F-15E: 81,000 lb (36,741 kg)
DIMENSIONS
  wingspan   42 ft 9 ¾ in (13.05 m)
  length   63 ft 9 in (19.43 m)
  height   18 ft 5½ in (5.63 m)
  wing area   608 ft² (56.50 m²)
PERFORMANCE
  max speed   at altitude: 1,433 kts (1,650 mph; 2,655 km/h) or Mach 2.5+
    sea level: 800 kts (921 mph; 1,482 km/h) or Mach 1.2
  approach speed   125 kts (144 mph; 232 km/h)
  time to 40,000 ft (12,200 m)   approx 1 min
  g limits   +9/−3

ceiling	60,000 ft (18,300 m)

max combat radius
F-15C: 1,062 nm (1,223 mi; 1,968 km)
F-15E: approx 1,000 nm (1,150 mi; 1,853 km)

range	2,500 nm (2,878 mi; 4,631 km)
armament	M61A1 20-mm Vulcan Gatling cannon with 940 rounds *and* 4 AIM-9 Sidewinder, 4 AIM-7 Sparrow, or 8 AIM-120 AMRAAM air-to-air missiles *and* up to 16,000 lb (7,258 kg) of nuclear or conventional bombs, rockets, or other ground-attack stores
radar	AN/APG-63 pulse-Doppler (original) *or* AN/APG-70 pulse-Doppler (retrofit)

Fighting Falcon (F-16)

The F-16 Fighting Falcon is a highly maneuverable, lightweight fighter aircraft flown in large numbers by the US Air Force and several other air forces. Originally intended primarily as a day fighter, the F-16 has proven to be an effective multipurpose, continually improving interceptor and strike aircraft.

The F-16 has a blended wing/body design in which the fuselage contributes lift, especially at high angles of attack. A prominent factor in the design is the acceptance of relaxed static stability, which reduces drag, by incorporating Fly-by-Wire (FBW) control through a Lear-Siegler quadruple-redundant flight control computer. As a result, the F-16 can attain 9 g in sustained turns; the maximum instantaneous turn rate at 400 kts (461 mph; 741 km/h) is 19°/sec.

The 11-spar, cropped delta wing is made primarily of aluminum alloy; its midfuselage location separates the large

F-16 Fighting Falcon
U.S. GOVERNMENT DEPARTMENT OF DEFENSE

engine intake and mount from the cockpit and nose. Narrow strakes extend forward from the wing root. Single-piece maneuvering flaps along the entire leading edge automatically deploy depending on the aircraft's angle of attack and Mach number. Flaperons occupy most of the wing's trailing edge, operating differentially for roll control and together to provide more lift at low speeds.

The single, tall fin and rudder and all-moving tailplanes also have aluminum structures, but have graphite-epoxy skin panels. Two trapezoidal ventral fins are located below and ahead of the tailplanes.

The fuselage has the cockpit well forward, ahead of the nose gear. The wide, ventral intake is not variable but is fitted with a boundary-layer splitter plate. The single engine is an afterburning turbofan.

Until FY1985, all F-16s were powered by the Pratt & Whitney two-shaft F100-PW-200 turbofan. Since FY1985, under the Alternate Fighter Engine, the F-16 has alternated engines with the General Electric F110-GE-100. The intakes on US F-16C/Ds and Netherlands Air Force F-16s have been fitted with Radar-Absorbing Material (RAM) designed to prevent radar glint on the turbine face.

The cockpit has a large bubble canopy, giving the pilot a 360° view in the upper hemisphere as well as excellent forward and downward visibility. US F-16C/Ds and Netherlands Air Force F-16s have received a gold-colored metal coating on the inside of the canopy to dissipate radar energy by reflecting it in all directions, giving the aircraft a stealth quality.

The seat back reclines 30°, the heel line is raised, and the conventional, centerline control stick is replaced by a side-stick controller located on the right console.

Primary avionics include a Westinghouse multimode, I/J-band pulse-Doppler radar, GEC Avionics Head-Up Display (HUD), angle-of-attack indicator, Combined Altitude Radar Altimeter (CARA), and Litton LN-39 Inertial Navigation System (INS).

F-16C/D aircraft have two Honeywell 4-in (102-mm) Multifunction Displays (MFD) located below the HUD, providing radar, navigation, and weapons system information. Pakistani aircraft carry the Thomson-CSF ATLIS laser target designation pods.

The F-16's Electronic Support Measures (ESM) equipment consists primarily of the Litton (or General Instruments) AN/ALR-46 or Litton AN/ALR-69 Radar-Warning Receivers (RWR) and Tracor ALE-40 chaff/flare dispensers. Air National Guard F-16s in Saudi Arabia flew with the Westinghouse AN/ALQ-119(V)15 jamming pod. The Belgian aircraft's ESM system is the Loral Rapport. Turkish aircraft are being fitted with the Loral AN/ALQ-178 Rapport III.

Standard internal armament consists of an M61 Vulcan Gatling cannon in the left LERX (Leading-Edge Root Extension). In addition to the centerline hardpoint and two stub pylons on the inlet, the F-16 has six wing pylons for external stores and two tip rails for Air-to-Air Missiles (AAM). The F-16A/B aircraft can fire only AIM-9 Sidewinder Infrared (IR) AAM; later models are capable of firing Beyond Visual Range (BVR) AAM such as the AIM-7 Sparrow, AIM-120 AMRAAM, and Sky Flash missiles. The F-16 has also test-fired Matra Magic 2 IR AAM.

Total weapons load on the F-16A/B is 15,300 lb (6,940 kg); F-16C/D weapons load capacity is 21,850 lb (9,911 kg) at 5.5 g, 13,750 lb (6,237 kg) at 9 g. F-16s fitted with Harpoon Interface Adapter Kit (HIAK) in weapons pylon are able to launch AGM-84D Harpoon antiship missiles.

DEVELOPMENT • The aircraft's initial operational capability was in 1979; its first flight was on February 2, 1974. In 1974, the YF-16 defeated the Northrop YF-17 in a US Air Force lightweight fighter competition.

Over 3,000 F-16s have been produced or ordered. Outside of the EPG production, each country purchasing F-16s is assigned a "Peace" name.

The F-16 is flown by over 15 other nations in Europe, Latin America, the Middle East and Asia.

VARIANTS • F-16A, F-16A (ADF), F-16B (trainer), F-16 Midlife Update (MLU), F-16C, F-16D (two-seat), F-16N (USN threat-simulate aircraft), F-16/79, RF-16 (reconnaissance), F-16X Agile Falcon, F-16AT/Falcon 21, A-16, F-16 (F/A-16) Close Air Support, FSX/SX-3 (Close Support fighter), F-16/AFTI, F-16XL/F-16E, NF-16D VISTA (Variable-Stability In-Flight Simulator Test Aircraft).

COMBAT EXPERIENCE • The Israeli Air Force used F-16s in the June 7, 1981, attack against the Iraqi Osirak nuclear reactor and the October 1, 1985, bombing raid against Palestine Liberation Organization forces in Tunisia. During the 1982 Peace in Galilee Offensive in Lebanon, Israeli F-16s were reported to have shot down 44 Syrian aircraft without loss to themselves.

Pakistani F-16 aircraft engaged in frequent combat with Afghan Air Force aircraft during the Afghanistan War, reportedly shooting down five MiG-21 Fishbeds and an unknown number of Su-25 Frogfoot aircraft.

In August 1990, F-16s from the 363rd Tactical Fighter Wing, Shaw AFB, South Carolina, were deployed to Saudi Arabia as part of Operation Desert Shield; several more active, Air Force Reserve, and Air National Guard squadrons followed.

After Operation Desert Storm began on January 17, 1991, 251 F-16As and Cs flew more than 13,500 sorties against targets in Iraq and Kuwait, 4,000 of them at night. Most of these sorties were flown against ground targets, as Iraqi Air Force resistance during the war was negligible; principal weapons were bombs and AGM-65 Maverick missiles.

F-16 reliability was high, even in the older Air National Guard F-16As; overall F-16 mission-capable rate was said to be 88%. Seven F-16s were lost during the seven-week war, five in combat and two in noncombat accidents.

In 1993, USAF F-16s conducted surveillance missions over Bosnia in support of international efforts to end the conflict in the former Yugoslavia.

SPECIFICATIONS •
MANUFACTURER   General Dynamics
CREW   1
ENGINES   1 Pratt & Whitney F100-PW-100 or -220 turbofan
or 1 General Electric F110-GE-100 turbofan
max power   F100-PW-220: 23,800 lb (10,796 kg) static thrust
F110-GE-100: 28,900 lb (13,109 kg) static thrust
internal fuel capacity
F-16C: 6,972 lb (3,162 kg) or approx 1,073 US gal (4,060 liters)
F-16D: 5,785 lb (2,624 kg) or approx 890 US gal (3,369 liters)
external fuel capacity
6,760 lb (3,066 kg) or approx 1,040 US gal (3,936 liters)
WEIGHTS
empty   18,238 lb (8,273 kg)
combat weight (50% fuel and 2 Sidewinder AAMs)
F100-PW-220: 26,250 lb (11,907 kg)
F110-GE-100: 27,350 lb (12,406 kg)

max takeoff 42,300 lb (19,187 kg)

DIMENSIONS

wingspan   to rails: 31 ft (9.45 m)
             with missiles: 32 ft 10 in
             (10 m)
length   49 ft 3 in (15.03 m)
height   16 ft 8 in (4.95 m)
wing area 300 ft² (27.87 m²)

PERFORMANCE

max speed more than 1,146 kts
             (1,320 mph; 2,124 km/
             h) or Mach 2
ceiling   60,000 ft (18,300 m)
radius   F-16A, with 6 500-lb (227-
             kg) bombs, hi-lo-hi,
             internal fuel: 295 nm
             (340 mi; 547 km)
             F-16C, weapons load
             unspecified: more than
             500 nm (575 mi; 925
             km)
ferry range more than 2,100 nm
             (2,420 mi; 3,891 km)
armament   1 M61 20-mm multibarrel
             cannon with 515
             rounds
             and 2 450-lb (204-kg)
             capacity wingtip launch
             rails for AAM
             and 6 wing, 1 belly, and 2
             inlet weapons stations
             for AAM, bombs, air-to-
             ground missiles, fuel,
             rockets, chaff/flare
             dispensers, or
             electronics pods; of
             these:
             2 700-lb (318-kg) capacity
             outer wing pylons for
             AAM only
             2 3,500-lb (1,588-kg)
             middle wing pylons
             AAM and other stores
             2 4,500-lb (2,041-kg)
             inboard wing pylons for
             other stores only
             1 2,200-lb (998-kg)
             capacity fuselage
             hardpoint for bombs,
             dispensers, or fuel

             2 900-lb (408-kg) inlet
             stub pylons for
             electronics pods
radar   AN/APG-68 pulse-
             Doppler

Hornet (F/A-18)

The F/A-18 Hornet is a strike-fighter air-craft in wide use by the US Navy and Marine Corps as well as several other air forces. In US service, the F/A-18 replaced the A-7 Corsair as well as some F-4 Phantoms in carrier air wings, while in Marine squadrons, it replaced the F-4 as well as some A-4 Skyhawk aircraft. The Night Attack variant is replacing Marine Corps A-6E Intruder aircraft.

The Hornet is flown in both single- and two-seat variants. It is characterized by high maneuverability, the ability to operate in either the fighter or attack role with only a change of weapons racks, and comparatively low maintenance requirements. The emphasis on easy access to aircraft systems is considered one of the aircraft's strongest points.

The Hornet has slightly swept wings with a relatively low aspect ratio, 20° sweep at the quarter-chord, 3° of anhedral, and Leading-Edge Root Extensions (LERX). The LERX allow flight at or beyond 60° angles of attack. Retrofitted fences on the LERX measure 32 in (813 mm) long by 8 in (203 mm) high. These fences generate vortices that reduce loads on the tail group and confer a six-times (and perhaps as high as 27-times) increase in the tail section's fatigue life. Leading-edge maneuvering flaps can be extended to 30° and be differentially deflected up to 3°. The trailing-edge flaps can be lowered to 45° and have 8° differential deflection.

The twin, swept fin-and-rudder surfaces are mounted forward of the swept, all-moving stabilators; the fins are canted 20° to the outside, and the stabilators have 2° of anhedral. A rectangular, front-

F/A-18 Hornet
U.S. GOVERNMENT DEPARTMENT OF DEFENSE

hinged speed brake is fitted between the vertical fins. Much of the wing, all of the tail surfaces, and the speed brake are composed of carbon/epoxy composites. All control surfaces are commanded by the AN/ASW-44 quadruplex fly-by-wire system.

The two low-bypass turbofan engines are fed by fixed pitot air intakes located under the wings; the exhaust nozzles extend to the rear of the stabilators. The intake ducts also house the main landing gear, each main wheel turning 90° during retraction. Finnish, Kuwaiti, Swiss, and US Navy aircraft delivered in 1992 and beyond are fitted with the F404-GE-402 Enhanced Performance Engine (EPE) variant, developing 17,600 lb (7,983 kg) static thrust with afterburning.

Approximately 50% of the structural weight of the aircraft is aluminum, 17% is steel, 13% is titanium, 10% is carbon/epoxy, and 10% other. The cockpit is located between the LERX and has excel-lent visibility; it is enclosed by a single-piece canopy that is hinged at the rear. The pilot sits in a Martin-Baker SJU-5/6 ejection seat.

Avionics in the F/A-18 include the Hughes AN/APG-65 digital, multimode air-to-air and air-to-ground radar, and Electronic Support Measures (ESM) equipment including the Magnavox AN/ALR-50 and Litton ALR-67 radar-warning receiver (some export aircraft may be retrofitted with the Litton AN/ALR-87 threat-warning system). Later aircraft are being fitted with the AN/APG-73 radar with three times the memory and a threefold increase in processing speed.

Other avionics include a centrally mounted 4.7 × 4.7-in (120 × 120-mm) Kaiser Cathode-Ray Tube (CRT) and AN/AVQ-28 Head-Up Display (HUD) with 20° field of view, and two additional Kaiser multifunction CRTs. Initial production F/A-18s were fitted with the Litton AN/ASN-130 Carrier Aircraft Internal Navigation System (CAINS), which uses gyros, accelerometers, a computer, and a platform. The Litton AN/ASN-139 CAINS II is a drop-in replacement for the ASN-130 and has an 11-in (280-mm) ring laser gyro, new accelerometers, and MIL-STD-1750-level processors.

In keeping with its dual role, the F/A-18 has a comprehensive weapons carriage capability. In addition to wingtip Sidewinder Air-to-Air Missile (AAM) stations, the aircraft can carry up to four Sparrow semiactive radar-homing AAMs on two outboard wing stations and two semirecessed fuselage hardpoints.

The M61 Vulcan gun system is mounted on a slide-in pallet in the nose. The centerline barrel mount in the airframe steadies the gun; vents to either side direct gases away from engine inlets. Firing rate is 4,000 or 6,000 shots per minute.

Three fuselage stations and four wing stations can carry Harpoon antiship and Maverick land-attack missiles, as well as the Walleye glide bomb, conventional bombs, up to three 330-US gal (1,250-liter) drop tanks, Loral (formerly Ford) Aeroneutronic AN/AAS-38 NITE Hawk Laser Target Designator/Ranger (LTD/R) pod with Forward-Looking Infrared (FLIR) system and Litton laser designator, Hughes AN/AAR-50 Thermal Imaging Navigation Set (TINS) pod with FLIR, or other stores.

DEVELOPMENT • The Hornet's initial operational capability was on January 7, 1983 and the F/A-18D in November 1989. Its first flight (F/A-18A) was on November 18, 1978; the F/A-18C's first flight was on September 18, 1987; the first flight of the F/A-18D night-attack variant was on May 6, 1988.

In production, with more than 1,070 delivered by early 1992 to US and international customers. The design's 1 millionth flight hour was registered by a US Navy pilot on April 10, 1990.

In early 1987, developmental models of the F/A-18 were assigned to the Blue Angels, the Navy–Marine Corps flight demonstration team (replacing A-4F Skyhawks).

At first, Iraq's August 1990 invasion of Kuwait seemed likely to doom Kuwaiti plans to acquire 40 F/A-18s. However, the US DoD authorized a $140-million advance on the contract to McDonnell Douglas in September 1990. The first of the order rolled out on October 8, 1991, for delivery in January 1992, with the entire purchase completed in fall 1993.

In May 1992, Finland announced a $2.5-billion deal to purchase 57 F/A-18C and 7 F/A-18D aircraft after an evaluation that included the Dassault Mirage 2000-5, the Swedish JAS 39 Gripen, and the MiG-29 Fulcrum.

Other countries operating the Hornet include Australia, Canada, South Korea, Spain, and Switzerland. Malaysia's mixed buy of 8 F/A-18s and 18 MiG-29s provided an opportunity for side-by-side comparisons.

VARIANTS • Northrop YF-17 (unsuccessful competition prototype with YF-16 Fighting Falcon ACF), YF-18, F/A-18A, EF-18 (Spanish designation), CF-18 (Canadian designation), TF-18 (initial designation for two-seat trainer aircraft; later F/A-18B), F/A-18C/D (single and two seats), F/A-18C/D Night Attack, F/A-18E/F (single and two seats), Hornet 2000, NASA HARV (NASA's High-Angle-of-Attack Research Vehicle), AF-18 (Australian), CF-18 (Canadian), EF-18/C.15/CE.15 (Spanish).

COMBAT EXPERIENCE • US Navy Hornets patrolled the Persian Gulf and Red Sea from US carriers as part of Operations Desert Shield/Desert Storm: 174 Navy and Marine Corps F/A-18s conducted both defense suppression and strike missions against Iraqi targets and proved to be among the most flexible and effective strike aircraft available. 90 Navy Hornets flew 4,431 sorties, and 84 Marine Corps F/A-18s flew 5,047 sorties.

In one instance, a Hornet en route to an air-to-ground attack shot down a MiG-21 Fishbed with an AIM-9 before continuing to its target. The aircraft's full-mission-capable rate averaged better than 90%, with each aircraft amassing an average of more than 90 flight hours per month.

Several F/A-18s were hit by surface-to-air missiles, but most were able to return to base flying on a single engine. A total of three US-flown Hornets were lost during the seven-week war, one to noncombat causes.

Canada deployed 26 CF-18s from Lahr, Germany, to the gulf.

SPECIFICATIONS •

MANUFACTURER McDonnell Douglas/ Northrop
CREW 1 (2 in F/A-18B/D)
ENGINES 2 General Electric F404-GE-400 turbofan
max power 16,000 lb (7,257 kg) static thrust each with afterburner
internal fuel capacity
approx 1,700 US gal (6,435 liters)
WEIGHTS
empty 23,050 lb (10,455 kg)
max weapons load
17,000 lb (7,711 kg)
takeoff fighter: 36,710 lb (16,651 kg)
attack: 49,224 lb (22,328 kg)
overload: 56,000 lb (25,401 kg)
DIMENSIONS
wingspan over AIM-9 missiles: 40 ft 5 in (12.32 m)
without missiles or tip launchers: 37 ft 6 in (11.46 m)
folded for storage: 27 ft 6 in (8.38 m)

length 56 ft (17.07 m)
height 15 ft 3½ in (4.66 m)
wing area 400 ft² (37.16 m²)
PERFORMANCE
max speed Mach 1.8+
launch Wind Over Deck (WOD)
35 kts (40 mph; 65 km/h)
recovery WOD
19 kts (22 mph; 35 km/h)
climb rate 45,000 ft/min (13,716 m/min)
acceleration from Mach 0.8 to Mach 1.6 at 35,000 ft (10,670 m)
less than 2 minutes
ceiling 50,000 ft (15,240 m)
combat radius
F/A-18A fighter: more than 400 nm (460 mi; 740 km)
F/A-18A attack: more than 575 nm (662 mi; 1,065 km)
F/A-18C with 4 1,000-lb (454-kg) Mk 83 bombs, 2 Sidewinders, 2 330-US gal (1,249-liter) drop tanks, and external sensors: 290 nm (334 mi; 537 km)
F/A-18C time on station at 150 nm (173 mi; 278 km) with 6 AAM, 3 330-US gal (1,249-liter) drop tanks: 1.4 hr
ferry range more than 2,000 nm (2,303 mi; 3,706 km)
armament M61 20-mm 6-barrel gun (570 rounds)
attack: 17,000 lb (7,711 kg) of bombs, rockets, AIM-7 Sparrow, AIM-9 Sidewinder, AIM-120 AMRAAM air-to-air missiles, AGM-65 Maverick land-attack, AGM-84 Harpoon antiship missiles

	fighter: 2 Sidewinder + 4 Sparrow AAM
radar	AN/APG-65 multimode digital

Lightning (Advanced Tactical Fighter/ATF/F-22A)

The US Air Force Advanced Tactical Fighter (ATF) program selected a front-line fighter to succeed the F-15 Eagle through a competition between the Lockheed/Boeing/General Dynamics YF-22A and the Northrop/McDonnell Douglas YF-23A designs, won by the YF-22A.

The Lockheed/Boeing/General Dynamics YF-22 design has near-delta double-taper wings with movable leading-edge flaps that extend from outboard of the intakes to the tips; at the inboard edge, both the flap and the fixed leading edge have a notch to reduce radar reflectivity when the flaps are deployed in combat maneuvers.

The forward-tapered trailing edges are lined with flaps and ailerons. In the prototype, leading-edge sweep is 48°, with the trailing edge sweeping forward at 17° angle.

All-moving horizontal stabilators are carried on short stubs outboard of the rectangular, thrust-vectoring engine nozzles. Their leading edges are parallel to the wing leading edges, just as their trailing edges parallel those of the main wing. From being roughly triangular in the prototype, the tailplanes are more lozenge-shaped in EMD design, but also measure about 68 ft² (6.32 m²). Each edge still parallels another horizontal or vertical surface.

On the prototype, a single-piece teardrop canopy is perched high on the blended wing/body and has a distinct peak. Forebody shaping consists of a deep-keeled lower half and rounded upper half with a "seam" or chine running along each side of the forward fuselage from the nose aft to the top of the intake.

Viewed from above, the wing/body blending shows a large fuselage area for engines, ducting, and fuel tankage behind the narrower forebody. Seen from the side, the large vertical tails and peaked canopy reduce the prototype's apparent size and give it a stubby look.

The developed aircraft looks leaner for several reasons: the nose is longer, the canopy is reshaped and moved forward, the intakes have been moved aft to behind the cockpit, the vertical tails are smaller, and the landing gear is relocated aft to maintain its relation with the aircraft's center of gravity.

The intakes lead aft and toward the centerline in an S-curve to feed the engines mounted side by side between the tails. Two Pratt & Whitney F119 two-spool, low-bypass turbofans with contrarotating high- and low-pressure turbines power the ATF.

The top surfaces of the intakes are positioned as Leading-Edge Root Extensions (LERX) for each wing; the forward upper edges have the same sweep as do the wing's leading edges.

Behind the missile bays are the main-landing-gear bays. The single-wheel gear extends down and slightly outward and is enclosed by doors with serrated edges to reduce their radar signatures. The single-wheel nose gear retracts to the rear under the cockpit in the prototype. Moving the nose gear aft from the prototype requires the gear to retract forward. Each wing skin is a single piece of thermoplastic composites; the midbody skin is a thermoset piece.

Reliability is also strongly stressed. Integrated combat turnaround time for the ATF should be half that of the F-15 Eagle. Fewer maintenance personnel and cargo aircraft will be required to support the ATF, much more of the equipment is intended to be field-repairable, and virtually all of the systems are at ground level. An Auxiliary Power Unit (APU) is fitted in the rear of the fuselage between the engines.

Principal requirements of the Electronic Combat (EC) suite will be to detect hostile emitters, counter them, and defeat hostile countermeasures; much of its operation will be passive. Many elements will use emitters and receivers that are also used by the navigation or radar systems. The aircraft's avionics have the Hughes Common Integrated Processor (CIP) with 32-bit technology, Harris databus interfaces, Sanders graphic-video interfaces, and General Electric liquid-crystal, flat-panel displays. Sanders and GE are teaming up on an Integrated Electronic Warfare System (INEWS) linked to the Hughes CIP. General Dynamics is leading development of the Inertial Navigation System (INS).

Armament will consist of BVR Air-to-Air Missiles (AAM) such as the AIM-120 AMRAAM as well as shorter-range dogfight AAMs and an internal gun. The dogfight missiles are housed in inlet sidewall bays. Two side-by-side belly bays have at least two weapons stations each for missiles the size of an AMRAAM.

DEVELOPMENT • The unofficial nickname for the YF-22 is Lightning 2, after the Lockheed-built P-38 twin-engine fighter of World War II. Rumors were that the chosen name was Superstar. The aircraft is in Engineering and Manufacturing Development (EMD). Selected over the YF-23A for EMD on April 23, 1991.

YF-22 (F120 engines) rolled out on August 29, 1990; taxi tests began September 19, leading to first flight on September 29, 1990. The second YF-22 prototype (F119 engines) first flew on October 30, 1990.

First flight in the second series of tests came on October 30, 1991. This aircraft crashed April 25, 1992, during a low-speed pass. Lockheed claimed that 90% of the program objectives had been met. The crash of the prototype was not immediately seen as damaging to the program, but the aircraft ultimately may never be built.

VARIANTS • Naval ATF.

SPECIFICATIONS •
MANUFACTURER   Lockheed/Boeing/ General Dynamics
WEIGHTS
operational empty
      34,000 lb (15,422 kg)
combat loaded
      62,000 lb (28,123 kg)
ENGINES   2 Pratt & Whitney YF119-PW-100 turbofan
max power   30,000-35,000 lb
      (13,608-15,876 kg)
      static thrust each
internal fuel capacity
      25,000 lb (11,340 kg)
DIMENSIONS
wingspan   prototype: 43 ft (13.11 m)
      EMD: 44 ft 6 in (13.56 m)
length   prototype: 64 ft 2 in (19.56 m)
      EMD: 62 ft ½ in (18.91 m)
height   prototype: 17 ft 9 in (5.41 m)
      EMD: 16 ft 6 in (5.03 m)
wing area   830 ft² (77.11 m²)
PERFORMANCE
max cruise without afterburner
      approx Mach 1.5
radar   Hughes AN/APG-77

Phantom (F-4)

The Phantom is one of the most versatile and widely flown fighter and attack aircraft of the jet era. It is a two-seat twin-engine, multirole fighter that is also often used as a reconnaissance aircraft. Originally developed for the US Navy, the Phantom was adopted by the Air Force as well as the Marine Corps and a number of other military forces.

The Phantom's design was governed by the need to combine high speed and long range, requiring a large and heavy aircraft, with the ability to take off and land on aircraft carriers. The resulting design has a tandem cockpit for the pilot and radar intercept officer, extensive internal fuel tankage, a large nose radar, and up to eight Air-to-Air Missiles (AAM), of which six can be medium-range AIM-7 Sparrows.

The configuration of the wings and tail group took unusual shape in an effort to obtain the desired low-speed handling. The wing planform is a swept delta, the leading edge having greater sweep than the trailing edges. The outer panels have 12° dihedral and 10% greater chord, creating a "sawtooth" leading edge. On naval Phantoms, the wings fold at the dihedral break for handling aboard carriers. The inboard leading edge was drooped at low speeds in the earlier variants; later versions have leading-edge slats on both inboard and outboard sections as well as drooping inboard "flaperons" on the trailing edge. The wings gain further lift at low speed through Boundary-Layer Control (BLC) that passes engine bleed air over the leading and trailing edges.

The short, sharply swept fin and rudder are mounted on a boom above and to the rear of the two variable-area nozzles. In line with the fin are the all-moving stabilators, which have a "cropped delta" planform and 23° anhedral; later variants have leading-edge slots in the tailplanes.

The two General Electric afterburning turbojets are housed side by side in the fuselage behind the cockpit. Air is fed through narrow "cheek" intakes that are headed by variable boundary-layer splitter panels. The aircraft can be refueled in flight, either through extendable probe (naval variants) or a boom receptacle located behind the cockpit.

The F-4's fire control radar has evolved in a series of Westinghouse radars beginning with the AN/APQ-72 and AWG-10 and passing through the APQ-100, -109, and -120. Avionics have been continually updated during the aircraft's lifetime. The GEC Avionics Standard Central Air Data Computer (SCADC) has been fitted. Many aircraft were fitted with General Electric AN/ASG-26A Lead-Computing Optical Sight (LCOS) and with Infrared (IR) scanners, and several hundred Northrop AN/ASX-1 Target Identification System Electro-Optical (TISEO) passive, daytime automatic target acquisition and tracking systems have been mounted on the port leading edge of US Air Force F-4s.

The F-4 was designed specifically for carrier operation as a missile or bomb carrier and was not initially fitted with an integral gun; F-4B/C/D/J variants often carried a Mk 4 gun pod bearing a Mk 11 twin-barreled 20-mm cannon on the centerline weapons station. F-4Es were built with a 20-mm M61 Vulcan Gatling cannon mounted in the nose below the radome. When armed as an interceptor, the F-4 carries four Sparrow AAMs in semi-recessed fuselage stations; two more Sparrows or four Sidewinder AAMs can be carried on the inboard wing pylons.

A centerline hardpoint and two pylons under each wing can carry up to 16,000 lb (7,257 kg) of bombs, land-attack missiles, rocket pods, and fuel tanks. Pylon-borne sensors include Ford Aerospace AN/AVQ-26 Pave Tack target designation pod, Westinghouse AN/ASQ-153 Pave Spike laser tracking and designator pod, Hughes AN/AXQ-14 weapons control system pod for the GBU-15 command-guided bomb, reconnaissance pods, and Electronic Countermeasures (ECM) pods.

The Phantom has been a landmark military aircraft whose design was the benchmark for every other fighter aircraft design for several decades. Its size allows it to carry large payloads over long distances, and its speed is still competitive with most operational fighters. The F-4 is ruggedly built, which increases its combat survivability and justifies rebuild programs that will carry it into the next century.

The Phantom's liabilities are its large

radar cross section, unstealthy angularity, smoky engines (in many earlier variants), utility hydraulics that failed regularly, and unwieldiness in tight-turning combat.

DEVELOPMENT • Initial operational capability was in 1961; first flight was on May 27, 1958. The original US Navy designation was AH-1; it was changed to F4H during development. The original US Air Force designation was F-110. All changed to F-4 series in 1962.

US production reached 75 aircraft per month in 1967 and ended in 1980 after 5,195 were produced. (Japanese production of 138 F-4EJs ended in 1981.) Almost 2,700 are still in service, and upgrade programs are under way in several countries.

The F-4 was still in service in the USAF, Air Force Reserve, Air National Guard, and USMC reserve units. The F-4 was phased out of US Navy service in late 1986 (its last carrier landing occur-

ring on October 18). The last active Marine Corps squadron converted to F/A-18 Hornets in February 1989. The Royal Air Force retired its last F-4 in September 1992. Other countries flying the F-4 are Greece, South Korea, Iran, Spain, Egypt, Israel, Turkey, Germany, and Japan.

VARIANTS • XF4H-1/YF4H-1 (prototypes), F-4A (development aircraft), F-4B (first production variant for USN and USMC), F-4C (first variant for US Air Force), F-4D, F-4E, F-4EJKai (Japanese), F-4EJ (reconnaissance), Israeli F-4E Wild Weasel (air defense suppressor), F-4F (Germany), F-4F Improved Combat Effectiveness (ICE), F-4G (carrier modification), F-4G Wild Weasel (Electronic Warfare/EW), F-4J (USN), F-4K/FG1 (Royal Navy), F-4M/FGR2 (RAF), F-4N, F-4S, RF-4 (reconnaissance), Kornas 2000/Super Phantom (Israeli-developed upgrade), F-4VG/F-4X (proposal).

U.S. Air Force F-4G Phantom II Wild Weasel

COMBAT EXPERIENCE • US Navy and Air Force Phantoms saw extensive combat service in Vietnam, Navy beginning on August 5, 1964, and Air Force in June 1965.

The Israeli Air Force (IAF) has used F-4s extensively in Middle East conflicts beginning in October 1969 during the "War of Attrition." In the Yom Kippur War of October 1973, F-4s flew most of the 500 deep-strike missions mounted by the IAF. During the 1982 Peace in Galilee Offensive into Lebanon, F-4s were credited with destroying most of the Syrian air defense network in the Bekaa Valley.

During the 1980–88 Gulf War with Iraq, the performance of Iranian Air Force F-4s was impeded by difficulties in obtaining spare parts, particularly for the radar and engines. One is said to have been shot down by an Iraqi Mi-24 Hind.

US Air Force F-4s stationed at Clark AB in the Philippines patrolled the airspace on December 1, 1989, during a coup attempt against the government. The F-4s were authorized to attack any rebel aircraft that launched from rebel-held Philippine airbases. No hostile action was necessary.

No F-4s were used by any country during Operations Desert Shield and Desert Storm; however, some RF-4C and F-4G Wild Weasel aircraft flew for the US Air Force.

SPECIFICATIONS (F-4S) •
MANUFACTURER   McDonnell Douglas
CREW   2 (pilot, radar intercept officer)
ENGINES   2 General Electric J79-GE-10 turbojet
  max power   17,900 lb (8,119 kg) static thrust each
  internal fuel capacity
    2,000 US gal (7,570 liters)
WEIGHTS
  empty   30,776 lb (13,990 kg)
  max takeoff   56,000 lb (25,455 kg)
DIMENSIONS
  wingspan   38 ft 5 in (11.71 m)

length   58 ft 3 in (17.76 m)
height   16 ft 3 in (4.96 m)
wing area   530 ft² (49.20 m²)
PERFORMANCE
  max speed   clean, at 36,000 ft (10,973 m): 1,260 kts (1,450 mph; 2,334 km/h) or Mach 2.2
  sea level, with Sparrows only: 790 kts (910 mph; 1,465 km/h) or Mach 1.2
  low-level penetration speed with 4,750-lb (2,155-kg) weapons load
    545 kts (628 mph; 1,010 km/h)
  climb rate   28,000 ft/min (8,534 m/min)
  ceiling   71,000 ft (21,641 m)
  radius   228 nm (262 mi; 422 km) (fighter role)
  136 nm (157 mi; 252 km) (attack role)
  range   1,600 nm (1,841 mi; 2,963 km) external fuel
  armament   various options, including:
    1 20-mm cannon (Mk 11 in Mk 4 external gun pod or internal M61 Vulcan Gatling)
    4 AIM-7 Sparrow + 4 AIM-9 Sidewinder AAM + 6 × 500-lb (227-kg) bombs
    or 4 Sparrow + 8 × 1,000-lb (454-kg) bombs
    or AGM-65 Maverick
  radar   Westinghouse series of digital radar/fire control systems

Tiger II/Freedom Fighter (F-5)

The F-5 is a lightweight, supersonic aircraft developed as an inexpensive, easily maintained fighter capable of operating from unimproved airfields. It was originally offered as a candidate for a US lightweight fighter but found virtually all of its market overseas. Although it is similar in appearance, the F-5E Tiger represented a significant improvement over the earlier F-5A. The T-38 Talon supersonic trainer is similar to the F-5 in most respects.

The F-5's small, thin wing is mounted low on the fuselage well aft of the cockpit. It has a 24° leading-edge sweep, leading-edge flaps, and single-slotted trailing-edge flaps inboard of the inset ailerons. The wingtips have long missile rails. On the F-5E Tiger, the leading- and trailing-edge flaps have automatic combat-maneuver settings to increase turn rate. The F-5E also has a Leading-Edge Root Extension (LERX) with compound sweep that improves the aircraft's handling at high angles of attack. Turn rates—both continuous and peak—increased by more than 30% over the F-5A.

The tail-group shape and position have remained constant throughout F-5 development. The double-taper fin has a two-section inset rudder; the cropped-delta, all-moving tailplanes are mounted at the bottom of the fuselage in line with the fin. Controls are assisted by two independent hydraulic systems, and the aircraft is fitted with a stability augmentation system.

The two J85 turbojet engines are buried side by side in the aft fuselage, with the afterburning nozzles extending well beyond the tail group. The air intakes are located low on either side of the fuselage. A boundary-layer splitter plate is fitted on the fuselage side of each intake, and the lip is curved aft as it moves away from the fuselage. The Tiger has uprated J85s and auxiliary inlet doors for takeoff and low-speed flight. Internal fuel tankage is confined to the fuselage. Iranian F-5s were fitted with a "buddy" refueling system in 1988 that permits one F-5 to refuel another.

The fuselage has a long pointed nose that slopes up to a low canopy; behind the canopy, a thick dorsal spine slopes down to the tail. The nose shape has varied, with some aircraft being fitted with a flattened "shark nose"; the RF-5E Tigereye reconnaissance variant has a chisel-shaped nose with an underslung pallet for cameras.

The main-landing-gear struts retract in from midwing pivots, the wheels being housed in fuselage wells. The nose gear in many F-5As and all F-5E/Fs has a two-position strut to raise the static angle of attack by 3⅓°, thereby increasing the wing's lift and shortening takeoff roll. Side-by-side air brakes are mounted on the fuselage bottom, forward of the landing gear.

The single-seat cockpit of the F-5A and F-5E is enclosed by a single-piece canopy that is hinged at the rear. The two-seat F-5B trainer and F-5F trainer-interceptor have two canopy sections that are hinged to the side.

The F-5E is equipped with an Emerson Electric AN/APQ-153 or -159 pulse-Doppler radar. The F-5F has the Emerson Electric APQ-157. In addition to a more comprehensive communications and navigation fit, the F-5E also has the General Electric AN/ASG-29 or -31 Lead-Computing Optical Sight (LCOS), a central air data computer, and an attitude and heading reference system. Several F-5E users have the Litton LN-33 Inertial Navigation System (INS); Saudi aircraft have General Instruments AN/ALR-46 Radar-Warning Receiver (RWR), Tracor AN/ALE-40 countermeasures dispenser, and Hughes AGM-65 Maverick missiles. Swiss and South Korean aircraft are being refitted with the Dalmo Victor AN/ALR-87 threat-warning system. Several air forces have avionics upgrades under way or planned (see Variants).

Armament consists of two Pontiac-built M39 20-mm cannon in the upper nose. (The F-5F has one M39 cannon, the other having been removed to make room for camera pallets.) Each wingtip missile launch rail carries an AIM-9 Sidewinder

Air-to-Air Missile (AAM). All variants have one centerline hardpoint and four wing pylons for external stores, including AAM, air-to-ground missiles, bombs, gun pods, rocket pods, and external fuel tanks.

DEVELOPMENT • The F-5A achieved its initial operational capability with the US Air Force in 1964; the F-5E in 1973. First flight of Northrop N-156 was on July 30, 1959. F-5A through D variants continue to serve with many other countries. The US Navy and Air Force have flown F-5E/F aircraft for aggressor training. The US Marine Corps adversary squadron replaced its F-21A Kfir fighters with F-5E aircraft, completing the changeover in fall 1989.

A total of 879 F-5A/Bs were built by Northrop, and 320 F-5A variants were built by Canadair in Canada and CASA in Spain. More than 1,400 F-5E/Fs were built, including license assembly by Korean Air in South Korea, F+W in Switzerland, and AIDC in Taiwan. 2,600 F-5s had been built in the US when production ended in February 1990; the last eight (for Singapore) were assembled from factory spares. More than 1,800 remain in service.

Ethiopian F-5A, -5E, and -5F aircraft had been unserviceable for several years before they were discarded in 1990. Royal Netherlands Air Force NF-5s were in service from 1969 to March 15, 1991. 60 Royal Netherlands AF NF-5s were donated to the Turkish Air Force, 12 to the Greek Air Force, and seven were sold to Venezuela.

The F-5 series is one of the most successful examples of a Western lightweight fighter design to have entered service. It is approximately the same size and weight as the MiG-21 Fishbed, but differs in having a lower maximum speed, higher weapons payload, and more tractable flying qualities at low fuel states.

The Freedom Fighter is flown by about 15 countries throughout the world; the Tiger is flown by over 20 nations.

VARIANTS • F-5A (Freedom Fighter), F-5B (trainer), CF-5A/D (Canadair/ CF-116), NF-5A/D (Canadair-built for the Netherlands), Norwegian F-5A/-5B Upgrade, Norwegian Tiger Upgrade Program for Avionics Weapon and Systems (PAWS), F-5E/F (Singapore Upgrade), SF-5A/D (CASA-built), F-5E Tiger II (second-generation), F-5F (trainer), Chegoong-Ho (Air Master/South Korean F-5F), Chung Cheng (Taiwanese F-5E), RF-5E Tigereye (reconnaissance), upgrade variants: Chile, Jordan, South Korea, Thailand, Venezuela; F-5G, T-38 Talon (trainer).

COMBAT EXPERIENCE • Saudi Arabian F-5Es flew training missions during the 1991 Operation Desert Storm; one F-5E was lost to noncombat causes.

SPECIFICATIONS •
MANUFACTURER   Northrop
CREW   1 (2 in F-5B/F)
ENGINES
   F-5A: 2 General Electric J85-GE-13 turbojet
   F-5E: 2 General Electric J85-GE-21B turbojet
   max power   F-5A dry: 2,720 lb (1,234 kg) static thrust each
      F-5A with afterburner: 4,080 lb (1,851 kg) static thrust each
      F-5E with afterburner: 5,000 lb (2,268 kg) static thrust each
   internal fuel capacity
      F-5A: 583 US gal (2,207 liters)
      F-5E: 677 US gal (2,555 liters)
WEIGHTS
   empty   F-5A: 8,085 lb (3,667 kg)
      F-5E: 9,723 lb (4,410 kg)
   max weapons load
      F-5A: 6,200 lb (2,812 kg)
      F-5E: 7,000 lb (3,175 kg)
   max takeoff   F-5A: 20,576 lb (9,333 kg)
      F-5E: 24,722 lb (11,214 kg)

DIMENSIONS

wingspan F-5A: 25 ft 3 in (7.7 m)
F-5E: 26 ft 8 in (8.13 m)

length F-5A: 47 ft 2 in (14.38 m)
F-5E: 47 ft 4 ¾ in (14.45 m)

height F-5A: 13 ft 2 in (4.01 m)
F-5E: 13 ft 4 in (4.06 m)

wing area F-5A: 170 ft² (15.79 m²)
F-5E: 186 ft² (17.3 m²)

PERFORMANCE *(at 13,350 lb/6,055 kg)*

max speed at 36,000 ft (11,000 m)
F-5A: 803 kts (925 mph; 1,489 km/h) or Mach 1.4
F-5E: 935 kts (1,077 mph; 1,733 km/h) or Mach 1.64

typical cruise 488 kts (585 mph; 904 km/h) or Mach 0.85

stall speed F-5A: 128 kts (147 mph; 237 km/h)
F-5E: 124 kts (143 mph; 230 km/h)

climb rate F-5A: 28,700 ft/min (8,748 m/min)
F-5E: 34,500 ft/min (10,516 m/min)

ceiling 51,800 ft (15,789 m)

radius F-5A, hi-lo-hi with max payload and combat reserves: 170 nm (195 mi; 314 km)
F-5E, lo-lo-lo with 5,200-lb (2,358-kg) payload and combat reserves: 120 nm (138 mi; 222 km)
F-5E at 15,000 ft (4,575 m), max fuel, 2 AAM, combat reserves: 570 nm (656 mi; 1,056 km)

ferry range, tanks dropped
F-5A: 1,359 nm (1,565 mi; 2,519 km)
F-5E: 1,545 nm (1,778 mi; 2,861 km)

armament 2 M239A2 20-mm cannon with 280 rounds each *and* 2 AIM-9 Sidewinder AAM on wingtip launchers *and* up to 6,200 lb/7,000 lb (F-5A/F-5E) of mixed ordnance on 4 underwing and 1 underfuselage stations including:
1 1,985-lb (900-kg) bomb
1 AGM-65 Maverick air-to-surface missile
9 500-lb (227-kg) bombs
submunitions dispensers
rocket pods
up to 3 GPU-5 30-mm gun pods
up to 3 150- or 275-US gal (568- or 1,041-liter) drop tanks

radar, F-5E AN/APQ-153 or -159 I/J-band pulse Doppler

ROTARY WING

Apache (AH-64)

The AH-64 is the US Army's principal gunship/antitank helicopter. It was the winner in the 1973–76 competition for an Advanced Attack Helicopter (AAH), beating out the Bell YAH-63 entry. The AH-64 is intended primarily for the antitank role, with an all-weather/night operating capability. It is relatively fast and maneuverable, carries a large antiarmor weapons load, has reduced radar and Infrared (IR) signatures, is damage-resistant against most small and medium antiaircraft artillery, and is crashworthy.

The four-blade main rotor assembly

consists of a hollow mast with an inertia-welded nickel-steel driveshaft. Each blade has five stainless-steel spars, steel leading edge, stainless-steel skin, and composite trailing edge. The blade design features a high-lift airfoil section and swept tips; the 20° sweep at the tips delays compressibility and improves the stability of both advancing and retreating blades.

The blades are linked to the hub arms with 22-ply-laminate strap packs. Two lead-lag dampers are fitted to each hub arm, and the flapping hinge is offset to 4% of blade radius to augment control power. The blades can be folded for transport by large cargo aircraft.

The antitorque rotor has two two-blade teetering rotors with a relatively low tip speed, which reduces tail rotor noise, and a 4,500-hour fatigue life. The titanium fork assembly carries one set of blades in elastomeric bearings above the plane of the other and at a 60°/120° angle. The tailplane had originally been mounted at the top of the tail. After tests, the broad, all-moving surface was relocated to near the base of the pylon. It adjusts automatically to provide a level attitude during Nap of the Earth (NOE) flight.

Primary flight control is by hydraulic actuation; a Sperry Fly-by-Wire (FBW) is provided as a backup. Stabilization is by the Sperry Digital Automatic Stabilization Equipment (DASE). Manufacturer McDonnell Douglas Helicopters claims that the AH-64 can move laterally and to the rear at speeds up to 45 kts (52 mph; 83 km/h). Maximum load factors are +3.5 g/−0.5 g; the positive load factor is reduced to 2.4 g with a 3,350-lb (1,520-kg) weapons load.

The two turboshaft engines are shoulder-mounted on the fuselage behind the main rotor mast. Each engine is fitted with a "black hole" passive IR exhaust suppressor.

The fuselage is designed to be crashworthy in vertical crashes of up to 42-ft/sec descent; the crew compartment is fur-ther protected by progressive deformation of the rest of the airframe, which absorbs additional energy. The entire airframe is designed to be invulnerable to 12.7-mm rounds. In addition, most vital components can sustain hits from 23-mm rounds and continue flying to a safe landing.

The pilot and copilot/gunner sit in tandem, Kevlar-armored seats surrounded by boron armor and under a heavily framed canopy. The canopy frame is designed to act as a roll cage, and the glazing between the crew members is impact-resistant; the glazing is not ballistically tolerant. The pilot is in the rear seat, which is 19 in (480 mm) above the copilot/gunner's. The front seat has a full set of flight controls that are typically stowed under the front sight.

The landing gear is fixed with the main, trailing-arm struts below the pilot's position and the tail gear extending beyond the tail rotor pylon. Detachable stub wings are fitted to the fuselage below the main rotor mast; each wing has two weapons pylons.

The core of the avionics fit is the Martin Marietta Target Acquisition and Designation Sight/Pilot's Night Vision Sensor (TADS/PNVS) linked to the Honeywell Integrated Helmet and Display Sight System (IHADSS) worn by both crew members. The turrets for the TADS and PNVS systems are fitted in the nose of the Apache. The upper PNVS turret contains a Forward-Looking Infrared (FLIR) sensor directly linked to the IHADSS and traverses with the user's head movements. Azimuth range is +/−90°; elevation is +20°/−45°. The lower TADS turret is divided vertically; the left half has direct vision optics with two fields of view (4° and 18°) above a daylight TV with 0.9° and 4° fields of view. The right half has a FLIR sensor. TADS is also fitted with a laser spot tracker and laser designator. Azimuth coverage is +/−120°, elevation is +30°/−60°. TADS imagery is relayed to the copilot/gunner through an optical relay "tube" that resembles a small console; it has both Head-Down and Head-Up Displays (HDD/HUD).

The three principal weapons systems on the Apache are the McDonnell Douglas Helicopters M230 30-mm Chain Gun, Rockwell AGM-114 Hellfire laser-guided antitank missiles, and Hydra 2.75-in (70-mm) rocket pods. The Chain Gun is fitted in a turret below the cockpit; turret traverse is +/−100°, elevation is +11°/−60°. Ammunition is fed from a 1,200-round pallet fitted under the main rotor assembly; operational experience has shown that a 380-round ammunition load is best. The stub pylons can carry up to 16 Hellfire missiles, although a load of eight is more typical. As an alternative load, up to four 19-rocket Hydra pods can be carried.

To improve its self-defense capabilities, the Apache was tested in November 1987 with Loral Aeroneutronic AIM-9 Sidewinder Air-to-Air Missiles (AAM) fitted on stub wingtip rails. The usual AAM fit, however, is the Air-to-Air Stinger (ATAS) adaptation of the General Dynamics FIM-92 Stinger shoulder-fired surface-to-air missile. Shorts (UK) Starstreak and Matra Mistral air-to-air and AGM-122 Sidearm antiradar missiles are also compatible.

DEVELOPMENT • The Apache's initial operational capability was in 1985. Its first flight was on September 30, 1975, and its first production rollout was in January 1984; the 500th production aircraft was rolled out on September 15, 1989. The first squadron of Apaches stationed in Europe arrived in August 1987 as part of REFORGER '87. A total of 975 AH-64A Apaches had been planned for procurement through FY1992, equipping 27 attack helicopter battalions. With the defense drawdowns following the collapse of the Soviet Union, the figure was again reduced under former Defense Secretary Cheney.

Since its service entry in 1985, the Apache has been the most advanced combat helicopter in service as well as plagued with reliability shortcomings in several key areas. Several studies conducted by the General Accounting Office (GAO) found many faults with the Apache, both mechanical and with its electronics.

Several countries have purchased the Apache: Bahrain, Egypt, Greece, Israel, Kuwait, Saudi Arabia, and the United Arab Emirates.

VARIANTS • Multistage Improvement Program (MSIP), AH-64B, AH-64C/D Longbow Apache (mast-mounted millimeter-wave radar), Naval Apache (shipboard/not funded).

COMBAT EXPERIENCE • In December 1989, 11 Apaches flew 200 hours of missions in support of the US military operation Just Cause to remove Panamanian General Noriega from power; 66% of the flying time was at night. According to the US Army, three AH-64s were damaged by ground fire and one aircraft took 32 7.62-mm hits, but they were back in service within 24 hours. The Army reported that Hellfire missiles used against fixed targets, including General Noriega's headquarters, were very accurate and effective.

In August 1990, Apaches from the 101st Airborne Division (Air Assault) were sent to Saudi Arabia as part of the US response to the Iraqi invasion and annexation of Kuwait. Accounts of their degree of readiness varied from 70% to 90%.

Eight Apaches were used to attack early-warning radar sites in western Iraq on a round-trip of 950 nm (1,094 mi; 1,759 km) that opened Operation Desert Storm's air war. The mission, which cleared an attack lane for precision strikes, achieved complete surprise and within two minutes had scored 15 hits with Hellfire missiles.

Additional reports during Desert Storm suggest that the Apache performed very well, whether alone or when flown in concert with the A-10. When the ground war was launched, Apaches led the 101st Airborne's airlift into Iraq. During the ground assaults against Iraq's Republican Guard formations, some AH-64s hit and destroyed several tanks with a single load of eight Hellfires. Overall, Apaches fired 2,876 Hellfires during Desert Storm. The 4th Battalion of the 229th Aviation Brigade was credited with 50 tanks in a single battle.

Serviceability reportedly remained high, and the Apache ended the campaign with an enhanced reputation.

SPECIFICATIONS •

MANUFACTURER   McDonnell Douglas Helicopters
CREW   2 (pilot, copilot/gunner)
ENGINES   2 General Electric T700-GE-701 or -701C turboshaft
  max power   1,695 shp (-701) or 1,890 shp (-701C) each
  internal fuel capacity
    376 US gal (1,422 liters)
WEIGHTS
  empty   10,760 lb (4,881 kg)
  primary mission gross weight
    14,445 lb (6,553 kg)
  with 3,350 lb (1,520 kg) weapons load and 2,500 lb (1,134 kg) of fuel
    17,650 lb (8,006 kg)
  ferry mission 21,000 lb (9,525 kg)
DIMENSIONS
  rotor diam   48 ft (14.63 m)
  length   48 ft 2 in (14.68 m)
  height   top of rotor: 12 ft 7 in (3.84 m)
    top of air data sensor: 15 ft 3½ in (4.66 m)
  disc area   1,809.5 ft² (168.1 m²)
PERFORMANCE
  (Army Hot day = 95° F/(35° C at 4,000 ft/1,220 m)
  speed   *max*
    clean: 164 kts (189 mph; 304 km/h)

Army Hot day: 147–155 kts (169-178 mph; 272-287 km/h)
Euro theater, 2,000 ft (610 m) at 70° F (21° C): 148–153 kts (170–176 mph; 274–284 km/h)
econ cruise
sea level, standard day: 128 kts (147 mph; 237 km/h)
Army Hot day: 119 kts (137 mph; 221 km/h)
rate of climb   *max*
standard day: 3,200 ft/min (975 m/min)
Army Hot day: 2,750 ft/min (783 m/min)
max, vertical
standard day: 2,460 ft/min (750 m/min)
Army Hot day: 1,450 ft/min (442 m/min)
ceiling   *standard day*
2 engines: 21,000 ft (6,400 m)
1 engine: 10,800 ft (3,292 m)
Army Hot day
2 engines: 10,300 ft (3,139 m)
1 engine: 6,400 ft (1,951 m)
hovering ceiling in ground effect, 14,445 lb (6,553 kg)
standard day: 15,000 ft (4,572 m)
Army Hot day: 10,200 ft (3,109 m)
hovering ceiling out of ground effect, 14,445 lb (6,553 kg)
standard day: 11,500 ft (3,505 m)
Army Hot day: 7,000 ft (2,134 m)
range   internal fuel: 260 nm (300 mi; 482 km)
ferry: 918 nm (1,057 mi; 1,701 km)

armament   1 M230 Chain Gun 30-
mm cannon in belly
turret with 1,200
rounds
4 wing pylons for up to
16 Hellfire antitank
missiles or 76 2.75-in
(70-mm) rockets in 4
pods
and 4 FIM-92 Stinger air-
to-air missiles

Sioux/Scout (OH-13)

The OH-13 (also known as the Bell 47) is one of the most widely used helicopters in history. It is a two-seat, light utility helicopter that has been adapted for use in the wire-laying, liaison, medical evacuation, training, and Antisubmarine Warfare (ASW) roles.

The OH-13 has a simple two-blade main rotor with a stabilizer bar mounted below the main rotor plane and at a 90° angle to it. Some variants have enclosed cabins, but most have a Plexiglas bubble canopy and an open lattice tailboom with an antitorque rotor on the right side. Twin-skid landing gear with two retracting wheels is standard, but some naval versions have pontoons for water operations. Medical evacuation versions carry two stretcher pods, one on either side of the cabin.

DEVELOPMENT • The OH-13's initial operational capability was in 1946. It is no longer in US military service or production but is still in service in many other countries. Over 6,000 had been produced when production ceased in 1973, a military-helicopter production run exceeded in the West only by the UH-1 Iroquois (Huey). The OH-13 was also license-built in Italy by Agusta, in Great Britain by Westland, and in Japan by Kawasaki.

The aircraft was operating in the mili-

tary services of about 25 nations, mostly in Africa and Latin America in the 1990s.

VARIANTS • YR-13/Bell 47A (proto-type), H-13B/Bell 47D, H-13D/Bell 47D-1 (two-seat), H-13E/OH-13E/Bell 47D-1 (three-seat), XH-13F (experimental), H-13G/OH-13G/Bell 47G, H/OH/UH-13H/Bell 47G-2, H/UH-13J (USAF), H/OH-13K/Bell 47G-3 (converted H-13H), TH-13L (USN trainer), TH-13M (trainer), TH-13N (trainer), UH-13P (USN utility), HH-13Q (USCG SAR), UH-13R, OH-13S/Bell 47G-3B, TH-13T/Bell 47G-3B-1 (US Army instrument trainer), HTL-3/Bell 47E (USN/Brazil trainer), HTL-7/Bell 47J Ranger (USN, USMC, and USCG), Agusta-Bell 47J-3 Super Ranger (Agusta-built shipboard ASW), Scout (British-built).

COMBAT EXPERIENCE • Used extensively in combat by US forces in the Korean War and by French forces in Algeria.

SPECIFICATIONS •
MANUFACTURER   Bell Helicopter
CREW   1
ENGINES
H-13H: 1 Lycoming VO-435 piston
OH-13S: 1 Lycoming TVO-435-A1A
piston
max power   H-13H: 200 hp
OH-13S: 260 hp
WEIGHTS
empty   H-13H: 1,564 lb (710
kg)
OH-13S: 1,936 lb (879
kg)
max takeoff H-13H: 2,450 lb (1,112
kg)
OH-13S: 2,850 lb (1,293
kg)
DIMENSIONS
rotor diam H-13H: 35 ft 1 in (10.69
m)
OH-13S: 37 ft 2 in (11.35
m)
length   H-13H: 27 ft 4 in (8.33 m)

	OH-13S:	32 ft 7 in (9.93 m)
height		9 ft 6 in (2.9 m)
disc area	H-13H:	966.1 ft² (89.8 m²)
	OH-13S:	1,089.1 ft² (101.2 m²)

PERFORMANCE

max speed	H-13H:	87 kts (100 mph; 161 km/h)
	OH-13S:	91 kts (105 mph; 169 km/h)
cruise speed		74 kts (85 mph; 137 km/h)
climb rate	H-13H:	770 ft/min (235 m/min)
	OH-13S:	1,190 ft/min (363 m/min)
ceiling	H-13H:	13,200 ft (4,023 m)
	OH-13S:	18,000 ft (5,486 m)
hovering ceiling in and out of ground effect		
	OH-13S:	18,000 ft (5,486 m)
range	H-13H:	261 nm (300 mi; 483 km)
	OH-13S:	281 nm (324 mi; 521 km)

Defender (MD 500/530)

The MD 500MD is a light, multipurpose helicopter adapted for observation, scout, special-operations, antiarmor attack, and Antisubmarine Warfare (ASW) roles. It is based on the earlier OH-6A Cayuse and its commercial derivative the Hughes 500. The Defender is an improved military variant of the Model 500 with uprated engine, T-tail, and heavier armament; it is the basis for all subsequent McDonnell Douglas scout helicopters.

The 500MD features a five-blade, fully articulated main rotor with cross-connected flap and feather straps. The slender tailboom extends aft from the roof of the egg-shaped fuselage pod to a narrow, swept fin; the fin extends below the boom and is fitted with a small tail skid.

The two-blade, antitorque rotor is mounted at the end of the boom on the left-hand side; a four-blade "quiet" rotor can also be fitted. The offset-V tail of the OH-6 has been replaced by a narrow horizontal stabilizer at the top of the fin; the stabilizer has tapered leading edges and small endplate fins.

The Allison turboshaft is carried behind the crew compartment, receiving air through a small intake on the cabin roof and exhausting through a nozzle at the aft end of the fuselage pod below the boom. The crew cabin features a glazed nose for maximum forward visibility. The 530 series (and the 500MG) have a pointed nose for streamlining. Engine access is through clamshell doors at the rear of the fuselage pod. The parallel-skid landing gear has internal oleo-pneumatic shock absorbers.

Variants of the 500MD have different armament configurations on detachable pylons. The Scout version is armed with a 7.62-mm minigun or Chain Gun pod, rocket pods, or 40-mm grenade launchers. The 500MD/TOW mounts a two-round TOW antitank missile launcher on each pylon. The 500MD ASW carries one or two lightweight ASW torpedoes between the skids.

DEVELOPMENT • The 500MD's initial operational capability was in 1976. It is produced primarily for export. The US Army purchased approximately 30 in the mid-1980s for 160th Aviation Group, a commando unit; additional orders brought the Army's total to at least 54.

Production of military variants was licensed to Kawasaki in Japan and Korean Air Lines in South Korea; civilian variants (including some purchased for military use) were also license-built by Breda Nardi of Italy.

Five Chilean MD530Fs were sold to a "Chilean sardine fishing concern" in 1988–89 but later discovered to be in Chilean Army service. When the transfer was revealed, the United States placed an embargo on spare parts.

The MD 500 and its variants have been in use in 17 foreign nations, primarily in Asia and Latin America. North Korea acquired at least 60 of the helicopters during the mid-1980s, reportedly through US dealers.

VARIANTS • OH-6A Cayuse, 500MD Scout Defender, 500MD ASW, 500MD/ TOW Defender, 500MD/MMS-TOW, 500MD Defender II, MD500E, NH-500E (Italian Army), MD530F Lifter, 530MG Defender, 500MG Defender, M/AH-6 "Little Bird," Nightfox (night vision equipment), NOTAR.

COMBAT EXPERIENCE • An undisclosed number of Task Force 160 "Little Birds" were deployed to Saudi Arabia as part of Operation Desert Storm.

SPECIFICATIONS •
MANUFACTURER   McDonnell Douglas
CREW   2 (pilot, copilot) + 6 troops
ENGINES
500MD/TOW: 1 Allison 250-C20B
   turboshaft
530MG: 1 Allison 250-C30 turboshaft
max power   500MD/TOW: 420 shp
   (derated to 375 shp)
   530MG: 650 shp (derated
   to 425 shp)
internal fuel capacity
   63 US gal (240 liters)
optional auxiliary tank
   21 US gal (79.5 liters)
WEIGHTS
empty   500MD/TOW: 1,976 lb
   (896 kg)
   530MG: 1,591 lb (722 kg)
max takeoff   500MD/TOW: 3,000 lb
   (1,361 kg)
   530MG: 3,550 lb (1,610 kg)

DIMENSIONS
rotor diam   500MD/TOW: 26 ft 4 in
   (8.03 m)
   530MG: 27 ft 4 in (8.33 m)
length   500MD/TOW 30 ft 10 in
   (9.4 m)
   530M: 32 ft 1 in (9.78 m)
height   500MD/TOW: 8 ft 8 in
   (2.64 m)
   530MG: to top of rotor
   head, 8 ft 7 in (2.62
   m); to top of Mast-
   Mounted Sight (MMS),
   11 ft 2½ in (3.41 m)
disc area   500MD/TOW: 544.6 ft²
   (50.6 m²)
   530MG: 586.8 ft²
   (54.5 m²)
PERFORMANCE
cruise speed   500MD/TOW: 119 kts
   (137 mph; 221 km/h)
   530MG: 135 kts (155
   mph; 250 km/h)
climb rate   500MD/TOW: 1,650 ft/
   min (503 m/min)
   530MG: 2,100 ft/min
   (640 m/min)
ceiling   15,800 ft (4,815 m)
range   330 nm (380 mi; 611 km)
armament   none integral to all
   variants, but optional
   armament includes:
   7.62-mm and .50-cal
   machine-gun pods
   7.62-mm Chain Gun
   7-tube or 12-tube 2.75-in
   rocket pods
   Stinger air-to-air missiles
   7.62-mm minigun
   40-mm grenade launcher
   TOW antitank missiles

Cobra/TOW (AH-1E/F/G/P/Q/S)

The AH-1 Cobra is an attack helicopter designed for close air support and antitank missions. The Cobra series was derived from the UH-1 Huey/Iroquois utility/transport helicopter, retaining the rotor, transmission, and engine in a completely redesigned fuselage. The manufacturer's designation is Model 209 HueyCobra.

The standard Cobra/TOW is the AH-1F, a redesignation of the modernized AH-1S; earlier AH-1 aircraft are being either retired or upgraded to the AH-1F level. The two composite blades are linked to the main rotor hub by "door hinges," creating a semirigid main rotor system.

The two-blade antitorque rotor is mounted on the starboard side of the tail pylon near the top. Short, slightly swept, horizontal stabilizers are midmounted on the fuselage approximately halfway between the engines and the tail rotor pylon.

The engine is mounted above the fuselage and behind the main rotor pylon. A cooled, plug-type, Infrared (IR) signature suppressor and cylindrical shroud is fitted to the engine exhaust.

The fuselage provides a minimal cross section (38 in; 0.99 m) with stub wings for carrying missiles, rocket packs, or gun pods, a nose turret with a 20-mm, 3-barrel Gatling gun, and tandem seating for a gunner/copilot (forward) and pilot. The landing gear consists of parallel skids on spring struts.

The fire control system has a Teledyne Systems digital ballistic computer and Kaiser Head-Up Display (HUD). Other avionics include the Singer-Kearfott AN/ASN-128 Doppler navigation system, E-Systems AN/APR-39 radar-warning receiver, Sanders AN/ALQ-144 IR countermeasures jammer, and a GEC Avionics IS 03-004 low-airspeed air data sensor, which is mounted on an outrigger on the starboard side.

Targeting for the TOW requires the M65 Airborne TOW missile system with the primary sensors fitted in the nose-mounted Telescopic Sight Unit (TSU). The TSU has a traverse of 110° to either side and an elevation range of −60°/+30°. Upgrades to the M65 include the Hughes Laser-Augmented Airborne TOW (LAAT) stabilized sight and the Rockwell AN/AAS-32 Airborne Laser Tracker (ALT).

Weapons include a chin-mounted General Electric Universal Turret capable of accepting Gatling-type guns ranging in caliber from 7.62 mm to 30 mm. The turret traverses 110° to either side and has an elevation range of −50°/+21°. Gun movement and targeting are controlled by the TSU or by a Helmet Sight Subunit (HSS) worn by either the gunner/copilot or the pilot. The stub wings have four weapons stations for up to a total of eight TOW or four rocket or gun pods.

DEVELOPMENT • The AH-1G's initial operational capability was in 1967. The prototype's first flight was on September 7, 1965. Over 1,450 single-engine Cobra models were built. License production by Mitsui in Japan continues.

The C-NITE Cobra variant entered service with the 77th Aviation Brigade in South Korea in 1990. Also in 1990, Pakistan agreed to purchase 24 C-NITE kits.

VARIANTS • Bell Model 209, AH-1G (US Army, USMC, Spain), AH-1Q (Improved Cobra Armament Program/ICAP), YAH-1R (Improved Cobra Agility and Maneuverability/ICAM), YAH-1S, AH-1S, AH-1P, AH-1E (US Army, Israel, Japan), AH-1P (Enhanced Cobra Armament System/ECAS), AH-1F (US Army/Army National Guard, Israel, Jordan, Pakistan, Thailand, South Korea), ARTI (Advanced Rotorcraft Technology Integration), C-FLEX (Cobra Fleet Life Extension), Z-16 (Spain).

COMBAT EXPERIENCE • Cobras have been used in combat by US forces in Vietnam, in Grenada, and in the December 1989 Operation Just Cause military ouster and capture of General Noriega. US Army Cobras were deployed to Saudi Arabia as part of Operation Desert Shield, and during Desert Storm AH-1s flew escort missions. A Cobra scored TOW hits on the lead vehicles in a 1,000-vehicle Iraqi column, blocking the rest of the force and leading to its capture or destruction.

Israeli Cobras have operated against Palestinian and Syrian targets in Lebanon's Bekaa Valley since 1982.

SPECIFICATIONS •

MANUFACTURER Bell-Textron
CREW 2 (pilot, gunner)
ENGINES
AH-1G: 1 Avco Lycoming T53-L-13 turboshaft
AH-1S: 1 Avco Lycoming T53-L-703 turboshaft
max power AH-1G: 1,400 shp
AH-1S: 1,800 shp
internal fuel capacity
AH-1G: 268 US gal (1,014 liters)
AH-1S: 259 US gal (980 liters)
WEIGHTS
empty AH-1G: 6,073 lb (2,735 kg)
AH-1S: 6,598 lb (2,993 kg)
useful load AH-1G: 3,427 lb (1,554 kg)
AH-1S: 3,402 lb (1,543 kg)
max takeoff AH-1G: 9,500 lb (4,309 kg)
AH-1S: 10,000 lb (4,535 kg)
DIMENSIONS
rotor diam 44 ft (13.41 m)
length 44 ft 7 in (13.59 m)
height AH-1G: 13 ft 6 in (4.12 m)
AH-1S: 13 ft 5 in (4.09 m)
disc area 1,520.5 ft² (141.3 m²)
PERFORMANCE
max speed AH-1G: 149 kts (172 mph; 277 km/h)
AH-1S: 123 kts (141 mph; 195 km/h) with TOW
climb rate AH-1G: 1,375 ft/min (419 m/min)

AH-1S: 1,620 ft/min (494 m/min)
ceiling AH-1G: 11,400 ft (3,475 m)
AH-1S: 12,200 ft (3,720 m)
hover in ground effect
AH-1G: 9,900 ft (3,015 m)
AH-1S: 12,200 ft (3,720 m)
range AH-1G: 325 nm (374 mi; 602 km)
AH-1S: 274 nm (315 mi; 507 km)
armament, AH-1G
M28 nose turret with 2 GAU-2B/A 7.62-mm miniguns
or 2 M129 40-mm grenade launchers
or 1 minigun and 1 M129 *and* stub wing pylons for 4 M157 pods with 76 2.75-in (70-mm) rockets
or 4 M157 pods with 28 rockets
or 2 M18E1 minigun pods
or M35 20-mm automatic cannon system
armament, AH-1S
M197 3-barrel 20-mm Gatling gun in nose turret
up to 8 Hughes BMG-71 TOW antitank missiles
or 4 LAU-68A/A (7-tube) 2.75-in rocket pods
or up to 4 LAU-61A/A (19-tube) 2.75-in rocket pods
or M181E minigun pods

SeaCobra/SuperCobra (AH-1J/T/W)

Note: Only differences from the basic AH-1G Huey are included in this entry.

These Cobra twin-engine variants are all assigned to the US Marine Corps. The main rotor system is based on the Bell 214 and is fitted with a rotor brake and has elastomeric bearings; the two broad-chord blades have swept tips.

The two turboshaft engines are mounted in separate nacelles located on either side of the main rotor pylon. The engines' air intakes are large, vertical rectangular inlets; the engine nacelles of the AH-1W are much larger and squarer than those of the AH-1J/T. In the AH-1W, the 73% increase in maximum rated power of the T700 engine installation has restored the operating capabilities found in the AH-1J at 50% greater maximum takeoff weight. The AH-1W's exhausts are fitted with large, boxy Infrared (IR) suppressors, and the fuel system can tolerate a direct hit from a 23-mm projectile.

The fuselage has a slender cross section (43 in; 1.09 m) that swells to 10 ft 9 in (3.28 m) across the engines; the AH-1T was stretched 12 in (305 mm) to account for the addition of TOW anti-tank missiles. The cockpit has tandem seating for a gunner/copilot (forward) and pilot.

The AH-1W's modest night-attack capability is currently limited to Night Vision Goggles (NVG) such as the AN/AVS-6 Aviator Night Vision Imaging System (ANVIS). In June 1994, the first AH-1W with the Taman Night Targeting System (NTS) upgrade entered service. The million-dollar improvement includes a gyro-stabilized Forward-Looking Infrared (FLIR) and laser designator system for night and adverse-weather targeting of the Hellfire missile.

DEVELOPMENT • The AH-1J's initial operational capability was in 1971. A total of 160 twin-engine Cobras were built for the United States; 202 AH-1Js were manufactured for Iran and eight for South Korea. Most Marine Corps SeaCobras are updated to the AH-1W level from the earlier AH-1T; the AH-1J remains in service in two other countries. Iran, South Korea, and Turkey operate the SeaCobra in addition to the US Army.

VARIANTS • AH-1J SeaCobra (USMC/Iran), AH-1T Improved SeaCobra, AH-1W SuperCobra, Four-Bladed Whiskey.

COMBAT EXPERIENCE • Cobras have been used in combat by US forces in the Vietnam War and in the 1983 Grenada operation. AH-1T and AH-1W helicopters were deployed in support of Operations Desert Shield/Desert Storm. The Marine Corps Cobras were particularly well suited to desert operations because their systems have been sealed against saltwater corrosion and thus are protected against sand infiltration as well. Approximately 78 USMC Cobras flew 1,273 sorties supporting the operations. One Marine Corps Cobra was lost during the seven-week war in a noncombat casualty.

SPECIFICATIONS •
MANUFACTURER   Bell Helicopter Textron
CREW   2 (pilot, gunner)
ENGINES
    AH-1J: 2 Pratt & Whitney T400-CP-400 turboshaft
    AH-1T: 2 Pratt & Whitney T400-WV-402 turboshaft
    AH-1W: 2 General Electric T700-GE-401 turboshaft
    internal fuel capacity
        304.5 US gal (1,153 liters)
    max power   AH-1J: 1,800 shp total
        AH-1T: 1,970 shp total
        AH-1W: 3,200 shp total
WEIGHTS
    empty   AH-1J: 7,261 lb (3,294 kg)
        AH-1T: 8,014 lb (3,640 kg)
        AH-1W: 10,200 lb (4,627 kg)
    max takeoff   AH-1J: 10,000 lb (4,535 kg)
        AH-1T: 14,000 lb (6,350 kg)
        AH-1W: 14,750 lb (6,690 kg)
DIMENSIONS
    rotor diam   AH-1J: 44 ft (13.41 m)

length	AH-1T/W: 48 ft (14.63 m)
	AH-1J: 44 ft 7 in (13.59 m)
	AH-1T/W: 48 ft 2 in (14.68 m)
height	AH-1J/W: 13 ft 8 in (4.15 m)
	AH-1T: 14 ft 2 in (4.32 m)
disc area	AH-1J: 1,520.5 ft² (141.3 m²)
	AH-1T/W: 1,809.6 ft² (168.1 m²)

PERFORMANCE

max speed	AH-1J: 180 kts (207 mph; 333 km/h)
	AH-1T: 149 kts (172 mph; 277 km/h)
	AH-1W: 189 kts (218 mph; 350 km/h)

max cruise at 3,000 ft (914 m) at 95°F (35°C)

	AH-1T: 135 kts (155 mph; 250 km/h)
	AH-1W: 160 kts (184 mph; 296 km/h)
ceiling	AH-1J: 10,550 ft (3,215 m)
	AH-1T: 11,000 ft (3,353 m)
	AH-1W: 17,500 ft (5,334 m)

hover in ground effect

	AH-1J: 12,450 ft (3,794 m)
	AH-1T: 4,500 ft (1,372 m)
	AH-1W: 14,750 ft (4,495 m)

hover out of ground effect

	AH-1J: 3,600 ft (1,097 m)
	AH-1T: 400 ft (122 m)
	AH-1W: 3,000 ft (914 m)
range	AH-1J: 335 nm (385 mi; 620 km)
	AH-1T: 310 nm (356 mi; 574 km)
	AH-1W: 343 nm (395 mi; 635 km)

armament, AH-1J

M197 3-barrel 20-mm cannon (750 rounds) in nose turret
wing pylons for 4

LAU-68A/A (7-tube) 2.75-in (70-mm) rocket pods
or up to 4 LAU-61A/A (19-tube) 2.75-in (70-mm) rocket pods
or M181E minigun pods

armament, AH-1T/W

in addition to AH-1S armament, can carry
8 BGM-71 TOW antitank missiles
plus in AH-1W:
2 AIM-9 Sidewinder air-to-air missiles
or 2 AIM-123 Sidearm antiradar missiles
or 8 AGM-114 Hellfire antitank missiles
or 4 CMU-55B fuel-air explosive weapons
or 16 5-in (127-mm) Zuni rockets
or 4 78-US gal (295-liter) or 2 100-gal (378-liter) auxiliary fuel tanks

Sea Knight (CH-46)

The Sea Knight has served as the medium assault helicopter for the US Marine Corps and as a Vertical On-Board Delivery (VOD) aircraft for the US Navy, and in a variety of other roles with several other countries.

The Sea Knight has two contra-rotating, three-blade main rotors mounted on rotor pylons atop the fore and after ends of the fuselage. When viewed from above, the forward blade rotates counterclockwise, the after blade clockwise, at a speed of 264 rpm.

The semimonocoque fuselage is an elongated, rounded box with a short nose, an extensively glazed, side-by-side flight deck, dorsal spine for the front rotor drive, and a loading ramp in the rear. The ramp forms the bottom of the fuselage as it tapers up to the tail. The fuselage is watertight and in later variants is also fitted with flotation bags. Troop access can be through the rear ramp or by the side doors, which can each mount a .50-cal machine gun.

The two General Electric turboshaft engines are mounted in faired nacelles on either side of the rear rotor pylon. 49 CH-46Es were fitted with 660-US gal (2,498-liter) fuel tanks that have a graphite-epoxy shell and Nomex honeycomb filler. The E's sponsons were enlarged to accept these tanks, which doubled the mission radius to 160 nm (184 mi; 296 km). Some are fitted with the Loral AN/AAR-47 electro-optical missile-warning system.

The fixed, two-wheel main-landing-gear main legs are mounted in sponsons on each rear side of the fuselage; the sponsons also carry fuel. The two-wheel nose-gear strut is centered under the flight deck.

The avionics fit was upgraded beginning in 1992 with the Rockwell Collins AN/APN-217 Doppler navigation system that has latitude-longitude positioning, ground and wind speed indicators, cross-track and track-angle error messages, and display of time, distance, course, and bearing to next target. Two Cathode-Ray Tube (CRT) displays, interface control units, and situation/hover indicator units are also installed in the lower console and instrument panel.

The US Army CH-47 Chinook is highly similar in appearance to the Sea Knight design but can be distinguished by quadricycle landing gear, a larger, boxier fuselage, and by the lack of the CH-46's landing-gear sponsons. The CH-46 is known in the fleet as Phrog.

DEVELOPMENT • The CH-46's initial operational capability was in 1962; the first flight of Model 107 was on April 22, 1958. Production ceased in the United States in 1971 after 666 units had been built for US service and for export. Kawasaki's 25 years of low-rate production

of KV-107 variants ended in February 1990 after 160 were built.

Fiberglass rotor blades were introduced as an upgrade in the late 1970s. In addition to the US Navy and Marines, Burma, Canada, Japan, Saudi Arabia, and Sweden have operated the CH-46.

In mid-May 1990, the Department of the Navy grounded all 261 US Marine Corps CH- and HH-46 and Navy UH- and HH-46 helicopters to correct a quill shaft problem "that could cause a loss of drive to the aft rotor."

VARIANTS • Model 107 (civilian), YHC-1A/CH-46C, HRB-1, CH-46A (SAR, utility), H-46B (not produced), CH-46D, CH-46E CILOP (Conversion in Lieu of Procurement CILOP), CH-46F, SR&M (Safety, Reliability, and Maintainability), CH-113 Labrador (SAR)/CH-113A Voyageur (transport) for Canada, HKP-4/HKP-7 (ASW/SAR), KV-107 (Japanese-built), KV107IIA (Kawasaki upgrade for Japan), KV107IIA-SM (Saudi Arabia).

COMBAT EXPERIENCE • The Sea Knight was used extensively by US Naval and Marine Corps forces in the Vietnam War. It also supported operations in Lebanon (1982–84) and Grenada (October 1983). In January 1991, CH-46s from the amphibious assault ship USS *Guam* (LPH 9) were diverted from Operation Desert Shield to participate in Operation Eastern Exit, which rescued 281 US and foreign nationals from the US embassy in Mogadishu during the bloody Somalian civil war.

In the fall of 1990, US Navy and Marine Corps CH-46s were deployed to the Persian Gulf as part of Desert Shield; 120 Marine Corps Sea Knights—60 operating from shore bases and 60 from ships—flew 1,601 sorties during Operation Desert Storm. They supported the drive into Kuwait that began the ground war on February 24, 1991. Two CH-46s were lost during the war for noncombat causes.

SPECIFICATIONS •

MANUFACTURER
Boeing Vertol
Kawasaki of Japan, under US license
CREW 3 (2 pilots, crewman) + 25 troops or 15 litters + 2 attendants
ENGINES 2 General Electric T58-GE-16 turboshaft
max power 1,870 shp each (transmission rating is 2,800 shp)
internal fuel capacity 380 US gal (1,438 liters)
extended fuel-capacity kit 660 US gal (2,498 liters)
WEIGHTS
empty operating, without armor or armament: 15,537 lb (7,047 kg) with armor, guns, and ammunition: 17,396 lb (7,891 kg)
payload without armor or armament: 5,166 lb (2,343 kg) with armor and armament: 4,153 lb (1,884 kg)
sling load 10,000 lb (4,536 kg)
max takeoff sea level, 59°F (15°C): 24,300 lb (11,022 kg) sea level, 90°F (32°C): 23,992 lb (10,883 kg)
DIMENSIONS
rotor diam 51 ft (15.54 m) each
length overall, rotors turning: 84 ft 4 in (25.72 m) fuselage: 45 ft 8 in (13.92 m)
width, fuselage 7 ft 3 in (2.21 m)
height 16 ft 8½ in (5.09 m)
disc area 4,086 ft² (379.6 m²)
PERFORMANCE *at max takeoff weight*
max speed 143 kts (165 mph; 265 km/h)
cruise speed 137 kts (154 mph; 248 km/h)
climb rate 2,045 ft/min (623 m/min)

service ceiling 14,000 ft (4,267 m)
hovering ceiling in ground effect standard day: 14,000 ft/4,267 m, 95°F/35°C 12,580 ft (3,834 m)
hovering ceiling out of ground effect standard day: 11,970 ft/3,649 m, 95°F/35°C 8,600 ft (2,643 m)
mission radius, with increased fuel-capacity kits 160 nm (184 mi; 296 km)
range at sea level on internal fuel 365 nm (420 mi; 676 km)
armament 2 .50-cal machine guns optional

Chinook (CH-47)

The Chinook medium transport helicopter is the largest helicopter in service with the US and British armies and is flown by several other nations. The Chinook is similar in basic design to the US Navy/ Marine Corps H-46 Sea Knight helicopter.

The Chinook features tandem, fully articulated, three-blade, contra-rotating main rotors on separate pylons. The forward rotor is located above the cockpit and rotates counterclockwise when seen from above; the aft rotor is on a taller pylon at the rear of the fuselage and rotates clockwise. The two engines are fitted externally on either side of the rear rotor pylon and drive a common transmission system. CH-47Ds are fitted with an Automatic Flight Control System (AFCS) that features dual, redundant control units and actuators.

Chinooks have fixed quadricycle landing gear; the rear, single-wheel units are fully castoring and steerable, and the forward legs have fixed, two-wheel units. The fuselage is designed around a cargo hold with a nearly square cross section. Ahead of the hold is a fully glazed flight deck with a short nose. The cargo ramp is in the rear of the fuselage and triple external cargo hook system; fore and aft hooks have 17,000-lb (7,712-kg) capacity, the center hook can hold 26,000 lb (11,793 kg), and dual-point capacity is 23,000 lb (10,433 kg).

The fuselage has external fuel tanks in sponsons along both sides and has a sealed lower half to permit water landings.

Defensive electronics and countermeasures are fitted to many Chinooks in various configurations.

DEVELOPMENT • The Chinook's initial operational capability was in 1962; its first flight was on September 21, 1961 (YCH-47A). The helicopter remained in production for foreign users after 736 were built by Boeing Vertol (later Boeing Helicopters) for the US Army. Over 200 have been built under license by Meridionali in Italy, and 54 were being built by Kawasaki in Japan.

The initial operational capability for the CH-47D was in February 1984.

In February 1991, the Canadian Air Command announced that it would dispose of its seven CH-147s by the middle of 1991 due to a series of comprehensive defense budget cuts.

All 264 US Army CH-47Ds were grounded in July 1989 and again in August 1989 after two aircraft suffered similar failures in the drivetrain for the aft oil-cooling fan assembly. In April 1990, the Army once again grounded its CH-47Ds because of possible cracked lock nuts in the forward transmission mounting.

In addition to the US Army, about 13 other countries throughout the world operate the Chinook.

VARIANTS • YHC-1B (prototype), CH-47A, CH-47B, CH-47C (BV 219) (US Army, Canada, China, Italy), Chinook HC Mk 1 (BV 352) (RAF), Chinook HC Mk 2, CH-47D (US Army, Germany, Greece, Spain), International Chinook (Model 414-100) (Japan, China), MH-47E (US SOF).

COMBAT   EXPERIENCE • Chinooks were widely used in the Vietnam War. Some were armed to act as gunships but were deemed unsuited to that role. In the Falklands War of 1982, the single available British Chinook—a survivor of the sinking of the requisitioned supply ship *Atlantic Conveyor* in which four other Chinooks were lost—flew 109 hours in combat conditions without spares or ground support; it carried up to 80 armed troops at a time.

169 US and 21 British CH-47s were deployed to Saudi Arabia in the fall of 1990 as part of Operation Desert Shield. Although at first beset by increased engine and rotor wear due to the fine sand, changes in operating and maintenance procedures improved reliability to acceptable levels.

US Chinooks flew hundreds of sorties before and during Operation Desert Storm. No CH-47s were lost during the war, although one was damaged, possibly by missile fire, on the first night of the war. A British Chinook HC 1 accidentally detonated a land mine near its touchdown point and was sprayed with fragments that left 77 holes and every tire flat. It managed to return to its base after a five-hour flight.

A CH-47 crashed, losing four crew members, a few days after the cease-fire took effect. After the cease-fire, Chinooks and other utility helicopters delivered supplies to several hundred thousand refugees massing near the Turkish border.

SPECIFICATIONS •
MANUFACTURERS
  Boeing Helicopters
  Elicotteri Meridionali, Italy
  Kawasaki Heavy Industries, Japan
CREW 3 (pilot, copilot, crew chief/
  combat commander) + 44 troops
  (see Operational Notes) or 24 litters
  and 2 attendants

ENGINES   2 Avco Lycoming T55-L-712
turboshaft
max power   3,750 shp each
internal fuel capacity
1,030 US gal (3,900 liters)
WEIGHTS
empty   22,452 lb (10,184 kg)
*internal payload over 100 nm (115 mi;
185 km) mission radius*
14,356 lb (6,512 kg)
*max external load over 30 nm (35 mi; 55
km) mission radius*
15,856 lb (7,192 kg)
external load capacity
28,000 lb (12,701 kg)
max useful load (internal and external)
26,679 lb (12,101 kg)
max takeoff   50,000 lb (22,680 kg)
DIMENSIONS
rotor diam   60 ft (18.29 m)
length   51 ft (15.54 m)
height   18 ft 8 in (5.68 m)
cargo hold   length: 30 ft 2 in (9.2 m)
width at floor: 8 ft 3 in
(2.51 m)
mean width: 7 ft 6 in
(2.29 m)
height: 6 ft 6 in (1.98 m)
volume: 1,474 ft^3 (41.7
m^3)
disc area   5,655 ft^2 (525.4 m^2)
PERFORMANCE
max speed   159 kts (183 mph; 295
km/h) no sling load
cruise speed, depending on conditions
120–138 kts (138–159
mph; 222–256 km/h)
max climb rate at 44,000 lb (19,958 kg)
1,980 ft/min (605
m/min)
ceilings at 50,000 lb (22,680 kg)
service: 8,500 ft (2,591 m)
hovering in ground
effect, ISA: 8,250 ft
(2,515 m)
hovering out of ground
effect, ISA: 4,950 ft
(1,509 m)
mission radius
23,030 lb (10,446 kg)

external load: 30 nm
(35 mi; 55 km)
14,728 lb (6,680 kg)
internal payload: 100
nm (115 mi; 185 km)
ferry range   1,111 nm (1,279 mi;
2,059 km)

Sea Stallion/Super Jolly (CH-53A/D)

The CH-53 is a heavy lift helicopter in
wide military use. Developed specifically
for the US Navy and Marine Corps, it is
employed for assault, vertical replenishment, and Mine Countermeasures
(MCM) operations. Some CH/HH-53B/
Cs have been modified for special operations and are known as the Pave Low III
series.

The CH-53 has a fuselage resembling
an enlarged US Air Force HH-3 "Jolly
Green Giant" with a six-blade, fully articulated rotor with aluminum blades that
fold under power. Later variants have
been retrofitted with composite blades
having titanium leading edges.

The main rotor mast rises out of a long
centerline hump that contains the Solar
T62T-12 Auxiliary Power Unit (APU).
The two T64 turboshaft engines are
shoulder-mounted on either side of the
centerline fairing. The inlets are protected by prominent debris screens. The
four-blade antitorque rotor is mounted
on the left side at the top of the slender
tailboom; the long-span, unbraced horizontal stabilizer extends to starboard opposite the antitorque rotor hub. The
tailboom has a strut-braced skid and can
be folded to starboard for shipboard
stowage.

The semimonocoque fuselage has a
blunt, almost stepless nose with tall
"cheek" windows as well as a split windshield and side windows. The large, unobstructed cabin is roughly square in cross
section—7 ft 6 in (2.29 m) wide and 6 ft 6

in (1.98 m) high. The original payload requirement was for 38 fully equipped troops, 24 litters, and four attendants, or 8,000 lb (3,629 kg) of cargo. In later variants, up to 55 troops can be carried, and the external hoist was ultimately rated at 20,000 lb (9,072 kg).

The after part of the cabin tapers up to the tailboom and holds the stern ramp, which is lowered for ground-loading or airdrops. The ramp opening is windshielded by small panels fitted to the fuselage sides below the tailboom.

Large sponsons are mounted on the lower aft fuselage sides; they have an airfoil cross section. The sponsons hold the two-wheel main-landing-gear struts, which retract forward behind the fuel tanks; additional fuel tanks are carried on semipermanent pylons mounted outboard of the sponsons. The two-wheel nose gear retracts forward.

DEVELOPMENT • The initial operational capability for the CH-53A was in 1966; its first flight was on October 15, 1964. Over 300 of these variants remain in service with the US Air Force, Navy, and Marines along with Germany and Israel; Iran's CH-53s are no longer operational. Also, eight Pave Low III and 31 Pave Low III-Enhanced Special Operations Command aircraft are operational.

VARIANTS • CH-53A, RH-53A (USN), HH-53B (USAF SAR), HH-53C, CH-53C, CH-53D (USMC), RH-53D (USN), CH-53E/MH-53E, CH-53G (110 license-built by Germany's VFW-Fokker), HH-53H/MH-53H Pave Low III, S-65-Oe (built for Austria, later transferred to Israel). Yasour 2000 (Israeli Air Force update program), MH-53J Pave Low III-Enhanced (modified hydraulic and electrical systems).

SPECIFICATIONS •
MANUFACTURER   Sikorsky Aircraft
CREW   3 (2 pilots, 1 crewman) + 38 troops or 24 litters

ENGINES   2 General Electric T64-GE-413 turboshaft
  max power   3,925 shp each
  internal fuel capacity
        622 US gal (2,354 liters)
WEIGHTS
  empty   23,628 lb (10,717 kg)
  max takeoff 50,000 lb (22,680 kg)
DIMENSIONS
  rotor diam   72 ft 3 in (22.04 m)
  length   67 ft 2 in (20.48 m)
  height   24 ft 11 in (7.59 m)
  disc area   4,100 ft² (380.9 m²)
PERFORMANCE
  max speed   171 kts (196 mph; 316 km/h)
  cruise   151 kts (173 mph; 279 km/h)
  climb rate   2,180 ft/min (664 m/min)
  service ceiling
        21,000 ft (6,400 m)
  hovering ceiling in ground effect
        13,400 ft (4,084 m)
  hovering ceiling out of ground effect
        6,500 ft (1,981 m)
  range   886 nm (1,020 mi; 1,640 km)

Super Stallion/Sea Dragon (CH-53E/MH-53E)

The E-series of the H-53 is the heaviest lift helicopter in service in the West. The H-53E series is similar to the CH-53A/D Sea Stallion helicopters in US Navy and Marine Corps service.

The airframe follows the pattern of the earlier CH-53 versions, having an unobstructed cabin with lowering rear ramp behind a blunt nose and flight deck and under the powertrain. The cabin is spacious enough to accept seven pallets measuring 3 ft 4 in × 4 ft (1.02 × 1.22 m); seating for 55 troops is also provided. A single-point cargo hook below the fuselage can carry a maximum 18-US ton (16.5-metric ton) sling load, although 16

CH-53E Super Stallion
U.S. GOVERNMENT DEPARTMENT OF DEFENSE

tons (14.5 metric tons) is more typical. The CH-53E flown by the Marine Corps can lift 93% of the heavy equipment of a Marine division compared to 38% for the CH-53D.

The biggest change is in the powertrain. A third T64 turboshaft engine is fitted behind the main rotor mast; it is fed by an intake located to the left of the rotor mast. The main transmission gearbox, located directly below the main rotor hub, is linked to the three engines by driveshafts that extend forward and outward to the outboard engines and to the rear for the third engine.

On either side of the fuselage are large fuel sponsons; the main gear units fold into the rear of the sponsons. The nose gear folds forward. Additional auxiliary fuel tank pylons can be fitted to the sponsons; the two 650-US gal (2,461-liter) drop tanks increase total fuel capacity by 127%. The aircraft is also fitted with a retractable in-flight refueling probe.

To absorb the increased power, a seventh blade was added to the fully articulated, titanium and steel main rotor hub. Each blade has a wider chord and greater length, a titanium spar, Nomex core, and fiberglass-epoxy skinning. The seven blades are power-folded.

DEVELOPMENT • The initial operational capability of the CH-53E was February 1981. The first flight of the prototype (YCH-53E) was on March 1, 1974, the CH-53E was in December 1980, and the MH-53E in September 1983. Over 100 CH-53Es and about 15 MH-53Es are in service with the US Navy and Marine Corps. The first delivery of the S-80-M-1 export version of the MH-53E was made to Japanese Maritime Self-Defense Force (JMSDF) in January 1989.

The tail section was altered several times during development, with the final arrangement having the tail rotor pylon canted 20° off vertical to port; the large four-blade antitorque rotor is fitted at the top. A long, strut-braced, gull-wing horizontal stabilizer extends to starboard opposite the antitorque rotor. The tail pylon power-folds to starboard, reducing overall height by 9 ft 9 in (2.98 m). Flight control is maintained by a Hamilton Standard FCC-105 Automatic Flight Control System (AFCS) with four-axis autopilot and two digital computers.

In 1987, the main transmission gearbox of the CH-53E was inspected and the bull gears replaced after inspections revealed excessive wear. The entire CH-53E fleet was grounded until the replacements could be made.

The MH-53E Sea Dragon is a minesweeping variant with larger fuel capacity.

The helicopter is used by the US Navy and Marines and by Japan.

VARIANTS • YCH-53E, CH-53E Super Stallion, MH-53E Sea Dragon, S-80-M-1 (Japan).

MH-53E Sea Dragon
UNITED TECHNOLOGIES/SIKORSKY

COMBAT EXPERIENCE • Three Marine Corps squadrons operating the CH-53E were deployed to the Persian Gulf in fall 1990 as part of Operation Desert Shield.

During the seven weeks of Operation Desert Storm, 75 Marine Corps Super Stallions—53 operating from shore bases and 22 from ships—flew 2,045 sorties supporting the preparation and execution of the Marine-Saudi drive up the coast.

MH-53s operating from amphibious ships in the Persian Gulf conducted antimine sorties to sweep Iraqi mines.

The MH-53J Pave Low transported covert reconnaissance teams into Kuwait and Iraq prior to ground war.

In January 1991, a small detachment was diverted to Mogadishu in Somalia to aid CH-46 Sea Knight helicopters in Operation Eastern Exit, which rescued 281 US and foreign nationals from the US embassy during the Somalian civil war.

SPECIFICATIONS •
MANUFACTURER   Sikorsky Aircraft
CREW   3 (2 pilots, 1 crew chief) + 55 troops
ENGINES   3 General Electric T64-GE-416 turboshaft
max power   4,380 shp each
internal fuel capacity
    1,017 US gal (3,849 liters)
WEIGHTS
empty   33,226 lb (15,071 kg)
max payload internal: 30,000 lb (13,607 kg)
    sling load: 32,000 lb (14,515 kg)
max takeoff internal payload: 69,750 lb (31,640 kg)
    external payload: 73,500 lb (33,339 kg)
DIMENSIONS
rotor diam   79 ft (24.08 m)
length   fuselage: 73 ft 4 in (23.55 m)
    tail and rotor pylon

    folded: 60 ft 6 in (18.44 m)
    overall: 99 ft 1.2 in (30.19 m)
height   27 ft 9 in (8.46 m)
cabin   length: 30 ft (9.14 m)
    width: 7 ft 6 in (2.29 m)
    height: 6 ft 6 in (1.98 m)
disc area   4,902 ft² (455.4 m²)
PERFORMANCE
max speed   at 56,000 lb (25,400 kg): 170 kts (196 mph; 315 km/h)
    at max takeoff, 4,000 ft (1,220 m): 154 kts (177 mph; 285 km/h)
econ cruise speed
    at 56,000 lb (25,400 kg): 150 kts (173 mph; 278 km/h)
    at max takeoff, 4,000 ft (1,220 m): 136 kts (157 mph; 252 km/h)
climb rate   at 56,000 lb (25,400 kg): 2,500 ft/min (762 m/min)
    at max takeoff: 1,630 ft/min (497 m/min)
service ceiling
    at 56,000 lb (25,400 kg): 18,500 ft (5,640 m)
    at max takeoff: 12,000 ft (3,658 m)
hovering ceiling in ground effect
    at 56,000 lb (25,400 kg), max power: 11,550 ft (3,520 m)
    at max takeoff, max power: 7,000 ft (2,134 m)
hovering ceiling out of ground effect
    at 56,000 lb (25,400 kg), max power: 9,500 ft (2,895 m)
    at max takeoff: 1,300 ft (396 m)
radius   50 nm (58 mi; 93 km) with 16-US ton (14.5-metric ton) sling load
    100 nm (115 mi; 185 km)

| | with max internal cargo |
| range | with 20,000-lb (9,072-kg) payload, external fuel: approx 450 nm (518 mi; 834 km) self-ferry with 4,408-lb (2,000-kg) payload: approx 1,000 nm (1,151 mi; 1,852 km) |

Chickasaw (H-19)

The H-19 Chickasaw is a 12-seat, multipurpose helicopter adapted for use in the Antisubmarine Warfare (ASW), troop and VIP transport, Search and Rescue (SAR), and general utility roles.

The H-19 has a fully articulated main rotor assembly that rotates counterclockwise when seen from above. The three all-metal blades have design lifetimes of 20,000 hours each. The two-blade anti-torque rotor is carried aft on a long tailboom; it is mounted on the left (tractor) side of the boom. Two small stabilizers are arranged in an inverted "V" on the underside of the boom ahead of the small tail skid.

The semimonocoque fuselage layout was dictated by a desire to place the main cabin under the main rotor, allowing a greater variety of payload configurations while remaining within the center-of-gravity envelope. The radial piston engine is located in the nose under a bulbous cowling; the driveshaft is led aft and up at a 45° angle under the flight deck to the main rotor. Its location permits easy maintenance through clamshell doors. The flight deck is located above the main cabin with the pilot and copilot sitting ahead of the main rotor mast; the flight-deck glazing is above the top line of the fuselage. The boxy main cabin is reached through a large sliding door on the starboard side. The rear of the cabin is vertical and has the narrow tailboom extending from the upper corners; a large triangular fillet was fitted to the rear of the fuselage to improve stability in production variants.

Landing gear is nonretracting quadricycle. The rear-landing-gear légs are outrigged on struts and have a wider track than the front pair. The front pair are fitted side by side under the front fuselage. All gear legs have shock absorbers. Floats can be fitted, as can amphibious landing gear.

DEVELOPMENT • The H-19's initial operational capability was in 1950; its first flight was on November 10, 1949. Sikorsky manufactured 1,067 H-19/S-55 helicopters from 1950 to 1959 and 1961 to 1962. Westland in Great Britain, Sud-Est in France, and Mitsubishi in Japan produced an additional 547; most of these were Westland Whirlwinds. The H-19 is no longer in production or in operational service with US military services. Only a few remain in service in Chile and Turkey, where they are operated as SAR aircraft.

VARIANTS • YH-19 (prototype), H-19A (USAF), HO4S-1 (USN/ASW), HRS-1 (production version/USMC), H-19B (USAF), HO4S-3 (USN ASW), HRS-2 (USMC; designation changed to CH-19E in 1962), HRS-3 (UH-19F in 1962), HO4S-3G (USCG SAR; redesignated HH-19G in 1962), H-19C (US Army), H-19D (US Army), HAR 21/HAS 22, Whirlwind, HAR1/HAR2 (Royal Navy/Air Force), HAR3/HAR4, HAR5/Whirlwind Series 2, HAR6, HAS7 (RN ASW), HCC 8 (Queen's Flight VIP aircraft), HAR9, HAR10/Whirlwind Series 3 (RAF), HCC12 (Queen's VIP aircraft), S-55 (commercial variant), S-55T (Chile), Elephant Joyeux (French-assembled), Simulated Hind (modified to simulate Russian Hind).

COMBAT EXPERIENCE • The Chickasaw was used extensively in combat by US and South Vietnamese forces in the early stages of the Vietnam War, by British forces in Malaysia, and by French forces in North Africa.

SPECIFICATIONS •

MANUFACTURER   Sikorsky Aircraft
CREW   2 (pilot, co-pilot) + 12 troops or 8 litters
ENGINES   1 Pratt & Whitney R-1340-57 radial piston
or 1 Wright R-1300 radial piston
  max power   R-1340: 600 hp
            R-1300: 700 hp
  internal fuel capacity
            185 US gal (700 liters)
WEIGHTS
  empty   4,795 lb (2,177 kg)
  max payload 2,855 lb (1,296 kg)
  takeoff   normal: 7,200 lb (3,266 kg)
          max: 7,900 lb (3,587 kg)
DIMENSIONS
  rotor diam   53 ft (16.16 m)
  length   fuselage: 42 ft 2 in (12.85 m)
          overall: 62 ft 7 in (19.07 m)
  height   13 ft 4 in (4.07 m)
  cabin   length: 10 ft (3.05 m)
          width: 6 ft (1.82 m)
          height: 5 ft 6 in (1.67 m)
          volume: 340 ft³ (9.63 m³)
  disc area   2,206.2 ft² (205 m²)
PERFORMANCE
  max speed   88 kts (101 mph; 163 km/h)
  cruise speed 74 kts (85 mph; 137 km/h)
  climb rate   700 ft/min (213 m/min)
  ceiling   10,500 ft (3,200 m)
  hovering ceiling in ground effect
          6,400 ft (1,951 m)
  hovering ceiling out of ground effect
          2,000 ft (610 m)
  range   352 nm (405 mi; 652 km)

Choctaw (H-34)

The H-34 Choctaw is a multipurpose helicopter that evolved from US Navy requirements for an Antisubmarine Warfare (ASW) helicopter. The H-34 series has been adapted for use in that role and for transport, utility, Search and Rescue (SAR), and Antarctic support operations.

The helicopter is similar in overall design to the H-19 Chickasaw but is larger and has a streamlined tail section. The Choctaw has a fully articulated, four-blade main rotor assembly that rotates counterclockwise when seen from above. The four-blade antitorque rotor is mounted on the left (tractor) side of the swept tail. A rectangular horizontal stabilizer extends from the leading edge of the fin.

The flight deck is located above the main cabin with the pilot and copilot sitting ahead of the main rotor mast; the flight-deck glazing is above the top line of the fuselage. The boxy main cabin is reached through a large sliding door on the starboard side. The fuselage is tapered from the rear of the cabin to the vertical tailboom.

The Wright radial piston engine is located in the nose, permitting easy maintenance through clamshell doors. The driveshaft is led aft and up at a 45° angle under the flight deck to the main rotor. The S-58T conversions have Pratt & Whitney Canada PT6T Twin Pac (two turbines coupled to single output shaft) in a lengthened nose that has a "lantern jaw" with intake "nostrils."

Landing gear is arranged in a "taildragger" layout. The main-landing-gear legs are outrigged on fixed struts below the cockpit. The fixed tailwheel is mounted under the fuselage just ahead of the vertical tail.

DEVELOPMENT • The Choctaw's initial operational capability was in 1955, and its first flight was on March 8, 1954. It is no longer in production or in US military service, but still in service with Argentina, Indonesia, Taiwan, Thailand, and Uruguay, the majority of the aircraft being S-58T conversions. A total of 2,187 were produced, of which Sud-Aviation of France assembled 135 and license-built an additional 166 aircraft. Westland produced its own turbine-powered version, dubbed the Wessex.

VARIANTS • XHSS-1 (prototype), HSS-1 Seabat (USN ASW), HSS-1N, HUS-1/ UH-34D Seahorse (USMC), HUS-1A/ UH-34E Seahorse, HUS-1G/HH-34F (USCG SAR), HUS-1L/LH-34D, HUS-1Z/ VH-34D (VIP), CH-34C, VH-34C, S-58T (flying crane), S-58B/C/D (commercial variants), Wessex.

COMBAT EXPERIENCE • CH-34 transport helicopters were widely used by the US Marine Corps in Vietnam.

SPECIFICATIONS •

MANUFACTURER   Sikorsky Aircraft

CREW
ASW: 4 (pilot, copilot, 2 sensor systems operators)
transport: 18 passengers or 8 litters

ENGINES
CH-34: 1 Wright R-1820-84 radial piston
S-58T: 1 Pratt & Whitney Canada PT6T-3/3B/6 coupled turboshaft
max power   CH-34: 1,525 hp
S-58T: 1,600 shp (-3/-3B) or 1,675 shp (-6)
internal fuel capacity
CH-34: 306 US gal (1,159 liters)
S-58T: 283 US gal (1,071 liters)

WEIGHTS
empty   8,400 lb (3,814 kg)
max payload 2,976 lb (1,350 kg)
max takeoff   CH-34: 13,300 lb (6,038 kg)
S-58T: 13,000 lb (5,896 kg)

overload   14,000 lb (6,350 kg)

DIMENSIONS
rotor diam   56 ft 0 in (17.07 m)
length   46 ft 9 in (14.25 m)
height   15 ft 11 in (4.86 m)
disc area   2,463 ft² (228.8 m²)

PERFORMANCE
max speed   CH-34 107 kts (123 mph; 198 km/h)
S-58T 120 kts (138 mph; 222 km/h)
cruise speed   CH-34 85 kts (98 mph; 158 km/h)
S-58T 110 kts (127 mph; 204 km/h)
econ cruise (S-58T)
80 kts (92 mph; 148 km/ h)
climb rate   1,100 ft/min (335 m/min)
ceiling   9,500 ft (2,896 m)
hovering ceiling in ground effect
CH-34: 4,900 ft (1,494 m)
hovering ceiling out of ground effect
CH-34: 2,400 ft (732 m)
S-58T (PT6T-3 engines): 4,700 ft (1,433 m)
S-58T (PT6T-6 engines): 6,500 ft (1,981 m)
range   CH-34: 158 nm (182 mi; 293 km)
S-58T PT6T-3: 260 nm (299 mi; 481 km)
S-58T PT6T-6: 242 nm (278 mi; 447 km)
armament (CH-34)
2 Mk-44 ASW homing torpedoes

Osage (H-55)

The Osage is a small, simply designed, two-seat training helicopter. Its fuselage is constructed of welded-steel tubes with an aluminum skin for the non-plexiglass portions of the cabin. A three-bladed, articulated main rotor of aluminum and a two-bladed steel and fiberglass tail rotor are powered by a single 180-hp Lycoming flat-four engine located below the cabin seats. The tailboom is a simple monocoque tube, and the landing gear is composed of skids mounted on shock absorbers.

DEVELOPMENT • The Osage's initial operational capability was in 1964; its first flight was in October 1956. Still in limited production for commercial customers. About 850 have been delivered to military customers in Latin America, Asia, and Europe.

VARIANTS • YHO-2 (US Army prototype), TH-55A, Hughes 269A/200/300 (commercial/export).

SPECIFICATIONS •
MANUFACTURER   Hughes
CREW   2 (pilot, student)
ENGINES   1 Lycoming HIO-360-B1A piston
max power 180 hp
WEIGHTS
empty   1,008 lb (457 kg)
max takeoff   1,850 lb (839 kg)
DIMENSIONS
rotor diam   25 ft 3 ½ in (7.71 m)
length   28 ft 11 in (8.8 m)
height   8 ft 3 in (2.5 m)
PERFORMANCE
max speed   75 kts (86 mph; 138 km/h)
cruise speed   57 kts (66 mph; 106 km/h)
ceiling   11,900 ft (3,625 m)
range   177 nm (204 mi; 328 km)

Chinook SOF (MH-47E)

The MH-47E Special Operations Forces (SOF) helicopter is a variation of the CH-47D Chinook medium transport helicopter. It was developed to achieve a 90% probability of completing a five-hour deep-penetration, clandestine mission over a 300-nm (345-mi; 556-km) radius. The aircraft must also be able to lift 30 fully equipped troops and hover out of ground effect at the midpoint of a specified mission during hot, adverse weather.

The MH-47E combines CH-47D and International Chinook upgrades with system improvements tested on Boeing's Model 360 demonstrator. Much of the avionics fit is common to both the MH-47E and the Sikorsky MH-60K variant of the UH-60 Blackhawk.

The two engines have been uprated to 7,500 shaft horsepower. The rotors can be stopped from full speed by rotor brakes in 45 seconds. Internal fuel is carried in lengthened external sponsons known as spontoons. A 28-ft (8.53-m) fixed refueling probe extends forward from the right spontoon and has a 300-US gal (1,136-liter)/min capacity. 1,700 US gal (6,435 liters) of auxiliary fuel can be carried in roll-in/roll-out fuel tanks in the cabin. The engines have Full-Authority Digital Engine Controls (FADEC) developed by Chandler Evans and Hawker Siddeley Dynamics.

To accommodate the longer spontoons, the front landing gear was moved forward 3 ft 4 in (1.02 m).

The nose of the flight deck on the SOF Chinook has been extended to accept a Texas Instruments AN/APQ-168 multimode terrain-following/terrain-avoidance radar and either a Hughes AN/AAQ-16 Forward-Looking Infrared (FLIR) turret or Texas Instruments AN/APQ-174 radar.

The MH-47E features a 600-lb (272-kg) capacity external rescue hoist that can also anchor a "fast-rope" rappelling system, on-board oxygen generation, and the AAR-Brooks & Perkins internal cargo handling equipment as well as 11 additional seats. An Electronic Flight Instrumentation System (EFIS) and mission-management system developed by IBM results in a flight deck having two full-color (inboard) and two monochrome (outboard) Multifunction Displays (MFD), an Allied Signal-Bendix digital moving map display, and two Control Display Units (CDU). Communications and navigation electronics are extensive. In addition to varied radio bands, equipment includes an Identification Friend or Foe (IFF) transponder, Airborne Target Handoff System (ATHS), satellite communications, ground communications, intercom, and personnel-locator system.

Navigation equipment goes beyond the basics, incorporating a Global Positioning System (GPS, Inertial Navigation System/INS), radar altimeter, Attitude and Heading Reference System (AHRS), and an air data computer.

DEVELOPMENT • The MH-47E's first flight was on May 31, 1990. Boeing received an $81.8-million contract in December 1987 to develop and qualify a prototype. 32 CH-47Ds were converted to MH-47D for operation by the US Army's Special Operations Force as an interim program. The aircraft would be replaced by the MH-47E.

SPECIFICATIONS •
MANUFACTURER   Boeing Helicopter
CREW   3 (pilot, copilot, crew chief/ combat commander) + 44 troops or 24 litters and 2 attendants
ENGINE   2 Avco Lycoming T55-L-714 turboshaft
  max continuous power
    4,110 shp each
  internal fuel capacity
    2,068 US gal (7,827 liters)
WEIGHTS
  empty   26,094 lb (11,836 kg)
  max takeoff 54,000 lb (24,494 kg)
DIMENSIONS
  rotor diam   60 ft (18.29 m)
  length   overall: 98 ft 11 in (30.15 m)
                 fuselage: 50 ft 9 in (15.47 m)
  height   18 ft 9 in (5.68 m)
  cargo hold   length: 30 ft 6 in (9.27 m)

width at floor: 8 ft 3 in (2.51 m)
mean width: 7 ft 6 in (2.29 m)
height: 6 ft 6 in (1.98 m)
volume: 1,474 ft³ (41.7 m³)
disc area   5,655 ft² (525.4 m²)
PERFORMANCE
cruise speed   138 kts (159 mph; 256 km/h)
rate of climb 1,841 ft/min (561 m/min)
ceiling   at 33,000 lb (14,969 kg): 15,000 ft (4,572 m)
                 at 50,000 lb (22,680 kg): 10,150 ft (3,094 m)
hovering ceiling in ground effect at 50,000 lb (22,680 kg)
                 standard day: 9,800 ft (2,987 m) ·
                 hot day: 7,900 ft (2,408 m)
hovering ceiling out of ground effect at 50,000 lb (22,680 kg)
                 standard day: 5,500 ft (1,676 m)
                 hot day: 3,300 ft (1,006 m)
mission radius, 12,000 lb (5,443 kg) payload
                 300 nm (345 mi; 556 km)
range, standard fuel, weight of 50,000 lb (22,680 kg)
                 612 nm (705 mi; 1,135 km)

Blackhawk SOF (MH-60)

Two MH-60 variants of the UH-60 Blackhawk tactical transport helicopter have been developed. The MH-60G Pave Hawk is a US Air Force night operations/ combat Search and Rescue (SAR) aircraft converted from the UH-60A. The MH-60K Special Operations Force (SOF) variant has been developed for Special Operations Command (SOC); it shares virtually all of its avionics design with the MH-47E Chinook SOF aircraft.

The MH-60K's avionics package is identical to the MH-47 Chinook SOF aircraft. Communications in the UHF, VHF, and HF bands are provided, with the UHF band being covered by Have Quick II frequency-hopping radios. Remaining communications electronics are also the same as the MH-47E.

The MH-60 also has extensive navigation equipment and self-defense capabilities integrated under the Aircraft Survivability Equipment (ASE) concept. It includes a Honeywell AN/AAR-47 missile-warning receiver, ITT AN/ALQ-136 pulse-radar jammer, Sanders AN/ALQ-144(V)1 pulsed IR jammer, Northrop AN/ALQ-162 Shadowbox Continuous Wave (CW) jammer, General Instruments AN/APR-39A(V)1 pulse-radar-warning receiver, AEL AN/APR-44(V)3 CW-radar-warning receiver, Hughes-Danbury Optical Division AN/AVR-2 laser-warning receiver, and CM-130 chaff/flare dispensers.

An external cargo hook will carry up to 8,000 lb (3,629 kg); typical sling loads include a 105-mm howitzer and 50 rounds of ammunition.

DEVELOPMENT • The MH-60G's initial operational capability was in September 1987, with the aircraft going to Air National Guard units.

The MH-60K program began in January 1988 with an $82.8-million contract to develop the prototype. It was rolled out in April 1990, with its first flight on August 10, 1990, and delivered to the 160th Aviation Regiment on August 20, 1991. The US Army operates the MH-60K variant, and the USAF operates the MH-60G.

VARIANTS • MH-60G Pave Hawk (special mission), MH-60K (basic variant).

COMBAT EXPERIENCE • MH-60Gs of the Special Operations Command's 55th Special Operations Squadron were airlifted to Saudi Arabia as part of Operation Desert Shield; during Operation Desert Storm, the MH-60Gs were used primarily for combat search and rescue as well as transporting covert reconnaissance teams into Kuwait and Iraq.

SPECIFICATIONS •

MANUFACTURER   Sikorsky Aircraft
CREW   3 (pilot, copilot, crew chief) + 7–12 troops
ENGINES   2 General Electric T700-GE-701C turboshaft
max power   1,900 shp each (transmission rating is 3,400 shp)
continuous   1,437 shp
internal fuel capacity   360 US gal (1,361 liters)
WEIGHTS
empty   hot and high mission (95°F/35°C at 4,000 ft/1,220 m): 15,966 lb (7,242 kg)
European mission (70°F/21°C at 2,000 ft/610 m): 16,239 lb (7,366 kg)
max takeoff   hot and high: 21,412 lb (9,712 kg)
European: 23,676 lb (10,739 kg)
self-deploy: 24,034 lb (10,902 kg)
DIMENSIONS
rotor diam   53 ft 8 in (16.36 m)
length   50 ft (15.26 m) without refueling probe
height   12 ft 4 in (3.76 m)
disc area   2,262 ft² (210.2 m²)
PERFORMANCE
never-exceed speed (Vne)   194 kts (225 mph; 361 km/h)
max cruise speed   sea level: 160 kts (184 mph; 296 km/h)
hot and high: 145 kts (167 mph; 269 km/h)

econ cruise speed, hot and high
    137 kts (158 mph; 254
    km/h)
hover ceiling out of ground effect
    (required)
        European mission: 2,000
        ft (610 m)
        hot and high: 4,000 ft
        (1,220 m)
*radius with 7 troops (hot and high) or 12
troops (European mission)*
        more than 200 nm (230
        mi; 370 km)
*self-deployment with 830 US gal (3,142
liters) auxiliary fuel*
        755 nm (869 mi; 1,398
        km)
armament   2 12.7-mm machine guns

Kiowa/JetRanger
(OH-58/Bell 206)

The OH-58 Kiowa is in widespread US Army and Navy service, as well as with a number of foreign military forces as the Bell 206 series. It is widely used for liaison, observation, fire direction, and training, with a few modified for the antitank role.

The Kiowa is a single-engine, general-purpose light helicopter. The semirigid, "seesaw" type two-blade main rotor has an aluminum spar and skin with a honeycomb core. The two-blade tail rotor is mounted on the left side of the shark-fin vertical tail; a fixed, rectangular horizontal stabilizer is mounted on the tailboom ahead of the fin.

The fuselage is in three sections: tailboom, semimonocoque center, and nose. The windshield is bulged and has a slight step down to the flattened nose; lower cheek windows in the nose aid in landing, takeoff, and hovering. Landing gear is parallel skids on struts extending from the fuselage.

Basic avionics consist of navigation and communications equipment. Beginning

OH-58 Kiowa Scout Helicopter
U.S. GOVERNMENT DEPARTMENT OF DEFENSE

in 1990, the older AN/ARC-114 radios in the US Army's OH-58Cs were replaced by the AN/ARC-201 Single-Channel Ground and Airborne Radio System (SINCGARS). In addition, many OH-58Cs are fitted with the AN/ALR-39 Radar Warning Receiver (RWR). Subsequently, the RWR was integrated with the AN/AVR-2 laser warning receiver.

Weapons may be added but are not integral to the design. For example, a few hundred OH-58Cs are being fitted with the Air-to-Air Stinger (ATAS).

DEVELOPMENT • The OH-58A's initial operational capability was in 1968. Its first flight as the Bell 206 JetRanger was on November 8, 1962. Originally designated as the OH-4A, it lost the US Army's competition for a Light Observation Helicopter (LOH) to the Hughes OH-6. A redesigned 206 then became a commercial success and was ordered by the US Navy as a training helicopter (TH-57, SeaRanger), after which the Army reopened the LOH competition and began purchasing the 206 as the OH-58A Kiowa.

Over 2,400 military 206 and 4,600 commercial JetRangers have been built; commercial production of JetRangers and LongRangers has been transferred to Bell Helicopter Canada with delivery of the first Canadian-built JetRanger occurring in December 1986. License production by Chincul SACAIFI in San Juan, Argentina, of the Bell 212 and 214 began in mid-1991.

In 1990, most of the US Navy's TH-57s were grounded to repair cracks on the landing skid supports, and over 80% were found to have the problem.

Approximately 600 US Army OH-58s are expected to remain in service into the 21st century. About 35 other nations fly the Kiowa and its variants, scattered throughout the Middle East, Asia, Europe, and Latin America.

Bell Helicopter Textron was awarded a contract to build 157 of its 206B JetRanger helicopters for military training.

The new helicopter, the first the US Army has bought "off-the-shelf," is designated the TH-67 Creek, and is assigned to the Army's helicopter training school at Fort Rucker, Alabama. Close to 8,000 of the basic Bell 206 airframes have been built.

VARIANTS • OH-4A (developmental), TH-57A SeaRanger (USN trainer), TH-57B, TH-57C (instrument trainer), OH-58A (US Army production model), OH-58A Plus, OH-58B (Austrian AF), 206B-1 (Australian-built), OH-58C, OH-58D Kiowa Warrior, TH-67 Creek (US Army), 206L-3 LongRanger (stretched version of 206 JetRanger), Cardoen 206L-3 Bichito (civilian), 206-L3 (gunship), 206L TexasRanger, CH-136 (Canadian), AB206A (Agusta-Bell), Zafar 300 (Iran).

COMBAT EXPERIENCE • OH-58s were deployed to Saudi Arabia during Operations Desert Shield/Desert Storm where they were used for reconnaissance, forward air control training, and personal transports for commanders. One aircraft was lost due to combat, one to noncombat causes.

SPECIFICATIONS •
MANUFACTURERS
  Bell Helicopter Textron
  Bell Helicopter Canada
  Agusta-Bell (Italy/AB206) licensed
  Chincul SACAIFI (Argentina/212, 214)
CREW   2 (pilot, copilot) + 2 troops
ENGINES
  OH-58A: 1 Allison T63-A-700 turboshaft
  OH-58C: 1 Allison T63-A-720 turboshaft
  max power   OH-58A: 317 shp (T63-A-700)
              OH-58C: 420 shp (T63-A-720)
WEIGHTS
  empty   OH-58A: 1,464 lb (664 kg)

OH-58C: 1,818 lb (825 kg)

normal   OH-58A: 2,768 lb (1,255 kg)

OH-58C: 2,890 lb (1,311 kg)

max takeoff OH-58A: 3,000 lb (1,362 kg)

OH-58C: 3,200 lb (1,451 kg)

DIMENSIONS

rotor diam   35 ft 4 in (10.77 m)

length   fuselage 32 ft 7 in (9.93 m)

overall 40 ft 12 in (12.49 m)

height   9 ft 6 ½ in (2.91 m)

disc area   980.5 ft² (91.09 m²)

PERFORMANCE

speed   never-exceed (Vne): 120 kts (138 mph; 222 km/h)

max range: 102 kts (117 mph; 188 km/h)

loitering: 49 kts (56 mph; 91 km/h)

max climb rate

OH-58A: 1,780 ft/min (543 m/min)

OH-58C: 1,800 ft/min (549 m/min)

ceiling   OH-58A: 18,900 ft (5,760 m)

OH-58C: 18,500 ft (5,640 m)

hovering ceiling in ground effect

OH-58A: 13,600 ft (4,145 m)

OH-58C: 13,200 ft (4,025 m)

hovering ceiling out of ground effect, at given weights

OH-58A, normal: 8,800 ft (2,680 m)

OH-58A, max: 6,000 ft (1,830 m)

OH-58C, normal: 9,700 ft (2,955 m)

OH-58C, max: 8,200 ft (2,500 m)

range   normal: both 260 nm (298 mi; 481 km)

max, OH-58C: 264 nm (305 mi; 490 km)

armament   XM-27 armament kit (7.62-mm minigun)

or BGM-71 TOW antitank missiles optional

Cayuse (OH-6)

The OH-6 is a light, multipurpose helicopter that has been adapted for observation, scout, special-operations, antiarmor attack, and Antisubmarine Warfare (ASW) roles. The OH-6, based on the successful Hughes 269 commercial helicopter, but turbine-powered and enlarged, won the US Army's 1962–63 competition for a Light Observation Helicopter (LOH). The OH-6 later developed into the commercial Model 500. The OH-6 features a four-blade fully articulated main rotor with cross-connected flap and feather straps; the light-alloy spar is wrapped with a single piece of light-alloy skin that is shaped into an airfoil.

The slender tailboom extends aft from the roof of the egg-shaped fuselage pod to a narrow, swept fin; the fin extends below the boom and is fitted with a small tail skid. The two-blade, antitorque rotor is mounted at the end of the boom on the left-hand side. On the starboard side is a broad-chord stabilizer held in at a sharp dihedral by a strut that connects it to the fin.

The Allison turboshaft, derated for greater reliability and lower fuel consumption, is carried behind the crew compartment and receives air through a small intake on the cabin roof and exhausts through a nozzle at the aft end of the fuselage pod below the boom. The crew cabin features a glazed nose for maximum forward visibility. Engine access is through clamshell doors at the rear of the fuselage pod. The parallel-skid landing gear has internal pneumatic shock absorbers.

The OH-6 has no integral armament, although it can accept gun pods or grenade launchers. Spanish 500Ms are fitted for Antisubmarine Warfare (ASW) with an AN/ASQ-81 Magnetic Anomaly Detector (MAD) and two Mk 44 lightweight antisubmarine torpedoes.

The OH-6A was often called the Loach by US soldiers in Vietnam, derived from a slurring of the letters LOH.

DEVELOPMENT • The OH-6's initial operational capability was in 1966; its first flight was on February 27, 1963. Its production for the US Army ended in 1970 after 1,434 were built; over 300 still serve in the Army National Guard. It is also assembled under license by RACA in Argentina, Breda Nardi in Italy, and Kawasaki in Japan.

The OH-6 is operated in over 20 countries throughout the world, primarily Latin America, the Middle East, and the Far East.

VARIANTS • YHO-6, OH-6A, OH-6C, Hughes 500 (commercial), 500M (Export Hughes 500, produced under license in Italy, Argentina, Japan, and South Korea), 500MD Defender, Super Cayuse (upgraded).

COMBAT EXPERIENCE • Many US Army OH-6 "Loaches" flew as observation aircraft during the Vietnam War.

SPECIFICATIONS •
MANUFACTURER   Hughes Aircraft (later McDonnell Douglas Helicopter)
CREW   2 (pilot, copilot) + 2 troops
ENGINES   1 Allison T63-A-5A turboshaft
max power   317 hp (derated to 252.5 shp)
WEIGHTS
empty   1,229 lb (557 kg)
takeoff   design gross: 2,400 lb (1,090 kg)
max overload: 2,700 lb (1,225 kg)

DIMENSIONS
rotor diam   26 ft 4 in (8.03 m)
length   30 ft 3 ¾ in (9.24 m)
height   8 ft 1 ½ in (2.48 m)
disc area   544.6 ft² (50.6 m²)
PERFORMANCE
max speed   130 kts (150 mph; 241 km/h)
cruise speed   116 kts (134 mph; 216 km/h)
climb rate   1,840 ft/min (560 m/min)
ceiling   15,800 ft (4,815 m)
hovering ceiling in ground effect
   11,800 ft (3,595 m)
hovering ceiling out of ground effect
   7,300 ft (2,225 m)
range at 5,000 ft (1,525 m) and 2,400 lb (1,090 kg)
   330 nm (380 mi; 611 km)
ferry range with approx 200 US gal (757 liters) of fuel
   1,354 nm (1,560 mi; 2,510 km)
armament   none integral to all variants but can be fitted with:
   2 twin 7.62-mm machine-gun packs
   or 2 M75 40-mm grenade launchers
   or a combination
   ASW: 2 Mk 44 torpedoes, AN/ASQ-81 MAD

Kiowa Warrior (OH-58D)

The OH-58D (Bell Model 406) is a conversion of the widely deployed OH-58A (Bell Model 206) Kiowa light observation helicopter, produced under the Army Helicopter Improvement Program (AHIP). It can perform reconnaissance and artillery spotting missions as well as search, classification, and designation of mobile targets. All AHIP helicopters are being fitted with Air-to-Air Missiles (AAM), antitank missiles, rocket pods, and gun pods. About 80 of these are being modified further to be multipurpose transport and reconnaissance aircraft.

Compared to the basic Kiowa, the OH-58D has a four-blade main rotor, more powerful engine, integrated navigation/attack equipment, and a Mast-Mounted Sight (MMS). As a result, the OH-58D empty weight is within 75 lb (34 kg) of the OH-58A maximum takeoff weight.

The main rotor has elastomeric bearings and a fiberglass yoke. The rotor's blades can be folded for transport. A Stability and Control Augmentation System (SCAS) combines with the four-blade rotor system to provide a much smoother ride than the earlier OH-58 variants. Like its parent's, the OH-58D's fuselage is in three sections. Its 650-shp Allison T703-AD-700 turboshaft engine is mounted in a large housing over the cabin. For the Kiowa Warrior upgrade, the engine is fitted with a new diffuser that results in a 15% power increase; the transmission is uprated as well to handle the increased power.

To reduce the aircraft's Radar Cross Section (RCS), a kit was developed to give the nose a sharper profile, the windshield was tinted, the passenger compartment given a cowling, and the rotor blade cuffs were enlarged and softened.

Cockpit avionics are based on dual MIL-STD-1553B databuses and feature two Multifunction Displays (MFD), one displaying the vertical situation and the other the horizontal (navigational) information. The AN/ASN-137 Doppler strapdown Inertial Navigation System (INS) is combined with the Litton LR-80 Attitude and Heading Reference System (AHRS) to generate very precise way-point navigation, often arriving within 110 yd (100 m) of a destination 54 nm (62 mi; 100 km) distant. Switches mounted on the control column handgrips permit head-up flying. Among the communications equipment is a secure UHF voice link.

Armament options include various combinations of four AGM-114 Hellfire laser-guided, air-to-ground missiles; four FIM-92 Air-to-Air Stinger (ATAS) Infrared (IR)-homing missiles, two Hydra 70 2.75-in (70-mm) rocket pods; or two .50-cal machine guns.

A Thomson-CSF VH-100 Head-Up Display (HUD), license-built by Hamilton Standard, is part of the targeting avionics. A 20-mm gun may be fitted as well as BGM-71 TOW antitank missiles. The Kiowa Warrior upgrade includes the addition of the Single-Channel Ground and Airborne Radio System (SINCGARS) and flight data recorder.

DEVELOPMENT • The OH-58D's initial operational capability was in 1986; its first flight was on October 6, 1983. The US Army had planned to convert at least 477 OH-58As to D standard to operate as "interim LHX" aircraft until the latter program begins production deliveries later in the 1990s; this total has been reduced to 279 funded and an overall goal of 375 conversions that may not be met.

The first OH-58D Kiowa Warriors to be sold for export were 12 ordered by Taiwan in December 1991, with another 14 put on option.

15 Model 406CSs were delivered to Saudi Arabia in October 1987. The helicopter is also flown by Norway, Singapore, and Taiwan.

VARIANTS • Kiowa   (OH-58A/C), Prime Chance (modification for Persian Gulf), Model 406CS (export version).

COMBAT   EXPERIENCE • Prime Chance conversions were deployed during the Iran-Iraq war against Iranian gunboats and minelaying craft. US Army OH-58Ds were deployed to Saudi Arabia as part of Operations Desert Shield/ Desert Storm. Saudi 406CS aircraft also operated during the war.

SPECIFICATIONS •
MANUFACTURER   Bell Helicopter Textron
CREW   2 (pilot, copilot) + 2 troops
ENGINES   1 Allison T703-AD-700 turboshaft
max power   OH-58D: 650 shp; transmission rating of 510 shp
Kiowa Warrior: 750 shp; transmission rating of 560 shp
internal fuel capacity
105.4 US gal (399 liters)
WEIGHTS
empty   2,825 lb (1,281 kg)
useful load   1,335 lb (606 kg)
max takeoff   4,500 lb (2,041 kg)
DIMENSIONS
rotor diam   35 ft (10.67 m)
length   fuselage: 33 ft 10 in (10.31 m)
overall: 42 ft 2 in (12.85 m)
height   to rotor head: 8 ft 6 in (2.59 m)
overall: 12 ft 9 ½ in (3.9 m)
disc area   962 ft² (89.38 m²)
PERFORMANCE
speed   never-exceed (Vne): 130 kts (149 mph; 241 km/h)
max level at 4,000 ft (1,220 m): 128 kts (147 mph; 237 km/h)
max cruise: 120 kts (138 mph; 222 km/h)
econ cruise at 4,000 ft (1,220 m): 110 kts (127 mph; 204 km/h)
max climb rate
ISA: 1,540 ft/min (469 m/min)
at 95°F (35°C) at 4,000 ft (1,220 m): more than 500 ft/min (152 m/min)
vertical climb rate
ISA: 760 ft/min (232 m/min)
at 95°F (35°C) at 4,000 ft

(1,220 m): more than 500 ft/min (152 m/min)
ceiling   17,200 ft (5,243 m)
hovering ceiling in ground effect
ISA: 13,800 ft (4,206 m)
at 95°F (35°C) at 4,000 ft (1,220 m): 10,700 ft (3,261 m)
hovering ceiling out of ground effect
ISA: 9,500 ft (2,896 m)
at 95°F (35°C) at 4,000 ft (1,220 m): 5,000 ft (1,524 m)
range   300 nm (345 mi; 556 km)
armament   2 FIM-92 Stinger missiles can be carried

S-76

The S-76 is a commercial helicopter (called Spirit) in limited military service as a transport and in variant form available as a military multirole helicopter. It is used for VIP transport, scout, medical evacuation, liaison, Counterinsurgency (COIN), and Search and Rescue (SAR) missions.

The S-76 bears a resemblance to the US H-60 Blackhawk series it was developed from. The S-76 has a scaled-down version of the Blackhawk's rotor system, featuring a fully articulated, forged-titanium main rotor hub with elastomeric bearings and four blades; the blades have a titanium core, are sheathed in composite materials, and have swept tips.

The tail pylon is set high on the fuselage and has a four-blade, composite-material antitorque rotor mounted on the left side. A double-tapered, all-moving horizontal stabilizer is fitted at the base of the tail pylon. The later S-76B and variants have tail pylons with 15% less fin area (taken from the trailing edge, which straightens the profile) and reshaped tailplanes with greater chord.

The sleek, semimonocoque fuselage has a flattened nose sloping gently up to a stepped windshield. The flight deck is accessible through doors on each side. The main cabin is open to the flight deck and has a constant cross section. Large side doors hinged at the front (or optional sliding doors) provide entry. The lower line of the after half of the fuselage tapers up to the tail pylon. The main-landing-gear legs retract to the rear into fuselage bays under the engines; the nose gear retracts to the rear.

Two turboshaft engines are mounted above the cabin and behind the main rotor mast. Allison- and Turbomeca-powered S-76s have small, raked rectangular intakes faired into the transmission hump and close-set exhausts. PT6B-powered aircraft have much larger engine nacelles set out from the hump on short stubs; each nacelle has its own upright, rectangular intake and exhaust duct.

Military variants of the S-76 have the Sikorsky designation H-76 and are available for both land-based and shipboard service. None are armed with internal weapons, but the AUH-76, H-76, and H-76N are fitted with external armament pylons that carry gun and rocket pods, antitank and air-to-ground missiles, air-to-air missiles, or antisubmarine torpedoes.

DEVELOPMENT • The S-76's initial operational capability was in 1979; its first flight was on March 13, 1977.

The S-76 is operated by Bahrain, Honduras, Hong Kong, Jordan, Philippines, Spain, and Trinidad and Tobago.

VARIANTS • S-76A, S-76A+ (Hong Kong), S-76 Mark II, S-76 Utility (Philippines), S-76B, S-76C (Hong Kong, Spain), S-76D, S-76 (SHADOW/Sikorsky Helicopter Advanced Demonstrator of Operator Workload), H-76 Eagle, H-76N (Navy).

SPECIFICATIONS •

MANUFACTURER   Sikorsky Aircraft

CREW   2 (pilot, copilot) + 12 passengers

ENGINES
  S-76A: 2 Allison 250-C30S turboshaft
  S-76B: 2 Pratt & Whitney Canada
    PT6B-36 turboshaft
  max power   S-76A: 557 shp each
            S-76B: 960 shp each
  internal fuel capacity
            281 US gal (1,064 liters)

WEIGHTS
  empty   S-76A: 5,600 lb (2,540 kg)
            S-76B: 6,548 lb (2,970 kg)
  max useful load
            S-76A: 4,700 lb (2,132 kg)
            S-76B: 5,250 lb (2,381 kg)
  max external load
            3,300 lb (1,497 kg)
  max takeoff S-76A: 10,300 lb (4,672
            kg)
            S-76B: 11,400 lb (5,171
            kg)

DIMENSIONS
  rotor diam   44 ft (13.41 m)
  length   fuselage: 43 ft 4 ½ in
            (13.22 m)
            overall: 52 ft 6 in (16.0
            m)
  height   14 ft 5 ¾ in (4.41 m)
  disc area   1,520.5 ft^2 (141.3 m^2)

PERFORMANCE
  never-exceed speed (Vne)
            sea level: 155 kts (178
            mph; 286 km/h)
            at altitude: 164 kts (189
            mph; 304 km/h)
  max cruise   145 kts (167 mph; 269
            km/h)
  econ cruise S-76A: 125 kts (144 mph;
            232 km/h)
            S-76B: 130 kts (150 mph;
            241 km/h)
  ceiling   15,000 ft (4,575 m)
  hovering ceiling in ground effect
            S-76A: 6,200 ft (1,890 m)
            S-76B: 9,400 ft (2,865 m)
  hovering ceiling out of ground effect
            S-76A: 2,800 ft (853 m)
            S-76B: 5,800 ft (1,768 m)
  range   S-76A, max load: 404 nm
            (465 mi; 749 km)

S-76A, max fuel, 8
passengers, offshore
equipment: 600 nm
(691 mi; 1,112 km)
S-76B, internal fuel, sea
level: 330 nm (380 mi;
611 km)
S-76B, auxiliary fuel at
best altitude: 416 nm
(479 mi; 771 km)

Seasprite (SH-2F/Seasprite)

The SH-2F is a US light Antisubmarine
Warfare (ASW) helicopter, adapted from
the earlier HU2K Seasprite utility helicopter. It is part of the Light Airborne
Multipurpose System (LAMPS I) that is
operated from surface combatants that
are too small to carry the larger Sikorsky
SH-60 Seahawk (LAMPS III).

The SH-2F has a four-blade main rotor
system with a titanium rotor hub and rotor brake. Most SH-2Fs have aluminum-
fiberglass blades; composite-construc-
tion blades were fitted beginning with
the aircraft delivered in October 1987.
The blade pitch is adjusted using a
unique midspan, trailing-edge servo flap
system.

The four-blade antitorque rotor is
mounted at the top of the tail pylon with
the rotor plane to port. Slim, strut-braced
horizontal stabilizers are fitted on each
side of the pylon near the fuselage; a portion of the pylon trailing edge is cam-
bered to port to aid antitorque control.

The SH-2F is powered by two GE turboshaft engines mounted on short stubs on
either side of the main rotor pylon. The
exhaust is directed to the side. The later
SH-2G is fitted with considerably uprated
and more reliable GE T700 turboshaft
engines. External fuel capacity is 200 US
gal (757 liters). The fuselage is a tapered,
semimonocoque structure with a watertight hull. The pilots are seated forward
of the main cabin, which holds the ASW
system operator's station and sonobuoy

rack. The aircraft can carry three passengers, two litters, or an instructor's seat
and is fitted with a 4,000-lb (1,814-kg)
external cargo hook and 600-lb (272-kg)
rescue hoist over the starboard door. The
retractable main-landing-gear struts have
two-wheel units and extend to the sides
when lowered, retracting inward and forward into exposed wells; the fixed tailwheel is located well forward of the tail
pylon. For hangar stowage, the main rotor blades fold back and the nose compartment splits into two folding halves.

The avionics fit includes a Canadian
Marconi LN-66HP surveillance radar in a
drumlike ventral radome located below
the cockpit, Teledyne Ryan AN/ASN-
123C tactical navigation system,
Rospatch AN/ARR-75 sonobuoy receiving set, and dual Collins AN/ARC-
159(V)1 UHF communications system.
The Honeywell AN/APN-171 radar altimeter fairings are located on both sides
near the tailwheel. Because the SH-2F
cannot process acoustical signals on
board the aircraft, it is also fitted with a
Rospatch AN/AKT-22(V)6 sonobuoy
data link and AN/ASA-26B sonobuoy recorder. The antennas for the General Instruments AN/ALR-66(V)1 Electronic
Support Measures (ESM) radar–warning
receiver are located in the nose avionics
compartment and the trailing edge of the
tail pylon. The sonobuoy rack dispenses
15 AN/SSQ-53 DIFAR or AN/SSQ-62
DICASS sonobuoys to port. Eight Mk 25
marine smoke markers are dropped from
a forward bay to port of the radome. A
stores station on either side carries a single ASW torpedo or a 100-US gal (379-
liter) drop tank.

DEVELOPMENT • The SH-2D's initial
operational capability was in December
1971; its first flight was on July 2, 1959
(HU2K-1). Between 1961 and 1966, 190
HU2K Seasprites were built; the 105 that
remained were converted to SH-2F by
1983. Subsequently, 54 new SH-2F helicopters were procured for a total LAMPS

I program of 159; six more requested in FY1987 as SH-2F were built as SH-2G Super Seasprite. Approximately 115 SH-2Fs are being upgraded to SH-2G at the rate of six to eight aircraft per year. An initial sale of five SH-2Fs to Portugal was announced in May 1989 but fell through; in June, a sale to Pakistan was announced. In September 1992, a $161-million sale of 12 SH-2Fs to Taiwan was announced.

VARIANTS • HU2K Seasprite, SH-2D, SH-2F, SH-2F MEF (Middle East Force), SH-2G Super Seasprite, SH-2H.

COMBAT EXPERIENCE • SH-2F helicopters were aboard *Belknap*-class cruisers, *Kidd*-class destroyers, and *Knox*-class frigates that deployed to the Persian Gulf during Operations Desert Shield/Desert Storm and used for maritime surveillance to enforce the economic sanctions imposed on Iraq.

SPECIFICATIONS •
MANUFACTURER   Kaman Aerospace
CREW   3 (2 pilots, 1 ASW systems operator)
ENGINES
SH-2F: 2 General Electric T58-GE-8F turboshaft
SH-2G: 2 General Electric T700-GE-401 turboshaft
max power   SH-2F: 1,350 shp each
SH-2G: 1,690 shp each
internal fuel capacity
276 US gal (1,045 liters)
WEIGHTS
empty, operating
SH-2F: 7,350 lb (3,334 kg)
SH-2G: 7,710 lb (3,497 kg)
normal landing weight, 20-min fuel reserve
SH-2F: 10,000 lb (4,356 kg)
SH-2G: 10,400 lb (4,717 kg)

max takeoff   SH-2F delivered before October 1985: 12,800 lb (5,806 kg)
SH-2F delivered after October 1985: 13,500 lb (6,123 kg)
SH-2G: 13,900 lb (6,305 kg)
DIMENSIONS
rotor diam   SH-2F: 44 ft (13.42 m)
SH-2G: 44 ft 4 in (13.51 m)
length, blades folded
38 ft 4 in (11.69 m)
length, blades turning
SH-2F: 52 ft 7 in (16.03 m)
SH-2G: 52 ft 9 in (16.08 m)
height   15 ft ½ in (4.58 m)
disc area   SH-2F: 1,520.5 ft² (141.25 m²)
SH-2G: 1,543.4 ft² (143.44 m²)
PERFORMANCE
max speed at max takeoff weight
SH-2F: 133 kts (153 mph; 246 km/h)
SH-2G: 135 kts (155 mph; 250 km/h)
max speed at landing weight
SH-2F: 140 kts (161 mph; 259 km/h)
SH-2G: 146 kts (168 mph; 271 km/h)
typical cruise speed
130 kts (150 mph; 241 km/h)
econ cruise   120-124 kts (138–143 mph; 222–230 km/h)
climb rate, average gross weight
SH-2F: 2,440 ft/min (744 m/min)
SH-2G: 2,360 ft/min (719 m/min)
climb rate, max takeoff weight
SH-2F: 1,600 ft/min (488 m/min)
SH-2G: 1,550 ft/min (472 m/min)

single-engine climb rate
SH-2F: 485 ft/min (148 m/min)
SH-2G: 1,260 ft/min (384 m/min)
ceiling at average gross weight
SH-2F: 15,250 ft (4,648 m)
SH-2G: 20,600 ft (6,280 m)
ceiling at max takeoff weight
SH-2F: 11,850 ft (3,612 m)
SH-2G: 16,700 ft (5,090 m)
Hovering in Ground Effect (HIGE), max takeoff weight, ISA
SH-2F: 10,100 ft (3,078 m)
SH-2G: 12,000 ft (3,658 m)
HIGE, landing weight, ISA
SH-2F: 18,100 ft (5,517 m)
SH-2G: 18,600 ft (5,669 m)
Hovering out of Ground Effect (HOGE), max takeoff weight, ISA
SH-2F: 4,700 ft (1,433 m)
SH-2G: 6,000 ft (1,829 m)
HOGE, landing weight, ISA
SH-2F: 14,500 ft (4,420 m)
SH-2G: 15,600 ft (4,755 m)
ASW patrol time on station at 30 nm (35 mi; 56 km), radius ISA, 20-min fuel reserve
with 1 torpedo
SH-2F: 2 hr 0 min
SH-2G: 2 hr 42 min
with 2 torpedoes
SH-2F: 1 hr 12 min
SH-2G: 1 hr 48 min
SAR search time, ISA, 20-min fuel reserve
at 30 nm (35 mi; 56 km) radius
SH-2F: 3 hr 0 min
SH-2G: 3 hr 42 min

at 100 nm (115 mi; 185 km) radius
SH-2F: 1 hr 30 min
SH-2G: 2 hr 18 min
Antiship Surveillance and Targeting (ASST) time on station ISA, 20-min fuel reserve
at 30 nm (35 mi; 56 km) radius
SH-2F: 3 hr 12 min
SH-2G: 4 hr 0 min
at 100 nm (115 mi; 185 km) radius
SH-2F: 1 hr 42 min
SH-2G: 2 hr 30 min
max ferry range, with 3 external tanks
SH-2F 425 nm (489 mi; 788 km)
SH-2G 505 nm (582 mi; 936 km)
armament   2 Mk 46 ASW torpedoes
radar   AN/APS-69 (LN-66) surface-search radar
EW   ALR-66(V)

Sea King/Pelican/Jolly Green Giant (H-3)

The H-3 is a relatively long-range, multi-purpose helicopter originally designed for the US Navy's Antisubmarine Warfare (ASW) role, but subsequently modified for combat Search and Rescue (SAR), minesweeping, troop transport, VIP transport, Airborne Early Warning (AEW), and general utility missions. The British Westland Sea King, although derived from the H-3, has a different powerplant and avionics.

The H-3 is a high-performance helicopter that set several speed and distance records soon after its first flight. Its large fuel capacity gives it high endurance or long range. Several variants have been produced.

The H-3 series features a fully articulated five-blade main rotor, mounted at the top of the boom; the rotor plane is to the left. A high-aspect-ratio, strut-braced horizontal stabilizer is fitted to the right of the boom at the same level as the tail rotor hub. Naval variants have folding rotors, land-based variants do not.

The fuselage of the naval ASW SH-3 is boat-shaped. The cabin section ends in a "boat tail" to which the fixed tailwheel is attached. The retractable main-landing-gear units are carried in outrigger pontoons located outboard of the lower fuselage behind the cockpit. The upper half of the fuselage is extended as a shallower semimonocoque structure that continues to the top of the slanting tail; most SH-3s have folding tailbooms to facilitate carrier storage.

The HH-3 Air Force variants have a revised fuselage that is not watertight. The fuselage width remains constant back to a hydraulically operated, full-width rear ramp. The ramp forms the floor of a section that slopes up to a slim boom that extends straight back. A more upright and distinct vertical tail than that of the SH-3 is mounted on the end of the boom.

The HH-3 landing-gear arrangement is tricycle and hence reversed from the SH-3. The nose gear retracts forward; the main gear retracts into large sponsons mounted on the lower fuselage behind the main rotor shaft line.

The US Navy's SH-3H and comparable foreign ASW models have sonobuoy dispensers, AN/AQS-13 dipping sonar, Magnetic Anomaly Detector (MAD), surface-search radar, and other submarine-detection gear. Brazilian Navy ASH-3Ds began carrying two AM-39 Exocet anti-ship missiles in 1991.

DEVELOPMENT • The Sea King's initial operational capability was in September 1961; the SH-3's first flight was on March 11, 1959. It is no longer in production in the United States but is still being built under license by Westland in Britain and by Agusta in Italy. Over 1,100 have been built; the 167th and last Mitsubishi-built SH-3 was delivered in March 1990.

The SH-3 is being replaced in US Navy

SH-3

service by the SH-60F CV-Helo; the US Coast Guard's HH-3F Pelicans are being replaced by the HH-60J. US-produced variants are operated by the US Air Force, Navy, and Coast Guard and in about 13 other countries throughout the world. The naval and some other models are named Sea King; the US Air Force HH-3 series is named Jolly Green Giant; the US Coast Guard HH-3F SAR aircraft are named Pelican.

VARIANTS • XHSS-2/YHSS-2, HSS-2/SH-3A (initial ASW version), CHSS-2/CH-124 (Canada), HSS-2B (Japanese license-built ASW), NH-3A (research), RH-3A (minesweeper), VH-3A (USMC White House VIP), HH-3A (USN SAR), CH-3B (US, Danish, Malaysian air forces), CH-3C (USAF), SH-3D (US, Spanish Navy, Argentina, Brazil/ASW), ASH-3D (Agusta), VH-3D (VIP), CH-3E, HH-3E Jolly Green Giant (USAF SAR), HH-3F Pelican (USCG SAR), AS-61R (Agusta), SH-3G, SH-3D AEW, SH-3H (USN ASW), ASH-3H (Agusta), YSH-3J, Westland Sea King HAS and HAR/Commando (British ASW/SAR), Nuri (Malaysian AF).

COMBAT EXPERIENCE • The British Westland Sea King saw extensive service in the 1982 Falklands War.

Five CH-124s deployed to the Persian Gulf in fall 1990 in the destroyer HMCS *Athabaskan* and the supply ship HMCS *Protecteur.* US Navy SH-3G/H helicopters were also deployed to the Persian Gulf; each US-deployed aircraft carrier had five SH-3Hs and several SH-3Gs from other ships. None were lost in combat, although the 30 carrier-based SH-3s flew 1,800 sorties. No Air Force HH-3s were deployed.

SPECIFICATIONS •

MANUFACTURER
Sikorsky Aircraft
Agusta SpA, Milan, Italy
Mitsubishi Heavy Industries, Tokyo, Japan
CREW   4 (2 pilots, 2 ASW systems operators)

ENGINES
SH-3H: 2 General Electric T58-GE-10 turboshaft
HH-3H: 2 GE T58-GE-100 turboshaft
max power   SH-3H: 1,400 shp each
HH-3H: 1,500 shp each
internal fuel capacity
840 US gal (3,180 liters)
WEIGHTS
empty   SH-3H: 11,865 lb (5,382 kg)
HH-3H: 13,255 lb (6,010 kg)
max takeoff   SH-3H for ASW mission: 18,626 lb (8,449 kg)
HH-3H: 22,046 lb (10,000 kg)
DIMENSIONS
rotor diam   62 ft (18.9 m)
fuselage length
SH-3H: 54 ft 9 in (16.69 m)
HH-3H: 57 ft 3 in (17.45 m)
height   SH-3H: 16 ft 10 in (5.13 m)
HH-3H: 18 ft 1 in (5.51 m)
disc area   3,019 ft² (280.5 m²)
PERFORMANCE
max speed   SH-3H: 144 kts (166 mph; 267 km/h)
HH-3H: 141 kts (162 mph; 261 km/h)
cruise speed
SH-3H: 118 kts (136 mph; 219 km/h)
HH-3H: 130 kts (150 mph; 241 km/h)
climb rate   SH-3H: 1,310–2,200 ft/min (400–670 m/min)
ceiling   14,700 ft (4,481 m)
hovering ceiling in ground effect
SH-3H: 8,200 ft (2,500 m)
HH-3F: 9,710 ft (2,960 m)
hovering ceiling out of ground effect
SH-3H: 3,700 ft (1,130 m)
range   540 nm (621 mi; 1,000 km)

armament 2 Mk 46 torpedoes in SH-3H; varies among license-built examples

Seahawk (SH-60)

The Seahawk, a multipurpose US Navy adaptation of the UH-60 Blackhawk tactical transport helicopter, was developed for Antisubmarine Warfare (ASW) and Search and Rescue (SAR) missions. The Seahawk is the helicopter component of the Navy's ship-based Light Airborne Multipurpose System (LAMPS) III, an over-the-horizon ASW and Antiship Surveillance and Targeting (ASST) system. A modified Seahawk, the SH-60F, is replacing SH-3s as the carrier-based inner-zone ASW helicopter.

The Seahawk has a forged titanium main rotor hub with elastomeric bearings and four blades; the blades have a titanium core, are sheathed in composite materials, and have tips swept at 20°. The main rotor shaft has a brake, and the blades are power-folded.

The tail pylon has a four-blade, composite-material antitorque rotor mounted on the right side and canted at 20° to increase vertical lift. The large, rectangular, variable-incidence stabilator is fitted near the base of the pylon and can set at +34° during hovering and −6° for autorotation. It also adds lift during cruise flight. The tail pylon has power-assisted folding that swings it to the left for stowage. The Automatic Flight Control System (AFCS) was expanded from that in the Blackhawk, adding an automatic altitude hold and approach to hover.

The SH-60's two turboshaft engines are mounted over the fuselage, separated from each other by the rotor drivetrain and transmission. The engines are uprated and "marinized" to resist corrosion. The aircraft can refuel during hover.

The fixed main-landing-gear legs trail back from a mount located below the cockpit; a second attachment point behind the sliding cockpit door bears the shock-absorbing strut that is fitted to the wheel hub. The fixed tailwheel is located just behind the cabin, considerably farther forward than in the Blackhawk and resulting in a wheelbase identical to that of the Kaman SH-2 Seasprite (LAMPS I). The landing gear is also lighter than that of the Blackhawk.

The fuselage has a side-by-side, two-seat flight deck forward; the pilot is seated to the starboard and the Airborne Tactical Officer (ATO) on the port. The Sensor Operator's (SO) position is located in the aft starboard side of the main cabin. The aircraft's electronics and sensors are linked and subdivided into four groups: navigation, mission avionics, data handling and display, and communications. Navigation equipment includes the Teledyne Ryan AN/APN-217 Doppler navigation radar, Honeywell AN/APN-194(V) radar altimeter, and Collins TACAN and UHF direction-finding equipment.

Mission avionics include the Texas Instruments AN/APS-124 360° search radar fitted under the flight deck, the Rospatch (now FlightLine) AN/ARR-75 sonobuoy receiving set, and the Raytheon AN/ALQ-142 omnidirectional Electronic Support Measures (ESM). A 25-tube pneumatic sonobuoy launcher is installed in the port side of the fuselage aft of the single cabin window.

An IBM AN/UYS-1(V)2 Proteus acoustic processor is linked to the ARR-75 and the AN/AYK-14 general-purpose digital computer. Sensor data is initially processed on board, then relayed to the Seahawk's "mother" ship over the Sierra Research AN/ARQ-44 data link. The Seahawk thus can act either as the forward-deployed "eyes and ears" of the comprehensive shipboard ASW and ASST processing center or as an independent unit. The aircraft's offensive armament is one or two Mk 46 lightweight ASW torpedoes.

The Norwegian AGM-119 Penguin short-range, antiship missile is being procured for the ASST mission.

Several Seahawks operating in the Persian Gulf in 1987–88 were fitted with dorsal and ventral AN/ALQ-144 Infrared Countermeasures (IRCM), AN/ALE-39 chaff dispensers on the port side of the cabin, Loral AN/AAR-47 electro-optical missile-warning system, and M60 7.62-mm machine guns in both cabin doors. Hellenic Navy S-70Bs operating from *Hydra*-class frigates will be fitted with the Litton AN/ALR-606(V)2 electronic support measures system as well as the Penguin antiship missile.

DEVELOPMENT • The SH-60's initial operational capability was in 1983; its first flight was on December 12, 1979. Still in production with over 470 aircraft ordered for the US Navy and four other navies. Six SH-60Bs were delivered to the Spanish V/STOL carrier *Principe de Asturias* in January 1989 at Patuxent River Naval Air Station, Maryland.

In addition to the US Navy, the S-60, or its commercial variant S-70, is flown by Australia, Greece, Japan, Spain, and Taiwan.

VARIANTS • SH-60B, Quick Reaction Forward-Looking Infrared (FLIR), SH-60F CV-HELO Ocean Hawk, HH-60H Rescue Hawk (USN SAR), HH-60J Jayhawk (USCG), VH-60A (USMC White House VIP), S-70 (military exports S-70A and S-70B), S-70B-2 (Australia), S-70B-3/SH-60J (Japan), S-70B-6 (Greece), S-70C(M)-1 (Taiwan Navy "commercial").

COMBAT EXPERIENCE • 12 SH-60Bs deployed to the Persian Gulf during 1987–88 and flew an average of over 100 hours per month, according to the US Navy.

34 US Navy SH-60Bs and three Australian S-70B-9s operated in Operations Desert Shield/Desert Storm; one was lost during the seven-week war to noncombat

causes. HH-60Hs were deployed in Saudi Arabia for combat SAR.

SPECIFICATIONS •
MANUFACTURER Sikorsky Aircraft
CREW 3 (pilot, copilot, sensor operator)
ENGINES 2 General Electric T700-GE-401 turboshaft
max power 1,713 shp each
internal fuel capacity
     360 US gal (1,361 liters)
WEIGHTS
empty 13,648 lb (6,204 kg)
mission gross weight
     ASW: 20,244 lb (9,183 kg)
     ASST: 18,373 lb (8,334 kg)
max takeoff 21,884 lb (9,927 kg)
DIMENSIONS
rotor diam 53 ft 8 in (16.36 m)
length operating: 64 ft 10 in
     (19.76 m)
     folded: 40 ft 11 in (12.47 m)
width operating: 53 ft 8 in
     (16.36 m)
     folded: 10 ft 8 ½ in (3.26 m)
height operating: 17 ft 0 in (5.18 m)
     folded: 13 ft 3 ½ in (4.04 m)
disc area 2,262 ft² (210.15 m²)
PERFORMANCE
never-exceed speed (VNE)
     sea level: 180 kts (207 mph; 334 km/h)
     at 4,000 ft (1,220 m): 171 kts 197 mph; 317 km/h)
dash speed sea level: 128 kts (147 mph; 237 km/h)
     at 5,000 ft (1,524 m), tropical day: 126 kts (145 mph; 233 km/h)
max climb rate
     sea level, ISA conditions: 1,330 ft/min (405 m/min)
     sea level, 90°F (32°C): 700 ft/min (213 m/min)

ceiling   13,800 ft (4,206 m)
hovering ceiling in ground effect
  ISA conditions: 6,500 ft
  (1,981 m)
  tropical day conditions:
  4,200 ft (1,280 m)
hovering ceiling out of ground effect
  ISA conditions: 3,400 ft
  (1,036 m)
  tropical day conditions:
  1,500 ft (457 m)
range at max takeoff weight, econ cruise,
no reserves
  internal fuel
  sea level: 437 nm (503
  mi; 810 km)
  at 4,000 ft (1,220 m):
  484 nm (557 mi; 897
  km)
  with auxiliary fuel
  sea level: 630 nm (725
  mi; 1,167 km)
  at 4,000 ft (1,220 m):
  678 nm (781 mi; 1,256
  km)
armament   2 Mk 46 torpedoes
radar   AN/APS-124 360° search
  AN/APN-217 Doppler
  (HH-60H/J)

Raven (H-23/UH-12)

The UH-12 (the H-23 Raven in US Army service) is an early-generation helicopter still in limited military and civilian service as an observation and light utility helicopter.

The UH-12 has a two-bladed main rotor with counterbalance weights, a two-bladed tail rotor on the right side of the pipelike tailboom opposite a stabilizer, twin-skid landing gear, and a bubble or "goldfish bowl" cockpit. The tailboom has a reinforcing strut to the top of the engine frame, which is set just behind the cockpit.

No armed versions have been manufactured.

DEVELOPMENT • The Raven's initial operational capability was in 1950; its first flight was in November 1947. It is no longer in production or in US military service, but about 40 remain in military service in Argentina, Colombia, Egypt, Mexico, South Korea, and Paraguay.

VARIANTS • Model 360 (prototype), UH-12A/HTE-1/H-23A Raven, UH-12B/HTE-2/H-23B, UH-12C/H-23C, UH-12D/H-23D, UH-12E/OH-23G/CH-112 (UH-12E/OH-23F, CH-112 [OH-23 in Canadian service]), UH-12E4/OH-23F, UH-12L4.

SPECIFICATIONS •
MANUFACTURER   Hiller
CREW   1 + 2 passengers
ENGINES   1 Lycoming VO-540 piston
  max power   340 hp
WEIGHTS
  empty   1,759 lb (798 kg)
  gross   2,800 lb (1,270 kg)
DIMENSIONS
  rotor diam   35 ft 5 in (10.8 m)
  length   fuselage: 28 ft 6 in (8.69 m)
    overall: 40 ft 8 in (12.4 m)
  height   9 ft 9 in (2.98 m)
PERFORMANCE
  max speed   83 kts (96 mph; 154 km/h)
  ceiling   16,207 ft (4,940 m)
  range   365 nm (420 mi; 676 km)

Huey/Iroquois (UH-1)

The UH-1, popularly called the Huey, is a general-purpose, multirole helicopter that has been produced in greater numbers and flown by more countries than any other helicopter in the West. The Huey has been adapted for air assault, gunship, medical evacuation, Search and Rescue (SAR), Antisubmarine Warfare (ASW), and general utility missions.

Both single- and twin-engine variants are in widespread service. A three-engine prototype was test-flown but not produced. The main single-engine variants are the UH-1B (Bell Model 204) and UH-1D/H (Bell Model 205). The two-blade, semirigid, all-metal main rotor has a stabilizer bar mounted above and at right angles to the blades and an underslung, feathering axis head. The rotor is mounted on the left side of the tail rotor pylon. The rectangular horizontal stabilizer in the tailboom, ahead of the antitorque rotor, is interconnected with the cyclic control and acts as a compensating elevator.

The single turboshaft engine is mounted in a slender housing behind the main rotor mast. The exhaust nozzle is tilted slightly upward.

The semimonocoque fuselage has a short nose, extensive glazing (including "chin" windows for look-down visibility) around the cockpit, and doors on both sides. The cockpit is open to the main cabin, which has large, rearward-sliding doors on both sides. The main cabin can carry troops in jump seats or litters in fold-down racks. Landing gear is parallel skids on tubular struts, with a tail skid at the end of the tailboom.

DEVELOPMENT • The Huey's initial operational capability was in 1958; first flight of the XH-40 was on October 22, 1956. Over 10,100 UH-1s have been built, and it is still in production by Agusta-Bell of Italy and Fuji of Japan and still in service with all US military forces and over 55 other countries.

VARIANTS • X/YH-40, HU-1, HU-1A, HU-1B, UH-1C, UH-1D, UH-1E (USMC), UH-1F (USAF), UH-1H, UH-1H Upgrade, EH-1H Quick Fix IA/IB (US Army Security Agency), EH-1U/EH-1X Quick Fix IIA, HH-1K (USN SAR/SEAL), UH-1L (USN), UH-1M, UH-1N/Model 212, UH-1P (special operations), UH-1V, Bell/Lycoming Fleet/Service Life Extension Program, T800 test bed, CH-118 (Canada), AB204/205 (Agusta-Bell),

204B-2/HU-1H Kai (Japan-Fuji), Bell 533 (three-engine research), AH-1G HueyCobra.

The Swedish designation for their AB205 aircraft is HKP-3.

COMBAT EXPERIENCE • In their assault role, Hueys have seen combat service with US forces in the Vietnam War (where the unarmed variants were known as Slicks) and in the 1983 operation in Grenada. They have also served in the Mideast in Israeli combat and in a number of other combat actions throughout the world. As a gunship, the Huey was used in Vietnam until the AH-1 Cobra series replaced it.

US Army UH-1Hs were deployed to the Persian Gulf as part of Operation Desert Shield. During Desert Storm, three UH-1s were lost, all to noncombat causes.

In February 1989, the UN Transitional Assistance Group (UNTAG) announced the purchase of eight AB205 helicopters to support their peacekeeping operations in Namibia. The aircraft were withdrawn when Namibia completed its transition to independence in March 1990.

In September 1989, 20 UH-1Hs were flown by cargo aircraft to Colombia to bolster antidrug forces in that country. The speedup in delivery of an existing order came after the assassination of a prominent presidential candidate and former guerrilla leader.

SPECIFICATIONS •
MANUFACTURER
Bell Helicopter Textron
Agusta SpA, Milan, Italy
Fuji Heavy Industries, Tochigo, Japan
CREW   2 (pilot, copilot); crewman optional + 11–14 troops
ENGINES   1 Lycoming T53-L-13 turboshaft
max power   1,400 shp
internal fuel capacity
211 US gal (799 liters)

WEIGHTS

empty operating
5,550 lb (2,517 kg)
max useful load
3,950 lb (1,792 kg)
max sling load
4,000 lb (1,814 kg)
max gross   9,500 lb (4,309 kg)
DIMENSIONS
rotor diam   48 ft (14.63 m)
length   41 ft 10 ¾ in (13.77 m)
height   13 ft 5 in (4.08 m)
disc area   1,809.6 ft² (168.1 m²)
PERFORMANCE
never-exceed (Vne), max level, max cruise,
and econ cruise speeds
110 kts (127 mph; 204 km/h)
max climb rate
1,600 ft/min (488 m/min)
service ceiling
12,700 ft (3,871 m)
hovering ceiling in ground effect, standard day
11,100 ft (3,383 m)
hovering ceiling in ground effect, 95°F (35°C)
5,000 ft (1,524 m)
hovering ceiling out of ground effect, standard day
6,000 ft (1,829 m)
range   sea level, standard tanks: 266 nm (306 mi; 493 km)
range at 4,000 ft (1,120 m) with auxiliary tanks: 675 nm (777 mi; 1,251 km)

Huey/Iroquois (UH-1N)

The UH-1N Huey is the twin-engine version of the Huey series of general-purpose helicopters.

The "Twin-Pac" turboshaft installation consists of two turbines driving a single output shaft, either being able to drive the rotor if the other fails. The turbines are mounted outboard of the main rotor mast with the nozzles carried side by side in a single housing. All other features of the Huey UH-1N are identical to the basic Huey.

DEVELOPMENT • The initial operational capability of the twin-engine Huey was in 1970; its first flight was in April 1969. It is still in production in Canada and by Agusta-Bell of Italy and Fuji of Japan and still in service with all US military forces except the Army.

As the Bell 212/412 and the Agusta-Bell AB212/AB212ASW/AB412 Griffon, the twin-engine variant is in service with numerous other countries. More than 1,500 212s and 250 4-blade 412s had been produced by 1992. Helikopter Service A/S of Sola, Norway, assembled 18 Bell 412SPs for the Royal Norwegian Air Force for delivery between late 1987 and April 1990.

In May 1990, Bell Textron and the Argentine firm Chincul agreed to license production of the Bell 212 and 412SP variants. In October 1990, Thailand announced a $330-million contract for 50 more Bell 412SP helicopters.

Poland became the first eastern European nation to order a Twin Huey, taking delivery of two 412s in 1991.

Canada's National Defense Department ordered 100 412HPs in April 1992 under a contract estimated at Can$1 billion. Aircraft deliveries will run from 1994 to 1997.

Over 65 countries throughout the world, in addition to the United States, operate the several Huey twin-engine variants.

VARIANTS • UH-1N/Model 212 (USAF, USN, Canada), Model 412, 412HP (High Performance), AB212ASW (Agusta-built ASW), Griffon/AB412 (Agusta), Model 214, AH-1J SeaCobra (Bell Model 209).

COMBAT EXPERIENCE • Hueys saw extensive combat service with US forces in Vietnam and Grenada. The Israelis have used them in the Middle East.

US Marine Corps UH-1Ns were deployed to Saudi Arabia in Operation Desert Shield. Two UH-1Ns flying from the USS *Okinawa* (LPH 3) were lost in the northern Arabian Sea in October 1990, and one from the USS *Tripoli* (LPH 10) crashed into the Pacific in December while the ship was en route to the Persian Gulf.

During Operation Desert Storm, the UH-1Ns were the Marine Corps' principal light utility helicopter. Some were fitted with Nite Eagle Forward-Looking Infrared (FLIR)/laser designator pods originally developed for the Aquila Remotely Piloted Vehicle (RPV) and used to designate targets at night. During Desert Storm, 50 Marine Corps UH-1Ns—30 flying from shore bases and 20 from amphibious ships—flew 1,016 sorties.

SPECIFICATIONS •

MANUFACTURER
Bell Helicopter Textron Canada, Mirabel, Quebec
Agusta SpA, Milan, Italy
CREW   2 (pilot, copilot); crewman optional + 11–14 troops
ENGINES
UH-1N: 2 Pratt & Whitney Canada PT6T-3B turboshaft
412: 2 Pratt & Whitney Canada PT6T-3B-1 turboshaft
412HP: 2 Pratt & Whitney Canada PT6T-3D turboshaft
max power   1,800 shp total, derated to 1,290 shp (UH-1N) or to 1,400 shp (412)
internal fuel capacity
standard
UH-1N: 215 US gal (814 liters)
412: 330 US gal (1,249 liters)
with optional auxiliary fuel
UH-1N: 395 US gal (1,495 liters)
412: 494 US gal (1,870 liters)

WEIGHTS
empty operating
UH-1N: 5,997 lb (2,720 kg)
412: 6,470 lb (2,935 kg)
412HP: 6,810 lb (3,089 kg)
max useful load
UH-1N: 5,033 lb (2,283 kg)
412: 5,390 lb (2,445 kg)
max sling load
5,000 lb (2,268 kg)
max gross   UH-1N: 11,200 lb (5,080 kg)
412: 11,900 lb (5,398 kg)

DIMENSIONS
rotor diam   UH-1N: 48 ft (14.63 m)
412: 46 ft (14.02 m)
length   41 ft 10 ¾ in (13.77 m)
height   13 ft 5 in (4.08 m)
disc area   UH-1N: 1,809.6 ft^2 (168.1 m^2)
412: 1,661.0 ft^2 (154.4 m^2)

PERFORMANCE
never-exceed (VNE), max level, max cruise, and econ cruise speeds
UH-1N: 100 kts (115 mph; 185 km/h)
max sea-level cruise
412: 124 kts (143 mph; 230 km/h)
range cruise
118 kts (136 mph; 219 km/h)
max climb rate
412: 1,420 ft/min (433 m/min)
412HP: 1,350 ft/min (411 m/min)
service ceiling
412: 13,200 ft (4,023 m)
412HP: 16,500 ft (5,029 m)
hovering ceiling in ground effect, standard day
UH-1N, max takeoff weight: 4,800 ft (1,463 m)

412 at 10,500-lb (4,762-kg) takeoff weight: 9,200 ft (2,805 m) 412HP at 11,900-lb (5,398-kg) takeoff weight: 10,200 ft (3,109 m)

hovering ceiling in ground effect, 95°F (35°C)
412: 2,500 ft (762 m)
412HP: 6,200 ft (1,890 m)

hovering ceiling out of ground effect, standard day
412HP: 5,200 ft (1,585 m)

range

sea level, standard tanks
UH-1N: 231 nm (266 mi; 428 km)
412: 354 nm (408 mi; 656 km)
412HP: 328 nm (380 mi; 607 km)
at 4,000 ft (1,120 m) with auxiliary tanks

UH-1N: 428 nm (493 mi; 793 km)
412: 590 nm (679 mi; 1,093 km)
412HP: 570 nm (656 mi; 1,055 km)
412 with max payload at 10,500 ft (3,200 m) and cruising at 118 kts (136 mph, 219 km/h): 375 nm (432 mi; 695 km)

Blackhawk (UH-60)

The Blackhawk is a multipurpose helicopter that serves as the US Army's principal tactical transport helicopter (replacing the UH-1 Huey series). The UH-60 has been adapted for medical evacuation, reconnaissance, night operations, Search and Rescue (SAR), Electronic Warfare/Electronic Intelligence (EW/ELINT), and general utility mis-

Blackhawk UH-60

sions, with naval variants employed for Antisubmarine Warfare (ASW) and SAR.

The Blackhawk has a forged-titanium main rotor hub with elastomeric bearings and four blades; the blades have a titanium core, are sheathed in composite materials, and have swept tips. The tail pylon has a four-blade, composite-material tail rotor mounted on the right side and canted at 20° to increase vertical lift. The large stabilator has forward swept trailing edges and is fitted near the base of the pylon; it can be pitched up to 40° during takeoff, hovering, and landing. The tailplane design also adds lift during cruise flight. The fixed main-landing-gear legs trail back from a point located below the cockpit; a second attachment point behind the half-door bears the shock-absorbing strut that is fitted to the wheel. The fixed tailwheel is fitted well aft of the cabin, ahead of the pylon-fold hinge.

The UH-60's twin engines are mounted over the fuselage, separated from each other by the rotor drivetrain and transmission. The rotor and engine installation is close to the fuselage; the rotor shaft can be lowered to allow shipment in transport aircraft as small as a Lockheed C-130 Hercules.

The fuselage has a side-by-side, two-seat flight deck forward, open to the passenger/cargo cabin, which has a volume of 410ft³ (11.61m³). Normal troop load-out is 11, but high-density seating permits 14 troops to be carried. For self-protection, 7.62-mm machine guns are fitted on pintle mounts at each cabin door.

The UH-60 has a high crashworthiness. The semimonocoque fuselage is designed to resist deforming in a lateral crash at 30 ft/sec (9.1 m/sec) and a vertical crash at 38 ft/sec (11.5 m/sec). It can also withstand a combined force of 20 g forward and 10 g downward. The main rotor blades are designed to have a 30-minute life after having the main spar severed by a 23-mm shell. The aircraft

also has low-reflectivity paint and a Hover Infrared Suppression System (HIRSS) to reduce its infrared signature, a Sanders AN/ALQ-144 IR countermeasures set, and an E-Systems AN/APR-39(V)1 radar-warning system; chaff and flare launchers provide deception.

Detachable External Stores Support System (ESSS) pylons can be fitted to points above the cabin doors. Up to four fuel tanks carrying a total of 1,360 US gal (5,148 liters) may be mounted for self-deployment up to 1,200 nm (1,380 mi; 2,220 km) away. The ESSS pylons can also carry rockets, four Volcano antitank mine dispensers, or up to 16 Hellfire antitank missiles. An external cargo hook will carry up to 8,000 lb (3,629 kg); typical sling loads include a 105-mm howitzer and 50 rounds of ammunition.

DEVELOPMENT • The UH-60's initial operational capability was in 1978. Its first flight was on October 17, 1974, as a competitor in the US Army's Utility Tactical Transport Aircraft System (UTTAS) program, which selected a successor to the Huey.

The 1,000th production helicopter was delivered to the Army in October 1988. It is still in production, and Sikorsky has a contract to develop, build, and test the MH-60K special-operations Blackhawk.

The S-70C commercial variant has been exported to China, Taiwan, and Thailand. Mitsubishi Heavy Industries (MHI) is producing 64 Japanese UH-60Js, the first of which was delivered in 1991. The Hong Kong Auxiliary Air Force ordered two S-70As in early 1992 for US$23.8 million.

38 Australian S-70A-9 aircraft were assembled by Hawker de Havilland; the first rolled out in April 1988. Also in 1988, Saudi Arabia ordered 13 S-70A-1 "Desert Hawks" from Sikorsky that were delivered in 1990.

In September 1990, South Korea announced plans to coproduce approximately 100 UH-60Ps. After years of competition, Turkey announced an $855-million contract in September 1992 in which Sikorsky would supply 25 UH-60s from its production facility in the United States and Turkish aviation facilities in Murted would coproduce 50.

The UH-60 is flown by the USAF and Army along with four Middle East nations, seven Asian nations, Australia, Colombia, and Turkey.

VARIANTS • UH-60A, UH-60A Credible Hawk (USAF updated to MH-60G Pave Hawk), UH-60L, UH-60P (South Korea), UH-60M (development only), EH-60C Quick Fix (US Army EW/ELINT), HH-60A/D/E Night Hawk (USAF, never operational), MH-60G Pave Hawk/MH-60K (special mission), CH-60 (USMC proposed), YEH-60B (canceled prototype), Embassy Hawk (European contingency aircraft), S-70 (export/commercial), S-70A-1 Desert Hawk (Royal Saudi Land Forces Army Aviation Command/RSLAV), S-70A-9 (Australian AF), S-70/UH-60J (Japanese Air Self-Defense Force/JASDF), WS-70A (Westland license-built).

COMBAT EXPERIENCE • Blackhawks were used during the US landings in Grenada in October 1983 and the military ouster of General Noriega in Panama in December 1989. A total of 25 UH-60s were damaged during the operation in Panama. All but one were back in service within a day.

During Operation Desert Storm, 489 UH-60s (46% of total Army inventory) were deployed to Saudi Arabia. A total of 44,000 flight hours were logged by the UH-60s fleet.

SPECIFICATIONS •
MANUFACTURER   Sikorsky Aircraft
CREW   3 (pilot, copilot, crew chief) + 14 troops
ENGINES   2 General Electric T700-GE-700 turboshaft
max power   1,622 shp each
(transmission rating is 2,800 shp)
continuous   1,324 shp
internal fuel capacity
360 US gal (1,361 liters)
WEIGHTS
empty   10,622 lb (4,818 kg)
takeoff mission
17,323 lb (7,858 kg)
max takeoff   20,250 lb (9,185 kg)
DIMENSIONS
rotor diam   53 ft 8 in (16.36 m)
length   50 ft (15.26 m) without refueling probe
height   12 ft 4 in (3.76 m)
disc area   2,262 ft^2 (210.2 m^2)
PERFORMANCE
never exceed speed (Vne)
194 kts (225 mph; 361 km/h)
max cruise speed
sea level: 160 kts (184 mph; 296 km/h)
hot and high (density altitude of 4,000 ft/1,219 m, 95°F/35°C): 145 kts (167 mph; 269 km/h)
econ cruise speed, hot and high
137 kts (158 mph; 254 km/h)
climb rate   1,600 ft/min (488 m/min)
ceiling   19,000 ft (5,791 m)
hover ceiling in ground effect
standard day 5,300 ft (1,615 m)
hot and high 3,600 ft (1,097 m)
hover ceiling out of ground effect
standard day 10,400 ft (3,170 m)
hot and high 5,600 ft (1,705 m)
range   max takeoff weight, max internal fuel: 324 nm (373 mi; 600 km)
with 460 US gal (1,741 liters) external fuel:

880 nm (1,012 mi; 1,630
km)
with 1,360 US gal (5,148
liters) external fuel:
1,200 nm (1,380 mi;
2,220 km)
armament   guns, Hellfire missiles,
mine dispensers,
rockets optional

Osprey (V-22)

The Osprey is a Vertical/Short Takeoff
and Landing (VSTOL) aircraft being developed for a variety of missions. It is designed to combine the independence
from airfields and the hover capability of
helicopters with the relatively high speed
of conventional aircraft. The V-22 design
evolved from the Bell XV-15 technology
demonstration aircraft. The multiuse aircraft would be deployed for troop carrier,
escort/gunship aircraft, combat Search
and Rescue (SAR), Antisubmarine Warfare (ASW), Air Force special operations
missions, and possibly Airborne Early

Warning (AEW). The Osprey has pivoting pods mounting Allison T406-AD-400
turboprops that drive large, three-blade,
graphite-epoxy rotors in opposite rota-
tions to provide both lift and thrust.
These pods are located at the tips of the
straight, high wing and are cross-
connected by a midwing transmission, so
that a single engine can turn both rotors
if necessary. The pods tilt to a vertical
position for VTOL, transitioning to a
conventional alignment for cruise flight.
Intermediate angles may be selected.

The forward-swept, composite-
material wing has two sections on the
trailing edge. The wing is carried on a
titanium ring above the fuselage that allows the entire wing to traverse 90° to
align with the fuselage for stowage.

The graphite-epoxy tail section consists of large endplate fins that have much
less ventral than dorsal area; each fin has
a rudder set in the upper half of the trailing edge. The stubby horizontal stabilizer
is mounted on the fuselage with an elevator along the entire trailing edge. In order to fold the Osprey into a compact

Bell Boeing V-22
BELL BOEING

package smaller than the SH-3 Sea King, the horizontal surfaces are reduced by 25%–30% and controlled by a GE triple redundant, digital Fly-by-Wire (FBW) flight control system that has triple Primary Flight Control System (PFCS) processors for the control surfaces and triple Automatic FCS (AFCS) processors for stability augmentation.

The Allison turboprops have intake screens and Infrared (IR) suppressors on the exhausts, and rotor brakes. They are equipped with full-authority digital electronic control. The fuselage is relatively conventional in layout but is made almost entirely of graphite-epoxy composites. It is designed to be crashworthy, although weight-reduction measures have reduced the level of protection. The flight deck will be protected against Nuclear, Biological, and Chemical (NBC) warfare effects through a slight internal overpressure.

The Osprey features a flight deck with side-by-side seating forward of an unobstructed, square-section main cabin. A cabin door is located forward, on the starboard side. The rear ramp is fitted in two sections and forms the bottom of the angled, "beavertail" rear fuselage. Cargo can be slung from one or two external hooks. The short, two-wheel main-landing-gear struts retract into the sponsons; the two-wheel nose gear folds to the rear under the cockpit.

The FCS, avionics, and displays are linked through triple redundant MIL-STD-1553B databuses; the aircraft has a built-in Vibration, Structural Life, and Engine Diagnostic (VSLED) system. The flight deck is integrated through a Cockpit Management System (CMS) that includes two AN/AYK-14 fully redundant mission computers, four Bendix Multifunction Displays (MFD), and two Control Display Units (CDU). The controls consist of a thrust/power lever, a cyclic lever, and the rudder pedals.

The radar is the Texas Instruments AN/APQ-168 terrain-avoidance/terrain-following radar; a Forward-Looking Infrared (FLIR) turret is fitted under the chin. The MFD can display a digital moving map system. The pilots will wear an integrated helmet display system that includes Night Vision Goggles (NVG) similar to a Head-Up Display (HUD), and FLIR output; the NVG, FLIR, and a gun turret would be slaved through the helmet. Electronic Support Measures (ESM) include the Honeywell AN/AAR-47 missile-warning system. The V-22 can be armed with a single, integral multibarrel gun and can carry a variety of weapons externally on sponson attachment points.

DEVELOPMENT • The Osprey is one of several controversial weapons systems of the early 1990s whose ultimate production is more dependent on political rather than military considerations. The V-22 is under development; the first prototype rolled out in late May 1988. Its first flight (hover mode only) was on March 19, 1989, after a nine-month delay, and its first full-conversion flight was on September 14, 1989. Four out of five prototypes were flying by the end of 1990; the fifth crashed during its maiden flight on June 11, 1991. The aircraft began rocking after hovering for about one minute; although the two crew members were not seriously injured, the aircraft was heavily damaged.

Flight testing stopped while the cause of the erratic flight and crash was investigated, eventually being attributed to incorrect wiring during manufacturing of the 120-wire wiring bundle for the cockpit interfaces, resulting in false information being fed to the flight control computers. Subsequently, the other four were grounded after more than 1,000 takeoffs and landings and 536 flight hours. Test-flying resumed on September 10, 1991. Bell Helicopter Textron is responsible for the design and fabrication of the wings, engine pods, and prop rotors. Boeing Helicopter Co. is responsible for the fuselage, including the avionics and cockpit design. Grumman Corp. designed the tail group as subcontractor.

In April 1989, the Bush administration eliminated all procurement funding for the V-22 in the FY1990–91 Biennial Budget. Before the cancellation, the Marine Corps had planned to acquire 552 aircraft. In addition, the aircraft's other potential roles were thought to bring the requirement to a total of 900–1,200 aircraft. Altogether, plans included 55 for Air Force use, 552 for Marine Corps use, and 50 for the Navy combat SAR role plus possibly 200–300 for other Navy roles.

The US Army vacillated on its procurement plans for the Osprey, eventually abandoning plans for 231 aircraft when the LHX scout helicopter was placed at a higher priority.

Supporters in Congress managed to secure $255 million in Research and Development (R&D) funding for FY1990. For FY1991, funding consisted of $237 million in R&D and $165 million in advance procurement funds for production-level aircraft that are used in operational testing. In June 1991, the Navy awarded a $36.5-million contract to Allison to improve its T406 engine and $163 million in two contracts to Bell-Boeing, including $88 million that had been rescinded in earlier actions.

An argument to continue developing the aircraft has been to exploit a technological area that the United States clearly leads. Persistent congressional support and the aging of the CH-46 led to further funding for low-rate production.

Japan included in its FY1991–95 five-year plan a request for two V-22s in FY1994 and two in FY1995 (SAR variant) if the aircraft is procured by US services. But funding cutbacks and delays meant no V-22s were procured under that five-year plan.

VARIANTS • JVX (developmental), EV-22 (US Army Special Electronic Missions), HV-22 (USN SAR), CV-22 (USAF), MV-22 (USMC), SV-22 (USN ASW), WV-22 (USN AEW).

SPECIFICATIONS •

MANUFACTURER
Bell Helicopter Textron
Boeing Helicopter

CREW 3 (2 pilots, crewman) + 24 troops

ENGINES 2 Allison T406-AD-400 turboprop
max power 6,150 shp each
internal fuel capacity
standard: 13,650 lb (6,192 kg)
with auxiliary: 29,650 lb (13,449 kg)

WEIGHTS
empty 31,772 lb (14,411 kg)
max internal load
10,000 lb (4,536 kg)
max sling load
2 hooks combined:
15,000 lb (6,804 kg)
2 separate hooks:
10,000 lb (4,536 kg) each
max takeoff 47,500 lb (21,546 kg) VTOL
55,000 lb (24,947 kg) STOL

DIMENSIONS
rotor diam 38 ft (11.58 m)
length 56 ft 10 in (17.33 m)
height 17 ft 4 in (5.28 m)
total disc area
2,268.2 ft² (210.7 m²)

PERFORMANCE
dash speed 315 kts (363 mph; 584 km/h)
cruise speed 275 kts (317 mph; 510 km/h)
ceiling 30,000 ft (9,144 m)
hovering ceiling out of ground effect at 91.5°F (33°C) at 44,980 lb (20,403 kg)
3,000 ft (914 m)
combat radius
HV-22 SAR, with 880-lb (400-kg) payload: 460 nm (530 mi; 852 km)
MV-22, VTOL weight of 44,980 lb (20,403 kg)

range

with 8,300-lb (3,765-kg) payload: 220 nm (253 mi; 408 km); with 24 troops or 6,000-lb (2,722-kg) payload: 430 nm (495 mi; 797 km) MV-22, STOL weight of 55,000 lb (24,948 kg) with 12,000-lb (5,444 kg) payload: 1,085 nm (1,249 mi; 2,011 km) 2,100 nm (2,417 mi; 3,889 km) ferry

Comanche (RAH-66)

The Comanche program is designed to replace the US Army's aging fleet of helicopters, particularly the OH-58 and AH-1. After some cutting back of the number of aircraft ultimately to be built, the program was delayed until at least the late 1990s, with funding directed for research and development.

A team composed of Boeing Helicopters and Sikorsky Aircraft, along with Germany's Messerschmitt-Bolkow-Blohm GmbH (MBB) and a team made up of Bell Helicopters Textron and McDonnell Douglas Helicopters won the contract for the helicopter.

The design calls for a sharklike airframe with a five-blade bearingless main rotor with a high hinge offset to greatly improve maneuverability. In September 1990, MBB was selected to design and produce the Comanche's main rotor, a design based on a prototype system that has a relatively high 9.5% hinge offset. A split torque transmission was adopted to reduce complexity. Also, the rotor head design was changed from a one-piece Pentaflex design to a type that has modular fittings for each rotor blade, permitting a much easier removal of a single blade in case of damage. The Comanche design also has an eight-blade fan-in-fin (also known as a Fantail) antitorque rotor and a T-tail.

To power the Comanche, the Army funded an effort in July 1985 to develop a 1,200-shp, advanced-technology engine (to be used in pairs in the LHX). Following a competition, a design by the Light Helicopter Turbine Engine Company (LHTEC), a joint venture of Allison and Garrett, was chosen. The T800-LHT-T800 powerplant is a dual-centrifugal-compressor design. Following initial design, the engine's output was raised by 12% (to 1,350 shp) to compensate for an increase in empty weight.

Infrared (IR) signature suppression is accomplished by mixing the engine exhaust with cool air drawn through grilles behind the engine.

The Boeing Aerospace/Hamilton Standard Fly-by-Wire (FBW) flight system has two modes: Automatic Flight Control System (AFCS), an altitude-priority mode in which the flight system holds the last-selected altitude even during pilot maneuvering, as in Nap of the Earth (NOE) flight, and Velocity Stabilization (VelStab), a ground- or airspeed-priority mode. Development of other automatic modes was deferred in 1992. Antitorque pedals have been eliminated, the yaw control being provided by twisting the right-hand sidestick controller.

A distinctive feature of the Comanche's airframe design is a composite-material internal box beam backbone that allows many more access doors to be cut in the skin than usual. The manufacturers claim that more than 50% of the surface area can be moved for access. Missile rails are stowed in bays enclosed by retractable doors that are strong enough to serve as work stands.

Avionics will be grouped into a Mission Equipment Package (MEP) featuring Very High Speed Integrated Circuitry (VHSIC). The MEP is expected to account for about 50%–60% of the unit flyaway cost of each unit and is considered as the most difficult element in the overall design.

The Comanche's standard self-defense

is primarily passive. This includes stealth fuselage shaping, a cockpit sealed against Nuclear, Biological, and Chemical (NBC) warfare effects, and the Infrared (IR) suppressors fitted on the engines. Many other elements were to be installed only on aircraft flying in high-threat areas.

Missile configuration ultimately resulted in a maximum of either:

• six AGM-114 Hellfire antitank and two FIM-92 Stinger antiair missiles
• four Hellfires and four Stingers
• two Hellfires and eight Stingers

A 20-mm three-barrel General Electric/GIAT Vulcan II Gatling gun turret is mounted under the cockpit.

DEVELOPMENT • The US Army announced on April 15, 1991, the designation of RAH-66 (for Reconnaissance-Attack Helicopter) and the name Comanche for the Boeing-Sikorsky LH. The Army explained that Comanche Indians were renowned for their skill as scouts and their fierceness as fighters. The initial operational capability for the Comanche is planned for the early 21st century. The award of the prototype contract to Boeing/Sikorsky was made on April 6, 1991.

The LHX competition entered its Demonstration/Validation (Dem/Val) phase in October 1988. In early 1990, the "X" was dropped from the designation to indicate the impending selection of the Full-Scale Engineering Development (FSED) team. In September 1990, however, the Defense Department (DoD) reintroduced a prototype phase in the aircraft's development, postponing FSED until the fall of 1994. Six prototype (four flying) aircraft were to be built at the Sikorsky plant.

Operation Desert Storm showed the Army that aircraft would have little opportunity to be fitted with sensor and survivability systems once fighting starts and

therefore needed to be carried on every flight. Thus, the basic survivability kit was upgraded to include floor armor and a radio-frequency interferometer as well as weight reservation for the IR Countermeasures (IRCM) and active radar jammer. As a result, an additional 144 lb (65 kg) was added for aircraft survivability upgrades and 130 lb (59 kg) for IRCM and the radar jammer.

At that time, the first prototype flight was planned for August 1994 and first delivery for FSED aircraft in October 1995, beginning low-rate initial production in October 1996 and initial deliveries in February 1998. Subsequent decisions by the DoD have pushed production back until the next century.

In September 1993, Army officials warned that the Comanche program may suffer the loss of some of its key features, such as its Longbow radar and stealth properties, because of cuts in the Army's budget.

SPECIFICATIONS •
MANUFACTURERS
    Boeing Helicopters, Sikorsky Aircraft, and Messerschmitt-Bolkow-Blohm GmbH
    Bell Helicopter Textron and McDonnell Douglas
WEIGHTS
    empty   original target: 7,055–7,500 lb (3,200–3,400 kg)
                 revised target: 8,224 lb (3,750 kg)
    mission   11,000 lb (4,990 kg)
ENGINES   2 LHTEC T800-LHT-800 turboshaft
    max power   1,200 shp each (increase to 1,479 shp planned)
DIMENSIONS
    rotor diam   39 ft ½ in (11.9 m)
    length   overall: 47 ft 6 in (14.48 m)
                    fuselage: 43 ft 4 ½ in (13.22 m)
    height   11 ft ¼ in (3.36 m)

disc area   1,197 ft² (11.2 m²)
PERFORMANCE
  minimum dash speed
      170 kts (196 mph; 315
        km/h)
  rate of climb at 4,000 ft (1,219 m) and
  95°F (35°C)
      minimum: 500 ft/min
        (152 m/min)
      max (with uprated
        LHTEC engines): 1,130
        ft/min (344 m/min)

ferry range with 2 450-US gal (1,703-
liter) external tanks
      1,260 nm (1,451 mi;
        2,335 km)
  armament   1 20-mm 3-barrel General
        Electric/GIAT Gatling
        cannon
      AGM-114 Hellfire
        antitank missiles
      AIM-92 Stinger ATAS air-
        to-air missiles

TANKERS

Extender (KC-10)

The KC-10 Extender is a military version of the McDonnell Douglas DC-10-30CF "wide body" civil air freighter. The aircraft is configured for use as a tanker and cargo aircraft, and it differs from the civil versions mainly in the communications and avionics suite, plus the refueling equipment. The KC-10 has the greatest transferable fuel capacity of any operational tanker as well as a cargo payload that was second only to the C-5A Galaxy among US military transports until the C-17 entered operational service in 1993.

KC-10

The low wing has a 35° quarter-chord sweep, incidence that washes out toward the tip, and two-stage dihedral in which the angle is greater inboard of the engines than outboard. The leading edge is lined with nine sections of slats, two inboard and seven outboard of the engine. The crescent-shaped trailing edge has two sections of double-slotted flaps flanking the cruise aileron; the outboard aileron operates at low speeds (i.e., only when the slats are deployed). Five sections of spoilers are mounted on the upper surface ahead of the outboard aileron; they are used both for roll control and for lift-dumping.

The swept fin and two-section rudder are mounted on top of the center engine nacelle, which is located on a short stub on the aft fuselage. The variable-incidence tailplanes are mounted on the fuselage below the engine; they have some dihedral and elevators with inboard and outboard sections. Controls, brakes, and high-lift surfaces are actuated by three fully independent hydraulic systems.

The wide-body fuselage has a constant, circular cross section aft of the pointed nose. The nose slopes up sharply to a nearly stepless flight-deck windshield. The main cargo hold is longitudinally divided with a cargo deck above and fuel cells below. An 11-ft 8-in (3.56-m) wide, 8-ft 6-in (2.59-m) high upper-deck cargo door is located to port and forward. Alternative upper-deck payloads include 75 passengers and 17 standard 463L cargo pallets, 20 passengers and 23 pallets, or a total of 27 pallets. (The C-5A has a max capacity of 36 pallets.) Cargo stores are shifted using powered floor rollers and winches.

Fuel is stored in seven bladders on the lower deck, and there is a refueling station well aft with three positions for the boom operator, instructor (for training), and observer. The refueling boom is located under the centerline of the aft fuselage. It is longer than that of the KC-135, has a maximum fuel transfer rate of 1,500 US gal (5,678 liter)/min, and is maneuvered through Sperry Flight Systems active Fly-by-Wire (FBW) controls. For aircraft equipped with refueling probes, a hose and drogue system with an 80-ft (24.4-m) long hose is fitted next to the flying boom station on the starboard side; it has a transfer rate of 600 US gal (2,271 liters)/min.

A General Electric turbofan engine is housed in a nacelle mounted on a pylon suspended from each wing. As noted above, the third engine is unusually located in a nacelle that stands proud of the aft fuselage. The main landing gear consists of two four-wheel bogies that retract inward into wing root bays and a centerline, two-wheel assembly that is in line with the outboard bogies and retracts forward. The two-wheel nose gear retracts forward.

The Bendix RDR-1FB (AN/APS-133) color weather radar is located in the nose radome. Three inertial navigation systems are provided, along with an Identification Friend or Foe (IFF) transponder and Tactical Air Navigation (TACAN) receiver.

DEVELOPMENT • The KC-10's initial operational capability was in 1981; its first flight was on July 12, 1980. The Air Force procured 60 aircraft under a multiyear procurement contract. The first KC-10 was delivered on March 17, 1981, and the last in April 1990. Since they entered service, KC-10s have sustained fully-mission-capable and mission-completion success rates of over 99%.

COMBAT EXPERIENCE • KC-10s delivered cargo and passengers to Saudi Arabia during Operations Desert Shield/Desert Storm. From August 7, 1990, to April 2, 1991, KC-10s flew more than 380 missions carrying over 1,000 passengers and 12,400 tons of cargo. All of these figures were less than 2 ½% of the airlift total.

However, KC-10s proved invaluable as tankers, especially on the long hauls between the United States and the Persian Gulf.

SPECIFICATIONS •

MANUFACTURER   McDonnell Douglas
CREW   3–6 (pilot, copilot, flight engineer + 3 refueling crew)
ENGINES   3 General Electric CF6-50C2 turbofan
max power   52,500 lb (23,814 kg) static thrust
internal fuel capacity
basic: 36,500 US gal (138,165 liters)
lower-deck fuel bladders: 18,125 US gal (68,610 liters)
WEIGHTS
empty   241,027 lb (109,328 kg)
max payload cargo: 169,409 lb (76,843 kg)
fuel: 356,065 lb (161,508 kg)
max takeoff   590,000 lb (267,620 kg)
DIMENSIONS
wingspan   165 ft 4 in (50.4 m)
length   181 ft 7 in (55.35 m)
height   58 ft 1 in (17.7 m)
wing area   3,958 ft² (367.7 m²)
PERFORMANCE
max speed   530 kts (610 mph; 982 km/h)
cruise speed
490 kts (564 mph; 908 km/h)
ceiling   33,400 ft (10,180 m)
range   max cargo: 3,797 nm (4,370 mi; 7,032 km)
with payload of 100,000 lb (45,359 kg): approx 6,000 nm (6,909 mi; 11,118 km)
refueling radius with fuel transfer
of 200,000 lb (90,718 kg): 1,910 nm (2,200 mi; 3,540 km)
of 100,000 lb (45,359 kg):

approx 3,250 nm (3,742 mi; 6,022 km)
ferry range   9,993 nm (11,500 mi; 18,507 km)
takeoff run   10,250 ft (3,124 m)
landing run 5,350 ft (1,630 m)

Stratotanker (KC-135)

The C-135 family of aircraft features a multitude of variants adapted to a variety of missions. This series is primarily used for in-flight refueling operations but has also been adapted for use as a cargo aircraft and in a variety of research and special-purpose electronics configurations. These aircraft are related to the Boeing 707 commercial airliner series, which evolved from the same design program.

The C-135 family has a conventional planform with low, swept wings swept 35° at the leading edge. Along the straight trailing edge are two sections of double-slotted flaps that flank the midspan flight aileron. The larger, low-speed aileron is outboard of the outer set of flaps. From 1975 to 1988, all KC-135s had their lower wing skins replaced to extend fatigue life to 27,000 hours.

The tall, slightly swept fin has an antenna extending forward from the tip, and a large, powered rudder. The swept tailplanes have inset elevators.

The four turbojet or turbofan engines are mounted on wing pylons. Most KC-135s have been refitted with CFM International F108-CF-100 engines, which give the aircraft a much needed 60% increase in takeoff thrust even as pounds of fuel burned per hour decreases. Others have received JT3D turbofan engines.

The KC-135 carries 31,300 US gal (118,471 liters) of transferable fuel that is passed to receiving aircraft through a Boeing-designed "flying boom." The boom is controlled by an operator lying prone in a compartment under the fuselage near the tail. An assessment of

KC-135
U.S. GOVERNMENT DEPARTMENT OF DEFENSE

KC-135 operations during Operations Desert Shield and Desert Storm in 1990–91 concluded that the KC-135E and KC-135R fleets require wing-mounted probe-and-drogue-type refueling pods.

DEVELOPMENT • The Stratotanker's initial operational capability was in 1957; its first flight was in July 1954. A total of 732 were completed before production ceased in 1966.

Accidents that occurred in September and October 1989 may have involved problems with the fuselage wiring and fuel cells. In the September accident, the aircraft crew was performing a final checklist after landing at Eielson AFB, Alaska, following a refueling flight when it exploded, killing two crewmen. In October, a KC-135 exploded in midair near the US-Canadian border in New Brunswick; four crew members were killed.

The first delivery of the KC-135E was on July 26, 1982, and the last of 186 conversion was in the summer of 1991. The

KC-135R's first flight was on August 4, 1982, and deliveries began in 1984. Most of them are expected to serve well into the 21st century.

The USAF's tanker force had been under the operational control of the Strategic Air Command since the command's inception. However, in the extensive reorganization of the Air Force effective June 1992, the tanker force was transferred to the new Air Mobility Command.

In addition to the United States, France also operates the tanker.

VARIANTS • KC-135A, KC-135E (upgraded tanker), KC-135R, C-135FR (French KC-135R).

COMBAT EXPERIENCE • Hundreds of US KC-135A/E/Rs supported the airlift to Saudi Arabia that initiated Desert Shield in August 1990. During Desert Storm, KC-135s and French C-135FRs refueled strike aircraft from several countries.

SPECIFICATIONS •

MANUFACTURER   Boeing Military Airplane

CREW   4 (pilot, copilot, navigator, boom operator)
3 (pilot, copilot, navigator) + 126 troops (C-135)

ENGINES
KC-135A: 4 Pratt & Whitney J57-59W or -43W turbojet
KC-135E: 4 Pratt & Whitney JT3D turbofan
KC-135R: 4 CFM International F108-CF-100 turbofan

max power   J57: 13,750 lb (6,233 kg) static thrust each
JT3D: 18,000 lb (8,165 kg) static thrust each
F108-CF-100: 22,000 lb (9,979 kg) static thrust each

WEIGHTS
empty   98,466 lb (44,664 kg)
max payload 89,000 lb (40,370 kg)
max fuel load
KC-135A: 189,702 lb (86,047 kg)
KC-135R: 203,288 lb (92,210 kg)
max takeoff KC-135A: 301,600 lb (136,800 kg)
KC-135R: 322,500 lb (146,285 kg)

DIMENSIONS
wingspan   130 ft 10 in (39.88 m)
length   134 ft 6 in (40.99 m)
height   38 ft 4 in (11.68 m)
wing area   2,433 ft^2 (226 m^2)

PERFORMANCE
cruise speed
461 kts (530 mph; 853 km/h)
max speed   508 kts (585 mph; 941 km/h)
climb rate at sea level, KC-135A
4 engines: 1,290 ft/min (393 m/min)
3 engines: 580 ft/min (177 m/min)
max climb rate, KC-135E
4,900 ft/min (1,494 m/min)
time to 30,500 ft (9,300 m)
27 minutes
ceiling   36,000 ft (10,900 m)
radius with transfer
of 120,000 lb (54,432 kg) fuel: 1,000 nm (1,150 mi; 1,853 km)
of 24,000 lb (10,886 kg) fuel: 2,998 nm (3,450 mi; 5,552 km)
ferry range   7,989 nm (9,200 mi; 14,806 km)

ARTILLERY/GUNS

AIRCRAFT GUNS

Several US automatic cannon are manufactured by Martin Marietta and operate on the Gatling principle. Three or more 20-, 25-, or 30-mm barrels are mounted on a geared rotor that is driven by an electric motor. As the rotor turns, the cam follower on the bolt of each rotating barrel follows a fixed cam path in the gun housing, opening and closing the bolt once per revolution. Firing only once per revolution reduces each barrel's rate of fire to below that of most single-barrel revolver cannon. Martin Marietta claims that this continuous rotary motion eliminates the impact loads on gun components and that sharing the thermal duty cycle among three barrels "significantly" increases barrel life. The use of external power eliminates jamming due to a misfired round.

The unusual mechanism of McDonnell Douglas Helicopters' externally powered "Chain Gun" consists of an endless roller chain riding in a "racetrack" around one driven and three idling sprockets. A chain drive slider mounted on the master link travels back and forth in a transverse slot on the underside of the bolt carrier. This reciprocal action opens and closes the breech on the single barrel. This design is said to be simpler and more reliable than other external-power mechanisms.

GECAL .50-Cal Gatling gun

The GECAL Gatling gun is a .50-cal 3- or 6-barrel weapon firing standard NATO .50-cal (12.7-mm) ammunition. Origi-

nally developed for the V-22 Osprey, the weapon requirement for that plane was dropped in 1985. The loss of nine helicopters in the 1983 Grenada invasion prompted the continued development of the GECAL as a means to upgun US utility helicopters.

Power can be obtained from external electric, hydraulic, or pneumatic sources. A self-starting gas drive and 4-ft 3-in (1.295-m) barrels weighing 10.4 lb (4.7 kg) each are also available.

The GECAL fires linkless ammunition. A delinking feeder can be installed to handle standard, linked ammunition.

No range for the GECAL is available, but comparable weapons have maximum ranges of about 7,330 yd (6,700 m).

DEVELOPMENT • Under development by Martin Marietta, Burlington, Vermont.

SPECIFICATIONS •
EMPTY WEIGHT 3-barrel 68 lb (30 kg); 6-barrel 96 lb (43.6 kg)
barrel 7.9 lb (3.6 kg) each
DIMENSIONS length overall 3 ft 10½ in (1.18 m), barrel length 3 ft (0.91 m), width (6-barrel) 8 in (203 mm)
MAX RANGE est. 7,330 yd (6,700 m); tracer burnout 1,750 yd (1,600 m)
MUZZLE VELOCITY 2,900 fps (884 mps)
RATE OF FIRE 3-barrel 4,000 rounds/min; 6-barrel 8,000 rounds/min time to reach max rate of fire: 0.3 sec

M61 Vulcan 20-mm Gatling gun

The 6-barrel M61A1 Vulcan 20-mm Gatling gun has been the standard self-defense gun armament on most US combat aircraft for over 30 years. (The self-powered GAU 4 is virtually identical.) Although used primarily as an air-to-air weapon, the Vulcan is effective against some types of ground targets. In addition, the gun has served as the basis for several land-based towed and tracked air defense weapons (M163 and M167) as well as shipboard Sea Vulcan and Phalanx close-in weapons.

Vulcans are very reliable weapons with long-lived barrels. Although the cannon's rate of fire is a very high 6,000 rounds/min, each barrel fires fewer rounds during an engagement than a high-speed revolver cannon. On the other hand, the revolver achieves its high rate of fire virtually instantaneously, while the Vulcan

has to "spin up," which takes 0.3–0.5 seconds. This spin-up reduces practical rate of fire to around 2,000 rounds/min as well as limiting accuracy during the first half second.

At first, most fighters carried the M61 in a SUU-16 or SUU-23 externally mounted pod, their designs providing little internal room. After experience in Vietnam showed that pod vibrations dispersed the gun's fire too widely, however, room was found within such aircraft as the F-4. Later aircraft were designed for internal cannon from the start.

The M61A1 internally mounted gun is driven by external electrical or hydraulic power; the GAU 4 is self-driven by gun exhaust gases. In most installations, the M56 armor-piercing ammunition is conveyed by a linkless feed from a 1,020–1,200-round storage drum.

In aircraft with the double-ended, hydraulically driven linkless feed system, rounds stored along longitudinal rails within the drum are moved to the gun

Vulcan Gun System
GENERAL ELECTRIC

end by a helix; the helix is made of Fiber-Reinforced Plastic (FRP) in the F/A-18. A rotating scoop disc assembly transfers the rounds to a rotating retaining ring. The rounds travel partway around the ring to the exit unit, which puts the rounds into the chute that feeds the gun. Empty cases are returned to the drum for storage.

DEVELOPMENT • Originally developed under Project Vulcan by General Electric in Burlington, Vermont, achieving initial operational capability on the F-105 Thunderchief in 1958. In production and in service with all US armed forces branches and with several foreign air forces as well.

The M61 gun is in widespread use by the United States and many other nations on the following aircraft (aircraft are listed by the country of manufacture):

USA: A-7 Corsair, AC-130 Spectre, F-4 Phantom, F-14 Tomcat, F-15 Eagle, F-16 Fighting Falcon, F-18 Hornet, F-111 "Aardvark"
Brazil/Italy: AMX attack
Italy: Aeritalia F-104S ASA Starfighter
Japan: F-1, T-2, SX-3 (FSX)
Many other aircraft can accept the M61 in the SUU-16 or SUU-23 externally mounted pods.

VARIANTS • Lightweight M61A1 has linear linkless feed system, AIM-GUNS fire control software changes that expand the effective gun envelope, and PGU-28/B Semi-Armor-Piercing High-Explosive Incendiary (SAPHEI) projectiles.

SPECIFICATIONS •
WEIGHT
SUU-16/A pod w/1,200 rounds: 1,719 lb (780 kg)
SUU-23/A pod w/1,200 rounds: 1,730 lb (785 kg)
GAU 4: 275 lb (125 kg)
M61A1 gun weight
standard: 252 lb (114 kg)
lightweight: 205 lb (93 kg)
DIMENSIONS
SUU-16/A, 23/A2: pod length 16 ft 7 in (5.05 m), diameter 22 in (560 mm)
M61A1: cannon length 6 ft 1.4 in (1.86 m), diameter 1 ft 1½ in (343 mm)
MUZZLE VELOCITY   M56 projectile 3,380 fps (1,030 mps); PGU-28/B 3,450 fps (1,052 mps)
RATE OF FIRE   6,000 rounds/min

M197 20-mm Gatling gun

This 3-barrel cannon is essentially half of an M61 Vulcan Gatling gun. It can be mounted in an M97 turret, an M197 pintle, or installed in the GPU-2/A Lightweight Gun Pod. The turret and pintle variants have linked-belt feed systems. In the GPU-2/A, ammunition is fed from a 300-round storage drum behind the gun; the feed is linkless.

DEVELOPMENT • Produced by Martin Marietta, Burlington, Vermont, with initial operational capability in 1969. Platforms include the AH-1 Cobra/TOW series, the AH-1J/T/W SeaCobra/SuperCobra series, and the OV-10D Bronco observation aircraft. Still in production to equip new AH-1W Whiskey Cobras.

SPECIFICATIONS •
FIRING WEIGHT   GPU-2/A 595 lb (270.0 kg)
gun   132 lb (59.9 kg)
DIMENSIONS
GPU-2/A: pod length 10 ft 8 in (3.25 m), diameter 19 in (483 mm)
M197 gun: overall length 6 ft (1.83 m), barrel 5 ft (1.52 m), diameter 10.8 in (274 mm)
MUZZLE VELOCITY   M197 with 6-in (152-mm) barrels 3,380 fps (1,030 mps)

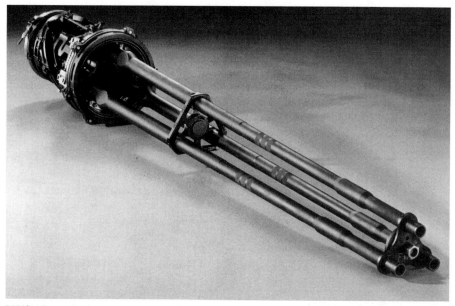

M197 20-mm Gatling Gun
MARTIN MARIETTA

RATE OF FIRE
linked feed   M97 turret: 750 rounds/
              min
              M197 pintle: 350 or 700
              rounds/min
linkless feed 750 or 1,500 rounds/min

GAU-12/U Equalizer

The 5-barrel GAU-12/U 25-mm Gatling gun is the principal gun armament of the AV-8B Harrier II. It is carried in a pod under the Harrier's belly; a linkless linear feed brings the round from the adjacent 300-round storage pod. A Sea Vulcan 25 variant was developed to protect small surface ships but has not entered service.

Compared to the M61 Vulcan 20-mm Gatling cannon, the GAU-12 weighs slightly more, has a lower maximum rate of fire, but fires a heavier round. Reliability was an important consideration, and the GAU-12's goals are a mainte-

nance cycle of 15,000 rounds and mean rounds between failure of more than 100,000 rounds.

At maximum rate of fire, the GAU-12 delivers 33 lb (15 kg) of armor-piercing projectiles per second. In 1985, the US Navy told Congress, in response to its questions, that the GAU-12's 25-mm ammunition was able to penetrate the armor of US M47 Patton and Soviet T-62 main battle tanks.

The gun fires High-Explosive Incendiary (HEI), HEI with Tracer (HEI-T), Armor-Piercing Incendiary (API), AP Discarding Sabot with Tracer (APDS-T), and Target Practice (TP) projectiles.

DEVELOPMENT • In production by the Aircraft Equipment Division, Martin Marietta, achieving initial operational capability in AV-8B in 1985. In service in US Marine Corps, Italian, and Spanish Navy AV-8Bs. (British Royal Air Force GR 5/7s have the Aden 25-mm revolver cannon.)

VARIANTS • Blazer 25 combines GAU-12/U gun (500 rounds ammunition) and eight Stinger SAMs, AN/VSG-2 Forward-Looking Infrared (FLIR) sensor as well as a digital fire control system. Selected for further development as armament for the eight-wheel LAV-AD variant in 1992.

COMBAT EXPERIENCE • The GAU-12 was the largest-caliber airborne gun in Marine Corps service during Operation Desert Storm, during which Harriers expended 83,373 rounds of 25-mm ammunition.

SPECIFICATIONS •
FIRING WEIGHT
system   1,231 lb (558 kg)
gun   270 lb (123 kg)
DIMENSIONS   length overall 6 ft 11 in (2.11 m), diameter 11 in (279 mm)

MUZZLE VELOCITY   APDS-T M791 4,412 fps (1,345 mps); HEI PGU-25 3,610 fps (1,100 mps); API PGU-20/U 3,281 fps (1,000 mps)
RATE OF FIRE   3,600–4,200 shots/min
PROJECTILE WEIGHT
    API PGU-20/U (round) 18.8 oz (533 g), (projectile) 7.6 oz (215 g)
    HEI PGU-22/M792 (M758 fuze) and PGU-25/Mk 210 (M505 fuze) (round) 17.7 oz (502 g) (projectile) 6.4 oz (184 g)
    APDS-T M791 (round) 16.0 oz (457 g) (projectile) 4.7 oz (134 g)

GAU-8/A Avenger

The GAU-8/A 7-barrel 30-mm Gatling cannon is the internal gun armament of the A-10 Thunderbolt II ("Warthog") ground-attack aircraft. It is the largest,

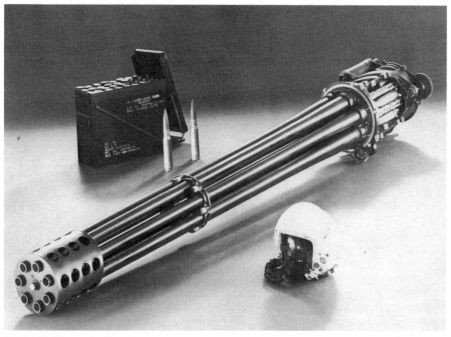

GAU-8/A 30-mm Gatling Gun
MARTIN MARIETTA

heaviest, most powerful aircraft gun in service.

The gun's great size and weight prevent it from being adapted to a gun pod, and no other aircraft has been built to accommodate it. The high rate of fire and weight of projectiles, however, have led to its adoption as the gun armament in the Goalkeeper shipboard Close-In Weapons System (CIWS).

The GAU-8/A was developed as an airborne "tank buster." Its success in that role depends on a high rate of fire and heavy ammunition with significant penetrating power. The gun is properly thought of as part of a system that includes Depleted Uranium (DU) ammunition and the A-10 attack aircraft, which was designed around the gun.

The GAU-8's 1,174 rounds weigh 1,800–2,000 lb (816–908 kg) depending on the mixture of Armor-Piercing Incendiary (API) and High-Explosive Incendiary (HEI) round types. Operating at maximum rate of fire (4,200 rounds/min), the GAU-8 can put approximately 65 lb (29.5 kg) of Kinetic Energy Projectiles (KEP) on a target every second. DU is pyrophoric as well, throwing off sparks as it penetrates armor and creating secondary incendiary effects.

Reliability goals include a maintenance cycle every 25,000 rounds.

DEVELOPMENT • Both candidates in the 1970 A-X competition—the Northrop A-9 and Fairchild Republic A-10—were designed around the Avenger. The A-10 was selected in 1973, and the aircraft (and gun) achieved initial operational capability in 1977. Produced by Martin Marietta. The GAU-8 is no longer in production as an airborne weapon but is being supplied as the gun used in the Goalkeeper shipboard CIWS.

COMBAT EXPERIENCE • The GAU-8 was effective against a variety of targets during Operation Desert Storm. See A-10 Warthog entry.

SPECIFICATIONS •
FIRING WEIGHT 3,798 lb (1,723 kg)
  gun 620 lb (281.2 kg)
DIMENSIONS length overall 21 ft (6.4 m), gun 9 ft 6 in (2.9 m), diameter 14 in (356 mm)
MUZZLE VELOCITY 3,215–3,375 fps (980–1,030 mps)
RATE OF FIRE 1,800–4,200 shots/min
AMMUNITION WEIGHT
  API round: 25.3–26.4 oz (717–748 g), projectile 13.8–15.2 oz (390–430 g)
  HEI round: 23.4 oz (662 g), projectile 12.7 oz (360 g)

GAU-13/A 30-mm Gatling gun

The US 4-barrel 30-mm GAU-13/A Gatling gun is a derivative of the 7-barrel GAU-8/A. It is usually mounted in the Pave Claw GPU-5/A external pod. It has also been developed as a vehicle-mounted weapon but is not in service in that configuration.

Deployment of the GPU-5/A on 18 F-16As during Operation Desert Storm showed some limitations in the installation similar to those exposed in the pod-mounted Vulcan during the Vietnam War. At the time, the F-16's computer couldn't provide the Continuously Computed Impact Point (CCIP) because there is no more room in the Fire Control System (FCS). Pilots resorted to less accurate manual techniques. Moreover, the gun's maximum 1.9-mi (3.05-km) stand-off range would have been too short had the Iraqis been able to use their short-range air defense missiles.

The gun can fire Armor-Piercing Incendiary (API), High-Explosive Incendiary (HEI), and Target Practice (TP) projectiles. These are conveyed to the breech by a linkless feed from double-layer helical tracks (353 rounds total) around the concentric aluminum inner tube housing the gun.

DEVELOPMENT • Built by the Aircraft Equipment Division, Martin Marietta, achieving initial operational capability in 1982.

COMBAT EXPERIENCE • When the Desert Storm ground war began, the 138th TFS (New York ANG) used the GPU-5/A during the first day of the offensive. In the absence of a CCIP, pilots guessed at the compensation for crosswinds and aimed by bullet impact, kicking the rudder to "stir" the stream. After one day's use, the pod was replaced by Rockeye cluster bombs, which appeared to be as effective and could be delivered from higher altitudes.

SPECIFICATIONS •
WEIGHT   loaded pod 1,900 lb (862 kg)
DIMENSIONS   pod length 14 ft 2 in (4.32 m), gun length 9 ft 2 in (2.79 m), diameter 24 in (610 mm)
MUZZLE VELOCITY
HEI PGU-13/B: 3,350 fps (1,021 mps)
API PGU-14/B: 3,225 fps (983 mps)
RATE OF FIRE   2,400 rounds/min; GPU-5/A pod 3,000 rounds/min, max
PROJECTILE WEIGHT   API PGU-14/B 15.0 oz (425 g); HEI PGU-13/B 12.6 oz (360 g)

M230 30-mm aircraft cannon

One of a series of "Chain Guns," the McDonnell Douglas Helicopters M230 is the main gun armament of the AH-64 Apache attack helicopter. It fires a significantly lighter projectile than the A-10's GAU-8 Gatling gun at a lower muzzle velocity. On the AH-64, the M230 is aimed with the Target Acquisition Designation Sight/Pilot Night Vision Sensor (TADS/PNVS).

This design is claimed to be simpler and more reliable than other external-power mechanisms, although vibrations from the M230 have caused circuit breakers to pop in Apaches, and the gun has fallen short of reliability standards. During a five-day exercise in January 1989, the principal cause of Apache groundings was the Chain Gun, which repeatedly jammed or broke down altogether; vibrations from the cannon were said to have tripped circuit breakers, shutting down the targeting systems.

Despite good reports from Operation Desert Storm about the gun's destructive power and general reliability, the General Accounting Office (GAO) reported in October 1991 and April 1992 that problems with the ammunition feed system still had not been resolved. In particular, carrier drive links, which take the ammunition from the box to the gun, bend or break, jamming the gun. In addition, the flex chute broke several times during reliability testing in December 1990–August 1991. GAO's report also stated that the gun had still not reached first article test levels of accuracy, even though the gun had been in production for several years.

The GAO noted some "work-arounds" used in Operation Desert Storm that appeared to reduce failure rates. These included selecting a burst length and holding the trigger until all rounds in the burst had been fired, reducing the ammunition load to 600–800 rounds, or using a different, commercially available lubricant.

Planned upgrades to the M230 hope to improve accuracy and reduce vibration. The Integrated Air-to-Air Weapons (INTAAW) program includes refinements to the turret, gun, and Apache sensors. Integrated Systems Inc. and HR Textron were funded under the subsidiary Precision Aircraft Armament Control Experiment (PAACE) to develop an active recoil attenuation system (HR Textron) and an all-digital turret control system (ISI).

HR Textron's design uses actuators to push the barrel in the direction of firing just before ignition with a force that reduces vibration, while retaining enough rearward force to return the gun to firing position.

The gun fires High-Explosive Dual-Purpose (HEDP) and Target Practice (TP) projectiles. Ammunition more suitable for air-to-air engagements is under development.

DEVELOPMENT • Hughes Helicopter (later acquired by McDonnell Douglas) tested its A-model prototype in July 1973, an improved B model following in 1974. Development of the gun and the helicopter was protracted, the system achieving initial operational capability in 1986. In production by McDonnell Douglas Helicopters Co. in Mesa, Arizona.

COMBAT EXPERIENCE • Eight Apaches struck two critical Iraqi early warning radars to open the air assault of Operation Desert Storm. In addition to the 27 AGM-114 Hellfire missiles and 100 Hydra 70 rockets, the AH-64s fired more than 4,000 rounds of 30-mm ammunition in the raid. In a more general comment, XVIII Airborne Corps officers found that the M230 was "excellent against all artillery pieces." Over 98,000 rounds were

expended altogether, including one that pierced the rear of a T-72 tank turret and thousands that devastated "soft-skinned" vehicles and other targets.

But the gun was very unreliable. In questioning 95 pilots and 82 maintainers for its April 1992 report, the GAO found that 56 pilots (59%) and 72 maintainers (88%) had encountered problems with the gun. Several battalion commanders reported breakdowns of over half of the guns during missions; in one case, all 18 guns suffered failures during the same mission.

SPECIFICATIONS •
TOTAL GUN SYSTEM WEIGHT   123 lb
(55.9 kg)
receiver   63 lb (28.6 kg)
barrel   35 lb (15.9 kg)
DIMENSIONS   length overall 5 ft 4 in (1.64 m), width 10 in (254 mm), height 11½ in (292 mm)
MUZZLE VELOCITY   2,641 fps (805 mps)
RATE OF FIRE   625 (+/−25) rounds/min, cyclic
AMMUNITION WEIGHT
round   12.3 oz (351 g)
projectile   8.3 oz (236 g)

MORTARS

M224 60-mm mortar

The M224 60-mm smoothbore mortar is one of the family of mortars developed to replace equivalent World War II–era weapons. The M224 benefits from US experience in the Vietnam War, which indicated the need for a reliable, lightweight weapon at the infantry company level. It can be fired from the standard baseplate and mount or handheld from a smaller baseplate. The mortar can weigh as little as 18 lb (8.2 kg) and be carried by one man.

The weapon can be either drop-fired or trigger-fired. Both the M64 optical

sight and the range indicator used for handheld firing are tritium-filled, giving good night-ranging visibility.

The M720 High-Explosive (HE) cartridge has four propellant increments that can be broken off to achieve the desired range. Other rounds include the M721 illuminating, M722 smoke, M723 White Phosphorus (WP) as well as two practice rounds. Handheld firing is restricted to a single-increment charge, which yields a 900-m range. The M734 fuze can be set for Proximity Burst (PRX), Near Surface Burst (NSB),

Impact Burst (IMP), or a half-second Delay After Impact (DLY) for ground penetration.

DEVELOPMENT • Begun in 1970 by the Watervliet Arsenal, Watervliet, New York, with design approval in 1973. Type classification came in 1977, the first unit equipping in 1981. The US Army procured a total of 1,590 M224s, with the Marine Corps purchasing an additional 698.

SPECIFICATIONS •
WEIGHT   conventional 46.5 lb (21.1 kg), handheld 18.0 lb (8.2 kg)
DIMENSIONS   bore 60 mm, barrel length 3 ft 4 in (1.02 m)
RATE OF FIRE   max 30 rounds/min for 4 min; sustained 20 rounds/min
ELEVATION   +45°/+85° (800/1,511 mils), traverse 7° (125 mils) to each side
RANGE (M720 HE ROUND)   conventional 3,817 yd (3,490 m); handheld 984 yd (1,340 m); minimum 76 yd (70 m)
SIGHTS   M64 with 17° (300-mil) field of view and 1.5-power magnification

M252 81-mm mortar

The M252 Improved 81-mm mortar is an "off-the-shelf" purchase of the British L16 mortar. The smoothbore, muzzle-loaded weapon replaced the M29 as the standard battalion-level mortar in the US Army and US Marine Corps.

The M252 combines the British barrel and bipod with a US-designed and -built M3A1 circular baseplate and M64A1 optical sight. The barrel has a distinctive flared blast attenuator; the lower half is finned to dissipate heat and reduce weight. Compared to the M29, the M252 is more stable and accurate and fires improved ammunition to a greater range.

Ammunition for the M252 includes not only all of the M29 projectiles but also the M821 High-Explosive (HE) bomb with the M734 multioption fuze and 49-yd (45-m) lethal radius, the M819 smoke

and M853 600,000-candlepower illumination projectiles. To gain a one-shot, non-line-of-sight antitank capability, the US Army tested the Royal Ordnance (in partnership with Alliant Techsystems) Merlin 81-mm terminal homing round beginning in 1991.

50 USMC LAV-25 light armored vehicles carry the M252 mortar mounted in the rear compartment and firing through roof hatches. The vehicle carries 90 mortar rounds. The first was delivered in July 1987.

DEVELOPMENT • US testing began in 1977 and led to type classification in 1984 and initial operational capability in 1987. Manufactured by Royal Ordnance, Great Britain, and Watervliet Arsenal, Watervliet, New York. The US Army procured nearly 1,100 M252s, while the Marines purchased 800.

COMBAT EXPERIENCE • LAV-Ms of the 1st Marine Expeditionary Force supported Marine Corps and Gulf State infantry units on their drive toward Kuwait City in February 1991.

SPECIFICATIONS •
CREW   5
WEIGHT   91 lb (41.3 kg)
DIMENSIONS   bore 81 mm, barrel length 4 ft 6 in (1.37 m)
RATE OF FIRE   sustained 15 rounds/min; max 33 rounds/min
ELEVATION   +45°/+85° (800/1,511 mils), traverse 7° (125 mils) to either side
RANGE   M29 ammunition 6,124 yd (5,600 m); M821 or M889 HE 6,151 yd (5,625 m); M835A1 5,960 yd (5,450 m); M819 5,577 yd (5,100 m); practice 437 yd (400 m)

M120/121 120-mm mortar

The M120 (towed) and M121 (mounted in the M1064 armored personnel carrier variant) mortars are "off-the-shelf" purchases (Nondevelopment Item/NDI) of Soltam of Israel's K6 and TT6 mortars. (The Israeli mortars were in turn derived from the Finnish Tampella designs.) The smoothbore, muzzle-loaded weapon replaces the rifled 4.2-in (107-mm) M30 that dates back to World War II.

Like the 81-mm M252 program, NDI selection strove to cut the deployment time for a new heavy mortar. Unfortunately, initial Army dissatisfaction with the three NDI candidates and funding cutbacks delayed procurement for several years.

The M120's smoothbore steel-alloy tube rests its breech on a circular baseplate and meets a broad-legged bipod about three-quarters up the barrel. Both the towed M120 and carrier-mounted M121 use many of the same components, the principal difference being a fully traversable base in the mortar carrier.

Ammunition consists of M933 High-Explosive (HE) set off by the M745 point-detonating fuze, M934 HE using the multioptional M734 fuze that is common to all new US mortars, M929 smoke, and M930 illuminating rounds. Probable range error amounts to 1% (80 yards at maximum range) while azimuth deflection is 0.45%. The Swedish Strix terminal homing antiarmor mortar round is being studied for possible use in the M120/M121.

M120 is the towed version mounted on a thick, 137-lb (62.1-kg) baseplate. It can be towed using the two-wheel, torsion-bar-sprung M286 trailer that also carries six rounds of ammunition. M121 is mounted in a modified M106A2 mortar carrier (part of the M113 family), which is upgraded to M113A3 standards. The M121 replaces the M30, while 69 120-mm rounds replace 88 107-mm rounds. Conversion plans envision 1,530 M106A1/A2s being converted to M1064 in FY 1993–98.

DEVELOPMENT • Because most of the world's heavy mortars use 120-mm ammunition, the US Army elected to replace the 107-mm M30 with a 120-mm NDI weapon in September 1984. US Army testing began in 1986 of NDI submissions from three teams: Spain's Esperanza y Cia, SA, and General Defense Corp.; France's Thomson Brandt and Honeywell Defense Systems; and Soltam International with Martin Marietta. Test results in 1986 showed that none of the three weapons met the Army's criteria and forced a delay of almost two years.

The Army chose the Soltam–Martin Marietta weapon in April 1988. Watervliet Arsenal, Watervliet, New York, builds the mortar under license while Martin Marietta supplies the ammunition. The 199th Infantry Brigade (Motorized), later the 2nd Armored Cavalry Regiment (Light), deployed the towed M120 in September 1991. An original goal of 2,606 mortars dropped to 1,725 with a decline in the force structure.

COMBAT EXPERIENCE • Israel has used its 120-mm mortars extensively in combat during the Arab-Israeli wars as well as in Lebanon.

SPECIFICATIONS •
CREW 4
WEIGHT total of towed version 709 lb (322 kg) including 390-lb (177-kg) M286 trailer; mortar 319 lb (145 kg)
DIMENSIONS bore 120 mm, barrel length 5 ft 9 in (1.76 m)
RATE OF FIRE sustained 4–5 rounds/min; max 19–20 rounds/min
ELEVATION +40°/+85° (711/1,511 mils), traverse 360° (6,400 mils) in M1064 vehicle
RANGE max 7,918 yd (7,240 m); minimum 197 yd (180 m)

NAVAL GUNS

Mk 15 20-mm Phalanx
Gatling single mount

The Phalanx Mk 15 Close-In Weapons System (CIWS) provides shipboard automatic defense against antiship cruise missiles. Virtually all US combatant and amphibious ships (as well as many auxiliaries) are fitted with the Phalanx. In addition, many foreign combatants are fitted with one or more Phalanx mounts.

The installation of Phalanx CIWS followed deployment of similar, larger-caliber rapid-fire gun systems in Soviet Navy surface warships; the Soviet weapons didn't have the colocated radar-spotting system, however. Most foreign CIWS designs include 25-mm or 30-mm rapid-fire guns rather than the smaller 20-mm cannon of the Phalanx.

Only one Mk 15 CIWS is installed per ship and consists of one or more Mk 16 Weapon Groups, the same number of Mk 339 local-control panels, and one Mk 340 remote-control panel. Thus, if a ship has a Mk 15 Mod 4 CIWS, she has four gun mounts.

The Mk 16 Weapon Group has a modified M61 Vulcan 6-barrel Gatling cannon assembly on a mount and train drive assembly, the search and J-band pulse-Doppler fire control radars housed in a domed cylinder located above the gun, barbette assembly containing the mount's digital computer, and the Weapon Group electronics enclosure. The basic mount does not require deck penetration and can be fitted to a wide range of ships.

The Mk 16's computer classifies threats detected by the search radar and lays the mount on the target azimuth. The J-band tracking radar follows both the target and the M61's bullet stream. The computer uses a closed-loop spotting technique to reduce the difference between the radar line of sight and the projectile trajectory to zero. The mount ceases fire when the target is out of range or destroyed.

Until the early 1990s, the only projectile was the dense Mk 149 subcaliber (12.75-mm) Depleted Uranium (DU) penetrator. A tungsten penetrator replaced the DU version, which lowered costs and simplified storage and handling.

Phalanx can be used against surface targets by using conventional optical target designators, although it is rare to do so.

DEVELOPMENT • Testing of closed-loop concept began in 1970; trials of operational suitability model began in 1976 in USS *Bigelow* (DD 942), achieving initial operational capability in 1980. In production by Pomona Division, Hughes Corp. (formerly General Dynamics Corp.), Pomona, California.

Besides the widespread distribution within the US Navy, ships of the following navies are also fitted with the Phalanx: Australia, Brazil, Canada, China, Great Britain, Greece, Israel, Japan, South Korea, Pakistan, Portugal, Saudi Arabia, and Taiwan.

VARIANTS • Block I, Mod 11 to Mod 14, replaces the parabolic search radar with four-plate back-to-back search radar array for better high-elevation coverage. The mount has greater ammunition stowage, higher rate of fire, and enhanced reliability and maintainability. In full production by October 1987, with all Block 0 to be upgraded to Block I standards by 1997.

COMBAT EXPERIENCE • In its only combat test, the CIWS on the USS *Stark* (FFG 31) did not engage the French-built Exocet AM-39 air-to-surface missiles launched against the ship by an Iraqi aircraft on May 17, 1987. The CIWS was not activated at the time for fear that a non-hostile ship might inadvertently trigger the system's automatic response. By the time the threat became apparent, no time remained to turn the system on.

SPECIFICATIONS •
CREW unmanned
LOADED WEIGHT   13,629 lb (6,182 kg) Mk 16 Block 1
ARMAMENT   bore 20 mm/76 cal
MUZZLE VELOCITY
  Block 0: 3,280 fps (1,000 mps)
  Block 1: 3,600+ fps (1,097+ mps)
RATE OF FIRE   (theoretical maximum) Block 0: 3,000 rounds/min, Block 1: 4,500 rounds/min
ELEVATION   Block 0: −10°/+70°; Block 1: −25°/+80° at 92°/sec
TRAVERSE   Block 1: +155° at 126°/sec
RANGE   1,625 yd (1,486 m)
MAGAZINE CAPACITY   Block 0: 980 rounds; Block 1: 1,562 rounds
FIRE CONTROL   VPS-2 pulse-Doppler, J-band search and track radar with closed-loop spotting, high-speed digital computer; 60-second reaction time from being switched on to being operational, 2 seconds from threat detection

30-mm Emerlec twin mount

The Emerlec mount, fitted with two Oerlikon 30-mm/75-cal rifled automatic cannon, is a US-built antiaircraft gun mount in service in several classes of non-US ships.

The gyro-stabilized mount puts the gunner's position between the two cannon, which are mounted on a trunnion that passes through the cabin behind the gunner. The two barrels elevate and tra-verse together. The front-entry cabin has a controlled environment and a daylight reflex sight or a image-intensifying night sight; the mount can also be operated under remote control.

The Oerlikon gas-operated cannon has a muzzle brake and fires from the open breech position, using propellant gas to unlock the bolt and breech during the firing cycle. It can be clip-fed or belt-fed, the belt feeds being set up from either the left or the right side.

The Oerlikon KCB fires High-Explosive Incendiary (HEI), HEI with Tracer (HEI-T), Semi-Armor-Piercing HEI (SAPHEI), and Target Practice (TP and TP-T) rounds. A below-decks maga-zine holds up to 1,970 rounds of ammuni-tion.

DEVELOPMENT • The Emerlec 30 be-gan as the EX-74 Mod 0, a mount devel-oped for the US Navy's Coastal Patrol and Interdiction Craft (CPIC) program in the early 1970s. Land testing began in 1972 with General Electric EX 28 30-mm ma-chine guns, which were replaced by the Oerlikons. Tests in the prototype CPIC began in 1975; neither was procured by the USN, but the mount design was ex-ported to several navies.

Produced by Emerson Electric, Gov-ernment and Defense Group (later ESCO) in St. Louis, Missouri.

In service with ships in the Ecuadorian, Greek, South Korean, Malaysian, Niger-ian, Philippine, and Qatari navies.

SPECIFICATIONS •
CREW   1
MOUNT WEIGHT   4,200 lb (1,905 kg), gun with feed mechanism 348 lb (158 kg)
DIMENSIONS   barrel length 7 ft 8 in (2.35 m), gun width 8.6 in (218 mm)
MUZZLE VELOCITY   3,543 fps (1,080 mps)
RATE OF FIRE   600–650 rounds/min per barrel
ELEVATION   −15°/+80°, traverse 360°

RANGE
max altitude
    11,483 ft (3,500 m)
max surface 10,936 yd (10,000 m)
AMMUNITION WEIGHT
round   1.9 lb (0.87 kg)
projectile   0.8 lb (0.36 kg)

Mk 75 76-mm/62-cal dual-purpose single mount

The Mk 75 dual-purpose, rapid-fire 76-mm gun is a license-built version of the Italian OTO Melara 76-mm/62 Compact gun. It has been installed in smaller US naval combatants and Coast Guard cutters.

The remotely controlled mount is normally unmanned, although local control through a stabilized optical sight is possible. Enclosing the mount is a lightweight, watertight, fiberglass-domed shield that provides protection against Nuclear, Biological, and Chemical (NBC) warfare effects. The 76-mm gun is water-cooled, has a fume extractor halfway along the barrel and a perforated muzzle brake. Be-

low the gun is a 70-round magazine with 10 additional rounds stored in the feeder drum and hoist.

DEVELOPMENT • The 76-mm Compact gun entered Italian service in 1964 and is in widespread use around the world; the first US Mk 75s, produced by FMC's Northern Ordnance Division, FMC Corp., Minneapolis, Minnesota, equipped *Oliver Hazard Perry* (FFG 7) class beginning in 1977. Some *Perry*s have the Italian-built gun.

Mk 75s also equip *Pegasus* (PHM 1) patrol hydrofoils and the US Coast Guard's *Hamilton* (WHEC 715) and *Bear*-class (WMEC 901) cutters. Two Saudi Arabian patrol craft classes built in US yards have the Mk 75—the *Badr*-class corvettes and the *As-Siddiq*-class missile boats.

SPECIFICATIONS •
CREW   none in turret, 4 below decks
MOUNT WEIGHT   13,680 lb (6,205 kg)
DIMENSIONS   bore 76 mm, barrel length 62 cal or 15 ft 5 in (6.95 m), rifling 13 ft 3.5 in (4.05 m)
MUZZLE VELOCITY   3,000 fps (914 mps)
RATE OF FIRE   75–85 rounds/min
ELEVATION   −15°/+85° at 35°/sec, traverse unlimited at 60°/sec
RANGE
max antiair   39,000 ft (11,888 m) approx at +85°
max surface   21,000 yd (19,202 m) approx at +45°
typical antiair
    18,991 ft (5,788 m)
typical surface
    17,391 yd (15,902 m)
AMMUNITION WEIGHT
complete round
    27.8 lb (12.6 kg)
projectile   14.0 lb (6.4 kg)
FIRE CONTROL   Mk 92 track-while-scan Gunfire Control System

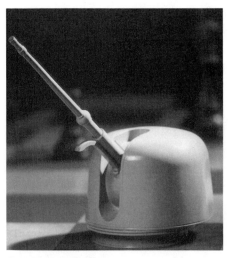

Gun Mount Mk 75
FMC CORPORATION

Mk 42 5-in/54-cal (127-mm) dual-purpose single mount

The US Mk 42 was the principal post–World War II 5-in (127-mm)/54-cal mount in surface combatants and aircraft carriers. It was replaced in new ships by the lighter Mk 45. Most mods have only a surface-fire capability.

DEVELOPMENT • Built by FMC Corp. in Minneapolis, Minnesota, achieving its initial operational capability in 1952 in USS *Mitscher* (DL 2).

No longer in production. In service in declining numbers in the *Belknap* (CG 26) class. The Mk 42 is fitted in ships of several other navies, some of which operate former *Adams*-class guided-missile destroyers and *Knox*-class frigates. These navies include those of Australia, Germany, Greece, Japan, Spain, Taiwan, and Turkey.

VARIANTS • Earlier variants are long out of service.

The Mod 7 was the principal model installed on new construction in the 1950s and 1960s; the Mod 8 added a Gunar Mk 3 radar antenna to the right of the gun.

The Mod 7's mount weight varies from 146,400 lb (66,407 kg) to 183,630 lb (83,294 kg). Mod 8 weights range from 144,900 lb (65,726 kg) to 201,195 lb (91,261 kg).

51 lighter-weight Mod 9 variants for the *Knox* (FF 1052)-class frigates have solid-state electronics for the ammunition handling system. Mount weight is 129,411 lb (58,700 kg).

Above-decks components built by Northern Ordnance Division, FMC Corp., Minneapolis, Minnesota, and below-decks equipment built at the US Navy's Naval Ordnance Station at Louisville, Kentucky.

Mod 10 designates conversions of Mods 7 and 8 that incorporate reliability and maintainability upgrades of Mod 9. Most US ships equipped with Mk 42 mounts received Mod 10 upgrades.

COMBAT EXPERIENCE • Four *Belknap*-class guided-missile cruisers, three *Adams*-class and three *Coontz*-class guided-missile destroyers, and 11 *Knox*-class frigates fitted with the Mk 42 as main gun armament were deployed in the Persian Gulf area during all or part of Operations Desert Shield and Desert Storm. A total of only 750 5-in/54-cal rounds from both Mk 42 and Mk 45 guns during Desert Storm, including practice rounds. The low expenditure indicates that the relatively small projectile and short range of the 5-in gun relegated medium-caliber surface-ship gunfire support to near invisibility compared to other weapons. By contrast, the two *Iowa*-class battleships fired more than 1,000 rounds of 16-in ammunition in three weeks.

In addition, the Australian *Perth*-class destroyer *Brisbane,* fitted with Mk 42 mounts, took part in Operation Desert Shield beginning in December 1990.

SPECIFICATIONS •
CREW   12–14 depending on Mod; Mod 10 has 12
WEIGHT
mount	139,000 lb (63,050 kg) Mod 10
gun	5,508 lb (2,498 kg) Mods 7–8

DIMENSIONS   bore 5 in (127 mm), bore length 54 cal or 22 ft 6 in (6.86 m), rifling 19 ft 1 in (5.82 m)
MUZZLE VELOCITY   2,650 fps (808 mps)
RATE OF FIRE   practical 20 rounds/min, max 40 rounds/min
ELEVATION   −7°/+85° at 25°/sec, traverse 360° at 40°/sec
RANGE
   max antiair   47,247 ft (14,401 m)
   max surface   23,936 yd (21,887 m)
   max with Rocket-Assisted Projectile (RAP) weighing 62 lb (29 kg)
            31,913 yd (29,181 m)

AMMUNITION
40 rounds in two ready service drums with dual-feed automatic loader weight: case 34.5 lb (16.8 kg), projectile 70.0 lb (31.75 kg)

FIRE CONTROL   Mk 68 Gun Fire Control System with SPG-53 radar (GFCS and radar subtypes vary with mod number and modernizations)

Mk 45 5-in/54-cal dual-purpose single mount

The Mk 45 is a lightweight development of the basic post–World War II Mk 42 5-in (127-mm)/54-cal single-barrel, dual-purpose mount. It is the main gun armament of all recent US cruisers and destroyers as well as the *Tarawa* class of helicopter carriers. It is also the largest-caliber naval gun mount in production and in service on US ships.

Compared to the older Mk 42, the Mk 45 mount is 62% lighter. To achieve this substantial reduction in weight (and crew), the design accepted a 20° lower maximum elevation as well as slower elevation and traverse speeds. Maximum rate of fire is cut in half, although typical rates of fire for both mounts are nearly identical. In addition, the conical gun house has been sneeringly described as "an upside-down Dixie cup."

On the other hand, the barrel has more than twice the firing lifetime (7,000 rounds vs. 3,070). Moreover, instead of the 12–14 crew of the Mk 42, the remotely operated Mk 45 has six crew including the four ammunition handlers below decks.

The Mk 19 Mod 0 or Mod 2 gun can fire any existing 5-in/54-cal round including the High-Capacity (HC), illumination, starshell, White Phosphorus (WP), and a lighter Rocket-Assisted Projectile (RAP). Two types of guided projectiles—the Deadeye Semiactive Laser-Guided Projectile (SALGP) and an

Infrared (IR) guided projectile—were canceled before development was complete.

DEVELOPMENT • Manufactured by Naval Systems Division, FMC Corp., Minneapolis, Minnesota. (General Electric's Ordnance Systems Division of Pittsfield, Massachusetts, was a second source during the 1970s.) Achieved initial operational capability in USS *California* (CGN 36) in 1974. Other US ship classes include *Virginia* (CGN 38), *Ticonderoga* (CG 47), *Spruance* (DD 963), *Kidd* (DDG 993), *Arleigh Burke* (DDG 51), and *Tarawa* (LHA 1).

Other navies using the Mk 45 include those of Australia, Greece, and Turkey.

VARIANTS • Mk 45 Mod 1 entered production in 1983 with a fire control system that automatically selects projectiles, sets fuzes electronically or mechanically, varies the firing rate to suit the projectile, and clears misfires. Drum holds 20 conventional rounds or 10 guided projectiles or a mixture of the two types. Other improvements included a fault-isolation system and solid-state optical system.

COMBAT EXPERIENCE • US cruisers and destroyers used the Mk 45 to bombard Lebanese targets several times from late 1983 to early 1984. In 1987–88, Iranian oil platforms were shelled by US destroyers firing Mk 45s. One of these absorbed 1,000 rounds in one bombardment, an expenditure that many argued showed the need for larger shipboard guns.

Many US warships deployed to the Persian Gulf in 1990 under Operation Desert Shield were fitted with the Mk 45 mount as the main gun. Altogether, 12 different *Ticonderoga-*, one *California-*, and three *Virginia-*class cruisers, one *Kidd-*class guided-missile destroyer, 13 *Spruance-*class destroyers, and two *Tarawa-*class amphibious assault ships operated in the area during part or all of Desert

Shield and Desert Storm. A total of 750 5-in/54 rounds were fired from both Mk 42 and Mk 45 guns during Desert Storm, including practice rounds. (See additional comments in the Mk 42 entry.)

SPECIFICATIONS •
CREW   none in mount; gun captain and 1 panel operator below decks plus 4 handlers in ammunition handling room
MOUNT WEIGHT   49,000 lb (22,226 kg)
DIMENSIONS   bore 5 in (127 mm), bore length 54 cal or 22 ft 6 in (6.86 m), rifling 19 ft 1 in (5.82 m)
MUZZLE VELOCITY   2,500 fps (762 mps)
RATE OF FIRE   16–20 rounds/min
ELEVATION   −15°/+65° at 20°/sec, traverse 170° to either side of centerline at 30°/sec
RANGE
antiair   47,245 ft (14,400 m)
surface   23,936 yd (21,887 m)
RAP   31,913 yd (29,181 m)
AMMUNITION WEIGHT
standard projectile weight 70.0 lb (31.75 kg), RAP 62.0 lb (28.12 kg) 20 rounds in ready service drum in mount; drum can be refilled during firing
FIRE CONTROL   Mk 86 digital Gun Fire Control System (GFCS) with SPQ-9 search and SPG-60 tracking radars; EP-2 operator's station; DDG-51s have Mk 160 using data from SPS-67 or SPY-1D radars

SELF-PROPELLED GUNS AND HOWITZERS

M44 155-mm howitzer

The M44 155-mm self-propelled howitzer began development immediately after World War II to incorporate lessons learned in that conflict. It uses several of the same chassis and automotive components as the M41 light tank and the M52 105-mm self-propelled howitzer, which were also developed shortly after the war.

The engine of the M44 is located in the front of the vehicle, with the open-top gun/crew compartment at the rear. The driver is seated on the left side, with the commander, who also acts as the antiaircraft gunner, directly behind him. When firing, the spade at the rear of the hull is lowered and the back of the gun compartment is folded down to form a platform for the crew to operate the gun.

The M45 23-cal howitzer has a Welin stepped-thread interrupted-screw breech and fires a variety of ammunition including High-Explosive (HE) M107 and M449, illuminating M118, and smoke White Phosphorus (WP) M110.

DEVELOPMENT • Began in 1947 as T99; adoption of M41 chassis led to its redesignation as T99E1. The first 250 built as T99E1 did not meet requirements and were modified as T194, which was later type-classified as M44 in 1953. 358 T194s were built, achieving initial operational capability in the early 1950s. A total of 608 T99E1/T194s (later designated as M44) were manufactured by Massey Harris.

No US M44s were substantially modified before they were replaced by M109s beginning in 1962, but Turkish M44s are getting diesel engines and a longer howitzer barrel.

VARIANTS • The M44A1, powered by a Continental AOSI-895-5 fuel-injected gasoline engine, entered service in 1956. Most M44s were later refitted with AOSI-895-5 engines.

M44T is a German-developed upgrade locally produced in Turkey that includes a 450-hp V-6 diesel engine and fuel capacity raised to 206 US gal (780 liters); cruising range is increased more than fivefold to 385 mi (620 km). The longer Rheinmetall 39-cal howitzer barrel can fire a standard HE projectile to 26,246 yd (24,000 m) and an extended-range projectile to 32,808 yd (30,000 m).

SPECIFICATIONS •

CREW 5

COMBAT WEIGHT 62,500 lb (28,350 kg)

ground pressure
9.40 lb/in² (0.66 kg/cm²)

DIMENSIONS
length 20 ft 2 in (6.16 m)
width 10 ft 8 in (3.24 m)
height 10 ft 2 in (3.11 m)
length of track on ground
12 ft 6 in (3.8 m)
ground clearance
19 in (483 mm)
track width 25 in (635 mm)

MAIN ARMAMENT M45 155-mm/23-cal rifled howitzer with 24 rounds
elevation −5°/+65° (−89 mils/1,156 mils), traverse 30° (533 mils) to either side

muzzle velocity
1,850 fps (564 mps)

rate of fire
1 round/min

max range 15,967 yd (14,600 m)

projectile weight
M118 101.0 lb (46.26 kg); M110 97.0 lb (44.40 kg); M449 94.2 lb (43.09 kg); M107 94.1 lb (42.91 kg)

SECONDARY ARMAMENT 12.7-mm antiaircraft machine gun with 900 rounds

ARMOR 12.7 mm

POWERPLANT Continental AOS-895-3 or AOSI-895-5 500-hp air-cooled, 6-cylinder gasoline engine, manual Allison CD-500-3 cross-drive transmission with 4 forward/2 reverse gears

power-to-weight ratio
17.63 hp/metric ton

SUSPENSION (EACH SIDE) torsion bar, 6 road wheels, front drive, sixth wheel acting as idler, 4 return rollers

SPEED 35 mph (56 km/h), range 76 mi (122 km)

OBSTACLE CLEARANCE vertical 2 ft 6 in (0.76 m), gradient 60%, trench 6 ft (1.83 m), fording 3 ft 4 in (1.01 m)

M109 Paladin 155-mm howitzer

The widely used M109 carries a 155-mm howitzer and has been the principal self-propelled artillery support for US Army divisions since the early 1960s. In addition, 30 other national armies operate one or more variants. It is a large, tracked vehicle with a fully traversable turret and prominent bustle. Early variants had a short, 23-cal barrel with a D-shaped fume extractor and single-baffle muzzle brake; later versions, including the M109A6 *Paladin,* have a 39-cal barrel with cylindrical fume extractor.

The M109A6 *Paladin* arises from the Howitzer Improvement Program (HIP) in which A2 hulls are refurbished and mated with a new turret being built by United Defense. The first armament modification phase substitutes the M284 gun for the A2/A3's M185 and strengthens the gun mount to prevent barrel rotation with maximum charge. Later armament options include the XM283, which has the same interior ballistics as the M284, but is more reliable, and the XM282, a 58-cal cannon capable of firing M864 base-bleed projectiles to 28 mi (45 km).

Paladin's Automatic Fire Control Sys-

M109 Paladin 155-mm Self-Propelled Howitzer
U.S. GOVERNMENT DEPARTMENT OF DEFENSE

tem (AFCS) permits 0.6 mi (1 km) separation between vehicles, improving battery survivability while still coordinating fires. At first, the AFCS was plagued by software problems and random computer lockups that could be solved only by shutting down the entire system and rebooting.

Du Pont Kevlar and rolled homogeneous steel armor were added and the suspension strengthened. Upgrades to cooling, electrical, and hydraulic systems as well as fire suppression and anti-NBC improve reliability and protection.

The gun fires rounds weighing between 94.6 and 103.2 lb (42.9 to 46.8 kg). These include High-Explosive (HE), M692/M731 HE Area Denial Artillery Munition (ADAM), M718/M741 Anti-tank Remote Antiarmor Mine System (AT-RAAMS), M549A1 Rocket-Assisted HE (HERA), M864 Dual-Purpose Improved Conventional Munitions (DPICM) carrying submunitions, Cop-

perhead Cannon-Launched Guided Projectiles (CLGP), nuclear, XM867 Artillery-Delivered Expendable Communications Jammer (ADEXJAM) submunitions, chemical, smoke, and illumination rounds.

DEVELOPMENT • The first M109s entered service in 1963. More than 2,000 were manufactured by three automobile companies. M109A1 and later variants have been built by BMY Combat Systems (formerly Bowen-McLaughlin-York) of York, Pennsylvania. Samsung Shipbuilding and Heavy Industries (SHI) is assembling up to 1,000 M109A2 howitzers. German, Italian, Norwegian, and Swiss M109s have been subjected to modification programs as well.

VARIANTS • M109A1   (1970)   with longer M185 155-mm gun and elevation, traversing, and suspension improvements; M109A2 (1978) features many detail improvements including larger turret bustle that carries 36 rounds; M109A3 (1980) has improved M178 mounting; designation also applies to retrofitted models; M109A4 737 US Reserve Component howitzers refitted under the NBC and Reliability, Availability, and Maintainability (RAM) program completed in FY1992; M109A5 further upgrade of M109A4 completed in FY1993 to bring the cannon and gun mount up to A6 standard.

COMBAT EXPERIENCE • M109s have seen service in many conflicts. Israeli forces have operated M109s in several Middle East wars, and Iranian and Iraqi forces (the latter through capture) battled each other in the 1980s. US operations include virtually the entire Vietnam War as well as Operations Desert Shield/Desert Storm.

Over 500 US and British M109s (including 24 Marine Corps vehicles) were employed in Desert Shield/Desert Storm. US forces found that the M185 howitzer's relatively short range put the Iraqi artillery out of reach of all but full-charge or rocket-assisted projectiles during the pre-ground war bombardment phase.

The range mismatch proved to be inconsequential once the land offensive began, however, as the Iraqi artillery was unable to maneuver under the coalition's air assault. The 155-mm M864 DPICM munitions were widely used and proved very effective against Iraqi artillery, especially when fired together with Multiple-Launch Rocket System (MLRS) batteries. The relatively few (90) Copperhead projectiles fired reflected the M901 Fire Support Vehicle's (FSV) difficulties in keeping up with the advance.

British 155-mm howitzers (most or all of them M109s) fired approximately 10,000 rounds during preparations for the ground war and the ground war itself.

In addition, Saudi M109s supported the US Marine Corps–Saudi offensive into eastern Kuwait.

SPECIFICATIONS •
CREW 6 (commander, gunner, 3 ammunition servers, driver)
COMBAT WEIGHT
M109A2/A3: 55,000 lb (24,948 kg)
Paladin: 63,300 lb (28,712 kg)
DIMENSIONS
hull length   20 ft 4 in (6.19 m); with gun forward A2/A3 29 ft 11 in (9.12 m), Paladin 32 ft 2 in (9.8 m)
width   10 ft 4 in (3.15 m)
height with Air Defense Machine Gun (ADMG)
A2/A3 10 ft 9 in (3.28 m), Paladin 10 ft 7 in (3.24 m)
length of track on ground   13 ft (3.96 m)
ground clearance   18 in (457 mm)
track width   15 in (381 mm)
MAIN ARMAMENT
A2/A3: 155-mm/39-cal M185 rifled howitzer with 22 "long wheelbase," 12 conventional, 2 Copperhead rounds
A6: 155-mm/39-cal M284 rifled howitzer with 39 rounds
elevation   −3°/+75° (−53/+1,333 mils), traverse 360° (6,400 mils)
muzzle velocity   2,244 fps (684 mps)
rate of fire (max)
A3: 4/min in first 3 min
Paladin: 3 rounds in 15 sec, 6 rounds/min
range   A2/A3 (full charge): 15,951 yd (14,586 m), max 19,400 yd (17,740 m); with M864 base-bleed 24,059 yd (22,000 m)

Paladin: max 26,247 yd (24,000 m); with M864 24,168 yd (22,100 m); with M549A1 HERA 32,808 yd (30,000 m)

FIRE CONTROL AFCS with ballistic computer/weapon controller, power conditioner, and an Inertial Reference Navigation Systems/Dynamic Reference Unit (IRNS/DRU)

ARMOR light alloy, 20 mm max

POWERPLANT General Motors 8V-71T 405-hp liquid-cooled, turbocharged 2-stroke V-8 engine

power-to-weight ratio
A2/A3 16.23 hp/metric ton; Paladin 14.11 hp/metric ton

SPEED 35 mph (56 km/h), range 214–220 mi (344–354 km)

OBSTACLE CLEARANCE vertical 1 ft 9 in (0.53 m), gradient 60%, trench 6 ft 0 in (1.83 m), fording 3 ft 3 in (1.0 m) without preparation, amphibious with airbags

M107 175-mm gun

The 175-mm M107 was the largest self-propelled gun (as opposed to howitzer) ever to be adopted by the US Army. The M113 gun's barrel extends for 60 calibers (i.e., a length 60 times the diameter), the highest of any mobile artillery piece ever deployed in significant numbers.

Changes in US artillery doctrine led to standardization on the 155-mm howitzer. Although many M110 8-in howitzers remained in service, the M107 had left US service by the early 1980s because of differing logistical requirements and rapid barrel wear caused by the high-velocity rounds. On the other hand, several non-US armies still field the M107.

The M107 shares a common chassis with the 203-mm M110 self-propelled howitzer and the M578 armored recovery

vehicle. The M113 gun's long, slender barrel extends well forward of the hull. Only the driver sits in the hull; his position is forward and to the left of the engine. The other crew members sit exposed around the breech of the howitzer. A hydraulically operated recoil spade can be lowered from the rear to brace the vehicle before firing the howitzer.

The M113 gun has a Welin step-thread interrupted-screw breech. It fires two variants of High-Explosive (HE) projectiles. The M437A1 has 30 lb (13.6 kg) of TNT, while the M437A2 has 31 lb (14.06 kg) of Composition B explosive. Two rounds travel with the gun; reload vehicles supply the rest.

DEVELOPMENT • First built by Pacific Car and Foundry (Renton, Washington), achieving initial operational capability in 1963. Later contracts were awarded to FMC (San Jose, California) and Bowen-McLaughlin-York (York, Pennsylvania). BMY alone built 524 between 1965 and 1980. The US Army and Marine Corps completed converting their M107s to M110s in 1981. Several countries, among them Israel, South Korea, and Turkey, still field the M107.

COMBAT EXPERIENCE • M107s served in several units during the US involvement in the Vietnam War, where their range and accuracy were especially prized for hitting targets in Laos and the Demilitarized Zone from within South Vietnam. M107/M110 commonality allowed some US artillery commanders in Vietnam to tailor their fire support by changing gun tubes on their mounts from one day to the next.

The M107 was the largest artillery piece in Israeli service during the 1973 Arab-Israeli war and saw action on both fronts. It has often fired in cross-border bombardments against Arab forces in Lebanon.

SPECIFICATIONS •

CREW   5 (commander, 3 gunners, driver), with up to 8 more
COMBAT WEIGHT   62,100 lb (28,168 kg)
ground pressure
          11.51 lb/in² (0.81 kg/cm²)
DIMENSIONS
hull length   18 ft 9 in (5.72 m), with gun forward 36 ft 11 in (11.26 m)
barrel length
          34 ft 6 in (10.5 m)
width   10 ft 4 in (3.15 m)
height to top of mount
          9 ft 3 in (2.81 m), traveling 12 ft 1 in (3.68 m) to top of barrel
length of track on ground
          12 ft 11 in (3.94 m)
ground clearance
          18 in (457 mm)
track width   18 in (457 mm)
MAIN ARMAMENT   M113 175-mm/60-cal rifled gun with 2 rounds
elevation   −2°/+65° (−35.5/+1,156 mils), traverse 30° (533 mils) to each side
max muzzle velocity
          3,028 fps (923 mps)
rate of fire
          1 round/2 min normal, 2 rounds/min intense
max range   Charge 1 (1,672 fps/509 mps): 16,951 yd (15,500 m)
          Charge 2 (2,303 fps/702 mps): 24,169 yd (22,100 m)
          Charge 3 (2,992 fps/912 mps): 35,761 yd (32,700 m)
ammunition weight
          147.2 lb (66.78 kg)
SENSORS AND FIRE CONTROL   M115 panoramic sight, infrared night vision devices
ARMOR   20 mm for the driver only

POWERPLANT   Detroit Diesel 8V-71T 405-hp liquid-cooled, 2-stroke, turbocharged V-8 diesel engine, Detroit Diesel Allison XTG-411-2A powershift crossdrive with 4 forward/2 reverse
power-to-weight ratio
          14.37 hp/metric ton
SUSPENSION (EACH SIDE)   torsion bar, 5 road wheels, front drive, last road wheel as idler, hydraulic cylinders as shock absorbers on each wheel, no return rollers, suspension lockout when firing, rear-mounted hydraulic spade lowered when firing
SPEED   35 mph (56 km/h), range 450 mi (725 km)
OBSTACLE CLEARANCE   vertical 3 ft 4 in (1.02 m), gradient 60%, side slope 30%, trench 7 ft 9 in (2.36 m), fording 3 ft 6 in (1.07 m)

M110A2 203-mm howitzer

The M110 8-in (203-mm) self-propelled howitzer is the heaviest field artillery piece in the US Army and Marine Corps. (It is not deployed in a towed version.) It is a large and mobile weapon but has no ballistic protection for its crew. Its numbers are declining because the US bases its artillery doctrine around the faster and more versatile 155-mm howitzer. The M110's partisans note that the 203-mm howitzer has a longer range, higher accuracy, and a more powerful warhead as well as being capable of firing an enhanced-radiation ("neutron") nuclear warhead. But its lower priority scrubbed needed fire control and ballistic-protection updates.

The M110 chassis is identical to that of the M107 175-mm self-propelled gun. In its M110A2 form, the vehicle is dominated by the long, thick barrel extending well forward of the hull. Only the driver sits in the hull; his position is forward and to the left of the engine. The other crew members sit exposed around the breech of the howitzer. A hydraulically operated recoil spade digs into the ground behind the vehicle.

The M201 howitzer has an interrupted-screw breech. Ammunition weighs 200–206 lb (90.72–93.66 kg) and includes M106 High-Explosive (HE), M404 Improved Conventional Munition (ICM) and the M509 Dual-Purpose ICM (DPICM), M650 Rocket-Assisted HE (HERA), M426 GB or VX chemical, and M422 and M753 nuclear rounds. The M404 ICM carries 104 M43A1 antipersonnel grenades; the M509 DPICM carries 180 M42 dual-purpose grenades. NATO nations began deleting nuclear warheads from the M110 arsenal in 1987 (Britain). Then-President Bush ordered the stand-down of all artillery-fired nuclear warheads in September 1991.

DEVELOPMENT • Prototypes were first tested in 1958, and first production units began in 1962. Built by Pacific Car and Foundry in Renton, Washington, FMC in San Jose, California (M110 only), and Bowen-McLaughlin-York in York, Pennsylvania (M110 and M110A1/A2 new construction and conversions). The M110 achieved its initial operational capability in 1963, with the M110A1 in 1977.

Construction of about 750 M110s ended in the late 1960s; the new M110A1/A2s were completed in the early 1980s. License production of 201 M110A2s in mid-1980s by Komatsu (vehicle) and Japan Steel Works (gun mount). Approximately 2,000 M110 series were built in all.

Although it is being phased out of US service, 15 other countries continue to operate the M110.

VARIANTS • M110 was the original production variant's howitzer with a shorter, 25-cal barrel and lower muzzle velocity and range. None remains in service.

M110A1/A2 has a 40-cal barrel with double-slotted muzzle brake and the ability to fire a Zone 9 charge for greater range than the Zone 8 charge of the A1.

Cost for converting each vehicle was $100,000.

COMBAT EXPERIENCE • The commonality of the M110 and M107 mounts and vehicles allowed some US artillery commanders in Vietnam to tailor their fire support by changing gun tubes on their mounts from one day to the next. Because they had no overhead protection, M110 crews usually created mobile foxholes on their vehicles with sandbags and fired from bunkered positions.

96 US Army and 12 Marine Corps M110 howitzers began shelling Iraqi positions in Kuwait soon after Operation Desert Storm began on January 17, 1991. The M509 DPICM round proved effective against Iraqi artillery and troop concentrations, often being fired in combination with the Multiple-Launch Rocket System (MLRS).

The Iraqi inability to locate coalition artillery and a lack of aggressiveness (as seen by US artillery personnel) outweighed the difficulties posed by a distinct range disadvantage and the prepared Iraqi fire positions. Massed US and British artillery barrages accounted for a high percentage of Iraqi artillery destroyed during the war. US 8-in ammunition expenditure has not been released; British M110s fired 2,500 rounds of 8-in projectiles.

US Marine Corps M110s were used in cross-border raids, a practice that initially discomfited the commander of the 5th Battalion, 11th Marines. He noted, however, that the 8-in DPICM had greater range and capacity than the 155-mm DPICM fired by other coalition howitzers, which made up for the longer emplacement time and slower rate of fire. The lack of any concerted Iraqi response reduced the risk.

SPECIFICATIONS •

CREW   5 (commander, driver, 3 gunners) + 8 in the associated M548 ammunition carrier

COMBAT WEIGHT   62,500 lb (28,350 kg)
ground pressure
          10.8 lb/in² (0.76 kg/
          cm²)
DIMENSIONS
hull length   18 ft 9 in (5.72 m), with
          gun forward 35 ft 2 in
          (10.73 m)
barrel length
          27 ft ½ in (8.24 m)
width   10 ft 4 in (3.15 m)
height   10 ft 4 in (3.15 m) to top
          of barrel
length of track on ground
          12 ft 11 in (3.94 m)
ground clearance
          15.4 in (393 mm)
track width   18 in (457 mm)
MAIN ARMAMENT   M201 203-mm/40-
cal rifled howitzer with 2 rounds
carried
elevation   −2°/+65° (−36/+1,156
          mils), traverse 30° (533
          mils) to each side
muzzle velocity
          2,333 fps (711 mps)
rate of fire   1 round/2 min normal,
          2+ rounds/min max
range   M650 HERA: 32,808 yd
          (30,000 m)

M509 DPICM: 24,606 yd
          (22,500 m) normal,
          26,247 yd (24,000 m)
          max charge
M106 HE, M404 HE,
          M426 CHEM: 23,293 yd
          (21,300 m)
SENSORS AND FIRE CONTROL   infrared
night vision equipment
ARMOR   20 mm max (est.)
POWERPLANT   Detroit Diesel 8V-71T 405-
hp liquid-cooled, 2-stroke, turbocharged V-8 diesel engine, Detroit Diesel Allison XTG-411-2A powershift
crossdrive with 4 forward/2 reverse
gears
power-to-weight ratio
          14.28 hp/metric ton
SUSPENSION (EACH SIDE)   torsion bar, 5
road wheels, front drive, last road
wheel acts as rear idler, shock absorber on each road wheel, no return
rollers
SPEED   on paved roads 34 mph (55.0
km/h), cross-country 9 mph (14.5
km/h); range 325 mi (523 km)
OBSTACLE CLEARANCES   vertical 3 ft 4 in
(1.02 m), gradient 60%, side slope
30%, trench 6 ft 3 in (1.90 m), fording 3 ft 6 in (1.06 m)

TOWED GUNS AND HOWITZERS

M167 20-mm Vulcan Gatling antiaircraft mount

The M167 Vulcan Air Defense System (VADS) is a US towed, antiaircraft system consisting of an M168 6-barrel 20-mm Gatling cannon with its own M61A1 fire control system mounted in a turret. M167A2 PIVADS (Product-Improved VADS) have a range-only radar, stabilized director-type gunsight, digital micro-processor, and improved elevation and traversing ability to reduce backlash. (Lockheed Electronics was awarded a contract for 285 kits in 1982.) The system is carried on the M42 one-axle trailer and is powered by two 24-volt Nickel-Cadmium (NiCad) batteries (one for the gun, one for the turret and radar).

The gun fires High-Explosive Incendiary (HEI), HEI with Tracer (HEI-T), and Armor-Piercing with Tracer (APT).

DEVELOPMENT • Original   variant achieved its initial operational capability in 1967; the PIVADS entered service in 1987. Manufactured by Martin Marietta; some also built by Daewoo Heavy Industries, Inchon, South Korea. Although it has left US service, the M167 serves in many other countries.

VARIANTS • Basic Vulcan has no range-rate radar, using a lead-computing gun-sight and range update computer. Many of these were exported.

SPECIFICATIONS •
CREW   1 (gunner in turret)
FIRING WEIGHT   3,450 lb (1,565 kg)
DIMENSIONS   6 × 20-mm barrels grouped on a geared rotor mounting with 500 linked ready rounds
length   traveling 16 ft 1 in (4.91 m), barrel 5 ft (1.52 m)
width   6 ft 6 in (1.98 m)
height   firing 5 ft 5 in (1.65 m); traveling 6 ft 8 in (2.04 m)
MUZZLE VELOCITY   3,379 ft/min (1,030 m/min)
RATE OF FIRE   antiair 3,000 rounds/min; ground target 1,000 rounds/min
SENSORS AND FIRE CONTROL   visual tracking and lead-computing gun-sight, VPS-2 radar supplies range and range rate in M167A2
ELEVATION   −5°/+80° (−89/+1,422 mils), traverse 360° deg
RANGE   antiair 3,937 ft (1,200 m); ground 2,406 yd (2,200 m)
PROJECTILE WEIGHT   APT 3.5 oz (100 g); HEI 3.52 oz (103 g); HEI-T 3.3 oz (94 g)

M101 105-mm howitzer

The M101 105-mm towed howitzer exemplifies the staying power of competent and reliable weapons. As the M1, this 105-mm howitzer was first designed in the 1920s but not produced in large numbers until World War II, under the designation M2. After World War II, the weapon was redesignated M101 and remained the principal 105-mm howitzer for several decades in the US Army and Marine Corps. The M101 has been replaced in US service by the M119 Light Gun.

The M2A1 or M2A2 barrel's rifling twists at a constant 1 in 20 rate and has 36 grooves. A horizontal sliding wedge seals the breech. Firing life is 7,500 Effective Full Charge (EFC) rounds.

Ammunition weighs between 38.25 and 46.40 lb (17.35–21.06 kg). Types of ammunition include High-Explosive (HE), antipersonnel grenades (HE-APERS), APERS with Tracer (APERS-T), Rocket-Assisted HE (HERA), smoke, chemical, illumination, leaflet, and practice projectiles. The M546 APERS-T sprays 8,000 flechettes. The M413 Improved Conventional Munition (ICM) carries 18 M35 antipersonnel grenades; the M444 ICM carries 18 M39 grenades.

DEVELOPMENT • Originally recommended by the Westervelt Board of 1919, the M1 was ordered in 1928, modified and redesignated M2 in 1935, began trials in 1938, entered production in 1940, and achieved initial operational capability in 1941. Production at the Rock Island Arsenal ended in 1953 after 10,202 weapons were built. Production to fill further foreign orders, however, did not end until November 1983. Very widely used by foreign military forces.

VARIANTS • The M101 original production model had the M2A1 carriage and the M2A1 model gun, which had a straight barrel.

M101A1 has an M2A2 carriage, which differs from the M2A1 chiefly in the amount of shielding, and the M2A2 gun with a thickened muzzle.

West German M101 modification featured a longer barrel with single-baffle muzzle brake, new breech ring, and new sights. Maximum range was extended 3,085 yd (2,821 m) to 15,420 yd (14,100 m).

COMBAT EXPERIENCE • The M101 saw extensive service in World War II and in numerous postwar conflicts including the Vietnam War. Eight M101s were deployed with Marine Corps units aboard amphibious ships in the Persian Gulf during Operation Desert Storm.

SPECIFICATIONS •

CREW 8

WEIGHT 4,980 lb (2,258 kg)

DIMENSIONS

bore	105 mm/24.5 cal
length	overall 19 ft 8 in (5.99 m), barrel 8 ft 5 in (2.57 m), rifling 6 ft 6 in (1.98 m)
width	firing 12 ft (3.66 m), traveling 7 ft 1 in (2.16 m)
height	firing 10 ft 3 in (3.12 m), traveling 5 ft 2 in (1.57 m)
ground clearance	14 in (356 mm)

MUZZLE VELOCITY M546 APERS-T 1,801 fps (549 mps); M548 HERA 1,798 fps (548 mps); HE, GB, HD, WP, HC, ILLUM 1,550 fps (472.4 mps)

RATE OF FIRE sustained 3 rounds/min; max 10 rounds/min

ELEVATION −5°/+66° (−89/+1,156 mils), traverse 23° (409 mils) to each side

RANGE M548 HERA 15,967 yd (14,600 m); M546 APERS-T 12,686 yd (11,600 m); HE, GB, HD, WP, HC, ILLUM 12,325 yd (11,270 m)

M102 105-mm lightweight howitzer

The M102 105-mm towed howitzer is a lightweight weapon used by US airmobile and airborne divisions. It replaced the M101 in those units.

The M102 features several improvements over the M101, such as longer range, lighter weight, prominent under-

M102 105-mm Lightweight Howitzer
U.S. GOVERNMENT DEPARTMENT OF DEFENSE

slung equilabrators, and a deep-section aluminum box trail that is joined at the rear. A roller at the rear of the trail allows unlimited traverse. In the firing position, the crew raises the two-wheel carriage, lowers a circular baseplate, and stakes it into the ground.

A vertical sliding wedge seals the breech. M137 barrel life is estimated at 5,000 Effective Full Charge (EFC) rounds.

Projectiles weigh between 38 and 42 lb (17.35–19.05 kg). Types of ammunition include High-Explosive (HE), Rocket-Assisted HE (HERA), Antipersonnel with Tracer (APERS-T) round with 8,000 flechettes, M413 or M444 submunition carrier with 18 M35 or M39 antipersonnel grenades, chemical, illuminating, smoke, and leaflet rounds.

DEVELOPMENT • The M102 achieved initial operational capability in 1965. Rock Island Arsenal produced more than 1,200 M102s from 1965 to 1971. 22 more were built for foreign armies in 1980; these services also fielded many surplus M102s.

COMBAT EXPERIENCE • US Army divisions, South Vietnamese, and Cambodian forces all used the M102 during the Indo-China wars. US artillerymen often broke up Viet Cong and North Vietnamese attacks with the devastating M546 APERS-T round, which was also known as the beehive for the furious humming created by 8,000 flechettes.

82nd Airborne and 101st Airborne (Air Assault) Divisions deployed 108 M102s during Operations Desert Shield and Desert Storm. To support the 101st ground campaign in February 1991, the division's artillery commanders used CH-47 Chinook helicopters to airlift the howitzers and 900 rounds of ammunition per battery. The CH-47s acted as prime movers and stayed with the battery. The fast pace of the ground attack meant that the air as-

sault leapfrogging occurred several times. (Obviously, the tactic succeeds best when hostile air or antiair power is virtually nil and ground defenses are in disarray.)

SPECIFICATIONS •

CREW 8

FIRING AND TRAVELING WEIGHT 3,400 lb (1,542 kg)

DIMENSIONS

bore	105-mm/32 cal
length	traveling 17 ft (5.18 m), barrel 11 ft 1 in (3.38 m)
width	6 ft 5 in (1.96 m)
height	5 ft 3 in (1.59 m)
ground clearance	13 in (330 mm)

MUZZLE VELOCITY APERS-T M546 1,801 fps (549 mps); HERA M548 1,798 fps (548 mps); all other rounds 1,620 fps (494 mps)

rate of fire sustained 3 rounds/min; max 10 rounds/min (for 3 min)

elevation −5°/+75° (−89/+1,333 mils), traverse 360° (6,400 mils)

range HERA 16,514 yd (15,100 m); HE 12,577 yd (11,500 m)

M119 105-mm howitzer

The US Army's M119 105-mm howitzer is a license-built variant of the British L118 Light Gun, which was developed to replace the British Army's Italian-made OTO Melara Model 56 105-mm pack howitzer. Airborne and light infantry divisions adopted it in place of the earlier M102, which in turn replaced the last of the M101 howitzers.

It is a relatively lightweight gun that offers a stable platform and good cross-country towing speed. It traverses easily, the gunners rolling the carriage's two wheels along the perimeter of the firing platform by lifting the tubular bow trail.

Helicopters such as the UH-60 Blackhawk (one gun) and the CH-47 Chinook (two guns and ammunition) can carry the M119 in slings. A C-130 Hercules can carry three M119s and drop them by conventional parachute or the Low-Altitude Parachute Extraction System (LAPES).

Supporters of Nondevelopmental Item (NDI) procurement, in which an existing system is bought "off-the-shelf" often point to the M119 as an example of its advantages. The gun required relatively few modifications, and few problems surfaced in testing. Time to field from concept definition was approximately five years, considerably less than similar US-developed weapons.

M119 differences from the L118 include a prominent single-baffle muzzle brake fitted to the muzzle of a shorter barrel (the L118 has a double-baffle brake). The ordnance is percussion-fired, the barrel has 36 grooves, and a twist increasing from 1 in 35 to 1 in 18 as the projectile moves down the tube. (The L118 has a constant twist, 28 grooves, and is fired electrically.) The breech is sealed by a vertical sliding wedge.

The M119 fires projectiles weighing 38.25–43.8 lb (17.35–19.89 kg). The standard M101 family includes High-Explosive (HE), M913 Rocket-Assisted HE (HERA), M546 Antipersonnel with Tracer (APERS-T), chemical, illuminating, smoke, and leaflet as well as M413 and M444 Improved Conventional Munition (ICM) rounds. The M760 cartridge is used to increase the basic HE range to 14,000 m. The XM915 Dual-Purpose Improved Conventional Munition (DPICM) with M80 antitank/antipersonnel submunitions is under development.

DEVELOPMENT • In December 1985, the US Army type-classified the L119 variant as the M119. The M119 achieved initial operational capability in December 1989. (Australia built a similar HAMEL gun for Australian and New Zealand forces, and South Korea manufactures the KH 178 using the L118 barrel.)

COMBAT EXPERIENCE • The British used the L118 during the Falklands War of 1982, firing more than 15,000 rounds. The gun demonstrated a long range for its caliber and proved itself to be accurate and reliable.

The M119 was not deployed to Southwest Asia during Operations Desert Shield and Desert Storm.

SPECIFICATIONS •
CREW 10
WEIGHT   4,100 lb (1,860 kg)
DIMENSIONS
  bore   105 mm/30 cal
  length   gun over trail 16 ft (4.88 m), rifling length 9 ft 1 in (2.78 m)
  width   5 ft 11 in (1.78 m)
  height   gun over trail 4 ft 6 in (1.37 m)
MUZZLE VELOCITY   M546 APERS-T 1,801 fps (549 mps); M548 HERA 1,798 fps (548 mps); HE, GB, HD, WP, HC 1,620 fps (494 mps)
RATE OF FIRE   sustained 3 rounds/min; for 1 min 8 rounds/min; for 3 min 6 rounds/min
ELEVATION   −5.5°/+70° (−98/+1,244 mils), traverse 5° (89 mils) to either side, 360° on firing platform
RANGE   M913 HERA 21,325 yd (19,500 m); HE 12,576 yd (11,500 m); with M760 charge 15,310 yd (14,000 m); minimum 2,734 yd (2,500 m)

M114 155-mm howitzer

The M114 155-mm towed howitzer was originally built as the M1 in World War II and redesignated M114 after the war. The gun was the US Army and Marine Corps' principal 155-mm howitzer until the introduction of the M198 in the early 1980's and was exported to many other countries as well. Although highly regarded for its accuracy and robustness, the M114 falls well short in range compared to later 155-mm howitzers with much longer barrels.

A stepped-thread, interrupted-screw mechanism seals the breech. M114 ammunition weighs between 94.5 and 95 lb (42.91–43.09 kg). The howitzer fires High-Explosive (HE), HE with Antipersonnel grenades (HE-APERS), nuclear, chemical, smoke, and illumination rounds. President Bush ordered the stand-down of all artillery-fired nuclear warheads in September 1991.

To bring the M114 up to date, RDM upgraded more than 200 M114s to an M114/39 standard in the late 1980s for the Netherlands, Denmark, and Norway. Features include a longer barrel (39 calibers vs. 23) with increased rifling twist, a three-port muzzle brake, beefier equilibrators and recoil system, an increase in maximum elevation, and a greater barrel chamber volume. The gun carriage has also been modified to handle the increased forces; as a result, the M114/39 is heavier than the US Army's M198. Unfortunately, the greater stress produced cracks and the Netherlands decommissioned its guns in 1994.

The new gun fires modern ammunition with improved ballistics at a higher muzzle velocity. For example, a Zone 9 charge kicks the 114/39's extended-range, full-bore high-explosive round (ERFB HE) out to 26,903 yd (24,600 m). Add a Base Bleed (BB) drag-reducing tail and an ERFB BB travels out to 33,246 yd (30,400 m), more than double the M114's range.

DEVELOPMENT • In 1919, the Westervelt Board recommended the development of a 155-mm howitzer. Unlike the 105-mm howitzer, which saw desultory development for most of the next two decades, the 155-mm howitzer only began development in 1939 as a departure from World War I–era French-designed equipment. The M1 achieved initial oper-

ational capability in 1942, and more than 6,000 were completed by the end of World War II.

Post–World War II redesignations transformed the M1 into the M114. No US formations use the M114 (having replaced it with the M198), but, like the smaller M101, it still serves in numerous countries. Before Yugoslavia's breakup, its arsenals built a copy of the M114 known as the M65. RDM's 39-cal makeover is the most elaborate updating of this venerable design.

VARIANTS • The M114 designation covers the M1 or M1A1 howitzer, recoil mechanism (M6), and its carriage (M1A1). M114A2 is the standard M114 fitted with the longer barrel of the newer M198.

COMBAT EXPERIENCE • Widely deployed in US divisions in World War II, the M1 gained a reputation for reliability and accuracy. Observers also commented favorably on the M114's accuracy during Korean War bombardments.

SPECIFICATIONS •
CREW   11
WEIGHT
  firing   M114: 12,787 lb (5,800 kg)
                M114/39: 16,755 lb (7,600 kg)
  traveling   M114 12,698 lb (5,760 kg)
DIMENSIONS
  bore   M114: 155 mm/23 cal
                M114/39: 155 mm/39 cal
  length, traveling
                M114: 24 ft (7.32 m)
                M114/39: 32 ft 10 in (10.0 m)
  barrel length
                M114: 12 ft 5 in (3.78 m)
                M114/39: 19 ft (6.045 m)
  width   8 ft (2.44 m)
  height   5 ft 11 in (1.8 m)
  ground clearance
                9 in (229 mm)

MUZZLE VELOCITY
M114: 1,850 fps (564 mps)
M114/39: 2,575 fps (785 mps)
RATE OF FIRE
2 rounds, 1st ½ min
8 rounds, 1st 4 min
16 rounds, 1st 10 min
40 rounds/hr sustained
ELEVATION M114 −2°/+63° (−36/
+1,120 mils), M114/39 −2°/+70°
(−36/+1,244, mils), traverse 25° (445
mils) right, 24° (427 mils) left
RANGE
M114: 15,914 yd (14,600 m)
M114/39   ERFB HE: 26,903 yd
(24,600 m)
ERFB BB: 33,246 yd
(30,400 m)

M198 155-mm howitzer

The M198 155-mm howitzer replaced the M114 as the principal towed 155-mm howitzer in the US Army and Marine Corps. Although the M198 has a leaner profile than the M114, it is 25% heavier and has a greater range. An interrupted-screw breech is fitted, as is a double-baffle muzzle brake.

The top carriage, which holds the gun tube and equilibrators, is anchored to the cradle's two curved arms; the equilibrators are secured to the top of the cradle arms. Twin, stalky elevating jacks are fastened to the bottom carriage and raise the front of the top carriage. A split, box-section trail with recoil spades stabilizes the gun.

The US Army Armament Munitions and Chemical Command (AMCCOM) at Rock Island Arsenal developed a System Improvement (SI) kit featuring 18 modifications, mostly to the gun carriage. Beginning in FY1991, all active M198s were retrofitted with these kits.

The gun fires rounds weighing between 94.6 and 103.2 lb (42.9–46.8 kg). Principal types include M107 High-

Explosive (HE), M692/M731 HE Area Denial Artillery Munition (ADAM), M718/M741 Antitank Remote Antiarmor Mine System (AT-RAAMS), M549 Rocket-Assisted HE (HERA), M864 Dual-Purpose Improved Conventional Munition (DPICM) carrying submunitions, Copperhead Cannon-Launched Guided Projectiles (CLGP), XM867 Artillery-Delivered Expendable Communications Jammer (ADEXJAM) submunitions, nuclear, chemical, smoke, and illumination rounds. The piece has a thermal warning system that monitors tube temperature; it is used to allow greater rates of fire if needed.

DEVELOPMENT • Development began in 1968, and the first prototypes were tested in 1972; initial operational capability came in 1979. In addition to US Army and Marine Corps units, the M198 has been deployed by Australia, Bahrain, Ecuador, Greece, Honduras, Lebanon, Pakistan, Saudi Arabia, Thailand, and Tunisia.

COMBAT EXPERIENCE • The M198's most extensive operational use came with Operations Desert Shield and Desert Storm. The Marine Corps deployed 180 M198 howitzers in Saudi Arabia and another 44 on landing ships in the northern Persian Gulf. 72 M198 howitzers served with the US Army's 18th Airborne Corps artillery during their flank-protection drive north into Iraq. These weapons first supported the French 6th Light Armored Division on the left flank, then shifted across the corps sector to support the US 24th Mechanized Infantry Division operations on the right flank. Operations entailed traveling 150 mi (241 km) cross-country in 36 hours.

As with self-propelled 155-mm and 8-in artillery units, the DPICM was the most highly valued round. Use of the Copperhead was limited by the poor mobility of the M981 Fire Support Team Vehicles (FIST-V) that carry the Ground/Vehicular Laser Locator Designator (G/VLLD). In one instance, however, an Iraqi unit attacked by DPICM took cover in a bunker that was hit almost immediately by a laser-guided Copperhead; the combination inspired a rapid surrender.

SPECIFICATIONS •

CREW 11

FIRING AND TRAVELING WEIGHT 15,791 lb (7,163 kg)

DIMENSIONS

bore   155 mm/39 cal

length   traveling 40 ft 6 in (12.34 m), firing 36 ft 1 in (11.0 m); barrel 20 ft (6.1 m)

width   traveling 9 ft 2 in (2.79 m), firing 28 ft (8.53 m)

height   traveling 9 ft 6 in (2.9 m), firing 5 ft 11 in (1.8 m)

ground clearance   13 in (330 mm)

MUZZLE VELOCITY HE 2,245 fps (684 mps); HERA 2,710 fps (826 mps)

RATE OF FIRE max 3 rounds/30 sec, 4 rounds/min during 1st 3 min, 2 rounds/min sustained

ELEVATION $-5°/+72°$ ($-89/+1,280$ mils), traverse 22.5° (400 mils) each side

RANGE HE 19,029 yd (17,400 m); M864 DPICM 31,933 yd (29,200 m); M549A1 HERA 32,808 yd (30,000 m)

VEHICLE GUNS

M242 Bushmaster 25-mm cannon

The M242 Bushmaster Chain Gun is the principal US light armored vehicle main armament. Although somewhat less powerful than the 30–40-mm cannon fitted in many light combat vehicles, the M242 has proven to be reliable and potent against many types of targets.

The LAV-25 uses the Delco turret, and the M2/M3 Bradley AFV series vehicles use the TBAT-II. Several other turret designs can accommodate the M242, including Creusot-Loire T.25 (France), SAMM TTB 125 (France), Helio FVT 925 (Great Britain), Arrowpointe (Southfield, Michigan), Cadillac Gage (Warren, Michigan), ESCO TAT-251 and TAT-252 (St. Louis, Missouri), and the FMC two-man autocannon turret.

The gun can fire M792 High-Explosive Incendiary with Tracer (HEI-T) and M758 Point Detonating Self-Destruct (PDSD) fuze, M791 Armor-Piercing Discarding Sabot (APDS-T), M793 Target Practice with Tracer (TP-T), and M910 TPDS-T projectiles.

DEVELOPMENT • Contract awarded to Hughes Helicopters (since acquired by McDonnell Douglas) in February 1976, with the first prototype beginning tests in early 1977. The gun achieved initial operational capability in 1983.

VARIANTS • Mk 38 Sea Snake is an M242 carried in a Mk 88 gun mount and fitted in patrol craft and new-construction amphibious and auxiliary ships as general-purpose, short-range armament.

Bushmaster II is a 30-mm cannon under development; 70% of the parts are from the original Bushmaster. It fires standard GAU-8 ammunition, or RARDEN and KCB ammunition with modification.

COMBAT EXPERIENCE • The Bushmaster cannon was said to have been very effective against many types of soft and light armored targets during Operation

Desert Storm's ground war in February 1991. Anecdotal reports even credited the M242 with knocking out some T-55 tanks with the APDS round. Nevertheless, some Army analysts were reported to be suggesting that the main gun be upgraded to 30- or 35-mm.

SPECIFICATIONS •

FIRING WEIGHT   244 lb (110.5 kg), barrel 95 lb (43.0 kg)

DIMENSIONS

length overall

9 ft 1 in (2.76 m), gun tube 6 ft 8 in (2.03 m)

width   12 in (330 mm)

height   15 in (380 mm)

EFFECTIVE RANGE   more than 2,187 yd (2,000 m) against BMP-1 armored personnel carrier

MUZZLE VELOCITY   APDS-T M791 4,412 fps (1,345 mps); HEI-T M792 3,609 fps (1,100 mps); API-T PGU/20 3,363 fps (1,025 mps)

RATE OF FIRE   100, 200, or 500 rounds/ min, cyclic

ROUND WEIGHT   API-T PGU/20 18.8 oz (533 g); HEI-T M792 17.7 oz (493 g); APDS-T M791 16.0 oz (454 g) with 3.7-oz (104.5-g) subprojectile

M68 105-mm tank gun

The M68 105-mm rifled gun is the American version of the British L7 gun and is the main armament of the US M60 Main Battle Tanks (MBT) as well as the first version of the M1 Abrams. It is also the main armament of the Israeli Merkava Mk 1 and Mk 2 MBT. In either its British or American version, the L7/M68 is the most effective tank gun of its generation and will remain a frontline weapon for the foreseeable future.

The 51-cal gun has a fume extractor and, in some installations, a thermal sleeve. The breech system is a drop-block type.

M68 Gun (on Abrams)

The M68 fires M392 Armor-Piercing Discarding Sabot with Tracer (APDS-T), M735 and M774 Fin-Stabilized APDS-T (APFSDS-T) with tungsten penetrators, M833 APFSDS-T with Depleted Uranium (DU) penetrator, M456 High-Explosive Antitank (HEAT), and M494 Antipersonnel with Tracer (APERS-T) projectiles. Chamberlain Manufacturing Corp. has also developed an M900 APFSDS-T round with a DU penetrator and the CMC105 APFSDS-T with a tungsten penetrator (20:1 length/diameter ratio) for export. Mecar's M1060 APFSDS with tungsten-nickel-iron (WNiFe) penetrator was purchased by the Saudi Army.

DEVELOPMENT • The M68 achieved its initial operational capability in the M60 in 1962. It was produced at the Watervliet Arsenal at Watervliet, New York, and in Israel.

VARIANTS • M68A1 was a low-recoil variant developed for the FMC Close Combat Vehicle-Light (CCV-L) and first shown in 1985; the Benet XM35 was later adopted for the production M8 AGS.

COMBAT EXPERIENCE • Like its British progenitor, the M68 proved very effective when used by Israeli M60 and Merkava tanks against Syrian T-72 tanks in 1982. APFSDS rounds sliced into the hull, hitting the carousel autoloader and detonating the ammunition with devastating results.

During the ground phase of Operation Desert Storm, which began on February 24, 1991, US Marine Corps M60A1s knocked out Iraqi T-55 and T-62 tanks in Kuwait, often firing at close range. Saudi tanks enjoyed particular success, with APFSDS ammunition believed to be the M1060 round.

SPECIFICATIONS •
FIRING WEIGHT   2,489 lb (1,128 kg), barrel 1,662 lb (754 kg)
DIMENSIONS   length, overall 18 ft 3 in (5.55 m), tube 17 ft 7 in (5.35 m), recoil 12 in (305 mm)
EFFECTIVE RANGE   APFSDS 90% hit probability 2,187 yd (2,000 m)
MUZZLE VELOCITY   APFSDS 4,921–4,955 fps (1,500–1,510 mps); APDS 4,783 fps (1,458 mps); M456/A2 HEAT-T 3,848 fps (1,173 mps); M494 APERS-T 2,693 fps (821 mps)
RATE OF FIRE   9 rounds/min sustained
AMMUNITION ROUND WEIGHT
M494 APERS-T: 55 lb (24.94 kg)
M456/A2 HEAT-T: 48 lb (21.78 kg)
M392A2 APDS-T: 41 lb (18.6 kg)
APFSDS rounds 37.8–39.7 lb (17.15–18 kg), APFSDS projectiles 12.79–15 lb (5.8–6.83 kg) (M1060 carries 7.3-lb/3.31-kg penetrator)

M256 120-mm tank gun

The Rheinmetall-designed 120-mm, 44-cal smoothbore tank gun is the main armament for the German Leopard 2 and US M1A1 Abrams Main Battle Tanks (MBT). The US Army's eventual adoption of the 120-mm gun reflected a belated concern that adversary tank armor might defeat the effective but smaller L7/M68 105-mm gun. Rheinmetall claims a 60% improvement in ballistic performance over the 105-mm.

The gun is the first heavy-caliber smoothbore gun in Western tanks, and its adoption (in preference to a rifled gun) was prompted by the desire to achieve high muzzle velocities without excessively shortening barrel life. High muzzle velocity, coupled with a higher cross-sectional loading (usually achieved by reducing the diameter of the Kinetic Energy Penetrator/KEP while retaining or increasing its mass), is currently seen as the most effective means of countering increases in armor thickness and quality.

The gun has a cold-drawn, seamless, autofrettaged tube with a chromium inner lining that improves wear resistance while firing fin-stabilized ammunition.

The gun tube's Effective Full Charge (EFC) life was originally set at 500 rounds, but upgrades extended the life to 750 and later 1,000 EFC rounds. Both the fume extractor and thermal sleeve are made of glass-reinforced plastic. The breech type is a semiautomatic vertical sliding wedge.

There is little difference between the original Rheinmetall gun and the American M256 produced under license at the Watervliet Arsenal. The M1 turret mantlet and trunnion bearings were redesigned to accept the M256.

Ammunition for the 120-mm gun is contained in semicombustible cartridges; German and US ammunition is similar. The M256 fires the M829 Armor-Piercing Fin-Stabilized Discarding Sabot (APFSDS-T) using a Depleted Uranium (DU) penetrator and the M830 High-Explosive Antitank, Multipurpose (HEAT-MP).

Olin Corp. developed the GD120 Kinetic Energy-Tungsten (KE-T) APFSDS-T round for export; Alliant Techsystems also has a KE-T round.

DEVELOPMENT • Development of the Rheinmetall gun began in 1964 at the same time the Soviet T-62 introduced the first Soviet smoothbore 115-mm gun into active service. Testing of the German gun began in 1974, and production started in 1979 for the Leopard tank. Testing in the M1E1 tank began in 1981, and production of the M1A1 tank was approved in 1984. First delivery of the M1A1 with the 120-mm gun—designated M256— occurred in 1985.

In production by Rheinmetall in Düsseldorf, Germany, and Watervliet Arsenal, Watervliet, New York. The Rheinmetall design is also fitted in Israel's Merkava 3, Japan's Type 90, and Korea's Type 88 tank.

COMBAT EXPERIENCE • The M256 established a convincing superiority over any other vehicle-mounted weapon during Operation Desert Storm. See M1 Abrams.

SPECIFICATIONS • Total system weight 6,649 lb (3,015 kg), gun 4,200 lb (1,905 kg), barrel 2,590 lb (1,175 kg)
DIMENSIONS
length   overall 18 ft 4 in (5.6 m), barrel 17 ft 5 in (5.3 m)
width   2 ft 5 in (0.73 m)
MAX EFFECTIVE RANGE (EXCEEDED IN COMBAT)
APFSDS-T: 3,281 yd (3,000 m)
HEAT-MP: 2,734 yd (2,500 m)
MUZZLE VELOCITY
APFSDS-T: 5,545–5,616 fps (1,690–1,712 mps)
HEAT-MP M830: 3,740 fps (1,140 mps)
AMMUNITION ROUND
HEAT-MP M830: 53.4 lb (24.2 kg) with 29.8-lb (13.5-kg) projectile
APFSDS M829: 41.2 lb (18.7 kg) with 15.9-lb (7.2-kg) projectile

GROUND COMBAT VEHICLES

AIR DEFENSE VEHICLES

Avenger

The US Avenger air defense system consists of an AM General High-Mobility Multipurpose Wheeled Vehicle (HMMWV or Humvee) fitted with a Boeing Aerospace/General Electric Pedestal-Mounted Stinger (PMS) system. The PMS consists of a GE one-man electrically driven, gyro-stabilized turret with a digital fire control processor. The turret bears two four-round Stinger Surface-to-Air Missile (SAM) Standard Vehicle Mount Launchers (SVML) and an FN M3P .50-cal (12.7-mm) machine gun located under the right launcher. The gunner sits in a compartment between the launchers, tracking through a CAI driven-reticle optical sight.

Under the left launcher are the Magnavox AN/VLR-1 Forward-Looking Infrared (FLIR) system and a Texas Instruments eye-safe CO2 laser rangefinder. In the armored cab is a General Electric Remote-Control Unit (RCU) that can be operated 55 yd (50 m) away from the vehicle.

The system is designed to function with some or all of the subsystems inoperative. The Avenger can fire a second missile at a target without losing the lock if the first round misses.

The Avenger system can be airlifted by several types of aircraft.

DEVELOPMENT • The Boeing/GE entry competed with the LTV Crossbow PMS (also mounted on a Humvee) for the US Army's Line-of-Sight-Rear (LOS-R) component of the Forward Area Air Defense System (FAADS) program. In a refreshing departure from the usual results of FAADS development efforts, both Avenger and Crossbow were reported to have exceeded requirements during testing. Boeing's bid was said to have been as much as $50 million less than LTV's.

In production by Boeing Aerospace in Huntsville, Alabama, achieving initial operational capability in April 1989.

COMBAT EXPERIENCE • Avengers were deployed with US Army units in Saudi Arabia as part of Operation Desert Shield. Because of the rapid disablement of the Iraqi Air Force during the first few days of Operation Desert Storm, no Avenger units fired on Iraqi aircraft.

SPECIFICATIONS •
CREW 3
COMBAT WEIGHT 8,600 lb (3,901 kg)
DIMENSIONS
  hull length 16 ft 3 in (4.95 m)
  width 7 ft 2 in (2.49 m)
  tactical height
    8 ft 8 in (2.64 m)
  ground clearance
    16 in (410 mm)
  wheelbase 10 ft 10 in (3.3 m)
MAIN ARMAMENT 8 Stinger SAM and 1 × 12.7-mm M3P machine gun with 200 12.7-mm rounds
  elevation −10°/+70°, traverse 360°
SENSORS AND FIRE CONTROL Digital fire control, FLIR, CO2 eye-safe laser rangefinder, driven-reticle optical sight, remote-control unit operable from Humvee cab or away from vehicle
ARMOR supplemental armor on cab

POWERPLANT   Detroit Diesel 135-hp air-cooled V-8 diesel
power-to-weight ratio
    38.6 hp/metric ton
SUSPENSION   independent double A-arm with coil spring on all wheels, front stabilizer bar
SPEED   60 mph (97 km/h), acceleration, 0–30 mph (48 km/h) 7 sec, 0–50 mph (80 km/h) 20 sec, range 300 mi (483 km)
OBSTACLE CLEARANCE   vertical obstacle 1 ft 10 in (0.56 m), gradient 60%, fording without preparation 2 ft 6 in (0.76 m), with preparation 5 ft (1.52 m)

M48 Chaparral

The US Chaparral short-range Surface-to-Air Missile (SAM) system consists of an M54 launcher bearing four modified AIM-9 Sidewinder Infrared (IR)-homing missiles that is mounted on the rear deck of a modified M548 tracked cargo carrier designated the M730 or M730A1. (It has also been deployed on a trailer and in ships.)

The powertrain was updated in the 1980s. Although newer vehicles were developed (notably the Americanized Roland and ADATS systems), teething problems and cost prevented a successor from entering service.

The full-width cab has a permanent blast shield on the rear. To prepare for firing, the crew folds down the windshield, side window frames, and roof, and covers the lower armored portion with a six-piece blast shield. An auxiliary power unit elevates and traverses the base and turret assembly.

Two vertically stacked missile rails are located on either side of the air-conditioned "gunner's" position. The gunner slews his turret onto a target bearing provided by a remote target-locating radar. Target acquisition and postlaunch tracking are by the missile's IR seeker,

conferring a "fire and forget" capability on the system.

The MIM-72 missiles have been upgraded several times; the current variant features the AN/DAW-2 Rosette Scan Seeker (RSS) two-color spectral discrimination detector that increases resistance to IR countermeasures, improves spatial discrimination and expands field of view without sacrificing sensor acuity.

VARIANTS • Night Chaparral (Chaparral FLIR) with forward-looking IR sight.

DEVELOPMENT • Installation of the MIM-72 missile (adapted from the AIM-7 Sidewinder) in 1969 was originally intended as a stopgap measure after the more sophisticated Mauler missile was canceled. The Regular Army achieved initial operational capability in 1969; the first National Guard unit (New Mexico) became operational with the Chaparral in FY1984.

The chassis is supplied by FMC of San Jose, California, and the missile system is manufactured by Loral's Aeroneutronics Division of Newport Beach, California.

In addition to US service, Egypt, Greece, Israel, Morocco, Taiwan, and Tunisia operate the Chaparral.

COMBAT   EXPERIENCE • Although Chaparrals were deployed with all major US Army units in Saudi Arabia during Operations Desert Shield and Desert Storm, the early achievement of air supremacy by the anti-Iraq coalition meant that no Iraqi aircraft came within the M48's range during the conflict.

SPECIFICATIONS •
CREW   4–5 (commander, driver, gunner, 2 loaders)
COMBAT WEIGHT   25,353 lb (11,500 kg)
ground pressure
    7.54 lb/in² (0.53 kg/cm²)
DIMENSIONS
hull length   19 ft 11 in (6.06 m)

Chaparral Air Defense Missile
U.S. GOVERNMENT DEPARTMENT OF DEFENSE

width   8 ft 11 in (2.69 m)
height   8 ft 10 in (2.68 m)
ground clearance
    16 in (400 mm)
length of track on ground
    9 ft 3 in (2.82 m)
track width   15 in (380 mm)
MAIN ARMAMENT   4 × MIM-72 Chaparral SAM with 8 rounds in reserve
elevation   −5°/+90°, traverse 360°
max range   3.2 nm (3.7 mi; 6 km)
max altitude
    9,843 ft (3,000 m)
minimum altitude
    164 ft (50 m)
rate of fire   4 rounds/min normal
SENSORS AND FIRE CONTROL   launcher has Forward-Looking Infrared (FLIR) thermal-imaging system with automatic target tracking and Identification Friend or Foe (IFF) interrogator; missile has passive IR homing with radar proximity fuze
POWERPLANT   Detroit Diesel 6V-53T 275-hp water-cooled 2-stroke V-6 diesel engine, X-200-4 fully automatic hydrokinetic crossdrive transmission with 4 forward/1 reverse gears
power-to-weight ratio
    23.9 hp/metric ton
SUSPENSION (EACH SIDE)   torsion bar, 5 road wheels, front drive, rear idler, no track return rollers
SPEED   38 mph (61 km/h), 3.5 mph (5.5 kmh) in water with tracks when fitted with flotation screen, range 313 mi (504 km)
OBSTACLE CLEARANCE   vertical 2 ft (0.62 m), gradient 60%, side slope 30%, trench 5 ft 6 in (1.68 m), amphibious

M42A1 Skysweeper

The M42A1 Skysweeper (usually known as the Duster) twin 40-mm self-propelled antiaircraft vehicle is obsolete in its primary role but remains useful against ground targets.

The Skysweeper has the same chassis as the M41 light tank and an open-top turret that houses four crew members. The driver of the M42 is located in the front left of the hull with the commander/radio operator seated to his right. The engine is at the rear of the vehicle.

The M42 is armed with twin 40-mm cannon that are mounted between a curved, scooped shield. The cannon fire a High-Explosive Tracer (HE-T) and Armor-Piercing Tracer (AP-T) round.

VARIANTS • Some Taiwanese M42s have been modified to carry and fire the TOW antitank guided missile.

DEVELOPMENT • Produced at Cadillac Motor Car's Cleveland (Ohio) Tank Arsenal from 1951 to 1956 and at ACF's Berwick, Pennsylvania, plant from 1952 to 1953. It achieved its initial operational capability in 1953. Production totaled 3,700 units. Not in service in active US units, but still in use in several other countries.

COMBAT EXPERIENCE • "Dusters" were often used by US forces in Vietnam against ground targets, in which the relatively heavy shell and high rate of fire proved effective. Very little shielding protected the crew, however, especially against threats from overhead.

SPECIFICATIONS: •
CREW   6
COMBAT WEIGHT   49,498 lb (22,452 kg)
ground pressure
    9.24 lb/in² (0.65 kg/cm²)
DIMENSIONS
hull length   19 ft 1 in (5.82 m), with guns forward 20 ft 10 in (6.36 m)
width   10 ft 7 in (3.23 m)
height   9 ft 4 in (2.85 m)

length of track on ground
          10 ft 8 in (3.25 m)
ground clearance
          17 in (440 mm)
track width   21 in (530 mm)
MAIN ARMAMENT   2 40-mm M2A1 automatic cannon with 480 rounds in the vehicle
elevation   −3°/+85°, traverse 360°
initial muzzle velocity
          HE-T: 2,887 fps (880 mps)
          AP-T: 2,860 fps (872 mps)
rate of fire   120 rounds/min per barrel, practical
SECONDARY ARMAMENT   7.62-mm M60 with 1,750 rounds
SENSORS AND FIRE CONTROL   mechanical computing sight, optical reflex sight
ARMOR HULL (GLACIS)   25.4 mm sloped at 45°, turret 9.52–15.87 mm
POWERPLANT   Continental or Lycoming AOSI-895-5 500-hp air-cooled 6-cylinder supercharged fuel-injected gasoline engine, Allison CD-500-3 powershift, crossdrive transmission with 4 forward/2 reverse gears
power-to-weight ratio
          22.26 hp/metric ton
SUSPENSION (EACH SIDE)   torsion bar, 5 road wheels, rear drive, front idler, 3 shock absorbers, 3 return rollers
SPEED   45 mph (72 km/h), range 100 miles (161 km)
OBSTACLE CLEARANCE   vertical 2 ft 4 in (0.71 m), gradient 60%, side slope 30%, trench 6 ft (1.83 m), fording 3 ft 4 in (1.02 m)

M163 Vulcan Air Defense System

The Vulcan air defense system consists of a modified M113 armored personnel carrier chassis (designated M741) mounting a turret fitted with a 6-barrel M61 Vulcan Gatling cannon and range-only radar.

The radar is similar to that used in the US Navy's Phalanx Close-In Weapons System (CIWS).

The 20-mm cannon fires Armor-Piercing with Tracer (AP-T) and High-Explosive Incendiary (HEI, HEI-T) projectiles weighing 3.3–3.5 oz (94–100 g). An AP Discarding Sabot round was developed for the Product Improved Vulcan Air Defense System (PIVADS).

PIVADS consists of a stabilized director-type gunsight, replacement of the analog computer with a digital microprocessor, and improved elevation and traversing ability to reduce backlash.

DEVELOPMENT • Like the Chaparral air defense vehicle, the M163 was an interim system, achieving initial operational capability in 1968. Manufactured by General Electric Co., Burlington, Vermont.

Cancellation of the Sergeant York Division Air Defense System (DIVADS) in 1986 meant that these 1960s-vintage systems remained in frontline service with the US Army until the 1990s. At that time, US service in Operation Desert Storm exposed severe shortcoming, in mobility. In addition, the M163 showed steadily declining effectiveness against modern targets and steadily increasing maintenance costs. As a result, the Army retired its M163s ahead of schedule, replacing them with M2 Bradleys fitted with Stinger missiles.

In service with 12 other countries.

COMBAT EXPERIENCE • Israeli M163s were credited with several Syrian aircraft destroyed during the 1982 Lebanese conflict.

US Army M163s deployed to Vietnam in the late 1960s encountered no North Vietnamese aircraft, but the high firing rate and relatively heavy rounds were effective against ground targets.

20 years later, M163s in Operations De-

sert Shield and Desert Storm likewise never engaged Iraqi aircraft or helicopters. During the 100-hour ground war, however, the system's 20-mm cannon proved effective against light armored vehicles, trucks and other unarmored vehicles, and Iraqi bunkers.

SPECIFICATIONS •

CREW   4 (commander, gunner, loader, driver)
COMBAT WEIGHT   27,478 lb (12,490 kg)
ground pressure
        8.68 lb/in² (0.61 kg/cm²)
DIMENSIONS
    hull length   16 ft 2 in (4.93 m)
    width   8 ft 9 ¾ in (2.69 m)
    height to turret top
        8 ft 8 ¾ in (2.64 m)
    length of track on ground
        8 ft 9 in (2.67 m)
    ground clearance
        16 in (406 mm)
    track width   15 in (381 mm)
MAIN ARMAMENT   M168 gun system consisting of 6 × 20-mm barrels grouped on a geared rotor mounting
    elevation   −5°/+80° at 60°/sec, traverse 360° at 75°/sec
    muzzle velocity
        3,379 fps (1,030 mps)
    rate of fire   antiair 3,000 rounds/min; ground target 1,000 rounds/min

magazine capacity
        1,100 ready rounds, linkless feed; 1,000 rounds more in hull
    max range   antiair 5,249 ft (1,600 m); ground 3,281 yd (3,000 m)
SENSORS AND FIRE CONTROL   visual tracking and M61A1 (US Navy Mk 20 Mod 0) lead-computing gunsight, AN/VPS-2 radar supplies range and range rate, AN/TVS-2B night vision sight
PROTECTION   5083 aluminum hull (12–38 mm), antimine appliqué armor on the bottom
POWERPLANT   Detroit Diesel model 6V-53 215-hp water-cooled 2-stroke V-6 diesel engine, Allison TX-100 automatic transmission with 6 forward/1 reverse gears
power-to-weight ratio
        17.47 hp/metric ton
SUSPENSION (EACH SIDE)   torsion bar, 5 road wheels, rear drive, front idler, 3 shock absorbers, no return rollers; suspension can be locked out during firing
SPEED   road 35 mph (56 km/h), cross-country 19 mph (30.6 km/h), acceleration 0–20 mph (0–32 km/h) 12 sec, 3.6 mph (5.8 km/h) in water, range 300 mi (483 km)
OBSTACLE CLEARANCE   vertical 2 ft (0.61 m), gradient 60%, side slope 30%, trench 5 ft 6 in (1.68 m), amphibious

ARMORED PERSONNEL CARRIERS

AAV7A1 (formerly LVTP-7A1)

The US Marine Corps AAV7A1 is a full-tracked, amphibian vehicle, providing an over-the-beach capability for landing troops and material through surf up to 10 feet high. The Marine Corps has often employed the AAV7A1 as an armored personnel carrier, although the vehicle has a high silhouette for this role and was not originally intended to move far inland from its assault beach.

Its mission dictates the AAV's bulk and unusual shape; the vehicle is taller and

AAV7A1
FMC CORPORATION

wider than any other APC. The bow is an upturned snout extending well forward of the tracks. Below the nose, the hull flares out in sponsons. This forward section of the hull houses the transmission and engine. The driver and commander are located to the left of the engine compartment, the gunner to the right in a slightly elevated weapons station. Farther aft, the crew compartment can hold 25 troops in three rows; the compartment's upper sides are sloped toward the centerline.

Propulsion is by tracks on land, twin water jets in the water. Afloat, the AAV is steered by a deflector's stream at the rear of each waterjet. Secondary track propulsion can be reverted to if necessary.

VARIANTS • 90 AAVC7A1 command, 61 AAVR7A1 recovery with crane.

DEVELOPMENT • The LVTP-7 was built by FMC Corp. (Ordnance Division) of San Jose, California, and achieved its initial operational capability in 1972. Production of the LVTP-7 ended in 1974 after 942 had been built.

Conversion of LVTP-7s to LVTP-7A1s (AAV7A1) came under a Service Life Extension Program (SLEP) with an initial operational capability for the LVTP-7A1 in 1982. The SLEP saw the Detroit Diesel powerplant replaced by the Cummins engine, a suspension upgrade, fully electric drive for the weapons station, new ventilation system, built-in test equipment, better night vision devices, secure voice radio equipment. The program was completed in 1986 after a total of 984 vehicles were modified. The production line was later reopened to produce an additional 333 new AAV7A1s for the Maritime Preppositioning Ships (MPS); first deliveries were made in October 1983.

Under a late-1980s Product Improvement Program (PIP), most AAV7s have been refitted with an "upgunned" weapons station carrying a 40-mm automatic grenade launcher and a 12.7-mm in new, all-electric turret. Another improvement is the Appliqué Armor Kit (AAK), consisting of two layers of corrosion-treated steel fastened to the hull sides. In addition, a bow plane has been added to improve water speed and safety, an Automatic Fire Sensing and Suppression System (AFSSS), and an improved transmission with double the reliability of the current transmission assembly.

Eight other countries operate the LVTP7 or AAV7. Many have been upgraded.

COMBAT EXPERIENCE • AAV7s landed Marines on Grenada in October 1983.

The AAV7s were among the first armored vehicles to be landed in Saudi Arabia after Iraq's August 1990 invasion and annexation of Kuwait. By the beginning of the Operation Desert Storm ground war in February 1991, the 1st Marine Expeditionary Force (MEF) had 225 AAV7s ashore. Another 115 were embarked in 31 landing ships in the northern Persian Gulf. The shore-based AAV7s served as one of two principal types of Marine Corps APCs (the LAV-25 being the other) during the drive to Kuwait City.

SPECIFICATIONS •

CREW   3 (commander, gunner, driver) + 25 troops

COMBAT WEIGHT   52,770 lb (23,936 kg)

ground pressure
7.82 lb/in² (0.55 kg/cm²)

DIMENSIONS

hull length   26 ft (7.94 m)

width   10 ft 9 in (3.27 m)

height   10 ft 8 in (3.26 m)

ground clearance
16 in (410 mm)

freeboard to driver's hatch
2 ft 3 in (0.85 m)

length of track on ground
12 ft 11 in (3.94 m)

track width   21 in (530 mm)

MAIN ARMAMENT   40-mm grenade launcher with 100 ready rounds, 12.7-mm machine gun with 200 rounds

elevation   −8°/+45°, 360° traverse

SENSORS AND FIRE CONTROL   infrared driving lights, passive night driving system, passive night firing system

ARMOR   30–45-mm hull armor, 6.72–12.7 mm on rear ramps

POWERPLANT   Cummins VT-400 400-hp water-cooled turbocharged 4-stroke V-8 diesel, FMC Corp. HS-400-3A1 hydraulic lock-up torque converter with 4 forward/2 reverse ratios

power-to-weight ratio
17.31 hp/metric ton

SUSPENSION (EACH SIDE)   tube-over-torsion bar, 6 road wheels, front drive, rear idler, 2 shock absorbers, no return rollers

SPEED   road 45 mph (72.5 km/h), cruising speed 20–30 mph (12.5–18.6 km/h), 8 mph (13 km/h) with 2 hydrojets, 4.5 mph (7.2 km/h) track-driven, road range 300 miles (482 km) at 25 mph (40 km/h), water range 7 hr

OBSTACLE CLEARANCE   vertical 3 ft (0.91 m), gradient 60%, side slope 40%, trench 8 ft (2.44 m)

LAV-25 Bison (in Canadian service)

Based on the Swiss MOWAG Piranha, the 8 × 8-wheeled LAV-25 was developed specifically for US Marine Corps use as an air-portable APC and reconnaissance vehicle. It has been built in several versions.

The LAV-25 has sloping hull sides and a severely sloped glacis; the four wheels on each side have no skirts or fenders. The driver sits at the front left of the hull with the engine to his right. The troop compartment is at the rear of the hull, with entry and exit through two rear doors that open outward. Two outward-opening roof hatches are located in the rear hull. The two-man, fully stabilized turret has an M242 25-mm Chain Gun.

VARIANTS • Canadian LAV-APC Bison, 96 LAV-AT Antitank with TOW, 50 LAV-M Mortar Carrier, LAV-AD Air Defense Vehicle with FIM-92 Stingers and GAU/12 5-barrel 25-mm Gatling cannon, LAV-AG Assault Gun Vehicle/LAV-105 with Benet EX-35 105-mm gun, 50 LAV-CC Command and Control, 94 LAV-L Logistics vehicles, 46 LAV-R Maintenance and Recovery Vehicle, 20 USAF MARV Mobile Armored Reconnaissance Vehicle, LAV-MEWSS (Mobile Electronic Warfare Support System).

DEVELOPMENT • After a competition, contract awarded to General Motors of Canada, Ltd., in London, Ontario, in September 1982. The vehicle achieved initial operational capability in 1984. A total of 758 were delivered to the USMC.

Other services using variants of the LAV-25 are the Australian Army, the Canadian Force's Ground Command, and Saudi Arabia's Army and National Guard.

COMBAT EXPERIENCE • The LAV was deployed on European exercises for the first time during "Teamwork 88" in northern Norway.

In operations in Panama beginning in May 1989, the wheeled LAVs proved versatile enough to travel on roads when tracked vehicles would do too much damage to the pavement or in water, often swimming across the canal to evade Panama Defense Force (PDF) surveillance. They also proved useful in breaking up barricades, often by using the LAV-Ls to pull them apart.

During the December 1989 Operation Just Cause—the actual military ouster of General Noriega—Marine Corps LAVs were used to take several positions, including the headquarters of the PDF. After the military operation, the LAVs were used to back up the successor government, often serving as a focal point for "nation-building" activities in small towns.

Marine Corps LAVs began landing in Saudi Arabia from Maritime Prepositioning Ships (MPS) within days after the US decision to begin Operation Desert Shield in August 1990. By the start of Desert Storm's ground war in February 1991, 372 were in the theater (193 LAV-25, 54 LAV-AT, 30 LAV-CC, 47 LAV-L, 26 LAV-M, and 22 LAV-R).

The LAV's strengths proved to be its dependability and speed. (The DoD's April 1992 summary was "flexible, responsive, and adaptable.") The vehicle's speed allowed units to flank fixed positions and evade superior forces. Although several LAV crews did score TOW missile hits on Iraqi tanks, the LAV did not seek out enemy armor.

The LAV-25's inherent weakness is its light armor. Ironically, the worst LAV casualties came three weeks before the ground war, when an Air Force A-10 Thunderbolt accidentally fired an AGM-65 Maverick at an LAV, killing seven of the eight men inside.

When the ground offensive began, the LAV's passive day/night sight proved inadequate. It required too much ambient light to be useful at night and was unable to penetrate the sand and oil-smoke fog that shrouded much of the battlefield.

After Desert Storm, one LAV commander contended that light armored infantry units often were not fully exploited because of a lack of understanding of the unit's reconnaissance capabilities. He also suggested upgrades to the LAV-25 including (among others) a thermal imaging sight for the 25-mm gun, redesign of the machine gun mount, and a redesign of the internal communications system in the basic vehicle to keep the scouts in the picture and in the C² vehicle to permit staff-only conferences (to avoid confusing the driver).

SPECIFICATIONS •

CREW   3 (commander, gunner, driver) + 6 troops

COMBAT WEIGHT   28,200 lb (12,791 kg)

DIMENSIONS

hull length   21 ft (6.39 m)
width   8 ft 2 in (2.5 m)
height   8 ft 10 in (2.69 m)
distance between axles
    1st to 2nd 3 ft 7 in (1.1 m), 2nd to 3rd 4 ft 5 in (1.35 m), 3rd to 4th 3 ft 5 in (1.04 m)
ground clearance
    20 in (508 mm)

MAIN ARMAMENT   25-mm M242 Chain Gun with 210 ready rounds, 420 stowed

elevation   −10°/+60° at 25°/sec, traverse 360° at 25°/sec

SECONDARY WEAPONS   7.62-mm M240 coaxial machine gun, pintle mount for 7.62-mm machine gun, 4,050 stowed rounds of 5.56-mm rifle ammunition

SENSORS AND FIRE CONTROL   M36E1 day/passive night vision sight for commander and gunner

ARMOR   ballistic protection against small arms and shell fragments

POWERPLANT   GM Detroit Diesel 6V-53T 275-hp liquid-cooled 2-stroke V-6 turbocharged diesel engine, Allison MT-653 DR automatic transmission with 5 forward/1 reverse gears

power-to-weight ratio
    21.5 hp/metric ton

SUSPENSION (EACH SIDE)   8 × 8 (8-wheel drive, front 4 steering); 4-wheel drive may be selected fully independent coil springs, twin shock absorbers on front 2 axles, trailing arm torsion bar on rear 2 axles

SPEED   62 mph (100 km/h), 6.2 mph (10 km/h) in the water with 2 propellers, range 410 mi (660 km)

OBSTACLE CLEARANCE   vertical 1 ft 8 in (0.5 m), gradient 70%, trench 6 ft 9 in (2.06 m)

V-300 Commando

The Commando V-300 6 × 6-wheeled Armored Personnel Carrier (APC) is a development of the earlier Commando V-150 4 × 4 armored reconnaissance vehicle, but is a larger vehicle similar to several models produced in Europe. A full glacis plate, second rear axle, and a wider range of turret options (from 7.62-mm machine guns to 90-mm cannon) are the principal changes. Despite its much greater gun power, the V-300 is still only lightly armored and has less cross-country mobility than tracked APCs.

The V-300 has a sloping frontal glacis plate and sloping sides. The turret is mounted toward the rear of the vehicle. The troop compartment is also in the rear; access is through two rear doors and two roof hatches.

Turret armaments range from 7.62- or 12.7-mm machine guns, through 20- or 25-mm automatic cannon, to the 76- or 90-mm gun. A retractable TOW antitank missile launcher with two missiles can also be fitted. The 90-mm Cockerill gun has a triple-baffle muzzle brake. A V-600, which featured a Cadillac Gage turret mounting the L7A1 105-mm/51-cal Low Recoil Force rifled tank gun ran trials but was not procured.

VARIANTS • APC, 81-mm mortar vehicle, recovery vehicle, ambulance.

DEVELOPMENT • Manufactured by Cadillac Gage, Warren, Michigan, achieving initial operational capability in 1983. Production has been limited, with Kuwait and Panama being the only buyers until early 1993, when the Philippines contracted for 24 through Foreign Military Sales. The Panamanian V-300 roster includes vehicles fitted with the Belgian Cockerill Mk 3 90-mm gun, APCs with two 7.62-mm machine guns, and armored recovery vehicles.

COMBAT EXPERIENCE • When Iraq invaded Kuwait in August 1990, very few of Kuwait's V-300s appear to have escaped.

SPECIFICATIONS •
CREW   3 (commander, gunner, driver) + 9–10 troops
COMBAT WEIGHT   32,000 lb (14,515 kg)
DIMENSIONS
 hull length   21 ft (6.4 m)
 width   8 ft 4 in (2.54 m)
 height   6 ft 6 in (1.98 m)
 distance between axles
         1st to 2nd 7 ft 3 in (2.21 m), 2nd to 3rd 5 ft (1.52 m)
 ground clearance
         14 in (356 mm)
MAIN ARMAMENT   Cockerill Mk 3 90-mm/36-cal rifled gun with 39 rounds of ammunition
 elevation   −8°/+28°, traverse 360°
SECONDARY WEAPONS   7.62-mm coaxial machine gun with 400 rounds, 7.62-mm antiaircraft machine gun with 200 rounds
SENSORS AND FIRE CONTROL   8-power monocular sight and 1-power periscope for gunner, 3 vision blocks for commander
ARMOR   CADLOY ballistic steel plate, proof against 7.62-mm ball ammunition (vision blocks and periscopes hardened to same level)
POWERPLANT   Cummins VT-504 270-hp liquid-cooled turbocharged V-8 diesel engine, Allison MT-643 automatic transmission with 4 forward/1 reverse gears
 power-to-weight ratio
         18.60 hp/metric ton
SUSPENSION
 6 × 6 (6 wheels driving, 2 wheels steering)

front axle has solid beam on trailing arms; coil springs, 2 telescoping shock absorbers, and antisway bars on each wheel
rear axles have independent trailing arm with coil springs and 1 shock absorber
SPEED   92 mph (57 km/h), water 3 mph (5 km/h) driven by wheels, range 435 mi (700 km)
OBSTACLE CLEARANCE   vertical 2 ft (0.61 m), gradient 60%, side slope 30%, amphibious

M113

The US M113 Armored Personnel Carrier (APC) is the most widely used of all non-Soviet APCs. Its hull and powertrain have been the basis for a great variety of battlefield vehicles, some modifications representing functional changes and others differences in locally available weapons, powerplants, or sensors.

In configuration, the M113 is a slimmed-down version of the earlier M59. The boxy hull is welded aluminum with a steeply sloped glacis and flat top. Although there is a roof hatch, troops enter the compartment on a lowered rear ramp. There are no firing ports or vision blocks.

In February 1987, the General Accounting Office contended that an M113A3 would be as mobile as the newer M2 Bradley and would be less likely to explode because of the less volatile ammunition it carries. Rebuttals to the report noted that the M113 was not as well armed or as easy for infantry to dismount from as the Bradley. US experience in Operation Desert Storm suggests that the Bradley's thermal sights and 25-mm Chain Gun, which the M113A3 does not have, were critical elements in the M2's success.

VARIANTS • M113 gasoline-powered APC derived from T113E1, M113A1 diesel-powered production model (25,459 produced), M113A2 (1978), M113A3 (1987).

M106 (107-mm), M125 (81-mm), M1064 (120-mm) mortar carriers.

Canadian M113A2s fitted with the Air Defense, Antitank System (ADATS) missile launcher.

M548 cargo carrier, M577 series command post, M1068 Standard Integrated Command Post Systems (SICPS).

M901 Improved TOW Vehicle (ITV) with two TOW antitank missiles.

M981 Fire Support Vehicle (FSV) with laser designator in erectable "hammerhead" mount.

M1015 Electronic Warfare (EW) systems carrier.

M1059 Smoke Generator Carrier.

DEVELOPMENT • Production began in 1959, with the M113 achieving initial operational capability in 1959, M113A1 in 1965. More than 78,000 were produced for over 50 countries by FMC Corp. of San Jose, California, with license production by OTO Melara of Italy and Thyssen-Henschel of Germany, with Pakistan assembly of 775 M113A2s beginning in 1990.

Known as the Zelda in Israeli service.

COMBAT EXPERIENCE • M113s were widely deployed in several versions, including the basic APC, with US, Vietnamese, Australian, and South Korean units in Vietnam. Experiments with camouflage and firing ports (to allow firing under cover) were short-lived and unsuccessful. A bridgelayer conversion, on the other hand, improved unit mobility in the marshes and defiles. M113s have also seen extensive service in several Israeli-Arab conflicts.

M901 ITVs, M981 FIST-Vs, and M577 command vehicles were deployed in US Army units in Saudi Arabia during Operations Desert Shield and Desert Storm. The M577s and the M981 FSVs were slowed down by the sand and proved to be the vehicles that most limited the tracked artillery's speed of maneuver and prevented greater use of Copperhead laser-guided projectiles. (The most effective laser platform was the OH-58D Kiowa AHIP helicopter.)

In fact, the M981 was the most severely criticized of all US military systems for its sluggishness in the sand, the need to be stationary to operate its "hammerhead," and its inferior optics, which often didn't see targets being engaged by M1A1 Abrams tank and M2/M3 Bradley fighting vehicles. In addition, having to orient the FIST-V's NSG added eight to 10 minutes to the time needed to provide targeting information, which was far too long in a fluid battlefield.

Saudi Arabian, Kuwaiti, and Egyptian M113s also participated in the ground war. None of the 50 M901 ITVs captured in Kuwait by the Iraqi Army took any part in the ground war.

A US M577 was accidentally struck by an AGM-114 Hellfire missile a week before the ground war began; several soldiers were wounded.

SPECIFICATIONS •
CREW 2 (commander, driver) + 11 troops
WEIGHT
M113A2: 24,986 lb (11,334 kg)
M113A3: 27,180 lb (12,339 kg)
ground pressure
M113A2: 7.96 lb/in^2 (0.56 kg/cm^2)
M113A3: 8.57 lb/in^2 (0.60 kg/cm^2)
DIMENSIONS
hull length M113A2: 15 ft 11 in (4.86 m)
M113A3: 17 ft 5 in (5.30 m)
width 8 ft 10 in (2.69 m)
height with air defense machine gun 8 ft 3 in (2.52 m)

M113A3
FMC CORPORATION

length of track on ground
        8 ft 9 in (2.67 m)
ground clearance
        17 in (430 mm)
track width   15 in (380 mm)
MAIN ARMAMENT   12.7-mm M2 HB machine gun with 2,000 rounds pintle-mounted at commander's hatch (M113A3 has armored gun shield)
        elevation   −21°/+53°, traverse 360°
ARMOR   5083 aluminum hull (12–38 mm), antimine appliqué armor on the bottom
POWERPLANT   Detroit Diesel model 6V53 215-hp (M113A2) or 6V53T 275-hp (M113A3) water-cooled 2-stroke V-6 diesel engine; M113A2 Allison TX-100-1 crossdrive transmission with 3 forward/1 reverse gears; M113A3

TX-200-4 hydrokinetic crossdrive transmission with 4 forward/1 reverse gears
power-to-weight ratio at combat weight
        M113A2 18.51 hp/metric ton; M113A3 22.45 hp/ metric ton
SUSPENSION (EACH SIDE)   torsion bar, 5 road wheels, front drive, rear idler, 2 shock absorbers, no return rollers
SPEED   road M113A2 38 mph (61 km/ h), M113A3 41 mph (65 km/h), cross-country (at 26,500 lb/12,020 kg), M113A1/A2 16.8 mph (27 km/ h), M113A3 22 mph (35.4 km/h); 3.6 mph (5.8 km/h) in water, acceleration 0–20 mph (0–32 km/h) at 26,500 lb (12,020 kg) M113A1/A2 11 sec, M113A3 9 sec

RANGE   M113A2 300 mi (483 km);
M113A3 309 mi (497 km)
OBSTACLE CLEARANCE   vertical 2 ft
(0.61 m), gradient 60%, side slope
30%, trench 5 ft 6 in (1.68 m), amphibious M113A2

M2 Bradley

The Bradley Mechanized Infantry Fighting Vehicle (MICV) supplements and will
eventually replace the M113 Armored
Personnel Carrier (APC). The Bradley
reflects the 1970s worldwide move away
from a troop "battle taxi" to a more flexible vehicle with better self-defense capabilities. The M3 Cavalry Fighting Vehicle
(CFV) variant is virtually identical, except
for the lack of firing ports and vision
blocks in the hull and more stowed TOW
antitank missile rounds.

The Bradley has been a controversial
design, criticized at first for being vulner-

able to small-arms fire and liable to catch
fire. It was also said to be less mobile than
the M113. In Operation Desert Storm,
however, Bradleys proved very reliable
and were far better at keeping up with
and actively supporting the M1 Abrams
tank during the ground war of 1991's Operation Desert Storm than were vehicles
based on the M113.

Viewed from above, the Bradley reveals
its asymmetrical hull layout; the left side
of the hull has a continuous in-sloping
upper section while the right is broken by
the engine compartment and ventilator
grille. Before the M2A2 variant, the hull
was shielded by spaced laminate armor;
the M2A2 has steel armor. The engine is
located in the front of the vehicle. The
driver's position is to the engine's left
and is covered by a low domed hatch with
vision ports.

Behind the engine and driver is the
TOW-Bushmaster   Armored   Turret
(TBAT-II), which mounts a 25-mm M242

M2 Bradley Fighting Vehicle
FMC CORPORATION

Chain Gun and a twin TOW antitank missile launcher. The gunner (on the left) has an integrated day/night sight with 4- and 12-power magnification and a thermal Imaging Infrared (IIR) device; the station also has a 5-power auxiliary sight with a 10° field of view. The commander (on the right) has a direct optical relay from the gunner's sight. Six troops ride in the rear compartment.

Some M2s are fitted with Stinger short-range SAMs to replace the elderly M163 Vulcan Gatling gun vehicles.

VARIANTS • M2 (2,300 produced), M2A1 (1,400 vehicles) with TOW 2 missiles, M2A2 with improved protection, suspension, more powerful engine. FM2 was ad hoc fire support vehicle created during Operation Desert Storm. M2A3 projected for 1990s but not produced. M1070 Electronic Fighting Vehicle System (EFVS).

DEVELOPMENT • An operational requirement (OR) for an M113 replacement was issued in 1964, but trials were unsatisfactory. 1970 OR led to 1973 selection of FMC, trials in 1975. Produced by FMC Ground Systems Division (later United Defense) in San Jose, California, the M2 achieving initial operational capability in 1983.

In April 1990, the Army reduced its requirement for 8,811 Bradleys to 6,882, with last delivery in December 1994.

COMBAT EXPERIENCE • Approximately 2,200 Bradleys were deployed to Saudi Arabia in the vehicle's first combat test. By the beginning of the ground war in February 1991, 33% of the force were A1s, 48% were A2s.

When the ground war began, the Bradleys proved reliable, effective, and highly mobile, according to Army reports. Vehicle commanders were pleased with the effect of the 600-hp engine on performance and welcomed the steel ap-pliqué armor. Crewmen felt that the Bradley needed a faster reverse gear to stay with the Abrams in all-azimuth fire-fights. In addition, the 25-mm Chain Gun, TOW launcher, and thermal sights were invaluable to the success of the Bradley/M1A1 Abrams armored sweeps.

The Bushmaster cannon was very effective against many types of soft and light armored targets. Nevertheless, some Army analysts suggested that the main gun be upgraded to 30- or 35-mm. The gunner's thermal sighting system was effective in near-zero visibility and permitted TOW missile firings at targets only the Bradley gunner could see. Only three Bradleys were reported destroyed by hostile fire; 17 more were destroyed by "friendly fire." According to the Army, the antispall liners and appliqué armor limited secondary damage and injury even when the vehicle was hit by a tank gun round. A Bradley was stopped when a 12.7-mm machine-gun round penetrated the hull and damaged the front transmission.

SPECIFICATIONS (M2A2) •
CREW 3 (commander, gunner, driver)
    + 6 (2 in M3 CFV) troops
WEIGHT M2A2 with armor kit 66,000 lb
    (29,937 kg)
    ground pressure
        10.20 lb/in^2 (0.72 kg/cm^2)
DIMENSIONS
    hull length 21 ft 6 in (6.55 m)
    width 11 ft 10 in (3.61 m)
    height 9 ft 9 in (2.97 m)
    length of track on ground
        12 ft 10 in (3.91 m)
    ground clearance
        18 in (457 mm)
    track width 21 in (533 mm)
MAIN ARMAMENT 25-mm/81.3-cal M242 Chain Gun with 300 ready rounds, 600 (1,200 in M3 CFV) reserve rounds
    elevation −10°/+60°, traverse 360°
    antitank missile
        2 × TOW antitank

missile launchers, 5 missiles in reserve (10 in M3 CFV)

elevation   −20°/+30°, traverses with turret

SECONDARY WEAPONS   7.62-mm M240C coaxial machine gun with 800 ready rounds, 1,400 (3,400 in M3 CFV) reserve rounds

SENSORS AND FIRE CONTROL   Integrated thermal imaging day/night sight with scan at 4-power, aiming at 12-power, AN/VVS-2 driver's night vision viewer with 38° × 45° field of view

ARMOR   5083 series aluminum covered by homogeneous steel plating to resist 30-mm ammunition, Du Pont Kevlar spall liner, attachment points for reactive armor tiles

POWERPLANT   Cummins VTA-903T 600-hp liquid-cooled 4-stroke turbocharged V-8 diesel engine, General Motors HMPT-500 hydromechanical transmission with 3 forward/1 reverse ranges

power-to-weight ratio   without armor kit 22.04 hp/metric ton, with armor kit 20.04 hp/metric ton

SUSPENSION (EACH SIDE)   torsion bar, 6 road wheels, front drive, rear idler, 4 shock absorbers (14-in/365-mm wheel travel), 3 return rollers

SPEED   42 mph (68 km/h), 5 mph (7.2 km/h) in water with tracks, range 300 mi (483 km)

OBSTACLE CLEARANCE   vertical 3 ft (0.91 m), gradient 60%, side slope 40%, trench 8 ft 4 in (2.54 m), amphibious

YPR765 Armored Infantry Fighting Vehicle (AIFV)

The Armored Infantry Fighting Vehicle (AIFV) is a modified M113 Armored Personnel Carrier (APC). The AIFV is also the basis for the 1,700-vehicle Turkish Armored Combat Vehicle (ACV) program. The design has been praised for its combination of effective gun armament, proven M113 components, and good cross-country mobility.

Principal differences from the M113 are the shape of the after hull, hull construction, and main armament. Spaced laminate steel armor is bolted over the standard aluminum hull sides and rear and forms the collars for the gunner's hatch and turret.

Main armament varies; several hundred of the Dutch AIFVs (and 75 of the Turkish ACVs) carry an Oerlikon 25-mm KBA automatic cannon in a boxy turret designed by FMC. The KBA 25-mm gun fires High-Explosive Incendiary with Tracer (HEI-T) and Armor-Piercing Discarding Sabot with Tracer (APDS-T) projectiles. After a Swiss-imposed embargo on supplying the KBA to Turkey, the remaining 575 ACVs have been fitted with the GIAT DRAGAR turret—60 with the McDonnell Douglas M242 25-mm Chain Gun, 515 with GIAT's M811 25-mm cannon.

VARIANTS •
Several Dutch YPR765 variants—cargo carriers, command vehicles, mortar carriers, radar carrier, recovery vehicle, TOW antitank missile carrier—are fitted with the standard M113 cupola mounting a 12.7-mm M2 HB machine gun. The ambulance is unarmed. Belgian variants are similar.

Turkish ACV family includes IFV, TOW 2, and mortar carriers.

DEVELOPMENT • Although failing to meet Army's 1970 Mechanized Infantry Combat Vehicle (MICV) requirement, other countries procured the AIFV, and over 2,000 have been built. Initial operational capability achieved in the Netherlands in 1978, Belgium in 1985. Dutch and Philippine vehicles manufactured by FMC Corp., San Jose, California; Belgian vehicles (AIFV-B) manufactured under license by Belgium Mechanical Fabrication, Grace-Hollogne, Belgium.

Turkish Defence Industry Development and Support Administration (DIDA) contracted with FMC/Nurol Insaat to build 1,698 vehicles for the Turkish Army. Nurol's Golbasi factory began delivering vehicles in 1991. Turret production manufactured in cooperation with Makina ve Kimya Endustrisi Kurunu (MKEK) in Ankara.

SPECIFICATIONS •

CREW 3 (commander, driver, gunner) + 7 troops

COMBAT WEIGHT 30,174 lb (13,687 kg)
  ground pressure
    9.53 lb/in² (0.67 kg/cm²)

DIMENSIONS
  hull length 17 ft 3 in (5.26 m)
  extreme width
    9 ft 3 in (2.82 m)
  overall height
    9 ft 2 in (2.79 m)
  length of track on ground
    8 ft 9 in (2.67 m)
  ground clearance
    17 in (432 mm)
  track width 15 in (381 mm)

MAIN ARMAMENT
  YPR765/first 75 ACV: 25-mm Oerlikon KBA-B02 cannon with 180 ready rounds, 144 in reserve
    elevation: −10°/+50°, traverse 360°
    secondary weapon: 7.62 coaxial machine gun with 230 ready rounds, 1,610 in reserve

  Turkish ACV: 25 mm/86-cal GIAT M811 with 220 rounds
    elevation: −10°/+45°, traverse 360°
    secondary weapon: 7.62-mm coaxial machine gun with 400 rounds; 5 firing ports in hull sides and rear

SENSORS AND FIRE CONTROL telescopic sights, optional integral night sight; Turkish IFVs have Cadillac Gage gun control equipment and Marconi Command and Control Systems thermal imager vehicle sight; Texas Instruments thermal sights being supplied to 650 vehicles

ARMOR aluminum alloy with spaced laminate steel bolted to sides and rear

POWERPLANT Detroit Diesel Allison 6V-53T 264-hp water-cooled turbocharged 2-stroke V-6 diesel engine, Allison TX-100-1A automatic transmission with 3 forward/1 reverse gears
  power-to-weight ratio
    19.29 hp/metric ton

SUSPENSION (EACH SIDE) tube-over-torsion bar, 5 road wheels, front driver, rear idler, 3 shock absorbers, no return rollers

SPEED 38 mph (61.2 km/h), up 10% grade 17.5 mph (28.2 km/h), 4 mph (6.5 km/h) in water with tracks, range 305 mi (490 km)

OBSTACLE CLEARANCE vertical 2 ft 1 in (0.64 m), gradient 60%, side slope 30%, trench 5 ft 4 in (1.63 m), amphibious

ARMORED RECONNAISSANCE VEHICLES

V150 (M706) Commando Series

The Commando series of light armored vehicles has been produced in a variety of configurations and is in widespread service. The basic Commando is a 4 × 4-wheeled vehicle with no vertical surfaces and a low superstructure or turret ring. Weapons fitted to the vehicle range from 7.62-mm machine guns to 90-mm cannon.

VARIANTS •
V-100 with Chrysler 191-hp gasoline engine; V-200 in several variants to Singapore; V-150 with gasoline or diesel engine, five-speed manual transmission replaced by two-speed automatic; V-150S with 18-in (0.46-m) stretch and system upgrades; Mexican-built DN-III/V Caballo. Also command, recovery, air defense, internal security, air force base security variants.

DEVELOPMENT • Manufactured by Cadillac Gage Co., Warren, Michigan, achieving initial operational capability in 1964. The original Commando was the gasoline-powered V-100 model. The V-200 was sold only to Singapore.
Since 1971, the four-wheel production model has been the V-150, a model with a loaded weight approximately halfway between the V-100 and the V-200 and powered by a diesel engine. In 1985, the V-150 was replaced in production by the longer V-150S.

In limited US Air Force service, but operated by more than 20 other countries.

COMBAT EXPERIENCE • V-100s were used by the United States Army and Air Force in the Vietnam War. Although troubled at first by rear-axle failure, they proved handy as light security vehicles. The turret's ability to accept a variety of weapons and the relatively high ground clearance were considered assets.

SPECIFICATIONS (V-150S) •
CREW   3 (commander, gunner, driver) + 2 troops
COMBAT WEIGHT   V-150 21,800 lb (9,888 kg); V-150S 24,000 lb (10,886 kg)
DIMENSIONS
  hull length   V-100/150 18 ft 8 in (5.69 m); V-150S 20 ft 2 in (6.14 m)
  width   7 ft 5 in (2.26 m)
  height to hull top
    6 ft 6 in (1.98 m)
  wheelbase   V-100/150 8 ft 9 in (2.67 m); V-150S 10 ft 3 in (3.12 m)
  ground clearance
    hull 25.5 in (650 mm), axles 15 in (380 mm)
MAIN ARMAMENT   (options fitted to V-150/150S)

# AND CALIBER	ELEVATION (DEG)	ROUNDS OF AMMUNITION
2 7.62 mm	−13/+55	800 ready, 3,000 in hull
2 12.7 mm	−10/+55	400 ready, 1,000 in hull
1 20-mm Oerlikon	−8/+55	200 ready, 200 in hull
1 25 mm	−8/+60	230 ready, 400 in hull
1 20-mm Vulcan		1,300
1 30 mm		
1 12.7-mm MG and 40-mm grenade		
launcher	−8/+45	100 (40 mm), 200 (12.7 mm)
1 76 mm		
1 90 mm	−8/+28	8 ready, 31 in hull
1 81-mm mortar	+40/+85	62 in hull
TOW antitank		7 missiles in hull

ARMOR   Cadloy steel armor plate protects against 7.62-mm fire

POWERPLANT
Chrysler 191-hp liquid-cooled V-8 gasoline engine; power-to-weight ratio 20.23 hp/metric ton *or* Cummins V-504 202-hp liquid-cooled V-8 automatic transmission with 4 forward/1 reverse gears; power-to-weight ratio V-150 20.43 hp/metric ton, V-150S 18.56 hp/metric ton

SUSPENSION   4 × 4 (all wheels powered, front wheels steering), solid beam axle, semi-elliptic multileaf springs, double-acting hydraulic shock absorbers

SPEED   55 mph (89 km/h), 3.1 mph (5 km/h) in water, road range 500 mi (800 km), cross-country range 400 mi (643 km)

OBSTACLE CLEARANCE   vertical V-100/150 2 ft 0 in (0.61 m), V-150S 3 ft 0 in (0.91 m), gradient 60%, 30%, amphibious

Commando Scout

The Scout is a small 4 × 4 Armored Reconnaissance Vehicle (ARV) developed as a private venture by Cadillac Gage. It is designed primarily for reconnaissance and security. No US units operate the Scout.

The Scout has a low silhouette with a long, sloping glacis. Viewed from the front, the hull's cross section is diamond-shaped, with both upper and lower hull halves sloping inward. Compared to other ARVs, the engine, driver, and turret are set farther to the rear of the vehicle. The one- or two-man turret is sited over the rear axle.

VARIANTS •
Command car and antitank vehicle with retractable TOW antitank missile launcher.

DEVELOPMENT • Manufactured by Cadillac Gage, Warren, Michigan, achieving initial operational capability in 1983. 28 in service in Indonesia and 112 in Egypt.

SPECIFICATIONS •
CREW   3 (driver, commander, gunner)
COMBAT WEIGHT   16,000 lb (7,258 kg)
DIMENSIONS
   hull length   16 ft 5 in (5.0 m)
   width   6 ft 9 in (2.06 m)
   height   7 ft 4 in (2.24 m)
   wheelbase   8 ft 10 in (2.74 m)
MAIN ARMAMENT   1-meter turret with 2 gun stations for twin 7.62 or 12.7-mm machine guns with 200 ready 7.62-mm rounds and 2,200 7.62-mm rounds stowed in hull; or 100 ready 12.7-mm rounds and 1,000 12.7-mm rounds stowed in hull. Turret can also

bear combination of 7.62-mm machine and 40-mm grenade launcher with 100 7.62-mm rounds ready, 200 stowed in hull
elevation   −10°/+55°, traverse 360° at 45°/sec
SENSORS AND FIRE CONTROL   8 vision blocks, M28C sight, 500,000-candlepower searchlight
ARMOR   Cadloy steel armor proof against 7.62-mm ammunition
POWERPLANT   Cummins 149-hp liquid-cooled V-6 diesel engine, Allison automatic transmission with 4 forward/1 reverse gears
power-to-weight ratio
        20.53 hp/metric ton
SUSPENSION   4 × 4 (4 wheels driving, 2-wheel steering), coil springs on all 4 wheels, front axle has solid swing arm, rear axle has independent swing arms
SPEED   60 mph (96 km/h), range 800 mi (1,287 km)
OBSTACLE CLEARANCE   vertical 2 ft (0.61 m), gradient 60%, side slope 30%, fording 3 ft 10 in (1.17 m)

M113C&R Lynx

The M113C&R (Command and Reconnaissance) is a shorter, smaller variant of the basic M113 tracked armored personnel carrier in service in the Dutch and Canadian armies. (The name Lynx applies only to Canadian vehicles.)

Although sharing many components with the M113, the Lynx has one less road wheel station per side. In place of the unbroken glacis of the M113 is a stepped profile that reduces the apparent size still more. Unlike the M113, the engine is mounted in the rear.

As delivered, the C&R had an M2 12.7-mm machine gun mounted ahead of the cupola. In the late 1970s, the Netherlands Army retrofitted a larger 25-mm Oerlikon KBA-B automatic cannon in a GDB-AOA turret; this gun fires High-Explosive (HE) and Armor-Piercing Discarding Sabot (APDS) rounds.

There are other, minor layout differences between the Dutch and Canadian vehicles. For example, the radio operator sits to the driver's right in the C&R; the Lynx radio operator sits behind the driver, to the left and rear of the commander.

DEVELOPMENT • Begun by FMC Corp. as a private venture in 1963, the M113C&R was passed over by the US Army in favor of the M114 APC. Manufactured by FMC, San Jose, California, achieving initial operational capability in the Netherlands (260 vehicles) in 1966, in Canada (174) in 1968.

SPECIFICATIONS •

CREW   3 (commander, driver, radio operator); radio operator is also gunner in Dutch M113C&R
COMBAT WEIGHT   19,345 lb (8,775 kg)
ground pressure
        6.83 lb/in² (0.48 kg/cm²)
DIMENSIONS
hull length   15 ft 1 in (4.6 m)
extreme width
        7 ft 11 in (2.41 m)
height to hull top
        5 ft 9 in (1.75 m)
length of track on ground
        7 ft 10 in (2.39 m)
ground clearance
        16 in (410 mm)
track width   15 in (380 mm)
MAIN ARMAMENT
    Lynx: 12.7-mm M2 HB machine gun in M26 turret with 1,155 rounds
        elevation: −15°/+55°, traverse 360°
        secondary armament:
        7.62-mm machine gun with 2,000 rounds
    M113C&R: 25-mm Oerlikon KBA-B automatic cannon with 120 HE, 80 APDS rounds
        elevation: −12°/+52°, traverse 360°
SENSORS AND FIRE CONTROL   M19 infrared periscope

ARMOR   all-welded aluminum armor
POWERPLANT   GMC Detroit Diesel Allison 6V-53 215-hp 2-stroke water-cooled V-6 diesel engine, Allison TX100 transmission with torque converter and 3 forward/1 reverse gears
power-to-weight ratio
24.5 hp/metric ton
SUSPENSION (EACH SIDE)   torsion bar, 4 road wheels, front drive, rear idler, no return rollers
SPEED   44 mph (71 km/h), water speed 3.5 mph (5.6 km/h) with tracks, range 325 mi (523 km)
OBSTACLE CLEARANCE   vertical 2 ft (0.61 m), gradient 60%, trench 5 ft (1.52 m), amphibious

M551 Sheridan

The M551 was developed to provide heavy firepower in a light, air-droppable armored reconnaissance vehicle. The aluminum-hulled Sheridan has an unusual main armament consisting of the M81 152-mm gun/missile launcher. The weapon fires conventional combustible-case ammunition and the MGM-51 Shillelagh antitank missile. The missile has Semiactive Command to Line of Sight (SACLOS) guidance using a two-way Infrared (IR) link. Conventional ammunition includes White Phosphorous (WP), canister, and High-Explosive Antitank with Tracer (Multipurpose)—HEAT-T-MP—projectiles.

The gun-tube-launched, antitank missile proved very troublesome and delayed widespread deployment for several years. By the time most of the bugs had been smoked out, the tube-launched missile had been supplanted by improved kinetic energy penetrators for conventional tank guns, and the Sheridan's potential declined rapidly. Disappointment with the Sheridan led to a phaseout from active US Army units beginning in 1978.

However, the 82nd Airborne Division retains these vehicles in active service; these will be replaced by M8 Assault Gun System vehicles. 330 Sheridans were "visually modified" to represent Soviet tanks and other armored vehicles and serve at the Army's National Training Center in Fort Irwin, California.

DEVELOPMENT • The M551 achieved initial operational capability in 1968, although it was several years after that before it was in regular service in large numbers. A total of 1,562 were built by the Allison Division of General Motors from 1966 to 1970.

COMBAT   EXPERIENCE • Although fast and apparently heavily armed, the 64 Sheridans deployed to Vietnam in 1968–69 revealed many deficiencies, most requiring extensive redesign work to rectify.

12 Sheridans were used in the December 1989 Operation Just Cause—the US ouster of Panamanian General Noriega—where it was said to have performed well. Eight were delivered using a Low-Velocity Airdrop (LVAD) technique. The design's weight allowed it to overrun makeshift street barricades, and the 152-mm bunker-busting rounds proved effective against reinforced-concrete walls. The one armor-piercing RPG-7 antitank rocket directed against a Sheridan missed its target.

In August 1990, Sheridans were deployed to Saudi Arabia with the 82nd Airborne Division as part of Operation Desert Shield. They were initially sent as a stopgap quick-strike force to forestall any Iraqi moves into Saudi Arabia in the first few weeks.

Although it was later fitted with thermal imaging sights for night fighting, the Sheridan's role in Operation Desert Storm was limited primarily to reconnaissance by its age and light armor. Nevertheless, several Shillelagh missiles were fired at Iraqi bunkers.

SPECIFICATIONS •

CREW 4 (commander, gunner, loader, driver)

COMBAT WEIGHT 34,900 lb (15,830 kg)

ground pressure
6.97 lb/in² (0.49 kg/cm²)

DIMENSIONS

hull length 20 ft 8 in (6.3 m)
width 9 ft 3 in (2.82 m)
height 9 ft 8 in (2.95 m)
length of track on ground
12 ft (3.66 m)
ground clearance
19 in (483 mm)
track width 17.5 in (444 mm)

MAIN ARMAMENT 152-mm M81 gun/missile launcher with 20 HEAT-T-MP rounds and 8 Shillelagh missile rounds
elevation −8°/+19.5°, traverse 360°

SECONDARY WEAPONS 7.62-mm M73 machine gun with 3,080 rounds and 12.7-mm M2 HB antiaircraft machine gun with 1,000 rounds

SENSORS AND FIRE CONTROL M129 gunner's telescope, magnification 8×, 8° Field of View (FOV), M44 gunner's IR night sight, magnification 9×, 6° FOV, IR SACLOS data link

ARMOR aluminum hull, steel turret

POWERPLANT Detroit Diesel 6V-53T 300-hp water-cooled turbocharged 2-stroke V-6 diesel, Allison TG-250-2A powershift crossdrive transmission with 4 forward/2 reverse gears
power-to-weight ratio
18.95 hp/metric ton

SUSPENSION (EACH SIDE) torsion bar, 5 road wheels, rear drive, front idler, 2 shock absorbers, no return rollers

SPEED 45 mph (72 km/h), 3.6 mph (5.8 km/h) in water with tracks, range 373 mi (600 km)

OBSTACLE CLEARANCE vertical 2 ft 9 in (0.84 m), gradient 60%, side slope 40%, trench 8 ft 4 in (2.54 m), amphibious

COMBAT SUPPORT AND SERVICE VEHICLES

M9 Armored Combat Earthmover (ACE)

The M9 ACE is a full-tracked, relatively fast armored earthmover capable of constructing weapons positions, building or clearing obstacles, and recovering other vehicles in combat areas.

The ACE is a combination of a bulldozer and a front-end loader, with the blade forming the front of a large "bowl" that holds up to 237 ft² (6.7 m²) of fill. The top corners of the dozer blade are mounted on heavy arms that lower the blade for dozing and raise it to expose the bowl for loading. The vehicle's hydromechanical suspension can tilt fore and aft or 5° toward one corner of the blade; dozing leverage can be increased by placing ballast in the bowl.

The engine is in the right rear with the driver seat to its left. A heavy armored cupola with vision blocks and a hatch protects the driver under fire. When overhead protection isn't necessary, the hatch pivots up and back to allow the driver to sit up.

The M9 is fully amphibious in all but fast-running rivers and can be airlifted by the C-130 Hercules and larger transport aircraft.

DEVELOPMENT • ACE began development in 1958 as All-Purpose Ballastable Crawler (ABC). Actual prototyping as the Universal Engineer Tractor (UET) started in 1962 with examples built by

Caterpillar Tractor and Universal Harvester, the latter winning the 1963 development award. Operational requirements kept changing, and at times two programs competed for attention.

PACCAR involvement began in 1975; testing of four prototypes ended in August 1976 with type classification to Standard A approved in February 1977. First production did not begin, however, until 1985, as funding was inadequate and the Army demanded further improvements and changes.

Finally, BMY of York, Pennsylvania, began production, with the ACE achieving initial operational capability in 1986. Although the Army originally planned to acquire 1,318 vehicles, ultimately 566 vehicles were to be purchased.

The US Marine Corps announced a requirement for 257 vehicles in 1986; later revisions reduced the number to 180. The first 41 were requested in the FY1993 defense budget.

An undisclosed "Far Eastern" nation ordered 18 ACEs.

COMBAT EXPERIENCE • 151 ACEs
were deployed with US units in Saudi Arabia during Operation Desert Shield. Most were shipped during December and January after being prepared by BMY, including 99 in a 10-day period in January 1991. 30 were "loaned" to the US Marine Corps, 24 of these being used in Operation Desert Storm.

M9s lived up to their job description, preparing US armor and artillery positions and demolishing the barriers raised by Iraqi forces. ACEs were praised as being fast, mobile, and effective. In fact, the 1st Infantry Division's technique for clearing Iraqi trenches centered on the ACE. The M9 drove down the trench escorted by M2 Bradley APCs on each flank, leaving "a smooth place where the trench had been." The ACE's only limitation is that the driver is effectively blind when under armor.

SPECIFICATIONS •
CREW   1 (driver in armored cab)
BALLASTED WEIGHT   54,000 lb (24,494 kg)
  ground pressure, loaded
    14.5 lb/in (1.02 kg/cm)
DIMENSIONS
  hull length   20 ft 6 in (6.25 m)
  width with dozer wings
    10 ft 6 in (3.20 m), over
    tracks 8 ft 10 in (2.69
    m)
  height to top of cupola
    9 ft 10 in (2.69 m)
  freeboard when fording
    11 in (279 mm) with
    4,000-lb (1,814-kg) load
    and armor partially
    removed
  ground clearance, sprung
    13½ in (343 mm)
  length of track on ground
    8 ft 9 in (2.67 m)
  track width   18 in (460 mm)
ARMOR   steel, aluminum, and Kevlar armor on engine, powertrain, and operator's position
POWERPLANT   Cummins V903C 295-hp liquid-cooled 4-stroke V-8 diesel engine, Clark Model 13.5 HR 3610-2 torque-converter manual transmission with 6 forward/2 reverse gears
  power-to-weight ratio, ballasted
    12.04 hp/metric ton
SUSPENSION (EACH SIDE)   hydropneumatic with rotary actuators, 4 road wheels, rear drive, no front idler or return rollers
SPEED   road 30 mph (48.3 km/h), water 3 mph (4.8 km/h) with tracks, range 200 mi (322 km)
OBSTACLE CLEARANCE   vertical 1 ft 6 in (0.46 m), ballasted gradient 60%, ballasted side 40% slope, trench 5 ft 2 in (1.57 m), fording 3 ft (0.91 m)

M88A1
The M88 is the principal US medium Armored Recovery Vehicle (ARV) and is based on the M48 Patton Main Battle Tank (MBT). It is capable of recovering

and evacuating all US armored vehicles except for some models of the M60 and the M1 Abrams MBT. Adoption of the Improved Recovery Vehicle (IRV) with an uprated engine in 1992 was unenthusiastic, but made necessary by the increasing weight of the Army's Abrams tank. Two M88A1s are needed to tow an M1 tank, a limitation that showed to the M88's disadvantage during Operation Desert Storm.

The hull is of cast and rolled armor welded together. The crew compartment is to the front, with the engine and transmission to the rear and doors on either side of the hull.

A blade mounted at the front is used for dozing operations and to stabilize the vehicle when using the winch or crane. The A-frame crane can hoist 12,000 lb (5,443 kg) with the dozer blade up, up to 40,000 lb (18,143 kg) with suspension locked out, and 50,000 lb (22,680 kg) with the blade down. The main winch has a 90,000-lb (40,824-kg) pull.

A fording kit is available which allows the vehicle to ford water 8 ft 6 in (2.6 m) deep. An auxiliary fuel pump can transfer fuel to other vehicles at a rate of 25 US gal/min (95 liters/min).

VARIANTS •
M88 (1,075 delivered from 1961) with Continental AVSI-1790-6A 980-hp V-12 gasoline engine, M88A1 (2,100 new, 875 converted) with diesel engine, NBC collective protection kit, M88A1E1/M88A2 Improved Recovery Vehicle (IRV) with nearly double crane and winch capacity.

DEVELOPMENT • M88 achieved its initial operational capability in 1961; M88A1 conversions began in 1977. Manufactured by BMY Corp., York, Pennsylvania (later United Defense). Production ended in 1989 but resumed in 1990 after the assembly line layout was reoriented to small-batch orders.

The Army's dissatisfaction with IRV trials led to the project's cancellation in April 1989, but lack of options led to development funding in September 1992. Production started in 1993 on 186 vehicles planned, with First Unit Equipped (FUE) planned for FY1994.

In service with the US Army and Marine Corps and over 20 other countries.

COMBAT EXPERIENCE • US units in Vietnam depended heavily on the M88 for recovery in the field, and the vehicle was widely deployed.

Although it was again widely deployed, the M88's performance in Operation Desert Storm earned unfavorable reviews. According to Defense News, 3rd Armored Division M88s could not tow M1A1 Abrams tanks and were said to have been "operational" only 60% of the time. The General Accounting Office reported in 1992 that in one brigade of the 24th Infantry Division (Mechanized), Abrams tanks more often towed M88s than the other way around. Moreover, a low towing speed of 5 mph (8 km/h) did not prevent engine and transmission breakdowns.

SPECIFICATIONS •
CREW
    M88A1: 4 (commander, mechanic, driver, co-driver)
    IRV: 3 (commander, mechanic, driver)
COMBAT WEIGHT
    M88A1: 112,000 lb (50,803 kg)
    IRV: 139,000 lb (63,049 kg)
    ground pressure
        M88A1: 10.86 lb/in² (0.76 kg/cm²)
        IRV: 13.40 lb/in² (0.94 kg/cm²)
DIMENSIONS
    hull length   27 ft 1 in (8.27 m)
    width   11 ft 3 in (3.43 m)
    height with machine gun
                     10 ft 3 in (3.12 m)
    length of track on ground
                     15 ft 1 in (4.61 m)
    ground clearance
                     17 in (430 mm)
    track width   28 in (710 mm)

ARMAMENT   12.7-mm M2 HB machine gun (1,500 rounds)

ARMOR   12.7–50-mm cast armor (IRV has 30-mm overlay), ballistic armor track skirts on IRV

POWERPLANT   Teledyne-Continental AVDS-1790-2DR (M88A1) or -8DR (IRV), 750-hp (M88A1) or 1,050-hp (IRV) air-cooled supercharged fuel-injected V-12 diesel engine, XT-1410-4 (M88A1) or -5A (IRV) crossdrive transmission with 3 forward/1 reverse gears

power-to-weight ratio
    M88A1 14.76 hp/metric ton, IRV 16.65 hp/metric ton

SUSPENSION (EACH SIDE)   torsion bar, 6 road wheels, rear drive, front idler, 3 shock absorbers, 3 return rollers

SPEED   27 mph (43.5 km/h), with towed load on level ground (M88A1) 18 mph (29 km/h) (IRV) 13–25 mph (21–40 km/h), range 280 mi (450 km)

OBSTACLE CLEARANCE   vertical 3 ft 6 in (1.07 m), gradient 60%, trench 8 ft 7 in (2.62 m), fording 4 ft 8 in (1.42 m)

M548 Cargo Carrier

The M548 is a full-tracked chassis based on the M113 armored personnel carrier and is used for ammunition resupply and cargo carriage. Although the M548 has proved valuable as an off-road resupply vehicle, it is easily overmatched by high cargo loads. Other M548 modifications carry missile systems and radar stations.

All vehicles in the M548 family have suspensions that differ from the M113 armored personnel carrier only in a thicker torsion bar and different final drive gear ratio. Physically, the M548 differs from the M113 in having a built-up cab and a low cargo deck protected by detachable hollow aluminum panels on the sides and a nylon cover supported by six aluminum bows. An optional cargo beam and traveling hoist can lift up to 1,500 lb (680 kg).

VARIANTS • M548 (4,970 delivered from 1965) and M548A1 (278 new, 2,806 upgrades) had engine cooling and suspension improvements.

Missile launcher variants include the M752 (launcher) and M688 (resupply) vehicles for the Lance short-range tactical missile, the M730 Chaparral air defense vehicle. (The M727 HAWK mobile surface-to-air missile system variant is out of service.) Israel's M548/LAR 160 Multiple Rocket Launcher System carries two 13-round pods or one 18-round pod of 160-mm bombardment rockets.

M1015 communications vehicles carry radio and electronic countermeasures equipment.

DEVELOPMENT • Initial operational capability in 1966. In production by FMC Corp., San Jose, California. In service with the US Army and more than 10 other countries.

COMBAT EXPERIENCE • US units operating in Vietnam found the unarmored M548s vulnerable to mines or artillery, but liked the vehicles' reliability, cross-country agility, and relative ease of handling.

20 years later, M548s served most of the US artillery units in Operations Desert Shield and Desert Storm. During the buildup, the M548 suffered at first from rubber separating from the road wheels and transmission case cracking. The consensus was that the vehicles had "excellent" cross-country mobility but that the engines tended to overheat.

After the February 1991 ground war, some Army units stressed two points: (1) the M548 performed its mission adequately after adjustments were made to accommodate its limitations, but (2) the Army needs to replace it. The 3rd Battalion, 41st Field Artillery of the 24th Mechanized Infantry Division, encountered "severe maintenance problems" with their 24 fully loaded M548s (96 rounds—

12 pallets—of ammunition). Battalion officers reduced the loads on each of the 24 M548s to seven pallets (56 rounds), which kept all of them running during the 200-mi (370-km) assault.

On the other hand, the 1st Infantry Division's action report singled out the M548 as "a piece of junk" when asserting the need to replace all but the M113A3. Other units found that maintenance personnel had to put too much effort into keeping the M548s running, which led to a call for more M985 Heavy Expanded Mobility Tactical Trucks (HEMTT).

SPECIFICATIONS •
CREW 4
WEIGHT
  combat   28,400 lb (12,882 kg)
  payload   12,000 lb (5,443 kg)
  ground pressure
               8.62 lb/in² (0.61 kg/cm²)
DIMENSIONS
  hull length   18 ft 10½ in (5.75 m)
  width, overall
               8 ft 10 in (2.69 m)
  height without machine gun
               8 ft 11 in (2.71 m),
               reducible to 6 ft 4 in
               (2.24 m)
  ground clearance
               17 in (430 mm)
  length of track on ground
               9 ft 3 in (2.82 m)
  track width   15 in (380 mm)
ARMAMENT fitted with ring mount for 7.62-mm machine gun (660 rounds) or 12.7-mm machine gun (300 rounds)
POWERPLANT GMC Model 6V-53 215-hp liquid-cooled 2-stroke V-6 diesel, Allison TX-100-1 3-speed transmission with torque converter with 6 forward/2 reverse gears
  power-to-weight ratio
               16.69 hp/metric ton
SUSPENSION (EACH SIDE) torsion bar, 5 road wheels, front drive, rear idler, 3 shock absorbers, no return rollers

SPEED 40 mph (64 km/h), acceleration 0–20 mph (0–32 km/h) 14 seconds, range 285 mi (458 km)
OBSTACLE CLEARANCE vertical 2 ft (0.61 m), gradient 60%, side slope 30%, trench 5 ft 6 in (1.68 m), fording 3 ft 3 in (1.0 m) (non-US M548s are amphibious, being propelled in the water by the tracks)

M578 Light Armored Recovery Vehicle

Based on the M107/M110 SPG chassis, the M578 is a light armored recovery vehicle used for recovering disabled vehicles as well as changing major subsystems in the field (engines, transmissions, and guns). It is used primarily for light armored vehicles and other support vehicles.

The hydraulic crane is housed in a turret mounted at the rear of the chassis. A stabilizing spade hydraulically lowers from the rear. Turret traverse is 360°, and the boom's capacity is 30,000 lb (13,607 kg). Towing winch capacity is 60,000 lb (27,030 kg), and the hoist winch can manage 20,500 lb (9,299 kg). Relatively thin steel armor offers splinter protection.

DEVELOPMENT • Designed and built by FMC of San Jose, California, achieving initial operational capability in 1963; 826 delivered by 1969. Bowen-McLaughlin-York (York, Pennsylvania) reopened production in 1971 and built 1,018 more by 1983. In service with the US Army and more than 10 other countries.

COMBAT EXPERIENCE • M578s were widely deployed in Vietnam during the eight-year-long US involvement. M578s supported US airborne, armored, and infantry units during Operation Desert Storm's ground war.

SPECIFICATIONS •
CREW 3
COMBAT WEIGHT   53,572 lb (24,300 kg),
air-portable 45,069 lb (20,443 kg)
ground pressure
9.95 lb/in² (0.70 kg/
cm²)
DIMENSIONS
length   hull 18 ft 4 in (5.59 m)
overall 21 ft 1 in (6.43
m)
width   10 ft 4 in (3.15 m)
height to top of cupola
9 ft 7 in (2.92 m)
length of track on ground
12 ft 4 in (3.76 m)
ground clearance
16 in (0.44 m)
track width   17 in (0.46 m)
ARMAMENT   12.7-mm M2 HB antiaircraft machine gun with 500 rounds
POWERPLANT   Detroit Diesel 8V71T
425-hp liquid-cooled turbocharged
V-8 diesel engine, Allison XTG-411-2A
powershift crossdrive transmission
with 4 forward/2 reverse gears
power-to-weight ratio
17.49 hp/metric ton,
loaded
SUSPENSION (EACH SIDE) torsion bar, 5
road wheels, front drive, no idler, no
return rollers
SPEED   34 mph (55 km/h), range 450
mi (725 km)
OBSTACLE CLEARANCE   vertical 3 ft 4 in
(1.02 m), gradient 60%, trench 7 ft 9
in (2.36 m), fording 3 ft 6 in (1.07 m)

M728 Combat Engineer Vehicle (CEV)

Based on the M60A1 main battle tank,
the M728 CEV recovers disabled vehicles,
clears and prepares obstructions, prepares firing positions for artillery, and
bombards hostile strongpoints at point-
blank range.

The hull is of cast sections welded together, with the engine, transmission,
and fuel tanks in the rear of the hull. A
25,000-lb (11,340-kg) capacity winch is
mounted in the bow.

The turret is cast in one piece. The
commander and gunner sit to the right of
the stubby main, "bunker-busting" M135
165-mm gun; the loader is to the left. This
demolition gun fires a 66-lb (30-kg)
round to a maximum range of 1,093 yd
(1,000 m). In addition to the gun, the
turret can support an A-frame crane with
35,000-lb (15,786-kg) capacity.

DEVELOPMENT • The T118 prototype
was constructed in 1960; the M728 entered production in 1965. 300 produced
at Chrysler Corp.'s Detroit Arsenal Tank
Plant, Warren, Michigan, with the M728
achieving initial operational capability in
1968. In addition to US Army service,
M728s are found in Saudi Arabian and
Singapore army service.

COMBAT EXPERIENCE • US Army
CEVs were used for a variety of tasks during Operations Desert Shield and Desert
Storm. During the ground war that began
on February 24, 1991, they broke through
berms and used their M135 demolition
gun against obstacles and bunkers. A CEV
of the 6th Battalion, 6th Regiment, 1st
Armored Division, fired 21 165-mm
rounds into the stubbornly defended
town of Al Busayyah: "That totally destroyed all the resistance in the town,"
according to the battalion commander.

After the cease-fire, CEV guns were
used to break up coke piles that had
formed around approximately 20% of
the burning oil wells in Kuwait. According to the US Army, the guns reduced the
time to break up coke formation from as
long as two days to 15 minutes.

SPECIFICATIONS •
CREW   4 (commander, gunner, loader,
driver)
COMBAT WEIGHT   117,286 lb (53,200
kg)

ground pressure
12.66 lb/in² (0.89 kg/cm²)

DIMENSIONS
hull length   29 ft 3 in (8.91 m)
width with blade
12 ft 2 in (3.7 m)
height   10 ft 8 in (3.26 m)
length of track on ground
13 ft 11 in (4.24 m)
ground clearance
15 in (381 mm)
track width   28 in (711 mm)
MAIN GUN   165-mm M135 demolition gun with 30 rounds
elevation   −10°/+20°, traverse 360°
secondary coaxial
7.62-mm M219 or M240 machine gun and 12.7-mm M85 antiaircraft machine gun
ARMOR
hull: 120 mm glacis, 76 mm sides, 44 mm rear, 57 mm top, 13 mm floor
turret: 120 mm front, 50 mm rear, 25 mm top
POWERPLANT   Continental AVDS-1790-2A or -2D 750-hp air-cooled 4-stroke V-12 diesel engine, Allison CD-850-6A powershift crossdrive transmission with 2 forward/1 reverse ranges
power-to-weight ratio
14.38 hp/metric ton
SUSPENSION   torsion bar, 6 road wheels, rear drive, front idler, 3 shock absorbers, 3 return rollers
SPEED   30 mph (48 km/h), range 280 mi (450 km)
OBSTACLE CLEARANCE   vertical obstacle 2 ft 6 in (0.76 m), gradient 60%, trench 8 ft 3 in (2.51 m), fording 4 ft (1.22 m), with fording kit 8 ft (2.44 m)

M977 Heavy Expanded Mobility Tactical Truck (HEMTT)

The M977 HEMTT (pronounced "hemmet") is the base vehicle for a series of 10-US ton 8 by 8 trucks that proved versatile, rugged, and reliable during Operations Desert Shield and Desert Storm. The cab seats two and is of heavy-duty, welded-steel construction. The spare wheel is mounted to the right rear of the cab. The cargo area is 17 ft 9 in (5.4 m) long and has drop sides to assist in loading/unloading.

A light-duty crane (capacity of 47,500 ft lb/6,567 kg m) is mounted on the rear of the truck for loading operations. All variants can be equipped with an optional 20,000-lb (9,072-kg) capacity self-recovery winch.

VARIANTS •
M978 2,500-US gal (9,500-liter) tanker, M983 tractor used with M989 Heavy Expanded Mobility Ammunition Trailer (HEMAT), M984A1 wrecker, M985 cargo with crane.

DEVELOPMENT • In production by Oshkosh Truck Corp., Oshkosh, Wisconsin, achieving initial operational capability in 1983. The original plan for 7,490 trucks was superseded by purchases that extended procurement to almost 13,000 vehicles.

COMBAT EXPERIENCE • Few of the US systems used in Operations Desert Shield and Desert Storm received such unconditional praise from their users as did the HEMTT. At the beginning of Operation Desert Storm in January 1991, the US Army had 11,177 HEMTTs in its inventory. 4,410 HEMTTs were deployed in Saudi Arabia, including 1,700 that were described as indispensable to the VII Corps sweep around the Iraqi right during Operation Desert Storm's ground war in February 1991. The HEMTTs were the only large cargo vehicles that could keep up with the advance.

A postwar review by officers of the 18th Field Artillery Brigade (Airborne) stated: "This vehicle was an outstanding asset. It could travel through all types of terrain— deep sand, mud, and rocks—with a full load. We loaded HEMTTs to their maximum gross weight capability. They never got stuck and didn't break down."

The commander of 1st Armored Division Artillery recommended that "all trucks that operate forward of a division's rear are either from the HMMWV [High Mobility Multipurpose Wheeled Vehicle] or HEMTT family of trucks." Some HEMTTs were converted to carry the artillery's Tactical Fire Direction System (TACFIRE) shelter.

The soft sand caused some problems at first for the HEMTTs of the 27th Field Artillery of the 42nd Field Artillery Brigade, however. When the support elements jumped off with the 3rd Armored Division, M985 HEMTTs with M989 HEMAT ammunition trailers each carrying four six-rocket MLRS pods struggled to keep pace with the M270 launcher vehicles. Within the first few hours, five driveshafts had snapped under the strain. A change in driving method to account for the unpredictable traction eliminated the problem.

SPECIFICATIONS •

CREW   2

GROSS VEHICLE WEIGHT RATINGS (GVWR)
62,000 lb (28,123 kg) except M984A1 95,000 lb (43,091 kg) and M985 68,000 lb (30,844 kg)
payload   22,000 lb (9,979 kg)

DIMENSIONS
length   33 ft 4 ½ in (10.17 m) except M983 29 ft 2 ½ in (8.9 m) and M984A1 32 ft 9 in (9.98 m)
overall width
8 ft (2.44 m)
cab height   8 ft 5 in (2.57 m)

distance between equalizer pivots
17 ft 6 in (5.33 m) except M983 15 ft 1 in (4.6 m) and M984 15 ft 11 in (4.85 m)

POWERPLANT   Detroit Diesel 8V-92TA 445-hp liquid-cooled 2-stroke V-8 diesel, Allison HT740D automatic transmission with torque converter, 4 forward/1 reverse gears
power-to-weight ratio
M977, M978, M983: 16.18 hp/metric ton
M984A1: 10.33 hp/metric ton
M985: 14.43 hp/metric ton

SUSPENSION   8 × 8 (8 wheels driving, 4-wheel steering), Hendrickson leaf spring with steel saddle, equalizing beams, and 10-in (254-mm) vertical travel on front and rear

SPEED   55 mph (88 km/h), range with full payload at 33.5 mph (54 km/h) 300 mi (483 km)

OBSTACLE CLEARANCE   gradient 60%

M992 Field Artillery Ammunition Support Vehicle (FAASV)

The FAASV (Fas-Vee) is a resupply vehicle based on the chassis of the M109 155-mm self-propelled howitzer. A covered superstructure protected by 32 mm of aluminum armor holds ammunition storage racks and a power-operated conveyor belt.

The FAASV carries 93 projectiles, 99 charges, and 104 fuzes in honeycomb storage racks. The on-board Ammunition Handling Equipment (AHE) uses a powered X-Y (Cartesian) stacker to pull rounds from the racks. After assembly and fuzing, the rounds travel to the M109 along a hydraulic conveyor at 6 rounds/ min. An Auxiliary Power Unit (APU) powers the conveyor, stacker, and vehicle electrical system.

The driver of the M992 is located on the left front of the hull with the engine to his right. At the forward part of the superstructure is a three-part resupply hatch behind which is the commander's cupola. The FAASV has an armored rear door that swings upward and outward to provide overhead protection between the FAASV and the howitzer during loading operations.

FAASVs in service with Egypt are fitted with a 1,500-lb (680-kg) capacity crane at the front of the hull.

VARIANTS •
Command post vehicle sold to Egypt (72), Greece (41), and Taiwan (six).

M1050 developed to support the M110 203-mm self-propelled howitzer but not funded.

DEVELOPMENT • Manufactured by BMY in York, Pennsylvania, and achieved its initial operational capability in 1985. Original US Army requirement was for one FAASV for each M109 (960 total vehicles), but budget limitations cut procurement to 675. Also in service in Saudi Arabia (60), Egypt (51), and Spain (six).

COMBAT EXPERIENCE • FAASVs accompanied several US artillery units during Operation Desert Storm. The commander of the XVIII Airborne Corps artillery commented that the one brigade with FAASVs didn't encounter the mobility problems that affected the others, which were supported by older, slower, unprotected M548 ammunition carriers.

Among the lessons learned was the need for better fire-extinguishing equipment in FAASVs. Although the Halon fire extinguishers operated properly when fire broke out in two vehicles after the ground war, the vehicles were destroyed when the fire reignited and reached the ammunition supply.

SPECIFICATIONS •
CREW   2 (commander and driver) + 6 troops
LOADED WEIGHT   58,500 lb (26,535 kg)
DIMENSIONS
length   22 ft 3 in (6.78 m)
width   10 ft 4 in (3.15 m)
height   10 ft 6 in (3.2 m)
ground clearance
                 14½ in (368 mm)
length of track on ground
                 13 ft (3.96 m)
track width   15 in (381 mm)
ARMOR   32 mm of alloy plate
POWERPLANT   Detroit Diesel 8V-71T 405-hp liquid-cooled turbocharged 2-stroke V-8 diesel engine, Allison XTG-411-2A crossdrive transmission with 4 forward/2 reverse gears
power-to-weight ratio
                 15.49 hp/metric ton
SUSPENSION (EACH SIDE)   torsion bar, 7 road wheels, front drive, rear idler, no return rollers
SPEED   road 35 mph (56.3 km/h), up 20% slope 12.5 mph (20 km/h), range 217 mi (350 km)
OBSTACLE CLEARANCE   vertical 1 ft 9 in (0.53 m), gradient 60%, side slope 40%, trench 6 ft (1.83 m), fording 3 ft 6 in (1.07 m)

M998 High-Mobility Multipurpose Wheeled Vehicle (HMMWV)

The US M998 "Humvee" is a 4 × 4-wheeled tactical vehicle being procured in large numbers to replace several older light trucks and cargo carriers in the US Army, Air Force, and Marine Corps. Like the earlier jeep, the Humvee is reliable, sturdy, capable of operating in all types of terrain, and readily adaptable to a variety of missions. Significant improvements over the Jeep include a better power-to-weight ratio, twice the payload, automatic transmission and power steering, and

HMMWV with Tow
U.S. GOVERNMENT DEPARTMENT OF DEFENSE

better ground clearance. The Humvee is also far less likely to roll over in a sharp turn than was the jeep.

The basic vehicle is a boxy truck using many commercial drivetrain components. Depending on its role, the HMMWV has a two- or 4-door cab with either a soft canvas top or a hard roof. In its basic configuration, the HMMWV is unarmored and unprotected against NBC warfare. The Humvee is large enough to carry several types of weapons systems, and its speed and cross-country mobility have led to its use as a reconnaissance vehicle.

The common chassis serves as a weapons carrier as well as utility vehicle, ambulance, squad carrier, shelter carrier, TOW antitank guided-missile carrier, and Pedestal-Mounted Stinger (PMS) surface-to-air missile system carrier. A C-130 Hercules cargo aircraft can carry three HMMWVs, a C-141B Starlifter holds six, and a C-5 Galaxy can transport 15.

VARIANTS • M966/M1036/M1045/M1046 TOW missile carrier, M996/M997/M1035 ambulance, M998/M1038 cargo troop carrier, M1025/M1026/M1043/M1044 armament carrier, M1028 AN/TRQ-32 Teammate Comint system, M1037/M1042 shelter carrier, M1069 light artillery prime mover, M1097 "Heavy Hummer" with uprated chassis.

DEVELOPMENT • After an early 1980s competition, the first AM General Humvee was delivered in 1985. More than 90,000 had been delivered by 1993, with production continuing. Later variants include the M1097 "Heavy Hummer" with an uprated Humvee chassis permitting a Gross Vehicle Weight (GVW) raised to 10,001 lb (4,356 kg) and payload increase for shelter carriers to 4,400 lb (1,996 kg). AM General also tested the Cab-Over Cargo Truck (COCT) with Heavy Hummer chassis adapted to lightweight, high-payload-capacity truck having a GVW of 12,000 lb (5,443 kg) and 5,000 lb (2,268-kg) payload.

Several other national armies and police forces operate Humvees, including Djibouti, Israel, Kuwait, Luxembourg, the Philippines, Saudi Arabia, and the United Arab Emirates. Civilian versions have been sold to the Chinese Ministry of Petroleum and the US Border Patrol, and a $40,000 commercial version became available in 1992.

COMBAT EXPERIENCE • More than 20,000 Humvees were deployed to Saudi Arabia in 1990 under Operation Desert Shield, where they lived up to their billing as the new jeep. The problems that cropped up were relatively minor, although annoying; these included steering gear box seals leakage, broken generator mounting bolts, and failure of a plastic speedometer gear in the transmission. Flat tires were a problem because the HMMWV doesn't have a spare wheel and tire as standard equipment.

After Operation Desert Storm began, "up-armored" Humvee scout cars were used by the US Army and Marine Corps to probe Iraqi positions. Many were armed with TOW antitank missiles and 12.7-mm machine guns; their passengers also had laser designators to support coalition air attacks. Marine Combined Antitank (CAT) teams consisted of six Humvees with TOW launchers.

When the ground war began, 50 Humvees of the 101st Airborne Division were airlifted by helicopter to establish a forward base in Iraq. Humvees of all descriptions accompanied the northern rush into Iraq and Kuwait, often taking the surrender of Iraqi units on their own.

SPECIFICATIONS •

CREW 1 (driver) + 3–7 troops or casualties

WEIGHT (lightest and heaviest of M998 series)
- *curb* basic cargo/troop carrier: 5,200 lb (2,359 kg) shelter carrier: 5,424 lb (2,460 kg)
- *payload* basic cargo/troop carrier: 2,500 lb (1,134 kg) shelter carrier: 3,176 lb (1,441 kg)
- *gross vehicle* basic cargo/troop carrier: 7,700 lb (3,493 kg) shelter carrier: 8,600 lb (3,901 kg)

DIMENSIONS
- *hull length* 15 ft (4.57 m) except ambulance 16 ft 9 in (5.11 m), shelter 15 ft 8 in (4.78 m)
- *width* 7 ft 1 in (2.16 m)
- *height (depending on role)* 5 ft 9 in (1.75 m) to 8 ft 8 in (2.64 m)
- *ground clearance* 16 in (406 mm)
- *wheelbase* 10 ft 10 in (3.3 m)

PROTECTION Armament, TOW, and PMS carriers have supplemental armor

POWERPLANT Detroit Diesel 150-hp air-cooled V-8 diesel, automatic transmission with 3 forward/1 reverse gears

SUSPENSION independent double A-arm with coil spring on all wheels, front stabilizer bar

SPEED 65 mph (105 km/h), range 300 mi (483 km)

OBSTACLE CLEARANCE vertical 2 ft 6 in (0.76 m), gradient 60%, side slope 40%, fording 2 ft 6 in (0.76 m) without preparation, 5 ft (1.52 m) with preparation

M1075 Palletized Load System

The Palletized Load System (PLS) was developed to simplify the handling of bulk resupply from rear areas to near the battlefield. The tractor vehicle is based on the Heavy Expanded Mobility Tactical Transport (HEMTT) and can carry one demountable cargo bed called a flatrack while towing an M1076 or M1077 trailer loaded with a second.

The all-wheel-drive truck has two axles just behind the cab and three more under the bed. The forward two axles and the rearmost axle are steerable, which improves maneuverability. A Central Tire Inflation System can be set to four preset levels—Highway (highest pressure), Cross-Country, Mud-Sand-Snow, and Emergency.

The key to the PLS is the multilift hoist located on the truck bed. Pairs of hydraulic rams extend the upper and lower arms back and down to position the fixed hook under the lift bar mounted on the forward edge of the flatrack. Once it has hooked the flatrack, the lower arm travels up and forward through a nearly 180° arc, pulling the flatrack onto the truck bed. Up to 24 pallets of ammunition and other heavy cargo can be loaded in one movement. As part of further development, the flatrack design was upgraded to allow use as an International Standards Organization (ISO) container, which simplifies transportation aboard train, truck, or ship. A 3,900-lb (1,769-kg) lifting capacity crane is also fitted.

DEVELOPMENT • Oshkosh Truck Corp. (Oshkosh, Wisconsin) is the builder, the PLS achieving initial operational capability in 1993. Development began in the early 1980s with first test funding requested in 1985; competition between Oshkosh, GM, and PACCAR. Originally decided in favor of the PAC-CAR entry, later retrials resulted in the award to Oshkosh in July 1990.

Army goals in 1992 set at 3,400 trucks, 1,521 trailers, and 63,418 flatracks, but likely to be reduced.

SPECIFICATIONS •

WEIGHT   gross vehicle 86,595 lb (39,290 kg), gross combination 136,970 lb (62,135 kg)

DIMENSIONS
   truck without flatrack
       length: 24 ft (7.34 m)
       overall width: 8 ft (2.44 m)
       height, cab: 9 ft 6 in (2.89 m)
   truck/trailer combination length, extended
       62 ft 1 in (18.943 m)
   wheelbase   18 ft 9 in (5.705 m)
   ground clearance
       15½ in (394 mm)

POWERPLANT   Detroit Diesel 8V-92TA 500-hp liquid-cooled 2-stroke V-8 diesel, Allison CLT-755 ATEC automatic transmission with torque converter and 5 forward/1 reverse gears

SUSPENSION
   10 × 10 (first, second, and fifth axles steer)
   front tandem: Hendrickson RT-340 walking beam
   third axle: Hendrickson Turner air ride
   rear tandem: Hendrickson RT-400 walking beam

SPEED   55 mph (90 km/h), range 336 mi (541 km)

OBSTACLE CLEARANCE   angle of approach 42°, angle of departure 62°, turning circle 96 ft (29.3 m), fording depth 4 ft (1.22 m)

M1078 Family of Medium Tactical Vehicles

The Family of Medium Tactical Vehicles (FMTV) is a series of 4 × 4 (Light Medium Tactical Vehicle/LMTV) and 6 × 6

(Medium Tactical Vehicle/MTV) trucks developed to replace aging 2½-ton ("deuce-and-a-half") and 5-ton trucks.

To reduce costs and speed up acquisition, bidders were required to use as many commercially available components as possible. The vehicle needed to show good cross-country and adverse-weather mobility, to share at least 75% of its components among variants, to be operated by both large male and small female drivers, and to be easily maintained and repaired.

The basis of Stewart & Stevenson's winning entry is the Austrian Steyr-Daimler-Puch 12 M 21 4 × 4 already in service in the Austrian Army. Given the extensive truck-building experience of its two competitors, the choice of Stewart & Stevenson surprised many observers. The size of the program was much larger than any other single effort the company had undertaken before. Stewart & Stevenson officials noted in rebuttal that the company has built many types of specialized vehicles and that the baseline FMTV truck was already in service.

In adapting the 12 M 21, Stewart & Stevenson sharply reduced the foreign content in the design by using US components, including the Allison MD-D7 seven-speed automatic transmission with integral transfer case in place of the nine-speed manual used by Austrian trucks.

The cab is designed to take three passengers. It has power-assist steering, fore and aft adjustable seat, tilt and telescoping steering wheel, and a Central Tire Inflation System (CTIS), which can remotely adjust tire pressure to one of five settings according to road conditions. A 12.7-mm machine-gun mount is fitted to the reinforced cab roof.

Some variants can be delivered to a landing area using the Low-Altitude Parachute Extraction System/Airdrop (LAPES/AD).

VARIANTS • LMTV 4 × 4 types include the M1078 cargo, M1079 van, M1081 LAPES-capable cargo, and M1080 chassis for other bodies.

FMTV 6 × 6 types include the M1083 cargo, M1084 cargo with crane, M1085 long-bed cargo, M1086 long-bed cargo with crane, M1087 expansible van, M1088 tractor, M1089 wrecker, M1090 dump truck, M1091 fuel tanker, M1092 chassis, M1093 cargo-LAPES/AD, and M1094 dump-LAPES/AD.

DEVELOPMENT • The FMTV program began in 1987 with prototype contracts awarded in October 1988 to BMY Tactical Truck Corp. of Marysville, Ohio, Stewart & Stevenson of Sealy, Texas, and Teledyne Continental Motors of Muskegon, Michigan. Stewart & Stevenson won the competition in October 1991, with the First Unit Equipped (FUE) in 1993.

Program goals originally set at 112,000 MTVs procured over a 30-year period. A June 1991 decision scaled the plan down to 89,000 trucks, with first five-year plan reduced from 19,000 to 14,000 and later to 11,000 trucks.

SPECIFICATIONS •
CREW 3
PAYLOAD   4 × 4, 5,000 lb (2,268 kg);
6 × 6, 10,000 lb (4,536 kg)
DIMENSIONS
overall length ·
LMTV: 21 ft 2 in to 21 ft 11 in (6.461-6.682 m)
MTV: 22 ft 10 in (6.961 m) (M1093) to 31 ft 9 in (9.689 m) (M1086)
width   8 ft (2.44 m)
height, max to top of cab
9 ft 1 in (2.76 m)
wheelbase   4 × 4: 12 ft 9½ in (3.9 m)
6 × 6: ranges from 13 ft 5 in (4.10 m) (M1083, M1090, M1093) to 18 ft ½ in (5.5 m) (M1086)
ground clearance
22 in (559 mm)
ANTIAIRCRAFT ARMAMENT   12.7-mm machine gun mount over cab

POWERPLANT   Caterpillar 3116 ATAAC 225-hp (LMTV), 290-hp (MTV) liquid-cooled turbocharged aftercooled in-line 6-cylinder diesel engine, Allison MD-D7 automatic transmission with 7 forward/1 reverse gears
power-to-weight ratio
18.9-23.7 hp/metric ton
SUSPENSION (EACH SIDE)
front: longitudinal leaf with shock absorbers
rear: longitudinal leaf with shocks (LMTV), bogie with leaf spring over walking beam (MTV)
SPEED   55 mph (88 km/h), range more than 400 mi (644 km) (LMTV), more than 300 mi (483 km) (MTV)
OBSTACLE CLEARANCE   approach angle 40°, departure angle 40° (LMTV), 63° (basic MTV), gradient 60%, side slope 30%, fording basic 3 ft (0.91 m), with preparation 5 ft (1.52 m)

Mk 48 Logistic Vehicle System (LVS)

The 8 × 8 Mk 48 LVS is an articulated cargo transporter that consists of the Mk 48 tractor and four types of Rear Body Units (RBU). Such a design permits much tighter turns (e.g., a turning radius up to 30% less than a conventional fixed-wheel-base truck) and better off-road mobility.

The tractor consists of a two-person cab ahead of the engine and is of heavy-duty, welded-steel construction. The powertrain is identical to that of the M977 Heavy Expanded Mobility Tactical Truck (HEMTT) series.

The tractor and RBU are linked through an articulated joint that transmits power to the rear two axles. The joint is also hydraulically driven to provide 32° of steering (yaw) motion to each side and 6° of roll freedom. The RBUs are quickly interchangeable among the platform, wrecker/recovery, tractor (i.e., fifth wheel), drop-side cargo with crane, and pivoting frame variants.

VARIANTS •
RBUs include 1,451 Mk 14 logistics platforms for cargo containers, 97 Mk 15 wrecker/recovery with crane and winch, 249 Mk 16 semitractors with standard fifth wheel, 277 Mk 17 cargo bodies with drop-down sides, and 530 Mk 18 tilting-bed platforms converted from Mk 14.

DEVELOPMENT • Marine Corps trials began in 1981. Production by Oshkosh Truck Corp., Oshkosh, Wisconsin, ran from July 1985 to September 1989, the LVS achieving initial operational capability in 1986. 1,682 Mk 48 front halves delivered. A total of 2,074 RBUs were delivered.

COMBAT EXPERIENCE • Between 800 and 1,000 Marine Corps LVSs were sent to Saudi Arabia in 1990 for Operations Desert Shield and Desert Storm. All variants except for the Mk 18 were used and performed well.

SPECIFICATIONS •
CREW   2
GROSS VEHICLE COMBINATION WEIGHT RATINGS (GVCWR)
on road   Mk 14: 150,000 lb (68,039 kg)
Mk 15 and 17: 153,971 lb (69,840 kg)
Mk 16: 188,000 lb (85,275 kg)
off road, all versions
105,000 lb (47,627 kg)
off-road payload
Mk 14, Mk 18: 25,000 lb (11,340 kg)
Mk 17: 20,000 lb (9,072 kg)
DIMENSIONS
length   Mk 14, Mk 17: 38 ft (11.58 m)
Mk 15: 37 ft (11.28 m)
Mk 16: 33 ft 1 in (10.09 m)
Mk 18: 35 ft 9 in (10.9 m)

overall width 8 ft (2.44 m)
cab height   8 ft 6 in (2.59 m)
distance between axles
1st to 2nd and 3rd to 4th:
all models 5 ft (1.52 m)
2nd to 3rd: 21 ft 7 in
(6.58 m) except Mk 16
19 ft 1 in (5.82 m)
POWERPLANT   Detroit Diesel 8V-92TA
445-hp liquid-cooled 2-stroke V-8 diesel engine, Allison HT740D automatic
transmission with torque converter, 4
forward/1 reverse gears

SUSPENSION   8 × 8 (8 wheels driving,
front axle and articulated-joint steering), Hendrickson leaf spring with
steel saddle, 6 torque rods and 14-in
(356-mm) vertical travel on front and
rear
SPEED   52 mph (84 km/h), range 300
mi (483 km)
OBSTACLE CLEARANCE   gradient 60%,
side slope 30%, angle of approach
45°, angle of departure Mk 14 45°, Mk
15 48°, Mk 16 65°, Mk 17 40°

LIGHT AND MAIN BATTLE TANKS

M1A1 Abrams

The M1 Abrams is the principal Main Battle Tank (MBT) of the US Army and Marine Corps. Originally developed as a
stopgap until a more advanced tank
could be fielded, the M1 struggled for
acceptance from its first trials in 1976. It
was criticized for high cost, high fuel consumption, and, especially, maintainability problems. Further criticism
focused on the 105-mm M68 gun, which
was initially chosen over the Rheinmetall
120-mm gun.

Many of the early problems have been
remedied, and, at its best, the M1A1
armed with the Rheinmetall-designed
120-mm smoothbore gun is possibly the
best combination of firepower, mobility,
and protection of any tank in service. Its
performance in Operation Desert Storm
demonstrated a convincing superiority
over the Soviet-designed T-72 (admittedly
an export variant) as well as relatively
high reliability and mobility.

The smoothbore gun (also fitted to the
German Leopard 2 and several other
MBTs) fires a broad range of projectiles
including two types of Armor-Piercing
Fin-Stabilized   Discarding   Sabot

(APFSDS) rounds. With upgrades, the
gun tube's Effective Full Charge (EFC)
life has risen from 500 to 1,000 rounds.

Fire control is sophisticated, relatively
simple to use, and a major contributor to
the tank's cost. In the M1A2, electronic
complexity and integration has become
"vetronics" (vehicle electronics), with
many of the systems linked through a
Texas Instruments MIL-STD-1553B digital databus. One of the most important
enhancements in the M1A2 is the Commander's Independent Thermal Viewer
(CITV), which permits the commander
to search and independently select new
targets.

The M1's relatively high mobility is
achieved through a high power-to-weight
ratio conferred on the tank by its 1,500-
hp gas turbine powerplant that is compact, starts more readily, and requires less
maintenance than a comparable diesel
but is noted for its poor fuel mileage. The
problem is significantly exacerbated by
the lack of an Auxiliary Power Unit
(APU) that would provide power to the
tank's electronics when stationary. (In
tanks produced after mid-1990, an Allied-

Bendix digital electronic fuel control system is claimed to reduce fuel consumption by 18%–20%.)

The suspension permits relatively high cross-country speeds. The M1's high weight (57–63 metric tons) limits the number of bridges it may cross and restricts its airportability to the Lockheed C-5 Galaxy (which can carry only one tank). Low mileage between track replacement also reduces the M1's mobility, although newer FMC-Goodyear T158 tracks have a claimed lifetime of 2,113 mi (3,400 km).

Protection is afforded by the spaced, laminate "Chobham" armor also found on the Leopard 2 and British Challenger MBTs as well as by the Abrams' low silhouette. The frontal armor is described as a semimobile matrix of aluminum, plastics, and glues in pockets that can be opened for improved combinations such as a steel-encased depleted-uranium mesh, which is said to produce an almost impenetrable carapace at the cost of an increase in weight.

Passive protection includes stowage of the main gun's ammunition in a bustle separated from the rest of the turret by fast-closing access doors and covered with blow out panels. The fire-suppression system has also proved effective.

VARIANTS • M1 (2,374 produced) with 105-mm/51-cal M68E1 rifled gun and 55 rounds. Improved M1 (IPM1) (894 produced) with cast trunnions for later refit with 120-mm gun.

M1A1 Block I introduced the 120-mm M256 gun, updated fire control system, collective overpressure NBC protection, stronger transmission and suspension.

M1A2 (M1A1 Block II) with vetronics integrated through MIL-STD-1553B databuses; Fire Control Electronics Unit (FCEU) coordinates CITV stabilization, primary sight, and gun turret drive.

DEVELOPMENT • The M1 with the 105-mm gun and weighing about 60 short tons achieved initial operational capability in 1983. Produced by the Land Systems Division of General Dynamics at the Lima Army Tank Plant in Lima, Ohio, and the Detroit Arsenal Tank Plant in Warren, Michigan. The original 1972 plan to procure 3,312 tanks was superseded several times until more than 8,131 had been delivered. 2,374 "basic" M1s and 894 Improved M1s (IPM1s) capable of being refitted with the 120-mm gun were produced by 1986.

Production then switched to the M1A1 Block I, which introduced the 120-mm main gun. 4,680 (221 for the Marine Corps) M1A1s were produced. The M1A2, which emphasized vetronics, was to be produced in large numbers, but production was curtailed to 62 by defense spending reductions. Many M1s are being upgraded to M1A1 standards.

Egypt is coproducing 555 M1A1s, while Saudi Arabia and Kuwait have procured several hundred M1A1s each. In 1993–94, Congress added funds to upgrade 210 M1 and M1A1 models to M1A2 standards. Plans called for nearly 800 more upgrades.

COMBAT EXPERIENCE • When Operation Desert Storm's ground war began on February 24, 1991, approximately 1,650 M1A1s (and another 300 M1s with 105-mm guns) were in Saudi Arabia; 60 of these were "loaned" to the Marine Corps, who used them effectively despite little time to prepare. Admittedly, assessments of the Abrams' performance must take account of unusually favorable conditions; thus, results were unusually positive. Still, the Abrams, handled by well-trained Army and Marine Corps crews, performed superbly in the battle it was asked to conduct.

During the tank battles, the M1's sighting and targeting systems performed well in haze, fog, and swirling sand. Unfortunately, lack of a means to identify targets positively led to the destruction of several "friendly" armored vehicles.

In tank-to-tank duels, M1s often beat T-72 tank crews to the first shot, and that shot often scored a fatal hit. (Many Iraqi tank turrets blew clear away from the chassis or flipped upside down.) Moreover, the 120-mm gun's much greater effective range kept the M1 well out of the 125-mm gun's killing range. Armor protection proved even more effective than expected, allowing few penetrating hits and no crew fatalities.

Concerns about mobility and reliability were met with a conservative refueling policy (every three to five hours) and high scheduled maintenance rates. As a result, the M1s set the pace during the advance into Iraq and Kuwait. One 120-mile (193-km) night move of several hundred Abramses ended successfully without a single mechanical casualty. Clearly, the success of the Left Hook owed much to the Abrams's good performance.

SPECIFICATIONS •

CREW   4 (commander, gunner, loader, driver)

COMBAT WEIGHT
M1A1: 126,000 lb (57,154 kg)
M1A2 with depleted-uranium armor: 139,080 lb (63,086 kg)
ground pressure
M1A1: 13.70 lb/in² (0.96 kg/cm²)
M1A2: 15.40 lb/in² (1.08 kg/cm²)

DIMENSIONS
length   26 ft (7.92 m), gun forward 32 ft 3 in (9.83 m)
width   12 ft (3.65 m) with skirts
height   9 ft 6 in (2.89 m) to top of cupola
length of track on ground
15 ft 3 in (4.65 m)
ground clearance
19 in (480 mm) center, 17 in (430 mm) sides
track width   25 in (635 mm)

MAIN GUN   120-mm/46-cal M256 smoothbore gun with 40 rounds
elevation   −10°/+20°, traverse 360°

SECONDARY WEAPONS   7.62-mm M240 coaxial machine gun, 7.62-mm M240 machine gun for loader, 12.7-mm M2 machine gun for commander

SENSORS AND FIRE CONTROL
M1A1: 12-kilobyte digital ballistic computer, primary stabilized sight with 3- and 10-power day optics, unity vision with 18° field of view, integrated Nd-YAG laser rangefinder, night vision/sight with thermal imaging
M1A2: CITV, Driver's Thermal Viewer, SINCGARS radio, eye-safe CO^2 laser rangefinder, position/navigation system, intervehicular information system

ARMOR   Chobham-type armor on glacis and turret and armored bulkheads between turret and engine, depleted-uranium armor in production in 1988

POWERPLANT   Avco-Lycoming AGT-1500 1,500-shp 2-spool free-shaft multifuel turbine, Detroit Diesel X-1100-3B hydrokinetic transmission with 4 forward/2 reverse gears
power-to-weight ratio
M1A1: 26.24 hp/metric ton
M1A2: 23.78 hp/metric ton

SUSPENSION (EACH SIDE)   torsion bar, 7 road wheels with 15-in (381-mm) travel, rear drive, front idler, 3 internal rotary shock absorbers, 2 return rollers

SPEED   road 41.5 mph (66 km/h), cross-country 30 mph (48 km/h), acceleration, 0–20 mph (32 km/h) 6.8–7.2 sec, range (M1A1) 289 miles (465 km) (M1A2) 243 miles (391 km)

OBSTACLE CLEARANCE   vertical 3 ft 6 in (1.07 m), gradient 60%, trench 9 ft (2.74 m), fording 4 ft (1.22 m) without preparation, 6 ft 6 in (1.98 m) with preparation

XM8 Armored Gun System

The FMC XM8 Armored Gun System (AGS) is designed to incorporate tank-level firepower in a compact, mobile, and airportable vehicle. The controversial AGS concept originated in the early 1980s as a means to provide more powerful direct support to rapidly deployable forces such as the US Army's light, mountain, and airborne divisions. Doubts remain about its ability to avoid engaging heavy forces while usefully supporting offensive action.

The M8's profile resembles a conventional tank, and the vehicle has a typical tank layout. The high engine compartment aft limits gun depression to a 270° arc. The large electrohydraulic, two-axis stabilized turret is asymmetrically laid out with the gun left of center in the mantlet and the turret slightly to the right of the centerline in the hull. (The combination of asymmetries repositions the gun on the vehicle centerline.)

The XM8's main armament is the 105-mm XM35 tank gun, a modified M68 that was turned upside down by Rheinmetall of Germany and fitted with a soft-recoil system that doubles the recoil length and buffers it through a rifled, multislotted muzzle brake that is 35% efficient. A fume extractor is fitted halfway up the barrel. When the gun is depressed, its breech recoils through hydraulically operated doors in the turret roof.

FMC Naval Systems Division supplies the 21-projectile autoloader; nine more rounds are stowed forward near the driver. The AGS can fire a full range of 105-mm ammunition, including Armor-Piercing Fin-Stabilized Discarding Sabot (APFSDS) rounds.

Fire control equipment includes the Computing Devices Corp. digital fire control system with 32-bit microprocessors and MIL-STD-1553B digital databus. The gunner's primary sensor is the Hughes Aircraft Co. day/night thermal sight and integrated laser range-finder in a two-axis stabilized mount on the right side of the turret. A relayed picture of the gunner's sight image can appear in the commander's sight.

To balance the contradictory demands imposed by airportability and the need for some level of protection, the AGS can be fitted with four levels of protection: none, Level 1 against splinters, Level 2 against armor-piercing small-arms and small-cannon fire, and Level 3 against cannon up to 30-mm. The crew compartment is sealed against Nuclear, Biological, and Chemical (NBC) warfare effects, even when the gun's recoil doors are open.

Vehicle mobility is aided by a relatively high power-to-weight ratio and relatively low ground pressure. Maintainability is enhanced by a powerpack that can be rolled out through a drop-down rear door for repair or replacement. An essential feature of the M8's design is its airportability: three can be loaded into a C-5 or C-17 transport, two into a C-141, and one in a C-130. The C-130 can deliver the "stripped" M8—lacking any armor and the commander's cupola—in a Low-Velocity Airdrop (LVAD).

DEVELOPMENT • In its earlier trials form, the M8 was known as the Close Combat Vehicle Light (CCVL). Development of the predecessor CCVL began in 1983, with prototype rollout on August 30, 1985. Interest in the AGS waxed and waned throughout the 1980s for many reasons; requirements were difficult to reconcile—the Army and Marine Corps had differing ideas.

After several changes and delays, a $27.7-million contract for Phase I was awarded on June 4, 1992, to FMC Corp. Defense Systems Group of San Jose, California (now United Defense); full Phase I contract amount was $119.6 million. Approximately 300 vehicles are planned, with an initial operational capability in 1996–97.

In September 1993, United Defense

and Taiwan's Hwa Fong Industries announced plans to build several hundred M8s for Taiwanese service.

COMBAT EXPERIENCE • None.

SPECIFICATIONS •
CREW   3 (commander, gunner, driver)
COMBAT WEIGHT   ranges from 36,900 lb (16,738 kg) (airdrop) to Level 3 armor 52,000 lb (23,587 kg)
ground pressure
12.16 lb/in² (0.86 kg/cm²)
DIMENSIONS
hull length   20 ft (6.1 m), with gun forward 30 ft 1½ in (9.18 m)
extreme width
8 ft 10 in (2.69 m)
height to top of turret
7 ft 9½ in (2.37 m)
ground clearance
16 in (406 mm)
length of track on ground
11 ft 10 in (3.61 m)
track width   15 in (381 mm)
MAIN ARMAMENT   Rheinmetall/ Watervliet 105-mm/51-cal rifled gun with 21 ready rounds in autoloader and 9 stowed in hull
elevation   −10°/+20°, traverse 360°
weapons   7.62 coaxial machine gun and 12.7-mm M2HB antiaircraft machine gun
SENSORS AND FIRE CONTROL   digital fire control computer, stabilized day/ night thermal sight and laser rangefinder for gunner, 8 periscopes for commander, 5 periscopes for driver with image intensifier in center
ARMOR   aluminum hull with steel armor modules
POWERPLANT   Detroit Diesel 6V-921A 550-hp liquid-cooled turbocharged 2-stroke V-6 diesel engine, General Electric HMPT-500-3EC hydro-mechanical, infinitely variable transmission with 3 forward/1 reverse ranges

power-to-weight ratio
30.47 hp/metric ton (Level 1) down to 23.32 hp/metric ton (Level 3)
SUSPENSION (EACH SIDE)   independent trailing arm torsion bar, 6 road wheels, rear drive, front idler, 5 linear shock absorbers, 10-in (254-mm) wheel travel, no return rollers
SPEED   43.5 mph (70 km/h), acceleration 0–20 mph (0–32 km/h) at Level 3 weight 6.5 sec, range 300 mi (483 km)
OBSTACLE CLEARANCE   vertical 2 ft 6 in (0.76 m), gradient 60%, side slope 40%, trench 7 ft (2.13 m), fording 3 ft 4 in (1.02 m)

M41 Walker Bulldog

The M41 is a light tank developed by the US Army in the late 1940s for reconnaissance and tank destroyer missions. Its armor is much heavier than contemporary light tanks such as the AMX-13 and the PT-76; the design of the latter two vehicles, however, more accurately presaged a postwar trend toward emphasizing firepower and mobility in a vehicle smaller than the M41.

The M41 has proved to be reliable and sturdy—except for its gasoline engine. It remains in service in several countries, although it was phased out of service in the US in the 1960s.

Upgrade programs concentrate on replacing the gasoline engine with a diesel engine (to achieve much greater range) and providing modern fire control equipment, such as a laser rangefinder, and more powerful ammunition. Among these are the Danish M41 DK-1, Taiwanese Yung Hu, and several dozen Brazilian M41s. Brazilian and Uruguayan tanks are armed with 90-mm guns.

The M41 hull and suspension were also used to mount twin 40-mm antiaircraft guns (M42 Skysweeper) and were built up into the M75 armored personnel carrier.

DEVELOPMENT • Manufactured at the Cleveland (Ohio) Tank Arsenal by Cadillac Motor Car Division of General Motors, achieving initial operational capability in 1951. Approximately 5,500 M41s were built.

Although long since phased out of the US Army, the M41 remains in service with several other countries.

COMBAT EXPERIENCE • The Army of the Republic of Vietnam (ARVN) operated M41s against Viet Cong and North Vietnamese forces during the 1960s and early 1970s.

SPECIFICATIONS •

CREW 4 (commander, gunner, loader, driver)
COMBAT WEIGHT 51,800 lb (23,497 kg)
ground pressure
      10.24 lb/in² (0.72 kg/cm²)
DIMENSIONS
hull length 19 ft 1 in (5.82 m), with gun forward 26 ft 11 in (8.21 m)
width 10 ft 6 in (3.2 m)
height to cupola top
      8 ft 11 in (2.73 m)
length of track on ground
      10 ft 8 in (3.25 m)
ground clearance
      17.8 in (450 mm)
track width 21 in (533 mm)
MAIN ARMAMENT 76-mm/60-cal M32 rifled gun with 57 rounds in M41, M41A1, 65 rounds in M41A2/A3
elevation −9¾°/+19¾°, traverse 360°
      Brazilian tanks have bored-out Ca 76/90 M32 BR2 that fires Belgian 90-mm Cockerill Mk III ammunition; Uruguayan tanks have Cockerill Mk III gun
SECONDARY ARMAMENT coaxial 7.62-mm M1919A4E1 machine gun with

5,000 rounds, 12.7-mm M2 HB air-defense machine gun with 2,175 rounds
SENSORS AND FIRE CONTROL commander has M20A1 periscope, gunner has M97A1 telescopic sight and M20A1 periscope, most have manual-hydraulic traverse and rack-and-pinion manual elevation
ARMOR
glacis: 25.4 mm at 30°
hull: 31.75 mm at 45° front, 19 mm rear, 9.25–31.75 mm floor, 12–15 mm top
turret: 38 mm mantlet, 25.4 mm front, 25 mm sides and rear, 12.7 mm roof
POWERPLANT
Continental AOS-895-3 (M41, M41A1) 500-hp air-cooled supercharged 6-cylinder gasoline engine
Continental AOSI-895-5 (M41A2, M41A3) fuel-injected gasoline engine
Allison CD-500-3 powershift crossdrive transmission with 4 forward/2 reverse gears
power-to-weight ratio
      21.31 hp/metric ton
SUSPENSION (EACH SIDE) torsion bar, 5 dual road wheels, rear drive, front idler, 3 hydraulic shock absorbers, 3 return rollers
SPEED 45 mph (72 km/h), range 100 mi (161 km)
OBSTACLE CLEARANCE vertical 2 ft 4 in (0.71 m), gradient 60%, side slope 30%, trench 6 ft (1.83 m), fording without preparation 3 ft 4 in (1.02 m), fording with preparation 8 ft (2.44 m)

M48 Patton

Once the principal Main Battle Tank (MBT) of the US Army and Marine Corps, the M48 was fully replaced by the M60 in US service. When it was introduced, the M48 represented a considerable improvement over the M47 Patton, having a better turret shape and less complicated sighting system but still having a relatively high profile and limited mobility. M48s have been the subject of several fire control update programs, and many now have laser rangefinders and thermal sights.

The M48A5 version is quite different from the original M48. As designed in the late 1940s, the M48 had a 90-mm M41 rifled tank gun and a Continental AV-1790 gasoline engine. The tank's mobility was severely limited by low fuel mileage, and, beginning with the M48A3, a diesel engine based on the AV-1790 was installed. The tank's power-to-weight ratio dropped, but its road range nearly quadrupled.

Raising firepower also proved possible with the retrofitting of the ubiquitous L7A3 (license-built as M68) 105-mm rifled tank gun to existing turrets. Fewer rounds can be stowed, but the increases in range and accuracy more than outweigh the loss of magazine capacity.

The conversion of earlier M48s to the M48A5 standard has proved to be a good solution to the need in many armies for a better tank at considerably less than the cost of a new one. The Turkish M48A5T1/T2 is the best M48 variant in service. T1 has a Turkish-built 105-mm gun and saw its first deliveries in September 1983. The T2 adds a laser rangefinder, Texas Instruments thermal sights for commander and gunner, Control Data Corp. solid-state ballistic computer, and Cadillac Gage Textron gun stabilization. Serial production began in 1987.

VARIANTS • M48 with 810-hp AV-1790 gasoline engine, 90-mm M41 rifled gun, and 60 rounds of ammunition.

M48A2 had higher-powered 825-hp gasoline engine, larger fuel tanks, fully automatic transmission, and suspension system modifications.

M48A3 rebuilt M48A1 and A2 with Continental AVDS-1790 diesel engine, fire control system updates, fuel capacity

increase. First examples introduced in 1964 with further large programs undertaken in 1967 and 1975.

M48A5 are M48A1 and M48A3 with the 105-mm M68 rifled gun and many changes to the fire control systems, engine air-cleaning system, and most other related systems. First deliveries 1975, last of 2,064 delivered in 1979.

M48 AVLB (Armored Vehicle Launched Bridge) that spans a 60-foot (18.29 m) gap.

(M67 series were flamethrower tanks used in Vietnam but no longer fielded.)

DEVELOPMENT • Production began at Chrysler Corp.'s Newark, Delaware, plant in 1950, the tank achieving initial operational capability in 1953 (M48).

11,703 M48 series tanks were produced, 6,000 by Chrysler, the others by American Locomotive Co. (Alco) in Schenectady, New York, and by General Motors at the Detroit Tank Plant in Warren, Michigan. More than 15 countries still operate the M48.

COMBAT EXPERIENCE • The M48 was the only medium-to-heavy tank to operate with US forces during the Vietnam War. It proved to be reliable and relatively rugged. Israeli M48s (many with diesel engines and 105-mm guns) met with considerable success against Arab tanks in the 1967 Six-Day War. On the other hand, Israeli gasoline-powered M48s acquired the nickname of Ronson, because they caught fire so easily after being hit.

SPECIFICATIONS (M48A5) •
CREW   4 (commander, gunner, loader, driver)
COMBAT WEIGHT   107,997 lb (48,987 kg)
ground pressure
12.51 lb/in^2 (0.88 kg/cm^2)
DIMENSIONS
hull length   21 ft (6.42 m), with gun forward 30 ft 6 in (9.31 m)

width   11 ft 11 in
(3.63 m)
height   10 ft 1 in
(3.09 m)
length of track on ground
13 ft 1 in (4.0 m)
ground clearance
16 in (406 mm)
track width   28 in (711 mm)
MAIN ARMAMENT   105-mm/51-cal M68 rifled gun with 54 rounds
elevation   −9°/+19°, traverse 360°
SECONDARY ARMAMENT   coaxial 7.62-mm M73 machine gun, antiaircraft 7.62-mm M60D machine gun with 10,000 7.62-mm rounds total
SENSORS AND FIRE CONTROL
M13 electromechanical ballistic computer, coincidence rangefinder, infrared driving lights and searchlights
Taiwanese and Turkish M48s fitted with AN/VSG-2 Tank Thermal Sights (TTS) that have laser rangefinder and Mercury-Cadmium-Telluride (HgCdTe) IR detector for passive night and dust vision
ARMOR
hull: 101/120 mm front, 76 mm sides (max), 44 mm rear, 57 mm top
turret: 110 mm front, 50 mm rear, 25 mm top
POWERPLANT   Teledyne Continental AVDS-1790-2D 750-hp air-cooled V-12 diesel, Allison CD-850 series automatic planetary transmission with 2 forward/1 reverse gears
power-to-weight ratio
15.89 hp/metric ton
SUSPENSION (EACH SIDE)   torsion bar, 6 road wheels, rear drive, front idler, 3 hydraulic shock absorbers, 5 return rollers (M48A3 has 3 return rollers)
SPEED   30 mph (48.2 km/h), range 309 mi (499 km)
OBSTACLE CLEARANCE   vertical 3 ft (0.92 m), gradient 60%, trench 8 ft 6 in (2.59 m), fording 4 ft (1.22 m) without preparation, 8 ft (2.44 m) with preparation

M60 Tank

M60 main battle tank

The M60 is in US service only in National Guard and Reserve units, but was the principal US Main Battle Tank (MBT) for two decades. It was developed from the earlier M48 Patton series. Although criticized for its high silhouette and limited cross-country mobility, the M60 is a rugged and reliable tank that has proved amenable to many updates over a long career; the M60A3 with the Tank Thermal Sight (TTS) is considered a frontline tank in most scenarios.

Firepower was increased over the M48 by adoption of the British-designed L7 105-mm/51-cal rifled gun with thermal sleeve and fume extractor in a reshaped turret. The turret permits high elevation and depression angles ($-10°/+20°$) but contributes to the high silhouette. The M60A3 TTS has a hybrid solid-state ballistic computer, laser rangefinder, tank thermal sight, and turret stabilization system.

Mobility and range were increased over that of the M48 by installing a diesel engine, but, compared to other contemporary tank designs, the M60 power-to-weight ratio is still relatively low and its ground pressure relatively high. Armor protection is considered quite good compared to its contemporaries.

VARIANTS •
M60A1 was the principal production version for 17 years.

M60A2 with 152-mm Shillelagh gun/ missile system; 13 missiles and 33 conventional 152-mm combustible charge.

M60 AVLB (Armored Vehicle Launched Bridge) spans a 60-ft (18.29 m) gap.

M728 Combat Engineer Vehicle (CEV). See M728.

DEVELOPMENT • Over 15,000 were built from 1960 to 1987 by Chrysler at Newark, Delaware, and Detroit Tank Plant in Warren, Michigan, with the De-troit plant building the great majority. The M60 achieved initial operational capability in 1961, M60A1 in 1963, M60A2 in 1974, and M60A3 in 1979.

M60A1 production (for the US Marine Corps) ended in 1980. M60A3 production for the US Army ended in 1983, and the last Foreign Military Sales (FMS) vehicles rolled out in late 1987. Conversion of 5,400 older models to M60A3 TTS ended in FY1990.

At its peak, the US Army's M60 inventory totaled 8,887 tanks, the first reductions coming in 1990 as part of the disposal of older US tanks in anticipation of a Conventional Forces in Europe (CFE) arms limitation. Also in service in more than 15 other countries.

COMBAT EXPERIENCE • The M60 was used extensively by Israeli forces in the 1973 Yom Kippur War in tank battles both in the Sinai and, more critically, in the Golan Heights.

210 M60A1s were fielded by the 1st Marine Expeditionary Force (MEF) during Operation Desert Storm in February 1991; another 39 were embarked on some of the 31 landing ships deployed in the northern Persian Gulf. The 1st MEF M60s, some equipped with mine-clearing rakes, supported the Saudi-Marine drive into eastern Kuwait that ended in Kuwait City.

As expected, the 105-mm gun proved effective against the Iraqis' Soviet-built T-55 and T-62 tanks. In addition, the commanding general of the 1st Marine Division stated that even T-72s had been destroyed by the M60A1. Most shots were fired from relatively short range (500 m), with at least one APFSDS round boring its way through a T-72's frontal armor and emerging from the rear engine compartment.

Given the M60's performance in Desert Storm, arguments against replacing it with the expensive M1A1 gained some strength. Despite these sentiments, however, all M60s were out of active Marine Corps service by the end of 1991.

SPECIFICATIONS (M60A3) •

CREW 4 (commander, gunner, loader, driver)

COMBAT WEIGHT 116,000 lb (52,617 kg)

ground pressure
   12.37 lb/in² (0.87 kg/cm²)

DIMENSIONS

length 22 ft 9 in (6.95 m) hull, 30 ft 11 in (9.44 m) gun forward

width 11 ft 11 in (3.63 m)

height 10 ft 9 in (3.27 m)

ground clearance
   18 in (457 mm)

length of track on ground
   13 ft 7 in (4.24 m)

track width 28 in (711 mm)

MAIN GUN 105-mm/51-cal M68 rifled gun with 63 rounds

elevation −10°/+20°, traverse 360°

SECONDARY WEAPONS 7.62-mm M240 coaxial machine gun with 5,950 rounds, 12.7-mm M85 antiaircraft gun with 900 rounds

SENSORS AND FIRE CONTROL M21 solid-state analog ballistic computer, AN/VVG-2 ruby laser rangefinder usable by both commander and gunner, AN/VSG-2 Tank Thermal Sights (TTS) with laser rangefinder and Mercury-Cadmium-Telluride (HgCdTe) IR detector for passive night and dust vision

POWERPLANT Continental AVDS-1790-2C 750-hp air-cooled 4-stroke V-12 multifuel engine, Allison CD-850-6/6A powershift crossdrive transmission with 2 forward/1 reverse gears

power-to-weight ratio
   14.24 hp/metric ton

SUSPENSION (EACH SIDE) torsion bar, 6 road wheels, rear drive, front idler, 3 shock absorbers, 3 track return rollers

SPEED 30 mph (48.3 km/h), range 298 mi (480 km)

OBSTACLE CLEARANCE vertical 3 ft (0.91 m), 60% gradient. 30% side slope, trench 8 ft 6 in (2.59 m), fording 4 ft (1.22 m) without preparation, 7 ft 10 in (2.4 m) with preparation

Stingray

The design goals for this light tank were to incorporate tank-level firepower in a compact, mobile, and airportable vehicle. Given the vehicle's small size and relatively low weight, a premium has been placed on firepower and mobility at the expense of protection (and perhaps some degree of ruggedness).

The Stingray's main armament is a low-recoil development (known as the Low-Recoil Force or LRF gun) of the widely used Royal Ordnance L7A3 105-mm rifled tank gun in a Cadillac Gage three-man turret. The LRF has a multislotted muzzle brake, concentric fume extractor, and thermal sleeve; it can fire a full range of 105-mm ammunition, including Armor-Piercing Fin-Stabilized Discarding Sabot (APFSDS) rounds.

A relatively high power-to-weight ratio and relatively low ground pressure contribute to mobility. The Stingray is transportable by C-130 Hercules transport aircraft.

For protection, the Stingray depends on Cadloy armor, ballistic shaping, small silhouette, and mobility. The low turret has many oblique angles that make a flush impact virtually impossible and also simplify adding more armor if needed. Soon after Stingrays entered service in Thailand, modifications began to add armor to the frontal arc, which increases the weight by approximately 4,400 lb (2,000 kg). Such reinforcement (and reportedly an exuberant driving style) led to the discovery of cracks in the hull that were repaired by FMC in 1993.

DEVELOPMENT • The first Cadillac Gage turret was tested in June 1984, and the first hull in August 1984. The complete vehicle began testing in 1985. A candidate for the US Army's XM4 Armored Gun System (AGS) light tank program, which was canceled, it lost to the FMC entry in the later XM8 program.

SPECIFICATIONS •

CREW   4 (commander, gunner, loader, driver)

COMBAT WEIGHT   44,500 lb (20,185 kg)
ground pressure
  9.81 lb/in^2 (0.69 kg/cm^2)

DIMENSIONS
hull length   20 ft 8 in (6.3 m), with gun forward 30 ft 5 in (9.27 m)
width   8 ft 10½ in (2.71 m)
overall height
  8 ft 4 in (2.55 m), reducible to 7 ft 10 in (2.4 m)
length of track on ground
  11 ft 11 in (3.63 m)
ground clearance
  18 in (457 mm)
track width   15 in (381 mm)

MAIN ARMAMENT   L7A3 LRF 105-mm rifled gun with 8 ready rounds, 24 stowed in hull
elevation   −7.5°/+20° at 8°/sec (unstabilized), 40°/sec (stabilized), traverse 360° at 25°/sec (unstabilized), 30°/sec (stabilized)

SECONDARY WEAPONS   7.62 coaxial machine gun with 400 ready rounds, 2,000 stowed; 7.62-mm air defense machine gun with 200 ready, 2,000 stowed rounds (or 12.7-mm air defense machine gun with 100 ready, 1,000 stowed rounds)

SENSORS AND FIRE CONTROL   Optic-Electronic Corp. M36E1 SIRE day/night sight with laser rangefinder for gunner and optional thermal sight, 7 periscopes for commander with optional NV52 day/night sight, optional Marconi digital fire control system, optional 2-axis turret stabilization

ARMOR   Cadloy steel armor; turret armor is reported to defeat 14.5-mm rounds over the frontal arc and 7.62-mm rounds from any angle

POWERPLANT   Detroit Diesel Allison 8V-92TA 535-hp liquid-cooled turbocharged 2-stroke V-8 diesel engine, Allison XTG-411-2A automatic transmission
power-to-weight ratio
  26.5 hp/metric ton

SUSPENSION (EACH SIDE)   independent trailing arm torsion bar, 6 road wheels, rear drive, front idler, 3 shock absorbers, 3 return rollers

SPEED   level road 42 mph (68 km/h), 10% slope 18 mph (29 km/h), 60% slope 3.7 mph (6 km/h), acceleration 0–20 mph (0–32 km/h) 7 seconds, range 300 mi (483 km)

OBSTACLE CLEARANCE   vertical 2 ft 6 in (0.76 m), gradient 60%, side slope 40%, trench 7 ft (2.13 m), fording 3 ft 6 in (1.07 m)

MISSILES/ROCKETS/BOMBS

ANTIAIR

AMRAAM (AIM-120)

The AMRAAM (Advanced Medium-Range Air-to-Air Missile) was developed jointly by the US Air Force and Navy as a follow-on to the AIM-7 Sparrow III AAM. The core of AMRAAM's performance specification is a high kill probability at short and long range under all weather conditions while subjected to heavy Electronic Countermeasures (ECM) and clutter. It is a "look-down, shoot-down" missile and can be launched at any aircraft speed or target angle. Although AMRAAM is to be more capable than the AIM-7, it is lighter and thinner and has a smaller warhead.

Unlike the AIM-7, whose target must be illuminated by the launch aircraft's radar, the AMRAAM is fitted with an active radar seeker whose 5-in (127-mm) antenna is energized by a small Traveling-Wave Tube (TWT) transmitter. To operate the missile most effectively, the launch aircraft needs a track-while-scan radar and the ability to assign targets simultaneously to more than one missile. The active monopulse seeker uses a pulse-Doppler programmable waveform to penetrate clutter and precipitation. Rapid automatic gain control and digital signal processing contribute to the seeker's Electronic Counter-Countermeasures (ECCM) capabilities.

After launch, the missile can operate autonomously, turning on its active seeker at a preset time or distance. Alternatively, AMRAAM can receive midcourse guidance updates to refine its terminal homing track. When presented with more than one target, AMRAAM will choose a particular target and ignore the others. The continuous-rod warhead of the AIM-7 has been replaced by a blast-fragmentation warhead with a "smart" fuze.

DEVELOPMENT • Full-scale development of the AMRAAM began in 1981, and its initial operational capability was in 1991. Flight tests began in 1985. The initial series production of 105 missiles began in October 1987. The Air Force received the first production AMRAAMs from Hughes and Raytheon in January 1989. The AMRAAM was originally intended for US and NATO service. AMRAAM is one of the US/European family of weapons first proposed in 1978. A 1980 Memorandum of Understanding (MoU) among the United States, Great Britain, and West Germany agreed that the medium-range missile would also be produced in Europe. Norway signed the MoU in 1989, and France has observer status within the European group. The US AMRAAM requirement had been 24,320 missiles, but later reviews reduced the total to 15,500 missiles.

The EURAAM joint venture was established in Britain in July 1987 to oversee European production of the AMRAAM. EURAAM consisted of AEG, British Aerospace, Marconi Defence Systems, and MBB. Responsibility for European production was reallocated to Germany in August 1988. In exchange, British Aerospace was named prime contractor on the ASRAAM—Advanced Short-Range Air-to-Air Missile.

In 1989, the AMRAAM's reliability was

rated 'clearly unacceptable,' and the production schedule was jeopardized. In February 1990, the US Air Force refused deliveries of the AMRAAM because of structural defects caused by vibrations and g-forces when carried on F-15s. In May 1990, the four-on-four test was conducted again and the missile performed successfully. The Air Force again accepted AMRAAM deliveries in mid-August 1990.

Germany ordered 200 ASRAAM missiles from Hughes. In May 1990, the US announced AMRAAM sales to Denmark (150 missiles and 70 launchers) and Norway (100 missiles and 132 launchers). In July 1990, a sale of 200 AMRAAMs and 55 launchers to Spain was announced. Norway ordered AMRAAMs in 1994 to outfit its ground-based Adapted HAWK missile batteries; the system, which entered service in early 1995, is called the Norwegian Advanced Surface-to-Air Missile System (NSAMS). Sweden bought 100 AMRAAMs in 1994 to equip its new JAS 39 Gripens and Turkey purchased 80 AMRAAMs.

VARIANTS • APREP (AMRAAM Producibility Enhancement Program), Preplanned Product Improvement (P3I) program, Advanced Tactical Fighter AMRAAM, Sea AMRAAM (proposed), Ground-Based AMRAAM (Norwegian).

COMBAT EXPERIENCE • During Operation Desert Storm, the Air Force deployed AMRAAMs as antiair and anti-Scud tactical ballistic missile weapons on F-15 aircraft, but none was fired.

SPECIFICATIONS •
MANUFACTURER
Hughes Aircraft
Raytheon (secondary)
MISSILE WEIGHT   345 lb (156.8 kg)
warhead   30–50 lb (13.6–22.7 kg)
DIMENSIONS
configuration
    resembles Sparrow III but smaller diameter; long

pointed nose, cruciform delta mainplanes indexed in line with steerable "cropped delta" tailplanes
length   12 ft (3.66 m)
diameter   7 in (178 mm)
wingspan   1 ft 9 in (0.53 m)
tail span   2 ft 1 in (0.63 m)
PROPULSION   Hercules high-thrust, reduced-smoke, solid-fuel boost-sustain rocket motor
PERFORMANCE
speed   approx Mach 4
max range   approx 40 nm (46.1 mi; 74.1 km)
WARHEAD   conventional high-explosive
SENSORS/FIRE CONTROL
Track-While-Scan (TWS) multiple-target tracking radar
inertial reference for each AMRAAM before launch
Nortronics midcourse updates to AMRAAM during flight terminal phase
Hughes I/J-band pulse-Doppler active radar with pulse compression and programmable waveforms, glint reduction

Phoenix (AIM-54)

The AIM-54 Phoenix was the US Navy's long-range fleet air defense missile against aircraft of the former Soviet Union. The Phoenix remains the most sophisticated and longest-range air-to-air missile in service with any nation. It is part of the Grumman F-14 Tomcat weapons system, which also includes the Hughes AWG-9 or AWG-17 radar/fire control system.

DEVELOPMENT • The initial operational capability for the AIM-54A was in 1974 and for the AIM-54C in December 1986. First flight tests were 1965 (AIM-54A), 1980 (AIM-54C), and August

1990 (AIM-54C+). The first flight test of a Raytheon-built AIM-54C was on June 6, 1989.

AIM-54A production was over 2,500, ending in 1980. AIM-54C in production beginning in FY1983, AIM-54C+ in production beginning in March 1986. The Phoenix is employed by the US Navy and on Iranian F-14A Tomcats.

The Phoenix has had a history of problems, including overpayments, schedule slippages, and unreliable fuzes.

Production funding was deleted from the FY1991 budget request.

VARIANTS • AAM-N-11, AIM-54A, AIM-54B (not produced), AIM-54C+, Phoenix Point Defense Missile System (PDMS) (not produced).

COMBAT EXPERIENCE • The AIM-54A was provided to the Imperial Iranian Air Force prior to the fall of the shah in 1979. However, the Iranian Air Force probably did not use Phoenix missiles in combat.

The Phoenix was deployed on US Navy F-14s during Operation Desert Storm, but none was fired.

SPECIFICATIONS •

MANUFACTURER
Hughes Aircraft
Raytheon (AIM-54C) (secondary)

MISSILE WEIGHT
AIM-54A: 985 lb (447 kg)
AIM-54C: 1,008 lb (457 kg)
warhead   135 lb (61 kg)

DIMENSIONS
configuration
resembles earlier Hughes Falcon (AIM-4); cylindrical body, pointed nose; extreme delta cruciform wings near tail with rectangular cruciform control surfaces just behind them

length   13 ft (3.96 m)
diameter   15 in (380 mm)
wingspan   3 ft (0.91 m)
PROPULSION   Aerojet Mk 60 or Rocketdyne Flexadyne Mk 47 long-burn-time solid-fuel rocket
PERFORMANCE
speed   Mach 5
max range   110 nm (127 mi; 204 km)
WARHEAD   expanding continuous-rod (AIM-54A), controlled fragmentation (AIM-54C)
SENSORS/FIRE CONTROL
digital electronics unit with software reprogrammability
Northrop strap-down inertial reference system
solid-state transmitter/receiver
Motorola DSU-28 Target Detecting Device (TDD)
semiactive radar homing (midcourse)
pulse-Doppler radar terminal homing
AWG-9 pulse-Doppler radar in F-14 can track 24 targets, select 6 targets, and guide 6 AIM-54s to interceptions

Sparrow III (AIM-7)

The Sparrow III is a radar-guided, medium-range air-to-air missile that has been in service for more than 30 years. The Sparrow III uses semiactive radar-homing guidance and either continuous-wave or pulse-Doppler radars for target illumination. Its guidance, warhead, and range have been improved to such an extent that later variants represent a new missile in the original airframe.

DEVELOPMENT • The AIM-7C's initial operational capability was in 1958, the AIM-7E in 1963, AIM-7F in 1976, and AIM-7M in 1983. The missile's first airborne test firing was in 1952. Over 40,000 have been manufactured. Three different Sparrow missiles were developed in the early 1950s, with Sparrow III by far the most massively produced.

AIM-7M production ended in 1990 while the AIM-7P was in development. In March 1990, Japanese license production of the AIM-7M was approved; Mitsubishi Electric Corp. (MELCO) is prime contractor. A Kuwaiti order for 200 AIM-7Fs was approved in August 1988.

In addition to the US Air Force, Navy and Marines, Sparrow missiles are operated by about 15 other nations in Europe, Asia, and the Middle East, along with Canada and Australia.

Although the US Navy requested no AIM-7 missiles in the Amended FY1988–89 Biennial Budget, delays in the Advanced Medium-Range Air-to-Air Missile (AMRAAM) program, which is planned to replace the Sparrow, resulted in the appropriation of $52.3 million in FY1989 to purchase 450 missiles.

VARIANTS • (Designation note: The first designation predated the 1962 tri-service redesignation scheme represented by the second.) AAM-N-2/AIM-7A Sparrow I, AAM-N-6/AIM-7B Sparrow II, AAM-N-6/AIM-7C Sparrow III, AAM-N-6B/AIM-7E, AIM-7F, AIM-7H, AIM-7M, AIM-7N, AIM-7P, (Missile Homing Improvement Program/MHIP), AIM-7R (proposed).

COMBAT EXPERIENCE • While the Sparrow saw combat experience in Vietnam, its experiences demonstrated the limitation of the AIM-7E and prompted the development of the -7E2 and -7F versions. The Sparrow has not been a good dogfighting missile, being much more effective in nonmaneuvering interceptions. In engagements against Libyan aircraft in 1981 and 1989 and an August 1987 interception of an Iranian F-4 well within the missile's stated range, five out of six Sparrows missed their targets for a variety of reasons. In the 1987 F-4 engagement, the first missile's motor failed to fire and the other was launched at nearly

its minimum range and missed the evading target. In January 1989, two F-14s from the aircraft carrier *John F. Kennedy* (CV 67) engaged two Libyan MiG-23 Floggers off the coast of Libya. The lead F-14 fired two Sparrows that failed to hold lock-on and missed the MiGs. The second F-14 downed one of the MiGs with a Sparrow. The other MiG was downed by a Sidewinder AIM-9.

In Operation Desert Storm, unlike its previous lack of success in combat, the Sparrow performed well. 23 Iraqi combat aircraft were shot down by AIM-7s during the seven-week war, 69% of the total Iraqi aircraft losses. Reports suggested that the missile operated reliably, due in part to better pilot training and solid-state electronics.

SPECIFICATIONS •
MANUFACTURER
    Raytheon
    General Dynamics (since 1977)
MISSILE WEIGHT   510 lb (231 kg)
    warhead   86 lb (39 kg)
DIMENSIONS
    configuration
        long cylinder with pointed nose, 2 sets of cruciform delta wings indexed in line, the steerable foreplanes at midbody, another fixed set at the tail
    length   11 ft 10 in (3.6 m)
    diameter   8 in (203 mm)
    wingspan   3 ft 4 in (1.02 m)
    tail span   2 ft 8 in (0.81 m)
PROPULSION   Hercules Mk 58 or Aerojet General Mk 65 boost-sustained solid-fuel rocket
PERFORMANCE
    speed   Mach 4+
    max range   approx 30 nm (34.5 mi; 56 km)
WARHEAD   Mk 71 controlled fragmentation high-explosive
SENSORS/FIRE CONTROL
    inverse monopulse semiactive radar-

homing seeker with digital signal processor, improved autopilot and fuze (which can work as contact or proximity type)

upgrades provide better electronic countermeasures resistance, improved look-down, shoot-down performance

Sidewinder (AIM-9)

The Sidewinder is a simple, effective infrared-homing, widely used Air-to-Air Missile (AAM), with over 110,000 produced. Its unique "rolleron" stabilization system consists of air-driven wheels fitted in the rear outside corner of the rear fins. The spinning wheels gyroscopically stabilize the missile effectively with few moving parts and at low cost.

The Sidewinder is used by a variety of Western fixed-wing combat aircraft and helicopters. As the Chaparral missile, it has been adopted for a surface-to-air mission.

DEVELOPMENT • The Sidewinder's initial operational capability as the AIM-9B was in 1956, the AIM-9E in 1967, the AIM-9H in 1973, the AIM-9J in 1977, the AIM-9L/P in 1978, and the AIM-9M in 1983. Development of the missile began in 1949 at the Naval Weapons Center in China Lake, California. Its first flight was on September 11, 1953.

The Sidewinder is operated throughout the world by 36 countries in South America, Europe, Asia, the Middle East, and Africa.

VARIANTS • XAAM-N-7 (prototype), SW-1 (production), AAM-N-7 (USN), GAR-8 (USAF), AIM-9 (assigned to all Sidewinders, 1962), AIM-9/A/B, AIM-9F, AIM-9C/D, AIM-9E, AIM-9G/H, AIM-9H (USN/USAF), AIM-9J/N, AIM-9L/M (third generation), AIM-9P, AIM-9Q, AIM-9R, AIM-9S, AIM-9X (USN/USAF Sidewinder successor), Box Office/

Improved Sidewinder, Boa, Helicopter-Launched Sidewinder, MIM72 (Chaparral).

COMBAT EXPERIENCE • The Sidewinder's first combat was in October 1958, when Taiwanese in F-86s launched them against Chinese MiG-17s, claiming as many as 14 shot down in one day. AIM-9s scored most of the air-to-air kills made by US Navy and Air Force aircraft in the Vietnam War, and by the Israeli Air Force in the 1967 and 1973 wars in the Middle East.

During the 1982 air engagements over Lebanon's Bekaa Valley, 51 out of the 55 Syrian-flown MiGs shot down were hit by Sidewinders.

In the 1982 conflict in the Falkland Islands, between Great Britain and Argentina, British Sea Harriers used AIM-9L Sidewinders for 16 confirmed kills and one probable against Argentine aircraft (of a total 20 air-to-air kills).

Ironically, the Sidewinder was used relatively little during Operation Desert Storm's air assault against Iraqi targets. However, Sidewinders fired by USAF F-15C Eagle jets downed six Iraqi combat aircraft. Two more Su-22 Fitters were shot down by AIM-9s three weeks after the cease-fire. A Saudi F-15 pilot downed two French-built Iraqi Mirage F1s with Sidewinders in a single attack. Two F/A-18 Hornets and an F-14 Tomcat scored with AIM-9s, the Hornets shooting down MiG-21 Fishbeds and the Tomcat downing a helicopter.

SPECIFICATIONS •
MANUFACTURER
Loral Aeronutronics
Raytheon
Bodenseewerk Geratetechnik consortium (Germany-Britain-Italy-Norway)
Mitsubishi Industries (Japan)
MISSILE WEIGHT
AIM-9H: 186 lb (84.4 kg)
AIM-9L/M: 191 lb (86.5 kg)

warhead   AIM-9B/E/J/N/P: 10 lb
             (4.5 kg)
             AIM-9D/G/H: 22.4 lb
             (10.2 kg)
             AIM-9L/M: 20.8 lb (9.4
             kg)
DIMENSIONS
configuration
             simple thin cylinder, 4
             cruciform "cropped
             delta" wings with
             stabilizing "rollerons"
             on the trailing edges,
             steerable cruciform
             foreplanes
length (AIM-9L/M)
             9 ft 6 in (2.85 m)
diameter   5 in (127 mm)
wingspan   2 ft 1 in (635 mm)
PROPULSION
solid-fuel rocket by Aerojet, Hercules,
    Rockwell, or Thiokol
Mk 17 on B/E/J/N/P
Mk 36 with flexadyne propellant on
    H/L/M
PERFORMANCE
speed   Mach 2+
max range 10 nm (11.5 mi; 18.5 km)
WARHEAD (AIM-9L/M)   annular blast
fragmentation wrapped in a sheath of
preformed rods
SENSORS/FIRE CONTROL
except for AIM-9C, all versions have
    used infrared homing
AIM-9L/M is the first with all-aspect
    seeker analog roll-control autopilot

Stinger (FIM-92A)

The FIM-92 Stinger is a lightweight, short-range surface-to-air missile that was initially deployed as a portable weapon by the US Army as the successor to the FIM-43 Redeye missile. It has also been deployed on several aircraft, including the AH-64 Apache and the OH-58D Kiowa Warrior.

The Stinger system consists of a reusable battery pack and gripstock with

sight. The launch tube is a "wooden round" requiring no field maintenance. The missile is a "fire and forget" weapon with a relatively simple firing sequence. After an Identification Friend or Foe (IFF) query confirms the target is hostile, the gunner cools the passive, all-aspect Infrared (IR) seeker and fires the missile when the seeker's "growl" tells him it has locked onto the target.

Most Stinger launchers have a simple plastic sight akin to the fixed "ring and bead" of older antiaircraft guns.

A gas generator pops the missile out of the tube; when it is a few yards away from the launcher, the dual-thrust main motor ignites and accelerates the missile to supersonic speed. Tail fins roll-stabilize the Stinger and an on-board processor uses twist-and-steer commands on two of the four canard surfaces. Proportional navigation with lead bias predicts an intercept point and guides the missile over the shortest path to that point. The missile has impact fuzing only.

DEVELOPMENT • The Stinger's initial operational capability was in 1981. It began advanced development in 1967, and engineering development began in 1972. Over 16,000 Stinger missiles have been produced.

In October 1988, the United States awarded a license to the Stinger Project Group (SPG) to produce missiles in Europe. SPG was formed following a 1983 Memorandum of Understanding (MoU) concluded among West Germany, Greece, the Netherlands, and Turkey. SPG's lead company is Dornier GmbH of Germany; subcontractors from the other MoU countries will also be involved. Manufacture of approximately 12,500 missiles was planned for the SPG countries, with low-rate production beginning in 1992; the license does not permit SPG to sell to non-SPG countries.

The Stinger is in service with the US Army, Navy, and Marine Corps and over 20 other countries and groups. When needed, Stingers are deployed on board US Navy ships, as in the August 1990 deployments for Operation Desert Storm.

In September 1988, Switzerland selected the Stinger over the French Mistral after a two-year evaluation, for approximately 2,500 to 3,000 missiles.

Iran and Qatar are known to have Stingers that they obtained through diversions from other users. The Stinger has also been used by Afghan Mujahideen rebels, UNITA antigovernment forces in Angola, and various factions in Lebanon. In the early to middle 1990s, the US attempted to recover the remaining Stingers held by the Afghan rebels.

In May 1990, two alleged Colombian drug dealers were charged with attempting to purchase Stingers for use against Colombian government aircraft.

VARIANTS • FIM-92C Stinger-POST (Passive Optical Seeker Technique), FIM-92C Stinger-POST RMP (Reprogrammable Microprocessor), FIM-92 Stinger Plus, Stinger Night Sight, Avenger Pedestal-Mounted Stinger (PMS), Setter, Air-to-Air Stinger (ATAS).

COMBAT EXPERIENCE • Afghan rebels received approximately 900 Stingers and used them effectively against Soviet helicopters, transports, and attack aircraft. The introduction of the Stinger in October 1986 had a significant effect on Soviet air tactics.

During the 1982 Falkland Islands conflict, the British Royal Marines' Special Boat Squadron employed Stinger missiles that were credited with destroying an Argentine aircraft.

Stingers were deployed on board US warships in the Persian Gulf in 1987–88 as a last-resort missile defense. However, the missile's lack of design for shipboard stowage or handling influenced the Navy to curtail its procurement in April 1988.

In April 1988, Israel reported that some Palestinian militia groups in Lebanon had obtained Stingers from Afghanistan or Iran and may have fired them at Israeli aircraft.

Although Stingers were deployed with both the ground and naval forces during Desert Storm, none was fired in combat, since no enemy aircraft came within range. Some Special Operations forces in Desert Storm were fitted with WASP-equipped Stingers.

SPECIFICATIONS •
MANUFACTURER
Hughes
Raytheon (second source, 1987)
WEIGHTS
system   34.5 lb (15.2 kg)
missile   22.0 lb (10.0 kg)
DIMENSIONS
configuration
              long cylinder with blunt
              nose, pop-out
              cruciform rectangular
              foreplanes, tapered
              exhaust with full-
              diameter nozzle,
              cruciform tailfins
length   5 ft (1.52 m)
diameter   2¾ in (70 mm)
PROPULSION Atlantic Research Mk 27
dual-thrust solid-fuel rocket
PERFORMANCE
speed   2,297 ft/sec (700 m/sec)
              or Mach 1+
max range   3 mi (4.8 km)
max altitude
              9,840 ft (3,000 m)
WARHEAD 2.2 lb (1.0 kg) penetrating
high-explosive
SENSORS/FIRE CONTROL
proportional navigation with lead bias
all-aspect automatic passive infrared
   homing
Identification Friend or Foe (IFF) interrogator
Magnavox M934 impact fuze

Patriot (MIM-104)

The Patriot is a US medium-to-high-altitude surface-to-air missile system developed as an area defense weapon to replace Nike-Hercules missile batteries in Europe. The Patriot gained widespread notoriety for its reported successes after being deployed in the early 1990s to Saudi Arabia, Israel, and Turkey as a defense against Iraqi-launched tactical ballistic missiles. A Patriot battery or fire unit consists of a phased-array radar, an Engagement Control Station (ECS), and electric generators (two 150-kW generators). Up to eight M901 trailer-mounted, four-tube launchers will be deployed; each tube is sealed at the factory and the missile requires no field maintenance.

The AN/MSQ-104 ECS includes the weapons control computer, and Identi-fication Friend or Foe (IFF) is performed by the colocated AN/TPX-46(V)7. The electronically steered phased-array radar is the trailer-mounted, G-band (4–6 GHz) AN/MPQ-53, which performs target acquisition, tracking, and missile guidance. The system can track more than 100 targets, interrogate, and assign priorities to those identified as hostile.

Patriots based in Saudi Arabia and Israel were linked to Defense Support Program (DSP) missile-warning satellites for launch warnings, increasing warning times to as much as five minutes.

Raytheon's upgrade to the ECS includes developing Very-High-Speed Integrated Circuit (VHSIC) technology to replace 200 modules in the ECS computer with 13 modules in a much smaller volume.

The Patriot system has the ability to guide several missiles simultaneously while tracking other targets, and also has a limited Anti-Tactical Ballistic Missile (ATBM) defense capability. In a 1986 test of its potential, a Patriot missile intercepted and destroyed a Lance tactical ballistic missile.

The Patriot's accuracy is due to its Track via Missile (TVM) terminal guidance method. Targets are selected by the system and illuminated by the GCS phased-array radars. Tracking "gates" in the software permit the radar to concentrate on a relatively small sector in which the missile is likely to appear next, which improves the precision of the tracking.

When the missile is launched, it maneuvers using tail control, with independently activated fins that move the after end of the body. Body lift generated by the missile's shape and speed steers the missile in the desired direction.

Typically, two missiles are automatically fired against a target missile in a "shoot-shoot" sequence to ensure interception. Later development could result in an earlier "shoot-look-shoot" sequence that allows counteraction at a greater distance from the target.

Patriot Missile
U.S. GOVERNMENT DEPARTMENT OF DEFENSE

The missile's on-board semiactive homing monopulse seeker senses the reflected energy from the target, establishes its position relative to the target, and relays that information to the ground-based AN/MSQ-104 ECS through a radio data link. At the same time, smaller ground-based radars are tracking the target. High-speed computers in the ECS compare the positions reported by the missile and the ground radars and calculate course corrections that direct the missile to fly the most efficient intercept course. If the ground-based system is jammed by Electronic Countermeasures (ECM), the TVM channel gives the system an alternate tracking mode.

The missile's warhead is designed to spray an aircraft with high-velocity fragments that are likely to hit vital systems. When used against a missile, the blast at least diverts the incoming missile and prevents the warhead from exploding; it is not usually massive enough to obliterate a missile.

DEVELOPMENT • The Patriot's initial operational capability was in 1985. Patriot development began as the Field Army Ballistic Missile Defense System (FABMDS) and Army Air Defense System of the 1970s (AADS-70) programs, which were combined into the SAM-D program in August 1965.

First flight tests began in 1970. Full-scale development began in 1972 but was delayed by a 1974 decision to incorporate a TVM ability into the system. In 1976 (the US bicentennial year), the name Patriot was selected and said to be an acronym for Phased-Array Tracking to Intercept of Target.

Limited production was authorized in August 1980, with first deliveries in 1982. The original plan was to procure 104 fire units but was later revised by budgetary constraints to 60 fire units planned.

In March 1988, Italy signed an air defense agreement that includes the purchase and coproduction of 20 Patriot missile batteries with 160 launchers and 1,000 missiles. A new consortium—Italmissile—composed of Selenia, BPD, and OTO Melara would coordinate Italian industrial participation and manufacture the missiles and launchers.

Japan signed a license-production agreement for 26 batteries (130 launchers and 1,300 missiles) in 1985; prime contractor is Mitsubishi Heavy Industries. Japan's first three fire units were declared operational in April 1990 with the 3rd Air Defense Missile Group (ADMG).

Siemens is prime contractor for German production. 36 fire units in six wings. 12 squadrons are owned and operated by the German Air Force. 12 will be owned by the US Army for 10 years and then turned over to the GAF, which has operated the batteries from the start. The last 12 are owned by the US Army but will be operated by the GAF until the year 2000. Four other squadrons (two "floating" and two training) are being fielded.

The Patriot is operational with the US Army and six other nations.

VARIANTS • PAC-1, PAC-2, quick-reaction upgrade, PAC-3/Advanced Tactical (AT) Patriot/Patriot Growth Missile (US/German), Launcher Improvement Program.

COMBAT EXPERIENCE • In August 1990, Patriot missile batteries were deployed to Saudi Arabia as part of Operation Desert Storm. Israeli Patriot batteries were delivered in early January 1991 and launched their first missiles on January 22.

A total of 158 Patriots from some of the more than 90 launchers deployed were fired at 47 TBM in both theaters; another 39 TBM were aimed at targets outside of the Patriot batteries' envelope.

In Saudi Arabia, the US Army claimed that more than 80% of the missiles that entered the Patriot's "coverage zone" were successfully engaged. This claim was hotly challenged by critics.

SPECIFICATIONS •

MANUFACTURER
Raytheon (prime)
Siemens (prime German contractor)
Japan (license producer)

WEIGHTS
missile   1,534 lb (700 kg)
warhead   198 lb (90 kg)

DIMENSIONS
configuration
long cylinder with cruciform "cropped delta" tailfins and ogival nose
length   17 ft 5 in (5.31 m)
diameter   16 in (406 mm)
fin span   3 ft (914 mm)

PROPULSION   Thiokol TX-486 single-stage solid-fuel rocket burns for 11 seconds

PERFORMANCE
speed   more than 1,722 kts
(1,983 mph; 3,191 km/h) or Mach 3 (sources report Mach 4 or 5)
range   max more than 43 nm (50 mi; 80 km)
min approx 1.6 nm (1.9 mi; 3 km)

WARHEAD   conventional blast fragmentation

SENSORS/FIRE CONTROL
AN/MPQ-53 phased-array radar
AN/TPX-46(V)7 IFF
AN/MSQ-104 ECS
Track via Missile (TVM) terminal guidance
M818E2 dual-beam fuze in PAC-2 variant

HAWK (MIM-23)

The HAWK and Improved HAWK (I-HAWK) are the primary US low-to-medium-altitude ground-based surface-to-air missile systems. It is carried on a

Launch of HAWK Air Defense Missile
U.S. GOVERNMENT DEPARTMENT OF DEFENSE

three-missile towed launcher. In the US Army, HAWK batteries consist of two platoons, each containing three three-missile launchers. The Triad battery, used to augment normal antiair capability, has three platoons. The US Army plans to retain HAWK missile batteries in active service indefinitely.

The MIM-23's name, HAWK, is said to be an acronym for Homing All the Way Killer.

DEVELOPMENT • The HAWK's initial operational capability was in August 1960. HAWKs for European countries were built by NATO HAWK Management Office established in the 1960s. Charter members, beginning in 1958, were Belgium, France, West Germany, and the Netherlands. Greece joined in 1972 and Denmark in 1974. In production and in service with several countries. Procurement by the United States was terminated in the FY1991 budget request. License-built in Japan by Mitsubishi and Toshiba.

In addition to the US Army and Marine Corps, over 20 other nations worldwide except for Latin America use the HAWK.

18 HAWK missiles were supplied to Iran from Israeli stocks in November 1985.

VARIANTS • I-HAWK (Improved), HAWK Mobility Enhancement (HME/Dutch and Raytheon), NOAH (Norwegian Adapted HAWK/Kongsberg Vapenfabrikk SA, Norway, and Hughes Aircraft), Israeli upgrades.

COMBAT EXPERIENCE • Israeli basic HAWKs succeeded in shooting down more than 20 MiG aircraft during the 1973 Yom Kippur War. In 1982, a HAWK missile guided by an Israeli-modified radar intercepted a MiG-25 Foxbat reconnaissance aircraft flying at 75,000 ft (22,860 m).

In September 1987, a French Army HAWK battery shot down a Libyan Air Force Tu-22 Blinder over Chad.

Although no HAWK missiles were fired by coalition forces during Operation Desert Storm, Kuwaiti missile batteries downed almost two dozen aircraft during the Iraqi invasion of August 1990. Iraqi forces subsequently captured HAWK missile batteries, but how many of Kuwait's five batteries and 150 missiles was never determined. In January 1991, the Iraqis claimed to have restored two batteries to service.

SPECIFICATIONS •
MANUFACTURER   Raytheon
MISSILE WEIGHT   1,383 lb (627.3 kg)
    warhead   120 lb (54.4 kg)
DIMENSIONS
    configuration
        cylindrical body, cruciform long-chord, "cropped delta" wings with control surfaces separated from trailing edges by narrow slot, ogival nose, narrowed nozzle at tail
    length   16 ft 6 in (5.03 m) diameter 14 in (360 mm)
    wingspan   3 ft 11½ in (1.21 m)
PROPULSION   Aerojet dual-thrust solid-fuel rocket
PERFORMANCE
    speed   Mach 2.5
    max range   21.6 nm (25 mi; 40 km)
    altitude   minimum: less than 98 ft (30 m)
        max: approx 60,000 ft (18,290 m)
WARHEAD   conventional high-explosive blast fragmentation with proximity and contact fuzes
SENSORS/FIRE CONTROL
    Hawk battery of 6 launchers is colocated with several radars and sensors
    2 acquisition radars, synchronized in azimuth: L-band Pulse Acquisition Radar (PAR) for high-to-medium targets and Continuous-Wave Ac-

quisition Radar (CWAR) for low-altitude detection through heavy clutter
2 High-Power Illuminators (HPI) operating in X band illuminate target for missile
K-band Range-Only Radar (ROR) used when other radars are jammed
Tracking Adjunct System (TAS) passive electro-optical tracker
missile has proportional navigation guidance coupled with CW and semiactive terminal homing

Sea Sparrow (RIM-7)

The Sea Sparrow naval Surface-to-Air Missile (SAM) system was originally developed in the late 1960s as an interim Basic Point Defense Missile System (BPDMS) against Soviet antiship missiles. Later versions include the Improved BPDMS and the NATO Sea Sparrow Surface Missile System (NSSMS). All use modified Sparrow III Air-to-Air Missiles (AAM) in an eight-cell launcher that can be fitted in a variety of ships.

The Mk 48 Sea Sparrow Vertical Launch System (VLS) was first tested on the Canadian destroyer *Huron* in April 1981. The system is designed to be assembled in groups of two vertical canisters and can be set either in the deck, exhausting vertically (Mod 0), on a bulkhead with overboard exhausting (Mod 1), or in a superstructure mount with vertical exhaust (Mod 2). The missile is fitted with Jet Vane Control (JVC) to quickly pitch the missile into cruise attitude from its vertical takeoff. Maximum missile turning rate during boost is 283°/sec.

The Mk 41 VLS, in US service on some *Ticonderoga* (CG 47)-class cruisers and *Spruance*-class destroyers, can also launch VL Sea Sparrows. Four Evolved Sea Sparrows (ESS) could fit in each Mk 41 VLS cell.

DEVELOPMENT • The BPDMS with RIM-7E initial operational capability was in 1969, NSSMS with RIM-7H around 1977, RIM-7M in 1983. International program was established by July 1968 Memorandum of Understanding (MoU) between Denmark, Italy, Norway, and the United States. Later, Belgium and the Netherlands in 1970, West Germany in 1977, Canada and Greece in 1982, and Turkey in 1986 signed.

The Sea Sparrow is mounted in several types of US Navy surface combatants, amphibious ships, and underway replenishment ships, fired from either the NATO Sea Sparrow Mk 29 launcher or the BPDMS Mk 25 launcher. Both launchers have eight cells, although some Mk 29 launchers will be refitted to fire RAM (RIM-116) missiles from two of the eight cells.

In production and in service with US Navy and other navies. In non-US navies the Sea Sparrow is mounted in Mk 29 launchers in destroyer and frigate classes except for Mk 48 VLS in new-construction ships. A launch system and 21 RIM-7M Sea Sparrow missiles will be fitted to the lead ship of the South Korean Destroyer Experimental (KDX) class, scheduled for service entry in 1995. Over a dozen other nations in Europe, Asia, and Canada have the Sea Sparrow system deployed on their destroyers and frigates.

VARIANTS • Basic Point Defense Missile System (BPDMS), NATO Sea Sparrow Surface Missile System (NSSMS), Guided Missile Vertical Launch System (GMVLS), RIM-7P, RIM-7R/Missile Homing Improvement Program (MHIP), Evolved Sea Sparrow (ESS).

COMBAT EXPERIENCE • Although Sea Sparrow launchers were the most widely deployed naval weapons system in Desert Storm, no missiles were fired against Iraqi aircraft or missiles.

SPECIFICATIONS •
MANUFACTURER
Raytheon (primary)
Hughes (secondary)

SUBCONTRACTORS
Belgium Manufacture Belge de
  Lampes et de Matériel (MBLE)
Canada EBCO
Raytheon Canada
Denmark DISA
NEA-Lindberg
Germany Motorenwerk Bremerhaven
  GmBH
Italy Selenia
Netherlands Bronswerk Fokker-VFW
Norway Norsk Forsvarsteknologi
  (NFT)
Turkey Aselsan Military Electronics
US Ball Aerospace

WEIGHTS

system	BPDMS 39,000 lb (17,690 kg)
	NSSMS 28,479 lb (12,918 kg)
	Mk 48 VLS (16 missiles)
	Mod 0
	above decks: 32,480 lb (14,896 kg)
	below decks: 1,793 lb (814 kg)
	Mod 1
	above decks: 29,960 lb (12,256 kg)
	below decks: 1,793 lb (814 kg)
missile	RIM-7H: 450 lb (205 kg)
	RIM-7M: 510 lb (231 kg)
	warhead: 88 lb (40 kg)

DIMENSIONS

configuration	long cylinder with ogival nose, cruciform, folding "cropped delta" mainplanes, clipped tail fins, JVC pack on tail of VLS variant
length	12 ft (3.66 m)
diameter	8 in (203 mm)
wingspan	3 ft 4 in (1.02 m)
tail span	2 ft (0.61 m)

PROPULSION   Hercules Mk 58 single-stage solid-fuel rocket (Mk 58 Mod 4 in RIM-7M)

PERFORMANCE

speed	Mach 2.5
max range	8 nm (9.2 mi; 14.8 km)

WARHEAD
RIM-7H: high-explosive continuous
  rod
RIM-7M: WAU-17/B high-explosive
  blast fragmentation

SENSORS/FIRE CONTROL

BPDMS	Continuous Wave (CW) illumination from Mk 51 radar
	Mk 115 manually operated fire control system
	Semiactive Radar (SAR) homing in RIM-7E
NSSMS	Mk 91 fire control system; Mod 0 has single director, Mod 1 has dual directors
	Ball Mk 6 Mod 0 LLLTV system
	Hughes Mk 23 Target Acquisition System (TAS) update

RIM-7M introduced inverse mono-pulse seeker, reprogrammable digital Missile-Borne Computer (MBC)

Rolling Airframe Missile— RAM (RIM-116)

The RAM (Rolling Airframe Missile) is being developed to provide a rapid-reaction, short-range Surface-to-Air Missile (SAM) for shipboard defense using "off-the-shelf" components. RAM has the Infrared (IR) seeker from the Stinger SAM and the rocket motor, fuze, and warhead from the Sidewinder Air-to-Air Missile (AAM).

The RAM is the first US Navy shipboard "fire and forget" missile and the only Navy missile that rolls during flight (i.e., is not aerodynamically stabilized).

In the initial flight phase, the missile uses passive Radio Frequency (RF) to home on target emissions to point its IR seeker at the target. RAM switches to IR homing during the terminal phase of flight. The guidance system measures the IR signal-to-noise ratio and determines when it is appropriate to switch to terminal IR homing. If the IR seeker cannot acquire the target, the missile continues on to target using the RF guidance.

There are three types of launchers. The production RAM Mk 31 launcher has 21 cells. Some NATO Sea Sparrow Mk 29 launchers will be modified so two of the eight cells would each launch five missiles. The RAM Alternative Launching System (RALS), a lighter, eight-round launcher for small combatants, is under development by TransLant Inc., a joint venture of General Dynamics and German RAM System.

DEVELOPMENT • The RAM's initial operating capability was originally planned for 1992–93. Funding for development was initially shared by the US, West Germany, and Denmark on a 49% 49% 2% basis. Denmark withdrew financial support from the project but participates on an ad hoc basis.

Although the RAM did not have immediate test success, with seven of 15 launched in an early 1985 series failing, later trials aboard the US destroyer *David R. Ray* (DD 971) from December 1986 to February 1987 resulted in 11 successes out of 13 attempts.

The US Navy established a requirement for 30 launchers and 4,900 missiles; the first allotment of 240 missiles is scheduled for the mid-1990s. Germany's requirement is for 55 launchers and 2,000 missiles.

The RAM will be deployed on US amphibious, command, and landing ships and frigates, German destroyers, frigates, and small combatants, and Danish frigates and small combatants.

Hughes and RAM System are working

separately to develop an improved seeker for the RAM. The new seeker would retain the dual RF/IR capability, but the IR seeker would use an image scanning concept to improve its field of view. The improvement will augment RAM's capability against antiship missiles using inertial guidance and IR homing.

SPECIFICATIONS •

MANUFACTURER
   Hughes (primary)
   RAM System (German consortium)
MISSILE WEIGHT   162 lb (73.5 kg)
   warhead   25 lb (11.3 kg)
DIMENSIONS
   configuration
      long, thin cylinder with blunt nose, 2 folding steerable foreplanes, small cruciform folding tailfins; EX-8 sealed canister round imparts a spin to the RAM as the missile is launched
   length   9 ft 3 in (2.82 m)
   diameter   5 in (127 mm)
PROPULSION   Mk 36 Mod 8 solid-propellant rocket
SPEED   supersonic
WARHEAD   conventional high-explosive
SENSORS/FIRE CONTROL   passive dual-mode RF/IR acquisition
MODIFIED MK 29 SEA SPARROW LAUNCHER
   capacity   10 RAM, 6 Sea Sparrow
MK 31 RAM STANDARD LAUNCHER
   weight   above decks: 11,424 lb (5,182 kg) with missiles
      below decks: 2,105 lb (955 kg)
   elevation   −25°/+80°
   traverse   360°
   capacity   21 rounds
RALS
   weight   above decks: less than 6,500 lb (2,950 kg) with missiles
      below decks: 1,600 lb (726 kg)

elevation	−25/+80°
traverse	175° to either side of centerline
capacity	8 rounds

Standard SM-1 MR (RIM-66B)

The Standard Surface-to-Air Missile (SAM) series was developed as a replacement for the three "T" missiles, the trouble-plagued Talos, Terrier, and Tartar. The Standard missile family was the result of an improvement program that began in the late 1950s. The SM-1 MR (Medium Range) is the oldest Standard type remaining in service, being a relatively short-range weapon with single-stage rocket propulsion.

The update program's emphasis was on the achievement of greater range and reliability than Tartar and Terrier. A more powerful dual-thrust rocket motor boosted intercept altitude by 25% and range by 45%. Reliability was enhanced by replacing vacuum-tube electronics and hydraulic controls with solid-state circuitry and electronically powered controls. Warm-up time was reduced from 26 seconds for the Improved Tartar to one second for the SM-1.

DEVELOPMENT • The SM-1's initial operational capability was in 1970. It is no longer in production but in service on destroyers and frigates in the US Navy and the navies of Australia, France, Germany, Italy, Japan, Netherlands, and Spain.

VARIANTS • RIM-66B, RIM-66E, RGM-66D Standard ARM, RGM-66E, RGM-66F, AGM-78 (air-launched ARM, see separate listing), RIM-67A, RIM-67B, RIM-67C, RIM-67D (rail-launched).

COMBAT EXPERIENCE • Although 13 *Perry*-class frigates participated in Operation Desert Storm, none fired its Standard missiles.

SPECIFICATIONS •
MANUFACTURER   Hughes
MISSILE WEIGHT   1,100 lb (499 kg)
DIMENSIONS
  configuration
    slim cylinder with pointed nose, cruciform narrow long-chord mainplanes indexed in line with steerable tailplanes
  length   14 ft 8 in (4.47 m)
  diameter   13½ in (342 mm)
  wingspan   3 ft 6 in (1.07 m)
PROPULSION   Mk 56 Mod 0 dual-thrust single-stage rocket motor
PERFORMANCE
  speed   Mach 2+
  max range   25 nm (28.8 mi; 46.3 km)
  max altitude
    60,000 ft (18,288 m)
  minimum altitude
    150 ft (46 m)
WARHEAD   conventional expanding, continuous rod
SENSORS/FIRE CONTROL
  missile guidance
  conical scan Semiactive Radar (SAR) homing
  single sideband receiver
  all-electric control surface actuation
  adaptive autopilot
  Motorola Mk 45 Target Detecting Device (TDD) proximity and contact fuze

Standard SM-2 MR (RIM-66C)

The SM-2 MR (Medium Range) has increased range over the SM-1 MR (about equal to the range of the SM-2 ER) as well as the addition of midcourse guidance and enhanced resistance to Electronic Countermeasures (ECM).

The SM-2 MR is being procured in several versions and Blocks, which has resulted in a proliferation of type designations. Block II and Block III variants are separated into three subtypes, each with a different letter suffix depending on

SM-2 MR
U.S. GOVERNMENT DEPARTMENT OF DEFENSE

whether the missile is intended for the Aegis missile system, a Vertical Launch System (VLS), or a Tartar guided-missile ship.

DEVELOPMENT • Initial operational capability was in 1981. Production by Hughes.

In service with US Navy *Ticonderoga-, California-,* and *Virginia-*class cruisers and *Kidd-* and *Burke-*class destroyers, Canadian *Iroquois-*class destroyers, and Japanese *Kongo-*class destroyers.

COMBAT EXPERIENCE • The first operational use of SM-2 missiles occurred on July 3, 1988, when two missiles were fired from the USS *Vicennes* (CG 49) at a target believed to be an Iranian F-14 Tomcat fighter. One or both missiles struck the aircraft, which was a civilian Iran Air Airbus 300 airliner carrying 290 passengers. All aboard were killed.

A total of 43 US, four Australian, two Netherlands, and two Spanish ships fitted with Standard SAM launchers deployed to the Persian Gulf during Operation Desert Storm. Because of the rapid destruction of Iraq's antiship weapons (principally the Mirage F1-EQ attack aircraft carrying Exocet missiles and the ground-launched Silkworm antiship missile), no Standards were launched during the deployments.

SPECIFICATIONS •
MANUFACTURER Hughes
Raytheon (secondary, Block II and III)
MISSILE WEIGHT
  Block I: 1,350 lb (613 kg)
  Block II/III: 1,556 lb (706 kg)
DIMENSIONS
  configuration
            cylinder with cruciform long-chord mainplanes, cruciform steerable tail fins, ogival nose
  length Block I: 14 ft 7 in (4.44 m)
            Block II/III: 15 ft 6 in (4.72 m)

diameter   13½ in (342 mm)
wingspan   3 ft 6 in (1.07 m)
PROPULSION   single-stage dual-thrust Aerojet Mk 56 Mod 2 (Block I) or Morton Thiokol Mk 104 (Block II/III) solid-fuel rocket
PERFORMANCE
  speed   Mach 2+
  max range Block I: approx 40 nm (46 mi; 74 km)
               Block II: approx 90 nm (104 mi; 167 km)
WARHEAD high-velocity controlled fragmentation conventional high explosive
SENSORS/FIRE CONTROL
  inertial navigation with 2-way communication link for midcourse guidance from warship
  digital guidance computer
  monopulse Semiactive Radar (SAR) homing
  Motorola Mk 45 Target Detecting Device (TDD) proximity and contact fuzes

Standard SM-2 ER (RIM-67A/B and 67C/D)

The SM-2 ER (Extended Range) version has extended range, midcourse guidance, an inertial reference system, and improved resistance to Electronic Countermeasures (ECM) compared to earlier missiles. The SM-2 ER is a two-stage missile that can reach an altitude of about 80,000 feet.

DEVELOPMENT • Initial operational capability was in 1981. The RIM-67A/B was deployed on the US Navy's *Bainbridge, Truxtun,* and *Long Beach-*class cruisers, and *Coontz-*class destroyers, and the RIM-67C/D was deployed on *Leahy-* and *Belknap-*class cruisers.

COMBAT EXPERIENCE • Three *Leahy-*class and four *Belknap-*class cruisers fitted with RIM-67C/D and three *Farragut-*class destroyers armed with RIM-67B missiles deployed during Operation Desert Storm, but no Standards were launched.

SPECIFICATIONS •

MANUFACTURER General Dynamics
MISSILE WEIGHT 2,920 lb (1,324 kg)
DIMENSIONS
  configuration
              cylindrical booster with
              cruciform steerable
              "cropped delta"
              tailplanes, necked top
              for mating to missile;
              cylindrical missile with
              cruciform long-chord
              mainplanes, cruciform
              steerable tailplanes,
              ogival nose
  length   27 ft (8.23 m)
  diameter   booster: 18 in (460 mm)
              missile: 13½ in (342 mm)
  wingspan   booster: 5 ft 3 in (1.6 m)
              missile: 3 ft 6 in (1.06 m)
PROPULSION
  two-stage solid fuel rocket
  Mk 70 booster in SM-2 ER
  Mk 56 or 104 sustainer
PERFORMANCE
  speed   Mach 2+
  max range   75–90 nm (86–104 mi;
              139–167 km)
  max altitude
              approx 80,000 ft
              (24,384 m)
WARHEAD conventional high-explosive
  controlled fragmentation
SENSORS/FIRE CONTROL
  inertial navigation with two-way communication link for midcourse
  guidance from warship
  digital guidance computer
  monopulse Semiactive Radar (SAR)
  homing
  Motorola Mk 45 Target Detecting Device (TDD) proximity and contact
  fuze

Standard SM-2 AER (RIM-67B)

The latest Standard variant is the Aegis Extended Range, which is considerably changed from earlier Standard missiles. Aegis ER launches from the Mk 41 Vertical Launching System on *Ticonderoga* and *Arleigh Burke* classes. The basic airframe resembles earlier Standards, although the dorsal fins have been enlarged.

The guidance, ECM equipment, and airframe improvements derived from several other Raytheon missile programs. Aegis ER's digital autopilot is based on Raytheon's AIM-120 AMRAAM Air-to-Air Missile (AAM) update design. The digital signal processor techniques are taken from AMRAAM and AIM-7 Sparrow AAMs and the ground-based MIM-104 Patriot SAM. Sparrow Electronic Counter-Countermeasures (ECCM) from Sparrow AAM. To cope with the heating imposed by a longer period of high-speed flight, the fused-silica radome developed for the Patriot has been adopted.

DEVELOPMENT • The SM-2 AER's initial operational capability was in 1992. This is the first Standard missile design for which Raytheon is prime contractor; all previous variants were led by General Dynamics. The missile is deployed on the US Navy *Ticonderoga*-class cruisers and *Arleigh Burke*-class destroyers.

SPECIFICATIONS •

MANUFACTURER Raytheon
MISSILE WEIGHT 3,200 lb (1,451 kg)
DIMENSIONS
  configuration
              cylindrical booster with
              necked top for mating
              to missile; cylindrical
              missile with cruciform
              long-chord mainplanes,
              cruciform steerable
              tailplanes, ogival nose
  length   missile only: 16 ft
              (4.88 m)

with booster: 21 ft 6 in
(6.55 m)
diameter   booster: 21 in (533 mm)
missile: 13.7 in (348 mm)
missile wingspan: 3 ft 6 in
(1.06 m)
PROPULSION
two-stage solid-fuel rocket
EX-72 booster
Mk 104 dual-thrust rocket motor sustainer
PERFORMANCE   larger envelope than
Block II/Block III
WARHEAD   conventional high-explosive
controlled fragmentation
SENSORS/FIRE CONTROL
inertial navigation with two-way communication link for midcourse
guidance from warship
digital guidance computer
monopulse Semiactive Radar (SAR)
homing

Nike Hercules (MIM-14)

The Nike Hercules Surface-to-Air Missile
(SAM) system is one of the oldest US-
designed SAMs still in active service. It is
capable of interceptions at relatively high
altitudes and long ranges but is not suitable for low-altitude defense. It can also
perform in a Surface-to-Surface Missile
(SSM) role. The fixed batteries that
formed part of the North American air
defense system have been dismantled;
mobile Nike batteries are still in service
in several other countries.

When targets are detected by the system's tracking radar, the Nike launcher is
elevated to 85° and the missile is fired.
After the boosters are spent and jettisoned, the missile-tracking radar guides
the missile to the target. Detonation of
the high-explosive or nuclear warhead is
by radio command.

DEVELOPMENT • The Nike's initial operational capability was in 1958. Although no longer in production or US

service, the Nike is in service in several
European and Asian countries.

VARIANTS • MIM-14C (1981 modification).

SPECIFICATIONS •
MANUFACTURER
Western Electric (prime)
Douglas Aircraft (missile)
Mitsubishi (Japanese license)
AT&T (upgrade prime)
MISSILE WEIGHT   10,710 lb (4,858 kg)
DIMENSIONS
configuration
2-stage missile, 4-booster
cluster, each booster with
cropped-delta stabilizer,
tapered cylinder, small
cruciform delta
noseplanes indexed in
line with extremely swept
delta mainplanes,
control surfaces joined
to mainplanes by
actuators
length   39 ft 8 in (12.1 m)
diameter   2 ft 7½ in (.8 m)
wingspan   6 ft 2 in (1.88 m)
PROPULSION
Hercules 4-motor solid-propellant
booster cluster
Thiokol solid-propellant sustainer
PERFORMANCE
speed   Mach 3.65
max range   more than 75 nm (87 mi;
140 km)
max altitude
more than 24.3 nm (28
mi; 45 km)
WARHEAD   conventional high-explosive
or nuclear
SENSORS/FIRE CONTROL
guidance   MIM-14A command and
control by Western
Electric
MIM-14C has Norden
DCS, General Electric
AN/MPQ-43 HIPAR

Super Falcon (AIM-4)

The Super Falcon is the final generation of one of the earliest Air-to-Air Missiles (AAM) in the US inventory. The AIM-4G has an all-aspect homing capability. The AIM-4D has only a tail engagement capability but has greater maneuverability and was designed as an antifighter weapon.

DEVELOPMENT • The Super Falcon's initial operational capability as the AIM-4 was in 1956, the AIM-4E in 1958, AIM-4F/G in 1960, and AIM-4D in 1963. Over 56,000 AIM-4-series missiles were built, most of which were AIM-4A/B/C variants. It is no longer in production but is still in service with the US Air Force and Air National Guard.

The Falcon's success was based on a light airframe containing a generous amount of Glass-Reinforced Plastics (GRP) and the best miniaturized electronics then available.

All Falcons were originally designated GAR (Guided Air Rockets); the AIM designation and revised numbering were instituted in 1962.

Super Falcons are operated by the air forces of Finland, Japan, Sweden, Switzerland, Turkey, and Taiwan.

VARIANTS • GAR-1/1D (AIM-4/4A), GAR-2 /2A (AIM-4B/4C), GAR-3/3A (AIM-4E/4F), GAR-4A (AIM-4G), GAR-2B (AIM-4D), XAIM-4H (test), XGAR-11/GAR-11/11A (XAIM-26/AIM-26A/26B), GAR-9 (AIM-47A), RB-27 (AIM-26B) and RB-28 (AIM-4D) (Swedish license-built).

SPECIFICATIONS •
MANUFACTURER
  Hughes Aircraft
  Saab-Scania (Sweden)
MISSILE WEIGHT
  AIM-4D: 135 lb (61 kg)
  AIM-4F: 150 lb (68 kg)
  AIM-4G: 145 lb (66 kg)

warhead   40 lb (18.14 kg)
DIMENSIONS
configuration
  cylindrical body with blunt nose (opaque for Semiactive Radar/SAR, clear for Infrared/IR seeker), four small aerial "ears" on forebody (AIM-4F/G only), extreme delta cruciform wings with large control services attached at trailing edge; AIM-4D has 4 fixed, semicircular canards near the nose, AIM-4F/G have long leading-edge extensions
length   AIM-4D: 6 ft 8 in (2.02 m)
  AIM-4F: 7 ft 2 in (2.18 m)
  AIM-4G: 6 ft 9 in (2.06 m)
diameter   AIM-4D: 6½ in (165 mm)
  AIM-4F/G: 6.6 in (168 mm)
wingspan   AIM-4D: 1 ft 8 in (0.51 m)
  AIM-4F/G: 2 ft (0.61 m)
PROPULSION   Thiokol M46 two-stage solid-fuel motor with first-stage thrust rating of 6,000 lb (26.7 kN) static thrust; second stage has lower rating for sustaining speed
PERFORMANCE
speed   Mach 3
max range   7 mi (11.3 km)
WARHEAD   conventional high explosive
SENSORS/FIRE CONTROL
  AIM-4D has an Infrared (IR) seeker
  AIM-4F has a Hughes semiactive radar-homing seeker
  AIM-4G has an all-aspect IR seeker

ANTIRADAR MISSILES

HARM (AGM-88)

The AGM-88 HARM missile was developed as a replacement for the AGM-45 Shrike and AGM-78 Standard Antiradiation Radar Missiles (ARM). It is an expensive missile, but one with a broad capability against ground- and ship-based radars.

The HARM can be fired in several modes: As a long-range standoff missile against preselected targets, HARM can delay acquisition of target until after launch. The all-aspect passive radar-homing seeker can be used to search for targets of opportunity; the missile is then fired manually. The missile can be launched in "range-known" and "range-unknown" and can home on back and sidelobe radiation. It can also be used as a self-defense missile in concert with aircraft Electronic Support Measures (ESM) equipment.

HARM has a digital autopilot and strap-down inertial navigation, a low-smoke solid-propellant rocket, and digital processing in both the missile and the launch aircraft, which allows the HARM to attack a broad frequency spectrum (four-octave bandwidth from 0.5 to 20 GHz) of hostile radars.

The high-explosive warhead is prefragmented into thousands of small steel cubes designed specifically to damage radar antenna and other fragile equipment.

DEVELOPMENT • The missile's initial operational capability was in 1984. It was developed by the Naval Weapons Center at China Lake, California; Texas Instruments began participation in 1974. A total of 14,000 were planned for the US services. West Germany ordered 1,000 HARMs in 1986 and took its first delivery

in November 1987. The 10,000th HARM was delivered in 1990.

In an attempt to increase the number of firms capable of producing antiradiation seekers, the Navy began developing the Low-Cost Seeker (LCS) program in 1984. While Texas Instruments continued developing the Block IV seeker, Ford Aerospace and Raytheon Corp. offered a competing LCS, with the Navy choosing the Ford design in 1988. (Ford Aerospace was later acquired by Loral Corp.)

Texas Instruments received a $459-million contract in February 1989 for the production of 2,449 missiles. Deliveries began in late 1990, to be completed by late 1991; the contract covers 1,319 missiles for the Navy, 950 for the Air Force, and 180 for Germany. In 1990, Spain ordered 200 HARMs for carriage by EF-18 Hornet aircraft.

The HARM has frequently been criticized for high cost, and in early 1986, the Navy briefly stopped accepting the missile because of quality control problems. Its future as the principal air-launched antiradar missile was assured, however, by its competent performance during the 1986 US naval air strikes against Libya.

Platforms for the HARM include fighters, electronic aircraft and attack (US), attack and electronic aircraft (Germany), and electronic (Spain).

VARIANTS • AGM-88A, AGM-88B, AGM-88C.

COMBAT EXPERIENCE • US Navy carrier-based aircraft launched 40 HARMs against Libyan surface-to-air missile radars, primarily SA-5s, in March–April 1986 air strikes against Libya.

When Operation Desert Storm's air

war began in January 1991, HARMs were a heavy contributor to the collapse of the Iraqi air defense radar network. Most of the more than 1,000 HARMs fired (661 by US Navy aircraft, 233 more by the US Marine Corps) were launched during the first half of the campaign.

SPECIFICATIONS •

MANUFACTURER   (see Development)
MISSILE WEIGHT   796–807 lb (361–366 kg)
warhead   145 lb (66 kg)
DIMENSIONS
configuration
    long cylinder with ogival nose, cruciform steerable double-delta foreplanes indexed in line with stubby fins at tail
length   13 ft 8½ in (4.17 m)
diameter   10 in (254 mm)
wingspan   3 ft 8½ in (1.13 m)
PROPULSION   Thiokol YSR-113-TC-1 dual-thrust reduced-smoke solid-fuel rocket (Hercules is second source)
PERFORMANCE
speed   Mach 2+
range   10 nm (11.5 mi; 18.5 km)
WARHEAD   conventional high explosive with prefragmented steel-cube warhead
SENSORS/FIRE CONTROL
    all-aspect passive radar homing
    Motorola DSU-19 active optical fuzing system

Shrike (AGM-45)

The AGM-45 is the first missile built specifically for the antiradar mission to enter mass production in the United States. It is based, in part, on the AIM-7 Sparrow air-to-air missile, which it resembles. It consists of four sections: a guidance system, the warhead, the control system, and the rocket motor.

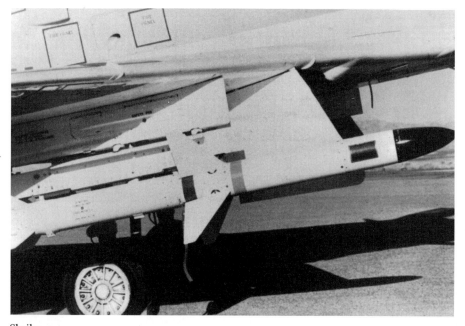

Shrike

The Shrike has had many subvariants, all of which differ principally in their seeker. It is gradually being replaced by the AGM-88 HARM missile.

DEVELOPMENT • The Shrike's initial operational capability was in 1963, and its first test flights were in 1962. Over 20,000 had been produced before production ceased.

The Shrike is deployed on US Air Force F-4Gs and F-16Cs and Ds, US Navy A-6Es, A-7Es, and F/A-18s, and Israeli F-4s and Kfirs.

The Shrike had several major limitations that reduce its effectiveness: it must be pointing at the target at the moment of launch and the target radar must be radiating throughout the missile's flight. Although upgrades have improved the Shrike's performance, the lack of a readily reprogrammable seeker remains an intrinsic limitation.

VARIANTS • AGM-45-9A Shrike G-Bias upgrade.

COMBAT EXPERIENCE • Shrikes were first used in combat in Vietnam in 1966. They were used extensively as a penetration aid by the US Air Force and Navy, but the missile's limitations—including a need for the target to continue radiating during the entire flight—led to many modifications.

The Israelis used the Shrike during the 1973 Yom Kippur War with success against SA-2 and SA-3 missiles, but ineffectively against the SA-6. It was also used by Israeli aircraft in the 1982 Lebanese conflict.

It was used ineffectively by British Vulcan bombers in the 1982 Falklands War and launched by the US Navy against Libyan radars in the 1986 US raid.

Although the AGM-88 HARM was used much more extensively in Operation Desert Storm, the US Air Force, Navy, and Marine Corps also launched Shrikes against Iraqi radars. Fewer than 100 were fired, however, and very little was said about their success rate.

SPECIFICATIONS •

MANUFACTURER
Texas Instruments
Sperry Rand/Univac
MISSILE WEIGHT   390 lb (176.9 kg), varies with subtype
warhead   145 lb (65.8 kg)
DIMENSIONS
configuration
resembles Sparrow AAM (AIM-7); long cylinder, ogival nose, cruciform delta steerable foreplanes at midbody, stubby tailfins
length   10 ft (3.05 m)
diameter   8 in (203 mm)
wingspan   3 ft (0.91 m)
PROPULSION   Rocketdyne Mk 39 or Aerojet Mk 53 polybutadiene solid-fuel rocket; Aerojet Mk 78 polyurethane dual-thrust solid-fuel rocket for AGM-45B
PERFORMANCE
speed   Mach 2
max range   approx 10 nm (11.5 mi; 18.5 km)
up to 25 nm (28.8 mi; 40.2 km) reported for improved rocket motor
WARHEAD   conventional high explosive/fragmentation
SENSORS/FIRE CONTROL
at least 18 variations, with over 13 variations on the seeker; other variations include increased range and safety features; AGM-45-9 and -10 have the widest range of coverage fuzing is proximity and contact

Sidearm (AGM-122)

The Sidearm is a short-range, antiradar missile developed to counter air defense weapons. It is an inexpensive self-defense missile for Marine Corps fixed-wing and helicopter aircraft.

The missile uses components from the AIM-9C Sidewinder, which has been in storage since the 1970s. The AIM-9C was a relatively unsuccessful Semiactive Radar (SAR)-homing variant of the Sidewinder; all other Sidewinders are Infrared (IR)-homing missiles.

The Naval Weapons Center at China Lake, California, modified the AIM-9C's narrowband semiactive seeker, creating a broadband passive seeker. The seeker achieves a conical scan by mounting the antenna off center on a spinning gyroscope wheel. The DSU-15A/B Target Detection Device (TDD) flown in the AIM-9L has also been modified for air-to-ground use.

Sidearm is intended primarily for low-altitude use, and the AIM-9C control system has been modified to cause the missile to pitch up soon after launch. This change allows aircraft to launch Sidearms while flying Nap of the Earth (NOE) profiles.

Former Soviet J-band tracking radars such as the Flap Wheel and Gun Dish were the principal targets.

DEVELOPMENT • Approximately 1,000 AIM-9Cs were converted to the Sidearm configuration before funding ended in FY1988 with the purchase of 276 units. The last was delivered in late 1990. The missile is deployable by any aircraft qualified to fire the Sidewinder.

The Marines have used the missile on its Harrier and Bronco planes and the Cobra helicopter.

SPECIFICATIONS •
MANUFACTURER   Motorola
MISSILE WEIGHT   200 lb (90.7 kg)
    warhead   22.4 lb (10.15 kg)
DIMENSIONS
    configuration
        thin cylinder with
        cruciform steerable
        delta foreplanes,

trapezoidal mainplanes at rear, hemispherical radome on nose
length   10 ft (3.0 m)
diameter   5 in (127 mm)
PROPULSION   Mk 36 Mod 9 or Mod 12 solid-fuel rocket
PERFORMANCE
    speed   Mach 2.5
    max range   9.6 nm (11 mi; 17.7 km)
WARHEAD   continuous rod, conventional high explosive
SENSORS/FIRE CONTROL   passive radar homing with broadband seeker

Standard Antiradar Missile (ARM) (AGM-78)

The US Standard Antiradar Missile (ARM) is a large, air-launched weapon based on the shipboard RIM-66A Standard SM-1 surface-to-air missile. It was developed to supplement the AGM-45 Shrike, which had shown range, seeker, and warhead-size limitations during early US use in Vietnam.

The first Standard ARM (AGM-78A) variant used the Texas Instruments seeker from the Shrike, which was pretuned to a given frequency band before fitting it to the aircraft. Later variants (from AGM-78B) used a Maxson Electronics wideband, gimballed seeker. This seeker does not require pretuning, can track a radar emitter from a wider range of attack angles, and has an on-board memory that allows it to continue attacks on shut-down radars. The Target Identification and Acquisition System (TIAS) on the launch aircraft provides targeting data to the Standard ARM before launch. When the missile hits, a smoke cloud reveals the impact point.

DEVELOPMENT • The missile's initial operational capability was in 1968, and its flight tests were conducted in 1967–68. It is no longer in production. It was retired from US Air Force service in 1984 with the last F-105 Thunderchief. In service only with the Israeli Air Force.

VARIANTS • AGM-78A, AGM-78B, AGM-78C, AGM-78D, Purple Fist (Israeli development).

COMBAT EXPERIENCE • Used by US Air Force and Navy aircraft against North Vietnamese radars. Purple Fist missiles (Standard ARMs with improved warheads) were launched by Israeli pilots against Syrian air defense radars in the Bekaa Valley during the 1982 Peace in Galilee invasion of Lebanon.

SPECIFICATIONS •
MANUFACTURER   General Dynamics
MISSILE WEIGHT   1,799 lb (816 kg)
warhead   215 lb (97.5 kg)

DIMENSIONS
configuration
thin cylinder with pointed nose, cruciform long-chord ultra-low aspect ratio lifting strakes indexed in line with trapezoidal steerable tailplanes
length   15 ft (4.57 m)
diameter   13½ in (343 mm)
tail span   3 ft 7 in (1.09 m)
PROPULSION   Aerojet General Mk 27 Mod 4 dual-thrust solid-propellant rocket motor
PERFORMANCE
speed   Mach 2.5
maximum range
16–30 nm (18.4–34.8 mi; 30–56 km)
WARHEAD   high-explosive blast/fragmentation
SENSORS/FIRE CONTROL
guidance: passive radar homing direct and proximity fuzes

ANTISHIP MISSILES

Harpoon (AGM-84/RGM-84/ UGM-84)

The series of AGM/RGM/UGM-84 Harpoons are long-range sea-skimming, antiship missiles that are the most widely used antiship missiles in the West. The ship-launched version of the Harpoon was originally conceived as an air-to-surface missile to attack surfaced Soviet Echo-class cruise missile submarines. The missile is deployed in surface ships and submarines, in land-based coastal defense positions, and on aircraft for a broad antiship role. All Harpoons in US service have been upgraded to AGM/RGM/ UGM-84D (Block 1C) level.

All Harpoons through Block 1C have the same missile body; different launch systems will use different body wings and fins, and restraint shoes. Harpoons launched from surface ships, submarines, or coastal defense platforms require a booster that is the same for all applications. Air-launched Harpoons do not require a booster and have pylon-attachment lugs instead of shoes. The Block 1D (AGM/RGM-84F) has a 23.2-in (592-mm) plug for more fuel capacity, relocated wings, and a Missile Guidance Unit (MGU) based on the AGM-84E SLAM.

Like the French Exocet missile, the Harpoon is a "fire and forget" weapon.

Target information is developed in different ways depending on the platform. Surface ships use the Harpoon Shipboard Command and Launch Control Set (HSCLCS, pronounced "Sickles"). Larger aircraft—P-3, F27 Maritime, B-52G, and Nimrod—are fitted with the "stand-alone" Aircraft Command and Launch Control Set (HACLCS or "Hackles"). Others—S-3 Viking and the Australian F-111C Pig—have a hybrid system that depends in part on the aircraft's weapons control system.

The F-16's Harpoon Interface Adapter Kit (HIAK) is a hybrid variant having software changes and a control box fitted in the underwing stores pylon. Full integration is also found on US, British Royal Navy, Australian, and Netherlands Navy submarines. Other non-US submarines are fitted with the Encapsulated Harpoon Command and Launch Control Set (EHCLS or "Eckles").

The MGU uses a Northrop or Smiths Industries (formerly Lear-Siegler) strapdown, three-axis Attitude Reference Assembly (ARA) to monitor the missile's relation to its launch platform (rather than in relation to the earth, as in inertial guidance). If terrain or nonhostile targets need to be avoided, a high-altitude flyout is preferred. A stealthier approach is to drop down to a presearch sea-skimming altitude.

The starting point for a circular search is offset from the target in the direction that offers the best chance of acquiring the intended target. The Bearing Only Launch (BOL) is used when the range to the target is not known or when target bearing or range is imprecisely known. In the Block 1C, the missile has improved Electronic Counter- Countermeasures (ECCM) as part of the missile upgrade.

Surface-ship-launched Harpoons are loaded into one of three types of reusable launch canisters at the factory or at a weapons station. The Harpoon can be fired from Mk 11 twin-rail and Mk 13 single-rail Surface-to-Air Missile (SAM) launchers, or from four cells (two outer on each end) of the eight-cell Mk 16 Antisubmarine Rocket (ASROC) launcher.

Submarine-launched Harpoons are carried in a buoyant capsule that is launched from a standard 21-in (533-mm) torpedo tube.

DEVELOPMENT • The missile's initial operational capability was in 1977 for surface ships and submarines, in 1979 in P-3C antisubmarine patrol aircraft, and 1981 in A-6E attack aircraft. Initial operational capability for AGM/RGM-84D was in 1984.

First air-launched tests were in 1972. Over 6,400 Harpoons and SLAMs had been ordered by the end of 1991. The missile is intended to continue in US service well into the 21st century.

The Harpoon has been deployed on US Air Force B-52G bombers and several US Navy aircraft. The missile is also deployed in the aircraft of eight European and Asian nations, as well as on board several classes of US Navy cruisers, destroyers, frigates, and small combatants, and the surface warships of 19 other nations. The UGM-84 is deployed in submarines of the US Navy and nine other navies.

The land-launched coastal defense missile variant of the Harpoon was ordered by South Korea (three batteries), Denmark, and Norway. This missile was identical to the production version, with quad canister and launched from a buyer-supplied vehicle.

VARIANTS • AGM/RGM-84A, UGM-84B (Sub-Harpoon, UK), RGM-84C, AGM/RGM-/UGM-84D, AGM/RGM-84F.

COMBAT EXPERIENCE • The first combat use of the Harpoon was by US naval forces against Libyan missile corvettes in the Gulf of Sidra in March 1986. During three separate incidents, at least two, and possibly an unconfirmed third, missile craft were destroyed by US Navy A-6E Intruders.

On April 18, 1988, US Navy frigate *Bagley* (FF 1069) launched a single RGM-84D Harpoon missile at the Iranian missile craft *Joshan* as she fired an RGM-84A Harpoon at US ships. Harpoons were fired on several occasions during the expanded US ship operations against Iraq that year.

During Operation Desert Storm, US Navy ships had very few chances for using Harpoons, as most Iraqi naval ships and craft were sunk by air-launched bombs and rockets. In late January 1991, the Saudis reported that one of their missile craft sank an Iraqi ship with a Harpoon.

SPECIFICATIONS •

MANUFACTURER McDonnell Douglas
MISSILE WEIGHT
AGM-84D: 1,172 lb (531.6 kg)
RGM-84D
Mk 11/13: 1,527 lb (692.6 kg)
Mk 16: 1,466 lb (665.0 kg)
canister/capsule: 1,530 lb (694.0 kg)
AGM-84F: 1,390 lb (630.5 kg)
RGM-84F: 1,757 lb (797.0 kg)
DIMENSIONS
configuration

thick cylinder with pointed nose, cruciform trapezoidal wings at midbody, cruciform in-line swept "cropped delta" control fins at tail; wings and control surfaces fold for storage, pop out after launch; engine has nearly flush ventral air intake; surface-launch version has short booster section with cruciform fins
length AGM-84D: 12 ft 7½ in (3.898 m)

RGM/UGM-84D/coastal:
15 ft 2½ in (4.635 m)
AGM-84F: 14 ft 7 in (4.445 m)
RGM-84F: 17 ft 2 in (5.232 m)
diameter 13½ in (340 mm)
wingspan 3 ft (0.914 m)
PROPULSION
booster (surface-/coastal-/submarine-launch): Aerojet or Thiokol solid-fuel rocket (avg 12,000 lb/5,444 kg static thrust)
Teledyne Continental CAE-J402-CA-400 turbojet sustainer developing 600 lb (273 kg) static thrust; 100 lb (45.4 kg) fuel (JP-10 in Block 1C/1D missiles)
PERFORMANCE
speed Mach 0.85
max range AGM-84D: 75–80 nm (86.3–92.1 mi; 139–148 km)
AGM-84F: approx 150 nm (173 mi; 278 km)
WARHEAD 500 lb (227 kg) conventional high explosive with some penetration capability
SENSORS/FIRE CONTROL
HCLS provides targeting data; no updates once missile is launched
on-board Midcourse Guidance Unit (MGU): IBM digital computer, Smiths Industries 3-axis ARA, and Honeywell AN/APN-194 short-pulse radar or Kollsman Frequency-Modulated Continuous Wave (FMCW) altimeter
Texas Instruments PR-53/DSQ-28 monopulse frequency-agile, jittered Pulse Repetition Frequency (PRF) active radar-homing seeker switched on at preplanned point

Skipper II (AGM-123)

The Skipper is a laser-guided standoff antiship missile originally based on existing missile and bomb components. The "body" is a standard Mk 83 1,000-lb (454-kg) bomb. The rocket motor is derived from the Shrike antiradar missile (AGM-45). The seeker, based on the Paveway II laser-guided bomb series, homes on a remotely designated laser reflected from the target.

DEVELOPMENT • The missile's initial operational capability was in 1985. In service with the US Navy on A-6E Intruder aircraft. The Skipper II was developed by the Naval Weapons Center at China Lake, California. Although the missile is comparatively low in cost and composed of already tested components, its deployment was delayed through a lack of strong support by the Navy.

The FOG-S (Fiber-Optic Guided Skipper) is a variation of the Skipper using US Army–developed fiber-optic data link for Non Line of Sight (NLOS) launch. After discouraging testing and other technical problems, the Navy abandoned the program in March 1991, and reprogrammed funding to support development of the Advanced Interdiction Weapons System (AIWS), which itself was later cancelled.

COMBAT EXPERIENCE • On April 18, 1988, a US Navy A-6 Intruder struck the Iranian frigate *Sahand* with an AGM-123 after the ship engaged US Navy warships in the Strait of Hormuz. The *Sahand* also sustained hits from an air-launched AGM-84 Harpoon and an RGM-84 launched by the USS *Joseph Strauss* (DDG 16) and sank later that night.

Three Skippers were launched by US Marine Corps aircraft in January–February 1991 during Operation Desert Storm.

SPECIFICATIONS •

MANUFACTURER
Aerojet General (rocket motor)
Emerson Electric (guidance)
MISSILE WEIGHT   1,283 lb (582 kg)
warhead   1,000 lb (454 kg)
DIMENSIONS
configuration

Mk 83 bomb has tapered body; guidance section pivots on nose, has cruciform fixed "cropped delta" fins, ringed tip; booster section at tail has cruciform, pop-out swept wings

length   14 ft (4.27 m)
wingspan   5 ft 3 in (1.6 m)
PROPULSION   Aerojet General solid-fuel booster
PERFORMANCE
speed   500 kts (575 mph; 926 km/h)
range   approx 5.2 nm (6 mi; 9.7 km) at 500 kts and 300 ft (91.4 m) launch altitude
WARHEAD   conventional high explosive with FMU-376 fuze
SENSORS/FIRE CONTROL   guidance: laser homing from remote designator

ANTITANK MISSILES

Copperhead (M712)

The M712 Copperhead Cannon-Launched Guided Projectile (CLGP) is a highly accurate, laser-guided projectile fired from standard 155-mm howitzers.

The projectile's semiactive laser seeker searches for a target illuminated by a forward ground- or aircraft-based observer using a coded laser. Copperhead aerodynamically adjusts its flight path to hit the target. The impact "footprint" is approximately 1,100 yd (1,000 m) from the nominal aim point. The Copperhead is biased to hit slightly above the aim point, the turret ring in the case of a tank, to ensure a hit. In one test at maximum range, the round dropped down the open hatch of a moving tank.

The warhead can penetrate every tank now in service. The standard CLGP has been modified with a time-delay fuze, which permits the warhead to penetrate reactive armor without detonating it.

The Copperhead can be fired using shallow flight path angles when cloud cover is below 3,000 ft (914 m). This increases guidance time below clouds, and consequently acquisition range is increased. The Copperhead can be fired from most US 155-mm towed and self-propelled howitzers, French GCT self-propelled gun, International FH-70, and Japanese Type 75 self-propelled howitzer.

DEVELOPMENT • The missile's initial operational capability was in 1982 following over 12 years in development. Its first tests were in 1974 between Martin Marietta and Texas Instruments prototypes, which ended with the selection of Martin Marietta. Full production began with FY1984 funding.

The Copperhead is operated by the US Army and Marine Corps and by Egypt.

VARIANTS • None operational.

COMBAT EXPERIENCE • During Operation Desert Storm, the VII Corps and XVIII Airborne Corps fired approximately 90 Copperheads against a variety of targets with "a high success rate." The principal constraint on Copperhead use came from the limited speed and mobility of the M981 FSV tracked vehicles used to designate targets; these vehicles often could not range far enough ahead of the artillery during the rapid maneuvers that characterized the ground war.

The commander of the 24th Mechanized Infantry Division's artillery claimed that every Copperhead fired during Desert Shield training had scored a hit.

SPECIFICATIONS •
MANUFACTURER   Martin Marietta
COMBAT WEIGHT   137.0 lb (63.0 kg)
  warhead   49.5 lb (22.5 kg)
  filler   14.0 lb (6.4 kg)
      Composition B
DIMENSIONS
  configuration
      kept in storage container until use; cylindrical body with rounded-cone nose; pop-out cruciform midwings; tail-mounted cruciform guidance fins
  length   4 ft 6 in (1.37 m)
  width   6 in (152 mm)
PROPULSION   launched by 155-mm howitzer
PERFORMANCE
  max range   17,498 yd (16,000 m)
  minimum range
      3,281 yd (3,000 m)
WARHEAD   49.6 lb (22.5 kg) High-

Explosive Antitank (HEAT), 14.1 lb (6.4 kg) explosive weight
SENSORS/FIRE CONTROL semiactive homing on laser designator

Dragon (M47)

The US M47 Dragon is a shoulder-fired, lightweight, antitank guided missile originally known as the Medium Assault Weapon (MAW). It is a short-range weapon needing only one soldier to fire.

The weapon consists of a tracker assembly and a discardable "packaged" missile. The missile has an unusual propulsion system consisting of 60 small rockets. The rockets are paired, with five such pairs making up a single longitudinal array along the missile's midbody. A total of six arrays are distributed evenly around the circumference of the midbody. These rockets provide thrust and stabilization, the latter in combination with three pop-out tailfins.

The missile uses Semiautomatic Command to Line of Sight (SACLOS) guidance with a Kollsman Infrared (IR) tracker following a flare in the missile's tail and bringing it to the gunner's line of sight. The original Dragon shaped-charge warhead was slimmer than the rocket section. Dragon Generation II has a full-diameter warhead.

DEVELOPMENT • The Dragon's initial operational capability was in 1971. Its series production ended in 1980. In January 1992, the US Army selected the Dragon II to serve as its interim short-range antitank missile until the Javelin (formerly the Advanced Antitank Weapons System-Medium/AAWS-M) is fielded in the late 1990s.

The Dragon is operated by the US Army and Marine Corps along with 10 other countries. Iraq is believed to have captured Dragons from Iran.

A major limitation of the Dragon is the SACLOS guidance. A Dragon gunner must remain exposed for approximately 16 seconds to obtain a hit. A 1990 Congressional Research Service report estimated that 33% of Dragon gunners would become casualties in a high-intensity war. This problem is not corrected in any of the improved versions. The Dragon has also been criticized for its inaccuracy.

The greatest limitation on Dragon III use, besides its still-modest maximum range, is its total weight of approximately 50 lb (22.5 kg). In practical use, the system's weight would prevent the operator from carrying any other equipment.

VARIANTS • B/B-77 (Swiss-made), Generation II Dragon, Generation III Dragon (USMC).

COMBAT EXPERIENCE • Although the Dragon was fielded with US Army and Marine Corps units in Operation Desert Storm, the rapid pace of the ground offensive in February 1991 meant that few Dragons were fired in combat. Some were used as "bunker busters" during attacks on machine-gun emplacements.

SPECIFICATIONS •
MANUFACTURER
McDonnell Douglas (original source)
Raytheon (second source)
Federal Aircraft Factory (Swiss license)
COMBAT WEIGHT   31 lb (14.1 kg)
round   25 lb (11.3 kg)
warhead   6 lb (2.72 kg)
DIMENSIONS
configuration
                 packaged ready-round
                 fiberglass tube
                 containing missile with
                 cylindrical body, 3
                 curved pop-out fins, 60
                 small sustainer rockets
                 which both propel and
                 control the missile
length   tube: 3 ft 8 in (1.12 m)
                 rocket: 2 ft 5 in (0.74 m)
warhead diameter
                 4 in (101.6 mm)

PROPULSION
Hercules motor
2 stages: gas generator expels missile from tube; 60 small rockets, firing in pairs, propel and control the missile in flight

PERFORMANCE

speed	launch: 260 fps (79 mps)
	flight: 328 fps (100 mps)
max range	1,094 yd (1,000 m)
minimum range	
	71 yd (65 m)
warhead	conical shaped-charge

SENSORS/FIRE CONTROL guidance: Semiautomatic Command to Line of Sight (SACLOS) with Kollsman Infrared (IR) tracker following flare in missile tail

Hellfire (AGM-114)

The Hellfire air-to-ground missile is the primary armament of several US attack/gunship helicopters. Although fielded as a laser-guided weapon, Hellfire accepts other guidance packages, including an Imaging Infrared (IIR) seeker, a Radio Frequency/IR (RF/IR) seeker, and a millimeter-wave seeker under development by Marconi Defense Systems.

The Hellfire can be launched in several modes. The Lock-On Before Launch (LOBL) has two modes. The first is ripple fire, in which several missiles are launched at one-second intervals at targets marked by different designators. The other LOBL mode—rapid fire—can be as fast as every eight seconds as the single designator shifts targets. Before Operation Desert Storm, this was the most common Hellfire sequence.

The missile can also be launched before its seeker locks onto a target. In this Lock-On After Launch (LOAL) mode, the missile will clear high or low obstacles (LOAL-H and LOAL-L) while seeking the coded laser designation, lock onto it, and dive on the target. Rockwell developed a hardened seeker that is more re-

sistant to being misled by beam attenuation due to dust, smoke, and haze or by active countermeasures; production since 1991 included this seeker.

The missile is capable of 13-g turns at supersonic speeds.

DEVELOPMENT • The Hellfire evolved from Rockwell International's earlier Hornet missile program. The name Hellfire is a nickname derived from "helicopter-launched fire and forget." The missile's initial operational capability was in 1986. The US services plan to purchase at least 60,000 missiles over the life of the program.

The Hellfire is deployed on US Army Apache, Blackhawk, Kiowa Warrior, and Defender helicopters, US Marine Cobras, and Israeli Apaches. Additionally, Sweden began receiving a total of 700 antiship Hellfires in June 1987 to be operated as a portable coastal defense system mounted on a Swedish-built, single-rail tripod launcher. The Swedish RBS-17 weighs 108.5 lb (49.3 kg) and has a range of 5.4 nm (6.2 mi; 10 km). The Bofors delayed-action warhead penetrates the superstructure or hull of a ship before exploding. The system was successfully tested in October 1989, when a target boat 3.1 mi (5 km) offshore was hit four times out of four launches.

In October 1989, Rockwell received a $500,000, 16-month contract to study the missile's ability to shoot down helicopters and slow-moving (less than 100 mph, 160 km/h) targets. The missile would be carried by the RAH-66 Comanche (formerly LH) helicopter, complementing or replacing the Stinger missile. A proximity fuze would be developed for the AAH. The system was first tested in air-to-air firings in July 1990 with direct hits against aerial drone targets traveling 60 kts (69 mph; 111 km/h) at 600 ft (183 m).

VARIANTS • AGM-114B (USN/USMC), AGM-114C (US Army), AGM-114D/F (US Army), AGM-114E/G (US Navy),

RBS-17 (Swedish coastal variant), Brimstone (proposed RAF), Ground-Launched Hellfire-Heavy (GLH-H), Ground-Launched Hellfire-Light (GLH-L), Sea-Launched Hellfire, Longbow Hellfire.

COMBAT EXPERIENCE • In December 1989, 11 Apaches flew 200 hours of missions in support of the US military operation Just Cause to remove Panamanian leader General Noriega. The Army reported that seven Hellfire missiles were used against fixed targets, including General Noriega's headquarters, and all were accurate and effective.

Eight Apaches were used to attack early-warning radar sites in western Iraq on a round-trip of 950 nm (1,094 mi; 1,759 km) that opened Operation Desert Storm's air war. The mission, which cleared an attack lane for precision strikes, achieved complete surprise and within two minutes had scored 15 hits with Hellfire missiles. Hellfires were launched at one-to-two second intervals from as far off as 3.8 nm (4.3 mi; 7 km), the pilot switching his laser designator from one target to the next. Apaches fired an estimated 5,000 Hellfires and destroyed an estimated 500 tanks.

During the attacks against Iraqi Republican Guard formations that prepared the way for the ground war, one AH-64 hit and destroyed seven tanks with seven Hellfires. The 4th Battalion of the 229th Aviation Brigade was credited with 50 tanks in a single battle. Army OH-58Ds carried Hellfires during their antiship patrols; at least one Silkworm antiship missile launcher was destroyed by a Hellfire.

Marine Corps AH-1T and -1W Seacobra gunships fired 159 Hellfires during Desert Storm against tanks and observation and command posts.

Hellfires were also involved in accidental hits on friendly light armored vehicles and resulted in several US and British deaths. Subsequent improved recognition techniques reduced the risk of repeating such accidents.

SPECIFICATIONS •

MANUFACTURER
Rockwell International (primary)
Martin Marietta (secondary)

MISSILE WEIGHT
Laser variant
    100.9 lb (45.7 kg)
RF/IR, IIR   105.6 lb (47.9 kg)
warhead   approx 18 lb (8 kg)

DIMENSIONS
configuration
    thick cylinder, blunt nose with laser seeker window, small cruciform steerable foreplanes, low-aspect-ratio mainplanes at the rear
length   laser variant: 5 ft 4 in (1.63 m)
    RF/IR: 5 ft 8 in (1.73 m)
    IIR: 5 ft 10 in (1.78 m)
diameter   7 in (178 mm)
wingspan   1 ft 0.8 in (0.326 m)

PROPULSION   Thiokol TX-657 reduced-smoke solid-fuel rocket (Navy designation is T773-3, Army motors designated M120E1)

PERFORMANCE
speed   Mach 1.1
max range   approx 4.3 nm (5 mi; 8 km)

WARHEAD   high-explosive shaped-charge

SENSORS/FIRE CONTROL
missile   Laser seeker has Cassegrain telescope in hemispherical glass nose, giving the missile broad window coverage and enhancing its autonomous search capability
    Analog autopilot in production version; digital autopilot in development

target designation
> TADS in AH-64 used by copilot to designate target itself or detect other designations and lock-on
> AN/TVQ-1 (G/VLLD) has range of 5,468 yd (5,000 m) against stationary target, 3,827 yd (3,500 m) against moving targets; designator weight is 28 lb (12.7 kg), total system weight is 51 lb (23.2 kg)
> AN/PAQ-3 MULE uses AN/PAQ-1 laser and designator and AN/GSV-5 rangefinder components; system weight is 37.5 lb (17 kg)

Javelin (AAWS-M)

The Javelin Advanced Antitank Weapons System-Medium (AAWS-M) is a man-portable antitank missile intended as a replacement for the M47 Dragon. Unlike the optically guided Dragon, the AAWS-M is an Infrared (IR) "fire and forget" system. It is a shoulder-fired missile coming in two parts: the disposable tube, which holds the missile, and the reusable Command Launch Unit (CLU).

The missile is designed to attack the top of tanks where the armor is thinner. The missile climbs 330–660 ft (100–200 m) after launch. As the missile approaches the target, it dives at a 45° angle. If the target is protected from above, the operator has the option of selecting a direct-flight mode.

The warhead is a tandem shaped-charge for penetrating reactive armor. The first charge detonates the armor and the second penetrates the vehicle.

The AAWS-M is guided by an imaging Long-Wave IR (LWIR) seeker in the missile's nose using a staring focal-plane array. The array is a 64 × 64 configuration containing 4,096 IR detectors. A scanning focal-plane array with 240 detectors is used in the CLU; both arrays are made of mercury-cadmium-telluride (mercad). The CLU's Field of View (FOV) varies according to type of sight and magnification. Day sight FOV at four power is 3° × 4°. The thermal sight's FOV at four power is 4° × 6°; at eight power it is 2° × 3°.

The missile has a two-stage propulsion system. The first low-power motor ejects the missile from the tube. The missile glides for 15–20 ft (4–6 m) and then the main motor ignites. This allows the AAWS-M to be fired from inside a building or from a prone stance.

DEVELOPMENT • The Javelin's initial operational capability was originally planned for 1994 but was later put off until later in the decade, probably 1996 at the earliest. The first guided test firing was at Huntsville, Alabama, in April 1991.

In mid-1990, Martin Marietta selected Hughes Aircraft Co. as the second source for the IR focal-plane arrays. The original $169.7-million development contract was in 1989, but an Army review in March 1991 raised cost ceiling to $370 million.

Both the US Army and Marine Corps are scheduled to receive the missile.

In February 1989, the TI/Martin Marietta design was selected over two other designs, one by Hughes/Honeywell and one by Ford Aerospace.

SPECIFICATIONS •
MANUFACTURER Texas Instruments
> Martin Marietta
COMBAT WEIGHT 41.9 lb (19.0 kg)
> *tube with missile*
>> 32.0 lb (14.5 kg)
> *missile* 27.0 lb (12.2 kg)
> *CLU* 9.9 lb (4.5 kg)

DIMENSIONS
  configuration
        cylinder with 4 folding
        control fins aft and 8
        folding wings at
        midpoint
PROPULSION
  Atlantic Research 2-stage motor system
  1st, low-power, motor ejects missile
  from tube at 164 fps (50 mps)
  2nd, main, engine then ignites for
  4.5–5 sec and boosts missile to
  1,804 fps (550 mps)
MAX RANGE   approx 2,871 yd (2,000 m)
WARHEAD   tandem, shaped-charge
SENSORS/FIRE CONTROL   focal-plane-
  array IR guidance

Tow (BGM-71)

The US BGM-71 TOW (Tube-Launched, Optically Tracked, Wire-Guided) is the most widely distributed antitank guided missile in the world. It is fired from tripods, ground-combat vehicles, and helicopters.

Six variants have been fielded. The Basic TOW has a 5-in (127-mm) diameter warhead, analog computer, and a 3,281-yd (3,000-m) range. Improved TOW (ITOW) added a telescoping standoff detonation probe. At launch, the two-section probe springs forward to provide the optimum distance between the armor and the exploding High-Explosive Armor-Piercing (HEAP) warhead. The TOW 2 has a three-section probe, a more powerful motor, and a 6-in (152-mm) diameter warhead. TOW 2A is similar to the TOW 2 except that it incorporates a tandem warhead to increase its effectiveness against reactive armor. The precursor warhead in the missile probe detonates the reactive armor, allowing the primary warhead to penetrate the tank.

The TOW 2B, a top-attack version, entered service in late 1992.

DEVELOPMENT • The initial operational capability for the TOW/BGM-71A was in 1970, ITOW/BGM-71C in 1982, TOW 2/BGM-71D in 1984, TOW 2A/BGM-71E in 1987, and TOW 2B/BGM-71F in 1992 (First Unit Equipped). Emerson Electric Co. builds the launcher, and Texas Instruments, digital guidance and the AN/TAS-4A night sight for TOW 2 retrofit. Over 500,000 TOWs have been built and are in service.

In January 1992, the Spanish joint-venture firm Guiado y Control (composed of Hughes and INISEL) won the Spanish Defense Ministry's $130-million contract to manufacture TOWs; additional orders were expected into the late 1990s.

In addition to the US Army and Marine Corps, over 36 other countries use the TOW missile. Although Brazil and Colombia are the only Latin American countries to receive the TOW, the missile is deployed extensively in countries in Europe, Asia, and the Middle East.

Many Western helicopters have been modified to fire TOWs. The Bell AH-1J, AH-1S, AH-1T, and AH-1W can carry TOWs as well as several versions of the McDonnell Douglas (formerly Hughes) 500MD, the MBB BO 105, Westland-Aerospatiale Lynx, Aerospatiale AS 350 Ecureuil, Agusta 109 Hirundo, and A129 Mangusta.

ISSUES • The controversial arms sales to Iran disclosed in late 1986 included over 500 TOW missiles from Israeli stocks. The missiles were reportedly Basic TOWs. A November 1987 report claimed that a further 20,000 TOWs contracted for in late 1984 were not delivered when the $264 million letter of credit disappeared with the Iranian contact. In July 1991, the *Financial Times* of London reported that London branches of the troubled Bank of Credit and Commerce International (BCCI) were used to bankroll the clandestine sale of 1,250 TOW missiles worth $9.375 million to Iran in 1985.

No TOW motors were produced at the Hercules-managed Radford, Virginia, plant between May and December 1986, because of problems in cold-weather firing and crumbling propellant. The delay affected almost 11,000 TOW missile bodies. Full production capacity was reached again in mid-1987.

Two TOW missile explosions in September 1986 were unrelated to the Hercules propellant problem, having occurred because of stress corrosion in the motor cases of TOWs produced before 1986. A plastic coating on new motor cases was recommended as a preventative measure.

Soon after the TOW 2A was announced in 1987, evidence suggested that some Soviet tanks have stacked reactive armor, the first layer of which detonates the probe, leaving the inner layer to deflect the HEAT warhead. Another armor option would be a light layer of laminate armor over the reactive armor. The TOW 2B is expected to be able to defeat such measures by virtue of its depressed angle of attack from above.

VARIANTS • Basic TOW, Improved TOW, TOW 2, TOW 2A, TOW 2B, Further Improved TOW (FITOW) (British MoD funded), MAPATS (Laser TOW) (Israeli), Hughes wireless TOW.

Major airborne TOW system-variants are the M65 Airborne TOW, M65L Laser-Augmented Airborne TOW (LAAT), TOW Roof Sight (TRS), C-NITE (Cobra-NITE), HELITOW (for Danish and Italian helicopters).

COMBAT EXPERIENCE • The TOW missile was first used in May 1972 near Hue, South Vietnam, by US Army and Marine Corps infantry and airborne units. The success rate for helicopter gunship launches was claimed to be 65 direct hits out of 81 launches (80%).

Israeli forces fired TOWs in the 1973 Yom Kippur War and the 1982 invasion of Lebanon. The Moroccan Air Force has used TOWs against Polisario units in the Western Sahara. Iranian forces used TOWs against Iraqi tanks during the 1980–88 Gulf War.

In 1987, Pakistan used TOW 2s against Indian forces in the conflict over the glacier region.

In Operation Desert Storm, beginning January 17, 1991, TOWs were deployed by the US Army and Marine Corps as well as by the British, Royal Saudi, Egyptian, and Kuwaiti armies in far greater numbers than any other ground- or vehicle-based antitank missile. In the Marine Corps alone, 582 M220E4 TOW launchers were deployed with the 1st Marine Expeditionary Force (MEF) in Saudi Arabia. Another 96 launchers remained with troops embarked on landing ships in the northern Persian Gulf.

During preparations for the ground war, TOW-equipped Marine Corps LAV-25s were used for reconnaissance of Iraqi border positions, using the missiles as "bunker busters" as well as against armored vehicles. At the battle of Khafji, January 30–31, Saudi TOW-equipped M113s engaged tanks as well as hitting bunkers.

Marine Corps Cobras also figured prominently in the Marine-Saudi drive on Kuwait City. Four Cobras attacked through breaks in the oily murk and destroyed several tanks with TOWs. Altogether, 250 TOWs were fired by Marine Corps units.

SPECIFICATIONS •
MANUFACTURER
  Hughes Aircraft (prime)
  McDonnell Douglas (secondary)
WEIGHTS
  on tripod launcher
    Basic TOW: 173 lb (78.5 kg)
    Basic with AN/TAS-4 night sight: 193 lb (87.5 kg)
    TOW 2: 205 lb (93 kg)

weight in container
    Basic TOW: 56.3 lb (25.5 kg)
    ITOW: 56.6 lb (25.7 kg)
    TOW 2: 62.0 lb (28.1 kg)
missile weight
    Basic TOW: 41.7 lb (18.9 kg)
    ITOW: 42.0 lb (19.1 kg)
    TOW 2: 47.4 lb (21.5 kg)
WARHEAD
    BGM-71A: 8.6 lb (3.9 kg)
    TOW 2/-71D: 13.0 lb (5.9 kg)
DIMENSIONS
configuration
    factory-sealed tube contains a cylindrical missile body; pop-out cruciform wings indexed 45° off line from cruciform rudders; 2 rocket exhausts at midbody; 2 guidance wire spools in tail
length   prelaunch: 3 ft 10 in (1.17 m)
    TOW 2, probe out: 4 ft 7 in (1.4 m)
diameter   missile: 6 in (152 mm) warhead Basic TOW, ITOW: 5 in (127 mm)
    TOW 2: 6 in (152 mm)
PROPULSION
2 Hercules solid-fuel rocket motors
1st motor has short burn to allow TOW to clear tube
2nd motor sustains TOW flight until impact
TOW 2 motor provides 30% greater impulse than Basic TOW
PERFORMANCE
speed   Mach 0.8–0.9
range (BGM-71D)
    max: 4,100 yd (3,750 m)
    minimum: 71 yd (65 m)
WARHEAD   High-Explosive Armor-Piercing (HEAP) shaped-charge; ITOW and TOW 2 have extendable

probes to enhance the hollow charge effect
ITOW probe length:
5 in (127 mm); standoff distance 15 in (381 mm)
TOW 2 probe length: 6 in (152 mm); standoff distance 21¼ in (540 mm)
penetration   classified but TOW 2 is intended to penetrate any 1990s tank
rate of fire
    3 launches in 90 sec
SENSORS/FIRE CONTROL
guidance: Semiautomatic Command to Line of Sight (SACLOS) wire guidance
automatic Infrared (IR) tracking of xenon or thermal beacon in missile tail
analog computer in Basic TOW
Texas Instruments dual digital programmable microprocessors in TOW 2
Texas Instruments AN/TAS-4 thermal night sight
Kollsman AN/UAS-12C thermal imager and missile guidance system for TOW 2
dual Thorn/EMI optical/magnetic proximity sensor for TOW 2B
CREW   4

Maverick (AGM-65)

The Maverick is a precision-guided, air-to-ground missile configured primarily for the antitank and antiship roles. Six models of Mavericks have been developed. The AGM-65A/B/D variants have a shaped-charge warhead and are used as antitank weapons; these dive on the tank at an angle to hit the more vulnerable top armor. The AGM-65E/F variants have a larger blast/penetration warhead and are used in the land-attack and antiship role; the -65F's terminal attack aims at the waterline of a ship.

In addition to the types of targets that can be engaged, the Maverick employs

Maverick AGM-65
U.S. GOVERNMENT DEPARTMENT OF DEFENSE

several different guidance methods. The AGM-65A/Bs are television-guided; the AGM-65C is laser-guided; the AGM-65D uses an Imaging Infrared (IIR) guidance system; the AGM-65E is the improved C model; and the AGM-65F combines the IIR seeker of the D model with the warhead and propulsion sections of the AGM-65E.

The Maverick is launched from a variety of fixed-wing aircraft and helicopters; the launch envelope varies slightly depending on warhead size.

DEVELOPMENT • The Maverick's initial operational capability was in 1972 for the AGM-65A, 1983 (AGM-65D), and 1985 (AGM-65E). The first test flights were in 1969. The AGM-65G completed its last test launch in October 1988. In August–September 1990, Hughes accelerated testing of the AGM-65D for launch from the AH-1W attack helicopter in re-

sponse to the August 1990 Iraqi invasion of Kuwait. Final manufacture and delivery of missile (5,225 AGM-65Gs and 36 AGM-65Fs to the US Navy) was in April 1994.

In addition to the Maverick being deployed on various US Air Force and Navy fixed-wing planes and helicopters, the missile is used by 19 other countries in Europe, Asia, and the Middle East.

VARIANTS • AGM-65A (TV), AGM-65B, AGM-65C, AGM-65D, AGM-65E, AGM-65F, AGM-65G, Rapid Fire.

COMBAT EXPERIENCE • The first combat use of the Maverick was in Vietnam in January–February 1973, where targets were hit in 13 of 18 launches.

During the 1973 Yom Kippur War, Israeli aircraft fired 50 AGM-65s and scored

42 hits and five deliberate near misses (to disable, not destroy). Later Israeli combat use (up through March 1983) experienced 20 missiles hit for 20 targets engaged.

In a June 1975 border clash, Iranian aircraft fired 12 missiles, all of which hit Iraqi tanks.

More than 5,100 Mavericks were fired during Operation Desert Storm, making the missile the Air Force's principal tank-killing missile during the conflict (although GBU-12 laser-guided bombs may have accounted for more armored vehicles).

An April 1992 official report on the conduct of the Persian Gulf War claimed an 80%–90% success rate (launch and guidance to target) for the TV and IIR Mavericks, and approximately 60% for the laser-guided variants.

SPECIFICATIONS •

MANUFACTURER
Hughes Aircraft (prime)
Raytheon (secondary)
Alenia (Italy, AGM-65D/G)

MISSILE WEIGHT
AGM-65A/B/D: 462 lb (210 kg)
65E/F: 637 lb (289 kg)
warhead   AGM-65A/B/D: 125 lb
(56.7 kg)
AGM-65E/F/G: 300 lb
(136.1 kg)

DIMENSIONS
configuration
Resembles an enlarged
Falcon AAM (AIM-4);
thick cylinder with
rounded nose,
cruciform extreme
delta wings with
rectangular control
surfaces immediately
behind

length   8 ft 2 in (2.49 m)
diameter   12 in (305 mm)
wingspan   2 ft 4½ in (0.72 m)

PROPULSION
Thiokol TX-481 or TX-633 2-stage
solid-fuel rocket; Aerojet is second
source
(Defense Department designation is
SR-109-TC-1)

PERFORMANCE
speed   between Mach 1 and 2
range   (launch aircraft speed of
Mach 0.9)
*at approx 3,000 ft (914 m)
launch altitude*
minimum; 2,000 ft (610
m)
max: 9 nm (10.4 mi; 16.8
km)
*at 10,000 ft (3,048 m)
launch altitude*
minimum: 5,000 ft (1,524
m)
max: 12 nm (13.8 mi;
22.2 km)
*at 30,000 ft (9,143 m)
launch altitude*
minimum: 3.5 nm (4.0
mi; 6.4 km)
max: 12.0 nm (13.8 mi;
22.2 km)
max with 300-lb (135-kg)
warhead: 13.5 nm (15.5
mi; 24.4 km)

warhead type
conventional high-
explosive
AGM-65A/B/D: shaped-
charge
AGM-65E/F/G: blast/
penetration

SENSORS/FIRE CONTROL   varies by
model

LAND-ATTACK MISSILES

AGM-130

The AGM-130 is a powered version of the US GBU-15 precision-guided modular glide bomb, which in turn evolved from the Mk 84 2,000-lb (907-kg) bomb. Commonality between the two weapons includes the TV seeker, body, and short-chord wings. Warheads for the GBU-15 are the Mk 84, a submunitions dispenser (SUU-54), or the more powerful BLU-109 (I-2000) unitary warhead.

In addition to its rocket motor, the AGM-130 differs from the GBU-15 in the provision of a digital autopilot and radar altimeter. The rocket motor extends the range of the AGM-130 up to three times farther than the GBU-15 under similar launch conditions.

The AGM-130 can be launched from low altitudes against high-value fixed targets. Its flight profile consists of a glide phase, a powered phase (after which the rocket separates from the missile), and a final glide phase. Midcourse corrections are passed through a jam-resistant data link that is an improvement over the GBU-15's AXQ-14. Targeting options can be Lock-On Before Launch (LOBL) or After Launch (LOAL), which provides for automatic tracking, or through joystick control by the weapons system operator on board the launch aircraft. The weapons systems officer can also update a locked-on AGM-130 during the flight.

GBU-15s have either a television (TV) (GBU-15(V)1/B) or Imaging Infrared (IIR) (GBU-15(V)2/B) seeker; the IIR seeker has 90% commonality with the AGM-65D Maverick IIR air-to-surface missile.

The AGM-130 serves as a standoff weapon for the F-4E, F-15E, and F-111F.

DEVELOPMENT • The initial operational capability of the GBU-15 (TV) was in 1983, the GBU-15 (IIR) in 1987. Air Force conducted nine initial operational test and evaluation launches, beginning in June 1989 and ending in January 1990. Eight of the nine launches were successful, with six scoring direct hits.

COMBAT EXPERIENCE • The GBU-15 was used effectively against Iraqi targets during Operation Desert Storm.

SPECIFICATIONS •
MANUFACTURER   Rockwell International (prime)
MISSILE WEIGHT
    GBU-15: 2,617 lb (1,187 kg)
    AGM-130: 2,980 lb (1,352 kg)
    warhead   2,000 lb (907 kg)
DIMENSIONS
    configuration
                    thick cylinders, with small cruciform foreplanes, and large rectangular mainplanes at the tail; AGM-130 has a strap-on ventral rocket
    length   GBU-15: 12 ft 10½ in (3.92 m)
                    AGM-130: 12 ft 11 in (3.94 m)
    diameter (both)
                    1 ft 6 in (460 mm)
    wingspan (both)
                    4 ft 11 in (1.50 m)
PROPULSION   Hercules solid-fuel booster weighing 480 lb (218 kg) with 9 in (0.27 m) diameter
PERFORMANCE
    max range   GBU-15: 4.3 nm (5 mi; 8 km)
                    AGM-130: 26 nm (30 mi; 48 km)

WARHEAD   Mk-84 conventional high explosive or SUU-54 explosive submunitions

SENSORS/FIRE CONTROL   guidance: manual command through 2-way data link or automatic TV or IIR guidance through pre- or postlaunch lock-on

Army Tactical Missile System (ATACMS)

The US Army Tactical Missile System (ATACMS) is a long-range tactical missile for deployment in modified M270 Armored Vehicle–Multiple Rocket Launchers (AVMRL), which are already used for the Multiple-Launch Rocket System (MLRS). The MLRS AVMRL is modified by changing the pods from two six-round to two M39 Missile/Launch Pod Assemblies (M/LPA) single-round units and updating the fire control software to Version 6. The Improved Stabilization Reference Platform (ISRP) provides more precise pointing, the Program Interface Module (PIM) allows the launcher and the missile to exchange more data, and the Improved Electronics Unit (IEU) gives better flexibility for processing types of munitions.

ATACMS is a semiballistic missile, with inertial guidance provided by a Honeywell H700-3A ring laser gyroscope system. Launch can be as much as 30° off axis, and the missile is steered aerodynamically by electrically actuated control fins during the descent, modifying the flight path from a ballistic parabola. Offsetting the launch angle and descending semiballistically complicates the enemy's ability to trace trajectory back to the launch vehicle. Its disadvantage is that accuracy is less precise than a straightforward flight path would achieve.

The missile was deployed with an M74 warhead that dispenses 950 M42 Antipersonnel/Antimatériel   (APAM)

submunitions that are cast forward at a 45° angle over the target area, producing a 600-ft^2 (183-m^2) footprint. Effectively, 18 ATACMS would equal the impact of 792 155-mm artillery rounds.

DEVELOPMENT • The Desert Storm conflict resulted in rushing the operational test battery, being deployed to Saudi Arabia in late 1990. The original, tightly scheduled development contract was awarded in late March 1986. The first flight test was on April 26, 1988. The development test phase ended in December 1989 after 26 missiles had been fired. The operational test phase ran from March to June 1990.

Delivery of the first production missile to the US Army was in June 1990. A $66.4-million contract for the low-rate initial production of 104 missiles was awarded in February 1990. The $126.3-million contract for full-scale production of 318 missiles was awarded in November 1990. First delivery from this lot occurred in June 1991. Further $30.5-million-contract modification in June 1991 added 55 missiles and some LPAs.

When the development test phase ended in December 1989, only 26 of 35 planned test launches had been conducted. South Korea, Japan, Saudi Arabia, France, Turkey, Italy, and Great Britain may purchase the ATACMS. Italy and France will participate in producing Block II warheads for the missile. ATACMS will also carry the brilliant antitank (BAT) missile as a submunition.

VARIANTS • Block II (follow-on warhead), Terminal Guided Warhead/TGW (US/German/French/British consortium), SADARM (Sense and Destroy Armor) submunition, Brilliant Antitank (BAT) submunition, AGM-137/MGM-137/TSSAM (Tri-Service Standoff Attack Missile).

COMBAT EXPERIENCE • The ATACMS was successful in Saudi Arabia during Desert Storm. More than 30 ATACMS missiles were launched against Iraqi fixed targets, mostly Russian-made SA-2 Guideline and SA-3 Goa missile launchers.

In at least one instance, 200 unarmored vehicles attempting to cross a bridge were also destroyed. According to official reports, all missiles hit, and destroyed or rendered inoperable, their targets, some of which were more than 54 nm (62 mi; 100 km) from the launch site.

SPECIFICATIONS •

MANUFACTURER   Loral Vought
WEIGHT WITH BLOCK 1 WARHEAD   3,687 lb (1,672 kg)
DIMENSIONS
   length   13 ft (3.96 m)
   diameter   24 in (610 mm)
PROPULSION   Atlantic Research 40,000-lb (18,144-kg) static thrust solid-propellant rocket
MAX RANGE   81 nm (93.2 mi; 150 km)
WARHEAD   M74 containing approx 950 M42 bomblets
SENSORS/FIRE CONTROL   missile guided

by Honeywell H700-3A ring laser gyro; overall ATACMS command and control managed by DEC MicroVAX computers

Multiple Launch Rocket System (MLRS)

The MLRS is a 227-mm system with tracked, self-propelled, launcher loader, disposable pods, and fire control equipment. The M270 Armored Vehicle–Mounted Rocket Launcher (AVMRL) consists of an M269 Launcher Loader Module (LLM) with two six-cell rocket Launch Pods/Containers (LP/C) mounted on an M993 carrier vehicle. Its mission is to bombard enemy field artillery and air defense systems as far as 20 mi (32 km) away. A full salvo of 12 227-mm ripple-fired rockets with the M77 submunition warhead will saturate a 60-acre (24-hectare) area with 7,728 antipersonnel bomblets in less than one minute. Other warheads include the AT2 antitank

A Multiple Launch Rocket System (MLRS)
U.S. GOVERNMENT DEPARTMENT OF DEFENSE

mine dispenser and a Terminally Guided Warhead (TGW).

The M993 vehicle is a modified M2 Bradley armored personnel carrier. Above the tracks, the superstructure has an armored cab forward and the bulky traversable launcher behind. When traveling, the cab and launcher roofs form a flat roofline. The M269 LLM has a twin-boom crane for reloading the six-round LP/C that requires no personnel other than the three-man crew. (One crew member can serve the launcher from emplacement to departure if necessary.)

US MLRS batteries are served by three ammunition sections, each of which has six Heavy Expanded Mobility Tactical Trucks (HEMTT) towing a Heavy Expanded Mobility Ammunition Trailer (HEMAT); total capacity is 108 LP/Cs. British MLRS reloads come on Reynolds Broughton two-axle trailers carrying specially adapted flatracks.

The entire fire mission can be conducted from within the cab. The Norden fire control system can be programmed with three different fire missions, each with 12 aim points. The maximum rectangular target size for each aim point is 2,187 yd × 1,094 yd (2,000 m × 1,000 m), square target is 1,094 yd (1,000 m) square, and maximum circular target radius is 547 yd (500 m).

The Fire Control System's (FCS) ballistic computer calculates the necessary trajectories. Operation is semiautomatic, the FCS leading the crew through the sequence and automatically reaiming the system during ripple fire. The crew can also designate targets manually. The FCS can also accept inputs from other battlefield surveillance radars and sensors. The FCS also controls the loading and unloading of launch pods.

Version 9 fire control software was introduced in 1990 for the battery's Fire Direction System (FDS) that links the launchers to the Tactical Fire Direction System (TACFIRE). Version 9 permits an MLRS fire direction specialist to control

launching in a Lance missile battery or to mix Lance and MLRS launchers. The FDS is now fielded at the platoon level, increasing flexibility and redundancy. In addition, the system can store four fire plans with up to 78 total targets and interact with the Airborne Target Handoff System (ATHS) on the OH-58D Kiowa and the Automatic Fire Control System (AFCS) developed for the M109A6 Paladin 155-mm self-propelled gun. Version 9 allows up to six firing units—platoons and batteries (depending on the size of the organization)—to mass their fires on a target.

DEVELOPMENT • The system's initial operational capability was in 1983, and it entered service in 1988. A year later, the Army awarded a five-year contract to the former LTV for the supply of 235 launchers and 127,000 rockets through 1995. The US Marines begin receiving their AVMRLs in 1995.

In December 1986, the Netherlands signed a $190-million agreement with the US government for 22 launchers, rockets, and spare parts. Its first units became operational in 1990.

In December 1987, the US government announced a 12-system sale to Turkey for $60 million. LTV (51%), EHY (34%), and MVKEK (15%) are shareholders in a program to produce 168 systems and 55,000 rockets over a 10-year period in a factory near Burda, Turkey.

A European Production Group (EPG) was established in 1981 with headquarters in Munich, Germany. The group was to produce MLRS systems for the nations in the consortium, Aerospatiale (France), RTG (Germany), Hunting Engineering (Great Britain), and SNIA BPD SpA (Italy). The first production contract was let on May 27, 1986. Aerospatiale began MLRS production for the EPG in October 1988; Wigmann is assembling German vehicles.

MLRS International Corp. (MIC), headquartered in London, England, is the marketing entity for all international sales. Vought Corp. (formerly LTV) owns

70% of the enterprise, with the EPG holding the other 30%.

The British (72 launchers), French (48 launchers), and Italian (22 launchers) armies have deployed their MLRS at the corps level. German MLRS is fielded in a nine-launcher battery composed of a four-launcher and a five-launcher platoon, two of which are assigned to each of eight division-level rocket artillery battalions. A US Army MLRS battery consists of nine AVMRLs.

Funding for Japanese production began in FY1991. As many as 150 launchers may be manufactured in Japan.

In addition to the US Army and Marine Corps, Bahrain, Japan, Netherlands, Saudi Arabia, and Turkey are or will be operating the US-produced MLRS.

VARIANTS • XR-M77 Extended Range, AT2 (Germany warhead), Terminal Guided Warhead (TGW), XM-135 Binary Chemical Warhead, SADARM (Sense and Destroy Armor) submunition, ABRS (shipboard).

COMBAT EXPERIENCE • Although the manufacturer claimed higher numbers, the official report on the conduct of the Persian Gulf War stated that 189 SPLLs had fired 9,660 rockets.

Most of the launchers were with US Army forces; the first US combat use came in mid-February as part of the preparation for the ground campaign. Generally, reports on the effectiveness of the weapon were very favorable, with a large percentage of Iraqi targets destroyed.

According to some reports, the rate of fire was described as "steel rain," allegedly coined by Iraqi soldiers to describe MLRS bombardments.

12 British MLRS launchers fired over 2,500 rockets during Desert Storm. As evidence of the system's destructive power, the British noted an Iraqi brigade that began with 80 artillery pieces and lost only 20 to air attacks over a period of weeks. After the MLRS barrages, only seven pieces remained operable.

SPECIFICATIONS •
MANUFACTURER
FMC (AVMRL chassis)
Loral Vought (MLRS)
European Production Group (EPG)
(see above)
Nissan Motors (Japan)
ROCKET ARMAMENT
number of cells
12
launcher elevation
+60° (+1,067 mils); rate 0.9° (15.5 mils)/sec
traverse   +/−194° each side of centerline; rate 5°/sec
rocket caliber
227 mm
weight   rocket
Phase I: 677 lb (307 kg)
AT2: 568 lb (257.5 kg)
warhead
Phase I: 339.5 lb (154 kg)
AT2: 236 lb (107 kg)
rocket length
Phase I: 12 ft 11 in (3.93 m)
diameter   9 in (227 mm)
max range   Phase I: 19.9 mi (32 km)
AT2: 24.8 mi (40 km)
rate of fire
less than 1 min for 12 missiles
LAUNCH VEHICLE
weight   combat: 55,536 lb (25,191 kg)
unloaded: 44,509 lb (20,189 kg)
launch pod: 5,004 lb (2,270 kg)
dimensions   hull length: 22 ft 10 in (6.97 m)
width: 9 ft 9 in (2.97 m)
height: 19 ft 5 in (5.93 m) elevated, 8 ft 7 in (2.62 m) traveling
length of track on ground: 14 ft 2 in (4.33 m)

track width: 21 in (530 mm)

ground clearance: 17 in (430 mm)

propulsion   Cummins VTA-903 903-in³ (14.8-liter) liquid-cooled 4-stroke turbocharged V-8 diesel engine

General Electric HMPT-500 hydromechanical transmission; 3 forward/1 reverse ranges (variable ratios)

max power: 500 hp at 2400 rpm

power-to-weight ratio 19.85 hp/metric ton

performance   speed: 40 mph (64 km/h)

range: 300 mi (483 km)

fuel capacity: 163 US gal (517 liters)

obstacle clearance: vertical 3 ft 3 in (1.0 m), trench 7 ft 6 in (2.29 m), fording 3 ft 7 in (1.1 m), gradient 60%

Sensors/Fire Control
Norden FCS
Bendix stabilization reference package/position determining system (SRP/PDS)

Crew   3 (section chief, gunner, driver); crew can fire entire load from cab and can reload MLRS without other help

Suspension   torsion bar, 6 dual road wheels, front drive, rear idler, 2 shock absorbers, 4 return rollers

Vehicle protection
armor against small-arms fire on cab and louvers on windows

overpressure protection against Nuclear, Biological, and Chemical (NBC) warfare electronics hardened against an Electromagnetic Pulse (EMP)

SLAM (AGM-84E-1)

The Standoff Land-Attack Missile (SLAM) is an Imaging Infrared (IIR) seeker, man-in-the-loop-terminally guided missile that is a derivative of the AGM-84A Harpoon antiship missile. SLAM is launched from aircraft and surface ships against high-value targets while maintaining collateral damage and risk to the launch aircraft and aircrew. The SLAM was developed by integrating the existing assets of the AGM-84 Harpoon, the Hughes Maverick IIR seeker, the Collins Global Positioning System (GPS), and the Walleye data link.

SLAM is capable of two modes of attack: Preplanned (PP) missions against high-value fixed or relocatable land targets and Target of Opportunity (TOO) missions against ships at sea.

The SLAM shares common control, warhead, and sustainer sections with the Harpoon. Its navigational heart is the 12.5-lb (5.67-kg) Rockwell-Collins single-channel GPS receiver/processor that determines the missile's three-dimensional location within 52 ft (16 m) and its velocity within 0.65 fps (0.2 mps).

In addition to using Harpoon-common components, SLAM adopts the IIR seeker of the AGM-65 Maverick and the AN/AWW-9 (later replaced by the more reliable AN/AWW-13) data link of the AGM-62 Walleye. The full-duplex

SLAM
U.S. GOVERNMENT DEPARTMENT OF DEFENSE

data link operates on one of eight transmit-and-receive frequency pairs, with the frequencies being widely separated.

Four missions (typically three PP and one TOO) can be loaded into the missile's Electronically Erasable Programmable Read-Only Memory (EEPROM) before takeoff, using a portable Prelaunch Data Memory Loader (PDML). The PDML can store up to 16 sets of mission data (64 missions) for an eight-hour period before self-purge occurs. Transfer of mission planning data to the missile takes about five minutes. At the same time, the missile's GPS clock data is updated. The pilot/weapons controller chooses one of the four missions before launch.

After launch, the SLAM flies autonomously to the area of the target via its GPS-aided inertial system. At a preprogrammed point approximately one minute before impact, the seeker turns on and, because of GPS-aided navigation

accuracy, should be looking directly at the target. The controller views the target scene and selects an aim point for the terminal phase via the SLAM's data link, and the missile flies autonomously to that point.

The missile can also be controlled from an aircraft other than the firing platform. Additionally, the SLAM provides the capability to attack targets of opportunity selected by scanning the missile's seeker at 4°/sec.

The combination of an A-6E launching a SLAM and an A-7 pilot performing the locking-on was used during its first operational flights against Iraqi targets in January 1991. F/A-18 Hornets have also successfully launched and guided the SLAM.

The SLAM incorporates a fuze-wiring modification into the same warhead used in the Harpoon to allow for instantaneous detonation (for certain land targets) and delayed detonation (for ship targets).

DEVELOPMENT • The SLAM's initial operational capability was in 1990. Its first test flight was in June 1989 launched from an A-6E Intruder. First production missile was delivered in November 1988. 160 missiles were funded in FY1991. After success in Desert Storm, FY1993 funding was appropriated by Congress but not authorized.

The missile is used on A-6E Intruder, F/A-18 Hornet, F-16 Fighting Falcon, P-3 Orion, and B-52 Stratofortress.

The first ship-launched SLAM test was conducted in June 1990 from the USS *Lake Champlain* (CG 57). Target lock-on was commanded by an air tactical officer flying in the ship's SH-60B Seahawk LAMPS III helicopter, which also served as data link for the ship's Combat Information Center (CIC).

VARIANTS • Ship Launch SLAM (SLS/cruise missile), SLAM-ER.

COMBAT EXPERIENCE • SLAMs were used during Desert Storm against Iraqi targets. Defense Department videos showed two SLAM strikes on a building, the second entering the hole made by the first. The SLAMs were launched from A-6E Intruders, but given midcourse corrections by A-7E Corsair pilots through the Walleye data link. Overall, seven SLAM missiles were successfully fired during the Persian Gulf conflict, even though the AWW-9 data link was very unreliable and required considerable maintenance.

SPECIFICATIONS •
MANUFACTURER Douglas Missile Systems
COMBAT WEIGHT 1,366 lb (619.5 kg)
warhead section
500 lb (226.8 kg)
DIMENSIONS
configuration
thick cylinder with rounded nose, cruciform trapezoidal wings at midbody,

cruciform in-line swept "cropped delta" control fins at tail; engine has nearly flush ventral air intake
length 14 ft 8 in (4.47 m)
diameter 13½ in (343 mm)
PROPULSION Teledyne Continental 660-lb (299-kg) static thrust CAE-J402-CA-400 turbojet sustainer burning JP-10 fuel
PERFORMANCE
speed Mach 0.85 (high subsonic)
range 60+ nm (69+ mi; 111+ km)
midcourse accuracy
52 ft (16 m)
WARHEAD DESTEX blast/fragmentation high explosive with preselected instantaneous or delay fuzing
DATA LINK AN/AWW-9, -13 Walleye datalink pods
SENSORS/FIRE CONTROL
on-board midcourse guidance unit
Rockwell Collins (R-2387/DSQ-51) Global Positioning System (GPS) receiver
IBM digital computer
Smith's or Northrop 3-axis attitude reference assembly
Honeywell AN/APN-194 short-pulse radar or Kollsman Frequency-Modulated Continuous Wave (FMCW) altimeter
terminal homing through AGM-65F Maverick Imaging Infrared (IIR) seeker (using -65G centroid-biased software developed to attack large targets) and Harris Corp. AGM-62 Walleye data link (RT-1608/DSQ-51)

Tomahawk (BGM-109)

The Tomahawk is a long-range cruise missile for both surface and submarine launch against both surface-ship and land targets. It was subsequently adapted for land launch as the US Gryphon Ground-Launch Cruise Missile (GLCM) as part of the US Intermediate-Range Nuclear Forces (INF) that were deployed in Western Europe.

Initially known as the Sea-Launched Cruise Missile (SLCM), the Tomahawk's principal roles are antiship (TASM), land attack with a conventional warhead (TLAM-C), and land attack with a nuclear warhead (TLAM-N). All versions operate at very low altitudes and have a radar cross section of approximately 10.76 ft^2 (1 m^2). The missile is sealed in its launch canister at the factory and can be treated as a "wooden round."

Both TLAM versions have an inertial guidance phase using a Litton P-1000 inertial platform and Litton LC-45/16/C computer, after which the missile's accuracy is updated using the McDonnell Douglas Electronics AN/DPW-23 Terrain-Contour Matching (TERCOM). TERCOM measures actual land contours with its on-board radar altimeter and compares them to stored digitized profiles. The profile's land area shrinks as the missile nears its target. TERCOM is also used to update the TERCOM-Aided Inertial Navigation System (TAINS).

While TLAM-N uses inertial and TERCOM guidance alone, TLAM-C uses a Loral Digital Scene-Mapping Area Correlator (DSMAC) as it nears the target for still greater accuracy. DSMAC correlates the optical view of the target area— obtained with a Fairchild Weston Schlumberger Charge-Coupled Device (CCD) sensor—with digitized target maps, refining the missile's terminal flight. For night flights, the DSMAC can flash a strobe light when needed.

Target map updating involves relatively simple DSMAC reprogramming. Either Tomahawk version can fly preprogrammed evasive flight paths between guidance updates; a "Flex-Targeting" upgrade, which permits retargeting during flight, has been tested. The antiship Tomahawk is fitted with a modified Harpoon active radar seeker. The missile flies a preprogrammed profile at sea-skimming height for most of its flight. When the missile nears the target's estimated position, the active radar seeker takes over. The latest antiship variant is reported to have a reattack mode.

The missile's great versatility and adaptability are based largely on having been constrained to the size of the standard 21-inch (533-mm) submarine torpedo tube. Later US submarines have 12 vertical-launch tubes for Tomahawks. The submarine-launch canister is made of stainless steel.

On board US Navy surface ships, the Tomahawk is launched from the four-missile Mk 143 Armored Box Launcher (ABL) or from the Mk 41 61-cell Vertical-Launch System (VLS). The ABL is deck-mounted and elevates hydraulically to 35° in 35 seconds to fire. As in the submarine-launched versions, a TRW Thrust Vector Control (TVC) system steers the missile during the first 15 seconds of flight.

The VLS combines weapons launcher and magazine and occupies the same below-decks volume as the 44-missile magazine of the older twin-rail missile launchers. In 1984, the Navy reported in congressional testimony that the nominal "load-outs" were 26 Tomahawks (6 TLAM-N) in the *Bunker Hill* (CG 52) and *Aegis* cruisers and 45 (two TLAM-N) in the *Spruance*-class destroyer VLS. Tomahawk load-outs for Operation Desert Storm were believed to be much higher in some ships.

DEVELOPMENT • The missile achieved initial operational capability in 1982 for TASM in surface ships, 1983 for TASM in submarines, 1984 for TLAM in surface ships, and 1987 for TLAM-N. On September 27, 1991, President Bush announced that all tactical nuclear weapons would be removed from US Navy surface ships and attack submarines. The order included all TLAM-Ns, which were placed in storage.

The 1,000th Tomahawk was delivered to the Navy by McDonnell Douglas on July 10, 1991. The missile is deployed on US Navy submarines, cruisers, and destroyers. Hughes became sole-source producer in 1994.

VARIANTS • BGM-109A/TLAM, BGM-109B/TASM, BGM-109C/TLAM Block IIA, BGM-109D/TLAM Block IIB, BGM-109E/TASM, BGM-109F/TLAM, BGM-109G/GLCM, Block III/TLAM, Block IV.

COMBAT EXPERIENCE • During Desert Storm, 264 BGM-109Cs (unitary warhead) and 27 BGM-109Ds (cluster bombs) were launched from the battleships *Missouri* and *Wisconsin*, several cruisers and destroyers, and at least two submarines, mostly in the early days of the war.

An analysis of Tomahawk results suggested that 85% of the 242 target aim points were hit. The United States suggested that two missiles may have been shot down.

Tomahawks attacked Iraqi targets twice more in 1993. The January attack directed 45 missiles against nuclear facilities (one hit a hotel instead). In June, 20 of 23 launched hit the Iraqi intelligence headquarters; three others landed in a residential area.

SPECIFICATIONS •
MANUFACTURER
Hughes (prime)
McDonnell Douglas Missiles (secondary)
WEIGHTS
VLS, loaded: approx 255.7 short tons (232 metric tons)
VLS, empty: approx 129 short tons (117 metric tons)
ABL: 55,000 lb (24,948 kg)
missile   2,650 lb (1,202 kg)
booster   550 lb (249 kg)
capsule   1,000 lb (454 kg) for submarine launch

warhead   1,000 lb (454 kg) TASM
DIMENSIONS
configuration
                torpedo-shaped fuselage with ventral pop-out turbofan intake, pop-out wings and tail surfaces
length   missile: 18 ft 2 in (5.54 m)
                booster: 2 ft (0.61 m)
diameter   21 in (533 mm)
wingspan   8 ft 8 in (2.64 m)
PROPULSION
Atlantic Research 6,000-lb (2,722-kg) static thrust solid-fuel booster that burns for 12 sec
Williams Research F107-WR-400 600-lb (272-kg) static thrust turbofan sustainer
PERFORMANCE
speed   331–496 kts (381–571 mph; 613–919 km/h) or Mach 0.50–0.75
cruise altitude
                50–100 ft (15–30 m)
max range BGM-109B: more than 250 nm (288 mi; 464 km)
                BGM-109C/D: approx 700 nm (806 mi; 1,297 km)
                BGM-109A: approx 1,350 nm (1,555 mi; 2,500 km)
WARHEAD conventional high-explosive in TASM; nuclear 5–150-kiloton W80 in TLAM-N
ACCURACY
Circular Error Probable (CEP)
TERCOM: less than 100 ft (30.5 m)
TERCOM + DSMAC: approx 33 ft (10.0 m)
GUIDANCE
Ships with Mk 143 ABL have AN/SWG-2 weapons control system
Ships with Mk 41 VLS have AN/SWG-3 weapons control system
Submarines have Mk 117 fire control system

TASM: inertial; terminal is active radar homing (similar to Harpoon)

TALM-C: inertial; terminal is Terrain Contour Matching (TERCOM) with Digital Scene-Mapping Area Correlator (DSMAC); Block IIA has a preselectable pop-up terminal maneuver

TLAM-N: inertial and TERCOM

Paveway Bomb Series (GBU-)

The Paveway II and III unpowered Precision-Guided Munitions (PGM) are based on the Mk 80 series low-drag general-purpose unguided bombs originally developed in the 1950s. The Mk 82 500-lb (227-kg) is the smallest of the three, followed by the 1,000-lb (454-kg) Mk 83 and the 2,000-lb (907-kg) Mk 84. This bomb series also formed the basis for the Destructor air-dropped bottom sea mines used extensively during the Vietnam War.

The first of the Paveway series of Laser-Guided Bombs (LGB) were originally given KMU designations but were later redesignated GBU. Paveways increased the standoff distance for attacking aircraft while improving bombing accuracy, which was unacceptably low. Using a spot seeker tuned to the 1.064-micron wavelength of the widely deployed Neodymium: Yttrium-Aluminum-Garnet (Nd:YAG) laser, Paveways entered service in Vietnam in the late 1960s. (25,000 Paveways were dropped for 18,000 targets claimed destroyed.)

In fundamental configuration and operation, these bombs have changed little since Vietnam. Each Paveway has several elements; from nose to tail they are: detector assembly, computer section, control section, the bomb itself, and the pop-out wing assembly. All are designated GBU-, the designation changing depending on bomb size and Paveway generation:

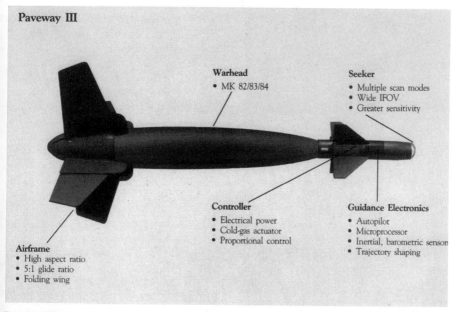

Paveway III

Warhead
- MK 82/83/84

Seeker
- Multiple scan modes
- Wide IFOV
- Greater sensitivity

Controller
- Electrical power
- Cold-gas actuator
- Proportional control

Guidance Electronics
- Autopilot
- Microprocessor
- Inertial, barometric sensor
- Trajectory shaping

Airframe
- High aspect ratio
- 5:1 glide ratio
- Folding wing

Paveway III
TEXAS INSTRUMENTS

Paveway II

GBU-10E/B	Mk 84
GBU-12E/B	Mk 82
GBU-16C/B	Mk 83

(British 1,000-lb Mk 13/18 bombs are similar to the GBU-16.)

Paveway II detector assemblies have a small seeker that swivels on a universal joint and has an annular ring that aligns it in the slipstream; it does not scan independently. The optical silicon detector staring array behaves analogously to a monopulse semiactive radar-homing seeker. The array is subdivided into four parts that receive reflected laser energy. A computer analyzes the relative reflection strengths and sends steering commands to the Airfoil Control Group system to the control fins. The fins operate on a full-on, full-off ("bang-bang") gas-operated system, adjusting the bomb's flight path until the reflections are equal in all four quadrants, thus refining its descent on the target. The pop-out rear wings stabilize the bomb and extend its range.

Paveway III

GBU-24A/B	Mk 84
	I-2000 steel-encased penetrator
GBU-27	steel-case 2,000-lb bomb delivered by the F-117

Paveway III GBU-24 Low-Level LGB (LLLGB) 2,000-lb bombs expand the launch envelope with a lower minimum altitude and greater standoff range. In addition, the more sensitive seeker has a wider field of view and several scan modes that move the seeker on gimbals in a search for the laser spot. The guidance electronics have a more powerful microprocessor that allows for delivery mode (level, loft, or dive) and trajectory shaping (to achieve the best terminal angle).

The midcourse autopilot is gyro-referenced (to establish its position relative to "up" and "level") and uses barometric sensors to determine the rate of descent. Texas Instruments claims that in the dive mode, the pilot only has to "place the target in the windscreen and "'pickle.'" The control system introduced proportional control with infinite fin-angle positioning in place of the bang-bang method. At the tail, much larger wings confer a glide ratio of 5:1 on the bomb.

GBU-24A/B Penetrators are the LLLGB with the BLU-109/B I-2000 warhead that has a hardened case and delayed fuze to greatly increase effectiveness against concrete bunkers and hardened aircraft shelters. In tests, the I-2000 penetrated up to 3 in (76 mm) of steel plates and 6 ft (1.83 m) of concrete.

GBU-27/B is a 2,000-lb penetrator with smaller wings and radar-absorbing materials delivered by the F-117A, and guided by a specially modified Paveway III guidance kit that ensured its accuracy. According to press reports, the kit has doubled the price of each bomb. 60% of GBU-27s in the inventory were used during Operation Desert Storm.

In January 1991, the GBU-28 didn't even exist. This is significant because during Desert Storm, the GBU-28 was developed, tested, shipped, and dropped by the time of the cease-fire at the end of February. The remarkable 17-day ad hoc effort combined the Air Force Systems Command, Watervliet Arsenal in New York, Lockheed Aeronautical and Space Systems, Texas Instruments, and LTV (now Vought).

At the suggestion of Lockheed engineers, who had been contemplating such an idea for approximately a year, Watervliet remachined surplus 8-in artillery piece tubes, boring them to 10 in (254 mm) and reshaping the outside.

As the casing took shape, Texas Instruments modified its GBU-27 Paveway III laser-guided-bomb guidance kit to account for the altered ballistics of the more cylindrical shape and greater weight of 4,700 lb (2,132 kg). Tests showed that the bomb could penetrate 100 ft (30.5 m) of earth or more than 22 ft (6.71 m) of concrete. (In the concrete test, the sled-driven bomb crashed through the 22-ft-thick slab and continued for another half mile before stopping.)

The bombs were then rushed to Eglin AFB, Florida, to be filled with 650 lb (295 kg) of explosive, a process so compressed that the bombs hadn't completely cooled before they were flown to Saudi Arabia. A total of 30 GBU-28s were made.

DEVELOPMENT • Initial operational capability for Paveway I was in the late 1960s. Paveway II went into production in 1977; Paveway III entered service in 1987.

In FY1988, the unit cost of a 2,000-lb hard target bomb was $12,686; in FY1992 the cost had dropped to $11,608. As of 1991, a standard "dumb" bomb cost roughly $2 per pound. A Paveway II costs between $10,000 and $15,000 depending on the length of the production run. Paveway IIIs cost approximately $40,000–$50,000.

VARIANTS • In addition to the variants listed above, three other members of the Paveway III family were proposed but not produced: GBU-21 (2,000-lb weapon), GBU-22 (500-lb, began development but not produced), GBU-23 (1,000-lb USN development variant).

COMBAT EXPERIENCE • During Desert Storm, 7,400 tons of precision-guided munitions were dropped on Iraqi targets. Most of the unpowered weapons were Paveways. In the official conduct of the Persian Gulf War report issued in April 1992, the totals were given as:

more than 2,500 GBU-10
more than 4,500 GBU-12
more than 200 GBU-16 (virtually all by USN aircraft)

almost 2,000 GBU-24/-27; 1,600 were penetrators

The US Air Force described how F-111s using GBU-12s destroyed 150 armored vehicles per night. Most of the large LGBs were GBU-10s, although hardened targets were reserved for the GBU-24 with the I-2000 warhead, the GBU-27, which was delivered solely by the F-117 Stealth fighter, and GBU-28. 60% of GBU-27s in the inventory were used.

Two GBU-28s were dropped by two F-111F Aardvarks on a command and control bunker in Baghdad only days before the cease-fire. One missed its mark (because of faulty laser spotting); the other penetrated, destroying the bunker and reportedly killing several Iraqi military leaders.

The US Navy reported delivering 202 GBU-10s, 216 GBU-12s, and 205 GBU-16s. An additional 611 LGB kits were fitted to other bombs. The British Royal Air Force reported dropping 1,000 LGBs.

SPECIFICATIONS •
DIMENSIONS

length	GBU-10: 14 ft 2 in (4.31 m)
	GBU-12: 10 ft 11 in (3.33 m)
	GBU-28: 18 ft 9 in (8.42 m)
bomb diameter	
	GBU-10: 1 ft 6 in (457 mm)
	GBU-12: 10 ¾ in (273 mm)
	GBU-28: 1 ft 4 ½ in (368 mm)
control fin span	
	GBU-10: 2 ft 7 ¼ in (794 mm)
	GBU-12: 1 ft 5 ⅔ in (448 mm)
wingspan	GBU-10: 5 ft 5 in (1.67 m)
	GBU-12: 4 ft 4 in (1.32 m)

AIRBORNE TARGETING PODS

AN/AAS-33 TRAM	A-6E Intruder
AN/AAS-37 IR detection set	OV-10D Bronco
AN/AAS-38 laser designating	F/A-18 Hornet
AN/ASQ-153 Pave Spike	British Buccaneers
AN/AVQ-14 LANTIRN	F-15E Eagle F-16A/C Fighting Falcon
AN/AVQ-26 Pave Tack	F-111 Aardvark
Mast-Mounted Sight	OH-58D Kiowa Warrior
TADS/PNVS	AH-64 Apache
ATLIS	French Jaguars
TIALD	British Tornados

GROUND-BASED DESIGNATORS

AN/PAQ-1 handheld laser target designator

AN/PAQ-3 Modular Universal Laser Equipment (MULE)

AN/TVQ-2 Ground/Vehicular Laser Locator Designator (G/VLLD)

Other aircraft such as the AV-8B Harrier, the A-10 Warthog, and the British Jaguar that did not have laser designators used their laser spot seekers to deliver LGBs against remotely marked targets.

GBU-15

The GBU-15 precision-guided modular glide bomb is based on the original Pave Strike GBU-8, which was used to great effect in the latter part of the Vietnam War. The weapon comprises a television (TV) or Imaging Infrared (IIR) seeker, warhead adapter section, warhead, fuze adapter, short-chord wings, and data link. Warheads for the GBU-15 are the Mk 84, a submunitions dispenser (SUU-54), or the more powerful BLU-109 (I-2000) unitary warhead. Midcourse corrections are passed through a jam-resistant AN/AXQ-14 data link.

Targeting options can be Lock-On Before Launch (LOBL) or After Launch (LOAL), which provides for automatic tracking, or through joystick control by the weapons system operator on board the launch aircraft. GBU-15s have either a TV (GBU-15(V)1/B) or IIR (GBU-15(V)2/B) seeker; the IIR seeker has 90% commonality with the AGM-65D Maverick IIR air-to-surface missile.

DEVELOPMENT • The initial operational capability for the GBU-15 (TV) was in 1983 and for the GBU-15 (IIR), 1987. In April 1989, the General Accounting Office criticized Rockwell for overstating prices on 13 material items by almost $5.6 million under a $114 million contract awarded in January 1984. Rockwell denied the criticism, arguing that although it had inadvertently failed to disclose some data, the contracting officer had not relied on Rockwell's information, an allegation denied by the contracting officer.

VARIANTS • GBU-15-I (with BLU-109 I-2000 penetrator warhead), AGM-130.

COMBAT EXPERIENCE • GBU-15s were delivered to F-15Es and F-111s during Operation Desert Storm, primarily to use against targets that were likely to be heavily defended or offering good contrasts to permit effective lock-on by the TV or IIR seekers. A typical GBU-15 payload was two weapons and a data link pod. A typical strike was flown at night using the IIR seeker, with a launch altitude between 10,000 and 23,000 ft (3,048–7,010 m).

To counter low visibility caused by bad weather, GBU-15s were dropped above the clouds but only locked onto their targets after they glided below the cloud deck.

The GBU-15s were effective against bridges, chemical plants, building complexes, command facilities, mine entrances, and bunkers and were also used to destroy the opened oil valves that were letting oil flow into the Persian Gulf. In the oil-manifold closure mission, one aircraft launched the missile, but a second one controlled it until impact.

SPECIFICATIONS •

MANUFACTURER   Rockwell International
MISSILE WEIGHT   2,617 lb (1,187 kg)
warhead   2,000 lb (907 kg)
DIMENSIONS
configuration
thick cylinder, small cruciform foreplanes, large rectangular mainplanes at the tail
length   12 ft 10½ in (3.92 m)
diameter   1 ft 6 in (460 mm)
wingspan   4 ft 11 in (1.5 m)
PROPULSION   GBU-15 is unpowered
PERFORMANCE
max range   4.3–22.6 nm (5–24.9 mi; 8–40 km), depending on launch altitude
WARHEAD   Mk-84 conventional high explosive or SUU-54 explosive submunitions
SENSORS/FIRE CONTROL   guidance: manual command through Hughes AN/AQX-14 2-way data link or automatic TV or IIR guidance through pre- or postlaunch lock-on

NAVAL MINES AND TORPEDOES

NAVAL MINES

The US Navy lays mines principally from aircraft and submarines. There are no surface minelaying ships in the fleet, and very few ships are fitted for minelaying. Attempts to replace the mines described below have met with little success. Several programs begun in the 1980s and early 1990s, the most promising a joint effort with Great Britain, were canceled when funding fell short and mines sank to their usual low priority. Remote Control (RECO) by acoustic signal has been developed for Captor and Quickstrike mines.

Mk 52

The Mk 52 is a modified 1,000-lb (454-kg) aircraft bomb deployed as an aircraft-laid bottom mine. Mods vary principally in their firing mechanism; in fact, most combinations of pressure, acoustic, and magnetic triggers were deployed: Mod 0 pressure, Mod 1 acoustic, Mod 2 magnetic, Mod 3 pressure-acoustic, Mod 4 pressure-magnetic, Mod 5 magnetic-acoustic, Mod 6 pressure-acoustic-magnetic, and Mod 11 seismic-magnetic.

It was rated as capable of detecting a submarine moving at three knots. Arming delays ran from one hour to 90 days and the mine could count up to 30 ships before detonating. It could also turn itself off between ship passages and self-sterilize at the end of its useful life.

DEVELOPMENT • The US Long-Range Mine Program began in 1948, with production of the Mk 52 getting under way in 1954 and testing starting in 1956. The weapon didn't achieve initial operational capability, however, until 1961. German production followed. Some may still be in service, although it is known that Mods 1 and 4 have been withdrawn.

COMBAT EXPERIENCE • Mk 52s were laid by US aircraft in North Vietnamese waterways as part of the late-1972 "Christmas offensive" mounted to persuade the government to return to end-of-war negotiations.

SPECIFICATIONS •
WEIGHT   1,130 (Mod 1) to 1,235 lb
(Mod 6) (513–561 kg)
warhead   595 lb (270 kg) of
conventional HBX-1
DIMENSIONS
length   5 ft 1 in (1.55 m)
diameter   19 in (477 mm), 2 ft 9 in
(0.84 m) over fins
MAX DEPTH   150 ft (45.7 m) (Mods 1, 3, 5, 6); 600 ft (183 m) (Mod 2)
SENSORS AND DETONATORS
Mod 1   acoustic
Mod 2   magnetic
Mod 3   pressure-magnetic
Mod 5   acoustic-magnetic
Mod 6   acoustic-magnetic/pressure
Mod 7   dual-channel magnetic
Mod 11   magnetic-seismic

Mk 55

The Mk 55 is the 2,000-lb bomb analogue to the Mk 52 and functionally resembles it. Many of the components were interchangeable.

DEVELOPMENT • Initial operational capability was in 1961. Probably still in service.

SPECIFICATIONS •

WEIGHT   2,039–2,128 lb (925–965 kg)

warhead   1,269 lb (576 kg) of HBX-1

DIMENSIONS

length   6 ft 7 in (2.09 m)
diameter   23.4 in (594 mm)
MAX DEPTH   150 ft (45.7 m) (Mods 3, 5, 6), 600 ft (183 m) (Mods 2, 7)

SENSORS AND DETONATORS
Mod 1   acoustic influence
Mod 2   magnetic influence
Mod 3   pressure-magnetic
Mod 5   acoustic-magnetic
Mod 6   acoustic-magnetic/pressure
Mod 7   dual-channel magnetic
Mod 11   magnetic-seismic

Mk 56/Mk 57

The Mk 56 is an aircraft-laid, moored US mine which was specifically designed for use against high-speed, deep-operating submarines. The Mk 56 has a nonmagnetic, stainless-steel case and is fitted with a magnetic firing mechanism. The Mk 57, launched by submarines, has a fiberglass casing.

DEVELOPMENT • Mk 57 achieved initial operational capability in 1964, the Mk 56 following in 1966.

SPECIFICATIONS •

WEIGHT   2,135 lb (968 kg); Mk 57 2,059 lb (934 kg)

warhead   357 lb (162 kg) of HBX-3; Mk 57 340 lb (154 kg)

DIMENSIONS

length   Mk 56: 9 ft 5 in (2.87 m)
Mk 57: 10 ft 8 in (3.25 m)
diameter   Mk 56: 23.4 in (594 mm) body
Mk 57: 21 in (533 mm)

MAX DEPTH   1,200 ft (366 m), also adjustable from 30–480 ft

SENSORS AND DETONATOR   magnetic dual-channel using total field magnetometer as detector

Mk 60 Captor (encapsulated torpedo)

The Mk 60 Captor is the US Navy's principal antisubmarine mine. Each Captor mine consists of a container that contains a threat analyzer and acoustic signature library, a Mk 46 Mod 4 Antisubmarine Warfare (ASW) torpedo, and an anchor. Captors are laid in a barrier pattern in deep water by aircraft or submarines; preferred drop points are straits and other "chokepoints."

As the container descends, it pays out the anchor, which drops to the seafloor. The container finds its preset surveillance depth and "floats" vertically at the upper end of its tether. Using a passive acoustic sensor, the Captor detects moving submarines while ignoring surface ships.

When the mine has established the submarine target's bearing, Captor begins active tracking using Reliable Acoustic Path (RAP) sound propagation. As the target comes within range of the torpedo's seeker, the container fills with water. The flooding is controlled in a way that tilts the canister to an angle 30° from the vertical. The torpedo is released, finds its own search depth, and searches with its passive acoustic homing seeker.

Despite its ability to be remotely activated and its "fire and forget" search and attack system, the Captor's punch is relatively light. This lack of explosive power concerned many in the US Navy during the days of Soviet submarine growth. A Captor would probably succeed in disabling or destroying most likely submarine targets, however.

DEVELOPMENT • Development of the Captor concept began in 1961; production started in March 1976 after several years of trials. The weapon achieved initial operational capability in 1979.

Produced by Goodyear Aerospace (now a division of Loral, Inc.), Akron, Ohio. Last authorization came in FY1986 at a unit cost of $377,000. Budget constraints cut Captor procurement in FY1985–87 from a planned 1,568 to 450. Total procurement fell short of the 4,109 originally stated as a requirement.

A modification program was planned but has not been funded.

SPECIFICATIONS •
WEIGHT   2,321 lb (1,053 kg)
  warhead   98 lb (44 kg) high explosive
DIMENSIONS
  length   12 ft 1 in (3.68 m)
  diameter   21 in (533 mm) mine, 12¾ in (324 mm) Mk 46 torpedo
MAX DEPTH   3,000 ft (914 m)
MAX DETECTION RANGE   3,281 ft (1,000 m)
SENSORS AND DETONATOR   passive acoustic monitoring switching to active once target is identified as submarine; monitoring is not continuous but turns on and off according to programmed schedule

Mk 62 Quickstrike

Quickstrike aircraft-laid bottom mines were converted from Mk 80 series bombs. They succeeded the Destructor series of conversions that were used to mine North Vietnamese harbors and rivers.

A Quickstrike conversion includes installation of a modular arming kit containing an arming device, fitting an explosive booster, and Mk 57 magnetic-seismic or Mk 58 magnetic-seismic-pressure Target Detection Devices (TDD). (Mk 70 and Mk 71 TDDs replaced Mk 57/Mk 58s in production in the mid-1980s.)

The Mk 62 is a modified Mk 82 500-lb (227-kg) bomb.

DEVELOPMENT • Began in the mid-1970s to replace the Mk 36 Destructor, achieving initial operational capability in 1980. Plans called for production of almost 40,000 TDDs, but only a small fraction was actually funded.

SPECIFICATIONS •
WEIGHT
  fixed conical tail
      531 lb (241 kg)
  low-drag tail
      570 lb (259 kg)
  warhead   192 lb (87 kg) of H-6 explosive
DIMENSIONS
  length   7 ft 5 in (2.25 m)
  diameter   10.8 in (274 mm)
MAX DEPTH   300 ft (91.4 m)
SENSORS AND DETONATOR   Target Detection Device TDD Mk 57/58 or TDD Mk 70/Mk 71, magnetic-seismic or magnetic-seismic-pressure firing mechanism

Mk 63 Quickstrike

Successor to Mk 40 Destructor series conversion of 1,000-lb (454-kg) bomb. Few of these seem to have been procured.

SPECIFICATIONS •
WEIGHT
  fixed conical tail
      985 lb (447 kg)
  low-drag tail
      1,105 lb (501 kg)
  warhead   450 lb (204 kg) of H-6 explosive
DIMENSIONS
  length   9 ft 5 in (2.86 m)
  diameter   14 in (356 mm)

Mk 64 Quickstrike

Successor to the Mk 41 Destructor, a modified Mk 84 2,000-lb (907-kg) bomb.

SPECIFICATIONS •
WEIGHT   2,000 lb (907 kg)
DIMENSIONS
  length   12 ft 8 in (3.83 m)
  diameter   18 in (457 mm)

Mk 65 Quickstrike

Although considered part of the Quickstrike series of bomb-to-mine conversions, the Mk 65 aircraft-laid bottom mine is substantially different from the Mk 84 2,000-lb (907-kg) bomb that is the basis of the Mk 64 and 65. The Mk 65 has a thin-walled mine-type case and several modifications to the arming mechanism, nose, and tail.

DEVELOPMENT • Production contract awarded to Aerojet Tech Systems, Sacramento, California, in April 1982. Achieved initial operational capability in 1983. 4,479 were produced under FY1983–86, FY1988–89 funding, very close to the 4,500 originally planned.

SPECIFICATIONS •
WEIGHT   2,390 lb (1,083 kg) including warhead with HBX explosive
DIMENSIONS
  length   9 ft 2 in (2.8 m)
  diameter   body 20.9 in (530 mm), across fins 29 in (734 mm)
MAX DEPTH   300 ft (91.4 m)
SENSORS AND DETONATOR   Target Detection Device TDD Mk 58/Mk 71 combination sensor, variable influence (magnetic-seismic-pressure)

Mk 67 SLMM

The Submarine-Launched Mobile Mine (SLMM) adapts a Mk 37 heavy torpedo to a self-propelled torpedolike mine that submarines can launch covertly into inaccessible waters. SLMM can also operate as a shallow-water bottom mine against surface ships.

The SLMM consists of a modified Mk 37 Mod 2 electrically powered torpedo with the wire guidance equipment removed and warhead replaced by a mine. The electronics are similar to those of the Quickstrike series. Honeywell Marine Systems proposed an Extended SLMM incorporating the NT-37E torpedo, but this was not developed.

DEVELOPMENT • Development began in 1977–78 with plans to produce 1,729 mines by the mid- to late 1980s. Delays in development and chronic funding problems pushed the service introduction date to 1992. By then only 889 had been produced under SLMM funding, although others may have been converted using torpedo refurbishment dollars. The prime contractor is Dewey Electronics of Oakland, New Jersey.

SPECIFICATIONS •
WEIGHT
  overall   1,759 lb (798 kg)
  warhead   529 lb (240 kg) of Mk 13 explosive
DIMENSIONS
  length   13 ft 5 in (4.08 m)
  diameter   21 in (533 mm)
MAX DEPTH   approx 328 ft (100 m)
SENSORS AND DETONATOR   Target Detection Device TDD Mk 71 combination sensor, variable influence (magnetic-seismic-pressure)

TORPEDOES

NT-37

The NT-37 medium-weight torpedo is an extensively reworked Mk 37 torpedo that is in service with several navies. It can be launched from surface ships or submarines. Alliant has offered several versions of the NT-37, including the digital NT-37E and the analog NT-37F.

The NT-37E proved to be too expensive for most prospective retrofit candidates. The costly strap-down guidance system provides more precision than the torpedo needs to get close enough for its terminal homing system. Therefore, Alliant claims that the NT-37F, which upgrades the analog system with gimballed gyros, achieves nearly the same performance and is more reliable than earlier Mk 37s while avoiding the expense of the digital system.

VARIANTS • NT-37C was developed in the early 1970s as an upgrade of the older Mk 37 torpedo. An Otto-fuel piston motor like that of the Mk 46 replaced the Mk 37's electric motor and battery. NT-37D used the NT-37C motor and replaced vacuum-tube acoustic technology with a solid-state acoustic processor system designed to improve antiship capability as well as doubling acoustic performance against submarine targets.

NT-37E replaces vacuum-tube analog guidance and control with strap-down solid-state digital equipment using Xylog processors and inertial navigation. Fitted with two-way communications link through the guidance wire. Improvements doubled the active detection range and nearly doubled the passive range. Reliability and logistical support also upgraded.

NT-37F was introduced in 1990 as a less expensive retrofit of Mk 37s. Original control system replaced by upgraded analog system controlled by computer having Intel 80186 processors; senses drift of less than one knot. After launch and immediately before turning on its homing sensor, the NT-37F takes background noise readings of itself and surrounding medium and can adjust seeker sensitivity accordingly.

The designation NT-37F is trademark-protected.

DEVELOPMENT • NT-37C/D kits developed and manufactured by Northrop Corp. from 1968 to 1980, achieving initial operational capability in 1974. The NT-37E/F developed by Honeywell Marine Systems (later Alliant Techsystems) in Everett, Washington. The NT-37E seeker was first tested in 1980, full kit tested in 1982–83.

Not in service in US ships but has replaced Mk 37 in several other navies. Canada, Norway, Peru, and Taiwan operated earlier NT-37 torpedoes; Israel (in 1986), Netherlands, and Taiwan also procured NT-37Es. Egypt (1991) was the first customer for the NT-37F.

SPECIFICATIONS •
WEIGHT   wire-guided 1,653 lb (750 kg),
free-running 1,415 lb (642 kg)
warhead   331 lb (150 kg)
DIMENSIONS
length   wire-guided 14 ft 9 in
(4.51 m), free-running
12 ft 7 in (3.85 m)
diameter   19 in (485 mm)
WARHEAD   conventional high explosive
GUIDANCE   solid-state acoustics designed to improve anti-surface-ship capability; solid-state, computer-driven guidance and control (NT-37E

is strap-down digital, NT-37F is analog with gimballed gyros); three search patterns: straight run (antiship), straight run with acoustic reattack, snake and circle, active for ASW, passive for antiship
POWERPLANT   90-hp thermochemical rotary piston cam motor using liquid monopropellant (Otto) fuel
SPEED   2 speeds selectable, max range 9.7 nm (11.2 mi; 18 km)

Mk 46 lightweight torpedo

The Mk 46 is the most widely deployed 12.75-in (324-mm) lightweight torpedo for use against submarines by helicopters, aircraft, and surface ships; it is also fitted in the Captor deep-water mine.

Development of the Mk 46 in the late 1950s as a successor to the Mk 44 addressed a design goal of a lightweight torpedo to counter nuclear-propelled submarines. Speed and range demands led to the substitution of a chemical-fuel motor in place of the Mk 44's battery-powered electric propulsion. The solid-fuel motor in the Mk 46 Mod 0 was not successful. The much more numerous Mod 1 (6,608 produced) is driven by a motor fueled by a liquid monopropellant.

A NEARTIP (Near-Term Improvement Program) and Mod 6 refit program began in the early 1980s to counter the loss in acquisition range due to introduction of anechoic hull coatings and to improve shallow-water capability. NEARTIP features an improved sonar transducer and a digital guidance and control system with correlation channel and second gyro; engine improvements included a slower search speed for greater range and lower self-generated noise.

Compared to the Mk 44, the Mk 46 is faster, dives deeper, and has approximately twice the range.

VARIANTS • Mk 46 Mod 2 (3,344 produced for Foreign Military Sales/FMS

customers) had improved Electronic Counter-Countermeasures   (ECCM) logic.

Mk 46 Mod 4 is used in the Captor mine, which is laid in geographic chokepoints and lies dormant until activated. Operating autonomously, the torpedo's seeker tracks ship noises and leaves the special capsule when a target is within range.

NEARTIP total of 4,922 kits was procured for the US Navy; refitted torpedoes were designated Mk 46 Mod 6. FMS production totaled 311.

Mk 46 Mod 5 are new-manufacture torpedoes with NEARTIP features that were first authorized for US Navy in the late 1970s as an interim measure (575 produced). As development of the Mk 50 Advanced Lightweight Torpedo (ALWT) hit delays, an additional 4,205 Mk 46 Mod 5 were authorized from FY1983 to FY1987. 1,278 were produced for FMS sales.

DEVELOPMENT • Aerojet Electro Systems Co. of Azusa, California, developed and produced both the Mod 0 and Mod 1. The Mk 46 achieved initial operational capability in 1966 for the Mod 0 and 1967 for the Mod 1. Honeywell Defense and Marine Systems of Everett, Washington (which became Alliant Techsystems, Inc., in September 1990), captured the later production contracts, completing the last Mod 1 in 1971 and the last of 23,000 Mk 46s in the mid-1990s. License production by Mitsubishi in Japan began in 1982.

Alliant also produced the Mk 46 Mod 2, Mod 5, and NEARTIP update kits. The last US Navy funding was authorized in FY1987, but FMS continued for almost another decade.

A list of aircraft and surface-ship classes that do *not* carry the Mk 46 would be far shorter than the list of those that do.

SPECIFICATIONS •

WEIGHT   508 lb (230 kg)
  warhead   95 lb (43 kg)
DIMENSIONS
  length   8 ft 6 in (2.59 m)

diameter 12¾ in (324 mm)
WARHEAD conventional PBXN-103 high explosive
GUIDANCE active/passive acoustic homing; capable of repeated attacks using "snake-search" method
POWERPLANT 5-cylinder cam engine with Otto liquid monopropellant fuel; contra-rotating propellers
SPEED 45 kts; max range 5.9 nm (6.8 mi; 11 km); max depth classified (greater than 984 ft/300 m)

Mk 48 heavyweight torpedo

The Mk 48 is a heavy, wire-guided, long-range, antisubmarine and anti-surface-ship torpedo that succeeded the Mk 37. The Mk 48 is generally considered the most advanced torpedo in Western naval inventories. Still, in the late 1970s, advances in Soviet submarine capabilities reduced its margin, leading the Navy to begin the Advanced Capability (ADCAP) program led by Hughes.

The Mk 48 is divided into five component groups. The nose group contains the sonar and homing equipment; next are the warhead, control (with gyro, command, and power units), and fuel tank groups. The fuel tank also holds the command wire dispenser. The afterbody/tailcone group consists of the engine and steering surfaces. The all-digital Mk 48 Advanced Capability (ADCAP) is virtually a new torpedo, possessing much greater "intelligence," speed, and range.

Following launch, the submarine performs a wire-clearance maneuver and the torpedo heads to a preselected "enable point." At the enable point, the acoustic search program guides the torpedo in a programmed search for the target. Once the target is acquired by the torpedo's sonar, the Mk 48 maneuvers to lock-on and accelerates to intercept.

The ADCAP effort suffered cost growth and delays during the first few years due in part to Hughes' inexperience in developing torpedo sensors as well as a continuing, and increasingly pessimistic, reassessment of the Soviet nuclear submarine threat. Each reassessment resulted in demands for more of every parameter.

For example, the Mk 48 Mod 4 interim ADCAP variant entered production at an accelerated rate in 1978 to take advantage of improvements in performance, active and passive acoustic search range, anti-surface-ship capability, and ease of operation studied. The later "Near-Term" Mod 5 ADCAP upgrades existing torpedoes to Mod 4 with a Hughes Aircraft electronically steered, higher-powered active sonar and a larger fuel supply.

Meanwhile, the "Full-Up" ADCAP continued development, spurred by continuing improvements in Soviet submarines. Further expansion of the operating envelope, higher fuel delivery rates and greater fuel capacity, further improvements in acoustics and electronics, thicker shell, speed increased to more than sixty knots were the result. The Hughes Guidance and Control subsystem has two computers, signal processor, digital-based, electronically steered active sonar, and Inertial Measurement Unit (IMU). It is capable of acoustic homing on fast-moving targets in shallow water and strong thermal gradients. Unfortunately, program delays continued as the Navy and Hughes played catch-up while tests to existing versions hit their inevitable snags.

US Navy apprehensions about the growing quality of Soviet submarines persisted right up to the moment of the Soviet Union's collapse. Almost overnight, that collapse alleviated the urgency of ADCAP development, and production withered.

VARIANTS • Mk 48 Mod 1 was the product of Gould (formerly Clevite Corp. and later Westinghouse) and Naval Surface Warfare Center at White Oak, Maryland, which began work on this variant in 1967. Propelled by a piston (swashplate) engine with a different acoustic homing system from the Mod 2. Mod 1 entered production in 1972.

Mk 48 Mod 3 was provided with TELE-COM (Telecommunications) two-way communications link that transmits 14 torpedo parameters once per second through the wire guidance path. Major production variant.

Closed-Cycle Advanced Capability Propulsion System (CCACPS) was a Product Improvement to the ADCAP torpedo with a propulsion system based on the Mk 50's Stored Chemical Energy Propulsion System (SCEPS). Full-Scale Development (FSD) was planned to start in March 1989 but was delayed several times and eventually canceled.

DEVELOPMENT • Development began in the early 1960s. The Ex-10 RETORC (Research Torpedo Configuration) turbine-propelled torpedo was the joint experimental project of Pennsylvania State University Applied Research Laboratory and Westinghouse Electric that began in the early 1960s. This led to the Mk 48 Mod 0/2 turbine-propelled variants; the Mod 2 lost in competition with Clevite's Mk 48 Mod 1, with the latter achieving initial operational capability in 1972. Production versions built by Westinghouse (formerly Gould, Inc.) Naval Systems Division in Cleveland, Ohio, and Hughes Aircraft Company in Forest, Mississippi.

Plans for 320 ADCAP torpedoes per year fell afoul of program problems as well as the diminution of the Soviet submarine threat. Until FY1992, production featured firm-fixed-price competition between Westinghouse and Hughes Aircraft Co.'s Undersea Weapons Division in Buena Park, California.

Beginning in FY1992, the production rate was reduced to minimum sustainable level for just one manufacturer. Hughes emerged the victor of a "winner take all" competition to produce 324 torpedos over a five-year period.

All US submarines (SSN/SSBN) carry the Mk 48 torpedo.

SPECIFICATIONS •
WEIGHT 3,450 lb (1,565 kg)
  warhead 650 lb (295 kg)
DIMENSIONS
  length 19 ft 2 in (5.84 m)
  diameter 21 in (533 mm)
WARHEAD conventional high explosive (PBXN-3)
GUIDANCE can be launched as free-running or wire-guided free-running; active or passive acoustic search and terminal homing
POWERPLANT 500-hp axial-flow, gas-piston (swashplate) pump-jet using Otto II monopropellant (nitrogen ester and Hydroxylamine Perchlorate/HAP oxidant) liquid fuel
SPEED 55 kts max; max range at 55 kts, 20 nm (23 mi; 37 km); range at 40 kts, 27 nm (31 mi; 50 km); max depth 2,500 ft (760 m)

Mk 50 lightweight torpedo

The Mk 50, formerly known as the Advanced Lightweight Torpedo (ALWT), is the successor to the Mk 46 for use by fixed-wing Antisubmarine Warfare (ASW) aircraft, helicopters, and surface ships. The Mk 50 is constrained by the need to stay within the Mk 46's weight and dimensions as well as having to fit within the length and width of the S-3A Viking's weapons bay. In addition, the Mk 50 will be carried in the Vertical Launch ASROC antisubmarine rocket launcher. (It was also to have been the conventional payload for the canceled Sea Lance ASW missile.)

Compared to the Mk 46, the Mk 50 is faster and will dive to a greater maximum depth. Its passive/active seeker can generate multiple, selectable transmit-and-receive beams and home on its target

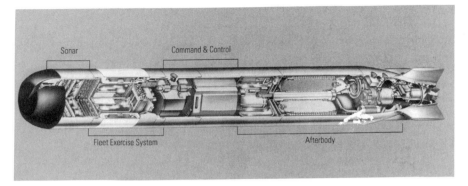

Mk 50 Advanced Lightweight ASW Torpedo
ALLIANT TECHSYSTEMS

from twice as far away as the Mk 46. The AN/AYK-14 on-board, programmable, digital computer analyzes signal returns in real time and provides mission control, navigation, and target detection and tracking.

The larger warhead was designed by the Naval Surface Warfare Center. The propulsion system is a closed, Rankine-cycle engine that uses a lithium-sulfur hexaflouride reaction to generate steam. The Mk 50 also has better counter-measures resistance and lower radiated noise than the Mk 46.

An earlier version of the ALWT was known as the Barracuda; the current Mk 50 logo shows the fish, but the name is not often used and is not official.

The Mk 50's size and weight constraints worried many late-1980s Western analysts who regarded the improving Soviet nuclear submarine fleet with increasing trepidation. Despite the real improvements in speed and operating depths, the Mk 50's warhead seemed too small to threaten the double hulls of Soviet boats. Use of a directed-energy warhead similar to the shaped charge found in antitank missiles would enhance performance, and development was believed to be under way.

VARIANTS • Mk 51 was the McDonnell Douglas/Raytheon entry in the 1979

"swim-off" with Honeywell/Garrett. (Gould/Hughes, Westinghouse offered a third contestant, but theirs was not selected for the swim-off.) Powered by silver-oxide electric battery (General Electric) and fitted with Raytheon side-looking linear or flank arrays.

DEVELOPMENT • Development began in August 1975. Alliant Techsystems (formerly Honeywell Underseas Systems Division) in Hopkins, Minnesota, is prime contractor. Westinghouse in Baltimore, Maryland, was selected as second source in May 1987; Martin Marietta supplies the command-and-control system for Westinghouse team.

Alliant and Westinghouse both received initial production contracts, but funding slipped in later years.

The Mk 50 was to replace the Mk 46 in many Western navies, but its cost seems likely to limit foreign sales.

SPECIFICATIONS •
WEIGHT   800 lb (363 kg)
  warhead   approx 100 lb (45.4 kg)
DIMENSIONS
  length   9 ft 6 in (2.9 m)
  diameter   12¾ in (324 mm)
WARHEAD conventional warhead; a directed-energy (shaped-charge) warhead has been considered

GUIDANCE   active and passive acoustic homing with multiple selectable transmit/receive beams; directed by AKY-14 programmable digital computer

POWERPLANT   Garret Pneumatic Systems Stored Chemical Energy Propulsion System (SCEPS) using a closed cycle steam turbine driving a pump jet

SPEED   50+ kts; max depth more than 1,968 ft (600 m)

SENSORS AND ELECTRONIC WARFARE

AIRBORNE RADARS

AAQ-13/AAQ-14 LANTIRN

The LANTIRN (Low-Altitude Navigation and Targeting Infrared System for Night) is a two-pod system fitted to F-15 Eagle and F-16 Fighting Falcon aircraft. It can also be operated by any aircraft that has a MIL-STD-1553B digital databus/multiplexer.

LANTIRN permits an aircraft to fly at very low levels at night or in limited-visibility conditions and conduct attacks with no external targeting data provided. Single-pilot operation is possible because of the high degree of automation and the integrated symbology. The pods are fitted under the engine intakes in both the F-15 and F-16.

The AAQ-13 is the navigation pod. It is fitted with a Texas Instruments J-band Terrain-Following Radar (TFR) that can be set in any one of five radar modes: manual TFR flight at preset altitudes from 1,000 ft (305 m) to 100 ft (30.5 m); Very Low Clearance (VLC) mode; weather mode permitting TFR flight in rain or other visible moisture; the Low Probability of Intercept (LPI) mode, designed to reduce detectability; and Electronic Counter-Countermeasures (ECCM) mode, which emphasizes immunity to ECM.

The navigational Forward-Looking Infrared (FLIR) has a selectable Field of View (FOV), using a wide, 6° FOV or the narrow, more precise 1.7° FOV. The FLIR can look into a turn or have its FOV offset 11° to either side for a "snap-look."

The AAQ-14 is the targeting pod and is also fitted with its own ECU (Electronic Control Unit) and pod control computer. The nose section rolls to allow targeting by the gimballed FLIR and Litton Laser Systems Laser Designator Rangefinder (LDR) in a wide range of flight attitudes. The FLIR has a selectable FOV and is capable of precision pointing and automatic tracking of designated targets; space and weight provisions have been made for an automatic target recognition capability.

A typical night-attack mission uses the targeting pod first by displaying a wide FOV image on the pilot's Head-Down Display (HDD). He switches to a narrow FOV for magnification and activates on the LDR. A Hughes missile boresight correlator allows the pod's targeting data to be handed off automatically to the Maverick's seeker. The LDR is also used as a target marker for LGB and as a rangefinder for unguided, free-fall ordnance.

VARIANTS • Sharpshooter is the targeting pod without the IR missile boresight correlator that is used with the Maverick IR missile.

Pathfinder is the simplified FLIR pod for close-air support missions in night or adverse weather conditions. Main component is the steerable, navigational FLIR from LANTIRN with dual FOV. It can be integrated with any aircraft equipped with MIL-STD-1553B digital databus and stroke/raster HUD.

DEVELOPMENT • Development began in 1980 by Martin Marietta in Orlando, Florida. US Air Force flight tests began in 1983 and totaled over 2,800 hours by the end of 1988. Development of the targeting pods experienced delays due to inability to meet AF performance requirements. As a result, the targeting pods began production at a slower rate than the navigational pods.

The first production navigation pod was delivered in April 1987; delivery of the first production targeting pod was delayed until June 1988.

Sharpshooter pods have been exported to Israel and Pathfinders to Egypt. Full LANTIRN outfits have been sold to the Turkish and South Korean air forces.

LANTIRN II is an upgraded version of the LANTIRN in development since late 1989. LANTIRN II is designed to be located in the nose of the aircraft. The system's dual-aperture design combines the navigation and targeting capabilities, and the system is guided by a head-steered helmet-mounted display.

COMBAT EXPERIENCE • LANTIRNs were deployed with the two squadrons of F-15Es that flew against Iraqi targets during Operation Desert Storm and were considered a great success. The combination of the aircraft's APG-70 radar, the navigation and targeting pods, and Paveway-series LGBs resulted in very precise strikes against bridges, command-and-control links, road networks, armored formations, airfields, and fixed and mobile Scud Tactical Ballistic Missile (TBM) sites by two-aircraft teams.

These teams consisted of one aircraft flying with both the navigation and targeting pod and the other carrying only the navigation pod (because of targeting pod shortages). Each aircraft carried eight GBU-12 500-lb (227-kg) LGBs; in some attacks, all 16 bombs were put on their targets, according to the Air Force. 72 F-16s carried only the navigation pod, which was credited with significantly

expanding the aircraft's night and adverse-weather capability. According to the US Air Force, LANTIRN reliability on these aircraft was over 98%.

SPECIFICATIONS •
LENGTH
    navigation pod
        6 ft 6.2 in (1.99 m)
    targeting pod
        8 ft 2½ in (2.5 m)
DIAMETER
    navigation pod
        12 in (305 mm)
    targeting pod
        15 in (381 mm)

APG-63

The AN/APG-63 multimode radar was developed for the F-15 Eagle fighter. The pulse-Doppler system uses a planar-array antenna and can operate on several selectable frequencies. The reliability goal of a 60-hour Mean Time Between Failures (MTBF) has proved elusive. In recent years, the average MTBF was 30–35 hours.

Four air-to-air modes include a search mode and three air-combat modes. Supersearch is the least discriminating, locking onto the first target to enter the F-15's Head-Up Display (HUD) field of view and marking it for the pilot. Vertical scan searches the vertical axis ahead of the aircraft. In the boresight mode, the antenna looks straight ahead and the radar notes any target coming into that cone.

The air-to-ground modes are ground mapping, an Inertial Navigation System (INS) velocity update mode, and an automatic bomb-release mode. The system also has Identification Friend or Foe (IFF) capability and automatic target acquisition out to 10 nm (11.5 mi; 18.5 km).

Hughes introduced a programmable signal processor with 96 kilobytes of memory in 1979 to improve ground mapping and close formation target discrimination capabilities. Further software updates provide Track-While-Scan (TWS) and compatibility with the AIM-120 Advanced Medium-Range Air-to-Air Missile (AMRAAM).

The APG-63 also flies in US Customs Service P-3A Orion maritime patrol craft for use against drug smugglers.

VARIANTS • APG-63 MSIP included more memory and a programmable signal processor as part of the F-15 Multistaged Improvement Program (MSIP).

APG-70 is the production version of a greatly enhanced APG-63 design; see APG-70 entry.

DEVELOPMENT • Production began in the early 1970s and ended in September 1986; manufactured by Hughes Aircraft Co.'s Radar Systems Group, Los Angeles, California. In service in US, Israeli, Japanese, and Saudi Arabian F-15s and in US Customs Service P-3s.

SPECIFICATIONS •
BAND   I/J

APG-65

The AN/APG-65 is the digital multimode radar in the US Navy's F/A-18 Hornet strike fighter. It can be used with the Sparrow and Sidewinder missiles and the 20-mm gun for air-to-air combat, and a variety of conventional and guided weapons for ground attack.

The system consists of five Line-Replaceable Units (LRU) including an elliptical, flat-plate, electrically driven planar-array antenna that has low sidelobes for better Electronic Countermeasures (ECM) resistance.

Two of the LRUs are a liquid-cooled, gridded Traveling Wave Tube (TWT) transmitter and a Receiver/Exciter that houses the analog-to-digital converter and uses Field-Effect Transistors (FET).

A general-purpose Radar Data Processor (RDP) has a 250,000-word 16-bit bulk storage memory. The digital Programmable Signal Processor (PSP) operates at 7.2 million operations per second.

The radar has a large variety of air-to-air and air-to-surface modes. In the air-to-air mode, the APG-65 presents a clean display in both look-up and look-down conditions and has all-aspect target detection. The radar can perform velocity search, Range-While-Search (RWS), monopulse single-target tracking, Track-While-Scan (TWS) of up to 10 targets simultaneously, raid assessment to distinguish among closely spaced targets and gun director using pulse-to-pulse frequency agility for short-range sighting for the 20-mm cannon. The short-range Air-Combat Maneuvering (ACM) target acquisition modes are displaying a target in the Head-Up Display (HUD) and vertical and boresight acquisition.

Surface-attack modes include real-beam ground mapping, Doppler beam sharpening, terrain avoidance, precision velocity update for the Inertial Navigation System (INS), sea surface search, air-to-surface ranging, fixed or moving target tracking, and a synthetic aperture mode.

DEVELOPMENT • Testing began in the mid-1970s, with the radar achieving initial operational capability in 1981. Manufactured by Hughes Aircraft Co., Radar Systems Group, El Segundo, California.

In addition to equipping most F/A-18s, the APG-65 replaced the AN/APQ-120 radar in German F-4F Phantoms under the Improved Combat Effectiveness (ICE) program. AV-8Bs of the US Marine Corps and the Spanish and Italian air forces are being fitted with a modified APG-65 with a smaller antenna; the first of these was delivered in the summer of 1993.

Extensive updates have resulted in the APG-73.

SPECIFICATIONS •

BAND I/J
WEIGHT 450 lbs (204 kg)
VOLUME OCCUPIED less than 14.8 ft³
(0.42 m³)

APG-66

The AN/APG-66 is a pulse-Doppler radar designed specifically for the F-16 Fighting Falcon fighter aircraft. It was developed from Westinghouse's WX-200 radar and is designed for operation with the Sparrow and AMRAAM medium-range and the Sidewinder short-range missiles. It is less capable than the F/A-18's APG-65 radar but weighs less, occupies less space, and is less expensive to acquire.

APG-66 uses a slotted planar-array antenna located in the aircraft's nose and has four operating frequencies within the I/J band. The modular system consists of the antenna, transmitter, low-power Radio Frequency (RF) unit, digital signal processor, computer, and control panel.

The system has 10 operating modes, which are divided into air-to-air, air-to-surface display, and submodes. The air-to-air modes are search (with Track-While-Scan/TWS) and engagement, each mode having several variations. Six air-to-surface display modes include real-beam ground map, expanded real-beam ground map, Doppler beam sharpening, beacon, and sea. APG-66 also has engagement and freeze submodes. Antenna size varies from the pocket version in New Zealand's upgraded A-4s to the larger-than-average APG-66J antenna in Japanese F-4EJs.

The system's displays include the control panel, Head-Up Display (HUD), and radar display, with all combat-critical controls integrated into the throttle grip and sidestick controller.

Line-Replaceable Unit (LRU) modularity allows for shortened Mean Time to Repair (MTTR), since they can simply be replaced, involving no special tools or

equipment. Westinghouse claims a 115-hour Mean Time Between Failure (MTBF), although the service average is 97 hours in service.

DEVELOPMENT • First design work began in the late 1960s, progressing to the WWX-200 in 1972. Development of the APG-66 began in 1975, with the radar achieving initial operational capability in 1979 in the F-16.

Besides the F-16, the A-4 Skyhawk (APG-66NZ), Japanese F-4EJ Phantom (APG-66J), and the British single-seat Hawk 200 carry the APG-66. Antidrug-patrolling aircraft such as the US Customs Service Cessna Citation IIs (six) and Piper Cheyenne (eight) as well as the Coast Guard's modified HU-25A Guardian aircraft. The APG-66 is the primary sensor of the Small Aerostat Surveillance System (SASS) as well, but the antenna is a solid banana-peel reflector.

SPECIFICATIONS •

BAND I/J
RANGE
  downlook   26 nm (30 mi; 48 km)
  uplook   39 nm (45 mi; 72 km)
PEAK POWER INPUT 3.58 kW
SYSTEM WEIGHT 296 lb (134.3 kg)
SYSTEM VOLUME 3.6 ft³ (0.102 m³)
ANTENNA BEAMWIDTH 3.2° × 4.8°
ANTENNA DIMENSIONS
  length   2 ft 5 in (0.74 m)
  width   1 ft 7 in (0.48 m)
MAX SCAN IN AZIMUTH 60° either side
  of vertical centerline
MAX SCAN IN ELEVATION 60° above or
  below horizontal centerline

APG-66(V)

The AN/APG-66(V) is a variant of the APG-66 pulse-Doppler radar with a Line-Replaceable Unit (LRU) containing the Signal Data Processor (SDP) that replaced the APG-66's computer and digital signal processor. The SDP performs their combined functions with increased memory, throughput capacity, and processing speed. APG-66(V)'s detection range is 20% greater than that of the APG-66.

The system has all of APG-66's operational modes and includes an additional 12 modes: Track-While-Scan (TWS), dual-target situational awareness, interleaved map, weather avoidance, advanced situation awareness, high accuracy track, Ground Moving Target Indication (GMTI), Ground Moving Target Track (GMTT), maritime target track, multitarget attack/reattack, High-Resolution Map Along Track (HRMAT), and Doppler Beam Sharpening (DBS).

DEVELOPMENT • Manufactured by Westinghouse Electronic Systems Group, Baltimore, Maryland. Intended primarily for export.

SPECIFICATIONS •
BAND I/J
PEAK INPUT POWER   2.204 kW
SYSTEM WEIGHT   240 lb (108.9 kg)
SYSTEM VOLUME   2.91 ft³ (0.08 m³)

GD-53 (APG-67) Golden Dragon

The AN/APG-67(V) multimode radar is a relatively lightweight and short-range system that fits into a small volume. Despite its merits, the APG-67 series has been unsuccessful in F-5A/E refit competitions. Only a derivative of the APG-67(C), which shares 90% commonality with the -67(F), met with success, being developed for the Taiwanese Ching Kuo Indigenous Defense Fighter (IDF) as the GD-53 Golden Dragon.

The APG-67 is a coherent pulse-Doppler system that uses a flat-plate, vertically polarized, slotted array antenna on a direct-drive, two-axis balanced-gimbal mount. The transmitter has variable output power, pulse widths, and Pulse Repetition Frequencies (PRF).

The radar data computer contains two MIL-STD-1750A central processing units that can execute 256-point Fast Fourier Transform (FFT) coherent integration. It can be integrated into an avionics system through an MIL-STD-1553B digital databus interface and has Built-In Test (BIT) capability.

Air-to-air modes include Range-While-Search (RWS), Velocity Search (VS), Adaptive Search Mode (ASM), air-combat (four submodes) Single-Target-Track (STT), Situational Awareness Mode (SAM), and Track-While-Scan (TWS).

Air-to-ground modes include Real-Beam Ground Mapping (RBGM), Doppler Beam Sharpening (DBS), and surface moving target indication.

VARIANTS • APG-67(E/F) is the export-oriented variant with lower weight, smaller antenna for the F-5E/F.

Golden Dragon GD-53 is Extended-Range Radar (ERR) APG-67(C) variant for operation in Taiwanese Ching Kuo IDF.

DEVELOPMENT • Development of the APG-67 began in the late 1970s for the Northrop F-20 Tigershark (formerly F-5G) aircraft, using technology derived from the Modular Survivable Radar (MSR) program. After the F-20's cancellation, GE developed the APG-67(E) and (F) for retrofit to non-US F-5 Freedom Fighter/Tiger aircraft. The only production version, however, is the GD-53 fitted in Taiwan's IDF.

SPECIFICATIONS •
BAND I/J
PEAK POWER   -67(E)/(F) 3.5 kW
TRANSMIT POWER   -67(V) 200 watts;
   -67(E)/(F) 160 watts
RANGE, APG-67(F)
   RWS, look-up: 27–31 nm (31.1–35.7
      mi; 50–57.4 km)

RWS, look-down: 17–21 nm (19.6–24.2 mi; 31.5–39.9 km)
Air Combat: 10 nm (11.5 mi; 18.5 km)
SMTI, patrol craft, sea state 4: 26 nm (29.9 mi; 48.2 km); tank 19 nm (21.9 mi; 35.2 km)
WEIGHT, -67(F)   189 lb (86 kg)
SYSTEM VOLUME   2.1 ft³ (0.060 m³)
ANTENNA SIZE, -67(F)
height   11 in (279 mm)
width   17 in (432 mm)

APG-68

The AN/APG-68 radar is derived from the AN/APG-66 but is substantially improved, making it capable of supporting the AIM-120 Advanced Medium-Range Air-to-Air Missile (AMRAAM). It supports the expansion of the F-16's mission from day fighter to multirole aircraft. Performance improvements include increased range; sharper resolution, especially in the ground-mapping modes; and the addition of several modes.

Other improvements include a gridded, multiple peak power Traveling Wave Tube (TWT) transmitter and programmable signal processor possessing a block-oriented, random-access 386Kword nonvolatile memory.

In the air-to-air mode, the APG-68 can perform velocity search, look-up search, Range-While-Search (RWS), Track-While-Scan (TWS) up to 10 targets simultaneously, raid assessment, and gun director, and three short-range Air-Combat Maneuvering (ACM) target acquisition modes including displaying a target in the Head-Up Display (HUD) as well as vertical and boresight acquisition.

Surface-attack modes include real-beam ground mapping with scan freeze, Doppler beam sharpening, terrain avoidance, terrain following, sea surface search, air-to-surface ranging, fixed and moving target tracking, and beacon homing.

The APG-68 also has improved Electronic Counter-Countermeasures (ECCM) including reduced sidelobes.

DEVELOPMENT • Upgrading of APG-66 design began in 1978, with the radar achieving initial operational capability in 1985. Manufactured by Westinghouse Electric Corp., Baltimore, Maryland. Fitted only to the F-16C/D Fighting Falcon; however, the APG-66(V) uses many of the same components and is intended for export. See APG-66(V).

SPECIFICATIONS •
BAND   I/J

APG-70

The AN/APG-70 is an improved version of the AN/APG-63 attack radar designed for the F-15E Eagle fighter aircraft. The system has improved software and hardware, with all hardware conforming to MIL-STD-1750A architecture. APG-70 also has growth provisions for increased memory capacity, processing speed, and mode enhancements.

Air-to-ground modes include precision velocity update and air-to-ground ranging. The APG-70 permits the crew, flying at a low altitude, to pick out targets from distances over 73 nm (80 mi; 135 km). It can freeze images of a particular area, allowing the radar to be turned off so the aircraft can close in on the target without being detected through its radar emissions. The APG-70's air-to-ground weapons delivery and high-resolution mapping modes can only be accessed by those F-15C/D and F-15E aircraft that have dual-role capability.

The system uses Synthetic Aperture Radar (SAR) imagery for better resolution in the real-beam ground mapping and high-resolution ground mapping modes. The original resolution specification of 8.5 ft (2.6 m) resolution at 20 nm (23 mi; 37 km) range was met and may have been surpassed.

The APG-70's search modes in the air-to-air role are Range-While-Scan (RWS) and velocity search. Three RWS modes use high, medium, or interleaved Pulse Repetition Frequency (PRF). The APG-70's Track-While-Scan (TWS) mode is accessed once targets are sorted. Other modes in the air-to-air role are single-target track, raid-assessment track, vertical search, super search, boresight, and auto-gun target acquisition modes.

VARIANTS • AN/APG-80 is the modified version of the APG-70 for the Air Force's AC-130U Spectre special-operations aircraft by Hughes Aircraft. Five additional operational modes: fixed target track, ground moving target indication and tracking, projectile impact point position, beacon track, and a weather mode for firing in poor visibility. Upgrades also include a digital scan converter and modifications to the APG-70 signal processor and antenna.

DEVELOPMENT • Initial operational capability in 1986, with flight tests beginning in 1986 and continuing through mid-1988. The first production system was delivered in December 1986, and the first production APG-70-equipped F-15C/D was delivered in June 1987.

APG-70 is part of the Multistaged Improvement Program (MSIP) for the F-15, replacing the AN/APG-63 already installed in the aircraft. Retrofitted into approximately 39 F-15C/D and approximately 392 F-15E aircraft. Manufactured by Hughes Radar Systems Group, El Segundo, California, with a coproduction agreement with Mitsubishi in Japan.

COMBAT EXPERIENCE • During Operation Desert Storm, the APG-70 proved as effective as had been hoped, with many observers calling the F-15E/APG-70 combination the best strike aircraft in the world. As an air-to-ground radar, its resolution was said to be excel-lent over a long range. The radar was also reported to be very reliable.

SPECIFICATIONS •
BAND I/J

APG-71

The AN/APG-71 fire control radar is an upgrade of the AWG-9 weapons control system used in the US Navy F-14 Tomcat. It also shares 86% of the Shop-Replaceable Assemblies (SRA) with the APG-70 flown in the F-15C/E. The APG-71 is basically a digital version of the AWG-9 but represents a reworking of virtually every part of the system; only the transmitter, power supply, and aft cockpit tactical information display are retained from the AWG-9. Detection and tracking ranges increase by 40%, while reliability is expected to double in hours between failures.

A new broadband radar master oscillator contributes to improved Electronic Counter-Countermeasures (ECCM) capabilities. The analog-to-digital converter is claimed by Hughes to be state-of-the-art. The antenna control allows for more flexible search patterns than those of the AWG-9.

The fully programmable, four-unit signal processor and improved radar data processor permit greater simultaneous coverage of opening (target moving away) and closing (target heading toward aircraft) speeds. Additional modes permit Beyond Visual Range (BVR) target identification, raid assessment with high-resolution Doppler techniques to distinguish among closely spaced targets, monopulse angle tracking to predict the future position of a single target during high-speed maneuvers, and distortion-less sector ground mapping of both ocean and land areas.

The APG-71 can also be linked to Infrared Search and Tracking (IRST) for passive, long-range search making little use of the active radar. Digital scan control and improved frequency agility are also part of the upgrade.

The advanced low-sidelobe antenna is more difficult to jam. Its mount is different, but the antenna retains the gimbal system used in the AWG-9.

Further improvements planned or proposed for the APG-71 cover virtually every operational facet. Budget stringencies battle with the newly enhanced air-to-ground role envisioned for the F-14 to determine which shall be funded. They include:

- adding a medium Pulse Repetition Frequency (PRF) capability for air combat maneuvering
- interleaving high- and low-PRF waveforms for improved detection at greater range
- modifying the frequency modulation of the ranging Doppler to operate over a greater range
- improving ground clutter definition and ground moving-target indication and tracking
- manual terrain avoidance and clearance
- improved look-down, shoot-down capability over land
- adding high-resolution synthetic aperture and inverse synthetic aperture modes

DEVELOPMENT • The   APG-71 achieved initial operational capability in 1991. Manufactured by Hughes Aircraft, Radar Systems Group, in Los Angeles, California.

SPECIFICATIONS •
BAND   I/J

APG-73

The AN/APG-73 is a US-Canadian program to greatly improve the F/A-18 Hor-

net's APG-65 radar by retaining the transmitter and antenna, but updating the Receiver/Exciter and developing new components that replace the general-purpose Radar Data Processor (RDP) and digital Programmable Signal Processor (PSP). Better resolution, added modes, and better ECCM are some of the benefits.

Processing speed and power increases are considerable. The PSP's speed jumps from 7.1 million complex operations per second to 60 million; spare capacity allows a later increase to 80 million. Memory capacity expands to one megaword in the PSP and two megawords in the RDP. RDP speed increases to 2 million instructions per second. Analog-to-digital converters also speed up several times.

A later phase upgrades Synthetic Aperture Radar (SAR) mode processing and a motion sensor subsystem that counteracts distortions from airframe bending that degrade accuracy in the current inertial reference unit. A third phase would introduce the active array antenna.

DEVELOPMENT • A $65.7-million Full-Scale Engineering Development (FSED) contract was awarded to McDonnell Douglas Aircraft (Hughes Aircraft is major subcontractor) in May 1990; later awards raised the value to $223 million. Five engineering development prototypes and the first 15 production sets were contracted for in 1991. Testing began in 1993, with first production delivery in June 1994.

All F/A-18s built for the US Navy after 1989 are to operate APG-73s as well as several foreign air force customers.

SPECIFICATIONS •
BAND   I/J
WEIGHT   approx 450 lbs (204 kg)
VOLUME OCCUPIED   less than 14.8 ft³
   (0.42 m³)

APQ-122(V)

The AN/APQ-122(V) dual-frequency radar is part of the Adverse-Weather Aerial Delivery System (AWADS) used in the C-130 transport aircraft. The radar's functions include long-range navigation, weather avoidance, and ground mapping.

In the (V)8 version, separate I-band and K-band receiver/transmitters feed a common solid parabolic antenna; the I-band transmitter can also energize a circular antenna used in Terrain Avoidance/Terrain Following (TA/TF) flight. (An additional "cross-scan" mode interleaves TA and TF in a time-sharing pattern.)

I-band is used for weather plotting, ground mapping, and ground beacon interrogation. K-band permits high-resolution ground mapping in adverse weather. APQ-122s received a Systems Research Laboratories scan converter in the late 1980s that converts radar range and bearing returns into signals suitable for high-resolution (1,024 × 810 pixels), raster-scan Cathode-Ray Tube (CRT) displays.

VARIANTS • APQ-122(V)1 was fitted in C-130Es, APQ-122(V)5 was an I-band-only radar that replaced the AN/APN-59 in the C-130 and E-4B, and APQ-122(V)7 is used in navigation training in the T-43 aircraft, but is otherwise similar to (V)5.

DEVELOPMENT • Approximately 250 units produced, 150 exported in C-130s. Being replaced by the ESCO AN/APQ-175. Manufactured by Texas Instruments in Dallas, Texas.

SPECIFICATIONS •
BAND   I and K
RANGE
  ground mapping: 200 nm (230 mi; 371 km)
  weather information: 150 nm (173 mi; 278 km)
  beacon interrogation: 240 nm (276 mi; 444 km)

APQ-153

The AN/APQ-153 is a lightweight airborne fire control radar used in the F-5E aircraft. Its principal operational modes are search, boresight missile, and air-to-air gunnery.

In search mode, target detection range is 20 nm (23 mi; 37 km) and the search pattern is space-stabilized to counter aircraft pitch and roll to prevent loss of target. In the boresight missile mode, the pilot can acquire targets out to ten nautical miles for the AIM-9 Sidewinder missile.

The two heads-up air-to-air gunnery modes, one of which is for use in dogfights, automatically acquire the first target encountered and provide range and range-rate information to the sight for all targets.

DEVELOPMENT • Achieved initial operational capability in the early 1970s. Currently in use in the F-5E aircraft in several countries.

SPECIFICATIONS •
BAND   I

APQ-156

The AN/APQ-156 is a multimode airborne radar that combines into a single radar the A-6A Intruder's AN/APQ-92 search and terrain-following radar and AN/APQ-112 target tracking and ranging radar.

The main antenna has an overhanging horn feed that generates a narrow beam with a cosecant-squared profile, reducing detectability and eliminating the need for the radar to scan in elevation. Modes include Track-While-Scan (TWS) and Airborne Moving Target Indicator (AMTI) processing, ground mapping, and beacon detection and tracking.

The APQ-156 radar added a Forward-Looking Infrared (FLIR)/laser Target Recognition Attack Multisensor (TRAM) system to the A-6E aircraft. An interferometer under the main parabolic reflector aids in terrain avoidance. In an antenna that is slaved to the main antenna in azimuth, 64 horns in two rows detect elevation changes along the aircraft's route by comparing the differences in phase delays between the upper and lower rows.

Plans to upgrade the system met with program redirection and budgetary cutbacks.

VARIANTS • AN/APQ-148 was the first version of the APQ-156. The AN/APS-130 is similar but is fitted in the EA-6B Prowler EW aircraft.

DEVELOPMENT • The APQ-148 was delivered in 1971, and the APQ-156 followed in 1981. Some were used for retrofit into the A-6A. APQ-148 systems in older A-6Es were upgraded to APQ-156 standard. Manufactured by Norden Systems, Norwalk, Connecticut.

SPECIFICATIONS •
BAND J

APQ-159(V)

The AN/APQ-159(V) series is a family of forward-looking multimode pulse radars. Used in the search mode, the APQ-159(V) series has a range of up to 40 nm (74 km). For shorter search ranges, the system conducts a space-stabilized two-bar scan of the planar-array antenna using an 8°-wide beam.

In the missile boresight mode, used with the Infrared (IR)-seeking AIM-9 Sidewinder air-to-air missile, the radar

locks onto the target and provides steering information to bring the aircraft within the missile seeker's boresight envelope. Off-boresight expands the radar's target search envelope at longer ranges. For gunnery, the array locks into boresight and searches through a range gate of 500–6,000 ft (152–1,830 m) at the rate of 22,000 ft/sec (6,706 m/sec), automatically locking onto the first target it sees.

In the Electro-Optical (E-O) mode, the system operates the AGM-65 Maverick missile, relaying the image from the missile's E-O seeker to the cockpit display.

A few of these radars were installed in MiG-21 Fishbed aircraft that the US acquired for evaluation.

VARIANTS • APQ-159(V)1–(V)4 are variants, with differences in the number of controls and video indicators. APQ-159(V)5 is described as having a 100% increase in the maximum track/acquisition range and a 100% increase in reliability. Used in "Red Flag" aggressor-squadron F-5Es.

DEVELOPMENT • Manufactured by Emerson Electric (later ESCO), St. Louis, Missouri. In February 1991, CESELSA, the Spanish electronics company, announced that it would be fitting Spanish Air Force Mirage IIID and IIIE with the APQ-159; this raised export hopes, but that program was later canceled for budgetary reasons.

SPECIFICATIONS •
BAND I/J

APQ-164

The AN/APQ-164 multimode, dual-channel, coherent pulse-Doppler radar is the Offensive Radar Subsystem (ORS) of the AN/ASQ-184 Offensive Weapons Control System of the B-1 bomber. Unlike many of the other B-1 systems, the

APQ-164 has encountered few service problems, possibly because it was derived from the proven AN/APG-68 radar flown in the F-16C/D Fighting Falcon.

Each channel of the APQ-164 has its own independent set of Line-Replaceable Units (LRU), which can back up the other set. The LRUs include a gridded, multiple peak power Traveling Wave Tube (TWT) transmitter, radar receiver/transmitter, and programmable signal processor, all originally developed for the APG-68, as well as a radar video signal processor.

The phased-array antenna has 1,526 phase control modules that can be scanned electronically in both axes to +/−60°. The dish can be locked into one of three positions (looking ahead or 45° to either side). When side-looking, the radar's field of view extends up to 105° aft of straight ahead.

The radar's four basic functions are navigation and weather detection, penetration through low-level terrain following/terrain avoidance, weapons delivery, and rendezvous for air-to-air refueling.

Navigation uses the synthetic aperture mapping mode with real-beam ground mapping for high-resolution images as well as strip mapping when the radar is slewed to one side or the other.

Terrain avoidance is manual, but terrain following is automatic. In velocity update, the radar emits a narrow "flashlight" beam periodically (the periodicity depending on selection of a given clearance altitude out of 11, ride levels, and nature of terrain).

Moving Target Indicator (MTI) processing allows detection of moving targets within ground clutter, and Moving Target Track (MTT) establishes a track file. Other modes can provide updates to the bomb delivery system's altimeter as well as target survey.

Air-to-air modes chiefly concern rendezvous for refueling, weather detection, and beaconing.

DEVELOPMENT • Derived from the APG-68 and EAR series. Development began in 1981. Achieved initial operational capability in 1986. Manufactured by Westinghouse Electric, Baltimore, Maryland.

SPECIFICATIONS •
BAND   I/J
SYSTEM WEIGHT   1,257 lb (570 kg)
ANTENNA DIMENSIONS
  width   3 ft 8 in (1.12 m)
  height   1 ft 10 in (0.56 m)

APQ-169

The APQ-169 is the latest of a series of forward-looking multimode attack radars flown in US Air Force F-111 strike aircraft. The system has been updated several times and has had several designators.

The air-to-air mode provides automatic range search, target acquisition and tracking, and plots angle tracks in a Track-While-Scan (TWS) mode. Air-to-air use is limited to the Infrared (IR)-guided AIM-9 Sidewinder missile, as the radar does not have a semiactive mode. The air-to-ground mode can be used for all-weather weapons delivery, navigational position fixing, and air-to-ground ranging.

The APQ-169 introduced pulse compression for better range resolution, a 0.25 pulse width, and a television raster-scan display. More important is the extensive reliability and maintenance upgrade that raised the mean time between failures substantially.

VARIANTS • APQ-113 (F-111A/E and RAAF F-111C), APQ-114 (FB-111A), APQ-144 (F-111F), APQ-161 (supports with AN/AVQ-26 Pave Tack electro-optical target designator system), APQ-163 (modified APQ-144 used in the B-1A bomber prototype program), APQ-165 (RAAF F-111C radar with Pave Tack and Harpoon antiship compatibility).

DEVELOPMENT • Began in the mid-1960s for the APQ-113/114. The APQ-169 achieved initial operational capability in the mid-1980s. Manufactured by GE in Utica, New York.

SPECIFICATIONS •

BAND   J
PULSE WIDTHS   0.2, 0.25, 0.4, 1.2, or 2.4 microsec
PRF   337–4,044 Hz

RANGE

I/J-band at 250 ft (76 m) above ground level, 20 nm (23 mi; 37 km); in 0.4-in (10-mm)/hr rainfall, 14 nm (16 mi; 26 km)

J-band can see coastlines at 50 nm (58 mi; 93 km), towers at 5 nm (5.8 mi; 9.3 km)

J-band radar beacon detection: 240 nm (276 mi; 444 km)

J-band, severe-weather cell: 150 nm (173 mi; 278 km)

APQ-170

The AN/APQ-170 was developed for the MC-130H Combat Talon II to support low-level, adverse-weather Special Operations Command missions. It is actually a combination of two radars: a flat, circular I/J-band (old X band) antenna and back-to-back, solid truncated paraboloid J-band (old Ku band) reflectors. The mount is fitted in the MC-130H's nose.

The I/J-band radar swivels through arcs of 90° horizontally, 75° vertically for terrain avoidance, terrain following, and beacon location. The J-band antennas rotate at up to 30 rpm for weather detection, ground mapping, and beacon location. If the J-band radars fail, the I/J-band system can take over weather detection and ground mapping.

Both radars are designed to see through rainfall, although at a reduced distance.

Software problems slowed acceptance of the APQ-170.

DEVELOPMENT • The APQ-170 achieved initial operational capability in 1993. Manufactured by ESCO in St. Louis, Missouri.

SPECIFICATIONS •

BAND

terrain avoidance/terrain following
I/J
weather   J

APQ-171

The AN/APQ-171 is the latest version of a series of dual-channel, multimode, forward-looking radars fitted in the F-111 deep-strike aircraft. Earlier models of the APQ-171 were the APQ-110 for the F-111A/C/E, APQ-128 for the F-111D, the APQ-146 in the F-111F, and the APQ-134 for the FB-111. The APQ-171 is similar in function to the earlier versions but is more reliable and more easily maintained. Compared to the original radar, the APQ-171 is a 75% redesign, with reliability improving sixfold.

Each version has a pair of multimode, forward-looking radars using identical antennas. The Terrain-Following Radar (TFR) automatically keeps the aircraft at a preset ground clearance by signaling the flight control system. Other TFR modes are terrain avoidance, ground mapping, and situation.

If the AN/APQ-169 attack radar should fail, the weapons control system can use the APQ-171 as a backup ground-mapping system by using its transmitter to drive the APQ-169's antenna. For air-to-ground ranging, the antennas are slaved to the lead-computing optical sight in elevation; their azimuth is corrected to the drift angle generated by the sight.

DEVELOPMENT • The APQ-110 entered service in the F-111A in 1967. After modifications to increase reliability and maintainability are completed, all earlier radars in the series are redesignated AN/APQ-171. Manufactured by Texas Instruments in Dallas, Texas.

SPECIFICATIONS •
BAND   J

APQ-174

The AN/APQ-174 Multimode Radar (MMR) was developed for the Special Operations Command MH-47E and MH-60K covert operation helicopters. It is based on the terrain-following radar found in the AAQ-13 navigation pod of the LANTIRN system. The small antenna means a relatively short range and lower resolution, but the APQ-174's compactness and low weight suit it well for volume-limited aircraft such as the MH-60.

Like the LANTIRN radar, the MMR modes include manual Terrain-Following Radar (TFR) flight, Very Low Clearance (VLC), weather, Low Probability of Intercept (LPI), and Electronic Counter-Countermeasures (ECCM). In addition, the APQ-174 offers Terrain Avoidance (TA), Ground Mapping (GM), and air-to-air ranging. Also, the APQ-174 can interleave the TF and TA modes as well as the TF and GM modes.

DEVELOPMENT • First funding came in 1990, with production contracts being awarded in 1992. Initial operational capability was achieved in 1994.

SPECIFICATIONS •
BAND   J

APQ-175

The AN/APQ-175 is the successor to the APQ-122 Adverse-Weather Aerial Delivery System (AWADS) radar set fitted in many C-130s. Like the AN/APQ-170, also produced by ESCO, the system combines two radars: an I/J-band (old X band) antenna for weather detection and long-range ground mapping and a K-band (old Ka band) for shorter-range precision ground mapping. The system also features dual independent high-resolution displays.

Both radars are designed to see through rainfall, although at a reduced distance.

DEVELOPMENT • First contracts awarded in mid-1980s for delivery of the first 50 production units beginning in 1990. The APQ-175 achieved initial operational capability in 1993. Manufactured by Electronics and Space Corp. (ESCO) in St. Louis, Missouri.

SPECIFICATIONS •
BAND
 long-range ground mapping and weather
   I/J
 precision ground mapping
   K
RANGE   I/J band long-range ground mapping: 175 nm (202 mi; 324 km)

APQ-181

The B-2's AN/APQ-181 radar emphasizes Low Probability of Intercept (LPI) design and operation and features 21 pulsed or pulse-Doppler search, detection, and track modes as well as penetration and navigation Synthetic Aperture Radar (SAR) modes.

Each B-2 has two fully redundant radar systems, each with five Line-Replaceable Units (LRU) and a MIL-STD-1553 digital databus. All LRUs except the antenna can function for both radars if necessary. Each system has a liquid-cooled, gridded Traveling Wave Tube (TWT) transmitter, air-cooled receiver that performs pulse compression and generates RF waveforms, fully programmable Radar Signal Processor (RSP), and Radar Data Processor (RDP) that develops the beam-steering commands used by the antennas' beam-steering computers.

The two liquid-cooled electronically scanned antennas are buried in the forward fuselage sides, each about 8 ft (2.44 m) from the aircraft's centerline and just behind the nose-gear compartment (which holds the other LRUs). Using a monopulse feed and steered in two axes, the radar achieves fractional beamwidth angular resolution. SAR operation requires correction for antenna movement, achieved through a Smiths Industries modified strap-down inertial platform.

DEVELOPMENT • Some modules were derived from the APG-70 and APG-71 fighter aircraft radars. The APQ-181 was first tested in the KC-135 Avionics Flight Test Bed (AFTB) in January 1987, amassing over 1,600 hours of operation—including more than 1,000 hours in 172 flights devoted to radar testing—up to January 1991.

Although the APQ-181 was tested on the first Air Vehicle (AV-1) to fly, the third, AV-3, is the avionics test bed. The radar is manufactured by Hughes Aircraft, Torrance, California.

SPECIFICATIONS •
BAND J (12.5–18 GHz)
WEIGHT
  system   2,100 lb (953 kg)
  antennas   575 lb (261 kg)
VOLUME 52.5 ft³ (1.49 m³)

APS-115

The APS-115 is an airborne search radar used primarily for maritime patrol and Antisubmarine Warfare (ASW) operations. The system uses two antennas, one in the nose and one in the tail of the P-3C Orion aircraft. The antennas scan 45° sectors and can be tilted through a −20°/+10° arc.

Also part of the system are two transmitter/receivers, an antenna position programmer, dual set controls, and a common antenna control unit. Long pulses at relatively low scan rates and Pulse Repetition Frequencies (PRF) aid long-range search. For target classification at shorter ranges, the radar switches to a short-pulse, higher-scan, higher-PRF mode.

DEVELOPMENT • Achieved initial operational capability in 1969 in early P-3C aircraft. Manufactured by Texas Instruments.

SPECIFICATIONS •
BAND I
PEAK POWER 143 kW
PULSE WIDTH 0.5 or 2.5 microsec
PRF 1,600 or 400 Hz
SCAN RATE 12 or 6 rpm
SYSTEM WEIGHT 523 lb (237 kg)
ANTENNA BEAMWIDTH 2.4° × 3.6°

APS-116
APS-137

The AN/APS-116 is a coherent, pulse-Doppler Antisubmarine Warfare (ASW) search radar designed to detect submarine periscopes and antennas in rough seas. It has been developed further as the export-oriented AN/APS-134 and the succeeding AN/APS-137(V), which has an added Inverse Synthetic Aperture Radar (ISAR) mode. The system's scanner is mounted in a nose radome, and the radar is integrated with the aircraft's data systems.

In its periscope-detection mode in high sea states, the radar uses high peak power, high scan rates (300 rpm) for high resolution, short pulse widths (2.5

nanoseconds), high Pulse Repetition Frequencies/PRF (2,000 Hz), pulse compression, and Moving Target Indicator (MTI) processing.

For navigation and surface search, the operator can select either a lower scan rate and low PRF with pulse compression for high resolution of maritime targets or Track-While-Scan (TWS) processing. A relatively slow scan rate, low PRF, and frequency agility serve for long-range search and navigation.

The APS-137 adds Inverse Synthetic Aperture Radar (ISAR) processing in which the radar acts as a searchlight, "staring" at a given point on a target. Processing the Doppler shifts of other parts of the target due to roll and pitch motion generates a two-dimensional image. Range resolution is nominally 6 ft (1.8 m) but can be reduced to 1.5 ft (0.46 m). Up to 32 ships can be tracked simultaneously. Subvariants include APS-137(V)1 (S-3), APS-137(V)2 (P-3C Update III aircraft), APS-137(V)3 (P-3C Update IV), APS-137(V)4 (Coast Guard HC-130 Search and Rescue/SAR aircraft), APS-137(H) (helicopter-based system).

DEVELOPMENT • APS-116 achieved its initial operational capability in 1974. Manufactured by Texas Instruments, Dallas, Texas. APS-137(V) is in production for P-3, S-3B.

SPECIFICATIONS •
BAND I (9.5–10 GHz)
WEIGHT   472 lb (214 kg)

APS-124

The AN/APS-124 radar is fitted in the US Navy's SH-60B Seahawk helicopter as part of the LAMPS III shipboard surveillance system. Designed primarily to detect submarine periscopes and masts, the APS-124 also searches for and acquires targets for antiship cruise missiles. It is not fitted in the SH-60F variant of this helicopter, which is the carrier-based model fitted with active dipping sonar, or other navalized SH-60 variants.

The APS-124 was configured for a "flat" radome that could be positioned under the forward fuselage of the SH-60. It is linked to other systems through its MIL-STD-1553 digital databus. The planar-array antenna rotates up to 120 rpm. Images can be displayed in the helicopter while in flight as well as being data-linked to surface-ship displays.

Three data modes using different pulse widths and Pulse Repetition Frequencies (PRF) provide for long- and medium-range search as well as fast-scan surveillance. An OU-103/A digital scan converter performs scan-to-scan integration of the returns, helping to screen out clutter.

DEVELOPMENT • The   APS-124 achieved initial operational capability in the SH-60B in 1983. Manufactured by Texas Instruments, Equipment Group, Dallas, Texas. All SH-60 operators use the APS-124.

SPECIFICATIONS •
WEIGHT   210 lbs (95 kg)
BAND   I/J
RANGE TO DETECT A 10.8-FT^2 (1-M^2) TARGET   16 nm (18 mi; 30 km)
PEAK POWER   350 kW
PULSE WIDTH
   long range: 2 microsec
   medium range: 1 microsec
   fast scan: 0.5 microsec
PRF
   long range: 470 Hz
   medium range: 940 Hz
   fast scan: 1,880 Hz
ANTENNA BEAMWIDTH   1.2° × 20°
ANTENNA DIMENSIONS
   width   6 ft (1.83 m)
   height   1 ft (0.31 m)

APS-125
APS-138
APS-139

This series of radars is the principal sensor for the E-2C shipboard Airborne Early Warning (AEW) aircraft. It can track 300 targets simultaneously at ranges of about 250 nm (288 mi; 463 km). The system is mounted in later E-2C Hawkeye aircraft and has a 24-ft (7.93-m) diameter rotodome mounted above the fuselage.

Some observers have contended that the APS-125 series radar system's range and processing capability, while impressive in the 1970s when the earlier variants were introduced, lagged behind the threat in the 1980s and 1990s. In many scenarios, the E-2 has come to rely on the radars of the scouting interceptors it was designed to support for initial detection of the enemy. During Operations Desert Shield and Desert Storm, moreover, the system proved relatively limited and inflexible, especially in comparison to the E-3 AWACS and Aegis ship-based sensor systems.

The APS-125 evolved from the APS-120 system found in the earlier E-2 aircraft but added the digital Advanced Radar-Processing Subsystem (ARPS) that coaxes targets out of clutter.

The APS-138 has an improved over-land/water capability through a Randtron Total Radiation Aperture Control Antenna (TRAC-A) that features low sidelobes. Using a Loral array track processor, the aircraft can simultaneously track more than 600 air targets and control up to 40 interceptions.

The APS-139, which was fitted to E-2Cs delivered from 1988 on, has an upgraded processor that allows tracking of more than 2,000 targets. In addition, the system has better Electronic Counter-Countermeasures (ECCM).

The rotodome revolves freely in the airstream at the rate of 6 rpm. It provides sufficient lift to offset its own weight in

flight and can be lowered to facilitate handling the aircraft aboard ship. To make the most effective use of the radar, the E-2 cruises with a 10° flap setting, which gives the rotodome the desired 3° of incidence for scanning.

DEVELOPMENT • The   APS-125 achieved initial operational capability in 1976, followed by the APS-138 in 1983 and the APS-139 in 1988. Manufactured by General Electric in Utica, New York. Four Customs Service P-3 anti-drug-smuggling surveillance aircraft use APS-138 systems.

SPECIFICATIONS •
BAND B/C (UHF)
RANGE 250 nm (288 mi; 463 km)
NUMBER OF TARGETS more than 300

APS-127

This search radar was built for use on the 41 US Coast Guard HU-25A Guardian surveillance aircraft; it also equips some aircraft in the Netherlands Air Force. It can be used in all weather conditions for search-and-rescue efforts as well as drug interdiction missions and enforcement of laws and treaties.

The APS-127 resembles the AN/APS-124 used on the SH-60B in that it has a lightweight, fast-scanning planar-array antenna, with scan-to-scan integration and direct-view displays for the pilot and surveillance system operator.

DEVELOPMENT • Achieved initial operational capability in 1982; produced until 1984. Manufactured by Texas Instruments, Fort Worth, Texas.

SPECIFICATIONS •
BAND I/J
RANGE AGAINST 10.8 FT^2 (1 M^2) TARGET 18 nm (20.7 mi; 33.3 km)
PEAK POWER 200 kW
PULSE WIDTH 0.5 or 2.0 microsec
PRF 1,600 or 400 Hz
SYSTEM WEIGHT 295 lb (134 kg)

ANTENNA BEAMWIDTH   5° × 6°
ANTENNA DIMENSIONS
   width   2 ft (0.62 m)
   height   2 ft 6 in (0.76 m)

APS-133(V)

The AN/APS-133(V) is one of the most widely used color weather radars in US military service. Based on the commercial RDR-1F radar, the APS-133(V) is fitted to most US Air Force transports as well as several Marine Corps aircraft.

The stabilized parabolic antenna can emit either a pencil or fan beam and has varying scan angle. In the Type 2, the sector scan control panel allows adjustment of the scan angle from 15° to 75° to each side of the centerline, and the centerline can vary up to 75° to the right or left of the aircraft's longitudinal axis.

The receiver/transmitter uses a solid-state modulator that transmits on three different pulse widths depending on its mode and has two Pulse Repetition Frequencies (PRFs).

DEVELOPMENT • First entered military service as part of C-141B upgrade in the 1970s. Installed on C-5, C-18, C-130, E-3, E-4, E-6, KC-10, and VC-25 (Air Force One) aircraft. The US Marine Corps introduced the later Type 2 in its aircraft in 1984.

SPECIFICATIONS •
BAND   I (9.375 GHz)
TRANSMIT POWER   65 kW
RANGE
   weather: 300 nm (345 mi; 556 km)
   mapping or beacon: more than 250 nm (288 mi; 463 km)
   skin painting/air-to-air: 30 nm (34.5 mi; 55.6 km)
PRF   200 or 800 Hz
PULSE WIDTH   0.4, 2.35, or 5.0 microsec
SYSTEM WEIGHT   104.4 lb (46.4 kg)
ANTENNA BEAM WIDTH   2.9° (30-in antenna), 4.4° (22-in antenna)
ANTENNA SCAN RATE   45°/sec

APS-134

The AN/APS-134 is a coherent, pulse-Doppler Antisubmarine Warfare (ASW) search radar derived from the AN/APS-116 radar for international sales. It is designed to detect submarine periscopes and antennas in rough seas. The system's scanner is mounted in a nose radome, and the radar is integrated with the aircraft's data systems.

In its periscope-detection mode in high sea states, the radar uses high peak power of 500 kW, high scan rates (150 rpm) with scan-to-scan processing for high resolution, short pulse widths, high Pulse Repetition Frequencies (PRF), pulse compression, and Moving Target Indicator (MTI) processing. Resolution is 1.5 ft (0.46 m).

For navigation and surface search, the operator can select a high scan rate, high PRF, and pulse compression for high resolution of maritime targets; Track-While-Scan (TWS) is also available. A relatively slow scan rate, low PRF, and frequency agility are used for long-range search and navigation. The system can also apply Inverse Synthetic Aperture Radar (ISAR) processing to identify surface-ship targets.

The antenna is a vertically polarized, heart-shaped parabolic dish with feed horn and pressurized waveguide.

DEVELOPMENT • In production; manufactured by Texas Instruments. Fitted in updated New Zealand P-3B Orion, German Atlantic, and US Coast Guard HC-130 aircraft as well as new Pakistani P-3Cs.

SPECIFICATIONS •
WEIGHT   522 lb (237 kg)
BAND   I (9.5–10 GHz)
POWER
   Peak   500 kW
   average   500 W

PULSE WIDTHS
periscope detection
2.5 nanosec
PRF
periscope detection
2,000 Hz
long-range, high-resolution or surveillance
500 Hz
ANTENNA BEAMWIDTH   2.4° × 4°
SCAN RATE
periscope detection
150 rpm
navigation/surface search
40 rpm
long-range search and navigation
6 rpm

APS-144

The APS-144 is one of the sensors developed for the US Army's Airborne Reconnaissance Low/ARL (formerly Grisly Hunter) program. ARL is being deployed in converted DHC-7 transports to aid in border surveillance. The small, low-power pulse-Doppler APS-144 should be able to detect small, slow-moving targets from the air. The usual benchmark is given as "a man leading a pack animal."

The radar was tested under the chin of a UH-60 helicopter, in a DHC-6 Twin Otter transport, and on board an Amber Unmanned Air Vehicle (UAV). Early versions had a 15.7-in (0.45-m) diameter antenna and an 8.1-nm (9.3-mi; 15-km) range.

DEVELOPMENT • First trials began in the late 1980s. Flight tests with the UH-60 occurred in 1991. Deployment of the ARL began in 1995–96. In production by AIL Systems.

SPECIFICATIONS •
WEIGHT   less than 100 lb (45 kg)
DIAMETER   2 ft 3½ in (0.7 m)
SEARCH RANGE   10.8 nm (12.4 mi; 20 km)
RESOLUTION IN "SPOTLIGHT" MODE   50 ft (15 m)

APS-145

The AN/APS-145 is an upgraded version of the AN/APS-125 surveillance radar fitted in US-built E-2C Hawkeye Airborne Early Warning (AEW) aircraft. It is likely to be the last of the series, with later shipboard AEW aircraft mounting conformal, or fixed, phased-array antennas.

The APS-145 introduced a lower Pulse Repetition Frequency (PRF) and rotodome rotation rate to extend the radar's range. Improvements in processing capability offset the coarsened velocity resolution that results from the lower PRF and rotation rate.

It also features "environmental processing" to screen out ground clutter. The search area is broken down into cells, each of which is assessed for clutter and target density. Sensitivity to clutter (both natural and man-made) can be adjusted by cell, which refines the system's Electronic Counter-Countermeasures (ECCM). Automatic scan-to-scan checking of the 10 available transmission channels avoids jamming.

The rotodome revolves freely in the airstream at the rate of 5 rpm.

DEVELOPMENT • Initial operational capability was achieved in 1991. Manufactured by Lockheed Martin Electronics Division, Utica, New York.

SPECIFICATIONS •
BAND   B/C
RANGE   350 nm (400 mi; 644 km)

APY-1/APY-2 AWACS

The APY-1 is the primary radar for the E-3A Airborne Warning and Control System (AWACS) aircraft.

The AWACS antenna is mechanically scanned in azimuth and electronically scanned in elevation. While in flight, but not in operation, the saucer- shaped, 30-ft

(9.14-m) diameter rotodome rotates at ¼ rpm to lubricate the bearings. Rotation speed climbs to 6 rpm during operation. The antenna is electronically scanned in elevation.

Most operational AWACS aircraft use an IBM CC-2 computer with a 665,360-word memory that is three times as fast as the earlier CC-1. Operating in the F-band, the radar uses pulse and pulse-Doppler modes as well as a high Pulse Repetition Frequency (PRF) for better look-down performance and higher resolution of targets with small Radar Cross Sections (RCS). The system can choose among several pulse widths depending on mode, and the antenna has low sidelobes, which reduces its sensitivity to jamming. Moveover, the radar's azimuthal scan can be broken into 24 sectors, some of which can be "blanked" (not scanned) to permit more detailed processing of other sectors.

Under the Radar System Improvement Program (RSIP), the system receives a new CC-2E system computer, new programming, a new surveillance radar computer, pulse compression, and the use of Fast Fourier Transform (FFT) processing to extract targets.

DEVELOPMENT • Development began in 1962, with the brassboard version entering test in 1971. Production began in 1975, and the first version achieved initial operational capability in 1978.

SPECIFICATIONS •
BAND   F
MAX RANGE
   bomber: 300 nm (345 mi; 556 km)
   fighter with 75.3-ft² (7-m²) radar cross section: 200 nm (230 mi; 370 km)

AWG-9

The AN/AWG-9 is the F-14 Tomcat's weapons control system that can simultaneously track up to 24 targets and guide missiles to six of them. Developed to control the AIM-54 Phoenix air-to-air missile, the AWG-9 can be used with AIM-7 Sparrow, AIM-9 Sidewinder, and AIM-120 AMRAAM, as well as for the F-14's M61 20-mm Gatling gun.

Although the AWG-9 has an impressive potential for fleet defense, the Phoenix has never been used in combat, and the F-14's success rate with Sparrows against hostile targets in the 1980s (four Libyan and one Iranian aircraft) was one out of six. In fact, three of four Libyan aircraft shot down by F-14s were hit by IR-guided Sidewinders at close range.

The slotted planar-array antenna has a 36-in (914-mm) diameter and two rows of six dipole arrays for the Identification Friend or Foe (IFF) system. It is raster-scanned in "bars." The AWG-9 radar can detect targets as low as 50 ft (15 m) and as high as 80,000 ft (24,384 m) at ranges over 115 nm (132 mi; 213 km), and across a front more than 150 nm (173 mi; 278 km) wide.

Its Traveling Wave Tube (TWT) transmitters can generate Continuous Wave (CW), pulse, and pulse-Doppler beams. One TWT provides CW illumination of a target for the Sparrow's Semiactive Radar (SAR) homing seeker. The other TWT provides either conventional pulse or pulse-Doppler beams and can operate in one of several modes.

Pulse modes include Search (PS) and Single-Target Track (PSTT). Pulse-Doppler modes include Search (PDS) for range rate and bearing, Range-While-Scan (RWS) that generates a range as well as range rate and bearing, Single-Target Track (PDSTT), and Track-While-Scan (TWS) for Phoenix missile targeting of up to 24 targets simultaneously. Time-sharing techniques permit simultaneous midcourse guidance of six Phoenixes at once against six different targets.

Other modes include a Vertical Scan Lock-on (VSL) with a lower threshold between 15° below the aircraft axis (ending at 25° above) and 15° above (ending at

55° above). Pilot Rapid Location (PRL) is effectively a boresight mode using a 2.3°-wide beam.

Both conventional and pulse-Doppler modes can be slaved to an Infrared Search and Tracking (IRST) system in which the IRST passively acquires a target and the radar illuminates the target at the appropriate time.

DEVELOPMENT • Development began in the mid-1960s as part of the abortive F-111B fleet defense aircraft program. Production of complete AWG-9 systems began in the early 1970s and ended in August 1988; spares manufacture ended in 1989. Manufactured by Hughes Aircraft Co. Radar Systems Group, El Segundo, California.

SPECIFICATIONS •
BAND   I/J
MAX RANGE
  pulse search: 63 nm (73 mi; 117 km)
  PSTT: 49 nm (56 mi; 91 km)
  PDS of 53.8-ft² (5-m²) target: 115 nm
    (132 mi; 213 km)
  RWS, TWS: 90 nm (104 mi; 167 km)
  VSL, PRL: 5 nm (6 mi; 9 km)
  CW illumination for Sparrow: 38 nm
    (44 mi; 70 km)
PEAK POWER   10 kW (7 kW in pulse-Doppler, 500 W in pulse)
PULSE WIDTH   0.4 and 50 microsec in pulse; 0.4, 1.3, 2.0, or 2.7 in pulse-Doppler
SYSTEM WEIGHT   1,300 lb (590 kg)
SYSTEM VOLUME   28 ft³ (0.79 m³)

GROUND RADARS

MPQ-53

The AN/MPQ-53 is the multipurpose assembly of radars that is part of the Patriot Surface-to-Air Missile (SAM) system. Emphasis is on real-time response, the ability to operate in a heavy Electronic Countermeasures (ECM) environment, and the flexibility to adapt to changing threats. During Patriot engagements in Saudi Arabia and Israel during Operation Desert Storm, the operators claimed that the radar was detecting targets at more than 54 nm (62 mi; 100 km). Upgrades will permit greater flexibility in launcher deployments and for a range increase. Later radars will have a dual Traveling Wave Tube (TWT) transmitter and low-noise exciter.

The upper half of the rectangular antenna mount is dominated by a large, G-band phased-array antenna that performs both surveillance and tracking. The roughly circular array consists of more than 5,000 phase-shifting elements. Below and to the outside of the lower arc

of the large array are two smaller arrays, each with more than 50 phase shifters. Above and to the outside of the upper arc are two covered antennas.

Dividing the rectangular mount in half is a row of 18 rectangular boxes. Below the row are access panels and four more planar arrays. Three are similar in size to the two sited below the large array. They are located at the bottom of the mount. A larger array of approximately 250 phase shifters is mounted just below the row of boxes. At least one array is the Hazeltine AN/TPX-46(V)7 Interrogation Friend or Foe (IFF) interrogator. The other planar antennas provide command guidance and receive signals from the missile.

The radars and missile launch controls are commanded by a computer housed in the trailer.

DEVELOPMENT • Raytheon began development of the radar in the SAM-D program of the late 1960s, achieving initial operational capability in 1985. In production by Raytheon Company, Andover, Massachusetts. In service in the US Army and several other countries.

SPECIFICATIONS •
BAND   G

MPQ-54/MPA-49/TPQ-32 FAAR

The Forward Area Alerting Radar (FAAR) is a family of air defense radars designed to provide early warning to air defense weapons systems such as the Vulcan, Chaparral, and Redeye. They are mobile, pulse-Doppler systems designed to detect low-flying aircraft in high-clutter environments. Specific FAAR systems are the AN/TPQ-32 (cabin- and trailer-mounted), AN/MPQ-54 (trailer-mounted), and the AN/MPA-49 (truck-mounted).

The FAAR system includes a primary open-mesh truncated paraboloid reflector and secondary Identification Friend or Foe (IFF) radar antenna assembly on a four-section telescoping mast. The operations shelter contains radar data extraction and processing units, operator's console, and VHF voice and data links.

DEVELOPMENT • Prototypes entered tests in 1968, with the system achieving initial operational capability in the early 1970s. Manufactured by Sanders Associates, Nashua, New Hampshire and Unisys, Great Neck, New York.

(CW) correlation techniques and coherent Doppler pulse modulation.

Detection logic uses both velocity and range gates. The "all-range" channel searches for moving targets, while the "discrete-range" channel (or range gate) detects a target moving into that range. When a target is found within the gate, the operator hears a rising tone and sees a lighted display.

DEVELOPMENT • Entered service in 1975. Manufactured by Amex Systems of Hawthorne, California (a subsidiary of General Dynamics). More than 1,650 had been sold before production ended. A later PPS-15B Model 386 had twice the maximum range, seven range gates, pseudo-random CW code modulation, and adjustable sector scan. It was not adopted for service, however.

COMBAT EXPERIENCE • PPS-15 radars were used by the US FBI for surveillance of the Lake Placid, New York, sites during the 1980 Winter Olympics. (So far as is known, they encountered no combat.)

SPECIFICATIONS •
BAND   J
RANGE
  vehicles   3,281 yd (3,000 m)
  personnel   1,640 yd (1,500 m)
SYSTEM WEIGHT   23.6 lb (10.7 kg)

PPS-15

The AN/PPS-15 is a lightweight, portable, short-range perimeter surveillance radar that can be remotely operated. The PPS-15 can be mounted on a tripod or vehicle and is battery-powered.

Its rectangular antenna can be set for automatic sector scan on a given bearing with a selectable scan azimuth width. The PPS-15 transceiver uses Continuous Wave

P-STAR

The Portable Search and Target Recognition Radar (P-STAR) is a lightweight surveillance radar for light infantry units. It is designed to detect both low-flying aircraft and helicopters.

The P-STAR's rectangular planar-array antenna has an integral Identification Friend or Foe (IFF) transponder and is sheathed in fiberglass. The Liquid-Crystal

Diode (LCD) display may be remotely located up to 109 yd (100 m) from the radar itself. The relatively powerful transmitter has 19 channels and Pulse Repetition Frequencies (PRF). The receiver's 60-dB subclutter visibility increases the range at which aircraft can be detected.

Signal processing places a premium on early target alerting and cuing to afford as much reaction time as possible. A primary channel detects both aircraft and helicopters; a secondary channel is designed to look for the peculiar Doppler returns from rotating helicopter blades.

To counter Electronic Countermeasures (ECM), the P-STAR employs frequency agility, sector blanking, strobe-on-jam, automatic search for a channel clear of jamming, and two sidelobe cancelers to block sidelobe jamming.

DEVELOPMENT • Development began in 1988; production prototype tested in May 1990, achieving initial operational capability in 1993. Manufactured by Sanders Associates Inc., a division of Lockheed, in Nashua, New Hampshire.

SPECIFICATIONS •

BAND   D
RANGE   11.9 nm (13.7 mi; 22 km)
HEIGHT COVERAGE   0–10,000 ft
   (3,054 m)
ACCURACY
   azimuth   +/−3° RMS
   range   +/−345 yd (300 m)
POWER
   peak   1,000 W
   average   50 W
SYSTEM WEIGHT   approx 300 lb (137 kg)
ANTENNA SCAN RATE   10 rpm
BEAM ELEVATION   −5°/+30°, adjustable over −5°/+5° range

TPQ-36 Firefinder

The AN/TPQ-36 is a member of the Firefinder family of mortar-locating radars, the other system being the longer-range and less mobile AN/TPQ-37. The short-range TPQ-36 replaced the AN/MPQ-4 mortar-locating radar, but it also locates rocket and artillery. The system can also be used to correct "friendly fire." A developed version is being produced as the AN/MPQ-64 Ground-Based Sensor (GBS).

This Three-Dimensional (3D), range-gated pulse-Doppler, vehicle-mounted system performs automatic scanning of a 90° sector of the horizon several times a second and can be expanded for 360° coverage when needed. Frequency shifts elevate the pencil beam, phase shifting steers it horizontally. The resulting beam-width is 2° in azimuth, 1.8° in elevation. A separate track channel for each projectile permits simultaneous tracking and measurement. This technique also allows the radar to designate another channel for uninterrupted scanning of the horizon. The TPQ-36 is effective in high-clutter environments.

The beams form a "fence" along the topographic horizon and "tag" every return. The system's processor calculates the projectile's origin by extrapolation of its trajectory and displays the firing weapon's coordinates and altitude on a grid. This data is stored, and subsequent projectiles fired from weapons that have been located are ignored. The data can be fed directly to artillery fire control centers.

The TPQ-36 is vehicle- and trailer-mounted, typically using the 2½-ton truck and more recently variants of the High-Mobility Multipurpose Wheeled Vehicle (HMMWV).

VARIANTS • AN/TPQ-36(A) is the Low-Altitude Surveillance Radar (LASR) that uses about 70% of the same components as the TPQ-36 from which it evolved. LASR, however, is a 3D, vehicle-mounted, air defense surveillance radar that detects and tracks helicopters and low-flying targets. First entered production for the US Army in 1987. NOAH is the LASR selected for the Norwegian Adapted HAWK (NOAH) surface-to-air missile program directed by a Norwegian fire control system.

DEVELOPMENT • Hughes Aircraft Ground Systems Group, Fullerton, California, won a full-scale, three-year contract from the US Army for development of the TPQ-36 in August 1978. TPQ-36 went into US Army service in 1981, with the US Marine Corps following; the Netherlands was the first foreign buyer in 1982, followed by 13 other countries.

The MPQ-64 Ground-Based Sensor (GBS) is based on the TPQ-36A and was selected in 1992 by the US Army as a nondevelopmental GBS for the Army's Forward Area Air Defense System (FAADS). 154 had been planned by 2001, but this number was later scaled back to 117, then to 85.

COMBAT EXPERIENCE • The TPQ-36 was used by the US Marine Corps peacekeeping force in Lebanon in 1983 and 1984. Thailand used the Firefinder during border disputes with Laos in the late 1980s and was reportedly dissatisfied with its performance.

TPQ-36s were deployed with US units in Saudi Arabia as part of Operation Desert Shield. Both Firefinder types received urgent software modifications that enabled them to plot launch points for Tactical Ballistic Missiles (TBM). 20 Army and Marine Corps Firefinders were modified on the day before the ground war began.

The "Q-36" became the "mainstay" of the XVIII Airborne Corps' artillery counterfire preparation when none of the larger TPQ-37s were able to complete the cross-country move because of "severe mobility problems." Accounts from several artillery units indicated that they regarded the system as indispensable.

On the other hand, the Q-36 often detected phantom targets. Conjecture suggested that the radar was picking up fragment trajectories and tracking those as well as real projectiles because the software was too sensitive. Further analysis added the possibility of a hitherto unsuspected bug in the system's software. Another explanation was that users had come to expect the radar to be more discriminating than was possible.

SPECIFICATIONS •
BAND I/J
RANGE 16.2 nm (18.6 mi; 30 km)
ACCURACY 0.2° × 0.17° (3.6 × 3 mils)
OPERATIONS CABIN WEIGHT 2,500 lb (1,136 kg)
SETUP TIME 20 min

TPQ-37 Firefinder

The AN/TPQ-37 and the shorter-range and more mobile AN/TPQ-36 make up the US Firefinder system of artillery-, rocket-, and mortar-locating radars. The TPQ-37 differs from the TPQ-36 in being capable of locating artillery and rocket launchers at their normal ranges.

The TPQ-37 was developed from the TPQ-36 and has an improved antenna, signal processor, and computer. It uses a phased-array antenna with Track-While-Scan (TWS) and simultaneous tracking capabilities using a separate track channel for each projectile.

The radar is generally deployed in conjunction with the TPQ-36, with three TPQ-36 and two TPQ-37 systems per division sector. The TPQ-36 is usually deployed 3.2–4.3 nm (3.7–5 mi; 6–8 km) from the Forward Edge of the Battle Area (FEBA), and the TPQ-37s at 4.3–5.4 nm (5–6.2 mi; 8–10 km).

The TPQ-37 is said to be reliable and capable of operating at a wide range of temperatures. Kevlar armor plating increases protection of the system from the environment.

DEVELOPMENT • Production of 72 systems was ordered in 1977 from Hughes

Aircraft, Ground Systems Group, Fullerton, California. In service in both the US Army and Marine Corps.

In 1981, a moratorium was placed on sales of the TPQ-37 to foreign buyers due to concerns regarding potential transfer and compromise of high technology. The moratorium was lifted and sales to foreign customers was authorized in 1983 after a study suggested that the risk was relatively small. As many as seven other countries may operate the TPQ-37.

COMBAT EXPERIENCE • US TPQ-37s were deployed to Saudi Arabia as part of Operation Desert Shield. Both Firefinder types received urgent software modifications that enabled them to plot launch points for Tactical Ballistic Missiles (TBM). 20 Army and Marine Corps Firefinders were modified on the day before the ground war began.

The commander of the 1st Armored Division Artillery said that the TPQ-37 "had no significant faults and was an extremely reliable source of enemy targeting information. It provided many more enemy artillery acquisitions during our counterfire battle than the [TP]Q-36 did." On the other hand, an officer of the XVIII Airborne Corps' artillery headquarters stated that the Q-37 "experienced severe mobility problems in cross-country movement. No Q37 [sic] radar played a significant role in the XVIII Airborne Corps eastern sector. All six radars were unable to complete the cross-country trek—the trailer must be replaced."

SPECIFICATIONS •
BAND I/J
RANGE 27 nm (31.1 mi; 50 km)

TPS-32/TPS-64

The AN/TPS-32 is a mobile, long-range, tactical, Three-Dimensional (3D) air defense radar used in the Marine Tactical Data System (MTDS). It is mounted in three shelters, with the antenna collapsible onto three pallets for movement.

The tall, narrow, horizontally polarized planar-array antenna rotates at 6 rpm. Subdividing a long pulse into five subpulses of differing frequencies creates five overlapping elevation beams that are step-scanned as a group through a $-1°$ to $+18°$ range. Returns are taken by five individual receivers, each of which is tuned to one of the five subpulses. The transmitter can vary the interpulse period and peak power to better illuminate targets at long ranges and lower elevations.

The receiver applies double-canceling Moving Target Indicator (MTI) processing for clutter rejection, automatic 3D target detection, automatic correlation of Identification Friend or Foe (IFF) and radar returns, and clutter censoring. A nine-channel video processor is also provided.

DEVELOPMENT • The TPS-32 began as the TPS-32 (XN-1) in 1958 and achieved initial operational capability in the US Marine Corps in 1969. Manufactured by ITT Gilfillan of Van Nuys, California; still in service. Turkey's sets were adapted for use within the NATO Air Defense Ground Environment (NADGE) system and designated AN/TPS-64.

COMBAT EXPERIENCE • The two Kuwaiti TPS-32 installations were destroyed during the Iraqi invasion in August 1990. As part of the US Marine Corps' mobilization during Operation Desert Shield, TPS-32s were deployed in Saudi Arabia.

SPECIFICATIONS •
BAND E/F (2.905–3.080 GHz)
RANGE 300 nm (345 mi; 556 km)
ACCURACY
  azimuth 0.5°
  height, at 100 nm (115 mi; 185 km)
    1,200 ft (336 m)

height, at 300 nm (345 mi; 556 km)
    3,000 ft (914 m)
range   750 ft (229 m)
PEAK POWER   2.2 MW
PULSE WIDTH   30 microseconds
INTERPULSE PERIOD   1,090–3,772 microsec
ANTENNA GAIN   at least 41 dB
ANTENNA SIDELOBE   at least 25 dB below peak of main beam

TPS-43E

The AN/TPS-43E is a three-dimensional, long-range, high-power, air defense radar that operates in the same frequencies as the Marine Corps' TPS-32. It is used as part of a ground-based air defense interceptor or missile system. The radar is palletized for ease of air or road movement.

The open-mesh, truncated paraboloid antenna has a stripline matrix array to create multiple height-finding beams. A separate Hazeltine AN/UPX-23 Identification Friend or Foe (IFF) interrogator with Interrogate Sidelobe Suppression (ISLS) sum/difference antenna is also mounted.

The linear-beam klystron transmitter with solid state creates the pulses. Electronic Counter-Countermeasures (ECCM) features include pulse-to-pulse frequency agility, staggered Pulse Repetition Frequencies (PRF), and sidelobe blanking. To reduce clutter and further enhance ECCM, the six-channel receiver/processor also applies digital coherent Moving Target Indication (DMTI) processing, Coded Pulse Anticlutter System (CPACS), and Jamming Analysis and Transmission Selection (JATS) that uses a small printed-circuit radar-sidelobe reference antenna.

DEVELOPMENT • More than 170 TPS-43 series radars produced for US and more than 20 other countries. Manufactured by the Westinghouse Defense and Electronics Center of Baltimore,

Maryland. US TPS-43s were modified as TPS-43E ULSA (Ultra-Low Sidelobe Antenna) radars (later redesignated TPS-75).

SPECIFICATIONS •
BAND   E/F (2.9–3.1 GHz)
RANGE   240 nm (276 mi; 445 km)
ACCURACY
    azimuth   0.35°
    height   +/−1,500 ft (457 m)
    range   350 ft (107 m)
PEAK POWER   4.0 MW, average 6.7 kW
PULSE WIDTH   6.5 microsec
ANTENNA BEAMWIDTH   1.1° × 0° to 20°
ANTENNA SCAN RATE   6 rpm
ANTENNA GAIN
    transmitting 36 dB
    receiving   40 dB
ANTENNA ELEVATION ANGLE   0°–20°
MEAN TIME BETWEEN FAILURES (MTBF)
    600 hr
MEAN TIME TO REPAIR (MTTR)   30 min

TPS-44 Alert

The AN/TPS-44 is a solid-state, air-transportable air surveillance radar used as the sensor component of the US Air Force's 407L forward air traffic control system.

Selection of a given Pulse Repetition Frequency (PRF) determines many of its performance attributes, including pulse width and average power.

Housed in a single operations shelter with large open-mesh truncated paraboloid antenna, the TPS-44 can be set up in about 40 minutes by a team of four persons.

DEVELOPMENT • Entered service in the 1970s. Manufactured by ISC Cardion Electronics of Woodbury, New York.

SPECIFICATIONS •
BAND   D (1.25-1.35 GHz)

ACCURACY
azimuth $+/-1°$
range   628 ft (191 m) at 533 and
800 Hz, 0.5 nm (0.6 mi;
0.9 km) at 400 Hz PRF
POWER
peak   more than 1 MW
average   745 W at 533 Hz PRF,
1.12 kW at 267 or 800
Hz PRF
PULSE WIDTH   4.2 (267 Hz PRF), 2.8
(400 Hz PRF), 1.4 (533 or 800 Hz
PRF) microsec
ANTENNA BEAMWIDTH   3.8° × 8° (cose-
cant squaring from 7° to 27° in elevation)

TPS-59

The AN/TPS-59 is a three-dimensional,
long-range, D-band air defense surveillance radar. The TPS-59 active phased-
array antenna is broken into two halves
for travel on trailers; the wing sections of
each row fold over the center section.
Setup time is about one hour.

The radar scans electronically in elevation while rotating in azimuth. The
TPS-59 antenna has 54 row feeds and
three column feeds; each row power assembly feeds two rows. The smaller
TPS-59M/34 has 34 row feeds. Above the
planar-array antenna is the Identification
Friend or Foe (IFF) antenna.

The transmitters have pulse-to-pulse
frequency agility over 14% of the bandwidth, being able to choose in a quasi-
random manner. The transmitters are
also capable of initiating psuedo-random
Pulse Repetition Frequency (PRF) and
pseudo-random beam positioning.

TPS-59 is transported on three trucks
or trailers; the antenna does not have to
be separated for travel.

DEVELOPMENT • General Electric began development in 1972. Marine Corps
acceptance trials came in 1976–77. 15
TPS-59s were built under a contract with
the US Marine Corps; four of these were
transferred to Egypt. Egypt later directly
purchased an additional TPS-59. "More
than one" TPS-59M/34 were purchased
by Egypt in 1991. Manufactured by Martin Marietta (formerly General Electric
Co.) of Syracuse, New York.

SPECIFICATIONS •
BAND   D (1.215–1.4 GHz)
COVERAGE
azimuth   360°
height   100,000 ft (30,480 m)
range   4–300 nm (4.6–345 mi;
7.4–556 km)

ACCURACY
azimuth   3 millirad (0.05°)
height   1,000 ft (3,048 m)
range   100 ft (30.5 m)
RESOLUTION
azimuth   3.4° (-59), 2.5° (-59M/34)
height   1.7° (-59), 2.7° (-59M/34)
range   140 ft (42.7 m)
PROBABILITY OF DETECTION OF 10.76-FT²
(1-M²) RADAR CROSS SECTION   more
than 90% within 200 nm (230 mi; 371
km); more than 70% at more than
200 nm
POWER
peak   46 kW (-59), 28 kW
(-59M/34)
average   8.3 kW (-59), 5 kW
(-59M/34)
prime power required
90 kW
CLUTTER REDUCTION   ground 53 dB;
weather 33 dB
ANTENNA BEAMWIDTH
-59 3.4° × 1.7° (monopulse) or 1.4°
(low-angle)
-59M/34 3.4° × 2.7° (monopulse) or
2.2° (low-angle)
ANTENNA DIMENSIONS
width   15 ft (4.57 m)
height   -59 30 ft (9.14 m),
-59M/34 19 ft (5.79 m)
ANTENNA SCAN RATE   6 or 12 rpm
ANTENNA SIDELOBE REDUCTION   55 dB
BEAM ELEVATION RANGE $-1°/+18°$ (depression angle through software)

MEAN TIME BETWEEN FAILURES (MTBF)
more than 1,000 hr
MEAN TIME TO REPAIR (MTTR)   less than
40 min

TPS-63

The AN/TPS-63 is a low-level, tactical air defense radar available in transportable or stationary configurations. The sectional antenna is stored in the operations shelter for movement and can be set up in about one hour. The original transmitter is a Traveling-Wave-Tube/Cross-Field Amplifier (TWT/CFA). A 100% solid-state transmitter is also available.

Most TPS-63s have a concave rectangular antenna that is taller than it is wide and has a central vertical feed. A Secondary Surveillance Radar (SSR) provides integral Identification Friend or Foe (IFF) interrogation. Also available is a Low-Sidelobe Antenna (LSA) that retains the central feed, but has 32 vertical columns in a reflector that is considerably wider than it is tall.

The operator is allowed 21 possible frequency-pair selections with dual diversity. Jamming effects are also reduced by several forms of frequency agility, including pulse-to-pulse, burst, and sector. The radar also uses a full array of clutter-reduction processing techniques and can initiate up to 600 targets automatically.

The Low-Altitude Surveillance Radar (LASS) system is a TPS-63 installed on a tethered balloon platform to provide stationary airborne surveillance for extended periods of time. It was originally developed by Westinghouse, but most LASS production came from TCOM. It is employed by the Saudi Arabian Air Force as a supplementary airborne early-warning radar.

DEVELOPMENT • More than 100 are in service in the US Army and Marine Corps

as well as in 10 other countries. Manufactured by Westinghouse Defense and Electronics Center in Baltimore, Maryland. Benha Company for Electronics Industry in Egypt began coproduction of 34 sets, with Benha assuming 90% production for any additional orders.

COMBAT EXPERIENCE • A LASS operated for the Kuwait Air Force by the US company TCOM detected the first surge of Iraqi armor that began the August 1990 invasion of Kuwait. The early warning is given credit for allowing the emir to escape to Saudi Arabia before Kuwait fell.

SPECIFICATIONS •
BAND   D (1.25-1.35 GHz)
RANGE   80–160 nm (92–184 mi; 148–296 km)
detection range of 10.76-ft² (1-m²) target, 90% probability and false-alarm probability of less than 1 in 10 million: 112 nm (129 mi; 207 km)
HEIGHT COVERAGE   0–40,000 ft (0–12,192 m), to 40° elevation angle
ACCURACY
    azimuth   0.35°
    range   492 ft (150 m)
RESOLUTION
    azimuth   2.7°
    range   1,200 ft (366 m)
POWER
    peak   100 kW
    mean   3 kW
PULSEWIDTH   39 microsec, dual-frequency selectable from 21 frequencies
PRF   774, fixed or staggered
RECEIVER DYNAMIC RANGE   123 dB
MOVING TARGET INDICATOR (MTI) IMPROVEMENT FACTOR   60 dB
SYSTEM WEIGHT   7,480 lb (3,400 kg)
ANTENNA GAIN   32.5 dB
ANTENNA SCAN RATE   6, 12, or 15 rpm
ANTENNA DIMENSIONS
    width   18 ft (5.5 m)
    length   16 ft (4.9 m)

TPS-65

The AN/TPS-65 is a variable-range air-search radar similar in characteristics to the earlier AN/TPS-63. The TPS-65 was developed as a military air traffic control radar featuring dual diversity within 51 channels with manual or automatic selection. The system is compatible with various subsystems designed for commercial air traffic control purposes.

The Moving Target Indicator (MTI) operates on a variable four-pulse transmission to eliminate ground clutter while maximizing moving aircraft detection. Dual-channel reception allows the addition of a secondary three-pulse transmitter to enhance capabilities in inclement weather. The system also features constant false-alarm rate generation and built-in test equipment.

DEVELOPMENT • In service with the Marine Corps as part of the US Air Traffic Control and Landing System and with several commercial users. Produced by Westinghouse Defense and Electronics Center, Baltimore, Maryland.

SPECIFICATIONS •
BAND D
RANGE COVERAGE 80–160 nm (92–184 mi; 148–296 km)
POWER
  peak 100 kW
  mean 3 kW
SYSTEM WEIGHT 13,669 lb (6,200 kg)
ANTENNA GAIN 32.5 dB
ANTENNA SCAN RATE variable to 15 rpm
ANTENNA DIMENSIONS
  width 18 ft (5.5 m)
  length 16 ft (4.9)

TPS-70

The AN/TPS-70 is a long-range tactical surveillance radar; it is also being studied as an Anti-Tactical Ballistic Missile (ATBM) radar. The highly mobile three-dimensional system consists of a planar-array antenna and an operations cabin.

The antenna has 36 waveguides with 96 slots each. The system produces very low sidelobes, reducing probability of detection by hostile sensors and minimizing vulnerability to antiradiation missiles. Moreover, the antenna radiates a lower temperature than most, reducing its heat signature. Other ECCM techniques include pulse coding, random and automatic frequency agility, and staggered Pulse Repetition Frequencies (PRF).

The TPS-70 uses six receive beams, each with its own receiver, to illuminate a target at a given elevation several times during a single antenna scan. A Digital Target Extractor (DTE) system provides automatic clutter mapping and filtering using four-pulse Moving Target Indicator (MTI) processing, radar plot extraction, Identification Friend or FOE (IFF) decoding/plot extraction, and radar/IFF correlation. MTI processing yields an improvement factor of 50 dB. The plot can maintain 500 tracks simultaneously.

DEVELOPMENT • The TPS-70 is in service in the US Army and Air Force. It is also the base for the US Caribbean Basin Radar Network (CBRN), which consists of eight radar sites.

Manufactured by Westinghouse Defense Electronics Center, Baltimore, Maryland. Westinghouse produces the TPS-70 in lots of four to six systems, which allows for the quick delivery of ordered systems. More than 10 other countries operate the TPS-70. Not all users have been identified.

SPECIFICATIONS •
BAND E F (2.9–3.1 GHz)
RANGE 240 nm (276 mi; 440 km)
  detection of target of 21.5-ft² (2.0-m²) cross section, probability of detection 75%, probability of false alarm less than 1 in 1 million: 175 nm (202 mi; 324 km)

ACCURACY
azimuth   0.25°
height at 180 nm (207 mi; 333 km)
           +/−1,500 ft (457 m)
range   350 ft (107 m)
RESOLUTION (50% probability for 21.5-ft²/2-m² target)
azimuth   2.4°
range   1,600 ft (488 m)
POWER
peak   3.5 MW
average   6.2 kW
PULSE LENGTH 6.5 microsec
PRF (AVERAGE) 250/275 pulses per sec
ANTENNA BEAMWIDTH azimuth 1.5°; elevation, transmit 0°–20°, receive 2.3°–6.0°
ANTENNA SCAN RATE 6 rpm
ANTENNA SCAN LIMITS azimuth 360°, elevation angle 0°–20°, altitude 99,500 ft (30,333 m)
ANTENNA DIMENSIONS
width   18 ft 2 in (5.55 m)
height   8 ft 4 in (2.54 m)
MEAN TIME BETWEEN FAILURES (MTBF)
600 hr
MEAN TIME TO REPAIR (MTTR) 0.5 hr

TPS-73

The AN/TPS-73 is a long-range tactical air traffic control radar that can also be used for gap-filling and surveillance duties. It is said to be the only E-band radar with a solid-state transmitter, which improves reliability. The system can be transported by a CH-53 helicopter or C-130 transport and can be set up within two hours.

The Alenia-built open-mesh, truncated paraboloid antenna is illuminated by dual E-band beams for better clutter performance.

The low-noise receiver applies Adaptive Moving-Target Detection (AMTD) and high-resolution ground-clutter maps to suppress clutter and range/azimuth adaptive threshholding of the Doppler filters to sharpen the radar's sensitivity

to targets. The autotracker can maintain 600 known tracks or 300 tentative tracks simultaneously. To resist Electronic Countermeasures (ECM), the radar applies pulse-to-pulse or burst-to-burst frequency agility as well as automatic selection of an unjammed frequency.

DEVELOPMENT • The TPS-73 was purchased by the Marine Corps in 1990. Manufactured by Paramax (a Unisys company) in Great Neck, New York, and Alenia SpA of Rome, Italy.

SPECIFICATIONS •
BAND E, F (2.7–2.9 GHz)
RANGE 60 nm (69 mi; 111 km)
detection of target of 10.8-ft² (1.0-m²) cross section, probability of detection 90%, probability of false alarm less than 1 in 1 million: 60 nm (69 mi; 111 km)
ACCURACY (RMS)
azimuth   0.18°
range   350 ft (60 m)
RESOLUTION (98% probability for 2 10.8-ft²/1-m² targets)
azimuth   3.5°
range   760 ft (230 m)
POWER
peak   10 kW
average   1.1 kW
ANTENNA BEAMWIDTH azimuth 1.45°, elevation 5°
ANTENNA SCAN RATE 12 or 15 rpm
MEAN TIME BETWEEN FAILURES (MTBF)
5,000 hr
MEAN TIME TO REPAIR (MTTR) 1.4 hr

TPS-75

The AN/TPS-75 is a three-dimensional, long-range, high-power, air defense radar that grew out of earlier updates of the TPS-43. It is used as part of a ground-based air defense interceptor or missile system. After the TPS-43's E-squared (-43E Enhanced) program began by improving signal processing, a second effort—Seek Screen—that developed the planar-array Ultra-Low Sidelobe Antenna (ULSA) was merged with it and the result redesignated the TPS-75. In turn, the smaller TPS-70 was developed as TPS-75's export variant. A physical difference between the -70 and -75 is the crease in the TPS-75's antenna, showing where it folds for transport.

The ULSA antenna uses a linear beam klystron transmitter and produces very low sidelobes, reducing probability of detection by hostile sensors. The low sidelobes also minimize the effect of signal jamming and reduce the ability of Antiradiation Missiles (ARM) to lock on, except at very short ranges where they would have already been detected and other defense systems activated. Moreover, the antenna radiates a lower temperature than most, reducing its heat signature. Other Electronic Counter-Countermeasures (ECCM) techniques include pulse coding, random and automatic frequency agility that steps through 12 frequencies, and staggered Pulse Repetition Frequencies (PRF).

A platform supports the antenna, and the whole unit may be mounted at fixed installations. A second antenna, for the Identification Friend or Foe (IFF) system, is located on top of the main array.

Like the TPS-70, the TPS-75 uses six receive beams, each with its own receiver, to illuminate a target at a given elevation several times during a single antenna scan. Data from the multiple beams are used for more accurate measurement of target elevation. Compared to the TPS-70, the TPS-75 has finer range and azimuth resolution.

A Digital Target Extractor (DTE) system provides automatic clutter mapping and filtering using four-pulse Moving Target Indicator (MTI) processing, radar plot extraction, IFF decoding/plot extraction, and radar/IFF correlation. The MTI improvement factor is 30 dB. As part of the processing system, Litton Data Systems' AN/GYQ-51 Advanced Tracking System (ATS) operates at the rate of 50 million instructions per second.

The radar is palletized for ease of air or road movement. Under the Seek Screen program, ITT began development of survivable decoys, with the first production examples being delivered in September 1992.

DEVELOPMENT • Initial operational capability in 1990. Manufactured by the Westinghouse Defense and Electronics Center of Baltimore, Maryland. 51 conversions from TPS-43E to TPS-75 funded through FY1991, with 12 in service by the end of 1991.

SPECIFICATIONS •
BAND E/F (2.9–3.1 GHz)
RANGE 240 nm (276 mi; 440 km) detection of target of 18.3-ft^2 (1.7-m^2) cross section, probability of detection 80%, probability of false alarm less than 1 in 1 million: 165 nm (190 mi; 306 km)
ACCURACY
  azimuth 0.35°
  range 350 ft (107 m)
  height +/−1,500 ft (457 m)
RESOLUTION
  azimuth 1.6°
  range 1,060 ft (323 m)
COVERAGE
  elevation 0°–20°
  azimuth 360°
POWER
  peak 4.0 MW
  average 6.7 kW
PULSE LENGTH 6.5 microsec
ANTENNA GAIN
  transmit 36 dB
  receive 40 dB
BEAMWIDTH
  azimuth 1.1°
MEAN TIME BETWEEN FAILURES (MTBF) 600 hr
MEAN TIME TO REPAIR (MTTR) 0.5 hr

TRACKSTAR

The Target Acquisition Radar System, or Trackstar, works with short-range air defense systems such as the Blowpipe, Chaparral, Stinger, and Vulcan. It is similar to the AN/MPQ-54 FAAR, but has many upgrades including an armored, self-contained, integrated radar/command-and-control system.

A folding antenna erects from the roof of the M577 command post carrier that houses the system electronics. Although a two- or three-person crew is required to operate Trackstar, erection, leveling, and stowage are automated.

Each Trackstar can operate in a network with three other systems, sharing targets through data links, which reduces the exposure of an individual radar to countermeasures. An individual radar can track up to 64 targets. The system rejects fixed clutter, ground traffic, weather and chaff using Digital Moving Target Indicator (DMTI) and Doppler processing while automatically transmitting target track cuing, allowing the system to operate in high-clutter environments. The digital signal processor can identify and classify rotary-wing aircraft even while homing in on the target at ranges up to 30 km.

DEVELOPMENT • First sale was to Egypt in 1990. Manufactured by Sanders Associates, Nashua, New Hampshire, and in service in Egypt.

SPECIFICATIONS •
BAND   D
RANGE   32.4 nm (37.3 mi; 60 km)

UPS-3 Sentry

The AN/UPS-3 Sentry Tactical Defense Alert Radar (TDAR) is a tactical, low-level air defense surveillance radar derived from the Israeli EL/M-2106H radar. It features a quadrapod-mounted antenna unit, remote-control operation, and remote-display unit.

The antenna has four slotted waveguides and has two rotation rates; GEC introduced a reduced sidelobe upgrade (−38 dB below main lobe) in 1988. The UPS-3's Track-While-Scan (TWS) mode can follow 40 targets simultaneously. A digital signal processor can apply Moving Target Indicator (MTI) processing to returns, improving the signal-to-noise ratio by 55 dB.

Early displays used Light-Emitting Diodes (LED) to indicate range and azimuth and if the target is fixed-wing (steady glow) or helicopter (flashing). Later displays use a more conventional Plan Position Indicator (PPI) screen. A single radar can cue as many as four displays.

DEVELOPMENT • First US buys came in 1990 by the US Marine Corps; later purchases supplied US Army light and airborne divisions. Manufactured by GEC (formerly Lear-Siegler) Astronics of Santa Monica, California; in production.

COMBAT EXPERIENCE • UPS-3 radars were deployed with the Marine Corps and the 82nd Airborne during Operations Desert Shield and Desert Storm in 1990–91.

SPECIFICATIONS •
BAND   D
RANGE   16.7 nm (19.3 mi; 31 km)
ACCURACY
    azimuth   2°
    range   656 ft (200 m)
    velocity   10 kts (11.5 mph; 18.5 km/h)
POWER
    peak   210 W
    average   18 W
SYSTEM WEIGHT   171 lb (77.6 kg)
SYSTEM GAIN   at least 22 dB
ANTENNA BEAMWIDTH   8° × 17°
ANTENNA SCAN RATE   10 or 15 rpm
ANTENNA ELEVATION   −3°/+10°

Vigilant

The Vigilant is a fully automated, mobile, three-dimensional, low-level air defense radar system. It is transportable by two vehicles or by aircraft and can be set up in about 30 minutes. The system is designed to operate as part of an air defense sensor network and can be remote-controlled.

The Vigilant features a planar array antenna with 36 slotted waveguides and low sidelobes. It generates seven stacked beams for height-finding and can track up to 1,000 targets simultaneously. The system has "look-down" capability and a variable data rate of three to six seconds for mountain deployment. To counter Electronic Countermeasures (ECM), Vigilant can apply pulse coding, staggered Pulse Repetition Frequencies (PRF), and random and programmed frequency agility. Moving Target Indicator (MTI) processing that results in a 48-dB improvement factor further weeds out clutter.

DEVELOPMENT • Manufactured by the Westinghouse Defense Electronics Center of Baltimore, Maryland. Switzerland procured five radars, the first being delivered in 1987.

SPECIFICATIONS •
BAND   E/F (2.9–3.1 GHz)
RANGE   60 nm (69 mi; 110 km)
ACCURACY
  azimuth   0.40°
  height   +/−902 ft (275 m)
  range   130 ft (45 m)
RESOLUTION
  azimuth   1.6°
  range   739 ft (225 m)
PEAK POWER   90 kW
ELEVATION COVERAGE   −3°/+20°

NAVAL RADARS

BPS-15/BPS-16

This is a low-power, surface search and navigation radar fitted in US nuclear-propelled submarines. The antenna is a horn array with a 40-in (1.02-m) aperture.

An update that improved the mechanical reliability of the radar mast resulted in the BPS-16.

DEVELOPMENT • Initial operational capability in the early 1960s. Manufactured by Unisys, Great Neck, New York.

The contract was awarded to Sperry Rand (later Unisys) after protest. The BPS-16 is currently in production for the Los Angeles (SSN 688)- , Seawolf, and Ohio-class submarines as well as already operating in Sturgeon (SSN 637)-class submarines.

SPECIFICATIONS •
BAND   I-J
PEAK POWER   35 kW
BEAMWIDTH   3° × 13°
PULSE LENGTH   0.1 or 0.5 microsec
PRF   1,500 or 750 Hz
SYSTEM GAIN   25 dB
RANGE RESOLUTION
  short-range mode
      90 ft (27.4 m)
  long-range mode
      300 ft (91.4 m)
SCAN RATE   up to 9.5 rpm

MK 23 Target Acquisition System (TAS)

The Mk 23 is a Two-Dimensional (2D), pulse-Doppler weapons direction radar for the NATO Sea Sparrow missile. It interfaces with the AN/SLQ-32 Electronic Countermeasures (ECM) system and with the Mk 68 gunfire control system. The Mk 23 automatically reacts to incoming sea-skimming, high-angle, or pop-up missiles launched from surface ships, high-altitude aircraft, or submarines. It is designed to operate in severe jamming and high-clutter environments, using digital signal and Moving Target Indicator (MTI) processing. A Traveling Wave Tube (TWT) is used to turn the radar on and off rapidly, increasing its ECM resistance. The system can track 54 missiles simultaneously.

Its linear-array antenna is mounted back-to-back with an Identification Friend or Foe (IFF) antenna on a roll-stabilized platform, which rotates for a 360° scan in azimuth. The main reflector is fed by 26 flared feed horns. Additional sidelobe-blanking and sidelobe-cancellation horns complete the array.

The Mk 23 has normal, medium-range, mixed, and emission control operational modes. The normal, or point defense mode, has a two-second data rate (30 rpm). Slowing the radar scan to 15 rpm allows for radar surveillance and aircraft control. These two modes are combined in the mixed mode for a high data rate providing rapid response and air control over a large area.

Emission control consists of several modes that are divided into the fully quiet modes or modes that narrow the sector to be scanned to a few degrees.

Although designed for total automatic operations, the Mk 23 has operator interface controls in the display unit for manual initiation of automation levels, override, and control. Only two crew members operate the Mk 23, one for fire control and the other for the improved point defense missile system.

TAS(I) is an improved 2D/3D system with a rotating phased-array (six-dipole) antenna fed by diode phase shifters that can steer two or more 11° beams simul-

taneously and much more powerful signal processing. Development began in 1986, but deployment was delayed by funding cutbacks and program reorientations.

VARIANTS •

Mod 0 had a Mk 158 computer and was the development model in the frigate *Downes* (FF 1070).

Mod 1 introduced the UYK-20 computer and is integrated into the Naval Tactical Data System (NTDS) in the *Spruance* class. Mod 3 is modified Mod 1 with AN/UYQ-21 display. Mod 5 is Mod 1 with AN/UYK-44 computer for *Spruance* class. Mod 7 is Mod 1 with UYK-44.

Mod 2 is a stand-alone model with AN/UYA-4 console (without NTDS); for major replenishment ships. Mod 4 is Mod 2 with UYQ-21 display. Mod 6 is Mod 2 with UYK-44. Mod 8 is Mod 2 with UYK-44 and UYQ-21 display.

DEVELOPMENT • Five different systems—Mk 20 through Mk 24—were evaluated, each succeeding Mk representating greater sophistication in some area. The Mk 23 was evaluated in the *Downes* (FF 1070) from 1975 to 1983, with the system achieving initial operational capability in 1980. Manufactured by Hughes Aircraft Co., Fullerton, California.

In service in all active aircraft carriers, *Spruance* (DDG 963)-class destroyers, *Wasp* (LHD 1)-class amphibious assault ships, and the *Sacramento* (AOE 1)-, *Supply* (AOE 6)-, and *Wichita* (AOR 1)-class auxiliary ships.

SPECIFICATIONS •
BAND   D
RANGE   30 rpm 20 nm (23 mi; 37 km);
15 rpm 90 nm (104 mi; 167 km)
PEAK POWER   200 kW
PRF   normal 4,000 Hz; medium-range 900 Hz
SYSTEM GAIN   21 dB

MTI CLUTTER REDUCTION   more than
50 dB
SYSTEM WEIGHT
topside   2,000 lbs (907 kg)
total   10,000 lbs (4,536 kg)
ANTENNA DIMENSIONS
width   19 ft 3 in (5.87 m)
height   10 ft 9 in (3.28 m)
ANTENNA BEAMWIDTH   3.3° × 75°

Mk 91

This continuous-wave fire control radar is associated with the short-range NATO Sea Sparrow Missile System (NSSMS). Side-by-side Mk 95 parabolic transmitting and Cassegrain lens receiving I-band antennas ride on a single pedestal mounted near the eight-cell launcher. The transmitter's radome is convex, the receiver's is concave.

To expand the tracker's field of view, the Mk 95 uses a wide-beam illuminator that allows the missile (a modified Sparrow III AAM) to use proportional navigation. An electro-optical tracker fitted between the Mk 95s provides an alternate tracking method in high-ECCM conditions.

VARIANTS •
Few ships use the single Mod 0. The dual Mod 1 equips ships in the Danish, Italian, Japanese, Norwegian, and US navies. A "Netherlands" form uses the Mk 73 fire control transmitter linked with the Dutch M25 fire control system; Belgian, German, Netherlands Navy, and Spanish ships use the Netherlands version.

DEVELOPMENT • Entered service in the 1970s. Manufactured by Raytheon, Wayland, Massachusetts. Used on many surface combatants as well as some amphibious and auxiliary ships of the US Navy. Also used in the Belgian, Danish, German, Italian, Japanese, Norwegian, and Spanish navies.

SPECIFICATIONS •
BAND   I/J
PEAK POWER   2 kW average, continuous-wave mode
ANTENNA DIAMETER   3 ft 3 in (1.0 m)
ANTENNA MOUNT DIMENSIONS   8 ft 4 in (2.54 m) × 8 ft (2.44 m)
ANTENNA WEIGHT   3,315 lb (1,504 kg)

MK 92

The Mk 92 is a gun and missile fire control system that performs tracking and illumination functions using two antennas in a Combined Antenna System (CAS) mounted above and below a supporting arm inside a distinctive egg-shaped dome. It is based on the Dutch WM28 fire control system and is produced in the United States under license from Hollandse Signaalapparaten.

The upper, inverted Cassegrain lens antenna uses monopulse tracking and Continuous-Wave Injection (CWI) for three-dimensional target acquisition and illumination. The lower, truncated paraboloid antenna uses a high scan rate (60 rpm) for search and includes a limited height-finding capability by shifting the beam in a spiral elevation pattern. The search radar also has 10 Identification Friend or Foe (IFF) dipoles across its face. Each antenna is capable of Track-While-Scan (TWS) processing, tracking two targets while scanning for others.

A Mk 106 Weapons Control Console (WCC) has a Plan Position Indicator (PPI) and two track displays. The Mod 2 variant adds the Separate Target Illumination Radar's (STIR) Mk 107 WCC with its own PPI.

In the late 1980s, Unisys developed a Coherent Receive/Transmit (CORT) kit to upgrade *Perry*-class Mod 2 radars. April 1989 tests showed that CORT provided a "significant improvement in clutter rejection" and showed increased resistance to jamming. In addition, the Mk 92 Mod 6 detected targets with much smaller radar cross sections at similar ranges, doubled the detection and tracking ranges of the Mod 2, and showed an improved ability to track and hold lock on targets as well as decreasing reaction times.

The *Ingraham* (FFG 61) was the only *Perry*-class ship completed with the CORT. Others are being upgraded, with six kits ordered in 1988 and seven more ordered in October 1990.

Mk 94 was a prototype fitted in the hydrofoil missile patrol boat *Pegasus*.

VARIANTS •

Mk 92 Mod 0 is the baseline variant that is capable of gun and missile control using one air-engagement channel and two surface-search, TWS channels.

Mk 92 Mod 1/5 are for gun control only. Mod 1 is fitted in the *Bear*-class cutters, the *Pegasus* (PHM 1) class (except for the lead ship *Pegasus*, which was fitted with the Mk 94 prototype), and modernized *Hamilton*-class cutters.

Mod 5 is fitted in Saudi Navy *Badr* and *Al-Siddiq* small combatant classes.

Mk 92 Mod 2 is combined in *Perry*-class frigates with the STIR radar (Mk 39 antenna on an SPG-60 pedestal) to provide a second missile guidance channel for engaging air targets. Also has two TWS, surface-engagement channels. The STIR system is fitted with the monopulse feed and CWI horns, making it similar to the targeting radar in the CAS radome.

DEVELOPMENT • Original Dutch
WM20 series entered service in the 1960s; Mk 92 achieved initial operational capability in 1977. Mod 6 CORT upgrade currently in production. Manufactured by Unisys, Great Neck, New York.

SPECIFICATIONS •
BAND I/J
WEIGHTS
  above decks: Mod 0/1 1,905 lb (865 kg); Mod 2 6,318 lb (2,866 kg)
  below decks: Mod 0 9,086 lb (4,121 kg); Mod 1 5,637 lb (2,557 kg); Mod 2

15,848 lb (7,189 kg); Mod 5 7,835 lb (3,554 kg); Mod 6 24,000 lb (10,886 kg)

SPG-51

The AN/SPG-51 is a target tracking and illumination radar used with the Tartar/Standard-MR Surface-to-Air Missile (SAM), in conjunction with the Mk 74 gun and missile fire control system. It was the first operational pulse-Doppler tracking radar.

The antenna is a parabolic dish reflector with offset horn feed. The Mk 74 uses two SPG-51 radar antennas per missile launcher; the antennas are stepped down from the air-search radar that first detects the target. Data goes from the air search radar to the Mk 74 digital fire control computer, which assigns a search pattern to the SPG-51 until the target is acquired.

The radar tracks the target, providing angle and range information to the missile launchers through the fire control computer; the operator can override angle and range tracking computation. Target tracking uses the differences in Doppler shifts in target returns, allowing experienced operators to hear as well as see the target picture.

Embedded I-band antennas in the SPG-51's reflector illuminate the target for the semiactive radar-homing seekers in the Standard missile.

VARIANTS •
SPG-51A replaced SPG-51's 2-kW illuminator with 5-kW module, while SPG-51B added velocity tracking using a narrowband Doppler filter.

SPG-51C added automatic acquisition and tracking, surface acquisition and track, horizon-search modes, and improved multiple-target resolution, clutter rejection, and electronic counter-countermeasures. Peak power is up to 30 kW. Updates replaced several vacuum-tube components with solid-state elements and substituted faster-acting, more reliable mount drives. Both the *Charles F. Adams* (DDG 2) and *Brooke* (FFG 1) classes operated this variant.

SPG-51D uses a more powerful, dual-channel, frequency agile (four changes per second) transmitter, more effective antenna with five times the gain, instantaneous electronic emission control on command.

DEVELOPMENT • After development, the SPG-51 achieved its initial operational capability in 1960. Raytheon Co., Wayland, Massachusetts, manufactured the SPG-51. In addition to Standard-armed guided missile destroyers in the US Navy, Standard-bearing ships in seven other navies use one or two SPG-51 pairs.

SPECIFICATIONS •

BAND G (tracking), I (illumination)
PEAK POWER tracking 81 kW; illumination 5 kW
PULSE WIDTH 2.1–3.2 microsec
PRF surface mode 4,100 Hz; air mode 9,500-17,700 Hz
SYSTEM GAIN tracking 39.5 dB; illumination 45 dB
ANTENNA BEAMWIDTH tracking 1.9° conical scan; illumination 0.9°
ELEVATION −30°-83°

SPG-53

The AN/SPG-53 is a fire control radar for the Mk 68 gunfire control system for use with Mk 42 5-in (127-mm) dual-purpose guns.

The SPG-53 uses a nutating feed in the center of a solid parabolic reflector for conical scanning. After acquiring a target using a 12° spiral scan, the radar switches to a 3° conical scan for target tracking; the transition between scanning modes takes approximately five seconds. Later variants of this radar provide monopulse tracking and clutter cancellation to allow low-elevation angle tracking.

VARIANTS •

SPG-35A operated in *Farragut*- and *Adams*-class missile ships. A 1970s program added Radar Signal Processing Equipment (RSPE) that eliminated two of the three operators while speeding up target acquisition and tracking. SPG-53E/F introduced monopulse tracking. The -53E wasn't deployed because the -53F also offered simulated ECM for training. Many SPG-53As were upgraded to this standard.

SPG-35B equipped four mid-1960s Tartar SAM destroyer conversions, SPG-53C has CWI and is fitted in the Spanish Navy *Baleares*-class guided-missile escorts, SPG-53D was similar to the -53C and was used in five US Navy *Knox*-class frigates fitted with Standard SAM missiles.

DEVELOPMENT • Prototypes developed in the early 1950s, with the first radars going into service in the *Forrest Sherman* class of all-gun destroyers in 1955. Manufactured by Western Electric.

Few active US ships still carry the SPG-53, but foreign navies operating former *Adams*-class destroyers and *Knox*-class frigates have it.

SPECIFICATIONS •

BAND I/J
RANGE 59.2 nm (68.2 mi; 110 km)
ACCURACY 30 ft (9.1 m)
RESOLUTION 240 ft (73.1 m)
PEAK POWER 250 kW
PULSE WIDTH 0.25 microsec
PRF 1,000 Hz
SYSTEM GAIN 39 dB
SYSTEM WEIGHT 5,000 lb (2,268 kg)
ANTENNA DIAMETER 5 ft (1.52 m)
ANTENNA WEIGHT 163 lb (74 kg)

SPG-55

The AN/SPG-55 "searchlight" illumination and guidance radar is fitted in ships armed with the Terrier/Standard-ER, surface-to-air missile, one radar unit per missile rail. These large, heavy assemblies succeeded the AN/SPQ-5 radars. The Mk 76 missile fire control system has progressed through several mods and is deployed in Mod 9 and Mod 10 variants. The current variant tracks and illuminates targets for the Semiactive Radar (SAR) homing seeker on the Standard-ER. The radar uses a G/H-band pulse tracking radar and I/J-band Continuous-Wave Illuminator (CWI). The radars are mounted as pairs; both reflectors can be energized by the same transmitter, should the other fail.

The 96-in (2.44-m) diameter Cassegrain antenna has two parabolic reflectors, one in front of the other, the distance between them being spanned by a casing that acts as a hyperbolic reflector. Pulse emissions from the G/H-band four-horn feed in the center of the rear (main) antenna strike the rear of the front antenna, reflect back onto the main antenna, and radiate out through the front reflector, which is polarized to become "invisible" to the beams.

The front dish serves as the parabolic reflector for the Continuous Wave (CW) I/J-band illuminator; at the same time, a broader beam radiates forward from the same feed horn to provide a rear reference signal for the missile's computer. An auxiliary Custer horn pillbox antenna on the side of the stabilized main antenna mount is used for tracking low, short-range targets such as antiship missiles.

The radar can operate in the presence of heavy jamming using a coast mode or range-rate prediction. The last of the beam-riding Terrier missiles, which required a conical scan with nutating feed, were retired in the late 1980s.

Refits and upgrades that replaced vacuum tubes with digital solid-state circuits greatly improved the SPG-55's reliability and its resistance and response to ECM and expanded its envelope to include surface targets and low-flying aircraft and missiles. Many passive techniques, including sidelobe canceling, passive angle tracking, and a radar silence mode that

features dummy loading of the transmitter's signal, counter the jamming target. The latest SPG-55 OrdAlts (field modification kits) permitted Continuous-Wave Angle Tracking (CWAT) that burns through jammers. To counteract the horizon-level targets, SPG-55s can search the horizon or a given sector, suppress clutter, and track a surface target continuously.

The last principal variants in service were the SPG-55C in the US *Bainbridge* and *Leahy* "double-ender" missile cruisers as well as the Italian *Vittorio Veneto* and *Andrea Doria* classes. *Long Beach* and the nine *Belknaps* had the -55D New Threat Upgrade (NTU) variant. (The recently retired *Farragut*-class guided-missile destroyers have -55Bs.)

DEVELOPMENT • Prototypes fielded in the late 1950s, with production beginning at Sperry Rand (later Unisys) in Great Neck, New York. Updates and OrdAlts began in the mid-1960s.

SPECIFICATIONS •
BAND   G/H (tracking) and I/J (CWI)
RANGE   148 nm (172 mi; 276 km); 49.3 nm (56.8 mi; 91.4 km) against 10.8-ft^2 (1-m^2), Mach 2 target
POWER
  peak   1 MW in G/H band
  average   5 kW in I/J band
PULSE WIDTH
  target acquisition and tracking
             26 or 1.6 microsec
  tracking   0.1 microsec
             (uncompressed or compressed from 12.7 microsec)
PRF
  target acquisition and tracking
             203-225 Hz
  tracking   427 Hz
SYSTEM GAIN   39 dB (G/H), 47 dB (CWI)
ANTENNA BEAMWIDTH
  G/H band: 1.6°
  I/J band: 0.8°

ANTENNA WEIGHT   12,970 lb (5,883 kg)
DIMENSIONS
   mount   14 ft 7 in × 23 ft 5 in
            (4.44 m × 7.14 m);
   antenna 8 ft (2.44 m)

SPG-60

The AN/SPG-60 is an automatic, scan-to-acquire, shipboard air target tracking radar that operates with the SPQ-9 in the Mk 86 fire control system and is used primarily to lay the ship's 5-in (127-mm) guns. It has a relatively high gain and a high Pulse Repetition Frequency (PRF) for precise velocity measurement.

Once a shipboard 2D or 3D search radar (e.g., the SPS-40 or the SPQ-9) designates the target area for the pulse-Doppler monopulse SPG-60 radar, it scans for, acquires, and tracks the target. Although primarily used against air targets, the SPG-60 can also operate in a horizon-search mode. To reduce the inherent range ambiguities of a pulse-Doppler radar, the Mk 86 computer varies the transmitter's pulse width and very high PRF. The radar can handle range rates of up to Mach 3.

When used for Sea Sparrow or Standard-MR SAM, the SPG-60 transmits a separate continuous-wave injection channel to illuminate the target. A closed-circuit television boresighted through the antenna allows passive tracking; it has a continuously adjustable field of view ranging from 2.1 to 21°. A separate optical sight provides visual fire control and damage assessment.

The SPG-60 is not used with the SPQ-9A and Mk 86 fire control system for the 5-in guns on *Ticonderoga* (CG 47)-class cruisers (antiair capability on those ships is provided by the Aegis AN/SPY-1 radars). The SPG-60's antenna mount carries the Separate Target Illumination Radar (STIR) and is fitted in the *Oliver Hazard Perry* (FFG 7) class to provide two missile control channels for the Mk 92 Mod 2 fire control system.

DEVELOPMENT • Development began in the late 1960s, with the first prototypes of the Mk 86 delivered to the US Navy in March 1970. Manufactured by Lockheed Electronics Co., Plainfield, New Jersey. In service in several US cruiser and destroyer classes as well as in US *Adams*- and *Perry*-design ships operating in the Australian, German, and Spanish navies.

SPECIFICATIONS •
BAND   I/J
RANGE
   instrumented: 49.3 nm (56.8 mi; 91.4
   km)
   detection of 10.8-ft^2 (1.0-m^2) target:
   41.9 nm (48.3 mi; 77.7 km)
   CW illumination of 10.8-ft^2 (1.0-m^2)
   target: 9.9 nm (11.4 mi; 18.3 km)
PEAK POWER   5.5 kW
PULSE WIDTH   0.27, 1, or 6 microsec
PRF   25,000–30,000 Hz
SYSTEM GAIN   41.5 dB
ANTENNA WEIGHT   4,015 lb (1,821 kg)
ANTENNA DIAMETER   13 ft 4 in (4.06 m)
ANTENNA BEAMWIDTH   1.2° × 1.2°

SPG-62

The AN/SPG-62 is a continuous wave, illumination radar for the Standard SM-2 missile in the Aegis air defense missile system. Three (DDG 51) or four (CG 47) Mk 99 missile control directors trigger the SPG-62's illumination signal as the Standard missile nears its target, bathing the target in a coded signal that the missile's semiactive homing seeker tracks until the missile explodes or hits the target.

DEVELOPMENT • Manufactured by Raytheon in Wayland, Massachusetts, and achieved initial operational capability in 1983 with the *Ticonderoga* (CG 47). Also fitted in *Arleigh Burke* (DDG 51)-class destroyers.

SPECIFICATIONS •
BAND I/J
AVERAGE POWER   10 kW
ANTENNA DIAMETER   7 ft 6 in (2.29 m)

SPQ-9A

The AN/SPQ-9A is a multipurpose US naval radar, operating with the AN/SPG-60 radar as part of the Mk 86 fire control system. This combination provides surface-search and low-level air coverage (up to 2,000 feet). The radar supports defenses against high-speed (up to Mach 3), low-flying missiles or aircraft, as well as tracking helicopters.

The SPQ-9 radar operates in a high-resolution, pulse-Doppler, track-while-scan mode. The Mk 86 FCS can handle up to 120 targets in the track-while-scan mode, handling two or three surface or low-flying target engagements simultaneously. The system can be integrated with the Naval Tactical Data System (NTDS).

A high scan rate of 60 rpm provides a one-second "data rate" to detect and more accurately track incoming missiles as well as surface targets. 167:1 optical pulse compression extends detection range. The basic SPQ-9 system provides low-altitude air-search (2,000 ft/610 m) and surface-search functions, and is enclosed by a radome; the other adds Identification Friend or Foe (IFF) and extends air coverage to an elevation of 25°.

The SPQ-9A provides pulse-to-pulse frequency agility in a choice of five frequencies to counter jamming and natural clutter, and to allow several radars to operate in a cluster without interfering with one another. Digital Moving Target Indicator (DMTI) processing added under a mid-1980s upgrade removes stationary objects from the target screen, reducing clutter. In addition, the upgrade introduced a Low-Noise Front End (LNFE), which increases effective system gain.

The SPQ-9A includes a separate radar beacon transmitter/receiver for accurate navigation during indirect shore bombardment, when the target is out of view of both the radar and optical sighting systems.

DEVELOPMENT • Prototypes tested beginning in 1967, with the first prototypes of the entire Mk 86 system being delivered to the US Navy in March 1970. Manufactured by Lockheed Electronics, Plainfield, New Jersey. In service on a variety of US surface combatants, the *Tarawa*-class amphibious assault ships, and Australian and German *Adams*-design destroyers.

SPECIFICATIONS •
BAND I/J
RANGE   20 nm (23 mi; 37 km) max; 450 ft (137 m) min
PEAK POWER   1.2 kW
PULSE WIDTH   0.3–16 microsec
PRF   3,000 Hz
SYSTEM GAIN   37 dB
ANTENNA WEIGHT   1,185 lb (537.5 kg) with radome
ANTENNA DIMENSIONS   7 ft 8½ in (2.35 m) wide × 2 ft 6 in (0.762 m)
ANTENNA BEAMWIDTH   1.35° × 3°

SPS-10

For decades, the AN/SPS-10 was the standard US Navy surface-search radar. Although considered a horizon-range navigation radar, it routinely detects targets at much greater ranges. Existing SPS-10s are being replaced by the solid-state SPS-67 that use the SPS-10's parabolic cylinder open-mesh antenna.

The original SPS-10 emitted 190–285-kW pulses. The next three versions used a more powerful 500-kW transmitter. SPS-10E/F versions offer a broader beamwidth of 1.9° × 16°.

DEVELOPMENT • Began in the early 1950s, with first deliveries in 1953, and achieved initial operational capability in 1955. Manufactured by Raytheon and GTE. Although long out of production, SPS-10 radars remain in widespread use.

SPECIFICATIONS •
BAND   G (5.45–5.825 GHz)
PEAK POWER   500 kW
PULSE WIDTH   0.25 or 1.3 microsec
PRF   625–650 Hz
SYSTEM GAIN   30 dB
ANTENNA BEAMWIDTH   1.5° × 16°
ANTENNA SCAN RATE   15 rpm
ANTENNA WEIGHT   442 lb (200 kg)
ANTENNA DIMENSIONS
   width   10 ft 6 in (3.2 m)
   height   6 ft 4 in (1.93 m)

SPS-40

The AN/SPS-40 is a family of long-range air-search and shipboard surveillance radars developed from the AN/SPS-31 and have been in US service since 1961. Although the SPS-40 was developed for use on destroyers, it is now the standard lightweight air-search system for the US Navy. It replaced the AN/SPS-6 and AN/SPS-29, and delayed the AN/SPS-49's introduction into service.

The Lockheed-developed family was replaced by an improved version, designated the SPS-40A, which in turn was replaced by the SPS-40B. Most SPS-40 systems now in use are the SPS-40D, an upgraded -40A that is fully solid-state.

The original SPS-40 had excellent range resolution, using a short transmitted pulse. The system uses a feed horn overslung on an open-mesh parabolic reflector antenna. Radar signals were originally emitted in the Ultra-High Frequency (UHF) band, using pulse compression for very long detection ranges.

Developments that resulted in the SPS-40A included a new broadband transmitter and solid-state receiver changes. Scan rate was a relatively low 6 rpm. Both the SPS-40 and -40A were un-reliable and had a low Mean Time Between Failure (MTBF) rate. These variants had difficulty spotting air targets closer than the radar's horizons (e.g., 300 ft/91.4 m to 18 nm/21 mi/33 km) when they flew at less than 50,000 ft (15,240 m).

The SPS-40B included an AIMS Identification Friend or Foe (IFF) system, 10 Radio Frequency (RF) operation channels, and a Low Flyer Detection Mode (LFDM). Some versions included a Minimum Range Modification (MRM) system that provided range and bearing data on low-flying aircraft in the SPS-40 and -40A's blind spot.

Modifications to the LFDM were included in the SPS-40C system that went into service in the early 1970s. The SPS-40C and its improved version, the SPS-40D, are solid-state systems with a 40% increase in reliability and maintainability over the previous SPS-40 versions. In addition, the Two-Dimensional (2D) SPS-40D has automatic target detection capability for use in a shipboard combat system, Digital Moving Target Indicator (DMTI).

DEVELOPMENT • Derived from the SPS-31, the SPS-40 was first delivered in June 1961. Older SPS-40s were upgraded to the C/D configurations, which use solid-state electronics to increase reliability from about 80 hours MTBF to about 200 hours. SPS-40E used a Westinghouse SSTx solid-state transmitter that powers up quickly and is much more reliable. Although envisioned for retrofitting into existing SPS-40 ships, the SPS-40E failed to attract funding and was canceled.

Manufactured by Lockheed Electronics, Plainfield, New Jersey. In service in many US ships as well as former US Navy ships transferred to other countries.

SPECIFICATIONS •
BAND   B (400–450 MHz)
PEAK POWER   225 kW; pulse-compressed 200 kW

PULSE WIDTH   3 or 60 microsec, compressed to 1 microsec (or 0.6 microsec) in some variants
PRF   278 or 300 Hz
SYSTEM GAIN   21 dB
ANTENNA BEAMWIDTH   11° × 19°
ANTENNA SIDELOBES
  horizontal   27 dB
  vertical   10 dB
ANTENNA SCAN RATE   7.5 or 15 rpm
WEIGHT
  antenna   1,728 lb (784 kg)
  below-decks equipment
        3,474 lb (1,576 kg)

SPS-48

The AN/SPS-48 is a Three-Dimensional (3D) FRESCAN (Frequency Scanning) radar used for long-range air search and for providing data to the Standard SM-2 series of medium- and long-range SAMs. The SPS-48 design eliminated the earlier SPS-39/42's mechanical stabilizer base, which was a principal source of weight, bulk, and equipment complexity.

The FRESCAN technique gives the system increased range and a high data rate that improve the probability of detecting a target. Using changes in frequency to steer the beam in elevation, the radar emits nine pulses of three microseconds each for a 6° elevation coverage. Each successive pulse stream shifts upward, providing coverage (in the earlier variants) from 0° to 45°. An antijamming mode transmits the signal in a single beam for 27 microseconds; processing compresses the return to three microseconds.

When the SPS-48 and SPS-48A were upgraded with Automatic Detection and Tracking (ADT) features and a Moving Target Indicator (MTI) capability, they were redesignated the SPS-48C. The SPS-48E encompasses elevation coverage of 0°–65°, has fewer components, lower sidelobes for greater ECM resistance, and better small-target performance.

DEVELOPMENT • Development began in 1959 with the radar achieving initial operational capabilities in 1962 (SPS-48), 1968 (SPS-48A), 1974 (SPS-48C), and 1983 (SPS-48E). The first SPS-48A production set was deployed on the cruiser *Worden* (CG 18) in March 1965; the *Biddle* (CG 34) was first with the -48E, completing installation in July 1987.

Under the New Threat Upgrade (NTU) program, the SPS-48E was fitted to all cruisers in the *Leahy, Belknap, California,* and *Virginia* classes as well as the cruiser *Long Beach* and the *Kidd*-class guided-missile destroyers. Manufactured by ITT Gilfillan in Van Nuys, California.

Plans in the 1980s to retrofit 12 aircraft carriers with the SPS-48E ran afoul of the $75 million per carrier cost ($12 million for the radar itself), and only the *Kitty Hawk* (CV 63) and *Constellation* (CV 64) actually received them.

SPECIFICATIONS •
BAND   E/F (2.9–3.1 GHz)
RANGE   220 nm (253 mi; 408 km); low angle 230 nm (265 mi; 426 km)
  accuracy   690 ft (210 m)
ELEVATION COVERAGE
  SPS-48C: +0°/+45°
  SPS-48E: +0°/+65°
MAXIMUM ALTITUDE   100,000 ft (30,480 m)
ELEVATION ACCURACY   1/6°
RESOLUTION IN RANGE   1,500 ft (457 m), in elevation 2°
POWER
  peak   2.2 MW
  average   SPS-48C: 15 kW
        SPS-48E: 35 kW
PULSE WIDTH   3 microsec
PRF   1,250–2,000 Hz
SYSTEM GAIN   38.5 dB
WEIGHT   (SPS-48C)
  total system   22,000 lb (9,979 kg)
  antenna   4,500 lb (2,041 kg)
ANTENNA BEAMWIDTH   1.5° × 1.6°
ANTENNA SIDELOBES
  SPS-48C: -23 dB
  SPS-48E: -33 dB

ANTENNA SCAN RATE 7.5 or 15 rpm
ANTENNA WIDTH
SPS-48C: 16 ft 2 in (4.93 m)
SPS-48E: 18 ft (5.49 m)
ANTENNA HEIGHT
SPS-48C: 17 ft 6 in (5.33 m)
SPS-48E: 18 ft (5.49 m)

SPS-49

The AN/SPS-49 is said to be the most effective rotating, Two-Dimensional (2D) search radar in US Navy service. Although developed in the 1960s, it did not enter service until the first *Oliver Hazard Perry*-class frigate was commissioned in 1977. In the next 15 years, the SPS-49 became the Navy's principal 2D air-search radar and has been produced in several variations.

An underslung, fan-shaped horn feeds the open-mesh, orange-peel parabolic antenna. A klystron amplifier maintains pulse-to-pulse stability of signal amplification while mechanical stabilization steadies the antenna.

A significant update entered service as the SPS-49(V)5. Improvement includes Automatic Detection Tracking (ADT), digital pulse-Doppler processing, Constant False-Alarm Rate (CFAR) processing, and clutter mapping. The system also uses frequency agility, four-loop Coherent Sidelobe Canceler (CLSC), an anti-chaff mode, and up-spotting (elevating the main beam) for better Electronic Counter-Countermeasures (ECCM) capability. In its (V)5 form, the radar's Mean Time Between Failure (MTBF) is a relatively healthy 600 hours.

VARIANTS • SPS-49(V)1 designates *Perry*-class ship installations.

SPS-49(V)2 replaces earlier 2D air-search radars in New Threat Upgrade (NTU) refit of cruisers and destroyers.

SPS-49(V)3 fitted in Canadian ships and has embedded ADT system.

SPS-49(V)6 designates installations in *Ticonderoga*-class cruisers.

DEVELOPMENT • The SPS-49 was evaluated in 1965 on board the experimental destroyer *Gyatt* (DDG 1/DD 712) but first became operational only in 1977. It is the principal 2D search radar in US service. Australian and Spanish *Perry*-design frigates also operate the SPS-49. Manufactured by Raytheon, Wayland, Massachusetts.

In 1990, the Navy canceled the SPS-49 SSTx with solid-state transmitter then under development by Westinghouse.

SPECIFICATIONS •
BAND C (851–942 MHz)
POWER
peak   280 kW (V)1, 360 kW (V)5
average   10 kW (V)1–4, 13 kW (V)5
PULSE WIDTH 125 microsec (with 83:1 compression) or 2 microsec
PRF 280, 800, or 1,000 Hz
SYSTEM GAIN 29 dB
RANGE ACCURACY 0.03 nm
AZIMUTH ACCURACY 0.5°
SYSTEM WEIGHT BELOW DECKS
SPS-49(V): 13,791 lb (6,255 kg)
SPS-49(V)5: 14,004 lb (6,325 kg)
ANTENNA BEAMWIDTH 3.4° × 30° cosecant^2
ANTENNA WEIGHT
SPS-49(V)1: 3,210 lb (1,456 kg)
SPS-49(V)5: 3,165 lb (1,425 kg)
ANTENNA DIMENSIONS
width   24 ft (7.3 m)
height   14 ft 3 in (4.3 m)

SPS-52

The AN/SPS-52 is a US three-dimensional air-search radar with electronic Frequency Scanning (FRESCAN) in elevation and mechanical rotation of the antenna in azimuth. It is an improved AN/SPS-39 (the first FRESCAN radar) that uses a similar klystron transmitter, a planar-array antenna, digital beam stabilization, parametric amplifier, and has a longer range. It is smaller and less capable than the AN/SPS-48.

For short-range tracking, a high-data-rate mode (15 rpm scan rate) supplies a high-PRF signal. The radar also uses high-angle, medium-range detection and tracking and long-range tracking; the -52B and C also have a Moving Target Indicator (MTI) mode that ignores clutter. Maximum range is 60 nm (111 km) against small, high-speed targets, and out to much greater distances against large, high-flying aircraft. Maximum viewing elevation is 42° with limited angles of 13° in the short and medium ranges, 4.5° in the long range.

The antenna is the AN/SPA-72B planar array, tilted back at an angle of 25° from the vertical, allowing coverage to a high angle of elevation. 60 stacked linear arrays, each with 98 radiating slots, make up the antenna and are energized by a deep serpentine feed along one vertical edge.

The SPS-52B introduced MTI clutter rejection for better low-altitude performance and the AN/UYK-15 computer. Peak power is 900 kW, low power level is 14.4 kW. The SPS-52C added Automatic Target Detection (ATD) that allows operation with a computerized combat system and an increase in claimed MTBF to 216 hours.

DEVELOPMENT • Development began in 1963 for the SPS-52 and 1973 for the SPS-52C, with the SPS-52C entering service in the late 1970s. Manufactured by Hughes Aircraft Co., Fullerton, California. The SPS-52 has been installed in several US warship classes (primarily the *Adams*-class destroyers and the *Tarawa* and *Wasp* amphibious assault ships). Australian and German *Adams*-design ships also use the SPS-52 as well as several Italian, Japanese, and Spanish ship classes. The sets in the older ships are being

modified to the current SPS-52C configuration to improve reliability and performance.

SPECIFICATIONS •
BAND   E/F (2.91–3.1005 GHz)
RANGE
  short, high-data-rate
             60 nm (69 mi; 111 km)
  high-angle 160 nm (184 mi; 296 km)
  long   240–245 nm (276–282
                mi; 444–454 km)
PEAK POWER   1 MW
LOW POWER MODE   16 kW
PULSE WIDTH   2.5, 4.6, or 10 microsec
SCAN RATE   15, 10, or 7.5 rpm
SYSTEM GAIN   39.5 dB
WEIGHT
  below-decks equipment
             SPS-52B: 15,934 lb (7,228
             kg);
             SPS-52C: 14,040 lb (6,368
             kg)
ANTENNA WEIGHT   3,200 lb (1,451 kg)
ANTENNA DIMENSIONS
  width   13 ft 9 in (4.19 m)
  height   13 ft 11 in (4.24 m)

SPS-53/SPS-60

This high-resolution surface search and navigation radar uses a 5-ft (1.5-m) slotted array antenna. The earlier SPS-53 has vacuum tubes, the SPS-60 solid-state circuitry. The chief difference among variants is the width (5 ft or 8 ft/1.52 m or 2.44 m) and height of the antenna.

The SPS-60 has solid-state components and uses a standard 8-ft (2.44-m) antenna.

DEVELOPMENT • Development began in the early 1960s, with the radar achieving initial operational capability in 1967. In some ships, it replaced the SPS-5. Manufactured by Sperry Rand (later Unisys), Great Neck, New York. Remains in service on auxiliaries such as the *Sacramento* and *Wichita* fast support ships.

SPECIFICATIONS •
BAND   I/J
PEAK POWER   40 kW
PULSE WIDTH   0.5 or 1.0 microsec
PRF   750 or 1,500 Hz
BEAMWIDTH   1.6° × 20°
SCAN RATE   15 rpm

SPS-55

This I-band surface search and navigation radar replaces the widely used C-band SPS-10. Because it operates in the I-band, the SPS-55 avoids interfering with C-band missile target trackers. It also tracks low-flying aircraft and helicopters.

The antenna has two end-fed slotted waveguide arrays arranged back-to-back and squint-compensated. Antenna polarization can be either linear or circular, the latter to screen out rain echoes. Sidelobes are approximately the same regardless of polarization. It is fed by a coaxial magnetron that generates two different pulse widths. At the longer (1.0 microsecond) pulse width, signals fainter than -102 dB below output can be detected.

The receiver is an image-suppression mixer preamplifier that has Automatic Frequency Control (AFC), Fast Time Control (FTC), Sensitivity Time Control (STC), and logarithmic/linear-logarithmic detection processing. Sector width can range between 10° and 180°, and coverage can start at any point around the horizon.

All components except the magnetron are solid-state, which contributes to higher Mean Time Between Failures (MTBF) and lower Mean Time to Repair (MTTR). Required MTBF was 500 hours; test results showed an MTBF of 1,200 hours.

VARIANTS • SPS-502 is a Canadian-built variant 95% compatible with SPS-55, but operating in the G-band and using the SPS-10B antenna truncated paraboloid antenna. The receiver has low-noise GAS Field-Effect Transistor (FET) RF amplifier ahead of the mixer preamp. Most characteristics are identical except: vertical antenna beamwidth is 12.5°, and noise figure is less than 5 dB.

DEVELOPMENT • Developed by Raytheon, but produced by Cardion Electronics (part of Ferranti International) in Woodbury, New York. The first production contract was placed in 1971. Several recent surface combatant classes as well as the *Avenger*-class minesweepers operate the SPS-55.

SPECIFICATIONS •
BAND   I (9.05-10 GHz)
PEAK POWER   130 kW
PULSE WIDTHS   1.0 microsec (+/−0.1 microsec) or 0.12 microsec (+/−0.03 microsec)
PRF   750 or 2,250 Hz
MINIMUM RANGE   long pulse 900 ft (274 m); short pulse 150 ft (46 m)
RESOLUTION   long pulse 650 ft (198 m); short pulse 75 ft (23 m)
RECEIVER BANDWIDTH   long pulse 1.2 MHz (+/−0.25 MHz); short pulse 10.0 MHz (+/−1.0 MHz)
RECEIVER NOISE FIGURE   10.5 dB maximum
ANTENNA SCAN RATE   16 rpm
ANTENNA GAIN
    linear polarization
        30 dB minimum at 9.5 GHz
    circular polarization
        no more than 4 dB less than linear
ANTENNA BEAMWIDTH   1.5° × 20°
ANTENNA SIDELOBES
    linear polarization
        −26° within 10°, −30° outside
    circular polarization
        −25.5° within 10°, −30° outside

SPS-59 (LN-66)

AN/SPS-59 is the US Navy designation for the LN-66 short-range navigation radar that is usually fitted in surface ships as a secondary, close-range navigation radar.

DEVELOPMENT • Manufactured by Marconi of Canada. In service in many US Navy ships as well as in the SH-2F LAMPS I ASW helicopter.

SPECIFICATIONS •
BAND I/J
PEAK POWER 10 kW
PULSE WIDTH 0.05 or 0.5 microsec

SPS-63

The AN/SPS-63 is a US license-built version of the Italian 3RM-20N surface-search radar. The antenna is a horizontally polarized slotted waveguide that produces a vertical beam pattern of 26°, shaped to 40°. The 20-kW transmitter has four Pulse Repetition Frequencies (PRF) and four pulse lengths.

DEVELOPMENT • Manufactured by the US firm Dynell Electronics under license from the Italian company SMA of Florence, Italy, to fit in the *Pegasus*-class patrol hydrofoil craft.

SPECIFICATIONS •
BAND I (9.375 GHz)
RANGE 40 nm (46 mi; 74 km) instrumented, 60 ft (18.3 m) minimum
BEARING ACCURACY 1°; resolution 1.2°
PEAK POWER 20 kW
PULSE WIDTH 0.05, 0.15, 0.5, or 1.5 microsec
PRF 6,000, 3,000, 1,500, or 750 Hz
SYSTEM WEIGHT 217 lb (98 kg)
SCAN RATE 25 rpm

SPS-64(V)

The AN/SPS-64(V) is a modular surface search and navigation radar that can operate in either F- or I-band. Depending on the variant, an SPS-64 set will combine elements of four I-band and one F-band slotted-waveguide antennas as well as three transmitter power levels emitting in either band.

In the F-band, the range is approximately 50 nm (92.6 km), and the radar can automatically track 20 targets simultaneously. I-band sets are used for navigation and feature higher resolution at a shorter range. RAYPATH, which plots and displays surface tracks, and RAYCAS, which tracks air targets, are also part of the system.

The commercial name for this radar is Pathfinder, and Raytheon designations include RM 1220 and RM 1620.

VARIANTS •
SPS-64(V)1/7/8/9: One 20-kW I-band transmitter, 6-ft (1.83-m) I-band antenna; Coast Guard; SPS-64(V)5 is similar to (V)1 for US Army ships; SPS-64(V)11 is (V)1 with RAYPATH; Coast Guard.

SPS-64(V)2: As (V)1, but with two 20-kW I-band transmitters and three displays; SPS-64(V)3 has two displays; SPS-64(V)10 has two 6-ft (1.83-m) I-band antennas.

SPS-64(V)4: One each of 20-kW I-band, 60-kW F-band transmitter, 6-ft (1.83-m) I-band, and 12-ft (3.66-m) F-band antenna; SPS-64(V)6 has 50-kW I-band transmitter and RAYCAS; Coast Guard (US Navy version is (V)15). SPS-64(V)16 is (V)6 with RAYPATH; US Army. SPS-64(V)18 is (V)15 with 9-ft (2.74-m) antenna.

SPS-64(V)12/13/14: As (V)5, but with 10-kW transmitter, (V)14 in radome; US Army.

SPS-64(V)17: 60-kW F-band transmitter, 12-ft (3.66-m) antenna, RAYPATH; US Army

DEVELOPMENT • Manufactured by Raytheon Co., Wayland, Massachusetts. Introduced in the early 1980s in US Navy ships and is the standard Coast Guard surface-search/navigation radar. Some US Army ships and craft also operate the radar, as do an assortment of foreign naval ships.

SPECIFICATIONS •

BAND   F (3.025–3.075 GHz) and/or I (9.345–9.405 GHz)

PEAK POWER   F band 60 kw; I band 20 or 50 kW

PULSE WIDTHS   0.06, 0.5, or 1.0 microseconds

PRF   3,600, 1,800, or 900 Hz

ANTENNA SCAN RATE   33 rpm

ANTENNA BEAMWIDTH (HORIZONTAL × VERTICAL)
F band: 2° × 25°
I band: 0.7°, 0.9°, 1.25°, or 1.9° × 22°

ANTENNA WEIGHT   6-ft 140 lb (63.5 kg); 12-ft 332 lb (150.6 kg)

SYSTEM GAIN   28 dB

SPS-58/SPS-65(V)

The AN/SPS-58/65 is a pulse-Doppler radar specifically adopted to detect antiship cruise missiles and for target acquisition for the Sea Sparrow point defense missile system.

Early variants had a 16-foot elliptical antenna, but later radars use an AN/SPS-10 antenna that had its original feed horn replaced by a dual-feed waveguide horn. The SPS-58 stands alone and, in some versions, has its own display; it uses a klystron transmitter. Taiwan Navy ships use the SPS-58 as the missile detector for the H930 combat system. Can apply both Automatic Target Detection (ATD) for a direct link to the H930 and Moving Target Indicator (MTI) processing to screen out clutter.

SPS-65 versions have a solid-state transmitter and feed their data into the ship's Naval Tactical Data System (NTDS), which combines the information with other sensor data and puts it up on integrated displays.

SPS-65(V)1 was designed as a detector rather than an engagement radar. SPS-65(V)2 adds autotracking (but operator must key it), a Fire Control Interface Group (FCIG), track history, target centroids (several previous recorded target positions rationalized into one), NTDS symbology, and output suitable for either gun or missile systems. SPS-65(V)ER operates in three modes using a more powerful transmitter, improved signal processing that includes digital MTI, stretch-pulsed transmission and pulse compression, and burst-to-burst frequency agility. The SPS-65(V)1 has a specified Mean Time Between Failure (MTBF) of 400 hours.

DEVELOPMENT • Development began in early 1967 after studies showed that existing radars would not detect low-flying missiles quickly enough. The sinking of the Israeli destroyer *Eilat* in December 1967 by an antiship missile gave an extra impetus to the project. Six different ideas or designs were considered before the Navy chose the Siemens MPDR-45 to be developed into the SPS-58 by Westinghouse Electric Corp., Baltimore, Maryland.

Those US ships fitted with SPS-58s saw them replaced by SPS-65(V) sets in the 1980s. In service in US aircraft carriers and command ships as well as in Taiwanese destroyers and ex-US *Knox*-class frigates in other navies.

SPECIFICATIONS •

BAND   D (1.215–1.365 GHz)

RANGE   (detection of 10.8-ft²/1-m² target)
-65(V)1/2: 23 nm (26.5 mi; 42.6 km)
-65(V)ER: 61 nm (70.2 mi; 113 km)

RANGE ACCURACY
-65(V)1/2: 1,500 ft (457 m)
-65(V)ER: 608 ft (185 m)

RANGE RESOLUTION   3,000 ft (914 m)

ELEVATION COVERAGE
-65(V)1/2: 16°
-65(V)ER: 30°

AZIMUTH ACCURACY   0.5°
AZIMUTH RESOLUTION
  -65(V)1/2: 5.8°
  -65(V)ER: 3.5°
PEAK POWER
  -65(V)1/2: 12 kW
  -65(V)ER: 25 kW
AVERAGE POWER
  -65(V)1/2: 260 W
  -65(V)ER: 1,200 W
PULSE WIDTH   7 microsec
PRF   -65(V)1/2 2,315 or 3,064 Hz, plus
  300–625 Hz in -65(V)ER
SYSTEM GAIN   23 dB
MTI IMPROVEMENT FACTOR   60 dB
SYSTEM WEIGHT, SPS-65   1,594 lb (723 kg)
ANTENNA WEIGHT, SPS-65   439 lb (199 kg)
ANTENNA BEAMWIDTH   3°
SCAN RATE   20 rpm (plus 10 rpm in (V)ER)

SPS-67(V)

The AN/SPS-67 naval surface search and navigation radar was developed as a successor to the long-serving AN/SPS-10 radar. Using the SPS-10 antenna, the SPS-67(V) replaces the vacuum-tube electronics with solid-state Standard/ Electronic Modules (SEM) vacuum tube technology to simplify repair and maintenance.

A digital noise suppressor and a very short-pulse mode improve performance, especially resolution of small targets at close range. This is in addition to the two existing SPS-10 modes. The (V)2 replaces the open-mesh, truncated paraboloid antenna with a linear array. The (V)3 has an add-on unit that provides for integration with the SYS-1 integrated automatic detection and tracking system, as well as providing automatic target detection and digital moving target indication.

DEVELOPMENT • Prototyping began in the 1970s, the SPS-67 achieving initial operational capability in 1982. Manufactured by Norden Systems, United Technologies Corp. The new antenna system, also built by Norden, was first tested in 1983.

Several surface combatant classes have been refitted with the SPS-67; the *Arleigh Burke*-class destroyers are receiving them during construction. In addition, later *Nimitz*-class carriers use the SPS-67, as do new amphibious and auxiliary ships.

SPECIFICATIONS •
BAND   C
PULSE WIDTHS   1, 0.25, or 0.10 microsec
PRF   750, 1,200, or 2,400 Hz
SCAN RATE   15 or 30 rpm

SPY-1 Aegis

The AN/SPY-1 multifunction, phased-array radar serves the Aegis Antiair Warfare (AAW) weapons system, which is composed of the SPY-1, a Command and Decision (C&D) element, fire control system, consoles and large-screen displays, air-search and fire control radars, missile launchers, and the RIM-66 Standard-MR and -ER antiaircraft missiles.

Aegis is certainly the most expensive shipboard sensor suite ever installed, and it has been criticized for its expense and for perceived shortcomings in service. Moreover, it is an electromagnetic beacon of prodigious size, beckoning anti-radar weapons launched from far-off platforms.

Nevertheless, as a fleet defense hub, the system provides far more capability than any other combination of systems. Moreover, the system has such signal processing power and range that it is being developed as a mobile Anti-Tactical Ballistic Missile (ATBM) system.

Most visible of all of these elements are the four octagonal fixed-array antennas mounted on superstructure faces, each measuring 12 ft 6 in (3.81 m) across. Each antenna is subdivided into 140 array modules of 32 radiating elements each; actual number of transmitting elements is 4,096 and receiving elements, 4,352. Each antenna covers a 110° arc to provide full 360° coverage with some overlap.

Aegis system computers process target track information and provide beam steering. Hundreds of targets can be acquired and identified simultaneously out to ranges of some 250 nm (288 mi; 463 km). The system provides terminal guidance for up to 20 missiles at one time through the associated Raytheon Mk 99 Standard SM-1/2 missile directors.

The Mk 1 C&D element can be programmed to select an appropriate and automatic response to any threat by any weapons system; these are called doctrine statements and are placed in a file until called by a ship's officer. During intense engagements, the combat system will handle most of the interceptions or other responses automatically. As we note below under Combat Experience, this is not immune to disastrous misuse.

Later Aegis ships fitted with the SPY-1B Baseline 4 have AN/UYK-43 computers and use the Advanced Combat Direction System (ACDS). The computers also run much faster and can maintain many more track files simultaneously.

Four Hughes AN/UYA-4 or -21 Large-Screen Displays (LSD), each measuring 3 ft 6 in (1.07 m) square, project processed information. The four LSDs can display ASW, AAW, and ASuW (Antisurface [ship] Warfare) information. Two sets of consoles face the LSD and five Automated Status Boards (ASTAB) perch above each pair of LSDs.

The SPY-1's ability to defeat ECM includes frequency diversity and jamming detection, which leads it to shift to frequencies that show less interference. Digital signal processing techniques counter or suppress jamming as well as sea clutter, allowing the system to spot sea-skimming missiles more easily.

VARIANTS • SPY-1B is a production version built for *Princeton* (CG 59) and later ships with upgraded antennae, improved transmitter with double-duty cycle and signal processor for increased effectiveness against low-flying and small radar-cross-section missiles, and enhanced ECM resistance including reduction of sidelobes by 15 dB.

SPY-1D is the single-deckhouse version in the *Arleigh Burke* class with two UY21 displays, three illuminators.

DEVELOPMENT • Development of the Aegis SPY-1 began in the late 1960s as a successor to the canceled Typhon system. The SPY-1 (one radar "face") began operation at the RCA development facility in Moorestown, New Jersey, in 1973, followed a year later by a single "face" being installed in the missile test ship *Norton Sound* (AVM 1). Lockheed Martin's Electronics Division at Moorestown produces the Aegis system, which achieved initial operational capability in *Ticonderoga* (CG 47) in 1983. LM (formerly GE) is prime contractor for the Aegis weapons system and "design agent" for the more comprehensive Aegis combat system.

A Unisys-Westinghouse team qualified in 1986 as the second source for the SPY-1D single-deckhouse version fitted in the *Arleigh Burke*-class destroyers, but fell victim to a March 1990 cancellation of plans to procure from two contractors.

US support of the Japanese Aegis destroyer program aroused significant criticism in Congress as well as in Japan. Concerns focused on the transfer of sensitive technology as well as the great cost. Despite the opposition, the program proceeded, and the first of four Japanese *Kongou*-class Aegis ships entered service in March 1993.

COMBAT EXPERIENCE • While providing gunfire support for the US Marines stationed in Beirut in 1983, the USS *Ticonderoga* (CG 47) used the SPY-1 radar to guard against suicide aircraft or small craft. Although most observers contended that the coverage was complete, a destroyer skipper claimed that the Aegis radar failed to pick up a Cessna light aircraft that was headed for the task force. The destroyer *Tatnall's* crew tracked the plane visually until it came within range of the destroyer's guns, while the Aegis radar allegedly never "saw" it.

On July 3, 1988, the *Vincennes'* (CG 49) SPY-1A detected a target that had just taken off from Bandar Abbas airfield in Iran. The *Vincennes'* captain, relying on SPY-1A data as well as IFF and unsuccessful attempts to communicate with the aircraft, launched 2 Standard-MR SM-2 missiles at the target. One destroyed the aircraft, killing the 290 passengers and crew on board the misidentified Airbus A300 commercial airliner.

11 different *Ticonderoga*-class cruisers were deployed in Operations Desert Shield/Desert Storm in 1990–91.

SPECIFICATIONS •
BAND   F (3.1–3.5 GHz)
POWER
  peak   4–6 MW
  average   58 kW
PULSE WIDTH   6.4, 12.7, 25.4, or 51 microsec
PULSE COMPRESSION RATIO   128:1
BANDWIDTH   sustained coherent 10 MHz; instantaneous 40 MHz
SYSTEM SCAN RATE   12 rpm air coverage; 1 rpm at the horizon
SYSTEM GAIN   42 dB
WEIGHT
  above decks, per face: SPY-1A 13,030 lb (5,910 kg); SPY-1B 7,900 lb (3,583 kg)
  below decks: SPY-1A 131,584 lb (59,686 kg)
ANTENNA BEAM WIDTH   1.7° × 1.7°

VPS-2

The AN/VPS-2 is a coherent pulse-Doppler range-only radar built into the Spanish Meroka naval Close-In Weapons System (CIWS) and the US Army's M163A2 self-propelled and M167A2-towed Vulcan Air Defense Guns (VADS). The VPS-2 antenna is mounted on the turret and moves with the barrel and sight mounts. The optical sight can be laid independently.

The radar operates autonomously to provide tracking of targets and the angular tracking rate. Moving Target Indicator (MTI) processing eliminates clutter. An automatic search and lock-on mode places the optical sight on the target for the gunner. Computation of the radar-measured range and range rate predicts future target position and adjusts the gun accordingly.

The Meroka CIWS uses the VPS-2 matched with the Alenia RAN-12L/X search radar through the Alenia PDS-10 tactical-data console.

DEVELOPMENT • Initial operational capability in the late 1960s. Manufactured by Lockheed Electronics Co., Plainfield, New Jersey. Shipboard use is confined to the Spanish *Perry*-design frigates to support the Meroka.

SPECIFICATIONS •
BAND   I (9,200–9,500 MHz; 6 crystal-controlled frequencies)
SEARCH RANGE   2.7 nm (3.1 mi; 5 km)
TARGET TRACKING   49–1,017 ft/sec (15–310 m/sec)
PEAK POWER   1.4 kW (average 10 watts)
ANTENNA BEAMWIDTH   4° conical beam
SUBCLUTTER VISIBILITY   40 dB or better

STRATEGIC WARNING RADARS

The United States Air Force Space Command (AFSPACECOM) is tasked with providing warning of strategic and tactical ballistic missile warning. Although the threat of such a missile attack is more remote than ever, many missiles still remain in various stages of operational capability throughout the world.

Therefore, USAF continues to operate radar and satellite systems to provide early warning and transmit critical data to senior decision makers in the National Command Authority (NCA). The sensors employed to provide warning are:

* **Defense Support Program (DSP):** This space-based system consists of satellites positioned about 22,300 miles above the equator. The satellites monitor areas known to have ballistic-missile launch capability along with large ocean areas. Satellite sensors detect the heat generated from a missile launch and transmit the data to ground stations that receive and provide analysis of the information. First launch of a DSP satellite was in the early 1970s.
* **BMEWS:** This radar system consists of 1950s-technology radars consisting of three large detection radars and a tracking radar located at three northern sites.
* **Pave Paws:** This system was developed in the mid-1970s to provide warning of a sea-launched ballistic missile threat. The system consists of a series of four sites located on the periphery of the continental United States.
* **PARCS:** PARCS (Perimeter Acquisition Radar Attack Characterization System) consists of a single radar located at Cavalier Air Force Station, North Dakota. This single-faced, phased-array radar provides warning and data on ICBM and SLBM attacks. It entered its present role in 1976 when the radar was transferred from the US Army.
* **Cobra Dane:** A single-faced, phased-array radar located at Shemya AFB, Alaska. It collects data on ballistic missile launches to the Northwest and over the Pacific.
* **Conventional Radars:** Two conventional radars are located at Pirinclik Air Station, Turkey, to collect space and missile activity data and provide limited warning. One radar provides tracking data and the other provides detection.

Ballistic Missile Early-Warning System/BMEWS (AN/FPS-49)

The BMEWS consists of three radar installations located at Fylingdales Moor, England; Thule, Greenland; and Clear, Alaska. Each site has radars used to detect land-based ballistic missile attacks against the United States, to track objects in orbit, and to monitor other Russian rocket launchings.

Each BMEWS site has different radar equipment. Fylingdales Moor has an AN/FPS-49 surveillance and tracking radar. Clear has an AN/FPS-92 tracking radar, an update of the FPS-49, as well as three large AN/FPS-50 surveillance radars. All three sites had their data processing and tactical control capabilities updated in the early 1980s.

Fylingdales is under the command and control of the Royal Air Force; the other two sites are under the US Air Force

BMEWS
U.S. GOVERNMENT DEPARTMENT OF DEFENSE

Space Command. All three are linked for data transfer between them.

The FPS-49 tracking radar has an 82-ft (25-m) parabolic dish housed in a 141-ft (43-m) diameter radome. Maximum range is approximately 2,700 nm (3,110 mi; 5,000 km), and the radar operates in the B/C (UHF) band. The radar was manufactured by RCA Corp.

The FPS-50 has a distinctive fixed parabolic-torus reflector that is 400 ft (122 m) wide and 165 ft (50 m) high. It operates in the B-band (425 MHz) at a peak power of 5 MW. Maximum range is 2,650 nm (3,052 mi; 4,910 km), and it covers an arc of 160° and has an elevation of +3.5° to +7°. The radar was built by General Electric Co.

Thule had four FPS-50s and one FPS-49A that were recently replaced with a solid-state, phased-array system built by Raytheon Corp., which is similar to the AN/FPS-115 PAVE PAWS installation. The radar began operations in July

1987, and the older antennas were dismantled.

The more recent Thule radar has two phased-array faces, each covering 120°, in a structure that stands 92 ft (28 m) high. Its maximum range is approximately 2,850 nm (3,280 mi; 5,280 km), and its beams can be elevated electronically from +3° to +85°.

DEVELOPMENT • The initial operational capability of the FPS-49/50 was in 1962; Thule's phased array was in 1987. The BMEWS is operated by the US Air Force Space Command.

The Fylingdales FPS-49 was replaced by a phased-array system in the early 1990s that became operational on October 1, 1992. Raytheon won the US Air Force $166.8-million contract for full system upgrade at Fylingdales in June 1988. Unlike the Thule system, the Fylingdales radar has three faces and offers full 360° coverage. Each face of the array consists of 2,560 active elements and is capable of tracking up to 800 objects simultaneously. Since becoming operational, the new radar averaged tracking about 6,000 satellite tracks a week, compared to 2,000 a week with the older system.

The Alaskan BMEWS site was upgraded in the early 1990s to a dual-faced, phased array.

The former Soviet Union had argued that the Thule and Fylingdales Moor radars violated the 1972 Anti-Ballistic Missile (ABM) agreement's provisions forbidding installation of ABM radars beyond a signatory's national borders. The Reagan administration countered that the Thule radar can be upgraded because the modifications are based on technology not understood in 1972. When the Soviets admitted that their Phased-Array Radar (PAR) at Krasnoyarsk violated the ABM treaty, they also contended the two US radars were in similar violation.

PAVE PAWS (AN/FPS-115)

The AN/FPS-115 Precision Acquisition Vehicle Entry Phased Array Warning System (PAVE PAWS) radar is a large, solid-state-technology, phased-array radar system with the primary role of detecting and tracking Submarine-Launched Ballistic Missiles (SLBM). It is a part of the North American Air Defense Command (NORAD) early-warning system as well as the Worldwide Military Command and Control System (WMCCS). These radars replaced the older FPS-85 and FSS-7 SLBM warning radars.

The four PAVE PAWS installations are located near the US coastlines. The first PAVE PAWS was erected at the former Otis AFB (now Cape Cod Air Force Station), Massachusetts, and covers most of the Atlantic Ocean area. The second, at Beale AFB in California, watches the Pacific Ocean. The third and fourth—at Robins AFB, Georgia, and Eldorado AFS,

PAVE PAWS
U.S. GOVERNMENT DEPARTMENT OF DEFENSE

Texas—cover the southern US coast. Some overlap in coverage occurs with the four sites.

Each radar installation is a 10-story building covering 76,732 ft² (7,129 m²) with three faces that tilt 20° from the vertical. Triangular segments fill in the sides such that the base is six-sided and the top is triangular. Two adjacent faces contain flat, octagonal, phased-array antennas measuring 102 ft (31.1 m) across.

Each electronically scanned and steered antenna has the capacity to hold approximately 5,400 individual elements. The Otis AFB installation has 1,792 active elements in each face, and Beale 3,584 after an update. Robins and Eldorado can use all 5,354 elements. Two computers direct each of the PAVE PAWS and are housed in the same structures.

An often-cited measure of the radar's capability is its ability to track a basketball-size object at distances up to 1,050 nm (1,200 mi; 1,931 km). This proves useful in its primary anti-Sea-Launched Ballistic Missile (SLBM) mission as well as in supporting the Air Force's Spacetrack satellite tracking system.

DEVELOPMENT • Initial operational capability at Otis AFB in 1979, Beale AFB in 1980, Robins AFB in 1986, and Eldorado Air Force Station in 1987. In February 1989, sources reported that the PAVE PAWS near Robins AFB had to be shut down periodically to eliminate the risk of detonating explosives on military aircraft that land at the base.

VARIANTS • PARCS (Perimeter Acquisition Radar Characterization System): Not a variant of PAVE PAWS but a predecessor that operates in the same band. Built to support the never-completed Safeguard anti-ballistic missile system installation at Grand Forks, North Dakota. Has one phased-array radar face with 110° coverage pointing northward and remains in service to supplement PAVE

PAWS. Compared to the PAVE PAWS, PARCS has a larger antenna (10,602.4 ft²/985 m²), a shorter pulse width (400–550 microseconds), slightly wider elevation arc (1°–90°), and a longer operating cycle (20–50%).

COMBAT EXPERIENCE • None.

SPECIFICATIONS •
MANUFACTURER   Raytheon
ANTENNA AREA   8,126.7 ft² (755 m²)
BAND   B (420–450 MHz)
COVERAGE
  azimuth   240°
  elevation   +3°/+85°
RANGE   approx 3,000 nm (3,455 mi; 5,560 km)
PEAK POWER PER ELEMENT   322 W
AVERAGE POWER   64–290 kW
PULSE WIDTH   300–5,000 microsec
BEAMWIDTH
  transmitting   2°
  receiving   2.2°
OPERATING CYCLE   11%–25%

Cobra Dane

The Cobra Dane is a large US phased-array radar located at Shemya AFB on Shemya Island in the Aleutian chain. It is used primarily for tracking objects in space and was formerly used to track Soviet missile test flights. In the flight-test tracking mode, Cobra Dane can follow 100 targets at once. As part of the early-warning network, the radar can provide tracking data on 200 targets, although this is not a major function. The computer, processing, and "back-end" radar equipment are being upgraded or replaced under a contract awarded in April 1990.

The single, circular, phased-array radar face is approximately 98 ft (30 m) in diameter and has about 35,000 elements, of which 15,000 are active. The radar faces southwest and covers an arc of 120°. The

Cobra Dane

Cobra Dane's Control Data Corp. Cyber 74-18 computer operates at 1 Million Instructions per Second (MIPS) and has a 131,000-word core memory. As part of the upgrade program, two Digital Equipment Corp. Vax 6000 series computers will replace the Cyber 74-18, one backing up the other. The DEC machines operate at 12 MIPS and have a main memory of 64 megabytes.

When upgrades were completed, the system improved its ability to catalog space objects from 5,000 separate objects to 12,000 initially and 15,000 if a growth option is exercised.

The Cobra Dane's range for space tracking is 25,000 nm (28,788 mi; 46,325 km). It is operated by the US Air Force Space Command.

DEVELOPMENT • The Cobra Dane's initial operational capability was in 1977. It was manufactured by Raytheon Co.

In April 1990, the Air Force awarded a contract worth up to $83.3 million to Raytheon to upgrade the digital signal and data processing. Raytheon is responsible for systems engineering and integration as well as developing radar-related software. TRW developed the application software for real-time mission operations, test and training simulation, and off-line data analysis. Control Data is responsible for technical support services development, operating systems, and applications.

Over-the-Horizon Backscatter Radar (AN/FPS-118)

The AN/FPS-118 radar system consists of a transmitter and a receiver located approximately 100 miles (161 km) apart. The OTH-B uses emissions bounced off the ionosphere to acquire targets up to 2,000 nm (2,303 mi; 3706 km) away; its dependence on atmospheric conditions has been a source of concern, but the

OTH-B is the only ground-based system with such a range. Minimum range is approximately 500 nm (576 mi; 927 km); the radar is blind to targets less than 500 nm away.

The first installation in Maine is a trial version (known as the Experimental Radar System/ERS) constructed by General Electric and, although a part of the operational system, it is less capable than those that had been planned for the North Central and West Coast. It is in limited operational use and has been renamed the East Coast Radar System (ECRS); the three sectors together cover a 180° arc from 16½° to 196½°, relative to true north.

There are 12 100-kW Continental Electronics/Varian elemental transmitters per 60° sector. The antennas can transmit in several different modes for surveillance and tracking. The emissions are received and processed by a 4,980-ft (1,518-m) receiver array at Columbia Falls.

DEVELOPMENT • The Maine site was accepted by the Air Force Operational Test and Evaluation Center in April 1990; the West Coast site was transferred to the Air Force in December 1990. Subsequently, USAF decided to shut down the West Coast system but maintain the site with a skeleton crew and reduce operations to 40 hours per week at the East Coast site, saving an estimated $37 million per year.

The Alaskan site was planned for completion in 1995. The first contract for the North Central site was planned for awarding in 1991. Both systems were canceled in late 1990.

VARIANTS • Preplanned Product Improvement (P3I) program began in FY1988 for the central US and Alaska systems, involving an upgrade of the system sensitivity. Hardware changes were also part of the program. The P3I was canceled when the OTH-B was cut back.

COMBAT EXPERIENCE • In late 1987 the Maine OTH-B radar had its first successful operational use when it picked up two Soviet Tu-142 Bear long-range antisubmarine aircraft at a range of 912 nm (1,050 mi; 1,690 km).

SPECIFICATIONS •
MANUFACTURER   General Electric
FREQUENCY   5–28 MHz
RANGE
  max   1,800 nm (2,073 mi; 3,335 km)
  minimum   500 nm (576 mi; 927 km)
EFFECTIVE RADIATED POWER   100 MW
BEAMWIDTH   7.5°
EAST COAST SITE
OPERATIONS CENTER
  size   32,500 ft² (3,019 m²)
  air-conditioning equipment
               180 US tons (163 metric tons)
               office 30 US tons (27 metric tons)
  power   normal: 2,000 kW
               standby: 1,200 kW
               UPS for 15 min: 465 KV ampere
  consoles   30 Aydin displays
  operators   officers: 37
               enlisted: 337
               civilian: 13
               support: 89
SOUNDER ANTENNAS
  tower height
               sector 1: 130 ft (40 m)
               sectors 2–3: 148 ft (45 m)
  pole height sector 1: 34 ft (10 m)
               sectors 2–3: 42 ft (13 m)
  foundations sector 1: 2,430 ft³ (69 m³)
               sectors 2–3: 1,161 ft² (33 m²)
TRANSMITTERS
  power   100 kW each

Transmitter Antenna Bands
A   5.00–6.74 MHz
B   6.74–9.09 MHz
C   9.09–12.25 MHz

D	12.25–16.50 MHz
E	16.50–22.25 MHz
F	22.25–28.00 MHz

RECEIVE ANTENNAS (MAIN ANTENNA)
tower height
  sectors 1–3 65 ft
  (20 m)
length   sectors 1–3 4,980 ft
  (1,518 m)
number of elements
  sectors 1–3 246

Seek Igloo (FPS-117/124)

Seek Igloo is a program to lower the operations and maintenance costs of the Alaskan early-warning radar network. The FPS-117 is part of the North Warning System (NWS) to replace the existing Distant Early Warning (DEW) Line, a series of bomber warning radars located along Canada's northern border. 15 FPS-117 radars replaced 31 AN/FPS-19 and AN/FPS-30 radars.

The FPS-117s have been mounted on existing DEW towers in Canada and Alaska, except for those at Baffin Island and two sites on the northeast coast of Labrador. The FPS-117 is a solid-state, three-dimensional, planar phased-array radar developed from the GE 592, an export-oriented, transportable variant of the AN/TPS-59 ground radar. The FPS-117 operates in the D-band and has a frequency bandwidth of 185 MHz. The radar scans electronically in elevation while rotating in azimuth. The radar requires no on-site personnel; maintenance is performed by three radar technicians who visit the site as necessary.

Unlike most radars, the FPS-117 has a distributed, redundant network of transceivers and power supplies connected directly to the antenna. Each transceiver requires relatively little power. Using distributed redundancy, the manufacturer claims higher reliability while retaining accuracy, range, and the ability to operate effectively in spite of heavy Electronic

Countermeasures (ECM) and environmental clutter. 44 row feeds and four column feeds constitute the surface of the antenna. Each row feed forms monopulse pencil beams with a linear, frequency-modulated waveform. Behind each row feed are the transistorized power generators, power modules (100-watt amplifiers), and receivers.

The transmitters have pulse-to-pulse frequency agility, being able to choose among 20 frequencies in a quasi-random manner. The transmitters are also capable of initiating pseudo-random Pulse Repetition Frequency (PRF) and pseudo-random beam positioning.

The receiver offers Moving Target Indicator (MTI) processing, Constant False-Alarm Rate (CFAR) processing, pulse compression, low sidelobes and sidelobe blanking, Doppler filtering for "lookdown" situations, and automatic environment clutter rejection.

The FPS-124 is a cylindrical phased-array radar that is approximately 12 ft (3.66 m) tall. It is cooled by 11 fans, which are the only moving parts in the system. FPS-124 is designed to be unattended, being monitored by a two-way link to satellites and having a mean time between critical failures of 4,000 hours (over 166 days). It will provide warning against small targets out to approximately 70 nm (81 mi; 130 km); coverage is 360°. The United States and Canada shared the approximately $640-million cost in a 60/40 ratio. Maintenance of the FPS-117 is contracted out to civilian firms.

DEVELOPMENT • The Seek Igloo's initial operational capability was in 1987. FPS-117 and FPS-124 developed by Unisys Defense Systems, McLean, Virginia. The 11 FPS-117s emplaced in Canada and four in Alaska are operational; four more were ordered in July 1991 for installation in Newfoundland, Nova Scotia, and British Columbia. The Unisys FPS-124 radar began Initial Operational Test and Evaluation (IOT&E) in the summer of 1988; further testing took place in June 1989. A $326.5-million contract for 37 production FPS-124s was awarded to Unisys in October 1990. In May 1991, the NORAD agreement was renewed for five years.

Three FPS-117s are also used by Germany in the NATO air defense network, and the US Air Force installed two FPS-117s in the northern part of Iceland.

Two FPS-117s were ordered by Saudi Arabia as part of the Peace Shield program, and a total of 17 FPS-117s are planned. Two FPS-117 systems are part of the $207-million Royal Thai Air Defense System (RTAD). RTAD, consisting of sensor systems and 31 microwave stations, was designed, developed, and tested over four years by Unisys. The $43-million cost of the FPS-117s is part of the US Military Assistance Program (MAP) to Thailand. The RTAD became operational in January 1990.

South Korea and Italy announced in February 1990 that they had ordered seven FPS-117 systems at a total cost of $130 million. South Korea ordered three systems, bringing the number of FPS-117s to eight. Italy ordered four systems, making them the seventh NATO nation to use the FPS-117.

Turkey signed a $15-million contract in October 1991 for one FPS-117 and an option for two more systems. Other operators of the system include Great Britain, Belgium, and Canada.

SPECIFICATIONS •

MANUFACTURER   General Electric
WEIGHTS
total   37,100 lb (16,828 kg)
transceiver group
              30,000 lb (13,608 kg)
process and control
              5,700 lb (2,585 kg)
operation control
              1,400 lb (635 kg)
DIMENSIONS
height   24 ft (7.32 m)
width   24 ft (7.32 m)

BAND   D
POWER
effective radiated
              125 MW
total system use
              70 kW max
peak   24.75 kW
duty factor 16%
RANGE
max   200 nm (230 mi; 371 km)
minimum   5 nm (5.8 mi; 9.3 km)
MAX ALTITUDE   100,000 ft (30,480 m)
ELEVATION   −6°/+20°
PULSE WIDTH
short range 51.2 microsec
compressed to
              0.8 microsec
long range   409.6 microsec
compressed to
              1.6 microsec
AZIMUTH   360°
ACCURACY
range at 200 nm
              0.25 nm (465 m)
azimuth   0.18°
altitude at 100 nm
              less than 3,000 ft (914 m)
elevation at 160 nm
              less than 6,000 ft
              (1,829 m)
MEAN TIME BETWEEN FAILURE (MTBF)
              1,076 hr
MEAN TIME TO REPAIR   30 min
PERIODIC MAINTENANCE TIME PER YEAR   35 hours

Relocatable Over-the-Horizon Radar (ROTHR/ TPS-71)

The AN/TPS-71 ROTHR is a tactical ionospheric backscatter radar system in development for the US Navy and similar in concept to the US Air Force AN/FPS-118 Over-the-Horizon-Backscatter (OTH-B) strategic early-warning radar system.

The ROTHR system consists of the transmitter and receiver sites. The transmitter installation uses two antenna arrays and a power generator. Each of the log periodic antennas uses 16 radiating elements. Each element or "curtain" consists of a series of dipole radiating elements hung at different lengths on a catenary (i.e., a wire suspended from a tower). Each dipole element is tuned to a specific frequency. The antennas transmit on a selected frequency using the arrays, which radiate throughout either the low or high band.

Power for the ROTHR is provided by generators housed in 10 shelters. Each generator uses four 5-kW amplifiers, producing up to 20 kW of power each. The amplifiers allow the generators to provide power for specific antenna elements. Power is fed unevenly to the antenna, with the outer elements receiving less power than the central elements, which receive the full 20-kW capacity. The antenna produces low sidelobes because of this gradual reduction of power. The lowered sidelobes reduce backscatter clutter, enhancing target detection. The receiving unit uses a single high-gain antenna with 372 dual monopole elements arranged in two rows that are 14 ft (4.27 m) apart. Each element pair uses a receiver to digitize incoming signals. The signals are then passed to a processor via a fiberoptic link. The processor forms the signal into a narrow receiving beam using digital beam-forming techniques. Targets are distinguished from clutter by their movement. Four computers are used to track detected targets. The system uses Digital Equipment Corp. Vax 8600 computers, which were to be replaced by newer Digital 6400 computers. Data is displayed in the Operations Control Center (OCC). ROTHR uses six interactive color workstations. Each workstation uses two raster displays and plasmas-touch screen controls. Frequencies available for use and locked-out frequencies can be displayed on a management spectral display system.

ROTHR differs from the strategic early-warning OTH-B system in that it has a tactical mission. The system is used to detect ships and aircraft beyond the horizon, supplementing surveillance by E-2C Hawkeye and E-3 AWACS airborne early-warning aircraft. The ROTHR enabled the Navy to detect former Soviet Union naval bombers and surface ships at a range up to 1,302 nm (1,500 mi; 2414 km). The total area that the ROTHR can monitor is 1.23 million nm^2 (1.63 million mi^2; 4.22 million km^2). This area is scanned in 176 sectors called Dwell Information Regions (DIR). DIRs are not uniform in size but vary according to distance from transmitter site. The system can concentrate on a specific DIR, or scan all DIRs, returning to specific ones as needed. The system may be moved but is not truly mobile. A system may remain at a site for periods of over one year. A ROTHR site may be prepared ahead of deployment and needs little maintenance. All antennas, operations control equipment, transmitters, and power sources can be moved to a site if required. The ROTHR is bistatic; its transmitting and receiving sites are separated by 50–100 nm (58–115 mi; 93–185 km), with the OCC colocated with the receiving site.

DEVELOPMENT • A prototype ROTHR was tested in Virginia and was moved to Amchitka Island in Alaska in 1989 to be the first operational ROTHR system. While in Virginia, the system fully tracked 24 of 25 ships in one region and partially tracked the 25th ship. It also demonstrated a 95% availability rate over a continuous two-week test period. The system's accuracy is classified, but the Wide Area Surveillance Systems program manager reported late in 1989 that the system had tracked an aircraft from flight through landing and only lost track as the aircraft entered a hangar. At least eight sites have been planned, including three on Guam, one in Hawaii, one in Virginia, and one in Europe.

The system's initial operational capability was in 1989. An engineering prototype was introduced in April 1984 and the operational evaluation in April 1989. Raytheon won a $273.7-million contract for the first three ROTHR systems in January 1990. The contract includes an option for another system and support equipment.

SPECIFICATIONS •
MANUFACTURER   Raytheon
ANTENNA ARRAY
    transmitting antenna
            length: 1,200 ft (365.8 m)
    receiving antenna
            length: 8,400 ft (2,560 m)
            height, monopole
            element: 19 ft (5.79 m)
    range   max: 2,000 nm (2,303 mi;
            3,706 km)
            minimum: approx 500
            nm (576 mi; 927 km)
AZIMUTH COVERAGE   60°
TRANSMITTING ANTENNA FREQUENCY
    low band   5–12 MHz
    high band   10–28 MHz
MAX POWER   20 kW per generator
AMPLIFIER POWER   5 kW each

Cobra Judy (SPQ-11)

The US AN/SPQ-11 Cobra Judy is a solid-state, phased-array radar fitted in the USNS *Observation Island* (T-AGM 23) operated in the Pacific. The operation monitors the exo- and endo-atmospheric portions of Russian and Chinese ballistic

missile test flights. Cobra Judy complements the Cobra Dane radar installed on Shemya Island in the Aleutians.

The Cobra Judy radar installation is a 250-ton, mechanically rotated, four-story-high structure on the afterdeck of the *Observation Island*. It has one octagonal radar face that measures 22 ft 6 in (6.86 m) across and contains approximately 12,000 elements. Detection and tracking are controlled by a Control Data Corp. CYBER 175-112 computer.

As originally designed, Cobra Judy operated only in the S (E/F) band. A recent modernization program added a parabolic dish antenna abaft the *Observation Island*'s funnel. This second radar operates in the X (I/J) band to gather higher-resolution data from the terminal phase of missile tests.

DEVELOPMENT • The Cobra Judy's initial operational capability was in 1981. The radar is operated by US Air Force and the ship operated by a civilian crew of the US Navy's Military Sealift Command (MSC).

SPECIFICATIONS •
MANUFACTURER   Raytheon
BAND
    phased-array
            S
    parabolic dish
            X

SONARS

ALFS

The Airborne Low-Frequency System (ALFS) is a dipping sonar designed to replace the AN/AQS-13F on the SH-60F carrier-borne helicopters. It will also be installed on the SH-60B Seahawks that are part of the surface combatant Light

Airborne Multipurpose System III (LAMPS III). Its active low-frequency sonar is said to defeat the anechoic coatings that were applied to many submarines in the 1980s.

After a long competition that faced

cancellation several times, a Hughes Aircraft Ground Systems/Thomson Sintra entry won in December 1991. The principal elements are the expandable sonar array and reeling winch originally developed by Thomson for their joint venture FLASH (Folding Light Acoustic System). FLASH operates in four low-frequency bands at considerable depths, the array arms extending on long arms at depth and retracting for insertion and retrieval.

The Hughes sonar processing system uses the controversial AT&T AN/UYS-2 Enhanced Modular Signal Processor (EMSP) whose development met delays and concerns that it would be incapable of performing some of the requirements. Congress mandated use of the UYS-2 in 1991 in an attempt to standardize signal processors. ALFS's UYS-2 variant has an input/output processor, three high-speed arithmetic processors, and two global memories. A 1553B digital databus links the processor to displays similar to those in service as well as a sonobuoy processor. A separate console controls the high-speed reeling mechanism.

DEVELOPMENT • In response to the rapidly improving Soviet submarine force that deployed in the 1980s, development of the AQS-13F's successor began in the mid-1980s. In addition to debates about the need within the Navy, the question of whether funding would come from the aviation or surface combatant budgets led Congress to delay funding altogether. When the SH-60B was added to the platforms that would carry the ALFS, future budget requirements grew at the same time that skeptics worried about the impact of the system's weight on SH-60B performance.

The December 1991 award funds five years of engineering development and has options for up to 50 production systems. At least 343 systems (185 for the SH-60B and 158 for the SH-60F) are planned at a cost of more than $1 billion.

AQS-13/AQS-18

The AN/AQS-13 active "dipping" sonar is fitted in the US Navy's SH-3H Sea King Antisubmarine Warfare (ASW) helicopters. These aircraft lower the transducer into the water to get below the zones where ship-generated noises are high (e.g., near a carrier battle group), and passive sonar or sonobuoy effectiveness is limited. Data gathered by the sonar includes bathythermal (depth vs. temperature) information, passive acoustic monitoring, and active echo determination of range and bearing.

The AQS-13F used on the SH-60F reaches much greater operating depths (up to 1,450 feet) using a high-speed cable-lowering system.

The AN/AQS-18 developed from the AN/AQS-13 and is a helicopter-borne, long-range, active, dipping sonar. Among the system features is a false-alarm filter to eliminate misleading indicators from the display screen. Target range, bearing, and identification data is provided at ranges up to 20,000 yards.

DEVELOPMENT • After development began in the mid-1960s, the AQS-13 came into widespread use on Sea Kings in the US Navy and several other countries. Manufactured by Bendix Oceanics Division of Sylmar, California. AQS-18 is in service in the German Navy.

SPECIFICATIONS •
FREQUENCY   9.23, 10, or 10.77 kHz
WEIGHT   30 lb (13.3 kg) sonar only
CABLE LENGTH   1,083 ft (330 m)

AQS-14

The AN/AQS-14 is an active, helicopter-towed mine-hunting sonar, initially developed for retrofit in the RH-53D Sea Stallion helicopter. Searching for mines requires a multibeam, side-looking sonar with electronic beam forming, all-range focusing, and an adaptive processor. The system uses a stabilized underwater vehicle to carry the transducer, an electromechanical tow cable, and an airborne electronic console.

The underwater vehicle cruises at a fixed point above the seafloor or below the surface, and the thin, coaxial cable is armored and nonmagnetic. Sonar data appears on the display as two continuous-moving televisionlike pictures.

DEVELOPMENT • The AQS-14 achieved its initial operational capability in 1984 in the RH-53D Sea Stallion. In production by Westinghouse Electric Corp., Annapolis, Maryland. Westinghouse, together with EDO and ARINC, are developing the AQS-20 to replace the AQS-14.

COMBAT EXPERIENCE • RH-53Ds first used the AQS-14 to clear mines from the Suez Canal in 1984. It was widely used in the Arabian Gulf to clear mines after the 1991 Operation Desert Storm. In that same year, an RH-53 used an AQS-14 to find four pesticide containers that had fallen off a barge at the mouth of Delaware Bay in stormy weather, the first nonmilitary use of this sonar.

BQQ-5

The AN/BQQ-5 multifunction, active/passive digital sonar system integrates the AN/BQS-11, -12, or -13 bow-mounted spherical transducer array, the conformal (hull-mounted) array, and the towed array. A computer-driven signal processor selects the hydrophones and steers the beams. Only computer capacity limits the number of beams that can be formed with this method.

The digital BQQ-5 suffers far less from internal noises than the AN/BQQ-2 that it replaced (which has manual switching). The BQQ-5 uses Digital Multibeam Steering (DIMUS) to enhance the detec-

tion of weaker acoustic signals. The BQQ-5 digital computer's processing also allowed a reduction in the number of operators compared to the BQQ-2.

Variants reflect continuing upgrades to the sonars or processing. Among the upgrades are the Steerable Hull-Array Beamformer (SHAB), first deployed in *Dallas* (SSN 700). BQQ-5C sets have Directional Frequency Analysis and Recording (DIFAR) reception using three AN/UYK-44 computers. First deployment came in the *Salt Lake City* (SSN 716); -5A and -5B sets in operation were upgraded to the -5C configuration.

Later additions include an integrated long-aperture, thin-line towed array and an improved handling system. All systems are now -5Es with an upgraded TB-12X thin-line array that emphasizes better localization.

DEVELOPMENT • The system achieved initial operational capability in 1976. The system was built into all *Los Angeles* (SSN 688)-class submarines through SSN 750 (the SSN 751 and later units being fitted with the AN/BSY-1 combat system that includes the BQQ-5C/D/E). Backfitted in the *Permit* (SSN 594) and *Sturgeon* (SSN 637) classes during overhauls. Manufactured by IBM Federal Systems, Owego, New York.

BQQ-6

The AN/BQQ-6 hull-mounted, passive sonar system was adapted from the AN/BQQ-5 passive/active sonar system to use in strategic missile submarines of the *Ohio* (SSBN 726) class. Given the Ohio's low self-noise, this system is likely to be a very effective self-defense sonar. It has 944 hydrophone transducers mounted on a sphere.

DEVELOPMENT • BQQ-6 achieved initial operational capability in 1981 with the commissioning of the *Ohio*. Manufactured by IBM, Bethesda, Maryland.

BQQ-9

The AN/BQQ-9 is a thin-line, towed-array sonar and signal processing system for *Ohio* (SSBN 726)-class ballistic missile submarines. The system processes signals received from the AN/BQR-15 passive towed array originally used in *Lafayette* (SSBN 616)-class submarines.

DEVELOPMENT • BQQ-9 achieved its initial operational capability in 1981 with the commissioning of the *Ohio.* Manufactured by Rockwell International, Columbus, Ohio.

BQR-15

The AN/BQR-15 passive detection system for submarines includes a towed array and the AN/BQR-23 signal processor. The array cable is 2,640 ft (800 m) long with a diameter of 0.5 in (12 mm) and can be streamed, retrieved, or adjusted through a hydraulic winch while the submarine is submerged.

DEVELOPMENT • Entered service in *Lafayette* (SSBN 616)-class submarines in 1974. Manufactured by Western Electric, Winston-Salem, North Carolina. The BQR-15A is fitted in some *Ohio* (SSBN 726)-class submarines.

BQR-19

The AN/BQR-19 is a mast-mounted active, short-range, rapid-scanning submarine sonar for collision avoidance, navigation, and other special applications, including upward-looking ice detection.

DEVELOPMENT • First entered service in 1970 in *Lafayette* (SSBN 616)-class submarines. Manufactured by Raytheon Submarine Signal Division, Portsmouth, Rhode Island.

BQR-21

The AN/BQR-21 is a hull-mounted passive detection and tracking sonar used in the *Lafayette* (SSBN 616)-class ballistic missile submarines. The transducers are arranged on a hull-mounted conformal array.

The BQR-21 uses DIMUS (Digital Multibeam Steering) in conjunction with the AN/BQR-24 signal processor. The system employs both analog and digital processing techniques and can detect targets at distances up to 87 nm (100 mi; 161 km), tracking as many as five at once.

DEVELOPMENT • Retrofitted in *Lafayette* beginning in 1977. No longer in series production. Manufactured by Honeywell, West Covina, California.

BQS-11/12/13

These are active detection, bow-mounted sonars for the AN/BQQ-5 system; they operate at the relatively low frequency of 3.5 kHz. The BQS-11 and -12 were upgraded as part of the program that retrofitted the BQQ-5 multi-sonar suite into older submarines such as the *Sturgeon* (SSN 637) class beginning in the mid-1980s. The BQS-13 is the active sonar used in later BQQ-5 variants found in *Los Angeles* (SSN 688)-class submarines.

DEVELOPMENT • BQS-11 first deployed in *Permit* (SSN 594)-class submarines in the mid-1980s. BQS-12 refitted to most *Sturgeon*s, except for the last two, which received BQS-13s. Manufactured by Raytheon Submarine Signal Division, Portsmouth, Rhode Island.

BQS-15

The AN/BQS-15 is an under-ice/mine avoidance, and target detection and tracking sonar developed for the *Los*

Angeles (SSN 688) class to allow safe navigation in heavily mined waters. It was integrated with the AN/BQQ-5 passive/active sonar system as a system upgrade.

DEVELOPMENT • Manufactured by Ametek Straza.

BSY-1

The AN/BSY-1 is an advanced US sonar/fire control system developed for the *Los Angeles* (SSN 688)-class submarines beginning with the *San Juan* (SSN 751). As designed, the system employs advanced computer hardware and software to exploit state-of-the-art acoustic sensors, such as Wide-Aperture Arrays (WAA), to analyze acoustic detection data, identify targets, and make fire control calculations. Altogether, the system software requires 4 million lines of code.

Originally there were to be three versions: the Basic version for SSN 751-759, the B version for SSN 760 (FY1986) and later *Los Angeles*-class submarines, and the B-prime for the SSN 21 class. Unfortunately for IBM and the Navy, the planned optical database (using fiberoptic technology) encountered difficulties, prompting a redesign effort to employ more conventional technology. There were subsequent difficulties in producing the multilayer computer circuit boards and other technical problems. The program was also sharply criticized for poor management, including lack of coordination that resulted in the inability to fit the system's cabling into the *San Juan*'s already cramped interior.

The BSY-1 employs several sonars:

The Submarine Active Detection System (SADS) includes a Medium-Frequency Active Capability (MFAC) spherical-array sonar mounted in the bow and a High-Frequency Active Capability (HFAC) mounted in the sail. The MFAC long-range panoramic sonar has a passive listening mode. The HFAC provides close-in, high-resolution detection of small targets including mines.

Two passive towed arrays supplement the active arrays: The TB-16 is a heavier array that is stored in a sheath along the submarine's hull. TB-23 is a thin-line array that can be reeled into the ship's main ballast tanks.

Beginning with the *Columbia* (SSN 771), the BSY-1 has the Lockheed Martin AN/BQG-5 Stand-Alone Wide-Aperture Array (SWAA); this system may also be backfitted into earlier BSY-1 level 688-class boats.

The Raytheon CCS Mk 2 upgrade includes an AN/UYK-43 computer in place of the AN/UYK-7, a Unisys AN/UYK-44 computer and Loral ASPRO high-speed parallel processor for tracking OTH contacts, and a single design for the graphics/display terminals in place of the 30 designs typically found on an SSN 688 boat.

DEVELOPMENT • The BSY systems were known as Submarine Advanced Combat System (SUBACS) until changed to the BSY series. Early development was plagued by severe technical and management problems, which delayed schedules, increased costs, and reduced the originally planned capability of the system.

In 1985, the Navy restructured the SUBACS program, breaking out the BSY-1 for the SSN 751 and later *Los Angeles*-class submarines. BSY-1 achieved limited initial operational capability in 1988. Several *Los Angeles* boats were delayed by the configuration problems mentioned above.

BSY-2

The BSY-2 (formerly FY1989 system in the Submarine Advanced Combat System/SUBACS program) is a more advanced version of the BSY-1 that operates in *Los Angeles* (SSN 688)-class submarines. It is being installed in *Seawolf* (SSN 21)-class submarines.

The BSY-2 emphasizes a distributed processing architecture integrating data from several sensors. These sensors include a BQG-5 Wide-Angle Array (WAA), sail-mounted BQS-24 Mine-Detection and Avoidance Sonar (MIDAS) active high-frequency sonar, active Large Spherical Array (LSA) and low-frequency array in the bow dome, and TB-16D and TB-29 towed arrays. Also supporting the system are a tactical situation plotter, 11 librascope combat system display consoles, transmit group, and librascope weapon launch system.

A 1989 General Accounting Office (GAO) report contended that developing software for the system would require 900 programmers to generate 3.2 million lines of Ada-language code. In October 1990, the Navy announced that it would purchase commercially developed, Motorola 68000-series microprocessors programmable in Ada as a means of cutting cost.

Like the troubled BSY-1 program, the BSY-2 has had problems. In December 1988, Newport News Shipbuilding complained to the Navy that integration of the BSY-2 into the *Seawolf* design was being hampered by delays in BSY-2 design. Newport News began its work using a generic combat system design until General Electric's design was selected. GE's design was significantly different and put the two programs out of phase by more than a year. Newport News also contended that direct interfaces between GE and itself were not permitted, which prevented coordination of design efforts.

DEVELOPMENT • In January 1988, General Electric/RCA (later Martin Marietta) was awarded a $13.6-million contract to develop and produce the BSY-2. GE/RCA competed with IBM for the contract. In October 1988, GE/RCA was awarded a contract to produce the BSY-2

for the SSN 21. Dramatic cutbacks in the *Seawolf* program will limit the number of BSY-2s to a handful.

CWE 610

The CWE 610 is an active, long-range, low-frequency, hull-mounted scanning sonar. This US-built sonar was designed for export and was fitted in several classes in the early 1970s.

Searches cover three 120° sectors. Signal processing allows the sonar to overcome the effects of heavy signal reverberation in shallow water. Search and tracking data can be displayed simultaneously, and a passive bearing-time display updates the operator.

DEVELOPMENT • The system achieved its initial operational capability in 1970. Manufactured by EDO Corp., Government Products Division, College Point, New York. Italian *Audace*-class and Dutch *Tromp*-class destroyers and Brazilian and Indonesian frigates use this sonar.

DE 1160

The DE 1160 series of hull-mounted sonars is a commercial version of the US Navy's AN/SQS-56 hull-mounted sonar. The active/passive, multifunction, digital sonar provides active echo ranging and passive panoramic surveillance (360° azimuth). The active array can search, track, classify, and give target information on several targets while the passive array maintains torpedo surveillance via a Digital Multibeam Steering (DIMUS) surveillance system. Most of the system's signal processing is accomplished using Navy's Standard Electronic Module Program (SEMP) components.

Several versions exist of the DE 1160: DE 1160B, DE 1160C, DE 1160LF, DE 1160LF/VDS, DE 1164, and DE 1167.

The DE 1160B is the standard active/passive sonar version of the system. It has a power output of 12 kW. The DE 1160C is identical to the DE 1160B except it is slightly larger and has a power output of 36 kW.

The DE 1160 is known as the DE 1164 when configured as a Variable-Depth Sonar (VDS). As a VDS, the sonar can descend to 656 ft (200 m) and be towed at speeds up to 20 knots.

The DE 1160 is capable of convergence zone performance when equipped with three additional transmitter cabinets (for a total of eight) and a larger, low-frequency transducer array. This configuration, which is fitted to the Italian aircraft carrier *Giuseppi Garibaldi,* is known as the DE 1160LF. The DE 1160LF/VDS combines the capabilities of the 1160LF with the VDS ability to adapt to the environment of the DE 1164.

The 1167 is smaller and less expensive. The sonar can be fitted in a hull dome or deployed as a VDS, or as an integrated hull dome and VDS. The VDS transmits at 12 kHz and the 36-stave circular, hull-mounted array transmits at either 12 or 7.5 kHz.

DEVELOPMENT • This system achieved its initial operational capability in 1977, with the 1167 following in 1984. Manufactured by Raytheon Co., Submarine Signal Division, Portsmouth, Rhode Island. In service in several export designs, including Spanish-built *Descubierta*-class frigates in Spanish service as well as those exported to Morocco.

Italian *De La Penne*-class destroyers and *Maestrale*-class frigates use the 1164 VDS. Egyptian *El Suez*-class frigates have the DE 1167 integrated 7.5-kHz hull-mounted and VDS version. Italian *Minerva*-class corvettes have the 7.5-kHz hull-mounted system only.

SPECIFICATIONS •
FREQUENCY   7.5 kHz, except DE 1160LF and 1160LF/VDS 3.75 kHz, and DE 1167 12 kHz (some installations)

SYSTEM WEIGHT
DE 1160B: 7,780 lb (3,536 kg)
DE 1160C: 9,037 lb (4,108 kg)
DE 1164: 63,604 lb (28,911 kg)
DE 1160LF: 31,359 lb (14,254 kg)
DE 1160LF/VDS: 85,926 lb (39,057 kg)

SQQ-14/SQQ-30

The AN/SQQ-14 is an obsolete dual-frequency, mine-detection and classification sonar used by minesweepers in shallow water against bottom mines.

The sonar is lowered from under the hull by a flexible cable that consists of 18-inch sections, connected by universal joints. This cable configuration allows the sonar to flex in any vertical plane, but prevents twisting.

The SQQ-30 is a digital descendant of the SQQ-14 that consists of an egg-shaped vehicle housing two sonars: a search sonar for mine detection and a high-frequency, high-resolution sonar for mine classification (each sonar has its own on-board display console). Because it was too limited to use against modern mines, the SQQ-30 was replaced by the SQQ-32.

DEVELOPMENT • The SQQ-14 was first deployed in 1960, the SQQ-30 following in 1983 in the *Avenger* (MCM 1). Manufactured by General Electric (later Martin Marietta), Syracuse, New York. Manufactured under license in Italy as the SQQ-14IT.

SPECIFICATIONS •
FREQUENCY   80 and 350 kHz

SQQ-23 PAIR

The AN/SQQ-23 Performance and Integration Retrofit (PAIR) is an upgrade of the AN/SQS-23 active/passive detection with improved passive detection. Each of the system's 48 staves has a single channel (versus two in the SQS-23).

The baseline SQQ-23A configuration used two sonar domes instead of one, with the second dome housing the passive transducer. All of the ships in this configuration—four *Charles F. Adams* (DDG 2)-class and two *Farragut* (DDG 37)-class destroyers—have been retired. The *Long Beach* (CGN 9), *Bainbridge* (CGN 25), and ships of the *Leahy* (CG 16) class had the SQQ-23B in a single dome.

A measure of the shrinkage in system weight and volume shows in the replacement of the 21 vacuum-tube cabinets and 10 motor generators of the SQS-23's transmission system with the three solid-state shipboard cabinets in the SQQ-23.

DEVELOPMENT • Retrofitted in ships beginning in 1972. Manufactured by Sperry (later Unisys).

SPECIFICATIONS •
FREQUENCY 4.3–5.7 kHz
PEAK POWER Omni-Directional Transmission (ODT) 160 kW for 160 microsec

SQQ-32

The AN/SQQ-32 is a mine-detection and -classification Variable-Depth Sonar (VDS) installed in the *Osprey* (MHC 51)- and *Avenger* (MCM 1)-class minesweepers. It replaces the less capable AN/SQQ-30 VDS in the *Avenger* minesweepers.

The SQQ-32 has improved discrimination between genuine mines and other objects, displays objects with near-picture quality, and has increased vertical coverage. The system uses a lower operating frequency for increased detection range. Like the earlier sonars, the SQQ-32 consists of two sonars: a search sonar for mine detection and a high-frequency, high-resolution sonar for mine classification. Each sonar has its own on-board dis-play console as well as variable-depth transducers. The consoles can display data from either of the two sonars.

The search sonar detects and displays the location of objects that are potential targets. The detected targets or their sonar shadows are then displayed by the classification sonar. The echo mode, which displays images of the detected target, is more effective for objects that are clear of the bottom. The shadow mode is suitable for objects on the bottom where there is interference from reverberations. A computer is used to help classify the targets, reducing operator workload.

DEVELOPMENT • Initial development began in 1982. Raytheon won the initial production contract in early 1989. Although originally intended to enter service with the first *Osprey*, deployment on the *Avenger* class was accelerated because of the increasing mine threat.

The detection sonar, computer system, and both consoles are manufactured by Raytheon Co., Portsmouth, Rhode Island, which is responsible for the overall system integration. The classification sonar is manufactured by Thomson CSF, Brest Cedex, France. The towed vehicle, cable, and towing winch were designed by Charles Stark Draper Lab, Cambridge, Massachusetts.

COMBAT EXPERIENCE • SQQ-32s deployed on the *Avenger* and on older *Aggressive* (MSO 421) minesweepers in the Persian Gulf during Operations Desert Shield and Desert Storm proved quite effective.

SQQ-89(V)

The AN/SQQ-89(V) combines sensors and weapons control systems with sophisticated data processing and display in the first integrated surface-ship ASW system. Known as the Squeak 89, the system correlates and manages acoustic sensor input from hull-mounted sonar and towed arrays to provide track data to the ship's combat direction center. The large, AN/SQS-53B/C hull-mounted sonars in cruisers and destroyers are integrated into the SQQ-89. *Ticonderoga* (CG 47)-class cruisers and *Spruance* (DD 963)-class destroyers have the SQS-53B, and the *Burke* (DDG 51)-class destroyers the SQS-53C.

All of the variants have the AN/SQR-19 towed arrays, the AN/SQQ-28 shipboard acoustic processing component of the LAMPS III helicopter system, the Mk 116 ASW weapons control system (*Perry*-class frigates use their Weapon Alternate Processors/WAP), AN/UYQ-21 displays, and the AN/UYQ-25 Sonar in Situ Mode Assessment System (SIMAS), which predicts acoustic environmental noise.

The limited-capability AN/SQS-56 sonar in frigates, however, is not integrated with the SQQ-89. The SQQ-89(V)2 is being installed in both active and Naval Reserve Force frigates of the *Perry* (FFG 7) class, the latter with the LAMPS I helicopter system.

The SQQ-89(V)6 features integration of AT&T's AN/UYS-2 Enhanced Modular Signal Processor (EMSP) and Diagnostic/Retrieval Systems CY-8571 (service designation AN/UYQ-21) Advanced Video Processor (AVP) color, raster-scan display system.

Development of the SQY-1, which began as the SQQ-89 Improvement (Q-89I or SQQ-89(V)10) program in 1986, envisaged using UYS-2 ESMP technology. Program slippage amounted to at least six years. Frequent changes in threat analysis, platform definitions, system specifications, and technical problems, particularly with the ESMP, created considerable turbulence, and the program was canceled in 1992.

DEVELOPMENT • SQQ-89 first deployed in the destroyer *Moosbrugger* (DD 980) in 1985. Navy plans call for 130 ships to be fitted with the SQQ-89 by 1995.

Manufactured by General Electric (later Lockheed Martin), Syracuse, New York and Westinghouse Electric, Baltimore, Maryland.

SQR-18A

The AN/SQR-18 series began with the SQR-18 Interim Escort Towed-Array Surveillance System (IETASS) that was developed to be a simpler version of the AN/SQR-14/15 long-range towed arrays for frigates and minesweepers. During tests, the SQR-18 towed array generated excess noise, which contributed to its unreliability in the first convergence zone.

The SQR-18A addressed these problems. It is a low-noise array with an improved tracker and an interference tracker. The (V)1 improves on the -18A with use of a noise cancellation feature to remove ship-radiated noise by subtracting measured self-noise of the towing ship from total noise output recorded by the array.

The (V)2 array does not require a VDS sonar fish for towing and is towed from a cable. It has its own towing and handling capability, enabling it to be streamed from ships without a VDS. The (V)2 array has 32 vibration-isolated hydrophones divided into eight hydrophone sections.

Both the (V)1 and (V)2 systems can be integrated with the AN/SQS-26 hull-mounted sonar and the AN/SQR-17 sonobuoy processor. They can also use the Advanced Modular Signal Processor (AMSP), which is a programmable system with interactive software.

DEVELOPMENT • Development on the SQR-18 began in FY1968. A Patterson Experimental Array (PEA) prototype of the SQR-18 was purchased by the US Navy in FY1972. An operational requirement for the system was placed in FY1973. Two IETASSs (SQR-18) were ordered in a contract awarded in August 1974. The Escort Towed-Array Sensor (ETAS) program was established in FY1975 after the IETASS had been tested on *Knox*-class frigates and a minesweeper. In turn, the Tactical Towed-Array Sonar (TACTAS) programs were developed from the ETAS. ETAS program established in FY1975. Production of SQR-18A began in spring 1978 and an improvement program in April 1981.

Developed and produced by EDO, College Point, New York. Also manufactured by Gould Electronics, Cupertino, California. Deployed on *Belknap* (CG 26)-class cruisers, *Spruance* (DD 963)-class destroyers, and *Oliver Hazard Perry* (FFG 7)- and *Knox* (FF 1052)-class frigates. Also fitted in Japanese destroyers and Indonesian *Ahmed Yani*-class frigates.

SQR-19 TACTAS

The Tactical Towed-Array Sonar (TACTAS) was developed as a component subsystem of the AN/SQQ-89 surface antisubmarine warfare combat system. It is also specifically intended for use with the LAMPS III airborne ASW system that features the SH-60B Seahawk helicopter. The towed array or "tail" consists of vibration-isolation modules; a telemetry drive module; heading, depth, and temperature units; and 16 acoustic modules comprising eight Very Low Frequency (VLF), four Low Frequency (LF), two Medium Frequency (MF), and two High Frequency (HF) modules. The modular construction of the array permits individual replacement of hydrophone components that fail or are damaged

The SQR-19 array can be effective at a relatively high ship's speed and in sea states up to four. Data storage (SQR-19A) and computing capacity (SQR-19B) have been improved.

DEVELOPMENT • The first production delivery occurred in July 1985, followed by the first SQR-19B in January 1991. In

service on some *Ticonderoga* (CG 47)-class cruisers, *Spruance* (DD 963)- and *Burke* (DDG 51)-class destroyers, and *Perry* (FFG 7)-class frigates. Installation in *Kidd* (DDG 993)-class destroyers is being considered.

Also in service in Canada's upgraded *Iroquois*-class destroyers and *Halifax*-class frigates, Japan's *Abukuma*-class frigates, and Spain's *Perry*-design *Santa Maria* class.

Manufactured by Gould Electronics and Lockheed Martin (formerly General Electric).

SQS-23

The AN/SQS-23 is a direct-path, active sonar with a range of some 10,000 yards that was intended to be compatible with the Antisubmarine Rocket (ASROC) weapon. It was fitted to a variety of ship classes, from World War II–era *Gearing*-class destroyers retrofitted under the 1959–65 Fleet Rehabilitation and Maintenance (FRAM) program to new-construction cruisers and destroyers. Most ships had sonar domes fitted under the hull, but several US destroyers had bow sonar mounts.

To generate a signal, a commutator mechanically scans two transducers on each of 48 staves at 150 cycles per second. Base frequencies can be varied by up to 380 Hz to reduce intership interference. The beam can be depressed electronically when closing a target. In a "lighthouse" Rotationally Directed Transmission (RDT) mode, a 60-kW beam is transmitted for 4.3 seconds. (This is obviously not a stealthy technique.)

The SQS-23 has been updated often, and a solid-state upgrade is offered for export as the DE 1190/DE 1191. In fact, the solid-state transmitter has been retrofitted into US ships, often in the successful SQQ-23 PAIR configuration.

Upgrades have added pulse variations and reliability improvements including the installation of assemblies of 1-kW solid-state transmitters, usually grouped in twelves. Designator series have run up to SQS-23H. DE 1190 has been exported in 12-, 24-, 36-, 48-, 72-, and 96-transmitter sizes. DE 1191 includes the DE 1190 SST and a slightly modified DE 1167 Receiver and Display.

DEVELOPMENT • The first SQS-23 achieved its initial operational capability in 1958. SQS-23 was manufactured by Sangamo and is no longer in production. The DE 1190/DE 1191 series is produced by Raytheon's Submarine Signal Division in Portsmouth, Rhode Island.

SQS-23 and DE 1190/1191 upgrades are widely deployed on former FRAM-type destroyers still serving in several navies. In addition, several warship classes built in Australia, Italy, Germany, and Japan in the 1960s are still fitted with the SQS-23.

SPECIFICATIONS •
BASE FREQUENCIES
   SQS-23: 4.5, 5, and 5.5 kHz
   PAIR, DE 1190: 4.3–5.7 kHz
PULSE LENGTHS
   SQS-23: 2, 30, and 120 millisec (2-
      millisec pulse later increased to 5)
PEAK POWER
   PAIR: 160 kW for 160 millisec in
      Omni-Directional Transmission
      (ODT) mode
   DE 1190: 28–56 kW
   DE 1191: 120 kW

SQS-26

The AN/SQS-26 is a high-power, active/passive sonar for surface warships and was the first major bow-mounted sonar in US ships. Delays in delivery and technical problems delayed approval for service use until November 1968. These shortcomings carried potentially embarrassing consequences. The more than 20 ships that carried the sonar had no long-

range sensor capability until the system was ready.

When solid-state electronics replaced vacuum tubes, the Navy designated the result AN/SQS-53.

DEVELOPMENT • Development began in the late 1950s and the first ship (*Bronstein* FF 1037) commissioned in 1962. 12 SQS-26AX sets and all examples of the later SQS-26CX were manufactured by General Electric, Syracuse, New York. 18 SQS-26BX sets were manufactured by EDO. Three nuclear-propelled cruisers (*Truxtun, California,* and *South Carolina*), eight of nine *Belknap*-class cruisers, and the *Bronstein-, Garcia-,* and *Knox*-class frigates all carried SQS-26s.

SPECIFICATIONS (CX VARIANT) •
FREQUENCY
   active mode   3–4 kHz
   passive mode
      1.5 kHz
RANGE
   direct path   9.9 nm (18.3 km)
   convergence zone or bottom bounce
      34.6 nm (64 km)
PEAK POWER   100 kW
TRANSDUCER WEIGHT   60,000 lb
   (27,215 kg)

SQS-38

The AN/SQS-38 is a keel-mounted, high-frequency sonar derived from the AN/SQS-35 Independent Variable-Depth Sonar (IVDS). Using more reliable solid-state technology, the SQS-38 replaced the vacuum-tube AN/SQS-36 keel-mounted sonar in the *Hamilton*-class Coast Guard cutters. This is the only sonar fitted in US Coast Guard cutters; conversely only the *Hamilton*s use the SQS-38.

The active/passive sonar operates in three frequencies.

DEVELOPMENT • 14 SQS-38 sets were manufactured for the 12-ship *Hamilton* class. The first set achieved initial operational capability in 1967. Manufactured by EDO Corp., College Point, New York.

SPECIFICATIONS •
FREQUENCY 11.9, 13, or 14 kHz

SQS-53

The AN/SQS-53 is a large active/passive submarine-detection sonar for surface warships. It is an improved version of the AN/SQS-26CX sonar and is housed in a bow dome.

The principal difference between the SQS-26CX and SQS-53 is the latter's digital computer interface with the shipboard Mk 116 Antisubmarine Warfare (ASW) weapons control system. The -53B extends the capability with the AN/UYS-1 acoustic signal processor, AN/UYK-44(V) digital computers in addition to the earlier AN/UYK-1s, and digital controls and displays that allow integration into the SQQ-89 system. The digital components allow less system degradation due to drift of calibration and alignment compared to analog; the system monitors itself to detect performance decreases. The system features multiple-target capability, automatic target tracking, and a higher systems availability (2,000 hours mean time between failure).

Continuing the line is the SQS-53C, which has shipboard electronics that are 50% smaller and lighter than the SQS-53B. The transducers have been modified to provide higher power and wider bandwidth, and the AN/UYH-1 mass memory was added.

DEVELOPMENT • The -53A achieved initial operational capability in 1975. Manufactured by General Electric (later Lockheed Martin) and Hughes.

The SQS-53A is fitted in the early *Ticonderoga*-class cruisers (CG 47 to 55). The SQS-53B was fitted in the later

Ticonderoga-class cruisers (CG 56 and on) as part of the AN/SQQ-89 ASW combat system, and is being backfitted in the *Spruance*-class destroyers. *Arleigh Burke*-class destroyers (DDG 51) introduced the SQS-53C. The first engineering development model of the SQS-53C was fitted in the *Spruance*-class destroyer *Stump* (DD 978) in late 1986.

SQS-56

The AN/SQS-56 is an active/passive, medium-frequency, hull-mounted submarine-detection sonar with limited capabilities. Its installation in the *Oliver Hazard Perry* (FFG 7)-class frigates represents an electronic example of Admiral Elmo Zumwalt's high-low mix policy of the early 1970s. Like the *Perry*s, the sonar is far less capable than the AN/SQS-26 and AN/SQS-53 sonars carried in several other classes of cruisers, destroyers, and frigates.

Use of the SQS-56 saved perhaps 600 tons of displacement in the FFG 7 and reduced electrical power requirments by almost half. The cost is effective range, however, with the SQS-56 being capable of detection only on the order of 5 nm (5.75 mi; 9.3 km)—far too little for effective use of ship-based Antisubmarine Warfare (ASW) helicopters. In fact, the *Perry*s' towed-array sonar and LAMPS III SH-60B Seahawk helicopter will often make the first contact.

The sonar provides active panoramic echo ranging and passive Digital Multibeam Steering (DIMUS) surveillance. Most of the system's signal processing is accomplished via the Navy's Standard Electronic Module Program (SEMP). A minicomputer provides system control, timing, and interface communication.

The display system is a single-operator Cathode-Ray Tube (CRT) console with both alphanumeric and symbol display. A remote display and loudspeaker/intercom system are optional features.

DEVELOPMENT • The SQS-56 achieved initial operational capability in 1977. Manufactured by Raytheon's Submarine Signal Division, Portsmouth Rhode Island. In addition to the 51 US Navy *Perry*-class ships, the SQS-56 equips locally built Australian, Spanish, and Taiwanese *Perry*-design ships as well as frigates and corvettes in the Greek, Saudi, and Turkish navies.

SPECIFICATIONS •
FREQUENCY   5.6, 7.5, and 8.4 kHz

UQQ-2 SURTASS

The Surveillance Towed-Array Sonar System (SURTASS) is an area surveillance system towed at slow speeds (about three knots) by civilian-crewed T-AGOS ships. The array is a flexible, tubelike structure about 2,600 feet long containing numerous passive hydrophones at the end of a 6,000-foot-long towing cable. Typical array towing depths are 500 to 1,500 feet.

Data from the hydrophone array is generated at a very high rate, preprocessed on the T-AGOS and sent at ¹⁄₁₀ the data rate by satellite to shore processors.

DEVELOPMENT • The first *Stalwart*-class T-AGOS ship entered service in 1984. The full 18-ship class was active for only a short time before the decline in the submarine threat led to the decommissioning or reassignment of most of the class. Several *Victorious* class SWATH (Small Waterplane, Twin Hull) T-AGOS ships also operate SURTASS.

Japan's *Hibiki*-class T-AGOS-type ships have a Japanese array.

SOSUS

The US Navy operates several seafloor Sound Surveillance Systems (SOSUS) in various parts of the Atlantic and Pacific oceans, as well as across the Strait of Gibraltar and off the North Cape north of Norway. (The locations of US SOSUS arrays have been identified in Soviet magazines.)

SOSUS is a series of passive arrays used to detect transiting submarines and, in wartime, would be used to direct air, surface, and submarine ASW forces to suspected submarine contacts.

Initially, a number of Naval Facilities (NAVFAC) were established as the shore terminals for SOSUS, with NAVFACs being located along both US coasts, in the Caribbean, Iceland, and Japan and at other overseas locations. Subsequently, more capable arrays and computers were developed, and NAVFACs in the United States and the Caribbean were consolidated.

SOSUS information is provided at several levels—to tactical as well as theater and national commanders—and for technical evaluation. Acoustic data from the NAVFACs and Regional Evaluation Centers (REC) is provided through the Ocean Surveillance Information System (OSIS) to the Atlantic, Pacific, and European area Fleet Command Centers (FCC), to the Naval Ocean Surveillance Information Center (NOSIC) in Suitland, Maryland, near Washington, DC, and to the National Command Authorities (NCA).

Published sources cite detection ranges of "hundreds" of miles by SOSUS, with arrays reported in the Atlantic and Pacific areas as well as in some regional seas. Several update programs have been announced, especially related to computer capability that can provide data more rapidly with an improved signal-to-noise ratio.

DEVELOPMENT • Immediately after World War II, the US Navy began development of deep-ocean arrays. By 1948, arrays were being tested at sea, and by 1951, the first SOSUS arrays were implanted.

Also termed Project Caesar, the first set of operational hydrophones was installed at Sandy Hook, south of Manhattan, followed in 1952 by a deep-water (1,200 feet) installation off Eleuthra in the Bahamas. That year the Chief of Naval Operations directed the establishment of six arrays in the Western Atlantic, all to be ready by the end of 1956. The first arrays in the Pacific were operational in 1958.

After the collapse of the Soviet Union and the related decline in the submarine threat, the Navy began using SOSUS to support civilian scientific research. In one project, a blue whale was tracked for 42 days. In another application, pinpointing the sounds of an erupting undersea volcano led to observations that had never been made before.

TABLE OF SONOBUOYS

DESIGNATION	MANUFACTURER	USE
SSQ-36	Sparton, Plessey	Aircraft-launched expendable Bathythermograph (AXBT). Transmits temperature data from the surface to 1,000 ft (3,048 m) to sonobuoy processors.
SSQ-41B Jezebel	Sparton, Magnavox	Omnidirectional passive detection. Emits on 31 or 99 VHF RF channels. -41B in service in 1964, -41B production between 1975 and 1982.
SSQ-47	Sparton	Active, nondirectional using continuous-wave keying. Short, 30-min life, 12 RF-channel, 6 sonic channel capacity. Production from 1965 to 1982, some later exported.
SSQ-53	Sparton, Magnavox	Active Directional Frequency Analysis and Recording (DIFAR). -53A had 31 RF channels, -53B/C have 99. Several hundred thousand produced from 1968 to 1993.
SSQ-57	Sparton	Passive, "special purpose" with 31 channels; mechanically similar to the SSQ-41. Production began in 1968; last procured in FY1989.
SSQ-62	Sparton, Magnavox	Directional Command-Activated Sonar System (DICASS), passively determines bearing and range. 31 channels. Production began in 1978, last procured in FY1991.
SSQ-71	Sparton	Air-Transportable Acoustic Communication (ATAC) for aircraft-friendly submarine contact. Replaced by SSQ-86.
SSQ-75	Bunker Ramo (for development)	Expendable Reliable Acoustic Path Sonobuoy (ERAPS) for deep-depth (down to 16,000 ft) detection. Development began in 1974, problems delayed deployment.
SSQ-77	Sparton, Magnavox, Sippican (one year only)	Vertical Line Array DIFAR (VLAD) with 11 omnidirectional, 2 DIFAR hydrophones for bottom-bounce returns; -77B has convergence-zone capability. 99 RF channels. Production began in 1978, continued into mid-1990s.
SSQ-86	Sparton	One-way communications link to friendly submarine. Coded message of 4 groups of 3 digits.

TABLE OF SONOBUOYS (continued)

DESIGNATION	MANUFACTURER	USE
SSQ-95	Litton	Active Electronic Buoy (AEB) to decoy antiship missiles.
SSQ-102		Air-Deployed Active Receiver Tactical Surveillance Sonar (ADAR TSS). Detects targets illuminated by other sonars.
SSQ-103		Low-cost sonobuoy. Canceled in early 1990s because of cost overruns.
SSQ-110	Sparton, Magnavox	Classified program. First contracts to Magnavox (6,000 units), Sparton (18,000 units).

TABLE OF ELECTRONIC WARFARE SYSTEMS

AIRBORNE ELECTRONIC WARFARE SYSTEMS

DESIGNATION	MANUFACTURER	PLATFORMS	NOTES
AAR-34	Cincinnati Electronics	F-111	Tail-mounted IR sensor to detect air-to-air missiles; interfaces with ALR-62.
AAR-44	Cincinnati Electronics	C-130, MC-130 Combat Talon, MH-53 Pave Low	Lower-hemisphere IR warner to detect SAMs, trigger chaff or flare response.
AAR-44FX	Cincinnati Electronics	fighters	Entrant in USAF Missile Approach Warning System (MAWS) trials.
AAR-47	Cincinnati Electronics	C-130, OV-10, AH-1T, CH-46, CH-53 series, MH-60, SH-2, SH-60, UH-1	Passive MAWS operating in ultraviolet band with 4 staring electro-optical receivers, processor to trigger countermeasures.
ALE-29	Loral, Tracor	A-6, F-14	2 30-cell chaff/flare/jammer dispensers, programmer.
ALE-38/41	Tracor	pod-mounted	Dispensers that cut chaff to length for corridor clearance.
ALE-39	Tracor, Loral	A-6, AV-8B, F-14, F/A-18, CH-46, CH-53, AH-1, SH-2, SH-60, UH-1	Derived from ALE-29 with greater flexibility in pattern and type of countermeasure.
ALE-40	Tracor	A-10, AMX, C-130, Mirage, F-5E, F-16	Modular chaff/flare dispensers. 30 chaff cells, 15 flare cells per unit.

DESIGNATION	MANUFACTURER	PLATFORMS	NOTES
ALE-45	Tracor	F-15	Microprocessor-controlled chaff/flare dispensers used with ALQ-135 TEWS.
ALE-47	Tracor, Loral	22 different aircraft	Updated ALE-40 with software-controlled dispensing patterns. Also exported as TACDS.
ALE-50	Raytheon	A-6	Advanced Airborne Expendable Decoy (AAED); towed jammer streamed from aircraft.
ALQ-99	Eaton-AIL	EA-6B, EF-111	Tactical Jamming System (TJS) with processor control, 10 jamming bands in pods (A-6) or converted weapons bay (EF-111).
ALQ-108	Magnavox	C-2, E-2C, EP-3E, S-3	Pod-mounted IFF jammer.
ALQ-119	Westinghouse	A-10, F-111, F-15	First dual-mode (noise and deception) jammer. Upgraded several times, last as ALQ-184.
ALQ-122	Motorola	B-52	Power-managed multiple false-target generator.
ALQ-126	Lockheed Sanders	A-6, F-14, F/A-18	Threat identification, priority setting, response through variety of jamming methods.
ALQ-128	Magnavox	F-15	H–J-band threat-warning receiver; part of ALQ-135 TEWS.
ALQ-130	Eaton-AIL	A-6, EA-6B	Tactical communications jammer.
ALQ-131	Westinghouse	A-10, AC-130, F-4, F-15, F-16, F-111	Pod- or internally mounted processor-controlled jammer using threat library, covers B–J radar bands. Exported to several countries.
ALQ-133 Quick Look	United Technologies	OV-1D, RV-1D	A–J-band passive locator, identifier of radars; relays information to ground stations.

AIRBORNE ELECTRONIC WARFARE SYSTEMS (*continued*)

DESIGNATION	MANUFACTURER	PLATFORMS	NOTES
ALQ-135	Northrop	F-15	Threat Evaluation and Warning System (TEWS). Receiver and jammer up through J band. Coordinates with ALE-45, ALR-56.
ALQ-136	ITT	AH-1, AH-64	Detects, analyzes, and jams SAM radars in I/J band.
ALQ-137	Lockheed Sanders	EF-111A	Power-managed, E–J-band jammer using several modes. Operates with ALR-62.
ALQ-142	Raytheon	SH-60B	E–K-band intercept, direction finder of submarine radars.
ALQ-144	Lockheed Sanders	AH-1, AH-64, SH-2, SH-60, UH-1, UH-60	Infrared Countermeasures (IRCM) system uses heated ceramic radiator to spoof heat-seaking missiles.
ALQ-147	Lockheed Sanders	OV-1, RV-1	Fuel-heated IRCM for aircraft with limited electrical supply.
ALQ-149	Lockheed Sanders	EA-6B	Communications, low-band (A/B) radar receiver, analyzer; complements ALQ-99 jammer.
ALQ-150 Cefire Tiger	GTE	RU-21	Communications intercept, jammer. Each of 3 bands covered in a different aircraft.
ALQ-151 Quick Fix	ESL, Tracor	EH-1, EH-60	Communications intercept (HF/VHF), VHF direction finding, VHF jamming.
ALQ-153	Westinghouse	B-52	Active pulse-Doppler radar MAWS that detects, classifies threats, automatically launches chaff/flares. Chosen over AIL's ALQ-154.
ALQ-155	Northrop	B-52	Receivers for ALT-28 noise jammer, power manager. Also links with ALR-46.

DESIGNATION	MANUFACTURER	PLATFORMS	NOTES
ALQ-156/-156A	Lockheed Sanders	A-6, CH-47, EH-1, EH-60, OV-1/RV-1, P-3C, RC-12, RU-21	Active pulse-Doppler radar MAWS. Automatically triggers ECM and IRCM. Can be used at high and low altitudes.
ALQ-157	Loral	CH-46, CH-53, C-130	Jams IR-homing missiles; uses 1 of 5 preset routines.
ALQ-158	Hazeltine	P-3C	Electronic Support Measures system with phased-array antenna.
ALQ-161	Eaton-AIL	B-1	A–K-band integrated airborne defensive avionics system. Severely troubled by technical glitches, threat changes; not fully operational.
ALQ-162 Shadowbox	Northrop	AV-8B, CF-18, Draken, EH-1, EH-60, EF-18, F-16, OV/RV-1D, RC-12, RF-4B, RU-21	Continuous-wave jammer developed to counter Soviet-designed SAM systems. Can identify and set threat priorities. Also exported to Canada (CF-18), Denmark (Draken), and Spain (EF-18).
ALQ-164	Lockheed Sanders	AV-8B	Pulse and continuous-wave jammer developed from ALQ-126.
ALQ-165 ASPJ	ITT-Westinghouse	A-6, AV-8B, EA-6B, F-14, F/A-18	Advanced C–J pulsed and CW jammer with microprocessor control. Canceled in 1991–92 but could be revived.
ALQ-172	ITT	B-52, AC-130U, MC-130E/H Combat Talon	ALQ-117 I/J-band jammer upgrade with phased-array antennas (in (V)2), power management, software updating.
ALQ-176	Hercules	various	Pod-mounted C–J-band jammer for training, combat evaluation.
ALQ-178 Rapport	Loral	F-16, Mirage III	Integrated radar warner and jammer fitted in export aircraft.

AIRBORNE ELECTRONIC WARFARE SYSTEMS (continued)

DESIGNATION	MANUFACTURER	PLATFORMS	NOTES
ALQ-184	Raytheon	A-10, F-111, F-4G, F-15, F-16	Repeater, transponder, noise-jammer upgrade of ALQ-119. Uses Rotman lens antennas for receiving, jamming.
ALQ-187	Raytheon	F-16	Active jamming pod for export.
ALQ-191	Perkin-Elmer	development	Laser warning receiver; 8–12-micron wavelength.
ALQ-192	Cartwright	proposed for F/A-18	Threat Missile Detection System (TMDS) MAWS.
ALQ-199	Loral	trials	Active pulse-Doppler MAWS based on Israeli EL/M-2160 system.
ALR-45/-45F	Litton	US Navy aircraft	Radar-Warning Receiver (RWR) with crystal-video receivers, software-programmable ATAC processor.
ALR-46	Litton	A-10, B-52, C-130, RF-4	E–J-band RWR that identifies up to 16 emitters (including frequency-agile) simultaneously.
ALR-52	Argo Systems	EP-3E	C–J-band Instantaneous Frequency Measurement (IFM) receiver, emitter analysis by digital computer.
ALR-53	Litton		Long-range homing receiver.
ALR-56A	Loral	F-15A	RWR with low-, high-band receivers; part of TEWS.
ALR-56C	Loral	F-15C	Upgrade of -56A; E–J-band, dual-conversion, wideband, agile scanning, super-heterodyne RWR.
ALR-56M	Loral, Litton	F-16C	ALR-56C reduced by 40%; replaces ALR-69 in earlier F-16s, to be fitted in B-1B.
ALR-58	Lockheed Sanders	P-3B	Electronic Support Measures (ESM) set.
ALR-59(V)	Litton	E-2C	C–J-band, 4-antenna radar receiver; replaced by ALR-73.

DESIGNATION	MANUFACTURER	PLATFORMS	NOTES
ALR-60 Deep Well	GTE/Sylvania	EP-3E	Communications intercept and analysis to track warships. 7 sets delivered.
ALR-62(V)	Litton	F-111	RWR that "looks through" own-aircraft jammers to detect emitters; ALR-62I proposed for F-111, B-1B upgrades.
ALR-64	Dalmo-Victor/ Litton	A-10, F-16	Compass Sail C/D-band RWR.
ALR-66(V)	Litton	P-3, SH-2, SH-3, C-130K, VC10, Tristar	E–J ((V)1), C–J (others) band RWR with 4 antennas, large threat memory. Variants expand band coverage, sensitivity.
ALR-67	Litton	A-6, AV-8B, F-14, F/A-18	D–J-band RWR; ALR-45F crystal-video receivers with a superheterodyne receiver, low-band receiver, and ATAC-16M processor. (V)3 is Advanced Special Receiver (ASR) upgrade.
ALR-68	Litton	German F-4 ICE	Updated ALR-46 digital Threat-Warning Receiver (TWS) for retrofit.
ALR-69	Litton	A-10, C-130, F-4, F-16	ALR-46 with ALR-64 and Frequency-Selective Receiver System (FSRS) for continuous-wave DF and pulsed emitter analysis. Exported to several countries.
ALR-73	Litton	E-2C	Passive Detection System (PDS) upgrade of ALR-59; 4-band frequency range through step-sweep, 4 receivers.
ALR-74	Litton	F-16	ALR-67/-69 update; lost competition to ALR-56M.
ALR-75	Scientific Communications	NKC-135, EC-24A	Surveillance receiver analyzing A–J bands simultaneously; 8 tuners.
ALR-76	IBM	S-3B, EP-3	RWR with extended frequency range, auto classification and location; replaced ALR-47.

AIRBORNE ELECTRONIC WARFARE SYSTEMS (continued)

DESIGNATION	MANUFACTURER	PLATFORMS	NOTES
ALR-77	Eaton-AIL	P-3C	ESM with IFM, DF, narrow-band analysis; replaced ALQ-78.
ALR-80(V)	Litton	C-101 Aviojet, F-5E, CN-235	Export-oriented digital, fully programmable ALR-66(V)3 upgrade.
ALR-85(V)	Litton	C-130, L-1011	Modular RWR for transports.
ALR-91	Litton	F-16	Replacement RWR for ALR-46 ((V)3), ALR-69 ((V)4) with 32-bit processor, all-band "staring" surveillance.
ALR-93	Litton	export	32-bit processor, super-heterodyne, IFM receivers can be added.
APR-38	McDonnell Douglas	F-4G	Emitter Location System (ELS) with 52 antennas. Planned upgrade to APR-47 canceled because of receiver problems, but much improved Weasel Attack Signal Processor (WASP) added to basic APR-38.
APR-39	E-Systems, Loral	OV-/RV-1D, most US helicopters, Lynx, Gazelle, BO-105, patrol craft	E–I-band RWR for helicopters with signal sorting, emitter identification, bearing computation.
APR-39A	Litton	C-130, OV-10, SEMA aircraft, AH-1, AH-64, UH-60, Hirundo	Expands APR-39 coverage to millimeter-wave bands (L, M). (V)3 adds crystal-video receivers for continuous coverage. Also serves as controller for AVR-2 laser warner, AAR-47.
APR-43	Loral, AEL	US Navy	RWR for C/D pulse, CW missile systems. Works with ALR-45/67, ALQ-126/-162.
APR-44	AEL	OH-58, UH-1N	Lightweight RWR that detects (in (V)3 version) H–J-band CW signals.

DESIGNATION	MANUFACTURER	PLATFORMS	NOTES
APR-46(V)	Watkins-Johnson	Special-operations aircraft	Wideband microwave receiver (30 MHz to 18 GHz) applicable to special-operations forces aircraft.
APR-50	IBM	B-2	ESM/Threat Warning suite using Very Large Scale Integrated (VLSI) and Gallium Arsenide (GaAs) circuitry.
ASS-2		UH-1	Infrared (IR) surveillance system.
ASS-24		OV-1	IR surveillance system.
ATRJ	ITT	development	Advanced Threat Radar Jammer suite for the AH-64.
ATIRCM	Lockheed Sanders, Loral, Northrop	development	(Advanced Tactical Infrared Countermeasures) Directed IRCM system using laser to jam IR seekers. Sanders uses coherent laser, Loral noncoherent, Northrop both.
AVR-2		transports	Laser-warning system.
P-MAWS 2000	Westinghouse	development	3rd-generation ultraviolet-band Missile Attack Warning System.
USA-4		OV-1	IR surveillance system.

GROUND-BASED ELECTRONIC WARFARE SYSTEMS

DESIGNATION	MANUFACTURER	PLATFORMS	NOTES
GLQ-3	Fairchild Weston	truck	VHF (20–230 MHz) tactical voice and data communications intercept and ECM system.
MLQ-33	GTE		Jams ground-to-air VHF/UHF communications.
MLQ-34 TacJam	GTE, AEL	M1015 tracked carrier	Jams most types of modulated signals in A–C bands; can direct 2,000 watts at each of 3 emitters simultaneously. Often deployed with TSQ-112.

GROUND-BASED ELECTRONIC WARFARE SYSTEMS (*continued*)

DESIGNATION	MANUFACTURER	PLATFORMS	NOTES
MSQ-103 Teampack	Emerson	truck (-103B) or M1015 (-103A/C)	Detects and provides Line of Bearing (LOB) on radars in C–K bands (0.5-40 GHz). Colocated with TSQ-114 COMINT system.
PRD-10		LAV MEWSS	SIGINT system.
PRD-12 LMRDFS	Watkins-Johnson	truck	Intercept, DF of hostile HF/VHF/UHF communications.
TLQ-15	AEL	various	2,000-watt jammer and "look-through" communications system.
TLQ-17 Traffic Jam Quickfix	Loral Fairchild	truck (-17A), EH-1, EH-160 Quickfix helo	Jamming/monitoring of HF/VHF systems. Can operate on up to 255 preset frequencies simultaneously. Sandcrab jammer developed for Operation Desert Storm.
TRQ-30		manpack	HF/VHF intercept and LOB. Known as Turkey 30.
TRQ-32 Teammate		truck	HF/VHF intercept and LOB. Known as Turkey 32. Replaced by TSQ-112.
TSC-109 Agtelis	Bunker Ramo	truck	C–J-band SIGINT DF (Direction Finding) system using 3 remote, 1 control stations; 1° RMS accuracy at 16 nm (30 km).
TSQ-112 Tacelis	GTE	truck	HF/VHF COMINT DF system; 2 remote master, 4 remote slave stations; deployed with MLQ-34.
TSQ-114 Trailblazer	ESL	M1015	HF/VHF/UHF search, intercept, and report sytem. Interoperates with Quickfix for DF in 20–80 MHz.
TSQ-152 Trackwolf		tracked	HF COMINT and auto DF, collection, processing.

DESIGNATION	MANUFACTURER	PLATFORMS	NOTES
TSQ-IEWCS	Electrospace	M2 tracked carrier, HM-WWV 5/4-ton truck	Intelligence and Electronic Warfare Common Sensor (COMINT/ECM/ELINT/ESM functions combined) to detect single channel and Low Probability of Intercept signals. Fielded in GBCS-Heavy (M2) and GBCS-Light variants. Replaces MLQ-34, MSQ-103, TLQ-17, TRQ-32, TSQ-114.
ULQ-19	Racal	mobile, helicopter	16-channel 100-watt communications jammer covering 20–80 MHz.
USD-9	ESL	RC-12	Airborne SIGINT system; with ELINT added, becomes Guardrail common sensor, works with TSQ-112.

NAVAL ELECTRONIC WARFARE SYSTEMS

DESIGNATION	MANUFACTURER	PLATFORMS	NOTES
BLD-1	Litton/Amecon	submarines (SSN 688, SSN 21)	Passive intercept and precise Direction Finding (DF) using phase interferometer.
BLQ-3	GE	submarines	Low-Frequency (LF) acoustic jammer.
BLQ-4	GE	submarines	High-Frequency (HF) acoustic jammer.
BLQ-5	GE	submarines	LF acoustic repeater.
BLQ-6	GE	submarines	HF acoustic repeater.
BLQ-8	Bendix, Aerojet	submarines	Acoustic Countermeasures (CM).
BLR 1-10	several	submarines	Radar-Warning Receivers (RWR).
BLR-13	Kollmorgen	submarines	ECM receiver.
BLR-14	Unisys	submarines	Basic Submarine Acoustic Warfare System (BSAWS) against torpedoes. Warns, analyzes, and launches CM.
BLR-15	Kollmorgen	submarines	Electronic Support Measures (ESM) receiver.
BRD-6/7	Lockheed Sanders	submarines	RDF, SIGINT receiver.

NAVAL ELECTRONIC WARFARE SYSTEMS (continued)

DESIGNATION	MANUFACTURER	PLATFORMS	NOTES
Mk 36 SRBOC	Loral Hycor	surface ships	6-barrel chaff/flare launcher deployed on ships in groups of 2 or 4.
Mk 70 MOSS		submarines (SSBN 726)	Tube-Launched Mobile Submarine Simulator.
SLQ-17	Hughes	aircraft carriers	ECM system that tracks, detects, and uses deception jamming against missile radars. Not regarded as a success.
SLQ-25 Nixie	Aerojet	surface combatants	Towed, electroacoustic torpedo decoy.
SLQ-29		aircraft carriers	Combines SLQ-17 with WLR-1/-8/-11 radar-warning/SIGINT systems
SLQ-32(V)1	Raytheon	auxiliary, amphibious warfare ships	Series uses Rotman lens technology for instantaneous bearing information. (V)1 passive H–J-band radar detection. Many installations upgraded to (V)2.
SLQ-32(V)2	Raytheon	destroyers, frigates	Expands passive detection to D–J-band spectrum. Many (V)2s also fitted with "Sidekick" jammer ECM, then designated (V)5.
SLQ-32(V)3	Raytheon	cruisers, destroyers, large amphibious, auxiliaries	(V)2 with ECM. Jammer can jam 75 pulsed and Continuous Wave (CW) emitters at once.
SLQ-32(V)4	Raytheon	aircraft carriers	(V)3 that replaces SLQ-17. SLQ-54 in development to replace SLQ-32 series.
SLQ-33		surface ships	Towed acoustic decoy.
SLQ-34 Outboard		28 surface ships	Intelligence collection system using SLR-16 and SRD-19 SIGINT.
SLQ-36		surface ships	Detects, decoys acoustic-/wake-homing torpedoes with variety of systems.
SLQ-39/-41 to -47			Chaff-dispensing (-39)/ expendable active EW buoys.

DESIGNATION	MANUFACTURER	PLATFORMS	NOTES
SLQ-49	Irvin	surface ships or aircraft	"Rubber duck" inflatable radar decoy. Developed in Great Britain.
SLQ-50 BGPHES	E-Systems	surface ship with aircraft	Battle Group Passive Horizon Extension System (pronounced "big feez"). Intercept antenna are airborne, info data-linked to shipboard processors.
SLR-16	Lockheed Sanders	surface ships	HF SIGINT using SRD-19 antennas. Part of SLQ-34/ SSQ-72 Classic Outboard systems.
SLR-21	E-Systems	PHM 1 hydrofoils	E–J-band radar intercept and DF.
SLR-22		aircraft carriers	Deception system.
SLR-23		surface ships	J-band radar intercept, DF; used with WLR-1, SLQ-32.
SLR-24		surface ships	On-board processor uses towed torpedo-detection array.
SLT-5, 8		surface ships	Communications jammers.
SRD-19 Diamond		surface ships	SIGINT in LF/MF/VHF bands; uses several types of antennas. Part of SSQ-72 Classic Outboard.
SRS-1		surface ships	Antiship missile radar detection emphasizing lower cost. Cost overruns reported.
SSQ-72/-74 /-108 Classic Outboard	ITT	surface ships	DF suite; -74 on 1 ship, -108 is most elaborate; uses SLR-16, SRD-19.
SSQ-82 Mute		surface ships	Emission control monitor.
ULQ-6	General Instrument	destroyers, frigates	Deception repeater jammer in older ships.
URD-9(V)		surface ships	A–B-band radar DF.
URD-27		surface ships	B–J-band SIGINT DF.
WLQ-4 Sea Nymph	GTE	submarines (SSN 637)	ESM detector/analyzer of radar, communications signals; -4(V)1 for use in *Seawolf*.
WLR-1H	ST Research	surface ships	HF to low-J-band RWR in early variants; 1H in H–J-band, has threat library, control of CM.

NAVAL ELECTRONIC WARFARE SYSTEMS (continued)

DESIGNATION	MANUFACTURER	PLATFORMS	NOTES
WLR-3	Jetonics	surface ships, submarines	RWR, SIGINT system.
WLR-4		surface ships, submarines	ESM receiver.
WLR-5		surface ships, submarines	Acoustic intercept receiver.
WLR-6 Waterboy		surface ships, submarines	Signal collection for reconnaissance.
WLR-8(V)	GTE	aircraft carriers, submarines	HF to J-band (except (V)2 C–J-band) signal surveillance and analysis with 7 superheterodyne tuners and 2 digital computers.
WLR-9	Norden	submarines	Acoustic Intercept Receiver (AIR); has 2 hydrophones, receiver processor for sonar intercept and analysis.
WLR-11	ARGO	aircraft carriers	H–J-band Instantaneous Frequency Measurement (IFM) to detect antiship missile radars. Used with WLR-1.
WLR-12	Norden	submarines	AIR with extended frequency coverage.
WLR-13		surface ships	Infrared, electro-optical warning receiver.
WLR-17	Norden	submarines	AIR derived from WLR-9.

SHIPS/SUBMARINES

AIRCRAFT CARRIERS

Enterprise (CVN 65)

The *Enterprise* was the world's second nuclear-powered surface warship and was the world's largest and most expensive warship when she entered service in 1961. The *Enterprise* was built to a modified *Kitty Hawk* design and features a fully angled deck with two C13 steam catapults, two more catapults at the bow, three elevators to starboard (two ahead of the island and one abaft it), and one elevator on the port quarter. Each elevator measures 85 × 52 ft (25.9 × 15.9 m).

The big difference from the *Kitty Hawk* was the machinery layout, with no fewer than eight reactors generating steam for four steam turbines. No other ship had even half as many nuclear reactors. Relatively small reactors and the immense size of the ship led to the complex arrangement.

In her original configuration, *Enterprise* was readily recognizable through the distinctive arrangement of "billboard" planar-array radar antennas and EW "beehive" on her island; these were removed in the late 1970s. Her flight deck has the greatest area of any aircraft carrier, her hangar is the largest and longest, she carries 8,500 tons of aviation fuel (approximately 2.72 million US gal/10,295,200 liters), and she has an ordnance capacity of 2,520 tons.

DEVELOPMENT • Enterprise was authorized in FY1958 and ordered from Newport News Shipbuilding in November 1957, completing in September 1960. Estimated construction cost was $444 million (contemporary conventional aircraft carrier construction costs in same-year dollars were estimated at $265 million). Hopes for five more in the class ran afoul of the high cost and complex reactor layout.

In January 1991, the *Enterprise* began a Refueling and Complex Overhaul (RCOH) at Newport News that included new reactor cores, overhauled propulsion plant, and modernization of the navigation, communications, and aviation support systems. Cost is estimated at between $1.5 and $2 billion to gain another 20 years. *Enterprise* was recommissioned in September 1994.

COMBAT EXPERIENCE • The *Enterprise* began flying air strikes against North Vietnam in November 1965, becoming the first nuclear-propelled ship to enter combat. She served two more tours off Vietnam but suffered a serious fire in January 1969 on her way out to a fourth tour.

In April 1988, A-6 and A-7 aircraft from the *Enterprise* attacked several Iranian Navy ships and craft in the Persian Gulf, sinking the frigate *Sahand* and several Boghammar fast attack craft and severely damaging the frigate *Sabalan*. (The *Enterprise* did not actually enter the gulf.)

SPECIFICATIONS •
DISPLACEMENT   90,970 tons full load
DIMENSIONS
length   1,101 ft 3 in (335.8 m)
                overall
beam   133 ft (40.5 m)

draft   39 ft (11.9 m)
flight deck width
             257 ft 2 in (78.4 m) max,
             area 4.94 acres (2
             hectares)
hangar deck length 860 ft (262.1 m),
             width 107 ft (32.6 m),
             height 25 ft (7.6 m)
MACHINERY   8 Westinghouse A2W
pressurized-water reactors, 4 Westing-
house steam turbines, 280,000 shp on
4 shafts=30+ kts, electric power
40,000 kW
CREW   3,208 + air wing 2,092
WEAPONS
  2 8-tube NATO Sea Sparrow
  launchers Mk 29
  3 20-mm Mk 15 Phalanx Gatling-type
  CIWS
AIRCRAFT   85
SENSORS
  SPS-48 3D air-search radar
  SPS-49 2D air-search radar
  SPS-64 surface-search radar
  SPS-65 threat-warning radar
  2 Mk 91 missile fire control systems
  SLQ-32(V)3 active/passive EW system

Forrestal (CV 59, AVT 59)

These four ships were the world's first
aircraft carriers to be built from the keel
up after World War II, construction beginning in the early 1950s. The *Forrestal*
introduced the basic supercarrier concept of four elevators and four catapults,
a vast, 8° angled flight deck, "hurricane"
bow for better seakeeping, a powerful
propulsion plant, and great increases in
fuel and ordnance storage capacity. Two
longitudinal bulkheads run from stem to
stern and extend from keel to waterline;
transverse bulkheads are placed approximately every 33 ft (10 m). This subdivision results in 1,200 watertight compartments under an armored flight deck.
    The elevator layout is the weakest point
of the design in that one is positioned at
the forward end of the angled deck, limit-

ing its use during flight operations. Each
elevator measures 62 ft × 52 ft 4 in (18.9
× 15.98 m). The island is midships in the
carrier's silhouette with one elevator
ahead and two astern along the starboard
side. The *Forrestal* has two inboard four-
blade propellers, two outboard five-blade
propellers, and three rudders.

DEVELOPMENT • Newport News Shipbuilding was the lead yard and constructed the *Forrestal* and *Ranger* from
1952 to 1957 while the Brooklyn Navy
Yard built the *Saratoga* and *Independence*
from 1952 to 1959.
    The 1980s Service Life Extension Pro-
gram (SLEP) updates include rehabilitation of the ship's hull, propulsion,
auxiliary machinery, and piping systems,
with improved radars, communications
equipment, and aircraft launch and recovery systems provided. Kevlar armor
was added to vital spaces, and more powerful C13 catapults, the Phalanx Mk 15
Mod 3 Close-In Weapons System (CIWS),
Mk 23 TAS radar, and Mk 29 Sea Sparrow
short-range Surface-to-Air Missile (SAM)
launchers were fitted.
    The *Saratoga* was first to enter the SLEP
(October 1980–February 1983), then the
Forrestal (March 1983–May 1985), and *Independence* (April 1985–February 1988).
The *Ranger* did not enter the SLEP program, getting instead a 1984–85 overhaul
that included many of the self-defense
sensor and weapons upgrades, an improved fire-fighting system, and improved evaporators.
    The *Forrestal* replaced *Lexington* (AVT
16) as the Navy's training carrier in February 1992. Her start in the new role was
delayed by her six-month deployment to
the Mediterranean in mid-1991. Later
cutbacks led to her being decommissioned in FY1994.
    The *Independence* shifted home ports to
Yokosuka, Japan, in September 1991, re-
lieving the USS *Midway* (CV 41). The
Ranger was decommissioned in 1993, the
Saratoga in 1994.

COMBAT EXPERIENCE • All four ships launched raids against North Vietnam in tours conducted from 1964 to 1975. The *Forrestal, Saratoga,* and *Independence* each had one tour; the *Forrestal* lost 134 crew dead to a fire in July 1967. The *Ranger* made four tours.

In August 1990, the *Independence* moved first to the northern Arabian Sea in response to Iraq's invasion of Kuwait and later (October 1990) became the first US carrier to enter the Persian Gulf since 1974. She was relieved by the carrier *Midway* in November.

The *Saratoga* arrived in the Desert Shield operating area in late August 1990 and remained in the Red Sea throughout Operations Desert Shield and Desert Storm. Her air wing flew 12,500 sorties during the deployment, more than 4,000 of them in Desert Storm, in which 2,025 tons of ordnance were delivered.

The *Ranger* reached the gulf a few days before Operation Desert Storm began. Her air wing delivered 2,110 tons of bombs and missiles.

SPECIFICATIONS •

DISPLACEMENT   78,200 tons full load (*Forrestal*); 79,200 tons full load (others)

DIMENSIONS
length   1,039 ft (316.7 m) overall (first 3); 1,046 ft 6 in (319.0 m) overall (*Independence*)
beam   130 ft (39.6 m)
draft   37 ft (11.3 m)
flight deck width
                  250 ft 3 in (76.3 m) (first 2); 270 ft (82.3 m) (last 2)
hangar deck   length 740 ft (225.6 m), width 101 ft (30.8 m), height 25 ft (7.6 m)
MACHINERY   8 Babcock & Wilcox boilers, 4 Westinghouse steam turbines, 260,000 shp (in *Forrestal*), 280,000 shp (others) on 4 shafts=33

kts (in *Forrestal*), 34 kts (others), range 12,000 nm at 20 kts
CREW   2,793–2,958 + air wing 3,400
WEAPONS
  3 8-cell NATO Sea Sparrow launchers Mk 29 in *Saratoga* and *Independence,* 2 launchers in *Ranger*
  3 20-mm Mk 15 Mod 3 Phalanx Gatling-type CIWS
AIRCRAFT   85
SENSORS
  SPS-48C (except SPS-49E in *Saratoga*) 3D air-search radar
  SPS-49 2D air-search radar
  SPS-10 surface-search radar
  3 Mk 91 missile fire control systems
  SLQ-29 (SLQ-17 jammer and WLR-8(V)4 radar-warning system)

John F. Kennedy (CV 67)

Officially a one-ship class that followed the three *Kitty Hawks* (CV 63), this ship has a distinctive single stack canted outboard. Her underwater protection layout also is different from earlier carriers. Otherwise, she resembles the *Kitty Hawks,* having the island set well aft and the four elevators at the deck edges. Three elevators are located on the starboard side, two ahead of the island and one abaft of it; the portside elevator is fitted on the port quarter. The elevators measure 85 × 52 ft (25.9 × 15.9 m).

The *Kennedy* was completed with a bow sonar dome, but, unlike the *America,* never had the SQS-23 sonar installed. The *Kennedy* originally had three Sea Sparrow Mk 25 launchers and Mk 115 FCS; she was later refitted with Mk 29 launchers.

DEVELOPMENT • The *Kennedy* was built by Newport News Shipbuilding and entered service in 1968; her construction was delayed by lengthy debates over whether the ship should have nuclear or conventional propulsion. (All subsequent large carriers built for the US Navy have been nuclear-powered.)

Her Service Life Extension Program (SLEP) refit was canceled in the FY1992 budget submitted in February 1991. A $400-million Complex Overhaul (COH) —a less elaborate refit—at Philadelphia was approved in the Operation Desert Storm supplemental funding bill passed in April 1991, with work beginning in 1993.

COMBAT EXPERIENCE • The *Kennedy* was deployed to the Sixth Fleet in August 1990 to replace the *Eisenhower* (CVN 69) and to support US forces in the Persian Gulf as part of Operation Desert Shield. The *Kennedy* was the only one of the six carriers not to embark F/A-18 Hornet dual-role fighters. Instead, she deployed the last A-7E Corsairs on active duty. Her CAW-3 air wing delivered 1,750 tons, including the only AGM-84E SLAMs used in the conflict. Altogether, more than 11,000 sorties left her deck during her deployment.

SPECIFICATIONS •

DISPLACEMENT   80,940 tons full load
DIMENSIONS
  length   1,050 ft 9 in (320.3 m)
  beam   128 ft 6 in (39.2 m)
  draft   36 ft 6 in (11.1 m)
  flight deck width
                  266 ft 11 in (81.4 m)
  hangar deck length 688 ft (209.75 m), width 106 ft (32.3 m), height 25 ft (7.6 m)
MACHINERY   8 Foster Wheeler boilers, 4 Westinghouse steam turbines, 280,000 shp on 4 shafts=30+ kts, range 12,000 nm at 20 kts, electric power 17,000 kW
CREW   3,045 + air wing 2,500
WEAPONS
  3 8-cell NATO Sea Sparrow launchers Mk 29
  3 20-mm Mk 15 Phalanx Gatling-type CIWS
AIRCRAFT   85

SENSORS
  SPS-48 3D air-search radar
  SPS-49 2D air-search radar
  SPS-10 surface-search radar
  3 Mk 91 missile fire control systems
  Mk 23 Target Acquisition System (TAS)
  SLQ-17 jammer and SLQ-26 EW systems

Kitty Hawk (CV 63)

These three ships have a modified *Forrestal* (CV 59) configuration, with improved elevator and flight deck arrangements, that would be the standard for all later Navy carriers. The island was moved farther aft; the new elevator layout placed all four at the deck edges. Three elevators are located on the starboard side, two ahead of the island and one abaft of it; the portside elevator is fitted on the port quarter. The elevators measure 85 × 52 ft (25.9 × 15.9 m).

The *America* has a bow sonar dome to house the SQS-23 sonar. She was the only postwar US carrier so fitted at the time; the set was removed in late 1981.

These ships were built with Terrier surface-to-air missile launchers (Mk 10 Mod 3 on starboard quarter and Mk 10 Mod 4 on port quarter) and SPQ-55B missile control "searchlight" radars that have been removed.

DEVELOPMENT • Delivery of the *Kitty Hawk* was delayed because of problems at New York Shipbuilding; her condition on delivery in 1961 was severely criticized by the Navy. The *Constellation* was delayed because of a fire on board while under construction at the Brooklyn Navy Yard, also completing in 1961. The *America*, built by Newport News Shipbuilding, entered service in 1965. (The *John F. Kennedy*, although similar, is considered a separate class; see the *John F. Kennedy* entry.)

The *Kitty Hawk* and *Constellation* SLEPs (Service Life Extension Program) at the

Philadelphia Naval Shipyard included rehabilitation of the ship's hull, propulsion, auxiliary machinery, electrical, and piping systems. Improved radars, communications equipment, and aircraft launch and recovery systems—including new blast deflectors, three-wire Mk 7 Mod 3 arresting gear, and new catapult rotary engines—were fitted as well as the Advanced Combat Direction System (ACDS).

Kitty Hawk's SLEP began in January 1988 with her first post-SLEP deployment coming in November 1992. The *Constellation*'s SLEP began in July 1990, with her first post-SLEP deployment coming at the end of 1993.

The *America*'s SLEP, planned for FY1995, was canceled as a part of force level cutbacks.

COMBAT EXPERIENCE • All three ships operated off the Vietnam coast from 1964 to 1975. *America* and *Kitty Hawk* served 3 tours each, while the *Constellation* saw duty on Yankee Station six times, the most of any supercarrier.

Aircraft from the *America* raided five Libyan airfields and other targets in 1986.

When Iraq invaded Kuwait in August 1990, both *Kitty Hawk* and *Constellation* were undergoing SLEPs. The *America* sailed from the West Coast in December, arriving in her launch area a few days before Operation Desert Storm began. Her CAW-1 flew more than 3,000 sorties during the air war and delivered 2,000 tons of ordnance.

In January 1993, aircraft from the *Kitty Hawk* struck at SAM sites in three raids intended to enforce a "no-fly" zone over southern Iraq.

SPECIFICATIONS •
DISPLACEMENT 80,800 tons full load
DIMENSIONS
length   1,045 ft 8 in (318.8 m)

(first 2); 1,047 ft 2 in (319.25 m) (*America*)
beam   129 ft 11 in (39.6 m)
draft   37 ft (11.3 m)
flight deck width
              251 ft 11 in (76.8 m)
hangar deck   length 740 ft (225.6 m), width 101 ft (30.8 m), height 25 ft (7.6 m)
MACHINERY 8 Foster Wheeler boilers, 4 Westinghouse steam turbines, 280,000 shp on 4 shafts=30+ kts, range 12,000 nm at 20 kts, electric power 15,000 kW (first 2), 18,000 kW (*America*)
CREW 2,773-3,017 + air wing 2,500
WEAPONS
    3 8-cell NATO Sea Sparrow launchers Mk 29
    3 20-mm Mk 15 Phalanx Gatling-type CIWS
AIRCRAFT 85
SENSORS
    SPS-48E 3D air-search radar (except SPS-48C in *America*)
    SPS-49(V) 2D air-search radar
    SPS-10 surface-search radar
    Mk 23 Target Acquisition System (TAS)
    SLQ-32(V)3 active/passive EW system

Nimitz (CVN 68)

These ships are the largest warships ever built and are the definitive supercarrier design. Construction of this class will cover more than 30 years, a record for a single class in the steam and steel age. The general arrangement of these ships is similar to the previous *Kitty Hawk* (CV 63) class with respect to flight deck, elevators (three to starboard, one on the port quarter), and island structure. Each elevator measures 85 × 52 ft (25.9 × 15.85 m).

The *Nimitz* was completed with two bridle retrieval horns extending forward from the bow catapults. Later ships in the class have only the starboard horn, as most Navy aircraft no longer require a wire bridle for launching. The number of arresting wires is being reduced from four to three during refit; the gear is currently produced by the Dutch firm Hydraudyne Systems and Engineering. The flight deck and hull are constructed from high-tensile steel. Protection includes 2 ½-in (63-mm) side armor, Kevlar armor over the magazines and engine rooms. 23 watertight transverse bulkheads and longitudinal bulkheads divide the hull into 2,000 watertight compartments. Payload includes up to 2,970 tons of aviation ordnance and 2.7 million US gal (10,219,500 liters) of aviation fuel.

These carriers have only two reactors compared to the eight in the first nuclear carrier, the *Enterprise* (CVN 65). The initial fuel cores in the *Nimitz*-class ships are estimated to have a service life of at least 13 years (800,000–1 million nm).

As designed, these ships can operate about 85 fighter, attack, antisubmarine, and airborne early-warning aircraft and helicopters. Beginning in 1993, US carriers sailed in some deployments as the flagship of a Joint Task Group of surface combatants and amphibious ships. Some of the normal aircraft were sent ashore to make room for a 600-person Marine Corps unit accompanied by six CH-53 transport and four UH-1N utility helicopters.

DEVELOPMENT • Six ships are in service, two more are under construction, and initial funding for a ninth was requested in the FY1993 budget. The first three (CVN 68–70) were delayed by shipyard problems and the fourth (CVN 71) by conflicts between the Congress and the Carter administration. The next four (CVN 72–75) were ordered in pairs in 1983 and 1988. CVN 76 was ordered in large part to maintain a US capability to build nuclear-powered surface ships.

COMBAT EXPERIENCE • In August 1981, *Nimitz*-based F-14 Tomcat fighters shot down two Libyan Su-22 aircraft during operations in the Gulf of Sidra.

In August 1990, the *Dwight D. Eisenhower,* which was nearing the end of a scheduled six-month deployment in the Mediterranean, entered the Red Sea as part of the US response to the Iraqi invasion and annexation of Kuwait. She was relieved in late September by the *John F. Kennedy* (CV 67).

The *Theodore Roosevelt* entered the Red Sea on January 15, 1991, and launched aircraft against Iraqi targets on January 17 as part of Operation Desert Storm, the only nuclear-powered carrier to participate in the air war. Her aircraft delivered approximately 1,615 tons of ordnance during the air war.

SPECIFICATIONS •

DISPLACEMENT   91,700 tons full load (first 3); 96,300–96,700 tons full load (later ships)

DIMENSIONS

length	1,089 ft (332.1 m) overall
beam	134 ft (40.85 m)
draft	37 ft (11.3 m) (first 3); 38 ft 5 in (11.7 m) (later ships)
flight deck width	
	252 ft 11 in (77.1 m) (first 3); 257 ft (78.3 m) (later ships)

HANGAR DECK   length 684 ft (208.5 m), width 108 ft (32.9 m), height 26 ft 5 in (9.5 m)

MACHINERY   2 Westinghouse pressurized-water reactors, 4 steam turbines, 260,000+ shp on 4 shafts=30+ kts, electric power 64,000 kW

CREW   3,000–3,200 + air wing 2,865

WEAPONS

3 8-cell NATO Sea Sparrow Mk 29 launchers

20-mm Mk 15 Mod 3 Phalanx Gatling-type CIWS 3 mounts in CVN 68 and CVN 69, 4 in later ships

AIRCRAFT   85 including 20 F-14 Tomcat, 20 F/A-18 Hornet, 16 A-6E Intruder, 5 EA-6B Prowler, 5 E-2C Hawkeye, 8 S-3 Viking, 6 SH-3 Sea King or SH-60F CV-Helo

CVN 71
U.S. GOVERNMENT DEPARTMENT OF DEFENSE

SENSORS

SPS-48B 3D air-search radar in CVN 68-70

SPS-48C in CVN 71-73 (to be replaced by SPS-48E)

SPS-49 2D air-search radar

SPS-10F surface-search radar in CVN 68-70

SPS-67(V) surface-search radar in CVN 71-73

SPS-64 surface-search radar in CVN 71 and later ships

SPS-65 threat-detection radar in CVN-71 and later ships

4 Mk 91 missile fire control systems

SLQ-29 (SLQ-17 jammer + WLR-8 radar-warning receiver)

WLR-1H radar-warning receiver

4 Mk 36 SRBOC 6-barrel chaff/flare launchers

AMPHIBIOUS SHIPS

Anchorage (LSD 36)

These five Dock Landing Ships (LSD) were part of the large amphibious ship construction program of the early 1960s. They resemble the earlier *Thomaston*-class (LSD 28) but have a prominent knuckle forward, a more rectangular superstructure profile, greater freeboard, and a more substantial helicopter landing area aft.

The docking well is 430 ft (131.1 m) long and 50 ft (15.24 m) wide; it was designed to accommodate four LCAC air cushion landing craft or three LCU utility landing craft or nine LCM-8 mechanized landing craft or 52 AAV amphibian tractors. Another 15 tractors can be stowed on a "mezzanine" deck, which when fitted allows only three LCAC air cushion assault craft to be embarked. A removable helicopter deck is fitted over the docking well, but the ships have no hangar or helicopter maintenance capability. Total vehicle storage space is 15,800 ft² (1,468 m²).

As built, these ships had eight 3-in guns in twin mounts; one amidships mount and the Mk 56 and Mk 63 gunfire control systems were removed in the late 1970s. One additional 3-in twin gun mount was deleted with installation of the two Phalanx Close-In Weapons Systems (CIWS) in the 1980s.

DEVELOPMENT • *Anchorage* was built by Litton's Ingalls yard at Pascagoula, Mississippi, from 1967 to 1969; the other four were constructed at General Dynamics' Quincy, Massachusetts, yard from 1967 to 1972.

COMBAT EXPERIENCE • *Anchorage, Portland, Pensacola,* and *Mount Vernon* all deployed to the Persian Gulf as part of Operation Desert Shield. *Portland* and *Pensacola* sailed with Amphibious Group 2, arriving in the theater in early September (*Portland* on the 3rd, *Pensacola* on the 6th). *Anchorage* and *Mount Vernon* were part of Amphibious Group 3, which entered the theater on January 12, 1991.

The threat of a large invasion force lying in the gulf east of Kuwait City was said to have been an important part of the deception that significantly reduced Iraqi armed forces' ability to react to the armored left hook that began the ground war in late February. All remained in the gulf as part of a potential invasion force until after the March 1 cease-fire.

SPECIFICATIONS •
DISPLACEMENT 14,000 tons full load
DIMENSIONS
length 553 ft 6 in (168.7 m) overall
beam 85 ft (25.9 m)
draft 18 ft 5 in (5.6 m)
MACHINERY 2 Foster Wheeler boilers (except Combustion Engineering in *Anchorage*), 2 De Laval steam turbines, 24,000 shp on 2 shafts=22 kts (20 kts sustained)
CREW 358 + 330 troops
WEAPONS
6 3-in (76-mm)/50-cal Mk 33 AA in twin mounts (4 guns in ships with Phalanx CIWS)
2 20-mm Mk 15 Phalanx Gatling-type CIWS
HELICOPTERS removable flight deck
SENSORS
SPS-40 air-search radar
SPS-10 surface-search radar
local fire control only for 3-in guns
SLQ-32(V)1 passive EW system

Austin (LPD 3)

These 12 ships are enlarged versions of the earlier three-ship *Raleigh*-class Lpds. They resemble dock landing ships but have a relatively smaller docking well and additional space for troop berthing and vehicle parks.

The LPD 7–13 are configured as amphibious squadron flagships and have an additional bridge level. All have a docking well that is 168 feet long and 50 feet wide; landing craft stowage in the well can be either two LCACs, one LCU with three LCM-6s or four LCM-8s, or 24 AAV7 amphibious assault vehicles. Two more LCM-6 or four LCVP or LCPL landing craft can be carried on the helicopter deck. Below decks is about 12,000 ft² (1,115 m²) of vehicle storage space and 40,000 ft³ (1,133 m³) of bulk cargo space.

These ships have a fixed flight deck above the docking well with two landing spots. All except the *Austin* are fitted with a helicopter hangar; an extension expands to provide a length of approximately 80 feet. As many as four CH-46s or CH-53s can be embarked at a time, but this can only be done with a helicopter carrier in company to provide sustained maintenance and support. As built, these ships had eight 3-in guns in twin mounts. The number was reduced in the late 1970s, and the associated Mk 56 and Mk 63 Gun Fire Control Systems (GFCS) were removed. Most have been fitted with two Phalanx Close-In Weapons Systems (CIWS).

DEVELOPMENT • Brooklyn Navy Yard built the first three, Litton's Ingalls yard in Pascagoula, Mississippi, the next two, and Lockheed Shipbuilding the last seven. Deliveries came between 1965 and 1971; LPD-16 was authorized, but not built. Plans in the 1980s for a Service Life Extension Program (SLEP) for this class were not funded by Congress. The first ships of this class began decommissioning in FY1993.

The *Coronado* (LPD 11) of this class was modified for use as a flagship in late 1980 and reclassified AGF 11. The LPD-17 follow-on class is planned for first order in FY1996. These 12 much bigger ships will displace 25,300 tons, measure 684 feet (208.4 m) long overall and have a 105-ft (31.9 m) beam. Each will carry 700 troops, two Landing Craft Air Cushion (LCAC), and have a hangar for helicopters or the MV-22 Osprey.

COMBAT EXPERIENCE • As with most of the US Navy's amphibious ships, these units frequently assist in disaster or humanitarian relief or evacuation of dependents. Six of the class participated in Operations Desert Shield/Desert Storm. The *Ogden* embarked part of the 13th Marine Expeditionary Unit (Special Operations Capable). The *Dubuque* was part of a small task force (ARG Bravo) that deployed to the Desert Storm theater for 35 days between September 9 and October 13, 1990.

Shreveport and *Trenton* lifted elements of the 4th Marine Expeditionary Brigade (MEB), reaching the theater of operations on September 3, 1990. *Denver* and *Juneau*, as part of Amphibious Group 3, transported the 5th MEB, arriving in the theater in mid-January 1991. All except *Dubuque* remained in the theater until well after the cease-fire.

SPECIFICATIONS •
DISPLACEMENT   16,900 tons full load
DIMENSIONS
　length　　568 ft 9 in (173.4 m)
　　　　　　overall
　beam　　84 ft (25.6 m)
　draft　　23 ft (7.0 m)
　well deck　length 393 ft 8 in (120.0
　　　　　　m), width 52 ft 3 in
　　　　　　(15.2 m), flight deck
　　　　　　area 15,000 ft² (1,394
　　　　　　m²)
MACHINERY   2 boilers (Foster Wheeler except Babcock & Wilcox in *Duluth* and *Shreveport*), 2 De Laval steam tur-

bines, 24,000 shp on 2 shafts= 20 kts, range 7,700 nm at 20 kts
CREW   425 + 930 troops in 5 ships; 840 troops + 90 flag in 6 ships
WEAPONS
   4 3-in (76-mm)/50-cal Mk 33 AA in twin mounts
   2 20-mm Mk 15 Mod 2 Phalanx Gatling-type CIWS in four ships
HELICOPTERS   flight deck with 2 landing spots and hangar
SENSORS
   SPS-40C air-search radar
   SPS-10F or SPS-67 surface-search radar
   LN-66 navigation radar
   local gunfire control only
   SLQ-32(V)1 passive EW system

Charleston (LKA 113)

These five ships carry heavy equipment and supplies to unload into landing craft and onto helicopters for opposed landings. Although they were the first US class to be built expressly for the attack transport role, they resemble conventional break-bulk freighters. But their prodigious hoisting capacity includes two 78-ton-capacity cranes and two 40-ton cranes; eight more 15-ton-capacity booms are also rigged.

These ships have a helicopter landing area aft, but no hangar or maintenance facilities. The landing area measures 6,082 ft² (565 m²). The *Charleston*s have approximately 33,000 ft² (3,065 m²) of vehicle storage space and almost 70,000 ft³ (1,982 m³) of bulk cargo space. Usual landing craft stowage includes four LCM-8s, five LCM-6s, two LCVPs, and two LCPs.

Two Phalanx Close-In Weapons Systems (CIWS) were fitted in the *Charleston* and *El Paso*.

DEVELOPMENT • Newport News Shipbuilding constructed all five ships, completing them from 1968 to 1970. The *Charleston* was decommissioned in FY1992 and the other four in FY1994.

COMBAT EXPERIENCE • To support Operations Desert Shield and Desert Storm, the *Durham* carried elements of the 13th Marine Expeditionary Unit (Special Operations Capable) from Okinawa to the Persian Gulf, arriving on September 7, 1990. The *Mobile* sailed with Amphibious Group 3, which arrived in the gulf on January 12, 1991 and remained until the cease-fire.

SPECIFICATIONS •
DISPLACEMENT   18,600 tons full load
DIMENSIONS
   length   576 ft (175.6 m) overall
   beam   62 ft (18.9 m)
   draft   25 ft 6 in (7.8 m)
MACHINERY   2 Combustion Engineering boilers, 1 Westinghouse steam turbine, 22,000 shp on 1 shaft= 20+ kts
CREW   360 + 225 troops
WEAPONS
   6 3-in (76-mm)/50-cal Mk 33 AA in twin mounts except 4 in *Charleston, El Paso*
   2 20-mm Mk 15 Phalanx Gatling-type CIWS
HELICOPTERS   landing area
SENSORS
   SPS-10 surface-search radar
   LN-66 navigation radar (except CRP-2900 in *Charleston*)
   local gunfire control only
   SLQ-32(V)1 passive EW system
   2 Mk 36 SRBOC 6-barrel chaff/flare launchers

Iwo Jima (LPH 2)

These seven ships were the first of any navy to be constructed specifically to operate helicopters. Unlike the Royal Navy's commando carriers of the 1960s and 1970s, and the later *Tarawa/Wasp* classes, however, these LPHs do not carry landing craft (except for the LCVP davits in the *Inchon*).

These ships represent an improved World War II–type escort carrier design with accommodations for a Marine battalion and supporting helicopter squadron. Up to seven CH-46 Sea Knight or four CH-53 Sea Stallion helicopters can operate from their flight decks. No catapults or arresting gear are fitted. The hangar deck, which is 229 ft 8 in (70 m) long, can accommodate 19 Sea Knights or 11 Sea Stallions or various mixes of these and other aircraft. The two deck-edge elevators measure 50 × 34 ft (15.2 × 10.4 m).

Below the flight deck, vehicle space amounts to 5,563 ft² (517 m²), and 40,000 ft³ (1,133 m³) of space is available for bulk cargo. These ships have extensive medical facilities with a 300-bed sick bay.

Between 1970 and 1974, all ships had two 3-in gun mounts replaced by Sea Sparrow missile launchers (one forward of the island and one on the port quarter). Still later, all ships were refitted with two Phalanx CIWS. The *Okinawa* had her forward Sea Sparrow launcher replaced by a Phalanx mount. The other six ships have one Phalanx on a sponson on the starboard side, forward of the Sea Sparrow launcher, a second Phalanx fitted on a sponson on the port side, aft. All gunfire control systems have been removed and only local control is now available for the 3-in guns.

Building on the *Tripoli*'s experience in Operation Desert Storm, the *Inchon* began testing a mine countermeasures support ship conversion in 1994. Success in these trials led to a $29-million conversion contract to Ingalls in December 1994. *Inchon*'s new designation is MCS-1.

DEVELOPMENT • Five of the class were built in naval shipyards (one at Puget Sound, four at Philadelphia) from 1961 to 1968; two were constructed at Litton's Ingalls yard in Pascagoula, Mississippi, and delivered in 1966 and 1970. *Iwo Jima* and *Okinawa* decommissioned in FY1993, *Guadalcanal* in FY1994.

COMBAT EXPERIENCE • These ships operated CH-53 helicopters in mine countermeasures operations off North Vietnam in 1973, in the Suez Canal in the late 1970s, and in the Persian Gulf in support of US Navy convoy operations during the 1980–88 Iran-Iraq war. They have also frequently participated in monitoring operations such as the Adriatic Sea patrol in 1992 and several evacuations.

The *Iwo Jima, Okinawa, Guam, Tripoli,* and *New Orleans* were deployed to the Persian Gulf region as part of Operation Desert Shield. The *Okinawa* was the first to arrive, on September 5, bringing a part of the 13th Marine Expeditionary Unit (Special Operations Capable). The *Iwo Jima* and the *Guam* lifted parts of the 4th Marine Expeditionary Brigade (MEB), arriving in the theater on September 8, 1990, and remaining until March 23, 1991. The *Tripoli* and the *New Orleans* were part of Amphibious Group 3, which reached the theater on January 12, 1991.

The *Tripoli* was named command ship of the Mine Countermeasures Group on January 17. On February 18, 1991, she struck a mine in the northern Persian Gulf, sustaining a 16 by 20-ft (4.88 by 6.1-m) hole 10 ft (3.05 m) below the waterline, but remained operational. She continued as flagship of the MCM force until June 18, when she was relieved by the cruiser *Texas* (CGN 39).

Cargo and utility helicopters flew 4,980 sorties from the *Tripoli*'s flight deck in support of Operation Restore Hope in Somalia in 1993.

SPECIFICATIONS •
DISPLACEMENT   18,300 tons full load
DIMENSIONS
length   602 ft 3 in (183.6 m)
                overall
beam   83 ft 8 in (25.5 m)
                waterline, extreme
                width 104 ft (31.7 m)
draft   26 ft (7.9 m)
MACHINERY   2 boilers (Combustion Engineering except Babcock & Wilcox in

Guam), 1 Westinghouse steam turbine, 22,000 shp on 1 shaft=22 kts (21 kts sustained, range 16,600 nm at 11.5 kts, 10,000 nm at 20 kts

CREW 685 + 2,000 troops

WEAPONS

    2 8-cell Mk 25 Sea Sparrow missile launchers (except *Okinawa*)

    4 3-in (76-mm)/50-cal Mk 33 AA in twin mounts

    2 20-mm Mk 15 Phalanx Gatling-type CIWS

HELICOPTERS 25 helicopters (class has operated AV-8B Harrier VSTOL aircraft but does not regularly embark them)

SENSORS

    SPS-40 air-search radar

    SPS-10 surface-search radar

    LN-66 navigation radar (except CRP-1900B in *Guam*)

    2 Mk 115 missile fire control systems

    SLQ-32(V)2 EW system (except WLR-1 in *Tripoli*)

Landing Craft Air Cushion (LCAC 1)

These 84 craft are the only US Navy air cushion landing craft in service. (The former Soviet Navy deployed several designs, many larger than the LCACs.) They are designed to transport troops and equipment from ships to over-the-shore during amphibious operations. Using the air cushion gives the LCAC the ability to carry approximately the same payload as an LCM-8-type landing craft at more than four times the speed and to travel inland over flat ground or marshes; they can clear land obstacles up to 4 ft (1.22 m) high.

The LCAC has more in common with a helicopter than with a landing craft. It is conned by a "craftmaster" using a yokelike control wheel (and earning "flight time") from a pilothouse on the starboard side; the navigator and craft engineer sit next to the operator in side-by-side seats. A fourth seat is provided for the group commander, who rides in one of three LCACs in a detachment. All five LCAC crew members are enlisted personnel, the craftmaster being most senior.

Typical payload is 60 tons (54.4 metric tons) of cargo, an M1 Abrams main battle tank (65 tons), or five light armored vehicles, or two M198 towed 155-mm howitzers and their prime movers, plus 24 combat-ready troops. Eight Marines ride below the pilothouse and 16 more sit in a deckhouse on the port side forward. The loadmaster rides in the port deckhouse and a deck hand/assistant engineer sits above. (During Operation Desert Storm, as many as 41 Marines were embarked.)

The cargo deck is 27 ft (8.23 m) wide and has an area of 1,809 ft² (168.1 m²); maximum cargo overload is 75 tons (68 metric tons). Along each side of the cargo deck are the crew and troop quarters (forward) and tandem engine units.

The craft are girdled with a "bag and finger" skirt that is inflated by the forward engine unit on each side. The Textron Lycoming gas turbines drive four lift fans through offset fan drive gearboxes. When the skirt is deflated, both bow and stern ramps can be used for loading and unloading.

The after engines on each side propel the craft with four-blade, reversible, 11-ft 9-in (3.58-m) diameter propellers through offset propeller drive gearboxes. Each propeller is housed in a deep-chord shroud that has five stators abaft the propellers and twin rudders. The engines also operate two bow thrusters that are used for propulsion and maneuvering.

DEVELOPMENT • LCAC 1 was delivered by Bell Textron in December 1984. The first operational deployment of the LCACs took place in August 1987 in *USS Germantown* (LSD 42). 107 had been planned, but only 84 were authorized, the last being ordered in 1992. The LCACs are evenly divided between Assault Craft

Unit 4 (ACU-4) of the Atlantic Fleet and ACU-5 in the Pacific. Japan ordered two LCACs in late 1993.

COMBAT EXPERIENCE • In August 1990, 17 LCACs were deployed to the Persian Gulf in several landing ships as part of Operation Desert Shield. Although a November 1990 landing rehearsal implied that LCACs might be limited by high waves, actual performance during Desert Storm was more gratifying. In a 24-hour period beginning on February 24, LCACs battled heavy seas and prevailing 40-knot winds to make 55 runs and carry more than 2,369 tons of vehicles and an entire MEB (7,300 men), an average of 43 tons and 132 men per run.

In May 1991, Amphibious Group 3, led by USS Tarawa (LHA 1), provided emergency aid to Bangladesh's cyclone victims as part of Operation Sea Angel. LCACs proved well suited for ship-to-shore transfers in the flooded and devastated river deltas.

SPECIFICATIONS •
WEIGHT   200 tons loaded
DIMENSIONS
  length   87 ft 11 in (26.8 m)
              overall on cushion
  beam   47 ft 0 in (14.3 m) on
              cushion
  draft   0 ft
MACHINERY 4 Textron Lycoming TF-40B gas turbines (2 for propulsion, 2 for lift), 31,640 ship= 50 kts max, 40 kts with payload, range 200 nm at 40 kts with payload
CREW   5 + 24 troops
SENSORS   1 navigation radar

Newport (LST 1179)

These 20 ships were the last large amphibious ships built for the US Navy that could beach themselves for unloading. The design has bow and stern ramps for unloading tanks and other vehicles. The bow ramp is 112 ft (34.14 m) long and is handled over the bow by twin, fixed derrick arms that are a distinctive feature of this class. Only the upper half of the bow has clamshell doors; the lower half has a raked stem to permit sustained speeds of 20 knots.

The block superstructure is amidships and is pierced by a vehicle passage connecting the main deck forward and aft. Abaft the superstructure is a broad stack on the port side and a smaller stack farther aft on the starboard side.

The ships have 17,300 ft^2 (1,607 m^2) of vehicle storage space. The tank deck is served by a 75-ton capacity turntable at each end; alternative loads include 41 2 ½-ton trucks, 29 M48-size tanks, or 23 AAV-7s. Four LCVPs (Landing Craft, Vehicle and Personnel) are carried in amidship davits.

These ships carry 2,000 tons when operated as a cargo ship, 500 tons of vehicles when beaching. Vehicle fuel capacity is 141,600 US gal (535,956 liters). Vehicles have 19,000 ft^2 (1,765 sq m^2) of main deck parking area; the helicopter landing area measures an additional 2,605 ft^2 (242 m^2). Two 10-ton cranes serve the main deck aft.

Replacement of the 3-in guns by two 20-mm Phalanx Gatling-type Close-In Weapons Systems (CIWS) was limited to less than half the class. Plans to fit all ships with two Phalanx CIWS were abbreviated by retirement of the class beginning in FY1992.

DEVELOPMENT • The first three ships were built by the Philadelphia Navy Yard and delivered in 1969–70. The other 17 ships were awarded as a block to National Steel and Shipbuilding in July 1966. This was the first naval ship construction block award to a US yard in the post–World War II era and presaged a pattern of large awards to single yards. The 17 ships were delivered in 1969–72.

Decommissioning these ships in the

early 1990s led to new careers for many of them in other navies. Argentina (1), Brazil (1), Chile (2), Malaysia (1), Morocco (1), Spain (2), Taiwan (3), and Venezuela (2) leased ex-Newports. Australia purchased 2 more for conversion to helicopter support ships.

COMBAT EXPERIENCE • The *Manitowoc, Peoria, Frederick, Schenectady, Cayuga, Saginaw, San Bernardino, Spartanburg County, La Moure County,* and *Barbour County* were among the amphibious ships that transported US Marines to the Persian Gulf area as part of Operation Desert Shield. Several remained in the region throughout Operation Desert Storm, although they never attempted to land troops in Kuwait.

Several ships were transferred to the Naval Reserve Force (NRF) beginning in 1980 with *Boulder.* Eight *Newports* (including the name ship) were decommissioned by FY1994.

SPECIFICATIONS •
DISPLACEMENT   8,450 tons full load
DIMENSIONS
length   561 ft 10 in (171.3 m)
               over derrick arms
beam   69 ft 6 in (21.2 m)
draft   17 ft 6 in (5.3 m)
MACHINERY   6 diesels (Alco 16-251 in first 3, General Motors 16-645-E5 in rest), 16,500 bhp on 2 shafts with controllable-pitch propellers=22 kts
CREW   253 + 400 troops
WEAPONS
    4 3-in 76-mm/50-cal Mk 32 AA in twin mounts in some ships
    1 20-mm Mk 15 Mod 1 Phalanx Gatling-type CIWS in some ships
SENSORS   SPS-10F surface-search radar

Tarawa (LHA 1)

These five amphibious assault ships combine the capabilities of several types of amphibious ships in a single hull. In addition, they are larger than virtually all non-US aircraft carriers and can operate AV-8B Harrier VSTOL aircraft, transport helicopters such as the CH-53 series, and gunships such as the AH-1 Supercobra. The first of a modified design—*Wasp* (LHD 1)—entered service in 1989.

In addition to a spacious flight deck, the design has 30,000 ft^2 (2,787 m^2) of vehicle storage decks connected by ramps to the flight deck and docking well, five cargo elevators that move equipment between the holds and flight deck, and approximately 110,000 ft^3 (3,115 m^3) of space for bulk cargo. Extensive command and communications facilities are provided for an amphibious force commander.

The stern docking well is 268 ft (81.7 m) long and 78 ft (23.8 m) wide and can accommodate four LCU 1610 landing craft or two LCUs plus three LCM-8s or 17 LCM-6s or 45 AAV/LVTP-7 amphibian tractors. Yet the docking well can accept only one LCAC air cushion landing craft because of the arrangement of the docking well.

A 900-horsepower through-tunnel thruster is fitted in the forward part of the hull. Other special features include an 18-foot section of the mast that is hinged to permit passage under bridges and a 5,000-ft^2 (464.5-m^2) training and acclimatization room to permit troops to exercise in a controlled environment. Extensive medical facilities include three operating rooms and bed space for 300 patients.

These are the only US amphibious ships currently armed with 5-in guns. The first ships fitted with the Phalanx were the *Saipan* and *Nassau.* The *Saipan* has a Phalanx mount replacing the Sea Sparrow launchers forward of the bridge; the *Nassau* has the Phalanx installed on a small deckhouse forward of the bridge structure and forward Sea Sparrow launcher.

DEVELOPMENT • Litton's Ingalls yard in Pascagoula, Mississippi, built all five ships. Nine were planned, but serious start-up problems and unanticipated inflation in the early 1970s resulted in cost overruns (the Total Package Procurement acquisition program was deemed the major culprit) and delays. Thus, funding authorized for nine ships could only pay for five. The *Tarawa* was completed in 1976. The others followed in 1976 to 1980.

COMBAT EXPERIENCE • These ships have participated in most of the major presence, combat, and humanitarian-aid operations the US Navy has mounted.

The *Nassau* was flagship of Amphibious Group 3 that operated in the Persian Gulf and northern Arabian Sea from September 7, 1990, until March 23, 1991, as part of Operation Desert Shield/Desert Storm. The *Tarawa* headed up Amphibious Group 2, which operated in the theater of operations from January 12 to late April 1991.

Like her sister ship's task force, the *Tarawa*'s group practiced amphibious landings and supported Marine Corps air operations during the Desert Storm air war. (Both *Tarawa* and *Nassau* served as aircraft carriers for AV-8B Harrier II and helicopter gunships.)

SPECIFICATIONS •

DISPLACEMENT   39,400 tons full load

DIMENSIONS

length	834 ft (254.2 m) overall
beam	105 ft 8 in (32.2 m) waterline, extreme width 131 ft 10 in (40.2 m)
draft	25 ft 11 in (7.9 m)
flight deck	length 820 ft (249.9 m), width 118 ft 1 in (36.0 m)

MACHINERY   2 Combustion Engineering boilers, 2 Westinghouse steam turbines, 70,000 shp on 2 shafts=24 kts (22 kts sustained), range 10,000 nm at 20 kts, electric power 14,600 kW

CREW   940 + 1,900 troops

WEAPONS
  2 8-cell Sea Sparrow missile launchers Mk 25 except 1 in *Saipan*
  3 single 5-in (127-mm)/54-cal Mk 45 dual-purpose
  1 20-mm Mk 15 Phalanx Gatling-type CIWS
  6 single 20-mm AA Mk 67

AIRCRAFT   35 Harrier VSTOL and helicopters

SENSORS
  SPS-52 3D air-search radar
  SPS-40 2D air-search radar
  SPS-53 surface-search radar
  Mk 86 gunfire control system with SPG-60 and SPQ-9 radars
  SLQ-32(V)3 active/passive EW system

Wasp (LHD 1)

These amphibious assault ships and the earlier *Tarawa* (LHA 1) class are the world's largest amphibious ships, and they dwarf all other conventional and VSTOL (Vertical/Short Takeoff and Landing) aircraft carriers save the Russian *Kiev*- and *Kuznetsov* (ex-*Tbilisi*)-class ships and the US Navy's supercarriers. As threats change and budgets decline, these ships increasingly are standing in for conventional aircraft carriers in forward deployments.

The design's primary role is to support Marine Corps amphibious operations and thus they are equipped with extensive Command, Control, Communications, and Intelligence (C3I) equipment. If deployed as the flagship of a surface action group, up to 20 AV-8B Harriers can be embarked as well as four to six SH-60B LAMPS III helicopters.

Differences from the *Tarawa* design reflect operational practice and growing acceptance of the AV-8B Harrier. The Combat Information Center (CIC) was relocated below the flight deck, permitting the island to be reduced in height by two decks. The island is also longer and narrower than that in the *Tarawas*. The hull retains the "clipper" bow and full-section after half, but the bow thruster has been deleted in favor of a bulbous forefoot.

The flight deck is constructed of high-strength HY-100 steel. It does not have a ski-jump ramp to assist VSTOL operations because the size of the flight deck is considered sufficiently large to enable rolling takeoffs for heavily laden VSTOL aircraft. (Despite the *Wasp*'s roominess, the Marine Corps has tested portable ski-jump assemblies.)

Helicopters use nine landing spots, six to port and three fore and aft of the island. The stern elevator has been moved to the starboard quarter, and the capacity of both deck elevators has been increased to 34 tons each. There are also six cargo and ammunition elevators.

The *Wasp* class has less vehicle storage space and bulk cargo space than the *Tarawas*, but carries more aircraft. The 270-ft (82.3-m) long docking well is narrower (having been reduced to a 50-ft/15.24-m width), but the removal of a longitudinal partition yields a greater unobstructed width, enabling the *Wasp* to embark three air cushion landing craft (LCAC). Medical facilities are double those of the LHA 1 class, with six operating rooms and facilities for 600 bed patients.

The self-defense armament has been modified by replacing the two 5-in (127-mm) guns with three Phalanx 20-mm Gatling-type Close-In Weapons Systems (CWIS). Two eight-cell NATO Sea Sparrow short-range surface-to-air missile launchers are also fitted; plans to fit vertical-launch Sea Sparrow were canceled.

Beginning with the *Essex* (LHD 2), these ships have composite armor built into the deckhouse to protect from small-caliber bullets and fire damage.

The Navy considered replacing the steam turbine propulsion plant with four gas turbines to increase the ships' speed to 25 knots and allow a longer range. Although the Navy estimated that gas tur-bines would be cheaper to install, operate, and maintain, the reengining was canceled when it appeared that the *Wasp* class would be limited to five ships.

DEVELOPMENT • The *Wasp* commissioned in July 1989. Although defense cutbacks were to limit procurement to five, later program revisions saw a sixth authorized in FY1993. Litton's Ingalls yard at Pascagoula, Mississippi, builds all LHDs.

COMBAT EXPERIENCE • The *Wasp*'s first deployment was in support of Operation Provide Comfort and Provide Comfort II in Turkey in June 1991. In a 1993 deployment, her AV-8B Harriers provided cover for UN forces operating in Mogadishu, Somalia, during 1992–93's Operation Restore Hope.

SPECIFICATIONS •
DISPLACEMENT   40,530 tons full load
DIMENSIONS
length   844 ft (257.3 m)
beam   106 ft (32.3 m) waterline, extreme width 140 ft (42.7 m)
draft   26 ft 1 in (8.0 m)
MACHINERY   2 Combustion Engineering boilers, 2 Westinghouse steam turbines, 71,000 shp on 2 shafts=22+ kts, range 9,500 nm at 20 kts, electric power 16,500 kW
CREW   1,081 + 1,875 Marines
WEAPONS
 2 8-cell Mk 29 launchers for NATO Sea Sparrow SAM
 3 20-mm Mk 15 Phalanx Gatling-type CIWS
AIRCRAFT   40 Harrier VSTOL and helicopters
SENSORS
 SPS-48 3D air-search radar (SPS-52 in *Wasp*)
 SPS-49 2D air-search radar
 SPS-64 surface-search radar
 2 Mk 91 fire control systems

Mk 23 Target Acquisition System
(TAS)
SLQ-32(V)3 active/passive EW system

Whidbey Island (LSD 41)

The *Whidbey Island*-class amphibious ships have replaced the 1950s-era *Thomaston* (LSD 28) class. The *Whidbey Island*s are similar to the earlier *Anchorage* class (LSD 36). However, the *Whidbey Island* design has a much larger, blockier superstructure; faired, rectangular-section diesel-engine stacks; a stump lattice foremast; and bulkier cranes amidships.

The docking well is 440 ft (134.1 m) long and 50 ft (15.2 m) wide and can accommodate 4 LCACs or 21 LCM-6 landing craft. There is approximately 12,500 ft² (1,161.7 m²) of vehicle storage space and 5,000 ft³ (141.6 m³) of space for bulk cargo. Cargo handling is aided by one 60-ton (54,432-kg) capacity and one 20-ton (18,144-kg) capacity crane.

The modified LSD 41CV (Cargo Variant) is similar to the *Whidbey Island* but emphasizes internal capacity at the expense of docking well room. Thus, bulk cargo space is increased eightfold to 40,000 ft³ (1,132.7 m³), while LCAC capacity in the well is cut in half to two.

DEVELOPMENT • Lockheed Shipbuilding at Seattle, Washington built the first three ships in the class, completing the first in February 1985. Avondale of Westwego, Louisiana, constructed all of the ships from the *Gunston Hall* on.

The number of big-well ships in Navy planning oscillated from nine to 10 up to 12 and back to eight. LSD 41CV construction began with the *Harpers Ferry* in April 1991. Five CVs were funded through FY1993.

COMBAT EXPERIENCE • In support of Operation Desert Shield, *Fort McHenry* arrived in the Gulf of Oman on September 7. *Gunston Hall,* which operated with Amphibious Group 2, entered the gulf four days later. *Germantown,* which operated with Amphibious Group 3, entered the gulf in mid-January 1991. All stood ready to launch invasion forces until after the cease-fire.

SPECIFICATIONS •
DISPLACEMENT   15,704 tons full load (LSD 41); 16,695 tons full load (LSD 41CV)
DIMENSIONS
length   609 ft 5 in (185.8 m) overall
beam   84 ft (25.6 m)
draft   20 ft (6.1 m) (LSD 41)
MACHINERY   4 Colt-Pielstick 16PC 2.5 V400 diesels, 33,600 bhp on 2 shafts=20 kts (21.6 kts for LSD 41CV), electric power 9,200 kW
CREW   342 + 500 troops with 64-man assault craft unit (LSD 41), 400 + 400 troops (LSD 41CV)
WEAPONS   2 20-mm Mk 15 Phalanx Gatling-type CIWS
HELICOPTERS   landing area
SENSORS
SPS-49 2D air-search radar
SPS-67 surface-search radar
SLQ-32(V)1 passive EW system

AUXILIARY SHIPS

Edenton (ATS 1)

These British-built ships are the only oceangoing tugs in active Navy commission. The design features a long forecastle that breaks abaft the superstructure, little sheer, a shallow knuckle forward, large open work spaces forward and aft, and a transom stern. The clipper bow curves up to a prominent sheave, which has a 272-ton dead-lift capacity. A tall vertical bridge face supports a 10-ton-capacity boom. Abaft the stack is the 20-ton crane.

The ships carry four mooring buoys to assist in four-point moors for diving and salvage activities. The ships have compressed air diving equipment and a through-bow thruster for precise maneuvering and station keeping.

DEVELOPMENT • The *Edenton* was funded in FY1966, the other two in FY1967, despite congressional opposition to procuring foreign-built ships. They were built at Brooke Marine in Lowestoft, England, from 1967 to 1972. Two more in the class were canceled in 1973 because of their high cost.

COMBAT EXPERIENCE • The *Beaufort* left Sasebo for the Persian Gulf on January 5, 1991, as part of Operation Desert Shield, arriving in the area on January 29. After the *Princeton* (CG 58) struck two mines in the northern gulf on February 18, the US minesweeper *Adroit* (MSO 509) led the *Beaufort* to the scene. *Edenton* supplied Navy divers to assess the damage and assisted the *Princeton* out of the area. Although the *Princeton* could steam, the *Beaufort* helped the cruiser to maneuver up the channel swept by the *Adroit*. The tense journey took all night and part of the next day.

The *Beaufort* remained in the area until mid-June, when she returned to Sasebo.

SPECIFICATIONS •
DISPLACEMENT   3,200 tons full load
DIMENSIONS
length   282 ft 8 in (86.2 m) overall
beam   50 ft (15.25 m)
draft   15 ft 2 in (4.6 m)
MACHINERY   4 Paxman 12 YLCM diesels, 6,000 bhp on 2 shafts with Escher-Wyss controllable-pitch propellers=16 kts, range 10,000 nm at 13 kts, electric power 1,200 kW
CREW   115
WEAPONS
2 twin Mk 24 20-mm cannon mounts in ATS 1
2 single Mk 68 20-mm cannon in ATS 2, 3
SENSORS
SPS-53 surface-search radar
SPS-64(V) navigation radar

Emory S. Land (AS 39)

These three ships are improved versions of the *L. Y. Spear*-class tenders that were expressly designed to support up to four *Los Angeles*-class nuclear-powered attack submarines simultaneously. These ships, the *Spears*, and the *Samuel Gompers*-class destroyer tenders are virtually identical in dimensions and propulsion machinery.

DEVELOPMENT • Lockheed Shipbuilding of Seattle built all three ships, laying down the *Land* in March 1976 and delivering the *Mckee* in August 1981.

SPECIFICATIONS •
DISPLACEMENT   22,650 tons full load

DIMENSIONS
length	645 ft 8 in (196.9 m) overall
beam	85 ft (25.9 m)
draft	25 ft (7.6 m)

MACHINERY   2 Combustion Engineering boilers, 1 De Laval steam turbine, 20,000 shp on 1 shaft=20 kts, range 10,000 nm at 12 kts

CREW   620

HELICOPTERS   VERTREP area

WEAPONS
4 20-mm Mk 67 in single mounts
2 40-mm Mk 19 grenade launchers in single mounts

SENSORS
SPS-10 surface-search radar
navigation radar

Hunley (AS 31)

The *Hunley* and *Holland* were the first tenders designed specifically to service Fleet Ballistic Missile (FBM) submarines. Each ship can service three SBBNs alongside simultaneously. Amidships are vertical tubes for 20 Poseidon submarine-launched ballistic missiles. 30-ton-capacity cranes move the missiles between submarine and tender.

The original armament for these ships was four 3-inch/50-cal antiair guns in twin mounts.

DEVELOPMENT • The *Hunley* was built by Newport News Shipbuilding from 1960 to 1962; the *Holland* came from Litton's Ingalls yard in 1963. *Hunley* was homeported at Holy Loch, Scotland, for many years until replaced by the *Simon Lake. Hunley* was decomissioned in FY1994.

SPECIFICATIONS •

DISPLACEMENT   19,819 tons full load

DIMENSIONS
length	599 ft (182.7 m) overall
beam	83 ft (25.3 m)
draft	24 ft (7.3 m)

MACHINERY   10 Fairbanks-Morse diesels turning electric motors; 15,000 bhp on 1 shaft=19 kts, range 10,000 nm at 12 kts

CREW   612-659

HELICOPTERS   VERTREP area

WEAPONS   4 20-mm Mk 67 in single mounts

SENSORS
SPS-10 surface-search radar
navigation radar

Impeccable (T-AGOS 23)

These ships were to have been the third generation of T-AGOS ships, an improved version of the *Victorious* (T-AGOS 19)-class SWATH (Small Waterplane Area Twin-Hull) ocean surveillance ships. Like the T-AGOS 19 class, the T-AGOS 23 class was to operate the US Navy's AN/UQQ-2 Surveillance Towed-Array Sonar System (SURTASS).

The T-AGOS 23 was based on the *Victorious* design. The design was to have twin, fully submerged hulls that resemble long torpedoes; these were to provide buoyancy, carry fuel, and have electric-drive propellers. The propeller was to be protected by a ring supported by four arms. Forward of the propulsion set were to be fins on the inboard sides of the hulls that help to control pitching. Rising up from each hull a thin side wall that broadens above the waterline to support the main deck and superstructure was planned. Above the waterline, the boxy hull was to have a broad bridge forward, abaft of which was to be the single, tapered engine stack. The SURTASS winch would sit on the fantail with a lattice cable boom extending aft from the stern.

The new design extended the original envelope of the SURTASS operations into higher-latitude sea states than the earlier class. And the addition of a second acoustic system resulted in greatly expanded acoustic collection capabilities.

The T-AGOS 23 was to displace 60% more than the older design and was intended to have an electric-drive propulsion plant. Steering was to be through angled canard surfaces well forward and angled rudders aft as well as two azimuthing thrusters forward.

DEVELOPMENT • The first ship was requested in the FY1990 budget, with the construction contract to be awarded in FY1990. The actual award of the lead ship (with options for up to five more) went to American Shipbuilding's Tampa Shipyards Division on March 28, 1991.

The delay in ordering the lead ship and a general cutback in planned defense procurement caused the elimination of two ships in the FY1992 and FY1993 budgets, leaving just one ship to be requested in FY1993. That ship was later moved forward to FY1992.

Contract problems led to this ship's cancellation in 1994.

SPECIFICATIONS •
DISPLACEMENT   5,370 tons full load
DIMENSIONS
length   281 ft 6 in (85.8 m)
           overall
beam   95 ft 9 in (29.2 m)
draft   26 ft (7.9 m)
MACHINERY   diesel-electric drive, 5,000 shp on 2 shafts=12 kts, range 3,000 nm, endurance 60 days
CREW   45
SENSORS
   navigation radar
   1 UQQ-2 SURTASS sonar

John McDonnell (T-AGS 51)

These burly ships collect hydrographic data in coastal and near-coastal areas for the US Navy's Oceanography Command. They are outfitted for shallow-water data collection in depths of 5.35 to 328 fathoms (10 to 600 m) and deep-water

data collection down to 2,187 fathoms (4,000 m).

One hydraulic crane stands on the forecastle ahead of the superstructure. A second hydraulic crane is mounted on the after deckhouse. The design has a total of 1,500 ft^2 (139.4 m^2) of working deck area. Laboratory work space is 700 ft^2 (65 m^2) and includes a wet lab, facilities for survey control, and space for electronic maintenance. Scientific storage amounts to 2,000 ft^3 (56.6 m^3). Helicopter facilities are limited to a hover-only resupply capability during daylight hours.

The extensive shipboard sonar survey systems include a shallow-water echo sounder operating at either 40 or 200 KHz, a 12-KHz deep-water echo sounder, a multibeam hydrographic survey system sounding at 95 KHz, and a towed side-scan sonar operating at 105 KHz. The 34-ft (10.3-m) survey launches also use the shallow-water sounder and the towed side-scan sonar.

Navigation and communications equipment include Global Positioning System (GPS) for mission-related location, short-range positioning (Microfix) for harbor surveying, and SatNav and Loran-C receivers.

DEVELOPMENT • Trinity Marine Group began building the first in the class. Original 1990 delivery dates slipped because of the contractor's termination of engineering drawing subcontractor services. Trials of the *John Mcdonnell* began in August 1991 with delivery following in December; *Littlehales* was delivered one month later.

SPECIFICATIONS •
DISPLACEMENT   2,000 tons full load
DIMENSIONS
length   208 ft 2 in (63.45 m)
           overall
beam   45 ft (13.72 m)
draft   22 ft 6 in (6.86 m)
MACHINERY   2 diesels, 2,000 bhp on 1

shaft= 12–16 kts sustained speed, 3–12 kts survey speed, range 13,800 nm
CREW   22 civilian + 11 survey party
SENSORS   1 navigation radar

L.Y. Spear (AS 36)

These were the Navy's first submarine tenders designed specifically to support SSNs; they can support four submarines alongside at one time.

As built, these ships each had two 5-inch/38-cal dual-purpose guns that were later deleted in favor of the minimal 20-mm gun armament.

DEVELOPMENT • Both ships in the class were built at General Dynamics' Quincy, Massachusetts, yard from 1966 to 1971. The AS 38 of this design was authorized in the FY1969 budget, but was not built because of funding shortages in other ship programs. *Dixon* (A537) is the first to decommission, leaving the fleet in FY1995.

SPECIFICATIONS •
DISPLACEMENT   23,493 tons full load
DIMENSIONS
  length   645 ft 8 in (196.9 m)
              overall
  beam   85 ft (25.9 m)
  draft   24 ft 8 in (7.5 m)
MACHINERY   2 Foster Wheeler boilers, 1 General Electric steam turbine, 20,000 shp on 1 shaft=18 kts, range 7,600 nm at 18 kts, 10,000 nm at 12 kts
CREW   532
HELICOPTERS   VERTREP area
WEAPONS   4 20-mm Mk 67 cannon in single mounts
SENSORS
  SPS-10 surface-search radar
  navigation radar

Mercy (T-AH 19)

These former *San Clemente*-class tankers were fully converted to hospital ships to support the US maritime prepositioning and intervention (amphibious) forces. They are the largest ships ever to be dedicated to hospital functions, which equal those of a very large city medical center.

Most of the visible changes have been made at the main deck level and above. The forward superstructure has much greater volume, its several-deck block overhanging the hull sides. Abaft the forward block is the large helicopter pad, a narrow superstructure section extending aft to a tall superstructure block and a single tapered stack. As hospital ships they have 12 operating rooms, four X-ray rooms, and an 80-bed intensive-care facility, with a bed care casualty capacity of about 1,000 patients; up to 1,000 more patients can be accommodated for limited care. The ships are intended to accommodate a peak admission rate of 300 patients in 24 hours with surgery required by 60% of the admissions and an average patient stay of five days.

The ships are designed to take aboard casualties primarily by helicopter; there is a limited capability for taking on casualties from boats on the port side.

DEVELOPMENT • Both ships were converted at the National Steel and Shipbuilding yard in San Diego; the T-AH 19 conversion was authorized in FY1983 (begun July 1984) and the T-AH 20 in FY1984 (begun April 1985). The *Mercy* operates out of Oakland, California, and the *Comfort* out of Baltimore, Maryland.

COMBAT EXPERIENCE • The *Mercy* was deployed to the Philippines in 1987 as soon as she was operational, carrying medical personnel from each of the US military services as well as from civilian organizations. The ship operated in the Philippines as a hospital facility from March to June 1987, after which the ship visited several South Pacific islands before returning to the United States in July 1987.

The *Mercy* and *Comfort* sailed for the Persian Gulf in August 1990 as part of Operations Desert Shield/Desert Storm. The *Comfort*, sailing from Baltimore, entered the theater on August 31; the *Mercy* followed two weeks later after a minor breakdown delayed her departure by a day. The two ships remained in the Persian Gulf until mid-March 1991.

Projections of thousands of casualties during a ground war against Iraq prompted fears that the two ships might be overwhelmed by the demand. The rapid course of Operation Desert Storm's ground war in February 1991 yielded unprecedentedly low casualties, however, which meant that the medical facilities were barely used.

SPECIFICATIONS •
DISPLACEMENT   69,360 tons full load (44,578 tons *Mercy*, 44,762 tons *Comfort* deadweight)
DIMENSIONS
length	894 ft (272.6 m) overall
beam	105 ft 9 in (32.3 m)
draft	32 ft 10 in (10.0 m)

MACHINERY 2 boilers, 1 General Electric steam turbine, 24,500 shp on 1 shaft=17.5 kts, range 13,400 nm at 17.5 kts, electric power 9,250 kW (including a 750-kW emergency diesel generator)
CREW   76 civilian + 1,083 Navy; patients 1,000 beds
HELICOPTERS   landing area
SENSORS   2 navigation radars

Pathfinder (T-AGS 60)

Known as the T-AGS (Ocean) type, these oceanographic survey and research ships are similar in design to the *Thomas G Thompson* (AGOR 23). The principal difference is in who operates them. An AGOR is operated by a private academic

institution, usually an oceanographic research institution. The T-AGS 60s operate under Military Sealift Command (MSC) direction.

The MSC mission statement gives an overview of the purpose of these ships:

"Conduct general-purpose oceanographic surveys and research worldwide and year-round in coastal and deep ocean areas.

—physical, chemical, and biological oceanography,
—multi-discipline environmental investigations,
—ocean engineering and marine acoustics,
—marine geology and geophysics,
—surveys (bathymetry, gravimetry, and magnetometry)."

The superstructure is centered in the profile, with the bridge level being considerably smaller than the upper deck, and bridge glazing affords a 360° view. Machinery consists of two steerable propellers aft (Z-drives) and a 1,140-horsepower bow thruster.

DEVELOPMENT • Halter Marine won the contract for the first two ships in January 1991; the option for the third was exercised in May 1992.

The *Pathfinder* replaced the *Lynch* (T-AGOR 7); the *Sumner* replaced the *De Steiguer* (T-AGOR 12); both ships operate in the Atlantic. The T-AGS 62 will relieve the *Bartlett* (T-AGOR 13). *Henson* (T-AGS-63) was ordered in 1994.

SPECIFICATIONS •
DISPLACEMENT   4,762 tons full load
DIMENSIONS
length	328 ft (100.0 m) overall
beam	58 ft (17.7 m)
draft	19 ft (5.8 m)

MACHINERY   diesel-electric, 8,000 shp with 2 Azimuth propellers=16 kts, range 12,000 nm at 12 kts, endurance more than 29 days

CREW   30

Safeguard (ARS 50)

These ships replaced the *Bolster* (ARS 38) class in the salvage and towing role. They are fitted for towing and heavy lift, with a limited diving support capability. Tall masts fore and aft bear crane booms, the after crane having the greater capacity. Bow and stern sheaves allow for towing. Maneuvering in restricted waters is aided by a 500-horsepower bow thruster

DEVELOPMENT • All 4 ships were built by Peterson Builders of Sturgeon Bay, Wisconsin from 1982 to 1986. One additional ship had been planned for the FY1990 program but was never requested.

SPECIFICATIONS •

DISPLACEMENT   2,880 tons full load

DIMENSIONS
  length   255 ft (77.8 m) overall
  beam   51 ft (15.5 m)
  draft   15 ft 5 in (4.7 m)

MACHINERY   4 Caterpillar geared diesels, 4,200 bhp on 2 shafts=13.5 kts, range 8,000 nm at 12 kts

CREW   90

WEAPONS   2 .50-cal machine guns in single mounts

SENSORS   SPS-55 surface-search radar

Samuel Gompers (AD 37)

These six ships were the Navy's first post–World War II destroyer tenders and were designed to support ships with nuclear and gas turbine propulsion. They are similar to the *L. Y. Spear* (AS 36)-class submarine tenders.

All ships have two 30-ton-capacity cranes and two 6.5-ton cranes. 65 storerooms occupying a total volume of 63,400 ft³ (1,795.3 m³) carry 60,000 different types of parts.

As built, the AD 37 and 38 had a single 5-in/38-cal dual-purpose gun forward with a Mk 56 gunfire control system; this armament was removed. Plans to install NATO Sea Sparrow missile launchers in these ships were dropped in the late 1980s.

DEVELOPMENT • Although grouped as a single class, the third ship was laid down nine years after the second was completed. Puget Sound Navy Yard built the first two ships in 1965–68. AD 39, authorized in FY1969, and AD 40, funded in 1973, were canceled before construction began.

National Steel and Shipbuilding constructed the remaining four from 1978 to 1983, delivering the *Shenandoah* in December 1983. An AD 45 was planned for the FY1980 program but was not funded and additional ships were dropped from Navy planning. The AD 41 and later ships are generally referred to as the *Yellowstone* class. The *Acadia* (AD 42) decommissioned in FY1995, the first of the class to do so.

COMBAT EXPERIENCE • The *Puget Sound, Yellowstone,* and *Acadia* were deployed to the Persian Gulf region as part of Operation Desert Shield.

The *Yellowstone* was in the theater from September 25 to October 13, 1990, and January 8 to February 27, 1991; she returned to Norfolk on March 23. The *Acadia* left for the theater on September 5, 1990, arriving on October 18; she left the area on March 12, 1991, and returned to Oakland on April 26. The *Puget Sound* arrived in the theater on February 18; she left the theater in May and returned to Norfolk on June 28.

SPECIFICATIONS •

DISPLACEMENT   20,500 tons full load (AD 37, 38); 20,225 tons full load (others)

DIMENSIONS

length	643 ft 4 in (196.1 m) overall
beam	85 ft (25.9 m)
draft	22 ft 8 in (6.9 m)

MACHINERY 2 Combustion Engineering boilers, 1 De Laval steam turbine, 20,000 shp on 1 shaft=20 kts (18 kts sustained), electric power 12,000 kW

CREW 1,367

HELICOPTERS landing area

WEAPONS

2 40-mm Mk 19 grenade launchers in single mounts

4 20-mm Mk 67 AA in single mounts on first 2, 2 20-mm in others

SENSORS

SPS-10 surface-search radar

LN-66 navigation radar

Simon Lake (AS 33)

These two large, high-freeboard tenders are designed to service simultaneously up to three Fleet Ballistic Missile (FBM) submarines moored alongside. In addition to regular AS (submarine tender) capabilities, FBM submarine tenders also store ballistic missiles.

These ships have side-by-side 30-ton cranes over 16 vertical cells that hold the missiles. Originally these were Polaris FBMs, but the *Simon Lake* was modified in 1970–71 and the *Canopus* in 1969–70 to support the Poseidon missile. At the end of the 1970s, the *Simon Lake* was again modified, this time to deal with the Trident C-4 missile; *Canopus* received her refit in 1984–85.

Note that the 3-in guns have been retained. Two Mk 63 directors for the 3-in guns were removed, leaving local gun control only.

DEVELOPMENT • *Simon Lake* was built by the Puget Sound Navy Yard in 1963–64. Litton's Ingalls yard constructed the *Canopus* in 1964–65. AS 35 of this design was authorized in FY1965, but construction was deferred and the ship was not built.

The *Simon Lake* left her home port at Holy Loch, Scotland, in March 1992 as the last overseas ballistic missile submarine base closed. The shrinking numbers of US Posiedon-launching SSBNs was given as the reason. *Canopus* (AS 34) was the first in the class to decommission, going into mothballs in FY1995.

SPECIFICATIONS •

DISPLACEMENT 19,934 tons full load (AS 33); 21,089 tons full load (AS 34)

DIMENSIONS

length	643 ft 9 in (196.3 m) overall
beam	85 ft (25.9 m)
draft	24 ft 6 in (7.5 m)

MACHINERY 2 Combustion Engineering boilers, 1 De Laval steam turbine, 20,000 shp on 1 shaft=18 kts, range 7,600 nm at 18 kts, electric power 11,000 kW

CREW 915 (AS 33), 660 (AS 34)

HELICOPTERS VERTREP area

WEAPONS 4 3-in (76-mm)/50-cal Mk 33 AA in twin mounts

SENSORS

SPS-10 surface-search radar

LN-66 navigation radar

Stalwart (T-AGOS 1)

These 18 Surveillance Towed-Array Sonar System (SURTASS) ships were developed to patrol vast regions providing passive surveillance of Soviet submarine forces. Early Navy planning envisioned 90-day patrol periods and eight days in transit, resulting in more than 300 days at sea per year. MSC rejected so intense a schedule as impractical and unrealistic. Actual patrol durations amounted to 60 to 74 days.

The decline of the naval threat after the collapse of the Soviet Union led to shrinkage in the active fleet and reassignment to several nonmilitary posts.

The hull is similar to that of the *Powhatan* (T-ATF 166) class; it is bluff with a high bow, short forecastle broken at the bridge, tall side-by-side stacks, and a reversed tripod mast with a WSC-6 Satcom link radome at top. The low fantail has a large winch drum for the AN/UQQ-2 SURTASS. Mothballed ships do not have either the UQQ-2 SURTASS or the WSC-6 Satcom link.

The civilian crew members enjoy a high degree of habitability, including single staterooms for all crewmen, with three single and four double staterooms for technicians.

A bow thruster powered by a 550-horsepower electric motor aids in station keeping. Special features reduce self-radiated machinery noise.

DEVELOPMENT • The lead ship, the *Stalwart*, was laid down in November 1982. The program suffered from significant cost increases over original estimates and equipment failures, resulting in a three-year delay over the original schedule. In particular, the Tacoma yard sought reorganization under bankruptcy laws, and some observers believed that the yard would not be able to complete its remaining two ships (T-AGOS 11 and 12). However, the Navy officially reordered these ships from Tacoma in September 1987, and the completion dates were pushed back one year to 1989 and 1990 respectively.

Halter's Moss Point, Mississippi, yard finished up the class, delivering T-AGOS 13 through T-AGOS 18 in 1988–90.

The T-AGOS fleet completed its 100th surveillance mission in October 1988.

Beginning with the *Tenacious* in April 1992, MSC began mothballing or transferring *Stalwart*s out of the MSC to other operations. *Adventurous* went to the National Oceanic and Atmospheric Administration (NOAA), *Contender* to the US Merchant Marine Academy at King's

Point. By the end of FY1994, ten more of the class had been laid up.

SPECIFICATIONS •

DISPLACEMENT   2,285 tons full load
DIMENSIONS
  length   224 ft (68.3 m) overall
  beam   43 ft (13.1 m)
  draft   15 ft (4.6 m)
MACHINERY   4 Caterpillar D-348B diesel generators with 3,200 bhp total turning 2 General Electric electric motors on 2 shafts=11 kts (array towing speed 3 kts), range 6,000 nm at 11 kts
CREW   21 civilian + 7 technicians
SENSORS
  2 Raytheon navigation radars
  UQQ-2 SURTASS

Victorious (T-AGOS 19)

These four craft are the world's first operational military ships with the Small Waterplane Area Twin-Hull (SWATH) design. Their mission is to stream the AN/UQQ-2 Surveillance Towed-Array Sonar System (SURTASS) in operations in high-latitude areas and in heavy weather. The SWATH design offers a high degree of stability and a large deck working area in comparison with conventional-hull designs. For example, a *Victorious*-class ship can maintain operations in all headings in sea state 6 and in the "best" heading in sea state 7.

Twin, fully submerged hulls resemble long torpedoes and provide buoyancy, carry fuel, and have electric-drive propellers. Forward of the propulsion set are fins on the inboard sides of the hulls that help to control pitching. Farther forward are canard surfaces and azimuthing thrusters.

Thin side walls support the main deck and boxy superstructure that has a broad bridge and side-by-side engine stacks. The SURTASS system's winch is mounted on the fantail with a lattice cable boom extending aft from the stern.

DEVELOPMENT • McDermott won in October 1986 for *Victorious'* detailed design and construction. She and her three sisters entered service in 1991–93. Five more were cut from the program in favor of the larger *Impeccable*-class ships.

SPECIFICATIONS •
DISPLACEMENT   3,384 tons full load
DIMENSIONS
  length   234 ft 6 in (71.4 m) overall
  beam   max 93 ft 6 in (28.5 m); of box at waterline 80 ft (24.4 m)
  draft   24 ft 11 in (7.6 m)
MACHINERY   4 Caterpillar 3512-TA diesel engines with a total of 4,800 bhp turning 4 Kato alternators (3,320 kW total) of which 2 drive propellers=9.6 kts, range 3,000 nm at 8.5 kts, electric power 1,970 kW
CREW   25
SENSORS
  navigation radar
  UQQ-2 SURTASS

Waters (T-AGS 45)

This built-for-the-purpose ocean survey ship replaces the outdated *Mizar* (T-AGOR 11). The T-AGS 45 conducts deep-ocean hydrographic, magnetic, and gravity surveys in support of strategic programs.

The T-AGS 45's environmental survey components will include the ability to:

• tow up to three acoustic projectors
• perform bathymetric, hydrographic, or oceanographic surveys
• launch, control, and recover a Remotely Operated Vehicle (ROV)

She is built to ABS/US Coast Guard standards and is ice-strengthened to ABS class C. Davits for Rigid Inflatable Boats (RIB) flank the narrowed forward superstructure abaft the bridge. Farther aft,

the after superstructure block is topped by a square-section, slightly raked stack. Well aft, handling gear for undersea surveillance gear and a ROV are mounted on the fantail.

DEVELOPMENT • Avondale Shipbuilding of Westwego, Louisiana, won the contract in April 1990 and delivered the ship in 1993. She operates in the Pacific.

SPECIFICATIONS •
DISPLACEMENT   12,208 tons full load
DIMENSIONS
  length   442 ft (135.6 m) overall
  beam   69 ft (21.0 m)
  draft   21 ft 2 in (6.45 m)
MACHINERY   5 GM 12-645-F3B diesel engines turning electric motors, 7,400 bhp on 2 shafts=13.2 kts
CREW   95
SENSORS   2 navigation radars

Wright

Roll-On/Roll-Off (RO/RO)-container merchant ships provide maintenance and logistic support for Marine aircraft in forward areas. They retain their RO/RO ability; vehicle storage space is 168,000 ft² (15,608 m²). In addition, they also pack 300 standard containers when deployed as maintenance ships. To speed setup on shore, many of the unit's facilities make up from standard container-size modules. These have access ladders, scaffolding, and shipboard electrical power and other services, which allow the unit to begin operation before disembarkation.

Some 300 of the troops embarked in the AVB are associated with the maintenance unit; the others serve in communications and other support capacities. Troop berthing and mess are installed above the number 7 hold.

Seven cargo holds are served by 10 30-ton-capacity booms (which can be joined for 60-ton lifts); a single 70-ton Stuelcken boom is also installed. Once the maintenance unit is disembarked, the *Wrights* can carry 684 standard containers.

The conversion included fitting a helicopter deck above the two forward holds; the deck can be removed to permit full access to the holds with the use of off-board cranes.

DEVELOPMENT • Both ships were converted at Todd Shipyards in Galveston, Texas. The *Wright* began conversion in June 1984, finishing in May 1986, and the *Curtiss* converted between December 1985 and March 1987. When not activated, the *Curtiss* is laid up in the Ready Reserve Force fleet at Suisun Bay, California; *Wright* is in the RRF fleet at James River, Virginia.

COMBAT EXPERIENCE • In August 1990, both ships were activated and sent to the Persian Gulf in support of Marine Corps aviation as part of Operation Desert Shield. Soon after she sailed on August 19, 1990, the *Curtiss* suffered a boiler failure; she put into Adak, Alaska, for repairs and arrived on September 10.

Once there, the two AVBs performed

"magnificently," according to a Marine general, judging the ships' AVB concept as "right on target." The *Wright* was based at Bahrain and supported A-6 Intruders and F/A-18 Hornets. The *Curtiss* supported primarily AV-8B Harriers and helicopters from her post at Jubayl, Saudi Arabia.

The *Wright* was returned to Marad control for layup on December 11, 1991, *Curtiss* joining her on December 17.

SPECIFICATIONS •
DISPLACEMENT   23,872 tons full load (15,694 tons deadweight)
DIMENSIONS
length	602 ft (183.49 m) overall
beam	90 ft (27.43 m)
draft	34 ft (10.36 m) (to summer freeboard)

MACHINERY   2 Combustion Engineering boilers, 2 General Electric steam turbines, 30,000 shp on 1 shaft=23.6 kts, range 9,000 nm at 23 kts, electric power 3,000 kW
CREW   41 civilian
HELICOPTERS   landing area
SENSORS   2 navigation radars

BATTLESHIPS

Iowa (BB 61)

The US *Iowa*-class ships were the world's last surviving battleships in naval service, having been returned to active commission in the 1980s. They were estimated to have a remaining service life of 10–15 years, and their main armament was conceded to have unmatched power within its range. On the other hand, they remained expensive to operate even with a slimmed-down crew. Moreover, the ships required unique knowledge, the lack of which could be fatal, as the turret explo-

sion in the *Iowa* showed. The four ships were stricken in 1995, forestalling any return to service.

These are the longest battleships ever completed, much of the length forward adopted to raise the maximum hull speed while retaining a broad beam across the citadel. Two of the three massive, three-gun turrets are superimposed ahead of the bridge; the third is in the main deck aft. They were by far the most heavily armored ships in any navy in the 1980s, having 12-in (305-mm) belt armor and 19.7-in (500-mm) armor on the turret face.

When reactivated in the 1980s, these ships underwent a limited modernization, including receiving updated communications and radars, sewage holding tanks, and habitability features. The Phalanx CIWS defensive system as well as Harpoon antiship and Tomahawk land-attack missiles were fitted. In 1987, the *Iowa* was trials ship for the Pioneer Unmanned Air Vehicle (UAV) system. The *Missouri* and *Wisconsin* subsequently employed Pioneer UAVs for gunfire spotting in Operation Desert Storm.

DEVELOPMENT • The *New Jersey* and *Missouri* were modernized and recommissioned at the Long Beach Naval Shipyard; the *Iowa* and *Wisconsin* were modernized at the Avondale and Litton/Ingalls shipyards. *New Jersey* recommissioned in December 1982; the last ship to recommission was the *Wisconsin*, in October 1988.

COMBAT EXPERIENCE • The *New Jersey* fired her 16-in guns against shore targets near Beirut for the first time on December 14, 1983. She was also the first US battleship to enter the Persian Gulf (December 1989).

The *Wisconsin* entered the Persian Gulf in August 1990 as part of Operation Desert Shield. Her main armament was the only artillery that could outrange the South African–designed G5 155-mm howitzers then deployed in Iraqi service.

When Operation Desert Storm began on January 17, 1991, the *Missouri* launched 28 Tomahawk cruise missiles at targets in Baghdad and other points; the *Wisconsin* launched 24 missiles. On February 4, the *Missouri* fired its guns in earnest for the first time since 1953, the *Wisconsin* joining on February 7.

During the next 3½ weeks, the two battleships fired 1,083 rounds of 16-in ammunition; the total included practice rounds. The *Missouri* fired 759 rounds in 41 Naval Gunfire Support Missions (NGFS), including 112 rounds in eight fire support missions in the first 48 hours. The *Wisconsin* undertook 34 NGFS and fired 324 projectiles.

Targets in Kuwait included bunkers, troop concentrations, artillery positions, SAM missile batteries, radar sites, and the Khawr al-Mufattah Marina (15 boats sunk). The Navy's battle damage assessment of 41 NGFS concluded that 32% of the 68 targets were destroyed, 10% neutralized, 26% heavily damaged, and 32% lightly to moderately damaged.

The bombardments represented the first combat use of the Pioneer UAVs for real-time targeting and damage assessment; just over half (52%) of the NGFS were "spotted" by the battleships' own UAVs. The small aircraft were claimed to have greatly improved the accuracy and effect of the 16-in guns. (Before long, Iraqi soldiers began showing surrender flags to the Pioneer's camera.)

The *Iowa* was decommissioned on October 26, 1990, with the *New Jersey* following on February 9, 1991, *Wisconsin* on September 30, 1991, and the *Missouri* on March 31, 1992.

SPECIFICATIONS •
DISPLACEMENT 57,350 tons full load
DIMENSIONS
  length   887 ft 3 in (270.6 m)
                 overall except *New Jersey*
                 887 ft 7 in (270.7 m)
  beam   108 ft 2 in (33.0 m)
  draft   38 ft (11.6 m)
MACHINERY 8 Babcock & Wilcox
  boilers, 4 steam turbines (General
  Electric except Westinghouse in *New
  Jersey*), 212,000 shp on 4 shafts=33 kts,
  range 15,000 nm at 15 kts, electric
  power 10,500 kW
CREW 1,570
WEAPONS
  16 Harpoon SSM in 4 quad canisters
  32 Tomahawk TASM/TLAM in 8
  quad Mk 143 ABL

9 16-in (406-mm)/50-cal Mk 7 guns in triple turrets
12 5-in (127-mm)/38-cal Mk 28 dual-purpose in twin turrets
4 20-mm Mk 15 Phalanx Gatling-type CIWS
HELICOPTERS   landing area
SENSORS
SPS-49 2D air-search radar

SPS-67 surface-search radar (except SPS-10F in *New Jersey*)
7 gunfire control systems (4 Mk 37 with Mk 25 radar, 2 Mk 38 with Mk 13 radar, and 1 Mk 40 with Mk 27 radar)
SLQ-32(V)3 active/passive EW system

COAST GUARD SHIPS

Bear (WMEC 901)

These 12 multipurpose cutters were designed to perform 14-day law enforcement patrols in areas out to 400 miles from base. Maximum normal at-sea endurance is 21 days. They have been criticized for being slow (although they match speeds with the similar-size *Reliance*-class cutters) and, despite fin stabilization, for riding poorly in heavy seas. According to one skipper, "A [*Bear*] is a tender ship" for winter Alaskan patrols.

The telescoping helicopter hangar and broad landing deck permit these cutters to handle any of the Coast Guard's helicopters as well as the Navy's SH-2F LAMPS I. In wartime, an SH-2F would be assigned to each ship for convoy escort. The Recovery Assistance and Traversing System (RAST) is fitted to facilitate helicopter operations in rough seas.

The Integrated Cutter Electronic Systems (ICES) includes the Command Display and Control (COMDAC) that is designed to integrate navigation, piloting, internal communications, and track and coordinate Search and Rescue (SAR) operations. The system suffered from teething troubles.

In wartime, these ships could be fitted with some combination of the following systems:

SH-2F LAMPS I antisubmarine helicopter
2 Harpoon antiship quad missile canisters
1 20-mm Phalanx Gatling-type CIWS
Tactical Towed-Array Sonar (TACTAS)
chaff launchers

DEVELOPMENT • The first four ships were ordered from Tacoma Boatbuilding. The remainder were planned for procurement also from the Tacoma yard; however, the Coast Guard was forced into competitive bidding. The subsequent ships were then awarded to the Derecktor yard of Middletown, Rhode Island. The *Bear*, originally scheduled for delivery in December 1980, was not delivered to the Coast Guard until February 1983; the last of the class completed in 1990.

COMBAT EXPERIENCE • Several of this class have operated in the Caribbean on anti-drug-smuggling and immigration control missions.

SPECIFICATIONS •
DISPLACEMENT   1,780 tons full load
DIMENSIONS
length   270 ft (82.3 m) overall
beam   38 ft (11.6 m)
draft   14 ft (4.3 m)

MACHINERY   2 Alco 18V-251 diesels, 7,000 bhp on 2 shafts=19.5 kts, range 3,850 nm at 19.5 kts, 10,250 nm at 12 kts, electric power 1,350 kW
CREW   109
WEAPONS
1 76-mm/62-cal Mk 75 dual-purpose gun
4 .50-cal (12.7-mm) machine guns
HELICOPTERS   1 light with hangar
SENSORS
SPS-64(V) navigation/surface-search radar
Mk 92 weapons control system
SLQ-32(V)1 passive EW system

Hamilton (WHEC 715)

These 12 cutters are the largest vessels in Coast Guard service except for the *Polar* (WAGB 10)-class icebreakers. They were among the first ships in any service to be driven by gas turbines, which operated in a Combined Diesel or Gas (CODOG) powerplant. For their peacetime, Coast Guard missions, the ships have oceanographic and meteorological facilities. One Coast Guard skipper has referred to them as "our Cadillac in terms of seakeeping capability and on-scene endurance. . . . A 378 [*Hamilton*] can sprint on its turbines to a hot area and then remain on the scene and do great work for an extended period of time."

The narrow helicopter hangars were used as balloon shelters before the class's modernization.

A late 1980s Fleet Rehabilitation and Modernization (FRAM) program addressed the imbalance between their handy size and capacity for operating a helicopter and their relatively dated combat systems. Under the FRAM, the Combat Information Center (CIC) has been relocated into the hull; the 5-in/38-cal main gun was replaced; communications, radar, sonar, and EW systems were modernized, and the flight deck was strengthened to handle the Coast Guard's HH-65 Dolphin or a Navy SH-2F LAMPS I ASW helicopter. In addition, several ships were fitted with Harpoon antiship missiles, and space and weight were reserved for the Phalanx Gatling-type Close-In Weapons System (CIWS).

DEVELOPMENT • 36 cutters of this class were planned in the 1960s, but only 12 were funded. All were built by Avondale of Westwego, Louisiana, completing in 1967–72. Planning for additional units was deferred in favor of retaining older ships and then was dropped with construction of the smaller *Bear* (WMEC 901)-class cutters.

FRAM work began in October 1985. Four East coast ships (*Hamilton, Dallas, Chase,* and *Gallatin)* frammed at the Bath Iron Works, Maine, the other eight ships at the Todd Pacific yard in Seattle, Washington. Delays hit the program and deliveries were spread out from November 1988 to April 1992.

SPECIFICATIONS •
DISPLACEMENT   3,050 tons full load
DIMENSIONS
length   378 ft (115.2 m) overall
beam   42 ft 8 in (13.0 m)
draft   20 ft (6.1 m)
MACHINERY   CODOG (2 Pratt & Whitney FT4-A6 gas turbines, 28,000 shp and 2 Fairbanks Morse 38TD8 1/8 diesels, 7,200 bhp) on 2 shafts with controllable-pitch propellers=29 kts, range 14,000 nm at 11 kts, 2,400 nm at 29 kts
CREW   148–165
WEAPONS
8 Harpoon missiles in 2 quad-canister mounts
1 76-mm/62-cal OTO Melara dual-purpose gun
2 40-mm Mk 19 grenade launchers in single mounts
2 20-mm Mk 67 cannon in single mounts
4 .50-cal machine guns in single mounts

6 12.75-in (324-mm) Mk 46 torpedos in triple mounts

HELICOPTERS   extendable helicopter hangar for SH-2F or HH-65

SENSORS

Lockheed SPS-40B air-search radar

SPS-64 with RAYCAS surface-search radar

SQS-38 keel-mounted sonar

Mk 92 gun/missile with fire control system

WLR-1C with Band 10 EW system

SLQ-32(V)2 active/passive EW system

2 Mk 36 SRBOC 6-barrel chaff/flare launchers

Healy (WAGB 20)

Construction of the Healy, a long-awaited replacement for several older icebreakers, was delayed by lack of Coast Guard funds. She's one of the largest icebreakers to be built.

The design resembles that of the *Polar* class but is 60 feet longer and has only a single stack. The hull form has been criticized for failing to take advantage of recent developments in icebreaking technologies. Instead of the *Polars'* gas turbine propulsion, the *Healy* is driven by large medium-speed diesels, which means a lower top speed but greater range. She can break 4-ft 8-in (1.4-m) ice at three knots or 8 ft (2.4 m) of ice by backing and ramming. Her hangar accommodates one or two helicopters and she has over 4,000 ft² (377 m²) of scientific labs.

DEVELOPMENT • The Coast Guard's chronic procurement penury delayed this ship for several years. Eventually, Congress voted $274.8 million in the *Navy*'s FY1990 authorization. When this proved insufficient to attract bids, another $62 million was added two years later. The first round of bids was canceled in March 1992 because no contestant would come within available funds. A second round ended with the selection of

Avondale Shipyard in Westwego, Louisiana, in July 1993 for completion in 1996.

SPECIFICATIONS •

DISPLACEMENT   17,710 tons full load

DIMENSIONS

length	459 ft 5 in (140.1 m) overall
beam	89 ft (26.85 m) waterline, 94 ft 6 in (28.8 m) extreme
draft	32 ft (9.75 m)

MACHINERY   4 Colt-Pielstick diesels, 40,000 bhp turning 4 10,000 kVa generators driving 2 shafts with controllable-pitch propellers=12.5 kts (cruising), range 34,000 nm at 12.5 kts, 37,000 nm at 9.25 kts, endurance 80 days, electric power 1,500 kW

CREW   133 (+ accommodation for 49 more)

WEAPONS   2 12.7-mm machine guns in single mounts

SENSORS

navigation radar

hydrographic mapping sonar

Island (WPB 1301)

The Coast Guard originally procured this class of 49 craft primarily for drug interdiction in south Florida and the Caribbean. The urgent need to replace 95-foot *Cape-* and 82-foot *Point-*class cutters, however, led to more general use. Secondary missions are offshore surveillance and search-and-rescue operations.

The 20-year-old design (based on Vosper Thornycroft 110-foot patrol boats) has a flush-deck, round-bilge hull with active fin stabilizers. The boats have a steel hull with aluminum deck and superstructure. They are expected to have only a 15-year life span because of the thinness of their hull plating.

Critics of the design note that these craft have a high minimum control speed of nine knots, making small-boat towing difficult. Also, early operational experience revealed hull problems—cracks developing in heavy seas. From the *Attu* (WPB 1317) on, the craft have heavier bow plating to correct the hull-cracking problem, and changes in operating procedures are claimed by the Coast Guard to reduce stress on the hull.

DEVELOPMENT • The *Farallon* (WPB 1301) was delivered for sea trials from Bollinger Machine Shop and Shipyard (Lockport, Louisiana) on November 15, 1985. WPB 1317 to WPB 1337 were ordered in two groups in February 1987: the first 16 were funded under the Coast Defense Augmentation Act, the last five under the Drug Omnibus Act. 12 more were ordered in December 1989, with the last being completed in 1992.

SPECIFICATIONS •
DISPLACEMENT   165 tons full load
DIMENSIONS
  length   109 ft (33.2 m) overall
  beam   21 ft (6.4 m)
  draft   7 ft 4 in (2.2 m)
MACHINERY   2 Alco-Paxman Valenta 16 RP200 diesels, 6,200 bhp on 2 shafts=26 kts
CREW   16
WEAPONS
  1 20-mm Mk 16 cannon
  2 7.62-mm M60 machine guns in single mounts
SENSORS   SPS-64(V) surface search radar

Mackinaw (WAGB 83)

The *Mackinaw* is the only icebreaker operating on the US-Canadian Great Lakes. The ship is homeported in Sheboygan, Michigan.

In designing the *Mackinaw* for Great Lakes service, many of the features of the earlier and more numerous *Wind* class were adopted. Compared to those oceangoing ships, however, she is longer and beamier but draws less. She can break 2 ft

(0.76 m) of ice continuously, and 11 ft (3.3 m) by backing and ramming.

DEVELOPMENT • Originally to be named *Manitowoc*, the *Mackinaw* was laid down in 1943 and completed at the end of 1944 by the Toledo Shipbuilding Corp. of Toledo, Ohio. She received a $100-million refit in 1982 but was put in "caretaker status" in 1988 because of a lack of operating funds. She was restored to service in 1989 and underwent another refit in 1991.

SPECIFICATIONS •
DISPLACEMENT   5,252 tons full load
DIMENSIONS
  length   290 ft (88.4 m) overall
  beam   75 ft (22.9 m)
  draft   19 ft (5.8 m)
MACHINERY   6 Fairbanks Morse 38D81/8 × 12 diesels turning Westinghouse electric motors generating 10,000 shp aft + 3,000 shp forward driving 2 shafts aft + 1 shaft forward=18.8 kts, range 10,000 nm at 18.7 kts, 41,000 nm at 9 kts, electric power 1,260 kW
CREW   127
SENSORS   2 SPS-64(V) surface search radar

Polar Star (WAGB 10)

Other than some icebreakers operated by the Russian Navy, these two ships are the largest icebreakers now in service. They've proved disappointing in some respects, particularly in the reliability of their cross-connected propulsion plants. Also, the ship has never achieved her design speed of 21 knots. Her great cruising range, however, is an asset.

One of the two ships deploys to the Antarctic each year, where they can break through six feet of ice while cruising at three knots and smash 21 feet of ice by riding up onto it.

The *Healey* (WAGB 20), a newer design, is under construction.

DEVELOPMENT • The *Polar Star* was ordered from Lockheed Shipbuilding in Seattle, Washington, in the early 1970s and delivered in 1976. The *Polar Sea* followed in 1978.

SPECIFICATIONS •
DISPLACEMENT   13,190 tons full load
DIMENSIONS
　length　　399 ft (121.6 m) overall
　beam　　　83 ft 6 in (25.5 m)
　draft　　　33 ft 6 in (10.2 m)
MACHINERY   CODOG: 6 Alco diesels, 18,000 bhp; 3 Pratt & Whitney gas turbines, 60,000 shp on 3 shafts=18 kts, range 28,000 nm at 13 kts, 16,000 nm at 18 kts
CREW   139
WEAPONS
　4 20-mm cannon in single mounts
　2 40-mm Mk 19 grenade launchers in single mounts
HELICOPTERS   2 HH-65 Dolphin
SENSORS   2 SPS-64(V) surface search radars

Reliance (WMEC 615)

These 16 medium-size patrol and search-and-rescue cutters have proven very useful since they entered service in the 1960s. They have a high bridge with nearly 360° visibility well forward and a long helicopter landing platform aft.

The first five cutters were completed with a Combined Diesel and Gas (CODAG) propulsion plant, but were converted to all-diesel propulsion in the late 1980s during their Major Maintenance Availability (MMA). All 16 cutters are being modified during their MMAs, an 18–21-month refit that reduces the helicopter deck space in favor of a tapered stack and enlarged superstructure, lessens topweight, increases at-sea endur-

ance by increasing provision storage, and upgrades the ship's fire-fighting capability.

The *Alert* was fitted with the Canadian-developed "Beartrap" helicopter hauldown system. No Antisubmarine Warfare (ASW) armament is provided.

DEVELOPMENT • The *Reliance* class provided one of the few opportunities for smaller yards to build combatants. American Shipbuilding in Lorain, Ohio, constructed eight ships, the Coast Guard yard at Curtis Bay, Maryland, built four, Todd Shipbuilding in Houston, Texas, constructed three, and Christy Corp. in Sturgeon Bay, Wisconsin, delivered one. All were commissioned between 1964 and 1969.

Curtis Bay conducted MMAs on the first five cutters to receive them. Colonna's Shipyard in Norfolk, Virginia, won the contract to refit the remaining 11. The program was originally scheduled to end in December 1990, but funding cuts forced a stretch-out to November 1996.

SPECIFICATIONS •
DISPLACEMENT   1,110 tons full load (615–619); 1,129 tons full load (others)
DIMENSIONS
　length　　210 ft 7 in (64.2 m) overall
　beam　　　34 ft 1 in (10.4 m)
　draft　　　10 ft 6 in (3.2 m)
MACHINERY   2 Alco 251B turbocharged diesels, 5,000 shp on 2 shafts with controllable-pitch propellers=18 kts, range 6,100 nm at 14 kts, 2,700 nm at 18 kts, endurance 30 days, electric power 500 kW
CREW   62–82
WEAPONS
　1 3-in (76-mm)/50-cal Mk 22 gun
　2 40-mm Mk 19 grenade launchers
　4 .50-cal machine guns
HELICOPTERS   landing area
SENSORS   2 SPS-64(V)1 surface-search radars

Sea Bird (WSES 2)

These Surface Effect Ships (SES) operate in the Caribbean as effective counter-drug-smuggling craft. In the mid-1980s, their annual usage averaged 3,000 hours under way. Trials with the earlier *Dorado* (WSES 1 or SES-200) proved convincing enough to prompt procurement of these three craft. The *Dorado* returned to naval control.

The SES is a mixture of catamaran and air cushion vehicle design ideas. The rigid side walls and flexible bow and stern seals contain the pressurized air cushion created by the two lift engines. Claims for the SES design include stability at high speeds because of their low (2.8:1) length-to-beam ratio, smooth ride in sea states lower than the freeboard, top speed of more than 40 knots, maneuverability, and shallow draft.

DEVELOPMENT • All three ordered from Bell Halter Marine, New Orleans, Louisiana, in 1981, delivered in 1982–83.

SPECIFICATIONS •
DISPLACEMENT 150 tons full load
DIMENSIONS
length 110 ft (33.5 m) overall
beam 39 ft (11.9 m)
draft 5 ft 6 in (1.7 m) on cushion, 8 ft 3 in (2.5 m) off cushion
MACHINERY 2 General Motors 16V 149TIB diesels, 3,600 bhp on 2 shafts, 2 General Motors 8V 92TIB diesels, 1,800 bhp driving 2 fans for lift, electric power 55 kW (2 GM diesels)
speed on cushion 33 kts in sea state 0, 30 kts in sea state 3; off cushion 19 kts in sea state 0, 15 kts in sea state 3; "best economical" 26 kts
range 1,100 nm on cushion in sea state 3 at 25 kts, mission endurance 7 to 10 days
CREW 17
WEAPONS 2 .50-cal machine guns
SENSORS 1 commercial navigation radar

COMMAND SHIPS

Blue Ridge (LCC 19)

These two large command ships are the only ships to be designed from the outset specifically for the amphibious command ship role. Both ships are now employed as fleet flagships.

The hull and propulsion machinery are similar to that of the *Iwo Jima* (LPH 2)-class helicopter carriers. Along each side of the hull, however, are long sponsons for landing craft and the ship's boats. The ships have large open deck areas resembling the *Iwo Jima*'s flight deck to provide for optimum antenna placement. A tall lattice antenna is stepped ahead of the bridge, a thick pedestal is placed farther aft. The superstructure "island" is amidships (both transversely and longitudinally).

Antiaircraft protection includes 76-mm twin gun mounts ahead of the island on each deck edge and Sea Sparrow octuple point-defense missile launchers abaft the island port and starboard. Both ships received two Mk 15 Phalanx Gatling-type Close-In Weapons Systems (CIWS) in the mid-1980s, one mounted forward on a small deckhouse fitted on the main deck, the other on a sponson at the stern (increasing length approximately 16 feet).

A helicopter landing area aft has no

hangar. (A small vehicle hangar is serviced by an elevator.) Davits provide stowage for five LCP/LCVP-type personnel craft plus a ship's launch.

DEVELOPMENT • *Blue Ridge* was built at the Philadelphia Navy Yard, *Mount Whitney* at Newport News Shipbuilding; completion came in 1970–71. *Blue Ridge* serves in Yokosuka, Japan, as flagship of the Seventh Fleet; *Mount Whitney* heads up the Second Fleet in Norfolk.

COMBAT EXPERIENCE • *Blue Ridge* was sent to the Persian Gulf under Operation Desert Shield. She served as the flagship for the commander of the US Naval Forces Central Command (NAVCENT) as well as the amphibious warfare command ship. She remained in the gulf until April 24, 1991, in the longest continuous deployment of any US ship in Operations Desert Shield/Desert Storm.

SPECIFICATIONS •

DISPLACEMENT   19,290 tons full load
DIMENSIONS
   length   636 ft 5 in (194.0 m) overall
   beam   82 ft (25.0 m), extreme width 108 ft (32.9 m)
   draft   27 ft (8.2 m)
MACHINERY   2 Foster Wheeler boilers, 1 General Electric steam turbine, 22,000 shp on 1 shaft=21.5 kts, range 13,500 nm at 16 kts
CREW   777–799 + 170–191 flagship staff
WEAPONS
   2 8-cell Mk 25 Sea Sparrow BPDMS launchers
   4 3-inch (76-mm)/50-cal Mk 33 AA in twin mounts
   2 20-mm Mk 15 Phalanx CIWS
HELICOPTERS   landing area
SENSORS
   SPS-48C 3D air-search radar
   SPS-40C 2D air-search radar
   SPS-65 threat-detection radar
   Marconi LN-66 navigation radar
   2 Mk 115 missile fire control systems
   SLQ-32(V)3 active/passive EW system

Coronado (AGF 11)

The *Coronado* is an *Austin*-class amphibious transport dock (LPD) modified for use as a fleet flagship. The conversion involved fitting the ship with command and communications facilities, a helicopter hangar, and additional air-conditioning.

Vice Admiral Jerry Tuttle, lamenting the *Coronado*'s absence from Operations Desert Shield and Desert Storm, spoke in 1991 of the ship's Command, Control, Communications, and Intelligence (C3I) facilities: "In my estimation, it is the finest system in the world. It has Inmarsat, SHF [Super High Frequency], UHF, and the first operational EHF [Extremely High Frequency]."

The *Coronado*'s hangar is 57 ft 9 in long and 20 ft 8 in wide. Phalanx Gatling-type Close-In Weapons System (CIWS) mounts stand on a "bridge wing" to starboard and just forward of the hangar to port.

DEVELOPMENT • *Coronado* replaced the destroyer tender *Puget Sound* (AD 38) as Sixth Fleet flagship and was home-ported in Gaeta, Italy, in October 1985. In July 1986 the *Belknap* became Sixth Fleet flagship and the *Coronado* shifted to the Pacific to become flagship for Commander, Third Fleet (based at Pearl Harbor).

SPECIFICATIONS •

DISPLACEMENT   17,000 tons full load
DIMENSIONS
   length   570 ft 2 in (173.8 m) overall
   beam   84 ft (25.6 m)
   draft   23 ft (7.0 m)
MACHINERY   2 Babcock & Wilcox boilers, 2 De Laval steam turbines, 24,000 shp on 2 shafts=20 kts, range 7,700 nm at 20 kts
CREW   516
WEAPONS
   4 3-in (76-mm)/50-cal Mk 33 AA in twin mounts
   2 20-mm Mk 15 Mod 2 Phalanx Gatling-type CIWS

HELICOPTERS   1 SH-3 Sea King
SENSORS
SPS-40 air-search radar
SPS-10 surface-search radar
Marconi LN-66 navigation radar
local gunfire control only
SLQ-32(V)2 radar intercept and jam-
mer
WLR-1H ESM
4 Mk 36 SRBOC 6-barrel chaff/flare
launchers

La Salle (AGF 3)

The *La Salle* was converted from one of three *Raleigh* (LPD 1)-class amphibious transport docks specifically to serve as flagship for the Commander, US Middle East Force (MEF).

Conversion came in 1972 and featured command and communications facilities, a helicopter hangar, and additional air-conditioning. The amidships hangar is 47 ft 5 in long and 19 ft 4 in wide.

Two Mk 15 Mod 2 Phalanx Close-In Weapons Systems (CIWS) have been installed amidships, port and starboard.

The *La Salle* is painted white with black numerals to reflect some of the Persian Gulf sun, giving rise to the nickname the Great White Ghost.

DEVELOPMENT • *La Salle* was originally built by the Brooklyn Navy Yard as the third in the *Raleigh* class of LPDs, completing in February 1964. Her conversion to AGF came in 1972. In November 1994, she became flagship of the U.S. Sixth Fleet at Gaeta, Italy.

COMBAT EXPERIENCE • The *La Salle* operated in the Persian Gulf/Indian Ocean area from 1972 to 1980, when she underwent an extensive overhaul at the Philadelphia Naval Shipyard from De-

cember 1980 to September 1982, returning to her flagship duties in June 1983.

Her post as flagship of the MEF inevitably meant involvement in several episodes during the Iran-Iraq war (1980–88). The *La Salle* was one of the first ships to respond when the USS *Stark* (FFG 31) was severely damaged by an Iraqi-fired Exocet antiship missile in May 1987. The *La Salle*'s crew provided damage control, emergency repairs, and berthing facilities for *Stark* crew members.

US interdiction of Iranian minelaying ships in September 1987 and an attack on an oil platform a month later were coordinated by the Commander, MEF, aboard the *La Salle*.

After the start of Operation Desert Shield, *La Salle* was soon joined by the command ship *Blue Ridge* (LCC 19), which has more extensive communications facilities.

SPECIFICATIONS •
DISPLACEMENT   14,650 tons full load
DIMENSIONS
length   521 ft 9 in (159.1 m)
                overall
beam   84 ft (25.6 m)
draft   21 ft (6.4 m)
MACHINERY   2 Babcock & Wilcox
boilers, 2 De Laval steam turbines, 24,000 shp on 2 shafts=21.6 kts, range 9,600 nm at 16 kts, 16,500 nm at 10 kts, electric power 4,600 kW
CREW   487 + 44 flag
WEAPONS
4 3-in (76-mm)/50-cal Mk 33 AA in twin mounts
2 20-mm Mk 15 Mod 2 Phalanx Gatling-type CIWS
HELICOPTER   1 SH-3 Sea King
SENSORS
SPS-40 air-search radar
SPS-10 surface-search radar
local gunfire control only
SLQ-32(V)2 EW system

CRUISERS

Bainbridge (CGN 25)

This was the US Navy's third nuclear-powered surface ship after the *Enterprise* (CVN 65) and the *Long Beach* (CGN 9). She differs from the later *Truxtun* (CGN 35) in being a "double-end" missile ship and in not having a 5-in gun and helicopter-support capability.

Her long-forecastle hull breaks just ahead of the aft twin-rail Surface-to-Air Missile (SAM) launcher. A split superstructure set well aft has short lattice masts carrying large radar antenna, and transom stern. Ahead of the superstructure is the forward SAM launcher and sloping reload house. Abaft the reload house is the eight-cell Antisubmarine Rocket (ASROC) box; no reloads are provided. Above the bridge are two SPG-55 missile guidance radar pedestals; two more SPG-55 pedestals are located abaft the mainmast.

The ship has a helicopter landing area on the fantail, but no hangar.

DEVELOPMENT • The *Bainbridge* was built by Bethlehem Steel in Quincy, Massachusetts, and commissioned in 1962. Her sensors were upgraded in 1983–85 and Phalanx Close-In Weapons Systems (CIWS) mounts were installed high in the after superstructure ahead of the mainmast at the same time. She was decommissioned in FY1994.

SPECIFICATIONS •

DISPLACEMENT   8,580 tons full load
DIMENSIONS
   length   565 ft (172.3 m) overall
   beam   58 ft (17.7 m)
   draft   29 ft (8.8 m)
MACHINERY   2 General Electric D2G pressurized-water reactors, 2 steam turbines, 60,000 shp on 2 shafts= 30 kts,

range 90,000 nm at 20 kts, electric power 14,500 kW
CREW   558
WEAPONS
   2 twin Mk 10 Mod 5/6 launchers for Terrier/Standard-ER SAM (80 missiles)
   8 Harpoon SSM Mk 141 (2 quad canisters)
   2 20-mm Mk 15 Mod 2 Phalanx Gatling-type CIWS
   1 8-cell Mk 16 ASROC launcher
   6 12.75-in (324-mm) Mk 32 torpedo tubes in triple mounts
HELICOPTERS   landing area
SENSORS
   SPS-48C 3D air-search radar
   SPS-49 2D air-search radar
   SPS-67 surface-search radar
   SQQ-23 bow-mounted active medium-frequency sonar
   4 Mk 76 missile fire control systems with 4 SPG-55B target-illuminating radars
   SLQ-32(V)3 active/passive EW system
   4 Mk 36 SRBOC 6-barrel chaff/flare launchers

Belknap (CG 26)

These nine "single-end" guided-missile cruisers were built to screen aircraft carriers. They were built to an improved *Leahy* (CG 16)-class design with a 5-in gun substituted for the after Surface-to-Air Missile (SAM) launcher. Like the *Leahy*s, the *Belknap*s have a long-forecastle hull with a cut-down fantail and transom stern. The Mk 10 Mod 7 twin-rail SAM launcher is mounted on the forecastle ahead of the bridge. A sloping reload deckhouse abaft the launchers leads to three 20-round magazine "rings" (one more "ring" than the earlier *Leahy*s to compensate for the reduction in launchers).

The superstructure is dominated by the superimposed SPG-55D target-illuminating radars, the combined mast stack ("mack") abaft the bridge bearing the SPS-48 planar-array antenna, and a short main mack topped by the SPS-49 truncated paraboloid antenna.

The helicopter hangar in these ships varies in size. Abaft the hangar is the flight deck, which extends the forecastle deck level aft of the hull plating break. On the fantail is the 5-in (127-mm) gun mount.

From 1986 to 1991, all *Belknap*s except the lead ship received the New Threat Upgrade (NTU), which greatly improves the ships' Antiair Warfare (AAW) capability to go with the Standard SM-2 ER Block II missile. In addition to upgraded radars, command and control as well as missile control systems were modernized.

The *Belknap* was modified to serve as a numbered fleet flagship in 1986. She has more superstructure and represents a separate class.

DEVELOPMENT • Five of the nine ships were built by Bath Iron Works; Todd's San Pedro yard built one, San Francisco Navy Yard built one, and Puget Sound Navy Yard constructed two. All were completed between 1964 and 1967. *Wainwright* and *Biddle* were the first of the class to be earmarked for decommissioning, their day coming in FY1994. The rest followed in 1994 and 1995.

COMBAT EXPERIENCE • In April 1988, *Wainwright* helped to sink the Iranian missile boat *Joshan* with Standard SAMs.

During Operations Desert Shield and Desert Storm, the *Jouett, Horne,* and *Biddle* operated in the Persian Gulf region. The *Jouett* escorted the carrier *Independence* (CV 62) from June to November 1990. The *Biddle* escorted the *Saratoga* (CV 60) from August 1990 to March 1991. The *Horne* served in the gulf-based Middle East Force from December 1990 to April 1991.

SPECIFICATIONS •
DISPLACEMENT 7,930 tons full load
DIMENSIONS
length   547 ft (166.7 m) overall
beam   55 ft (16.7 m)
draft   28 ft 10 in (8.8 m)
MACHINERY   4 boilers (Babcock & Wilcox in all but CG 29–31 and 33, which have Combustion Engineering), 2 steam turbines (GE in all but CG 29–31 and 33, which have De Laval), 85,000 shp on 2 shafts=33 kts, 2,500 nm at 30 kts, 8,000 nm at 14 kts, electric power 6,800 kW
CREW   492
WEAPONS
  1 twin Mk 10 Mod 7 launcher for RIM-67C Standard SM-2 ER SAM (60 missiles)
  8 Harpoon SSM (2 quad canisters Mk 141)
  1 5-in (127-mm)/54-cal Mk 42 dual-purpose gun
  20-mm Mk 15 Mod 2 Phalanx Gatling-type CIWS
  ASROC ASW missiles launched from Mk 10 missile launcher
  6 12.75-in (324-mm) Mk 32 torpedo tubes in triple mounts
HELICOPTERS   1 SH-2F/G LAMPS I
SENSORS
  SPS-48E 3D air-search radar
  SPS-49(V)3 2D air-search radar
  SPS-67 surface-search radar
  Mk 68 gunfire control system with SPG-53F radar
  2 SPG-55B illuminating radar
  SQS-53A bow-mounted active sonar in *Belknap*
  SQS-26AXR bow-mounted active sonar in *Josephus Daniels*
  SQS-26BX bow-mounted active sonar in remaining ships
  SLQ-32(V)3 passive/active EW system
  SLQ-34 Outboard jammer in 6 ships
  4 Mk 36 SRBOC 6-barrel chaff/flare launchers

California (CGN 36)

These two ships—*California* and *South Carolina*—represented the US Navy's hope that experimentation with nuclear power in surface ships could be supplanted by series production. It was a vain hope, partly because of their cost and because of steady changes in weaponry and threats to the fleet. This class is fitted with single-rail Mk 13 launchers for the Standard SM-1 MR missile system, rather than the twin-rail Mk 26 found on most US cruisers. Refits and modifications have been limited; for example, these ships do not carry Tomahawk land-attack cruise missiles.

The low, split superstructure is set relatively far aft. Each superstructure block is topped by a conically tapered, plated mast. These ships have a large helicopter landing area aft, but no hangar or maintenance facilities. They have separate AS-ROC (Antisubmarine Rocket) "box" launchers because their Mk 13 launchers cannot accommodate the Antisubmarine Warfare (ASW) weapons.

In addition to the two single 5-in/54-cal Mk 45 gun mounts, Mk 15 Mod 2 Phalanx Close-In Weapons System (CIWS) multibarrel mounts were fitted ahead and outboard of the mainmast.

DEVELOPMENT • Both ships were originally classified as guided-missile frigates (DLGN) but were changed to CGN on June 30, 1975. They were built by Newport News Shipbuilding and delivered in 1974 and 1975. The construction of additional units was deferred in favor of the more capable *Virginia* class.

COMBAT EXPERIENCE • The *South Carolina* sailed to the Mediterranean in September 1990, accompanying the carrier *Saratoga*'s (CV 60) battle group in the Desert Shield theater of operations from October 23 to December 11. Then, as flagship of Cruiser-Destroyer Squadron 24 (CruDesRon 24), the *South Carolina*

coordinated antiair warfare operations in the Mediterranean to forestall intervention from states allied with Iraq.

SPECIFICATIONS •

DISPLACEMENT   10,530 tons full load
DIMENSIONS
　length　　　596 ft 6 in (181.8 m) overall
　beam　　　61 ft (18.6 m)
　draft　　　31 ft 6 in (9.6 m)
MACHINERY   2 General Electric D2G pressurized-water reactors, 2 steam turbines, 60,000 shp on 2 shafts=30+ kts
CREW   595–603
WEAPONS
　2 single Mk 13 Mod 3 launchers for RIM-66C/E Standard SM-1 MR SAM (80 missiles)
　8 Harpoon SSM (2 quad canisters Mk 141)
　2 single 5-in (127-mm)/54-cal Mk 45 dual-purpose guns
　2 20-mm Mk 15 Mod 2 Phalanx Gatling-type CIWS
　1 8-tube ASROC launcher and 4 fixed 12.75-in (324-mm) Mk 32 torpedo tubes
HELICOPTERS   landing area
SENSORS
　SPS-48 3D air-search radar
　SPS-49 2D air-search radar
　SPS-67 surface-search radar
　2 SPG-51D missile control radars
　Mk 86 gunfire control system with SPG-60 and SPQ-9 radars
　SQS-26 series bow-mounted active sonar
　SLQ-32(V)3 active/passive EW system

Leahy (CG 16)

These nine cruisers are "double-enders," having twin-rail Surface-to-Air Missile (SAM) launchers fore and aft and no gun armament larger than a 20-mm Mk 15 Phalanx Gatling-type Close-In Weapons System (CIWS). Their lack of gun armament and the relatively low-

powered sonar underscore their principal role as Antiair Warfare (AAW) fleet
escorts. In tonnage and length, they are
the smallest US Navy ships currently classified as cruisers.

This class introduced the "mack" superstructure (combination masts and exhaust stacks) to US warships. A split
superstructure, each with its own mack,
long-forecastle hull, and missile
launchers with sloping reload houses
mark the design. Each launcher has two
20-missile "rings" below. The forward
black-capped mack has the SPS-48E
planar-array antenna stepped forward
and a tall topmast abaft the mack. The
short main mack is topped by the SPS-49
truncated paraboloid antenna; the topmast is stepped ahead of the exhaust up-
take. Above the bridge are two SPG-55
missile guidance radar pedestals; two
more SPG-55 pedestals are located abaft
the mainmast. Some ships have been fitted with the Hughes Aircraft Naval Mast-
Mounted Sight (NMMS).

As built, all ships of this class had two
3-in/50-cal twin antiaircraft mounts
amidships. These were removed and Harpoon missile canisters were fitted in their
place. The *Leahy*s also received the New
Threat Upgrade (NTU), which greatly
improves the ships' AAW capability to go
with the Standard SM-2 ER Block II missile. In addition to upgraded radars, command and control as well as missile
control systems were modernized.

DEVELOPMENT • All nine ships were
built as DLGs (guided-missile destroyer
leaders), being reclassified as cruisers in
1975. Bath Iron Works of Bath, Maine,
built three, New York Shipbuilding of
Camden, New Jersey, two; Puget Sound
Shipbuilding (later Lockheed), Todd's
San Pedro, California, yard, and the navy
yards at San Francisco and Puget Sound
all had one. Completions came between
August 1962 and May 1964.

First retirements in the class were the
Leahy, Harry E. Yarnell, Worden, and *Reeves*

in FY1994. *Richmond K. Turner* was the last
in FY1995.

COMBAT EXPERIENCE • The *Worden,*
Richmond K. Turner, and *England* were deployed to the Persian Gulf region during
Operations Desert Shield and Desert
Storm. The *England* operated with the
Gulf-based Middle East Force from June
to 3 November 1990, and was succeeded
by the *Worden. Turner* sortied as part of
the *Theodore Roosevelt*'s (CVN 71) battle
group in December 1990, arriving in the
theater on January 14.

SPECIFICATIONS •
DISPLACEMENT 8,200 tons full load
DIMENSIONS
length 533 ft (162.5 m) overall
beam 55 ft (16.8 m)
draft 25 ft (7.6 m)
MACHINERY 4 boilers (Babcock &
Wilcox in CG 16–18, Foster Wheeler
in CG 19–24), 2 steam turbines (General Electric in CG 16–18, De Laval in
CG 19–22, Allis-Chalmers in CG 23–
24), 85,000 shp on 2 shafts=32 kts,
range 8,000 nm at 20 kts, electric
power 6,800 kW
CREW 423
WEAPONS
2 twin Mk 10 Mod 5/6 launchers for
RIM-67C Standard-ER SAM (80
missiles)
8 Harpoon SSM in 2 quad canisters
2 20-mm Mk 15 Mod 2 Gatling-type
CIWS
1 8-cell ASROC launcher
6 12.75-in (324-mm) Mk 32 torpedo
tubes in triple mounts
SENSORS
SPS-48E 3D air-search radar
SPS-49(V)3 2D air-search radar
4 Mk 76 missile fire control systems
4 SPG-55B target-illumination radars
SPS-10F or Norden SPS-67 surface-
search radar
CRP-1900 ND navigation radar (CG
16), LN-66 navigation radar (CG 17,

21, 23), CRP-2900 navigation radar (CG 22, 24)
SQS-23 bow mounted active medium-frequency sonar except SQQ-23B PAIR in CG 17
NMMS in some ships
SLQ-32(V)3 active/passive EW system
4 Mk 36 SRBOC 6-barrel chaff/flare launchers

Long Beach (CGN 9)

The *Long Beach* was the world's first nuclear-powered surface warship. Although originally intended to be the first of the nuclear "frigates" (e.g., what was eventually realized in the *Bainbridge*), she became instead the nuclear-powered equivalent of a traditional heavy cruiser. The design kept growing as more and more systems were added. In the end, like an all-gun heavy cruiser in the battleship era, the missile-laden *Long Beach* was designed to support aircraft carriers while being capable of operating on her own. Her cost, however, as well as the limitations of the Surface-to-Air Missiles (SAM) then in service made her a one-of-a-kind ship.

As completed, *Long Beach* had a long-range Talos twin-rail launcher aft and stepped twin-rail Terrier launchers forward. In the late 1970s, Congress proposed fitting the *Long Beach* with the Aegis phased-array radar and weapons system; the FY1978 budget provided $371 million to begin Aegis conversion. Navy fears that such a conversion would imperil construction of new nuclear-propelled cruisers, combined with a Carter administration reluctance to take on the expense of this one-ship program, killed the plan.

She retained her original weapons and electronics until 1979, when the Talos system (launcher and radars) was removed, the space later being filled by two quad Armored Box Launchers (ABL) for Tomahawk cruise missiles. A year later came the dismantling of the "billboard" antennas for the electronically scanned AN/SPS-32/33 3D radars that gave the bridge superstructure its unusual (and quite unstealthy) profile; the plating is now protected by 1.75 in (45 mm) of armor. Forward of the bridge are the stepped pedestals fc. two SPG-55 missile guidance radars, a twin-rail Standard-ER SAM launcher on the 01 level, and, well forward, another twin-rail launcher on the main deck. Two more SPG-55s are mounted on stepped pedestals on the bridge roof.

Between the block bridge and the quadrapod lattice mainmast are the AS-ROC eight-cell box launcher and side-by-side 5-in (127-mm) single gun mounts; the 5-in guns addressed the embarrassing lack of close-in defense against small craft. As part of the major refit in the 1980s, Harpoon quad canister launcher groups to port and starboard of the mainmast and stepped Phalanx Gatling-type Close-In Weapons System (CIWS) mounts were added aft.

DEVELOPMENT • *Long Beach* was ordered from Bethlehem Steel's Quincy, Massachusetts, yard in October 1956 and completed in September 1961. The *Long Beach* had been scheduled for a New Threat Upgrade beginning in FY1993, but this was later canceled. She was instead earmarked for retirement in FY1994.

SPECIFICATIONS •
DISPLACEMENT   17,100 tons full load
DIMENSIONS
length   721 ft 9 in (220.0 m) overall
beam   73 ft 2 in (22.3 m)
draft   28 ft 10 in (8.8 m)
MACHINERY   2 Westinghouse C1W pressurized-water, 4 General Electric steam turbines, approx 80,000 shp on 2 shafts=30+ kts, range approx 90,000 nm at 30 kts, 360,000 nm at 20 kts, electric power 17,000 kW

CREW 958
WEAPONS
8 Tomahawk land-attack in 2 quad
  ABL
8 Harpoon antiship missiles in 2 quad
  canisters
2 twin Mk 10 Mod 1/2 launchers for
  Terrier/Standard-ER SAM (120
  missiles)
2 5-in (127-mm)/38-cal Mk 30 dual-
  purpose guns in single mounts
2 20-mm Mk 15 Phalanx Gatling-type
  CIWS
6 12.75-in (324-mm) Mk 32 torpedo
  tubes in 2 triple mounts
1 8-cell ASROC launcher
HELICOPTER   landing area
SENSORS
SPS-48C 3D air-search radar
SPS-49 2D air-search radar
SPS-67 surface-search radar
4 Mk 76 missile fire control systems
  with SPG-55B target-illumination
  radars
2 Mk 56 gunfire control systems with
  Mk 35 radar
LN-66 navigation radar
SQQ-23 PAIR keel-mounted sonar
SLQ-32(V)3 active/passive EW system

Ticonderoga (CG 47)

These 27 ships are the most complex and capable surface combatants the US Navy has deployed. In effect, they summarize US Navy developments in Antiair and Antisubmarine Warfare (AAW/ASW) over the past three decades. In addition to the Aegis air defense radar and command and control system, the design also features 122 Vertical Launch System (VLS) cells (except in the first five ships, which have two twin-rail Surface-to-Air Missile/SAM launchers). A VLS ship can launch Standard SM-2 MR or ER SAM, Tomahawk land-attack cruise missiles, and ASROC ASW missiles. Other weapons and sensors include a powerful bow sonar, Harpoon antiship missiles,

two 5-in (127-mm) guns, two Light Airborne Multipurpose System (LAMPS) III helicopters (SH-60B), and antisubmarine torpedo tubes.

All of these weapons are deployed in a hull and propulsion system derived from the *Spruance* (DD 963)-class destroyer design. Changes included a bow bulwark to reduce wetness forward and higher exhaust stacks. The superstructure has been enlarged to accommodate the Aegis/SPY-1 system, with two fixed phased-array radar antennas on the forward deckhouse facing forward and to starboard, and two on the after deckhouse, facing aft and to port. Internal changes include limited armor plating for the magazine and critical electronic spaces, increases in the ship's three service generators from 2,000 kW to 2,500 kW, additional accommodations, and additional fuel tanks.

The size and duration of the Aegis cruiser program has resulted in the subdivision of the class into five blocks or "baselines," representing points at which upgrades were introduced into new construction. Baseline 0 covered the first two ships. Baseline I (CG 49) introduced LAMPS III, improved SAMs, and better displays. Baseline II (CG 52) has VLS, better sonars, Baseline III (CG 59) an improved (SPY-1B) radar and displays, and Baseline IV (CG 64) faster, more capable computers.

The LAMPS III ships have the Recovery Assist Secure and Traversing (RAST) helicopter-hauldown system, which improves capability to operate helicopters in rough seas.

DEVELOPMENT • Begun as conventionally powered guided-missile destroyer counterparts (DDG 47) to a projected series of nuclear-powered strike cruisers, the *Ticonderoga*s replaced the strike cruisers in force planning after costs spiraled unacceptably. Litton's Ingalls yard at Pascagoula, Mississippi, was the lead yard, winning the order in Sep-

CG 52

tember 1978 and completing the ship in January 1983. Ingalls then built 18 more ships. Bath Iron Works completed its first ship (CG 51) in August 1987 and built seven more.

COMBAT EXPERIENCE • First combat action for the class came in April 1986, when *Yorktown* (CG 48) fired two Harpoons at a Libyan missile boat, damaging or possibly sinking it. The *Vincennes* (CG 49) incurred notoriety in July 1988 when her crew mistook an Iranian airliner for a hostile combat aircraft and shot it down with Standard missiles, killing 290 passengers and crew.

At the start of Operation Desert Storm in January 1991, seven VLS-equipped *Ticonderogas* launched Tomahawks against Iraqi targets. They were: *Bunker Hill* (28 missiles), *Mobile Bay* (22 with one failure), *Leyte Gulf* (2), *San Antonio* (14 with one failure), *Philippine Sea* (10), *Princeton* (3), and *Normandy* (26).

Princeton later struck a mine, which severely damaged her hull; nevertheless, the Navy claimed her AAW systems were back in service within hours.

In January 1993, *Cowpens* launched Tomahawks against an Iraqi nuclear research facility, and *Chancellorsville* fired nine TLAM (one more failed to launch) against Iraq's military intelligence headquarters in June 1993.

SPECIFICATIONS •
DISPLACEMENT   9,400–9,530 tons full load
DIMENSIONS
length   565 ft 10 in (172.5 m) overall
beam   55 ft (16.8 m)
draft   31 ft 6 in (9.6 m)
MACHINERY   4 General Electric LM 2500 gas turbines, 80,000 shp on 2 shafts with controllable-pitch propellers=30+ kts, range 6,000 nm at 20 kts, electric power 7,500 kW

CREW 364
WEAPONS
2 twin Mk 26 Mod 1 launchers for
Standard SM-2 MR SAM, ASROC
(88 missiles) in CG 47-51
2 61-cell Mk-41 VLS for Standard
SAM, Tomahawk land-attack, and
Vertical-Launch ASROC (VLA) in
CG-52 and later ships
8 Harpoon antiship missiles in 2 quad
canisters
2 5-in (127-mm)/54-cal Mk 45 dual-
purpose in single mounts
2 20-mm Mk 15 Phalanx Gatling-type
CIWS
6 12.75-in (324-mm) Mk 32 torpedo
tubes in triple mounts (36 torpedoes)
HELICOPTERS 2 LAMPS I (SH-2F) in
CG 47–48, 2 LAMPS III (SH-60B Sea-
hawk) in CG 49 and later ships
SENSORS
4 Aegis multifunction phased-array
(SPY-1A in CG 47-58, SPY-1B in CG
59-73)
SPS-49(V)6 2D air-search radar
SPS-55 surface-search radar in CG
47-48
SPS-64 surface-search radar in CG
49-73
4 Mk 99 missile directors with SPG-62
radar
1 Mk 86 gunfire control system with
SPQ-9A radar
SQS-53A bow-mounted active sonar in
CG 47–55
SQQ-89(V)3 in CG 56–73 includes:
SQS-53B in CG 56–68,
SQS-53C in CG 69–73
SQR-19 TACTAS towed-
array sonar
SQQ-28 Shipboard Sonar
Processing System for
LAMPS III
Sonar in Situ Mode
Assessment System
(SIMAS) with UYQ-25
data processing system
SLQ-32(V)3 active/passive EW system
SLQ-25 Nixie torpedo decoy

4 Mk 36 SRBOC 6-barrel chaff/flare
launchers

Truxtun (CGN 35)

The *Truxtun* was the fourth nuclear-
powered surface combatant built for the
US Navy. Like the *Long Beach* (CGN 9)
and *Bainbridge* (DLGN 25, later CGN 25),
Truxtun reflected an inability (for many
reasons) to stabilize nuclear-propelled
surface combatant design. She was a stopgap while development continued on the
long-range Typhoon missile system,
which used an early version of the Aegis
radar; that program was later canceled.

Truxtun was built to a modified *Belknap*
(CGN 26)-class design with the gun and
missile launcher positions reversed (gun
forward, missiles aft) to accommodate
the SQS-26 sonar in a bow dome. The
ship's distinctive appearance comes from
four-legged lattice masts that faintly resemble the "cage" masts of early US battleships.

The *Truxtun* has a long-forecastle hull
with raked bow, little sheer, forecastle
break abaft the helicopter platform and
abreast of the twin-rail Surface-to-Air Missile (SAM) launcher, and transom stern.
Ahead of the superstructure is the single
5-in/54-cal Mk 42 gun mount and a low
deckhouse. Above the bridge is the pedestal for the SPG-53 gunfire control radar.

The tall lattice foremast has a short
pole topmast; the large planar-array antenna serves the AN/SPS-48E system.
The lattice mainmast (equal in height to
the foremast and also fitted with a pole
topmast) is stepped into the after superstructure block; the truncated parabolic
antenna is part of the AN/SPS-49 radar
system. The *Truxtun* is also fitted with the
Hughes Aircraft Naval Mast-Mounted
Sight (NMMS) electro-optical surveillance system that has TV, Forward-
Looking Infrared (FLIR), and laser designator in a traversable ball.

Abaft the mainmast are the hangar and

flight deck for the SH-2F Seasprite (LAMPS I) helicopter.

Harpoon missile canisters were emplaced in the positions originally occupied by two 3-in/50-cal AA single gun mounts. Two Phalanx Gatling-type Close-In Weapons Systems (CIWS) are forward of the bridge.

DEVELOPMENT • *Truxtun* was built by New York Ship and commissioned in 1967. She was decommissioned in FY1995.

SPECIFICATIONS •
DISPLACEMENT   8,800 tons full load
DIMENSIONS
   length   564 ft (172.0 m) overall
   beam   58 ft (17.7 m)
   draft   31 ft (9.5 m)
MACHINERY   2 General Electric D2G pressurized-water nuclear reactors, 2 steam turbines, approx 60,000 shp on 2 shafts =30+ kts, electric power 14,500 kW
CREW   591 (39 Off + 552 Enl)
WEAPONS
   1 twin Mk 10 Mod 8 launcher for Terrier/Standard-ER SAM and ASROC ASW missiles (60 missiles)
   8 Harpoon antiship missiles in 2 quad canisters
   1 5-inch (127-mm)/54-cal Mk 42 dual-purpose gun
   2 20-mm Mk 15 Phalanx Gatling-type CIWS
   4 fixed 12.75-in (324-mm) Mk 32 torpedo tubes
HELICOPTER   1 LAMPS I (SH-2F)
SENSORS
   SPS-48C 3D air-search radar
   SPS-49 2D air-search radar
   SPS-67 surface-search radar
   2 Mk 76 missile fire control systems with 2 SPG-55B target-illumination radars
   1 Mk 68 gunfire control system with SPG-53F radar
   SQS-26BX bow-mounted active sonar
   NMMS electro-optical surveillance system
   SLQ-32(V)3 active/passive EW system

Virginia (CGN 38)

These four nuclear-powered ships are based on the previous *California* (CGN 36)-class cruisers, but with the ASROC launcher deleted, Mk 26 twin-rail missile launchers, and provision for a helicopter hangar and elevator in the stern. They constituted the largest class of nuclear-propelled surface combatants, but are likely to be the last nuclear-propelled surface ships (other than aircraft carriers) to be built by the US Navy.

As in the *Californias*, the flush-deck design has a split superstructure set relatively far aft with each block topped by a tapered, plated mast. As originally built, the ships had a stern hangar with a folding hatch cover and elevator arrangement to accommodate a single SH-2F LAMPS (Light Airborne Multipurpose System) helicopter.

After encountering problems with the elevators, and in keeping the hangars watertight, the Navy deleted the helicopters in the early 1980s in favor of two Tomahawk Armored Box Launchers (ABL) on the fantail, aft of the second Mk 26 launcher. Earlier proposals to provide a Vertical Launch System (VLS) for Tomahawk missiles in place of the hangar were dropped. Side-by-side Phalanx Close-In Weapons System (CIWS) mounts were added abaft the tower foremast during refits.

DEVELOPMENT • CGN 38-40 were originally classified as "frigates" (DLGN 38–40); they were changed to cruisers on June 30, 1975. The *Arkansas* was ordered as CGN 41. All were built at Newport News Shipbuilding and entered service from 1976 to 1980. *Virginia* and *Texas* were the first to decommission in 1994, less than 20 years after they entered service.

COMBAT EXPERIENCE • The *Virginia* and *Mississippi* were deployed to the Mediterranean and Southwest Asia in late 1990 as part of Operation Desert Shield.

The *Virginia* launched two Tomahawks at Iraqi targets from the Mediterranean. The *Mississippi* operated with the *John F. Kennedy*'s (CV 67) task force from September 14, 1990 to March 13, 1991.

The *Texas* arrived in the Persian Gulf with the *Nimitz* (CVN 68) in June 1991, replacing the *Tripoli* (LPH 10) as flagship of the multinational mine countermeasures task force that swept the northern Persian Gulf after the cease-fire.

SPECIFICATIONS •
DISPLACEMENT   11,300 tons full load
DIMENSIONS
length   585 ft (178.4 m) overall
beam   63 ft (19.2 m)
draft   29 ft 6 in (9.0 m)
MACHINERY   2 General Electric D2G pressurized-water reactors, 2 steam turbines, 60,000 shaft hp on 2 shafts=30+ knots
CREW   562–613
WEAPONS
2 twin Mk 26 Mod 0/1 launchers for RIM-66D/J Standard SM-2 MR SAM (68 missiles)

8 Tomahawk TASM/TLAM (2 quad ABL Mk 143)
8 Harpoon SSM (2 quad canisters Mk 141)
2 single 5-in (127-mm)/54-cal Mk 45 dual-purpose
2 20-mm Mk 15 Mod 2 Phalanx Gatling-type CIWS
ASROC ASW missiles fired from forward Mk 26 launcher
6 12.75-in (324-mm) Mk 32 torpedo tubes in triple mounts
SENSORS
SPS-48 3D air-search radar
SPS-49 2D air-search radar
SPS-55 surface-search radar
4 SPG-51D missile control radars
Mk 86 gunfire control system with SPG-60 and SPQ-9 radars
SQS-53 series bow-mounted active sonar
SLQ-32(V)3 active/passive EW system
Naval Mast-Mounted Sight (NMMS) electro-optical surveillance system in *Arkansas*

DESTROYERS

Arleigh Burke (DDG 51)
These complex destroyers (28 authorized by the end of FY1994) were designed from the outset to be smaller and less expensive (by 25%) than the *Ticonderoga* (DDG/CG 47) design. Even so, they represent a significant investment and show an unmatched flexibility in their seakeeping and weapons layout. The design's one weakness is the lack of helicopter capability in the original design, which is being remedied in later ships.

The *Burke*'s design is unlike previous US destroyer construction, especially in its broad waterplane hull, which is beam-

ier than any other US destroyer design, its phased-array radar, and its Vertical Launching System (VLS). In addition, these are the first US destroyers in 50 years constructed of steel, which provides increased blast, fire, and fragment resistance as well as protection from Electromagnetic Pulse (EMP). The *Burke* has 130 tons of Kevlar armor plating to protect vital spaces, and for the first time in a US warship design, a Nuclear, Biological, and Chemical (NBC) Collective Protective System (CPS) is fitted from the outset.

Each angled bridge face bears a fixed

antenna for the Martin Marietta (formerly General Electric/RCA) AN/SPY-1D Aegis radar. The after corners of the forward superstructure also have SPY-1D antennas. Beginning with *The Sullivans* (DDG 68), a Track Initiation Processor (TIP) permits better tracking, especially of slow-moving targets, and reduced clutter. A 29-cell VLS is fitted in the deck forward of the bridge, a 61-cell VLS is well aft.

A helicopter landing deck and limited support capability are provided, but no hangar. Instead of providing a full Light Airborne Multipurpose System (LAMPS III/SH-60B) helicopter capability to these ships, as Congress at one point directed, funding limitations inspired a modest $10-million package that was added to the DDG 52 and later ships while under construction.

Flight II (beginning with DDG 72 *Bernard L. Austin*), is fitted with the Joint Tactical Information Distribution System (JTIDS) command-and-control processor, Tactical Information Exchange System (TADIX), Tactical Data Information Link (TADIL J), Combat Direction Finding, the Aegis Extended-Range Standard SAM, and AN/SLQ-32(V)3 ESM.

Flight IIA (formerly Flight III) ships (beginning with DDG 79) will have full helicopter facilities including a hangar for two LAMPS III helicopters, blast-hardened transverse bulkheads, and the Kingfisher mine-detection module for the SQS-53C sonar. The Phalanx system will be beached in favor of Evolved Sea Sparrow SAMs fired from VLS cells. To compensate, the Harpoon missiles and SQR-19 towed-array sonar will be removed and less expensive commercial color displays fitted.

DEVELOPMENT • Studies for a smaller Aegis ship began in 1979. Planned numbers in the class have ranged from 29 to 63 ships, with at least the minimum certain to be built.

Bath Iron Works of Bath, Maine, is the lead yard, being awarded the contract for the *Arleigh Burke* in April 1985. The *Burke* was commissioned on July 4, 1991 and began her first operational deployment in February 1993. Litton's Ingalls yard in Pascagoula, Mississippi, received its first contract (for the *Barry*) in May 1987; the *Barry* commissioned in December 1992. In the shrinking defense budgets of the 1990s, the *Burkes* were likely to be the only surface combatants funded for several years.

SPECIFICATIONS •

DISPLACEMENT   8,315 tons full load
DIMENSIONS
length	504 ft 6 in (153.8 m) overall
beam	59 ft (18.0 m)
draft	30 ft 7 in (9.3 m)

MACHINERY   4 General Electric LM 2500 gas turbines, 100,000 shp on 2 shafts with controllable-pitch propellers = 30+ kts, range 4,400 nm at 20 kts
CREW   340
WEAPONS
90-cell VLS for Standard-MR/Tomahawk/Vertical Launch ASROC
8 McDonnell Douglas Harpoon SSM (2 quad canisters Mk 141)
1 5-in (127-mm)/54-cal Mk 45 dual-purpose
2 20-mm Mk 15 Phalanx Gatling-type CIWS
6 12.75-in (324-mm) Mk 32 torpedo tubes in triple mounts
HELICOPTERS   flight deck aft through DDG 78, hangar for 2 SH-60B LAMPS III in DDG 79 and later
SENSORS
4 SPY-1D multifunction radar antenna
SPS-67(V) surface-search radar
SPS-64 navigation radar
3 Mk 99 illuminators with SPG-62 radar
SQS-53C bow-mounted active sonar
SQR-19 TACTAS towed-array sonar
SLQ-32(V)2 active/passive EW system
SLQ-25 Nixie towed torpedo decoy
4 Mk 36 SRBOC 6-barrel chaff/flare launchers

Kidd (DDG 993)

Also known colloquially as the Ayatollah class, these four guided-missile destroyers were part of a six-ship order by the Imperial Iranian Navy in the 1970s; they were purchased for the US Navy after the fall of the shah of Iran. Until the commissioning of the *Arleigh Burke* (DDG 51) in July 1991, these were the most capable destroyers in US service, having excellent Antiair Warfare (AAW) and Antisubmarine Warfare (ASW) capabilities.

The *Kidd*s are based on the *Spruance* (DD 963)-class ASW destroyers, which were designed from the beginning to have a SAM-capable variant (DXG). These ships have a considerably higher displacement than do the *Spruances* and have more aluminum-alloy and Kevlar armor.

The superstructure is composed of large, unstealthy blocks dominated by heavy lattice fore- and mainmasts and two gas turbine stacks arranged in echelon (the forward stack to port, after stack to starboard). Abaft the after stack are the side-by-side helicopter hangars and landing platform.

The machinery is quiet and has proved to be very reliable, with a Mean Time Between Overhauls (MTBO) for the LM 2500 of 9,000 hours. These ships are reported to be very quiet during ASW operations, a condition achieved in part through use of the Prairie-Masker bubbler system. Iranian government requirements that these ships be provided with increased air-conditioning capacity and dust separators for their engine air intakes have been welcome by their US Navy operators.

These ships were completed with the Light Airborne Multipurpose System (LAMPS) I, which uses the SH-2F Seasprite helicopter. Two larger SH-60B LAMPS III helicopters could also be embarked.

All ships have received the New Threat Upgrade (NTU), the foremast being fitted with an additional platform over the SPQ-9A radome for the SPS-49(V)2 two-dimensional search antenna. In addition, command-and-control as well as missile control systems were modernized. The *Kidd* was fitted with the Naval Mast-Mounted Sight (NMMS) electro-optical surveillance system that has TV, Forward-Looking Infrared (FLIR), and laser designator in a traversable ball.

DEVELOPMENT • Six of this design were ordered by the shah's navy in 1973–74. Delays in contract signing and rising cost had cut the buy to four, which had barely begun production when the shah's empire fell. After a congressionally mandated purchase in July 1979, Litton's Ingalls yard in Pascagoula, Mississippi, built all four ships, commissioning them between July 1981 and March 1982.

COMBAT EXPERIENCE • The *Scott* was part of the *Dwight D. Eisenhower*'s (CVN 69) carrier battle group that sailed in the Red Sea from August 8 to 24 as part of the initial US response to Iraq's invasion and annexation of Kuwait.

The *Kidd* arrived in the Operation Desert Storm theater on February 1, 1991, as part of a regular rotation of ships for the permanently based Middle East Force; she remained until mid-June.

SPECIFICATIONS •
DISPLACEMENT   9,574 tons full load
DIMENSIONS
length   563 ft 8 in (171.8 m) overall
beam   55 ft 1 in (16.8 m)
draft (including sonar dome)
                33 ft (10.1 m)
MACHINERY   4 General Electric LM 2500 gas turbines, 80,000 shp on 2 shafts with controllable-pitch propellers= 30+ kts, range 6,000 nm at 20 kts, 3,300 nm at 30 kts, electric power 6,000 kW
CREW   339

2 twin Mk 26 Mod 3/4 launchers for Standard SM-2 MR SAM (52 missiles)

8 Harpoon SSM (2 quad canisters Mk 141)

2 5-in (127-mm)/54-cal Mk 45 dual-purpose guns in single mounts

2 Mk 15 Mod 2 Phalanx Gatling-type CIWS

6 12.75-in (324-mm) torpedo tubes in 2 triple mounts

ASROC ASW missile fired from forward Mk 26 launcher (16 missiles)

HELICOPTERS 1 SH-2F LAMPS I

SENSORS

SPS-48E 3D air-search radar

SPS-49(V)2 2D air-search radar

SPS-64(4) surface-search radar

SPS-55 surface-search radar

2 Mk 74 missile fire control systems with SPG-55D illuminating radars

1 Mk 86 Mod 5 gunfire control system with SPG-60 and SPQ-9A radars

SQS-53A bow-mounted active sonar

NMMS electro-optical surveillance system

SLQ-25 Nixie towed torpedo decoy

SLQ-32(V)2 radar intercept and jammer EW system

4 Mk 36 SRBOC 6-barrel chaff/flare launchers

Spruance (DD 963)

These 31 large destroyers were originally built as specialized Antisubmarine Warfare (ASW) ships with only point-defense missiles for the Antiair Warfare (AAW) role. Although their AAW capability remains limited, the *Spruance*'s surface warfare punch was greatly enhanced by adding Harpoon antiship and Tomahawk land-attack missiles. Their great assets are their considerable size, quietness, and modular weapons layout.

As a class, they are the most numerous Western destroyer class completed since World War II. Moreover, the basic hull and powerplant have been used in four *Kidd*-class AAW destroyers and the 27 ships of the *Ticonderoga*-class Aegis missile cruiser class. (*Hayler*, the 31st ship, was originally authorized as a helicopter-capable destroyer with enlarged hangar and flight deck, but completed to the *Spruance* design.)

The ship's profile has large superstructure blocks dominated by heavy lattice fore- and mainmasts and two stacks arranged in echelon (the forward stack to port, after stack to starboard). Farther aft are side-by-side helicopter hangars and landing platform. Although bulky, the *Spruance*'s interior volume is considerable and her bunkerage gives her a good range at cruising speed.

The four General Electric LM 2500 gas turbines are connected in pairs to shafts that drive controllable-pitch propellers. The quiet machinery has proved to be very reliable, showing a Mean Time Between Overhauls (MTBO) for the LM 2500 of 9,000 hours. Use of the Prairie-Masker bubbler system decreases the ship's already low acoustic signature.

Armament includes Harpoon antiship missiles, two 5-in guns, an ASROC "pepperbox" ASW launcher, and Sea Sparrow SAM launcher. The ASROC launcher is automatically reloaded from a vertical magazine providing 16 reloads. A total of 24 Sea Sparrow missiles are normally carried.

Seven ships carry two Tomahawk Armored Box Launchers (ABL); these will be replaced by the 61-cell Mk 41 Vertical Launch System (VLS) that is being fitted in the other 24 ships. *Merrill* was the first *Spruance* fitted with the ABL in October 1982; *Spruance* completed the first VLS installation in June 1987. Refitting the other ships (including those with ABLs) will take until the turn of the century.

These ships were completed with the Light Airborne Multipurpose System (LAMPS) I but have been upgraded to

LAMPS III level, which uses the SH-60B Seahawk.

All *Spruances* are being fitted with the SQQ-89 integrated ASW system, which includes several other systems such as the SQR-19 Tactical Towed-Array Sonar (TACTAS).

Several *Spruances*, including *Elliott, David R. Ray, O'Brien,* and *Leftwich,* have Hughes Aircraft Naval Mast-Mounted Sight (NMMS) electro-optical surveillance system that has TV, Forward-Looking Infrared (FLIR), and laser designator in a traversable ball.

DEVELOPMENT • All 31 ships were built at Litton's Ingalls yard at Pascagoula, Mississippi. Under the Total Package Procurement policy adopted in the late 1960s, Litton was awarded all 30 ships at once (although funding was spaced out over several years). Far from achieving the hoped-for economies of scale, the program hit rapid cost growth and serious delays. Nevertheless, average construction time was a creditable three years, with the first ship completing in September 1975 and the *Fletcher* (DD 992) in July 1980. The *Hayler,* procured separately, was commissioned in March 1983.

COMBAT EXPERIENCE • Throughout the 1980s, *Spruance*-class destroyers supported US naval action in Lebanon, Grenada, the Persian Gulf in 1987–88, and in Operations Desert Shield and Desert Storm. In most of these deployments, the *Spruances* used their 5-in guns against shore targets or oil platforms.

A total of 11 *Spruances* supported Desert Shield, and five of them launched Tomahawks against Iraqi targets in January 1991; *Fife* launched 60 (59 successes), *Foster* sent up 40 (38 successes). Almost exactly two years later, *Caron* (which had launched two TLAMs in January 1991) and *Stump* launched Tomahawks against an Iraqi nuclear research facility, followed in June 1993 by the *Peterson's* 14-missile contribution to the attack on the headquarters of Iraqi military intelligence.

SPECIFICATIONS •

DISPLACEMENT   8,040 tons full load
DIMENSIONS

length	563 ft 4 in (171.8 m) overall
beam	55 ft (16.8 m)
draft	29 ft (8.8 m)

MACHINERY   4 General Electric LM 2500 gas turbines, 80,000 shp on 2 shafts with controllable-pitch propellers=32.5 kts, range 6,000+ nm at 20 kts, 3,300 nm at 30 kts, electric power 6,000 kW
CREW   334
WEAPONS
  8 Tomahawk TASM/TLAM (2 quad ABL Mk 143) in DD 974, 976, 979, 983, 984, 989, 990
  61-cell Mk 41 Mod 0 VLS for Tomahawk/VLA being fitted in other 24 ships
  8 Harpoon SSM in 2 quad canisters
  1 8-cell NATO Sea Sparrow launcher Mk 29
  2 5-in (127-mm)/54-cal Mk 45 dual-purpose in single mounts
  2 20-mm Mk 15 Mod 2 or Mod 12 Phalanx Gatling-type CIWS
  1 8-cell ASROC launcher Mk 16 (being removed from ships receiving VLS) (24 missiles)
  6 12.75-in (324-mm) Mk 32 torpedo tubes in triple mounts
HELICOPTERS   2 SH-60B Seahawk LAMPS III
SENSORS
  SPS-40B/C/D 2D air-search radar except SPS-49 in DD 997
  SPS-55 surface-search radar
  Mk 86 gunfire control system with SPG-60 and SPQ-9A radars
  Mk 91 missile fire control system for Sea Sparrow
  Mk 23 antiship missile Target Acquisition System (TAS)
  SPS-53 or LN-66 navigation radar

SQS-53 series bow-mounted sonar
SQQ-89(V) ASW combat system
NMMS electro-optical surveillance system
SLQ-25 Nixie torpedo decoy

SLQ-32(V)3 active/passive EW system
4 Mk 36 SRBOC 6-barrel chaff/flare launchers
WLR-1 in DD 971, 975

FRIGATES/CORVETTES

Knox (FF 1052)

These 46 large antisubmarine frigates constituted the most numerous class of surface combatants built in the West since World War II until the advent of the *Oliver Hazard Perry* (FFG 7) class. When the *Knox*es entered service, they were criticized for their relatively low speed, single screw, and light armament. Over their operational lifetime, however, most received new weapons systems and were not notably unreliable.

The superstructure is topped by a distinctive cylindrical "mack" that combines mast and stacks. The hull design proved wet forward, so the Navy fitted bulwarks and bow strakes in the 1970s. The helicopter deck aft, originally intended for Drone Antisubmarine Helicopters (DASH), was strengthened to operate the manned SH-2 Light Airborne Multipurpose System (LAMPS) I.

Evidence of the class's ASW orientation lies in the emphasis on ASW sensors and weapons and the fitting of such systems as the Prairie-Masker bubbling system that reduces self-generated noise. The ASROC eight-cell box launcher can launch ASROC ASW rockets or Harpoon antiship missiles; a 16-round reload magazine replenishes the system.

DEVELOPMENT • The first 26 ships were ordered in August 1964 from four yards: lead yard Todd Shipyard in Seattle, Washington (six ships), Todd in San Pedro, California (eight ships), Lock-

heed in Seattle (five ships), and Avondale in Westwego, Louisiana (seven ships). This traditional pattern of dividing an order among several yards (a tradition within US naval shipbuilding) was broken with the August 1966 follow-on bulk order of the last 20 ships from Avondale.

All yards suffered delays, strikes, materials shortages, and price inflation, leading to a marked cost and schedule overrun. The first delivery came in April 1969, the last in November 1974.

COMBAT EXPERIENCE • 10 *Knox*-class frigates were deployed to the Persian Gulf in 1990–91's Operations Desert Shield/Desert Storm as escorts to carrier battle groups or ships assigned to the gulf-based Middle East Force (MEF). They were:

Reasoner (*Independence* Battle Group/ BG)
Stein (*Eisenhower* BG)
Marvin Shields (MEF)
Francis Hammond (*Ranger* BG)
Vreeland (*Theodore Roosevelt* BG)
Paul (*Eisenhower* BG)
Elmer Montgomery (*John F. Kennedy* BG)
Brewton (*Independence* BG)
Barbey (MEF)
Thomas C. Hart (*Saratoga* BG)

The class's high-pressure boilers and steam turbines doomed them to early retirement from a navy that was increasingly powered by gas turbines. *Knox*-class frigates have been leased to the Royal Hellenic (*Connole, Vreeland,* and *Trippe*), Taiwanese (*Robert E. Peary, Brewton,* and *Kirk*), and Turkish (*Capodanno, Fanning, Reasoner, Thomas C. Hart*) navies. All of the other ships were due to be decommissioned by FY1995. Eight ships, redesignated FFT, were to remain active with cadre crews, but they too were mothballed under the FY1994 budget.

SPECIFICATIONS •
DISPLACEMENT   4,250 tons full load
DIMENSIONS
length   438 ft (133.6 m) overall
            (439 ft 8 in/134.0 m
            with bulwarks)
beam   46 ft 9 in (14.3 m)
draft   24 ft 9 in (7.5 m)
MACHINERY   2 Combustion Engineering boilers, 1 Westinghouse steam turbine, 35,000 shp on 1 shaft=27+ kts, range 4,500 nm at 20 kts
CREW   282
WEAPONS
Harpoon antiship missiles fired from ASROC launcher
1 5-in (127-mm)/54-cal Mk 42 dual-purpose gun
1 20-mm Mk 15 Phalanx Gatling-type CIWS
4 fixed 12.75-in (324-mm) Mk 32 torpedo tubes
1 8-tube ASROC launcher Mk 116
HELICOPTER   1 SH-2F Seasprite (LAMPS I)
SENSORS
SPS-40B air-search radar
SPS-58 threat-warning radar in some ships
SPS-67 surface-search radar
1 Mk 68 gunfire control system with SPG-53A/D/F radar
Mk 23 Target Acquisition System (TAS) in *Downes*
SQS-26CX bow-mounted active sonar
SQS-35 variable-depth sonar or SQR-18A(V)1 TACTAS towed-array sonar
SLQ-32(V)1 or SLQ-32(V)2 EW system

2 Mk 36 SRBOC 6-barrel chaff/flare launchers

Oliver Hazard Perry (FFG 7)

The 51 ships in this class constitute the most numerous class of major surface warships built in the West since World War II; only the Soviet *Skoryy* destroyer class was larger. First designed as austere sea control ships with a single screw, relatively low-powered sonar, and little protection in the early 1970s, the *Perrys* acquired a Surface-to-Air Missile (SAM) launcher at congressional insistence. The *Perrys* proved versatile and suprisingly hardy ships, their modular construction making repairs from severe combat damage a practical proposition.

Although considered a single class, these ships were built in "flights," which allowed for upgrades to the design during the run of the program. Many of the updates raised the design's ASW and long-range surveillance capabilities. Some of the updates were refitted to ships of a given flight during their Post-Shakedown Availability (PSA) periods; ships of the next flight had these upgrades included during construction.

After the lead ship, Flight 1 was the basic production configuration and covered FFG 8 through FFG 18. The first two Flights were equipped with SH-2F Seasprite helicopters as part of the Light Airborne Multipurpose System (LAMPS) I.

Flight 2 (FFG 19 to FFG 35) saw the introduction of the SLQ-32(V)2 EW system, the 20-mm Gatling-type Phalanx Close-In Weapons System (CIWS), and the SRBOC chaff/flare launchers.

Flight 3 (FFG 36 to FFG 49) represented a considerable augmentation when the LAMPS III suite with two SH-60B Seahawk helicopters were embarked after a PSA retrofit. Fin stabilizers were fitted after completion, and the Recovery Assist Secure and Traversing (RAST) helicopter handling system was installed on a lengthened flight deck that resulted in a raked stern. Link 11 tactical data transfer system was also fitted during construction.

Flight 4 (FFG 50 to FFG 61) was equipped with LAMPS III, RAST, and fin stabilizers during construction (except FFG 52, which received LAMPS III and RAST during her PSA). AN/SQR-19 TACTAS towed-array sonar was fitted during PSAs for FFG 55-FFG 58; FFG 59-FFG 61 received TACTAS during construction.

Only the FFG 61 (*Ingraham*) received the Mk 92 Mod 6 CORT (Coherent Receiver/Transmitter) fire control system that offers improved capabilities in bad weather and improved reliability. 11 other ships (*Taylor, Gary, Underwood, Reuben James, Vandegrift, Nicholas, Hawes, Ford, Elrod, Kauffman,* and *Carr*) will have received similar upgrades by 1995. In addition, 10 more ships will get a more modest "CANDO" (Commercially Off-the-Shelf Affordable Near-Term Deficiency-Correcting Ordalts) upgrades.

DEVELOPMENT • *Perry* was built as a prototype by Bath Iron Works, being commissioned in December 1977. The 50 that followed were built by three yards: Bath (23 ships), Todd's San Pedro, California, yard (18 ships), and Todd's Seattle yard (nine ships). The last ship commissioned in August 1989.

Todd Seattle constructed four more ships of the same design for the Royal Australian Navy (RAN) as the *Adelaide* class. Two more Australian, six Spanish, and at least eight Taiwanese Navy *Perry*-design ships have been built in those respective countries.

Most of the Flight I and II *Perry*s have been shifted to the Naval Reserve Force (NRF).

COMBAT EXPERIENCE • Two ships— *Stark* (FFG 31) and *Samuel P. Roberts* (FFG 58)—were severely damaged by hostile action in the Persian Gulf. *Stark* was hit by Exocet antiship missiles in May 1987; *Roberts* triggered a mine in April 1988. Both were nearly lost, but both rejoined the fleet after repairs. (The *Roberts* repair involved modular hull replacement for the first time.)

13 US, three Australian, and two Spanish *Perry*-class ships were deployed to the Persian Gulf region at some time during Operations Desert Shield and Desert Storm in 1990–91. They conducted maritime sanction patrols and operated light US Army helicopters as well as their Seahawks. Most often cited in dispatches was the *Nicholas,* which raided Iraqi oil platforms on January 18, taking 23 Iraqis prisoners; she later escorted first the *Missouri* (BB 63), then the *Wisconsin* (BB 64), to their bombardment missions off Kuwait.

SPECIFICATIONS •

DISPLACEMENT 3,658 tons full load (FFG 7, FFG 9–FFG 35); 3,900–4,100 tons full load (FFG 8, FFG 36, and later)

DIMENSIONS
length   445 ft (135.6 m) overall except 453 ft (138.2 m) overall for ships with LAMPS III modification
beam   45 ft (13.7 m)
draft   24 ft 6 in (7.5 m)

MACHINERY 2 General Electric LM 2500 gas turbines, 40,000 shp on 1 shaft with controllable-pitch propeller=28+ kts sustained, 4,500 nm at 20 kts (2 electrically driven APU; 650 hp for restricted area maneuvering), electric power 3,000 kW

CREW 206 in active ships, 114 active + 76 reservists in NRF ships

WEAPONS
1 Mk 13 Mod 4 single launcher for Standard SM-1 MR SAM and RGM-84 Harpoon antiship missiles (40 with typical missile loadout of 36 SM-1 MR and 4 Harpoon)
1 76-mm/62-cal AA Mk 75 gun

1 20-mm Mk 15 Phalanx Gatling-type
  CIWS
6 12.75-in (324-mm) Mk 32 torpedo
  tubes in triple mounts for Mk 46
  torpedoes (14 torpedoes)
HELICOPTER   1 or 2 SH-2F LAMPS I
ASW in NRF ships, 2 SH-60B LAMPS
III Seahawk ASW in active ships
SENSORS
  SPS-49(V)2 2D air-search radar
  (-49(V)5 in FFG 61)

SPS-55 surface-search radar
Mk 92 Mod 4 weapons fire control sys-
  tem (Mod 6 in FFG 61)
STIR targeting radar
SQR-18A towed array in NRF ships
SQR-19 towed array in active ships
SQS-56 keel-mounted sonar
Naval Mast-Mounted Sight (NMMS)
  electro-optical system in 19 ships
SLQ-32 (V)2 EW system
2 Mk 36 chaff/flare launchers

MINE WARFARE SHIPS

Avenger (MCM 1)

These 14 relatively large Mine Countermeasures (MCM) ships locate and destroy mines that cannot be countered by
conventional minesweeping techniques
or minesweeping helicopters. The basic
MCM design is similar to previous MSO
(Ocean Minesweeper) classes. The long-
forecastle hull has a low magnetic signature, being constructed of fiberglass-
sheathed wood (laminated oak framing,
Douglas fir planking, and deck sheathing
with reinforced fiberglass covering). A
degaussing system further reduces the
signature.

One or two Honeywell AN/SLQ-48
Mine Neutralization System (MNS) vehicles are carried in addition to conventional sweep gear.

The ships are fitted with Magnavox
AN/SSN-2(V) Precise Integrated Navigation System (PINS). The MCMs were initially fitted with the AN/SQQ-30 variable-
depth sonar. This equipment was succeeded in later ships by the AN/SQQ-32.
Influence mines are swept by the AN/
SLQ-37(V)2 magnetic/acoustic sweep
equipment; the mechanical sweep is the
Oropesa Type 0 Size 1.

All ships have four very-low-magnetic

diesel engines for propulsion; the original engine design had several defects.
Electrical power for minesweeping gear is
provided by gas turbines.

DEVELOPMENT • When laid down in
1983, the *Avenger* was the first large minesweeper under construction for the US
Navy since the *Assurance* (MSO 521) was
completed 25 years earlier; she entered
service in 1987. Peterson of Sturgeon
Bay, Wisconsin, built all but three of the
class; Marinette constructed the *Defender,*
Champion, and *Patriot.* The program suffered delays (especially due to engine
problems) and the last of 14 wasn't due to
commission until 1995.

COMBAT EXPERIENCE • The *Avenger*
cleared traffic lanes near the Kuwaiti
coast for combatants during Operations
Desert Shield/Desert Storm, especially
the battleships *Missouri* and *Wisconsin.* After the cease-fire, she and a large international minesweeping flotilla cleared
more than 1,200 mines. She was relieved
in June 1991 by the *Guardian,* which remained in the Persian Gulf until February 1992.

SPECIFICATIONS •

DISPLACEMENT   1,312 tons full load
DIMENSIONS
   length   224 ft 4 in (68.4 m)
              overall
   beam   39 ft (11.9 m)
   draft   11 ft 6 in (3.5 m)
MACHINERY   4 diesels, Waukesha L-1616
2,600 bhp (first 2 ships), Isotta-
Fraschini ID36 SS-6V AM 2,720 bhp
(remaining ships), 2 shafts with
controllable-pitch propellers=13.5
kts, (max minehunting speed is 5
kts), low-speed maneuvering by 2 220-
hp electric motors turning propellers,
1 350-hp bow thruster, electric power
1,125 kW
CREW   72
SENSORS
   SPS-55 surface-search radar
   SQQ-30 mine-detecting sonar in first 9
   SQQ-32 mine-detecting sonar in last 5

Osprey (MHC 51)

These 12 coastal minehunters are based
on the Italian-designed *Lerici*-class coastal
minehunter design. After the expensive
failure of the *Cardinal* (MSH 1) surface-
effect minehunter in the mid-1980s, these
ships were procured virtually as a Nondevelopmental Item (NDI) to shore up
the Navy's weak mine warfare capability.

*Osprey*s have a Glass-Reinforced Plastic
(GRP) monohull single-skin structure
and operate the remotely operated underwater vehicle known as the AN/
SLQ-48 Mine Neutralizing System
(MNS). Mechanical and influence minesweeping systems are being developed
independently. The ships are capable of
coastal mine clearance operations of up

to five days without replenishment. In the
translation of the Italian design to US
requirements, full-load displacement
climbed to almost 900 tons.

DEVELOPMENT • The contract for
adapting the *Lerici* design was awarded in
August 1986 to Intermarine USA (established by Intermarine Sarzana of Italy,
builders of the original *Lerici* design),
which was chosen in May 1987 to con-
struct the lead ship of this class. The first
ship was laid down in May 1988 and was
scheduled for delivery in April 1991. Almost immediately (and inevitably) delays
crept into the schedule and none of the
original target dates was met. Intermarine contracted for eight of the 12
craft, and Avondale of Westwego, Louisiana, received contracts for the other four.

SPECIFICATIONS •

DISPLACEMENT   895 tons full load
DIMENSIONS
   length   187 ft 10 in (57.25 m)
                overall
   beam   35 ft 11 in (10.95 m)
   draft   9 ft 6 in (2.9 m)
MACHINERY   2 Isotta-Fraschini ID 36 SS
   6V-AM diesels, 1,160 bhp driving 2
   Voith-Schneider vertical cycloidal pro-
   pellers=12 kts, range 2,500 nm at 12
   kts (2 180-bhp hydraulic motors for
   minehunting, 1 180-hp bow thruster),
   electric power 600 kW
CREW   51
WEAPONS
   1 30-mm or 40-mm gun
SENSORS
   SPS-64(V)9 surface-search radar
   SQQ-32 mine-detection sonar
   SLQ-48(V) MNS

SEALIFT AND PREPOSITIONED SHIPS

New-Construction Sealift Ships

Desert Shield mobilization experience and the likelihood that US forces would have to build up rapidly at remote locations in the future led to a considerable expansion of the US sealift fleet. In addition to the conversion of five commercial Roll-On/Roll-Off (RO/RO) ships by Newport News Shipbuilding and NASSCO, 12 new ships (*Bob Hope* class) were ordered in September 1993. An award for six (one confirmed plus five options) went to Avondale, followed by a similar award to NASSCO.

The design resembles that of the *Algol* class, having about the same length and beam. It is slower, however, with a maximum speed of 26 knots. (Experience with the *Algol*s shows that the extra six to eight knots requires expensive, fuel-inefficient, and unreliable machinery.)

DEVELOPMENT • The Avondale and NASSCO contracts require delivery of the first ships in October 1997 and the last ships by April 2001.

Algol (T-AKR 287)

These eight Fast Sealift Ships were built in West Germany and the Netherlands for the US Sea-Land Services, Inc., of Port Elizabeth, New Jersey, as commercial container ships. Originally delivered in the early 1970s, they are the fastest commercial cargo ships ever built. The penalties for such high-speed capability are heavy fuel consumption even at slower cruising speeds and machinery unreliability.

The relatively quick and simple conversion to Fast Sealift Ships included the addition of a RO/RO ramp forward and aft, and a LO/LO (Load-On/Load-Off) capa-

bility aft for containers. Paired 35-ton cranes and twin 50-ton cranes serve the holds.

Each ship has a RO/RO capacity of 185,000 ft² (17,187 m²), and a LO/LO capacity of 26,000 ft² (2,415 m²) for containers or vehicles containerized in flatracks. A 35,000-ft² (3,252-m²) helicopter flight deck strong enough for the heaviest US military helicopters is located between the forward and after deckhouse. Four cargo decks beneath the flight deck are connected by ramps and can accommodate helicopters as well as vehicles, the first deck with a height of 19 ft 6 in (5.94 m) and the others 13 ft 6 in (4.11 m).

DEVELOPMENT • The US Navy purchased the eight ships in 1981–82 for a total of $272 million, including procurement of 400 containers and 800 container chassis and spare parts. Each ship cost approximately $60 million (FY1982 dollars) to convert to RO/RO vehicle cargo ships for use by the Military Sealift Command's (MSC) Rapid Deployment Force (RDF). NASSCO of San Diego, California, converted three, as did Avondale of Westwego, Louisiana. Penn Ship of Chester, Pennsylvania, handled the other two.

These ships are maintained at East Coast and Gulf Coast layberths, ready for rapid loading of Army or Marine equipment and sailing to crisis/war areas.

COMBAT EXPERIENCE • All eight ships left US ports in August 1990 to support Operation Desert Shield. *Antares* broke down in the Atlantic and had to be towed to Spain. Seven arrived in Saudi Arabia, taking an average of two weeks for the 8,800-nm voyage.

Altogether the seven ships made 32 "lifts" to the region by the end of April 1991, delivering 321,940 short tons of dry cargo. The value of their great size and speed is best seen in a comparison with the smaller, slower ships of the Ready Reserve Force, which averaged less than two trips per vessel and carried 45% less cargo per lift.

In December 1992, *Altair, Bellatrix, Capella, Denebola,* and *Pollux* were activated to support the movement of supplies to Somalia as part of the Restore Hope humanitarian relief operation.

SPECIFICATIONS •
DISPLACEMENT   55,350 tons full load (22,279–25,915 tons deadweight)
DIMENSIONS
  length   946 ft 6 in (288.5 m) overall
  beam   105 ft 8 in (32.2 m)
  draft   36 ft 9 in (11.2 m)
MACHINERY   2 Foster Wheeler boilers, 2 General Electric steam turbines, 120,000 shp on 2 shafts=33 kts, range 14,000 nm at 33 kts (unloaded), 12,200 nm at 27 kts (loaded), electric power 8,000 kW
CREW   45 civilian + 56 troops
HELICOPTERS   flight deck
SENSOR   navigation radar

2nd Lt. John P. Bobo

These five ships are part of the Maritime Prepositioning Squadron (MPS) force. Three MPSs are stationed in areas well away from the United States where support of US intervention may be required quickly. Each ship carries about a quarter of the equipment and supplies needed to support a 15,000-Marine force (known in 1990 as a Marine Expeditionary Brigade) in a forward area for 30 days. Four of the *Bobo* class form MPS 3, based in Guam, while the name ship is grouped with three *Kocak*-class ships in MPS 1 in the eastern Atlantic. Although built specifi-

cally for the MPS role, the *Bobos* are owned by private interests and are under 25-year-term charter to American Overseas Marine. They are the only class built expressly for MPS service.

These ships have an immense storage capacity: 150,000 ft² (13,935 m²) of vehicle deck; storage space for 522 standard 20-ft (6.1-m) and 41 refrigerated containers; almost 300,000 ft³ (8,495 m³) of dry storage capacity for ammunition, general cargo, standard military rations, and refrigerated storage, and over 1.5 million gallons of liquid storage.

All cargo can be unloaded onto a pier in three days; from a four-point mooring, discharge takes five days. On deck are four powered causeways, six unpowered causeways, two LCM-8 landing craft, one side-loading warping tug, and three hose reels. A Navire stern ramp is fitted for unloading vehicles into landing craft and onto piers. Five 40-ton capacity cranes are fitted ahead of the bridge on three pedestals (one single boom, two double booms). A 1,000-horsepower bow thruster is fitted to permit maneuvering alongside a pier without the aid of tugs.

Crisis Action Modules (CAM) and Deterrence Force Modules (DFM) are alternative loading packages, developed beginning in 1989, that can be loaded and unloaded quickly to tailor an individual ship or a partial squadron for different requirements ranging from a contingency Marine air ground task force to a full 15,000-man force. The *Lummus* was fitted with a CAM after her initial deployment to Saudi Arabia during Operation Desert Shield.

All MPS ships have berths for a Marine "surge team"—known as the Off-Load Preparation Party (OPP)—that prepares vehicles and other materiel for unloading while the ships move from their bases to the disembarkation port.

DEVELOPMENT • *Bobo* and *Williams* were ordered in August 1982, the others in January 1983. All were built at General

Dynamics' Quincy, Massachusetts, yard and delivered in 1985–86. They are also known as the Braintree class, connoting the shipyard's actual location in Massachusetts.

COMBAT EXPERIENCE • These ships supported the Marine Corps buildup ashore as part of Operation Desert Shield. MPS 3 off-loading in Saudi Arabia was complete by September 4, 1990. MPS 1, which included *Bobo*, arrived in December and finished off-loading in four days.

Once the MPS deployment was complete, *Button* and *Williams* were retained as sea-based logistics ships that provided environmentally controlled storage space, *Lopez* was put in service in "common user status," and *Lummus* was "reconstituted" with a CAM prepositioning loadout sufficient to support a Special-Operations-Capable Marine Expeditionary Unit/MEU(SOC) or an air contingency battalion. *Bobo* provided Assault Follow-On Echelon (AFOE) support to the 5th Marine Expeditionary Brigade (MEB). All MPS ships were restored to peacetime condition by November 1991.

Lummus was also used to support relief efforts in Bangladesh after a May 1991 typhoon and in the Philippines in June after the eruption of Mount Pinatubo. *Lummus* also landed equipment for the Marine force that deployed to Somalia in December 1992.

SPECIFICATIONS •
DISPLACEMENT   40,846 tons full load (26,523 tons deadweight)
DIMENSIONS
length   671 ft 2 in (204.6 m) overall
beam   105 ft 6 in (32.2 m)
draft   29 ft 6 in (9.0 m)
MACHINERY   2 Stork Werkspoor 18TM410V diesels, 26,040 bhp on 1 shaft=18 kts, range 12,840 nm at 18 kts, electric power 7,850 kW
CREW   30 civilian + 25 maintenance personnel (flagship also has 7 Navy-civilian and 8 Navy communications personnel)
HELICOPTERS   landing area
SENSORS   2 navigation radars

Cpl. Louis J. Hauge, Jr.

These five ships are former Maersk Line combination container and Roll-On/Roll-Off (RO/RO) vehicle cargo ships that were acquired by the US government specifically for conversion to the Maritime Prepositioning Squadron (MPS) role. Each ship transports one-fifth of the equipment and supplies needed to support a Marine Expeditionary Brigade (MEB).

During conversion, a new 157 ½-ft (48-m) midsection was added to each ship. The result was 120,080 ft^2 (11,156 m^2) of vehicle storage space and three vehicle parking decks. Each ship can carry up to 413 standard 20-ft (6.1-m) freight containers subdivided into 280 ammunition, 86 general cargo, 23 fuel-drum, and 24 refrigerated containers. Nearly 1.3 million US gal (mostly bulk fuels) is carried, and dry cargo capacity is 524,000 ft^3 (14,838 m^3). The Navire slewing ramp, two 36-ton and four 30-ton cranes serving eight hatches provide a limited self-unloading capability.

(For more information about the MPS program, see the *2nd Lt John P. Bobo* class.)

DEVELOPMENT • The first three ships were ordered in August 1982, the latter two in January 1983. The *Hauge, Anderson,* and *Phillips* were converted at the Bethlehem Steel yard at Sparrows Point, Maryland; the *Baugh* and *Bonnyman* at the Bethlehem Steel yard in Beaumont, Texas. They are owned by private interests and operated by the Maersk Line. The five ships form MPS 2, based in Diego Garcia in the Indian Ocean.

COMBAT EXPERIENCE • Two and a half weeks after Iraq invaded Kuwait in August 1990, *Hauge, Anderson,* and *Bonnyman* were unloading equipment in Saudi Arabia as part of Operation Desert Shield. (The other two ships were undergoing MPS Maintenance Cycle/MMC refits in the United States.) The Off-Load Preparation Parties (OPP) were credited with having the equipment at a 99.9% readiness rate when it was disembarked. The *Fisher* (later renamed *Franklin S. Phillips*) arrived on August 24 and the *Baugh* on September 7. Altogether, the nine ships of MPS 2 and MPS 3 (see the *Bobo* class) delivered equipment and stores to support 33,000 Marines in combat for 30 days.

SPECIFICATIONS •

DISPLACEMENT   46,552 tons full load (20,718–23,138) tons deadweight)

DIMENSIONS

length	755 ft 6 in (230.3 m) overall
beam	90 ft 1 in (27.5 m)
draft	32 ft 1 in (9.8 m)

MACHINERY   1 Sulzer 7RND 76M diesel, 16,800 bhp on 1 shaft=17.5 kts, range 10,800 nm at 17.5 kts, electric power 4,250 kW

CREW   30 civilian + 20 civilian maintenance personnel (7 Navy-civilian + 8 Navy communications in *Bonnyman*)

HELICOPTERS   landing area

SENSORS   2 navigation radars

Sgt. Matej Kocak

These three ships were acquired for conversion to MPS ships soon after their completion for the Waterman Lines; they never entered commercial service. They are civilian-crewed and -operated under contract by Waterman Steamship Co. (For more on the MPS program, see *2nd Lt. John P. Bobo* class.)

As part of their conversion, a 126-ft

(38.4-m) midbody section was added primarily for hospital and troop spaces. Each ship carries one-fourth of the equipment and supplies needed to support a 15,000-Marine landing force.

The ships were reconfigured for 152,524 ft² (14,170 m²) of vehicle cargo space, 682,000 ft³ (19,312 m³) of dry cargo storage space, and 540 standard cargo containers, and they carry more than 1.6 million US gal of liquids, mostly bulk fuels.

To aid unloading, the ships are fitted with vehicle ramps including a jackknife-style stern ramp. Ahead of the bridge are back-to-back 30-ton cranes on the after pedestal, back-to-back 50-ton cranes farther forward, and a full-beam traveling gantry for hoisting containers; the gantry has a 30-ton capacity.

DEVELOPMENT • All three ships were converted to the MPS role by the National Steel and Shipbuilding Co. (NASSCO) in San Diego, California. The contract for the first two was awarded on August 17, 1982; conversion of the *Charles Carroll* (renamed *Major Stephen W. Pless*) was ordered on January 14, 1983.

This class and the *Bobo* form the MPS 1 based in Norfolk, Virginia. All 13 MPS ships are named for US Marine Corps Medal of Honor winners.

COMBAT EXPERIENCE • All three *Kocak*-class ships and the *Bobo* arrived in Saudi Arabia on December 13, 1990. The *Pless* and *Kocak* were then reassigned to "common user status" for the US Transportation Command, while the *Obregon* joined the *Bobo* as on-station repositories of Assault Follow-On Echelon (AFOE) equipment to support the 5th Marine Expeditionary Brigade (MEB).

SPECIFICATIONS •

DISPLACEMENT   48,754 tons full load (21,189–23,653 tons deadweight)

DIMENSIONS

length	821 ft (250.3 m) overall

beam   105 ft 6 in 32.2 m)
draft   32 ft 4 in (9.9 m)
MACHINERY   2 boilers, 2 General Electric steam turbines, 30,000 shp on 1 shaft=20 kts, range 13,000 nm at 20 kts

CREW   39 civilian + 25 civilian maintenance personnel (plus 7 Navy-civilian + 8 Navy communications in 1 ship)
HELICOPTERS   landing area
SENSORS   2 navigation radars

SMALL COMBATANTS

Cyclone (PC 1)

These 13 fast patrol craft are the first of their kind to be built for the US Navy since the Vietnam War and are among the largest ever procured for that service. They are based on the British-built Egyptian Navy *Ramadan*-class missile boats, but are gun-armed craft intended to patrol US coastlines as well as covertly deploying US Navy Sea-Air-Land (SEAL) teams.

The stern is cut away to form a boat-landing dock for Rigid Inflatable Boats (RIB). Below decks are four Paxman Valenta diesels, each driving a fixed-pitch propeller through Reintjes reverse-reduction gearboxes; the gearboxes have a trolling valve for slow speeds and loiter.

A RIM-92 Stinger short-range surface-to-air missile system is mounted in a Stabilized Weapons Platform System (SWPS) on the fantail. Additional weapons include two Mk 88 mounts bearing Mk 38 Sea Snake 25-mm Chain Guns, two Mk 19 40-mm grenade machine guns, and two 12.7-mm and two 7.62-mm machine guns.

DEVELOPMENT • The Patrol Boat Coastal (PBC) program was funded in FY1989 at the insistence of Congress as a considerably larger successor to the failed Sea Viking program. Delays in the selection of engine and hull builders postponed the first lay-down to June 22, 1991. Bollinger Machine Shop and Shipyard of Lockport, Louisiana, built 13 PBCs (16 were originally planned).

SPECIFICATIONS •
DISPLACEMENT   315 tons full load
DIMENSIONS
length   170 ft 7 in (52.0 m)
beam   25 ft (7.6 m)
MACHINERY   4 Paxman Valenta diesels, 13,400 bhp on 4 shafts=35 kts, range 2,000 nm at 12 kts, endurance 10 days
CREW   28 + 9 SEALs
WEAPONS
  2 Stinger SAM in twin mount
  2 25-mm Mk 88 Sea Snake cannon in single mounts
  2 40-mm Mk 19 grenade machine guns in single mounts
  2 12.7-mm machine guns in single mounts
  2 7.62-mm machine guns in single mounts
SENSORS
  RASCAR surface-search radar
  Wesmar side-scanning sonar

Pegasus (PHM 1)

These six high-speed, heavily armed hydrofoil missile craft were originally built to trail and attack hostile warships in "chokepoints" or other restricted areas; they were to have been based in the Mediterranean. They saw their most extensive service, however, as part of the US drug interdiction effort in the Caribbean.

These are speedy and highly maneuverable craft, capable of more than 50 knots and able to turn more than 8°/sec. All foils are fully submerged foils (as opposed to surface-piercing). A broad delta bow foil providing one-third the total lift is carried on a single strut on the centerline; this strut swings 90° forward for hullborne operations. The rectangular foil is carried by two struts, one on each stern quarter; these pivot back 90°. Trim tabs on the foils aid lift.

Propulsion comes from three water jets driven by a Combined Diesel or Gas (CODOG) set of two diesels and one gas turbine. The gas turbine uses reduction gears to drive a single water jet pumping up to 141,000 US gal (533,685 liters) of water per minute. Off-foil, the diesels each drive 30,000-gal/min (113,550 liter/min) water jets. A through-bow thruster is provided for low-speed maneuvering.

Harpoon antiship missiles provide the main punch; up to eight can be carried. Main gun armament is a 76-mm gun mount forward. No antisubmarine warfare capability and no secondary gun battery are provided. The PHM design provides for two 20-mm Mk 20 single gun mounts to be fitted abaft the mast.

DEVELOPMENT • Originally ordered in the early 1970s, these craft were to be a part of a trinational (US, Italy, and West Germany) program; the US was to supply five six-craft squadrons. Cost growth, delays, and a high degree of skepticism about their mission soon drove the other navies out. After a change of administrations, the *Hercules* and following craft were canceled in April 1977. Congress insisted on their being built and they entered service in 1981–83 after their construction by Boeing Marine of Seattle, Washington.

All six craft were based at Key West, Florida, in PHM Squadron 2. Fleet reductions that began in the early 1990s led to decommissioning all the PHMs on July 30, 1993.

SPECIFICATIONS •
DISPLACEMENT   265 tons full load
DIMENSIONS
length   147 ft 4 in (44.9 m) overall (foils retracted), 131 ft 7 in (40.1 m) overall (foils extended)
beam   28 ft 2 in (8.6 m)
draft   6 ft 4 in (1.9 m) (foils retracted), 23 ft 3 in (7.1 m) (foils extended)
MACHINERY   CODOG (1 General Electric LM 2500 gas turbine, 16,767 shp and 2 MTU 8V331 diesels, 1,630 bhp), 2 water jets hullborne=12 kts, 1 waterjet foilborne=50 kts, range 1,225 nm at 11 kts hullborne, 600+ nm at 40+ kts foilborne
CREW   25
WEAPONS
   8 Harpoon antiship missiles in 2 quad canisters
   1 3-in (76-mm)/62-cal Mk 75 AA gun
SENSORS
   SPS-63 surface-search radar
   Mk 92 gunfire control system
   SLR-20 EW system

ATTACK SUBMARINES

Los Angeles (SSN 688)

The 62 boats in this class represent the largest class of nuclear-powered submarines to have been built to a single basic design. Initially developed in the late 1960s to counter the Soviet *Victor*-class fast attack submarines, production carried on far longer than originally expected, setting a construction duration record for submarines of any type.

As built, the *Los Angeles* class subs were about five knots faster than the earlier US *Sturgeon* (SSN 637) class. Like all US submarines, the *LA* is a single-hulled design, which is quieter than a comparable double-hull boat, but also more vulnerable to ASW weapons. The speed advantage was later diminished by upgrades in weaponry, sonars, and survivability. Those upgrades have also eliminated a 250-ton reserve designed into the class. The *LA*s were significantly quieter than Soviet submarines until improved Soviet design (and propeller-milling machinery from Norway and Japan) helped to narrow the gap in the mid-1980s.

One of the most apparent changes is the 12-tube Tomahawk Vertical Launch System (VLS) in the bow introduced in *Providence* (SSN 719). The troubled BSY-1 advanced sonar and fire control system was potentially so great an advance that boats so equipped—*San Juan* (SSN 751) and later—are described as a subclass—Improved 688 or ISSN 688. Other ISSN 688 features include modifications to permit minelaying and an under-ice capability with retractable bow planes. (Virtually all other US submarines had diving planes on the sail.)

In addition to the large BQQ-5 series bow sonar, a large towed-array passive sonar is carried in a sheathlike housing fitted to the upper starboard side of the hull. Later boats have the BSY-1 sonar system.

DEVELOPMENT • As with most US shipbuilding programs begun in the late 1960s, the *Los Angeles* class had a rocky start with cost overruns, material price inflation, and rancorous fault-finding between the Navy and the builders. Newport News Shipbuilding was lead yard and was awarded 29 boats. General Dynamics' Electric Boats contracted for 32 submarines. The *Los Angeles* was commissioned in November 1976.

Problems with integrating the BSY-1 system were so nearly intractable that average building times stretched out considerably. Incorrect engineering drawings, delays by the sonar's contractor, and Navy changes were blamed. The last boat—*Greeneville* (SSN 773)—will complete in late 1996.

Los Angeles Submarine
U.S. GOVERNMENT DEPARTMENT OF DEFENSE

Meanwhile, defense cutbacks caused the Navy to begin retiring *Los Angeles* class submarines early. The *Baton Rouge,* due for an expensive refueling, was "inactivated" instead in September 1993, 16 years after her commissioning.

COMBAT EXPERIENCE • In November 1986, as the *Augusta* operated submerged (playing "cat and mouse") in the Atlantic in October 1986, she collided with an apparently undetected Soviet attack submarine while evading another. Both submarines survived the collision with no personnel losses. The *Augusta* returned to Groton, Connecticut, where her damage (external ballast tank and bow sonar cap) cost about $2.7 million to repair. Other such collisions may have contributed to the loss of one or more Soviet submarines.

The first known operational use of submarine-launched Tomahawks was the launch by *Louisville* (SSN 720) during Operation Desert Storm; approximately 12 were fired by submarines. The *Pittsburgh* was later revealed to have launched Tomahawks from the Mediterranean. The *Philadelphia, Chicago,* and *Newport News* were also reported by the Navy as having supported Desert Shield. Altogether 13 submarines, most or all of them *Los Angeles*-class ships, were reported to have been deployed to the region.

The *Topeka* was the first US submarine to enter the Persian Gulf, visiting Saudi Arabia in January 1993 in response to the delivery of the first Russian-built *Kilo*-class attack submarine to Iran.

SPECIFICATIONS •
DISPLACEMENT   6,080 tons standard, 6,927 tons submerged
DIMENSIONS
  length   360 ft (109.7 m) overall
  beam   33 ft (10.1 m)
  draft   32 ft (9.8 m)
MACHINERY   1 General Electric S6G pressurized-water nuclear reactor, 2 steam turbines, approx 30,000 shp on 1 shaft=30+ kts submerged

CREW   133
WEAPONS
  4 21-in (533-mm) Mk 67 torpedo tubes amidships for Mk 48 torpedoes (total stowage 26 torpedoes/missiles)
  Harpoon anti-ship and Tomahawk land-attack launched from torpedo tubes
  12 vertical launch tubes for Tomahawk in SSN 719 and later submarines
SENSORS
  BPS-15A surface-search radar
  BQQ-5A/B/C/D multifunction bow-mounted low-frequency sonar (being upgraded to BQQ-5E)
  BSY-1 multifunction sonar in SSN 751 and later submarines
  TB-16 or TB-23 towed-array sonar
  BQS-15 under-ice/mine–detection high-frequency sonar
  Mine and Ice Detection System (MIDAS) in SSN 751 and later submarines
  BRD-7 direction finder
  WLR-8(V) radar-warning receiver
  WLR-9 sonar receiver
  WLR-12 ESM receiver

Seawolf (SSN 21)

This attack submarine design was intended to succeed the *Los Angeles* (SSN 688) class. Reflecting increased concern over the quieter Soviet submarines, the emphasis in this class lay on improved machinery, quieting (especially in machine isolation from the hull), and improved combat systems, both sensors and additional weapons.

The result was a large, plump boat with a relatively low length-to-beam ratio that was the largest attack submarine to be built outside of the Soviet Union. Despite its size, the most powerful US submarine nuclear reactor propels the submarine at a maximum speed slightly faster than the *Los Angeles* (SSN 688) class (making it the fastest US submarine design).

One Navy design goal was a high maximum "acoustic speed" of more than 20 knots (i.e., the speed at which the submarine can transit while maintaining a sufficiently low noise level to employ passive sonar; 1980s-era Soviet submarines had a maximum acoustic speed of six to eight knots). The pump jet propulsors, designed in Great Britain, are the same as those used in the very quiet British *Trafalgar*-class SSNs.

Bow-mounted diving planes retract into the bow for under-ice operations. The forward edge of the sail-hull joint is covered by a "cusp," or fairing, that is similar in appearance to the dorsal fillet on an airplane. It distributes the stresses imposed by surfacing through the ice.

Installation of *Seawolf*'s BSY-2 sonar/ fire control system was delayed by a variety of technical and programmatic problems. In addition, construction delays and early problems with the propulsor played their parts in raising the cost to over $1 billion per boat.

Armament has more torpedo tubes and internally stowed weapons than in existing subs, but no external Tomahawk Vertical Launch System (VLS) tubes like those in the later units of the *Los Angeles* class. 30-in (762-mm) diameter tubes allow a quiet, "swim-out" torpedo launch.

The *Seawolf*'s place as the core of the 21st-century Navy's nuclear-powered attack submarine force eroded during continuing, at times acrimonious, debate over its design and increasing resistance to its cost. Further weakening the case was the collapse of the Soviet Union and the apparent diminution of the successors' submarine fleet.

Critics strongly disagreed with the emphasis on size and weapons load, arguing that the cost per boat would make it impossible to respond to the high building rates established for Soviet *Akula* and *Sierra* nuclear attack boats as well as the very competent *Kilo*-class diesel-electric design.

DEVELOPMENT • Despite the debate over its size and cost, *Seawolf* began con-

struction at Electric Boat in Groton, Connecticut, in 1990. Delivery fell behind by more than a year when inspectors discovered cracks in many of the *Seawolf*'s hull welds; all welds had to be inspected and many redone.

Attempts by Newport News Shipbuilding to share construction were frustrated by a sharply declining building rate. By the mid-1990s, the program had been scaled down from a 30-boat force to fewer than five (probably no more than three), and studies had already begun of a smaller, less expensive design known as the Centurion.

Seawolf, which had been canceled by the Bush administration in FY1992, was revived in the election year of 1992, primarily as an industrial-base preservation program. Naming the SSN 22 *Connecticut* honored the sub's home state even as it ignored a recent policy directive that reestablished the names of fish as proper for submarines.

SPECIFICATIONS •

DISPLACEMENT   9,150 tons submerged
DIMENSIONS
  length   350 ft (106.7 m) overall
  beam   40 ft (12.2 m)
  draft   35 ft 11 in (10.9 m)
MACHINERY   1 pressurized-water nuclear reactor, 2 steam turbines, approx 60,000 shp on 1 propulsor = 35 kts submerged, diving depth over 1,500 ft (460 m)
CREW   approx 130
WEAPONS
  8 30-in (762-mm) torpedo tubes amidships (50 weapons)
  Harpoon antiship and Tomahawk land-attack missiles launched from torpedo tubes
  Mk 48 torpedoes
SENSORS
  surface-search radar
  BSY-2 suite with bow-mounted transducers, wide-aperture array, and towed-array sonar
  TB-16 towed-array sonar
  TB-23 towed-array sonar
  WLQ-4(V)1 passive EW system

Sturgeon (SSN 637)

These 37 submarines are improved versions of the *Permit* (SSN 594) class, with a taller sail structure, an improved electronics suite, under-ice operational capability, and low-mounted sail planes for better depth-keeping when near the surface. They are slower than the *Permits* because the same propulsion machinery drives a bigger, heavier hull. This is accentuated in the last nine boats, which are 10 ft (3 m) longer than the others.

Interest in Arctic Ocean operations is reflected by the attention given to operating under the ice. Both the sail and rudder were reinforced, the sail planes can be rotated 90° to slice upward, and upward- and forward-looking navigational sonars allow safer operations between the seafloor and the jumbled blocks of ice.

Many, if not all, of these submarines have an acoustic device known as GNAT fitted just forward of the upper rudder fin.

Many *Sturgeons* have been modified for a variety of purposes. Some have been modified to carry the the Deep Submergence Rescue Vehicle (DSRV). Others, including the *Cavalla,* were altered to support covert swimmer-delivery concepts and equipment such as a removable Dry Deck Shelter (DDS) hangar that permits loading and deployment of a group of free-swimming divers or a Swimmer Delivery Vehicle (SDV) while fully or partially submerged.

DEVELOPMENT • The *Sturgeon* was ordered in November 1961 and delivered in March 1967; the last in the class was completed by Newport News Shipbuilding in August 1975. Sharing the yards with the higher-priority *Lafayette*-class ballistic missile boats slowed the pace. Electric Boat in Groton, Connecticut, built 13 altogether. Other yards included Newport News (10), General Dynamics' Bethlehem yard at Quincy, Massachusetts (two), Litton's Ingalls yard at Pascagoula, Mississippi (five plus one begun by New York Shipbuilding), Mare Island Navy Yard (five), and Portsmouth Navy Yard (two).

COMBAT EXPERIENCE • The *Whale* became the first of the class to operate under the Arctic ice pack for more than a brief period. In late 1989 and early 1990, the *Silversides* (SSN 679) became the first ship since the *Nautilus* (SSN 571) to circumnavigate the North American continent. The trip took 89 days and included surfacing at the North Pole.

Several *Sturgeon*-class submarines were reported to have supported US naval forces during Operations Desert Shield and Desert Storm in 1990–91. In March 1993, the *Grayling* collided with a CIS (Commonwealth of Independent States) Navy Delta III-class ballistic missile submarine in the Barents Sea. Although such meetings are thought to have occurred often, very few were publicized before the collapse of the Soviet Union.

The *Queenfish* was the first of the class to be decommissioned (October 1990), followed by nine more by the end of FY1994.

SPECIFICATIONS •

DISPLACEMENT   4,250 tons standard except SSN 678–687 4,460 tons; 4,780 tons submerged except SSN 678–687 4,960 tons

DIMENSIONS
length   292 ft 0 in (89.0 m) overall (except SSN 678–687 302 ft (92.1 m))
beam   31 ft 8 in (9.7 m)
draft   28 ft 10 in (8.8 m)

MACHINERY   1 Westinghouse S5W pressurized-water nuclear reactor, 2 De Laval or General Electric steam turbines, 15,000 shp on 1 shaft, approx 15 kts surface, approx 30 kts submerged

CREW   129

WEAPONS
4 21-in (533-mm) Mk 63 torpedo tubes amidships
Mk 48 wire-guided torpedoes

Harpoon antiship and Tomahawk land-attack missiles launched from torpedo tubes

SENSORS
BPS-14/15 surface-search radar
BQQ-5 multifunction bow-mounted sonar

BQS-14 mine-avoidance/under-ice sonar
TB-16 or TB-23 towed-array sonar
WLR-9 sonar receiver

STRATEGIC SUBMARINES

Lafayette (SSBN 616)

These 31 submarines were the definitive production launch platforms for the Polaris Submarine-Launched Ballistic Missile (SLBM) design. The program is nearly unique in its success in getting so many complex ships in service in so short a time.

These submarines are enlarged and improved versions of the previous *Ethan Allen* (SSBN 608) class. Their main armament upon completion was the Polaris A-2 and A-3 SLBMs. From 1970 to 1978, all 31 boats were converted to fire the Poseidon C3, which was fitted with Multiple Independently Targetable Reentry Vehicles (MIRV). *James Madison* (SSBN 627) deployed on the first Poseidon patrol in March 1971. In a second upgrade, 12 submarines were upgraded to fire the longer-range Trident C-4 missile from 1979 to 1982. *Francis Scott Key* (SSBN 657) was the first to deploy Tridents in October 1979, the *George Bancroft* (SSBN 643) the last of the 12 in June 1989.

As in the *Ethan Allen* class, the pressure hulls are constructed of HY-80 steel. The *Lafayette*-class operating depth is probably deeper than that of the later *Ohio* (SSBN 726) class. The last 12 submarines of this class had quieter machinery installations and other minor differences and were officially designated as the *Benjamin Franklin* class. (The *Daniel Webster*/SSBN 626 had bow-mounted diving planes instead of sail planes as in all other US SSBNs; she was retrofitted with sail planes before her decommissioning.)

Lafayettes navigated through two Mk 2 Mod 6 Ship's Inertial Navigation Systems (SINS), which were augmented by an Electrostatically Supported Gyro Monitor (ESGM) fitted first to the Trident boats and later to the 19 Poseidon craft.

DEVELOPMENT • An indication of the urgency with which they were procured is the furious building rate, with the first being ordered in July 1960 (completion in April 1963) and the 31st finishing up less than seven years later, in April 1967. Four shipyards participated in the program: General Dynamics' Electric Boat in Groton, Connecticut (13 boats), Newport News Shipbuilding (10), Mare Island Navy Yard (six), and Portsmouth Navy Yard (two).

Designed originally for a 20-year service life, most of the class was retired well before their 30th birthday.

The *Mariano Vallejo* (SSBN 658) was credited with completing the 2,500th SSBN patrol on April 4, 1987. Decommissioning of this class began in 1986 with the *Nathan Hale* (SSBN 623) and *Nathanael Greene* (SSBN 626). The last went into mothballs in 1994.

SPECIFICATIONS •
DISPLACEMENT   surfaced 7,310–7,350 tons; submerged 8,260 tons (SSBN 616–626), 8,240 tons (627–639), 8,250 tons (640–659)

DIMENSIONS
length   425 ft (129.6 m) overall
beam   33 ft (10.1 m)
draft   31 ft 6 in (9.6 m)
MACHINERY   1 Westinghouse S5W
pressurized-water reactor, 2 steam tur-
bines, 15,000 shp on 1 shaft=20 kts
(surfaced), 25 kts (submerged)
CREW   140-146
WEAPONS
16 tubes for Poseidon C-3/Trident
C-4 SLBM
4 21-in (533-mm) Mk 65 bow torpedo
tubes with Mk 48 torpedoes
SENSORS
BPS-11/11A or BPS-15 surface-search
radar
BQR-7 passive sonar
BQR-15 towed-array sonar
BQR-19 navigation sonar
BQR-21 passive array sonar
BQS-4 active/passive detection sonar
WLR-8 passive intercept EW system

Ohio (SSBN 726)

These 18 launch platforms for Trident
Submarine-Launched Ballistic Missiles
(SLBM) are the largest submarines built
in the United States, although the Soviet
Typhoon SSBNs are almost half again as
large. The *Ohio*s have four more missile
launch tubes than the *Typhoon*s, but, unlike the Russian boats, are of an evolu-
tionary, rather than radically new, design.
For example, they retain the bow sonar
dome and amidships torpedo tubes of
later attack submarines (SSN).

The first eight *Ohio*s are armed with the
Trident C-4 missile, which was also deployed on 12 *Lafayette*-class SSBNs. The
Tennessee (SSBN 734) and later boats have
the Trident D-5 missile, which was to be
fitted into the earlier craft during subsequent overhauls. Those refits were canceled due to the decline in the nuclear
deterrent posture as well as the cessation
of the D-5's W88 warhead production because of safety problems at the Rocky
Flats plant. In fact, only 400 W88 war-

heads were completed, not enough to
outfit all D-5s being built.

The first eight boats have two Mk 2
Mod 7 Ship's Inertial Navigation Systems
(SINS) with the Electrostatically Supported Gyro Monitor (ESGM). Beginning with the *Tennessee,* the heart of the
navigation system is the Electrostatically
Supported Gyro Navigator (ESGN). The
Navigation Sonar System (NSS), also fitted to these boats, has a better ability to
measure velocity than earlier systems.

Reportedly, the *Ohio* is significantly quieter than the ship's design goals for self-
quieting. At low speeds, when using natural convection rather than pumps for the
circulation of pressurized water in the
primary loop, the *Ohio* may be the qui-
etest nuclear submarine yet constructed.
As the nuclear threat waned, this attri-
bute, and the class's relative youth, led to
a suggestion that some of the earlier
boats be retired or rearmed as Tomahawk
cruise missile carriers.

DEVELOPMENT • A force of 20 *Ohio*-
class Trident submarines was originally
planned. Because of budget cuts and the
uncertainty of SSBN force requirements
in light of ongoing arms control talks, the
number of submarines was cut to 18. The
Ohio was ordered in January 1974 but
wasn't commissioned until April 1981 because of design changes, program mis-
management, and problems at the
Electric Boat shipyard in Groton, Connecticut. A late-1980s Navy attempt to
force competition between Electric Boat
and Newport News Shipbuilding failed
when EB's edge as lead yard proved too
great to overcome.

The first squadron of *Ohio*s (Submarine Squadron 17) operates in the Pacific, based at Bangor, Washington, and
established on January 5, 1981. The second *Ohio*-class submarine squadron was
formed in the Atlantic, based at Kings
Bay, Georgia; the *Tennessee* (SSBN 734)
was the first submarine to be assigned
there. These submarines conduct 70-day

patrols interrupted by 25-day overhaul/ replenishment periods, during which time the blue/gold crews change over. Under this schedule the submarines undergo a lengthy overhaul and reactor refueling every 10 years.

SPECIFICATIONS •

DISPLACEMENT 16,764 tons standard, 18,750 tons submerged

DIMENSIONS
  length 560 ft (170.7 m) overall
  beam 42 ft (12.8 m)
  draft 36 ft 5 in (11.1 m)

MACHINERY 1 General Electric S8G pressurized-water reactor, 2 General Electric steam turbines, 60,000 shp on 1 shaft=18 kts surface, 30 kts submerged

CREW 155

WEAPONS
  24 tubes for Trident C-4 SLBM in SSBN 726–733
  24 tubes for Trident D-5 SLBM in later units
  4 21-in (533-mm) Mk 68 torpedo tubes amidships for Mk 48 torpedoes

SENSORS
  BPS-15A surface-search radar (being replaced by Sperry BPS-16)
  BQQ-6 bow-mounted sonar
  BQR-19 navigation sonar
  BQS-13 active detection sonar
  BQS-15 under-ice sonar
  TB-16 or TB-29 towed-array sonar
  WLR-8 (V)5 radar-warning system

UNDERWAY-REPLENISHMENT SHIPS

Cimarron (AO 177)

These five fleet oilers are designed to provide two complete refuelings to a conventional aircraft carrier and six to eight accompanying escort ships. As completed, they proved too small and were stretched 108 ft (32.9 m) to increase petroleum product capacity by 50%. After their "jumboizing," the *Cimarrons* carry 183,000 barrels of petroleum products—F76 (DFM) marine fuel and F44 (JP-5) gas turbine fuel. Five Standard Tensioned Replenishment Alongside Method (STREAM) fuel delivery rigs are arranged in pairs at the forecastle break and near the superstructure face; a third portside STREAM rig was added during the jumboization. The stretched *Cimarrons* can transfer up to 9,000 US gal/min (34,065 liters/min) of JP-5 and 15,000 US gal/min (56,775 liters/min) of DFM.

Original Navy manning was to be approximately 135; it was increased to provide improved maintenance self-sufficiency for prolonged deployments.

Avondale also fitted AN/SLQ-32(V)1 and AN/SLQ-32 Nixie Electronic Warfare (EW) systems in the ships during the jumboizing.

DEVELOPMENT • These ships were built by Avondale Shipyards of Westwego, Louisiana, from 1978 to 1983. In 1988, the same yard began stretching the five-ship class, delivering the last one (*Platte*) in December 1992.

COMBAT EXPERIENCE • *Cimarron* operated with the *Independence*'s (CV 62) battle group (AO 177) from the beginning of Operation Desert Shield until November 1990, when the battle group was relieved by that of the *Midway* (CV 41). *Platte* supported the *Theodore Roosevelt*'s (CVN 71) battle group from January to April 1991.

SPECIFICATIONS •

DISPLACEMENT　37,866 tons full load

DIMENSIONS

　length　　708 ft 6 in (215.95 m)
　beam　　88 ft (26.8 m)
　draft　　33 ft 6 in (10.2 m)

MACHINERY　2 Combustion Engineering boilers, 1 steam turbine, 24,000 shp on 1 shaft=19.4 kts, electric power 8,250 kW

CREW　212

HELICOPTERS　landing platform

WEAPONS

　2 20-mm Mk 15 Phalanx Gatling-type CIWS in AO 178–180, 186

SENSORS

　SPS-10B or SPS-55 surface-search radar
　1 navigation radar
　SLQ-32(V)1 passive EW system
　SLQ-25 torpedo decoy

Henry J. Kaiser (T-AO 187)

These fleet oilers are based on the earlier *Cimarron* (AO 177) design but are being built to civilian specifications and are intended for civilian (Maritime Sealift Command/MSC) manning. Compared to the *Cimarron*s, the *Kaiser*s are longer and beamier and are propelled by diesels instead of a single steam turbine. In addition, *Kaiser*-class ships have outside single staterooms for all permanent crew members; the crew also have a gymnasium, hobby shop, and library.

These are midsize petroleum carriers with a 180,000-barrel cargo capacity, divided between F76 marine distillate (DFM) and F44 jet fuel (JP-5). A 60% DFM/40% JP-5 load proportion is typical, but tankage can be converted to a maximum of 70% DFM or a maximum of 52% jet fuel. These ships have five Standard Tensioned Replenishment Alongside Method (STREAM) fuel delivery rigs with a delivery capacity of 9,000 US gal/min (34,065 liters/min) of JP-5 and 15,000 US gal/min (56,775 liters/min) of DFM.

Water tankage includes 88,000 US gal (333,080 liters) of feed water and 105,000 US gal (397,425 liters) of potable water as well as 25,000 US gal (94,625 liters) of lube oil.

These ships have a limited Underway Replenishment (UNREP) capacity for dry stores as well as fuels, using a pair of Cargo STREAM 10-ton-capacity rigs. As lead ship in the class, the T-AO 187 suffered from several problems that were resolved during shakedown trials. Vibration levels were excessive at higher speeds, and general vibration levels were unsatisfactory as well. Reduction gears and their bearings suffered from alignment problems and backlash. PTO bearings wore quickly, fuel oil injectors and pumps did not work properly, and several items of underway replenishment equipment were not acceptable.

Space and weight are reserved for the AN/SLQ-25 Nixie torpedo countermeasures, and 20-mm Phalanx Close-In Weapons System (CIWS) mounts could be fitted for wartime service.

DEVELOPMENT • The lead ship was laid down by Avondale on August 29, 1984, and delivered in 1987. Avondale built all but four of the 18 ships in the class. Pennsylvania Shipbuilding had won contracts for the others but proved unable to complete any of them. Avondale finished the *John Ericsson* and *Kanawha*, while Tampa Ship took over construction of the *Benjamin Isherwood* and *Henry Eckford*. In September 1993, however, the Navy canceled its contract with Tampa Ship because of the yard's lack of progress and financial problems, and the ships were left incomplete.

The *Kaiser* and the *Higgins* were ticketed for inactivation in FY1995 as part of the scaling-down of the US fleet.

COMBAT EXPERIENCE • Five *Kaiser*-class oilers supported Operations Desert Shield/Desert Storm. The *Henry J. Kaiser*, *Joshua Humphreys*, and *John Lenthall* refueled ships in the Mediterranean and Red Sea; the *Kaiser* conducted 188 underway refuelings altogether. The *Humphreys* operated in the Desert Shield theater of operations from January 15, 1991, to April 23. The *Andrew J. Higgins* supported the *Independence*'s (CV 62) battle group from September to November 1990 and conducted many other subsequent refuelings. The *Walter S. Diehl* sailed with the *Midway*'s (CV 41) battle group.

SPECIFICATIONS •

DISPLACEMENT   40,700 tons full load (27,761 tons deadweight)
DIMENSIONS
length   677 ft 6 in (206.6 m) overall
beam   97 ft 6 in (29.7 m)
draft   35 ft (10.7 m)
MACHINERY   2 Colt-Pielstick 10P C4.2V diesels, 32,000 bhp on 2 shafts=20 kts, range 6,000 nm at 20 kts, electric power 10,600 kW
CREW   98 civilian + 21 Navy
HELICOPTERS   landing area
SENSORS   2 navigation radars

Kilauea (AE 26)

These high-capability ammunition-resupply ships are especially tailored for underway replenishment. The *Kilauea* design provides for the ship's main cargo spaces forward of the superstructure with a helicopter landing area aft. Six constant-tension replenishment stations stand in a kingpost frame forward, side-by-side rigs farther aft, and staggered rigs near the superstructure. Some stations have been deactivated to permit a reduction in crew.

The after superstructure holds a helicopter hangar for two UH-46 Vertical Replenishment (VERTREP) helicopters. Cargo capacity is approximately 6,500 tons.

As built, the ships had eight 3-in guns

in twin mounts with two Mk 56 gunfire control systems. *Kilauea* lost her guns when she transferred to the Military Sealift Command (MSC). The others saw the armament cut in half; the last four then received two Phalanx Close-In Weapons System (CIWS) mounts each.

DEVELOPMENT • These ships were funded over four fiscal years (1965–68) in groups of two. Bethlehem in Quincy, Massachusetts, built the first two; Bethlehem, Sparrows Point, Maryland, the second pair, and Litton's Ingalls yard in Pascagoula, Mississippi, constructed the last four. They entered service from 1968 to 1972.

Kilauea was transferred to the Military Sealift Command in October 1980. She is officially a United States Naval Ship (USNS) and has a civilian crew.

COMBAT EXPERIENCE • Six of the class were deployed to the Persian Gulf region as part of Operations Desert Shield and Desert Storm. The *Flint* was already in the Indian Ocean with the carrier *Independence*'s (CV 62) battle group when the Iraqi invasion occurred. She entered what was later designated as the Desert Shield/Storm Theater of Operations on August 5, 1990, remaining on station until November 4. After a rapid turnaround on the West Coast, the *Flint* reentered the theater on January 21, 1991, and operated in the area until mid-March.

The *Kiska* operated with the *Midway*'s (CV 41) battle group in the Desert Storm theater from November 2, 1990, to March 14, 1991. The *Shasta* sailed from the West Coast with the *Ranger*'s (CV 61) battle group in December 1990, arriving in the theater on January 13, 1991, not leaving until April 29.

The *Santa Barbara*'s tour with the *Theodore Roosevelt*'s (CVN 71) battle group included service in the Persian Gulf and Mediterranean from mid-January 1991 to the beginning of June.

The *Mount Hood* was not attached to a particular battle group. She arrived in the theater on February 1, 1991, and departed on March 13.

The *Kilauea* operated in a shuttle between the Persian Gulf and the northern Arabian Sea from September 3, 1990, to March 8, 1991.

SPECIFICATIONS •
DISPLACEMENT   19,937 tons full load (8,593 tons deadweight)

DIMENSIONS

length	564 ft (172.0 m) overall
beam	81 ft (24.7 m)
draft	25 ft 9 in (7.8 m)

MACHINERY   3 600-psi Foster Wheeler boilers, 1 General Electric steam turbine, 22,000 shp on 1 shaft=22 kts (20 kts sustained), range 18,000 nm at 11 kts, 10,000 nm at 20 kts, electric power 5,500 kW

CREW   navy ships 385; *Kilauea* 123 civilian + 37 Navy

WEAPONS
4 Mk 33 3-in (76-mm)/50-cal guns in twin mounts (except none in *Kilauea*)
2 20-mm Mk 15 Phalanx CIWS in AE 32–35
2 12.7-mm machine guns in *Kilauea*

HELICOPTERS   2 UH-46 Sea Knight

SENSORS
1 SPS-10 surface-search radar
SLQ-32(V)1 passive/active EW system
2 6-barrel Mk 36 SRBOC chaff launchers

Mars (AFS 1)

These seven large, built-for-the-purpose underway-replenishment ships combine the capabilities of store ships (AF), stores-issue ships (AKS), and aviation store ships (AVS). They were among the first to be ordered of the large fleet of underway-replenishment ships procured during the 1960s. Five cargo holds (one refrigerated) have a 7,000-ton cargo capacity and a total volume of 586,118 ft³

(16,597 m³). Fore to aft, the holds contain: (1) spare parts, (2) aviation parts, (3 and 4) provisions, and (5) spare parts. 40,000 bins and racks carry up to 25,000 types of spare parts. The holds are served by five M-shaped cargo masts (three forward, two aft) with constant-tension gear. Ahead of the large helicopter deck over the fantail is the hangar for two utility helicopters.

These ships entered service armed with four 3-in twin gun mounts. Half of these mounts were deleted from all ships but the *White Plains* during the late 1970s; all ships lost their Mk 56 gunfire control system as well as their SPS-40 air-search radar. In the mid-1980s, the *White Plains* beached two of her mounts in favor of two Phalanx Close-In Weapons Systems (CIWS).

DEVELOPMENT • Construction of the class lasted from 1962 to 1970 at National Steel and Shipbuilding in San Diego. NASSCO won the order for the *Mars* in July 1961; the other six ships followed at the rate of one per fiscal year (except FY1963).

The *Niagara Falls*, *White Plains*, and *San Jose* are homeported in Guam.

Three additional ships originally planned for the FY1977–78 shipbuilding programs were not requested.

In FY1993, ships of this class began transferring to Military Sealift Command (MSC) control, where they would have civilian crews. The *Mars*, *Sylvania*, *San Diego*, and *Concord* were the first to be reassigned.

COMBAT EXPERIENCE • The *San Jose* was the first ship to assist the *Samuel B. Roberts* (FFG 58) after she struck a mine in the Persian Gulf in 1988.

All but one of the *Mars* ships deployed to the Desert Storm theater at some point during Operations Desert Shield and Desert Storm. The *White Plains* operated with the *Independence*'s (CV 62) carrier battle group from August 17 to October 15, 1990. The *San Jose* served the longest period in the theater, arriving September 24, 1990, and leaving March 13, 1991.

The *Sylvania* had two tours—October 8–13, 1990, and January12–February 17, 1991—during which her crew delivered 20,500 tons of supplies (in effect, three full shiploads), once resupplying four ships simultaneously, and filled more than 30,000 requisitions. Her helicopters transferred another 5,000 tons of supplies.

The *Mars* operated in the region from December 21, 1990, to March 22, 1991, the *Niagara Falls* from January 15, 1991, to the end of March, and the *San Diego* from January 14, 1991, to April 6.

SPECIFICATIONS •
DISPLACEMENT   16,070 tons full load
DIMENSIONS
  length   581 ft 3 in (177.3 m) overall
  beam   79 ft (24.1 m),
  draft   24 ft (7.3 m)
MACHINERY   3 Babcock & Wilcox boilers, 1 steam turbine (De Laval except Westinghouse in AFS 6), 22,000 shp on 1 shaft=21 kts, range 18,000 nm at 11 kts, 10,000 nm at 20 kts, electric power 4,800 kW
CREW   435
WEAPONS
  2 twin Mk 33 3-in (76-mm)/50-cal AA gun mounts
  2 20-mm Mk 15 Phalanx Gatling CIWS mounts in AFS 4
HELICOPTERS   2 UH-46 Sea Knight helicopters
SENSORS
  1 SPS-10 surface-search radar
  SLQ-32(V)1 passive EW system

Sacramento (AOE 1)

These are the world's largest Underway Replenishment (UNREP) ships, designed to provide a carrier battle group with full fuels, munitions, dry and frozen provisions, and other supplies. They are also among the fastest naval auxiliaries in commission.

These ships can carry 194,000 barrels of fuels (more than the *Kaiser-* and *Cimarron*-class oilers), 2,100 tons of munitions and 250 tons each of dry and refrigerated stores. Between the superstructure blocks is a forest of cargo transfer rigs, alternating between long-armed fuel hose rigs and shorter stores and ammunition derricks. All are constant-tension devices.

A large helicopter deck extends aft of a three-bay hangar for UH-46 Vertical Replenishment (VERTREP) helicopters.

The canceled *Iowa*-class battleship *Kentucky* (BB 66) supplied propulsion machinery for the first two ships, while her barely started sister *Illinois* (BB 65) produced machinery for AOE 3 and 4.

The octuple Sea Sparrow short-range Surface-to-Air Missile (SAM) launcher is forward of the bridge. The 2 Phalanx Close-In Weapons System (CIWS) mounts are fitted up in the after superstructure, abaft and outboard of the stack.

DEVELOPMENT • Puget Sound Navy Yard built all but the *Seattle*, which was delivered by New York Shipbuilding in Camden, New Jersey. The *Seattle*, delivered in 1968, was the last ship completed by New York Ship, and the *Detroit*, delivered in 1970, represents the last new construction by Puget Sound Navy Yard.

A fifth ship of this design was originally planned for the FY1968 shipbuilding program and subsequently for the FY1980 shipbuilding program, but the ship was never built. Instead, the smaller and less expensive *Wichita* (AOR 1) design was developed.

The later *Supply* class (AOE 6) is somewhat smaller and powered by gas turbine engines.

COMBAT EXPERIENCE • Three of the four ships in the class supported US and coalition navy fleets during Operations

Desert Shield and Desert Storm. The *Sacramento* sailed with the battleship *Missouri*'s (BB 63) surface action group, arriving in the region on January 1, 1991, and leaving on March 24. The *Seattle* supported the carrier battle group headed by the *John F. Kennedy* (CV 67); she arrived on September 14, 1990, and departed March 11, 1991. The *Detroit* operated with the *Saratoga* (CV 60) and her battle group, which deployed in the region three separate times: August 24–September 21, 1990, November 7–December 16, 1990, and January 6–March 6, 1991.

The *Camden* supported the carrier *Nimitz* (CVN 68) and her battle group, which relieved forces in the Persian Gulf in April 1991.

SPECIFICATIONS •

DISPLACEMENT   53,600 tons full load
DIMENSIONS
  length   794 ft 9 in (242.4 m) overall
  beam   107 ft (32.6 m)
  draft   39 ft 4 in (12.0 m)
MACHINERY   4 Combustion Engineering boilers, 2 General Electric steam turbines, 100,000 shp on 2 shafts= 27.5 kts (26 kts sustained), range 10,000 nm at 17 kts, 6,000 nm at 26 kts
CREW   594-612
WEAPONS
  8-tube NATO Sea Sparrow launcher Mk 29
  2 Mk 15 Phalanx Gatling-type CIWS
HELICOPTERS   2 UH-46 Sea Knight
SENSORS
  SPS-40 air-search radar in AOE 1, 2
  SPS-53 surface-search radar
  Mk 91 Sea-Sparrow missile fire control system
  Mk 23 Target Acquisition System (TAS) Mod 2 in *Seattle*
  SPS-10 surface-search radar
  SLQ-32(V)3 active/passive EW system

Supply (AOE 6)

These are large Underway Replenishment (UNREP) ships designed to provide a carrier battle group with fuels, munitions, provisions, and other supplies. They are based on the design of the slightly larger *Sacramento* (AOE 1)-class fast combat support ships but have gas turbine propulsion instead of steam turbine.

The profile is of a flush-deck hull with a split superstructure. A large helicopter deck extends aft of a large three-bay hangar for UH-46 Sea Knight Vertical Replenishment (VERTREP) helicopters.

These ships can carry 156,000 barrels of fuels, 1,800 tons of munitions, 250 tons of dry stores, and 400 tons of refrigerated stores. They have highly automated cargo-handling equipment.

The first name for the AOE 7 was later seen as more properly belonging to a destroyer (DDG 60), and *Rainier* was substituted. Considering the names of the first three ships, the naming pattern for this class is inscrutable.

DEVELOPMENT • The Navy had planned the construction of at least seven AOEs of this class, but rising costs, serious delays, and construction problems, as well as a declining active fleet, seem likely to abbreviate the program at the four authorized by 1994. National Steel won the AOE 6 contract in 1987 with an option for three additional ships. The Navy exercised options on AOE 7 and AOE 8 in 1988 and 1989.

NASSCO had difficulty completing the first two ships, with some reports claiming that the company underbid the ships and could not make a profit. In September 1991, the General Accounting Office (GAO) noted that planned delivery dates had slipped by almost two years in the case of the *Supply,* 13 months for the *Rainier,* and 10 months for the *Arctic.* The delay stemmed primarily from problems with the reversing reduction gears, which were a new design being manufactured by Cincinnati Gear Co.

When funding for the AOE 9 was withdrawn from the FY1992 budget, NASSCO's option expired. As often happens with canceled hull numbers, the Navy skipped to AOE 10 for the FY1993 ship (effectively the FY1992 ship delayed a year) rather than reusing the canceled hull number.

SPECIFICATIONS •
DISPLACEMENT   48,800 tons full load
DIMENSIONS
   length   755 ft (230.1 m) overall
   beam   107 ft (32.6 m)
   draft   39 ft (11.9 m)
MACHINERY   4 General Electric LM 2500 gas turbines, 100,000 shp on 2 shafts=26 kts, electric power 12,500 kW
CREW   660
WEAPONS
   1 8-cell Mk 29 launcher for NATO Sea Sparrow SAM
   2 20-mm Mk 15 Phalanx Gatling-type CIWS
   2 25-mm Mk 88 Chain Gun AA in twin mount
HELICOPTERS   3 UH-46 Sea Knight
SENSORS
   SPS-67 air/surface-search radar
   SPS-64(V)9 navigation radar
   Mk 91 missile fire control system
   Mk 23 Target Acquisition System
   SLQ-32(V)3 passive/active EW system
   4 6-barrel Mk 36 SRBOC chaff/flare launchers

Suribachi (AE 21)

These ships were the first to be designed specifically for underway replenishment of munitions. Cargo capacity is 7,500 tons and is handled by three large kingpost masts (two forward, one aft). The profile has an almost straight stem, short forecastle, single block superstructure with a slender tapered stack amidships, canoe-shaped stern, and long helicopter platform.

All five ships were extensively modernized during the 1960s. They were fitted to carry and transfer guided missiles; their after 3-in gun mounts were removed and a helicopter deck installed. The three later ships are also referred to as the *Nitro* class.

DEVELOPMENT • These were among the first post–World War II auxiliaries to be authorized, the *Suribachi* and *Mauna Kea* being ordered from Bethlehem's Sparrows Point, Maryland, yard in 1954. *Nitro* and *Pyro* followed in 1957 and *Haleakala* in 1958. Deliveries came in 1957–59.

Pyro was the first to be decommissioned, leaving the active fleet in FY1994. The *Haleakala* was homeported in Guam.

COMBAT EXPERIENCE • The *Suribachi*, *Nitro*, and *Haleakala* deployed to the Persian Gulf region as part of Operation Desert Shield. The *Suribachi* moved with the carrier *Eisenhower*'s (CVN 69) battle group from the Mediterranean to the Red Sea in August 1990.

Nitro sailed with the carrier *America*'s (CV 66) battle group in December 1990, arriving in the theater on January 10, 1991. She operated with the battle group until it left the theater on April 10, 1991.

The *Haleakala* was independently deployed from Guam on January 22, 1991, and arrived in the theater on February 9. She resupplied ships in the region until March 14.

SPECIFICATIONS •
DISPLACEMENT   17,500 tons full load (AE 21, 22); 17,450 tons full load (AE 23–25)
DIMENSIONS
   length   512 ft (156.1 m) overall
   beam   72 ft (22.0 m)
   draft   29 ft (8.8 m)
MACHINERY   2 Combustion Engineering boilers, 1 steam turbine supplied by the builder, 16,000 shp on 1 shaft=20.6 kts,

range 12,000 nm at 15 kts, 10,000 nm at 20 kts

CREW 348

WEAPONS

4 3-inch (76-mm)/50-cal Mk 33 AA in twin mounts

HELICOPTERS landing area only

SENSORS

SPS-10 surface-search radar

SLQ-32(V)1 passive EW system in some ships

Wichita (AOR 1)

These are large combination petroleum-munitions Underway Replenishment (UNREP) ships, smaller and slower than the *Sacramento* (AOE 1) class, but still larger than any foreign ship other than the Soviet replenishment oiler *Berezina.*

They resemble the *Sacramentos*, having the same split-superstructure layout, helicopter flight deck aft, and array of transfer rigs amidships. There are many detail differences, however. The ships can steam at 18 knots on two boilers while the third is being maintained.

These ships can carry 160,000 barrels of petroleum, 600 tons of munitions, 200 tons of dry stores, and 100 tons of refrigerated stores. Except for the forward station, which is a single liquid-stores derrick extending to port, all stations serve both sides. An upright solid-stores frame with port and starboard stations is followed by two liquid-stores frames (long arms joined by truss girder), another solid stores frame, and a final liquid-stores station structure.

All ships except the *Roanoke* were built with helicopter decks but without hangars; all later received two-bay hangars. Installation of the hangars led to striking the two twin 3-in/50-cal twin antiaircraft gun mounts aft and the Mk 56 gunfire control system. Several ships received the 20-mm Phalanx Gatling-type Close-In Weapons System (CIWS).

DEVELOPMENT • Bethlehem's Quincy, Massachusetts, yard built the first six ships, receiving contracts in 1965–67 and completing the orders in 1969–73. NASSCO began the *Roanoke* in 1974 and delivered her in 1976.

The *Wichita* and *Milwaukee* were the first to be mothballed, being decommissioned in FY1993; the *Wabash* followed in FY1994.

COMBAT EXPERIENCE • Three of the class supported US and coalition navy operations during the 1990–91 Operations Desert Shield and Desert Storm. The *Kansas City* sailed with the carrier *Ranger*'s (CV 61) battle group, operating in the Desert Storm theater from January 13, 1991, to April 19. The *Savannah*'s visit to the region lasted only from October 8 to 13, 1990. The *Kalamazoo* supported the carrier *America*'s (CV 66) battle group from January 15, 1991, to March 30.

SPECIFICATIONS •

DISPLACEMENT   41,350 tons full load

DIMENSIONS

length	659 ft (201.0 m) overall
beam	96 ft (29.3 m)
draft	33 ft 4 in (10.2 m)

MACHINERY   3 Foster Wheeler boilers, 2 General Electric steam turbines, 32,000 shp on 2 shafts=20 kts, range 10,000 nm at 17 kts, 6,500 nm at 20 kts, electric power 8,000 kW

CREW   approx 450

WEAPONS

1 NATO Sea Sparrow launcher Mk 29 except in *Wichita*

20-mm Mk 15 Phalanx Gatling-type CIWS except in *Wichita*

HELICOPTERS   2 UH-46 Sea Knight

SENSORS

SPS-10 surface-search radar

LN-66 or SPS-53 surface-search radar

Mk 91 missile fire control system except in *Wichita*

Mk 23 Mod 2 TAS in *Kalamazoo*

SLQ-32(V)3 passive/active EW system

APPENDIX I

STRATEGIC MISSILES

Armed with powerful nuclear warheads and poised to attack strategic targets in the Soviet homeland, these weapons were in many ways the symbols of the Cold War, and they often stimulated the greatest controversy. But unlike many of the other weapons and weapons systems described in this book, their use ultimately proved unthinkable. Moreover, in the span of a few years, strategic missiles have gone from being the most urgent, ready-to-go-to-war weapons to a dormancy matched by few other systems. Although modest upgrades go on, there is a real possibility that strategic nuclear weapons will fade out of the U.S. inventory sometime early in the next century. Therefore, we've included six strategic systems still in the inventory as of early 1995 as an appendix, rather than as an integral part of the US military weapons system complex.

ADVANCED CRUISE MISSILE (AGM-129)

The AGM-129 Advanced Cruise Missile (ACM) is a low-observable ("stealth") missile intended for launching by strategic bomber aircraft. Fewer than one-quarter of those originally planned were delivered; these would be carried by B-52H Stratofortresses, but are not usually mounted on the bombers' pylons.

The ACM uses both composite materials and design characteristics to lessen its radar signature. Forward-swept, pop-out wings are fitted just aft of midbody, high on the fuselage. Three control surfaces are visible: two downward-folding elevators that have no dihedral when extended, and a folding ventral rudder that is offset to one side to place it clear of the exhaust. Like the exhaust, the inlet is underneath the missile and of flush design. The exhaust exits through a slot underneath the tail.

The stealth features are concentrated on the forward and top aspects, which is from where the missile is most likely to be detected. The lower half of the nose is boatlike, having a broad "stem" sweeping up from the flat bottom to a sharp chine line at midheight. (The flat bottom provides additional lift.) The upper half of the nose is also divided into two planes. The inlet, exhaust, and rudder are shielded by the afterbody. The radar cross-section from the side is probably large, but ground clutter would shield the missile from detection at this angle.

The Northrop guidance system is probably similar to that in the AGM-86 Air Launched Cruise Missile, only with a larger memory, a radar altimeter with a low-probability of intercept, a Kearfott Inertial Navigation System (INS), and a Hughes Aircraft laser Doppler velocimeter ranging system for navigation and targeting. A 1991 *Krasnaya Zvezda* (Soviet Army newspaper) reported estimates of the ACM's accuracy as 5 meters (16 ft), Circular Error Probable (CEP).

VARIANTS • AGM-129B was officially described as "AGM-129A modified with structural and software changes and an alternate nuclear warhead for accomplishing a classified cruise missile mission."

Development began in 1988. First flight planned for December 1992, but the program was cancelled in November 1991.

DEVELOPMENT • Originally planned to total approximately 2,000, this program's total cost was estimated at $7 billion before cutbacks announced in 1991–1992. But ACM production was repeatedly cut back both because of quality control problems as well as changes in force planning. At one point (November 1987) a USAF lieutenant general described the overall status of the program as "very poor." Although later Air Force reports were more reassuring, the General Accounting Office (GAO) singled out the "sensor, guidance set, forward and aft avionics units, actuators, altimeter, and deployment system" as presenting "significant reliability concerns." The missile also suffered from fuel leaks, and several subsystems were reportedly hard to reach for maintenance. The Air Force agreed that reliability was below the planned level, but that all of the problems had been identified, and most rectified. A 26-flight schedule of Full-Scale Development (FSD) testing ended in September 1990. The first operational AGM-129 was delivered to the US Air Force on January 29, 1991.

As with all strategic weapons, debate over the cost and use of the ACM seemed irrelevant as the dissolution of the Soviet Union became irrevocable. Development of the AGM-129B was cancelled in November 1991 and only 461 AGM-129As were delivered.

SPECIFICATIONS •

MANUFACTURER   General Dynamics Convair Division, San Diego, Calif.
MISSILE WEIGHT   3,709 lb (1,682 kg)

DIMENSIONS
length   20 ft 10 in (6.35 m)
depth of lower fuselage
              2 ft 1 in (639 mm)
radius of upper half of fuselage
              14.45 in (367 mm)
wingspan   10 ft 4 in (3.16 m)
PROPULSION   Williams International F112-WR-100 turbofan
CRUISING SPEED   Mach 0.9
MAX RANGE   approx 2,000 nm (2,300 mi; 3,700 km)
WARHEAD   W80 nuclear, 5–150 kiloton
SENSORS/FIRE CONTROL   TERCOM (Terrain Contour Matching) with terminal active radar or laser-assisted guidance

ALCM (AGM-86)

The AGM-86 ALCM (Air-Launched Cruise Missile) is a long range, air-to-ground cruise missile originally designed to be launched by manned bombers and attack strategic targets. The ALCM (pronounced Al-kum) has many of the attributes of the earlier Hound Dog cruise missile but is slower, longer range, and much more accurate. Flying at a very low altitude, ALCM relies on its small radar signature and surrounding ground clutter to defeat enemy air defenses. A conventional version using Global Positioning System (GPS) navigation was secretly developed in the mid–1980s and used in Operation Desert Storm in 1991.

The missile's fuselage is a welded assembly of four segments, each machined from a cast aluminum block, that serves as a virtually leak-proof fuel tank. The slender wings are swept at 25 deg; additional lift is generated by the "beluga whale" nose. Flight surfaces and the dorsal air intake pop out at launch, the intake being first, elevons and vertical tail next, followed by engine start, and deployment of the wings. Unlike the original ALCM-A, the ALCM-B is too long to fit in standard B-52 or B-1 weapons bays, having been stretched by 30% to achieve a 100% increase in range. Eight will ride on a rotary launcher fitted in modified B-52 or B-1 bays. Others are carried on wing pylons.

The aircraft's Inertial Navigation System (INS) aligns the ALCM platform at the beginning of a mission; position updates are provided automatically every 60 seconds until launch. In the missile, the McDonnell Douglas Terrain Contour Matching (TERCOM) software compares sensor input with digitized Defense Mapping Agency data, interprets differences through Kalman filtering, and corrects the missile's flight. As the missile nears its target, TERCOM progressively reduces the land area to be compared. The missile descends to a low penetration altitude and may begin using ECM against air defense radars until a fuze detonates the nuclear warhead.

The AGM-86C, which has a conventional blast/fragmentation warhead, shorter range, but greater accuracy, uses GPS navigation in addition to the TERCOM.

DEVELOPMENT • ALCM had its origins in SCAD (Subsonic Cruise Armed Decoy), which was designed to be launched from strategic bombers penetrating Soviet air space to confuse and overwhelm enemy air defenses while the bombers launched their supersonic AGM-69 Short-Range Attack Missiles (SRAM). Both SCADs and SRAMs were to fit on the same rotary launchers.

SCAD development ended in 1973 when the Air Force chose a purely attack weapon, the ALCM-A, which was essentially the SCAD with better guidance. ALCM-A flew in March 1976, but was superseded by the longer ALCM-B.

ALCM-B was chosen in March 1980 to equip B-52G and B-52H bombers after competing against the AGM-109, an air-launched variant of the Tomahawk cruise missile. Initial operational capability came in December 1982. Production

ended with 1,715 built. Unit cost was $1.352 million in FY1982 dollars. ALCM-C development began in June 1986 to contribute to the conventional stand-off attack capability of B-52G bombers. It secretly entered service in January 1988. On September 28, 1991, all US strategic bombers were taken off 24-hour ground alert status. All nuclear weapons, including the ALCMs, were removed and placed in storage.

COMBAT EXPERIENCE • Only the conventionally armed AGM-86Cs have seen combat. Seven B-52Gs left Barksdale AFB in Louisiana at 6:35 AM CST (1235 GMT) on January 16, 1991 and flew to launch positions near Iraq. An hour and a half after Operation Desert Storm's air assault began, the B-52s launched a total of 35 AGM-86C at eight power generation and transmission facilities and military communications sites.

SPECIFICATIONS

MANUFACTURER Boeing Aerospace
   Company, Seattle, Washington
WEIGHT 3,150 lb (1,429 kg)
DIMENSIONS
   length   20 ft 9 in (6.32 m)
   diameter   2 ft 0 in (0.69 m)
   height on launcher
                     2 ft 2 in (0.65 m)
   wingspan   12 ft 0 in (3.66 m)
PROPULSION Williams Research F-107-WR-100 600-lb (272-kg) static thrust turbofan
   engine burning JP-10 fuel
SPEED Mach 0.7
MAX RANGE over 1,350 nm (1,550 mi; 2,500 km)
CIRCULAR ERROR PROBABLE (CEP)
   approx 98 ft (30 m)
WARHEAD AGM-86B one 200-kiloton W-80-1 oralloy/supergrade plutonium with tritium
AGM-86C conventional blast/fragmentation

SENSORS/FIRE CONTROL   AGM-86B INS
with TERCOM
AGM-86C INS with TERCOM, GPS

MINUTEMAN (LGM-30)

The Minuteman III (LGM-30G) ICBM is the most numerous US land-based strategic missile with 500 missiles currently deployed in fixed silos that are hardened to withstand 2,000 psi (140 bar) of blast overpressure. Minuteman was the first solid-fuel rocket ICBM and the first with Multiple Independently targetable Re-entry Vehicles (MIRVs). Development of the MIRV in the late 1960s was criticized as accelerating the US–Soviet arms race, while supporters noted the greater numbers of Soviet missiles and a similar drive for greater accuracy.

The third stage solid-propellant rocket uses fluid-injection thrust vector control for greater range and accuracy. The post-boost vehicle, which holds the MIRVs, uses eleven small rockets for post-boost control. Of the 500 Minuteman IIIs, the 300 fitted with the highly accurate Mk 12A MIRVs are the most modern of the deployed Minuteman force. These introduced remote retargeting through the Command Data Buffer System (CDBS), which allows the missiles to be remotely retargeted before launch in less than a half hour.

In the late 1980s, the Air Force began the REACT (Rapid Execution and Combat Targeting) upgrade program to support rapid message processing and missile retargeting; establish commonality among Minuteman III, fixed and rail-mobile Peacekeeper, and small ICBM launch control systems; provide a logistically supportable system past the turn of the century, and improve crew effectiveness and crew environment. Other life-extension efforts included clean-out and repouring of second-stage motors, the re-manufacture of third-stage motors, and the development of new penetration aids.

DEVELOPMENT • Minuteman I (LGM-30A/B) saw its Initial Operational Capability (IOC) in 1963. Minuteman II (LGM-30F) with a 1.2-megaton warhead followed in 1966. Minuteman III's IOC came in 1970; the first Mk 12A MIRVs achieved IOC in 1979. Production ended in 1977.

The 450 Minuteman II missiles were scheduled to be deactivated and dismantled over a seven-year period under the terms of the 1991 Strategic Arms Reduction Treaty (START) once the treaty was ratified.

Minuteman IIIs are at four bases (Malmstrom, Grand Forks, Minot, and F.E. Warren) in Montana, North Dakota, and Wyoming.

VARIANTS • The earliest version was the single-warhead Minuteman I, none of which remain in service. 450 single-warhead Minuteman IIs were decommissioned as part of President Bush's massive scaledown of the US nuclear deterrent in September 1991.

SPECIFICATIONS •

MANUFACTURER   Boeing Aerospace, Seattle, Washington

WEIGHT
  missile   78,000 lb (35,380 kg)
  throwweight 2,400 lb (1,089 kg)

DIMENSIONS
  length   59 ft 10 in (18.21 m)
  diameter at first interstage
              5 ft 6 in (1.68 m)

PROPULSION
  1st stage   Thiokol M-55 210,000 lb
              (95,255 kg) static
              thrust
  2nd stage   Aerojet-General SR-19-
              AJ-1 60,300 lb (27,352
              kg) st
  3rd stage   Thiokol SR73-AJ-1, 34,400
              lb (15,604 kg) st

MAX RANGE   more than 6,950 nm
  (8,000 mi; 12,875 km)

CIRCULAR ERROR PROBABLE (CEP)   605
  ft (185 m)

WARHEADS   3 General Electric (GE) Mk
12 MIRVs with W62 170-kiloton warheads or 3 GE Mk 12A MIRVs with
W78 330-kiloton warheads

SENSORS/FIRE CONTROL   Rockwell
NS-20 inertial guidance GE1 MIRV
using Bell Aerospace post-boost control system; penetration aids include
decoys and chaff

PEACEKEEPER (LGM-118)

The LGM-118 Peacekeeper was developed to replace the LGM-30 Minuteman
as the US land-based ICBM. Better
known under its development name MX,
the Peacekeeper is a large and very accurate missile that reflected 20 years of US
ICBM design practice with the most significant improvements coming in guidance and warhead technology.

A big change was the adoption of a
cold-launch technique. A small gas generator pops the missile out of its silo after
which the first stage ignites. This technique, never before used to launch a US
ICBM, was developed to enable the MX
to be deployed as a mobile system.

The solid-propellant missile has three
boost stages and a powered Post-Boost
Vehicle (PBV). All 3 motor cases are
made of wound Kevlar aramid fibers.

The PBV can carry up to ten Multiple
Independently targetable Reentry Vehicles (MIRVs). Achieving unprecedented
accuracy was the role of the Rockwell Au-
tonetics Missile Guidance and Control
Set (MCGS), of which the Northrop Advanced Inertial Reference Sphere (AIRS)
Inertial Measurement Unit (IMU) is a
prominent component. The IMU is a
sphere that floats in fluorocarbon 77 and
contains approximately 14,000 components, including three gyroscopes and
three sophisticated accelerometers
known as Specific Force Integrating Receivers (SFIR), which update an onboard
digital computer.

Of equal importance in the program
were the efforts to protect the MX from
preemptive attack by moving the missile
around. As originally proposed during
the Carter Administration, the MX program called for 200 missiles, each to be
deployed in one of several hardened shelters located on large tracts of land in remote western areas. At random intervals,
special carriers would move from one
shelter to another.

By the early 80s, procurement plans
had been scaled back to 100 missiles, but
the basing issue persisted in vexing DoD,
the Air Force, and Congress. Proposals
for a "dense pack" silo plan, deep silos,
and finally a rail garrison mode encountered criticisms over cost, feasibility, and
their chilling effects on arms-control negotiations. Proponents of the program
pointed to the large Soviet SS-24 Scalpel
ICBMs, which began their rail-based deployments at this time, as well as deployment of the smaller, but even more
mobile SS-25 Sickles.

With a further, Congress-mandated
limit of 50 deployed missiles being imposed, Rail Garrison MX gained momen-
tum. Twenty-five, nine-car trains were
planned, one for every two missiles. On
word of a high alert status, the trains
would move from their protective "ig-
loos" onto the US rail network to "hide"
from Soviet ICBMs. The trains were to be
capable of independent operations for
one month before requiring resupply
and crew relief.

Basing 50 Peacekeepers in modified
Minuteman silos at F. E. Warren Air Force
Base in Wyoming was to be a temporary
measure. But the basing discussion was
overtaken by events, as the threat of Soviet missile attacks against the United
States declined rapidly in 1989–1991 due
to the demise of the Warsaw Pact and the
subsequent dissolution of the Soviet
Union itself. President Bush's September
1991 cancellation of rail garrison development reflected the declining threat of
a surprise Soviet nuclear weapons strike

against the United States as well as lack of Congressional support.

DEVELOPMENT • Full scale development began in 1979 with the first test flight coming on June 17, 1983. Testing was greatly delayed by problems with the IMU, reduced funding for missile procurement, and Congressionally imposed delays on testing until the basing mode question was satisfactorily addressed. Initial operational capability came in December 1986, with all fifty missiles in place by December 1988. START II arms-control limitations call for the gradual removal of MX from the silos, beginning in the year 2000 and ending in 2004.

SPECIFICATIONS •
MANUFACTURER   Martin Marietta
TOTAL MISSILE WEIGHT   195,000 lb (88,450 kg)
post-boost vehicle
        3,000 lb (1,361 kg)
throwweight 8,000 lb (3,629 kg)
DIMENSIONS
overall length
        71 ft (21.64 m)
PBV   4 ft (1.22 m)
diameter   7 ft 8 in (2.34 m)
PROPULSION   first 3 stages are solid-propellant rockets (Morton-Thiokol, Aerojet, Hercules); fourth stage is a Rocketdyne storable-liquid rocket
MAX RANGE   more than 6,000 nm (6,909 mi; 11,118 km)
CIRCULAR ERROR PROBABLE (CEP)   394 ft (120 m)
WARHEADS   10 Avco Mk 21 MIRV, each armed with one W87 300–475 kiloton nuclear warhead
SENSORS/FIRE CONTROL   Northrop AIRS IMU, PBV has guidance and control section to deploy MIRVs on ballistic trajectories

TRIDENT I (UGM-96)
The US Navy's Trident I (C-4) Submarine-Launched Ballistic Missile (SLBM) succeeded the Poseidon (C-3) SLBM in *Lafayette* and *Ohio*-class ballistic missile submarines. In fact, the original design criteria for the Trident was primarily to obtain an increase in range over the Poseidon while remaining compatible with existing Poseidon submarine launch tubes.

The Trident's Multiple Independently targetable Reentry Vehicles (MIRV) have twice the yield and twice the accuracy of those of the Poseidon. The Trident C-4 was designed to alternatively carry the Mk 500 Evader Maneuvering Reentry Vehicle (MaRV) warhead. This was designed to overcome ballistic-missile defenses; it was not deployed. Trident was the first US SLBM to be able to hit targets in the Soviet Union while its launch boat operated near US waters.

DEVELOPMENT • Development began in the early 1970s with the missile achieving initial operational capability in October 1979. The last *Lafayette*-class Trident boat was decommissioned in 1994. The eight *Ohio*-class boats were to have been retrofitted with the larger Trident D5, but this program was curtailed.

SPECIFICATIONS
MANUFACTURER   Lockheed Missiles and Space Company, Inc, Sunnyvale, Calif.
WEIGHT
missile   65,000 lb (29,484 kg)
throwweight more than 3,000 lb (1,361 kg)
DIMENSIONS
length   34 ft 0 in (10.36 m)
diameter   6 ft 2 in (1.88 m)
PROPULSION   3-stage solid-propellant rocket
MAX RANGE   approx 4,000 nm (4,606 mi; 7,412 km)

CIRCULAR ERROR PROBABLE (CEP)
approx 0.25 nm (460 m)
WARHEADS   eight Mk 4 MIRV, each carrying a W76 100-kiloton nuclear warhead
SENSORS/FIRE CONTROL   stellar inertial guidance

TRIDENT II D-5 (UGM-133A)

The Trident II D-5 SLBM is a significantly more capable version of the Trident I C-4 and was the first SLBM to have a "hard target" (e.g., an ICBM missile silo) kill capability. It is estimated that a D-5 W88 warhead has an 88% probability of kill against a target hardened to 7,200 psi (506 kg/sq cm). In addition to outfitting later US *Ohio*-class missile boats, Trident II missiles carrying a British warhead will arm the Royal Navy's class of four 16-tube *Vanguard* ballistic missile submarines.

Although it is more accurate and carries a larger MIRV warhead than any previous SLBM, Trident II shares some of the limitations of its predecessors. Reaction time suffers from the difficulty of submarine communications and the dormant guidance system of the missile, which takes several minutes to activate. Also, Trident II's missile footprint is three times smaller than the MX Peacekeeper's footprint, which is the target area into which a Multiple Independently targetable Reentry Vehicle (MIRV) can be guided. This creates limitations on the Trident force when planning targets. The smaller footprint is a result of the solid-fueled Post Boost Vehicle (PBV) in the Trident. (MX has a liquid-fueled PBV.)

Trident II's range depends on the type and number of warheads carried; typical range is 4,000 nm (4,606 mi; 7,412 km) and the maximum range with a reduced payload is 6,000 nm (6,909 mi; 11,118 km). Plans to test a D-5 with 12 Mk 4 MIRVs each carrying a W76 100 kiloton nuclear warhead ran afoul of arms-control counting rules.

DEVELOPMENT • Prior to the first submarine test launch, the D-5 was reported to be within schedule and cost projections parameters. For example, the first D-5 test launch on January 17, 1987 was within two hours of the target date set four years earlier.

However, a February 1989 DOD audit found that more than $11 billion of expected costs had been excluded from Navy estimates given to the Defense Acquisition Board (DAB) during its March 1987 production review. The $11 billion included $6.9 billion in Trident submarine modifications and $4.1 billion in research and development costs needed to deploy the system.

Compared to the land-based test series, the first of nine scheduled submarine launches (held on March 21, 1989) had a less auspicious conclusion. After ejection from the launch tube of the USS Tennessee (SSBN-734), the Trident broke the water's surface as planned, but a malfunction during the first stage of powered flight caused the missile to veer off course, pinwheel, and self-destruct after four seconds of flight. Other test problems led to fixes that slightly delayed the Initial Operating Capability (IOC) to March 1990.

Plans to outfit eighteen *Ohio*-class boats, a total of 432 Trident II missiles (with a potential for 3,456 warheads) changed rapidly for two reasons. One was the September 1991 decision to scale back US nuclear weapon deployments in response to reduced threats. This included a decision to "download" Trident II missiles. British Prime Minister Major's government announced similar plans in 1992.

Such restraint may have been inevitable. Serious production and environmental problems at the Rocky Flats, CO, plutonium processing plant led to its closing in November 1989. As the scope of the cleanup at Rocky Flats became clearer, its reopening prospects dimmed appreciably. As a result, only about 400

W88 warheads had been manufactured. Similarly, management problems and staff shortages delayed completion of the new Aldermaston warhead facility in England.

SPECIFICATIONS •

MANUFACTURER   Lockheed Missiles and Space Company, Sunnyvale, Calif.

WEIGHT
missile   130,000 lb (58,967 kg)
throwweight 6,170 lb (2,800 kg)

DIMENSIONS
length   44 ft 0 in (13.40 m)
diameter 6 ft 11 in (2.11 m)

PROPULSION   3-stage solid-fuel rocket; 1st and 2nd stage, each with 65-sec burn time, are manufactured by Hercules or Morton Thiokol; 3rd stage, with burn time of 40 seconds, comes from United Technologies

MAX RANGE   more than 6,000 nm (6,909 mi; 11,118 km)

CIRCULAR ERROR PROBABLE (CEP) 295-395 ft (90-120 m)

WARHEADS   8 W88 300-475 kiloton MIRVs in a solid-fuel Mk 5 PBV

SENSORS/FIRE CONTROL   dormant stellar inertial guidance

APPENDIX II

REGISTER OF SHIPS

AIRCRAFT CARRIERS

SHIP NAME	TYPE	HULL BUILDER	LAID DOWN D M Y	LAUNCHED D M Y	COMPLETED D M Y
FORRESTAL	CV	59 Newport News	14 07 52	11 12 54	01 10 55
FORRESTAL—SLEP	CV	59 Phila NY	21 01 83		19 05 85
SARATOGA	CV	60 Brooklyn NY	16 12 52	08 10 55	14 04 56
SARATOGA—SLEP	CV	60 Phila NY	01 10 80		01 02 83
RANGER	CV	61 Newport News	02 07 54	29 09 56	10 08 57
INDEPENDENCE	CV	62 Brooklyn NY	01 07 55	06 06 58	10 01 59
INDEPENDENCE— SLEP	CV	62 Phila NY	18 04 85		16 05 88
KITTY HAWK	CV	63 NYSB, Camden	27 12 56	21 05 60	29 04 61
KITTY HAWK— SLEP	CV	63 Phila NY	28 01 88		02 08 91
CONSTELLATION	CV	64 Brooklyn NY	14 09 57	08 10 60	27 10 61
CONSTELLATION— SLEP	CV	64 Phila NY	02 07 90		05 03 93
ENTERPRISE	CVN	65 Newport News	04 02 58	24 09 60	25 11 61
ENTERPRISE— RCOH	CVN	65 Newport News	08 01 91		27 09 94
AMERICA	CV	66 Newport News	09 01 61	01 02 64	23 01 65
JOHN F. KENNEDY	CV	67 Newport News	22 11 64	27 05 67	07 09 68
NIMITZ	CVN	68 Newport News	22 06 68	13 05 72	03 05 75
DWIGHT D. EISENHOWER	CVN	69 Newport News	14 08 70	11 10 75	18 10 77
CARL VINSON	CVN	70 Newport News	11 10 75	15 03 80	13 03 82
THEODORE ROOSEVELT	CVN	71 Newport News	31 10 81	27 10 84	25 10 86
ABRAHAM LINCOLN	CVN	72 Newport News	03 11 84	13 02 88	11 11 89
GEORGE WASHINGTON	CVN	73 Newport News	25 08 86	21 07 90	04 07 92
JOHN C. STENNIS	CVN	74 Newport News	13 03 91	26 03 94	
HARRY S TRUMAN	CVN	75 Newport News	03 08 92	16 03 96	
RONALD REAGAN	CVN	76 Newport News			

SLEP: Service Life Extension Project.
RCOH: Refueling and Complex Overhaul.

AMPHIBIOUS SHIPS

SHIP NAME	TYPE	HULL BUILDER	LAID DOWN D M Y	LAUNCHED D M Y	COMPLETED D M Y
TARAWA	LHA	1 Litton/Ingalls	15 11 71	01 12 73	29 05 76
SAIPAN	LHA	2 Litton/Ingalls	21 07 72	18 07 74	15 10 77
BELLEAU WOOD	LHA	3 Litton/Ingalls	05 03 73	11 04 77	23 09 78
NASSAU	LHA	4 Litton/Ingalls	13 08 73	28 01 78	28 07 79
PELELIU	LHA	5 Litton/Ingalls	12 11 76	06 01 79	03 05 80
WASP	LHD	1 Litton/Ingalls	30 05 85	04 08 87	29 07 89
ESSEX	LHD	2 Litton/Ingalls	20 03 89	02 03 91	17 10 92
KEARSARGE	LHD	3 Litton/Ingalls	06 02 90	26 03 92	24 09 93
BOXER	LHD	4 Litton/Ingalls	01 04 91	28 08 93	10 06 94
BATAAN	LHD	5 Litton/Ingalls	25 04 94		12 96
BONHOMME RICHARD	LHD	6 Litton/Ingalls			
CHARLESTON	LKA	113 Newport News	05 12 66	02 12 67	14 12 68
DURHAM	LKA	114 Newport News	10 07 67	29 03 68	24 05 69
MOBILE	LKA	115 Newport News	15 01 68	19 10 68	20 09 69
ST. LOUIS	LKA	116 Newport News	03 04 68	04 01 69	22 11 69
EL PASO	LKA	117 Newport News	22 10 68	17 05 69	17 01 70
RALEIGH	LPD	1 Brooklyn NY	23 06 60	17 03 62	08 09 62
VANCOUVER	LPD	2 Brooklyn NY	19 11 60	15 09 62	11 05 63
LA SALLE	LPD	3 Brooklyn NY	02 04 62	03 08 63	22 02 64
AUSTIN	LPD	4 Brooklyn NY	04 02 63	27 06 64	06 02 65
OGDEN	LPD	5 Brooklyn NY	04 02 63	27 06 64	19 06 65
DULUTH	LPD	6 Brooklyn NY	18 12 63	14 08 65	18 12 65
CLEVELAND	LPD	7 Litton/Ingalls	30 11 64	07 05 66	21 04 67
DUBUQUE	LPD	8 Litton/Ingalls	25 01 65	06 08 66	01 09 67
DENVER	LPD	9 Lockheed, Seattle	07 02 64	23 01 65	26 10 68
JUNEAU	LPD	10 Lockheed, Seattle	23 01 65	12 02 66	12 07 69
CORONADO	LPD	11 Lockheed, Seattle	03 05 65	30 07 66	23 05 70
SHREVEPORT	LPD	12 Lockheed, Seattle	27 12 65	25 10 66	12 12 70
NASHVILLE	LPD	13 Lockheed, Seattle	14 03 66	07 10 67	14 02 70
TRENTON	LPD	14 Lockheed, Seattle	08 08 66	03 08 68	06 03 71
PONCE	LPD	15 Lockheed, Seattle	31 10 66	30 05 70	10 07 71
IWO JIMA	LPH	2 Puget NY	02 04 59	17 09 60	26 08 61
OKINAWA	LPH	3 Phila NY	01 04 60	14 08 61	14 04 62
GUADALCANAL	LPH	7 Phila NY	01 09 61	16 03 63	20 07 63

SHIP NAME	TYPE	HULL BUILDER	LAID DOWN	LAUNCHED	COMPLETED
			D M Y	D M Y	D M Y
GUAM	LPH	9 Phila NY	15 11 62	22 08 64	16 01 65
TRIPOLI	LPH	10 Litton/Ingalls	15 06 64	31 07 65	06 08 66
NEW ORLEANS	LPH	11 Phila NY	01 03 66	03 02 68	16 11 68
INCHON	LPH	12 Litton/Ingalls	08 04 68	24 05 69	20 07 70
ANCHORAGE	LSD	36 Litton/Ingalls	13 03 67	05 05 68	15 03 69
PORTLAND	LSD	37 GD/Beth, Quincy	21 09 67	20 12 69	03 10 70
PENSACOLA	LSD	38 GD/Beth, Quincy	12 03 69	11 07 70	27 03 71
MOUNT VERNON	LSD	39 GD/Beth, Quincy	29 01 70	17 04 71	13 05 72
FORT FISHER	LSD	40 GD/Beth, Quincy	15 07 70	22 04 72	09 12 72
WHIDBEY ISLAND	LSD	41 Lockheed, Seattle	04 08 81	10 06 83	09 02 85
GERMANTOWN	LSD	42 Lockheed, Seattle	05 08 82	29 06 84	08 02 86
FORT McHENRY	LSD	43 Lockheed, Seattle	10 06 83	01 02 86	08 08 87
GUNSTON HALL	LSD	44 Avondale	26 05 86	27 06 87	22 04 89
COMSTOCK	LSD	45 Avondale	27 10 86	16 01 88	03 02 90
TORTUGA	LSD	46 Avondale	23 03 87	15 09 88	17 11 90
RUSHMORE	LSD	47 Avondale	09 11 87	06 05 89	01 06 91
ASHLAND	LSD	48 Avondale	04 04 88	11 11 89	09 05 92
HARPERS FERRY	LSD	49 Avondale	15 04 91	16 01 93	
CARTER HALL	LSD	50 Avondale	08 11 91	23 11 93	
OAK HILL	LSD	51 Avondale	21 11 92		15 01 95
PEARL HARBOR	LSD	52 Avondale			
——	LSD	53			
——	LSD	54			
NEWPORT	LST	1179 Phila NY	01 11 66	03 02 68	07 06 69
MANITOWOC	LST	1180 Phila NY	01 02 67	04 06 69	24 01 70
SUMTER	LST	1181 Phila NY	14 11 67	13 12 69	20 06 70
FRESNO	LST	1182 National Steel	16 12 67	20 09 68	22 11 69
PEORIA	LST	1183 National Steel	22 02 68	23 11 68	21 02 70
FREDERICK	LST	1184 National Steel	13 04 68	08 03 69	11 04 70
SCHENECTADY	LST	1185 National Steel	02 08 68	24 05 69	13 06 70
CAYUGA	LST	1186 National Steel	28 09 68	12 07 69	08 08 70
TUSCALOOSA	LST	1187 National Steel	23 11 68	06 09 69	24 10 70
SAGINAW	LST	1188 National Steel	24 05 69	07 02 70	23 01 71
SAN BERNARDINO	LST	1189 National Steel	12 07 69	26 03 70	27 03 71
BOULDER	LST	1190 National Steel	06 09 69	22 05 70	04 06 71
RACINE	LST	1191 National Steel	13 12 69	15 08 70	09 07 71

AMPHIBIOUS SHIPS (continued)

SHIP NAME	TYPE	HULL BUILDER	LAID DOWN D M Y	LAUNCHED D M Y	COMPLETED D M Y
SPARTANBURG COUNTY	LST	1192 National Steel	07 02 70	11 11 70	01 09 71
FAIRFAX COUNTY	LST	1193 National Steel	28 03 70	19 12 70	16 10 71
LA MOURE COUNTY	LST	1194 National Steel	22 05 70	13 02 71	18 12 71
BARBOUR COUNTY	LST	1195 National Steel	15 08 70	15 05 71	12 02 72
HARLAN COUNTY	LST	1196 National Steel	07 11 70	24 07 71	08 04 72
BARNSTABLE COUNTY	LST	1197 National Steel	19 12 70	02 10 71	27 05 72
BRISTOL COUNTY	LST	1198 National Steel	13 02 71	04 12 71	05 08 72

AUXILIARY SHIPS

SHIP NAME	TYPE	HULL BUILDER	LAID DOWN D M Y	LAUNCHED D M Y	COMPLETED D M Y
SAMUEL GOMPERS	AD	37 Puget Sound NY	09 07 64	14 05 66	01 07 67
PUGET SOUND	AD	38 Puget Sound NY	15 02 65	16 09 66	27 04 68
YELLOWSTONE	AD	41 National Steel	27 06 77	21 01 79	28 06 80
ACADIA	AD	42 National Steel	14 02 78	28 07 79	06 06 81
CAPE COD	AD	43 National Steel	27 01 79	02 08 80	17 04 82
SHENANDOAH	AD	44 National Steel	02 08 80	06 02 82	17 12 83
SAFEGUARD	ARS	51 Peterson	02 11 82	12 11 83	17 08 85
GRASP	ARS	52 Peterson	30 03 83	21 04 84	14 12 85
SALVOR	ARS	53 Peterson	24 10 83	28 07 84	12 08 86
GRAPPLE	ARS	54 Peterson	25 04 84	08 12 84	15 11 86
HUNLEY	AS	31 Newport News	28 11 60	28 09 61	16 06 62
HOLLAND	AS	32 Litton/Ingalls	05 03 62	19 01 63	07 09 63
SIMON LAKE	AS	33 Puget Navy	07 01 63	08 02 64	07 11 64
CANOPUS	AS	34 Litton/Ingalls	02 03 64	12 02 65	04 11 65
L. Y. SPEAR	AS	36 GD/Beth, Quincy	05 05 66	07 09 67	28 02 70
DIXON	AS	37 GD/Beth, Quincy	07 09 67	20 06 70	07 08 71
EMORY S. LAND	AS	39 Lockheed, Seattle	02 03 76	04 05 77	07 07 79
FRANK CABLE	AS	40 Lockheed, Seattle	02 03 76	14 01 78	05 02 80
McKEE	AS	41 Lockheed, Seattle	14 01 78	16 02 80	15 08 81
EDENTON	ATS	1 Brooke Marine	01 04 67	15 05 68	23 01 71
BEAUFORT	ATS	2 Brooke Marine	19 02 68	20 12 68	22 01 72
BRUNSWICK	ATS	3 Brooke Marine	05 06 68	14 11 69	19 12 72
STALWART	T-AGOS	1 Tacoma Boat	03 05 82	12 11 83	09 04 84

SHIP NAME	TYPE	HULL BUILDER	LAID DOWN D M Y	LAUNCHED D M Y	COMPLETED D M Y
CONTENDER	T-AGOS	2 Tacoma Boat	10 01 83	20 12 83	29 07 84
VINDICATOR	T-AGOS	3 Tacoma Boat	14 04 83	01 06 84	20 11 84
TRIUMPH	T-AGOS	4 Tacoma Boat	13 07 83	07 09 84	19 02 85
ASSURANCE	T-AGOS	5 Tacoma Boat	16 04 84	12 01 85	01 05 85
PERSISTENCE	T-AGOS	6 Tacoma Boat	22 10 84	06 04 85	14 08 85
INDOMITABLE	T-AGOS	7 Tacoma Boat	26 01 85	16 07 85	01 12 85
PREVAIL	T-AGOS	8 Tacoma Boat	13 05 85	07 12 85	28 02 86
ASSERTIVE	T-AGOS	9 Tacoma Boat	30 07 85	20 06 86	12 09 86
INVINCIBLE	T-AGOS	10 Tacoma Boat	08 11 85	11 11 86	30 01 87
AUDACIOUS	T-AGOS	11 Tacoma Boat	29 02 88	28 01 89	12 06 89
BOLD	T-AGOS	12 Tacoma Boat	13 06 88	22 05 89	29 09 89
ADVENTUROUS	T-AGOS	13 Halter	19 12 85	23 09 87	19 08 88
WORTHY	T-AGOS	14 Halter	03 04 86	06 02 88	16 12 88
TITAN	T-AGOS	15 Halter	30 10 86	18 06 88	08 03 89
CAPABLE	T-AGOS	16 Halter	17 10 87	02 10 88	09 06 89
INTREPID	T-AGOS	17 Halter	26 02 88	17 02 89	29 09 89
RELENTLESS	T-AGOS	18 Halter	22 04 88	12 05 89	12 01 90
VICTORIOUS	T-AGOS	19 McDermott	12 04 88	02 05 90	13 08 91
ABLE	T-AGOS	20 McDermott	23 05 90	16 02 91	24 03 92
EFFECTIVE	T-AGOS	21 McDermott	16 02 91	26 09 91	28 01 93
LOYAL	T-AGOS	22 McDermott	02 10 91	18 09 92	01 07 93
IMPECCABLE	T-AGOS	23 Tampa Ship	01 02 93	CANCELLED	
INTEGRITY	T-AGOS	24 Tampa Ship	01 02 93	CANCELLED	
WATERS	T-AGS	45 Avondale	16 05 91	06 06 92	19 03 93
McDONNELL	T-AGS	51 Halter	03 08 89	13 12 90	15 11 91
LITTLEHALES	T-AGS	52 Halter	25 10 89	14 02 91	10 01 92
PATHFINDER	T-AGS	60 Halter	18 08 92	07 10 93	31 10 94
SUMNER	T-AGS	61 Halter	18 11 92	19 05 94	30 04 95
BOWDITCH	T-AGS	62 Halter	17 06 93		
HENSON	T-AGS	63 Halter		05 07 94	30 11 95
MERCY	T-AH	19 National Steel	20 07 84		08 11 86
COMFORT	T-AH	20 National Steel	02 04 85		24 09 87
WRIGHT	T-AVB	3 Todd, Galveston	14 12 84		14 05 86
CURTISS	T-AVB	4 Todd, Galveston	07 12 85		03 87

BATTLESHIPS

SHIP NAME	TYPE	HULL BUILDER	LAID DOWN D M Y	LAUNCHED D M Y	COMPLETED D M Y
IOWA	BB	61 Brooklyn NY	27 06 40	27 08 42	22 02 43
IOWA—update	BB	61 Avon/Ingalls	01 10 82		13 02 84
NEW JERSEY	BB	62 Phila NY	07 12 40	07 12 42	23 05 43
NEW JERSEY— update	BB	62 Long Beach NY	01 10 81		28 12 82
MISSOURI	BB	63 Brooklyn NY	06 01 41	29 01 44	04 06 44
MISSOURI—update	BB	63 Long Beach NY	01 10 84		10 05 86
WISCONSIN	BB	64 Phila NY	25 01 41	07 12 43	16 04 44
WISCONSIN— update	BB	64 Avon/Ingalls	15 08 86		21 10 88

COAST GUARD

SHIP NAME	TYPE	HULL BUILDER	LAID DOWN D M Y	LAUNCHED D M Y	COMPLETED D M Y
MACKINAW	WAGB	4 Toledo SB	20 03 43	04 03 44	20 12 44
POLAR STAR	WAGB	10 Lockheed	15 05 72	17 11 73	19 01 76
POLAR SEA	WAGB	11 Lockheed	27 11 73	24 06 75	23 02 78
HEALY	WAGB	20 Avondale	22 04 91	25 07 92	18 09 93
HAMILTON	WHEC	715 Avondale	15 01 65	18 12 65	20 02 67
DALLAS	WHEC	716 Avondale	07 02 66	01 10 66	01 10 67
MELLON	WHEC	717 Avondale	25 07 66	11 02 67	22 12 67
CHASE	WHEC	718 Avondale	27 10 66	20 05 67	01 03 68
BOUTWELL	WHEC	719 Avondale	05 12 66	17 06 67	14 06 68
SHERMAN	WHEC	720 Avondale	23 01 67	23 09 67	23 08 68
GALLATIN	WHEC	721 Avondale	27 02 67	18 11 67	20 12 68
MORGENTHAU	WHEC	722 Avondale	17 07 67	10 02 68	14 02 69
RUSH	WHEC	723 Avondale	23 10 67	16 11 68	03 07 69
MUNRO	WHEC	724 Avondale	18 02 70	05 12 70	10 09 71
JARVIS	WHEC	725 Avondale	09 09 70	24 04 71	30 12 71
MIDGETT	WHEC	726 Avondale	05 04 71	04 09 71	17 03 72
RELIANCE	WMEC	615 Todd, Houston	25 09 62	25 05 63	20 06 64
DILIGENCE	WMEC	616 Todd, Houston	12 12 62	20 07 63	26 08 64
VIGILANT	WMEC	617 Todd, Houston	25 09 62	24 12 63	03 10 64
ACTIVE	WMEC	618 Christy	29 07 63	31 07 65	17 09 66
CONFIDENCE	WMEC	619 Curtis Bay SY	15 01 63	08 05 65	19 02 66
RESOLUTE	WMEC	620 Amship, Lorain	09 12 63	30 04 66	08 12 66

SHIP NAME	TYPE	HULL BUILDER	LAID DOWN D M Y	LAUNCHED D M Y	COMPLETED D M Y
VALIANT	WMEC	621 Amship, Lorain	21 01 80	14 01 67	28 10 67
COURAGEOUS	WMEC	622 Amship, Lorain	19 10 81	18 05 67	10 04 68
STEADFAST	WMEC	623 Amship, Lorain	20 10 82	24 06 67	25 09 68
DAUNTLESS	WMEC	624 Amship, Lorain	14 04 83	21 10 67	10 06 68
VENTUROUS	WMEC	625 Curtis Bay SY	31 08 84	11 11 67	16 08 68
DEPENDABLE	WMEC	626 Amship, Lorain	11 01 84	16 03 68	27 11 68
VIGOROUS	WMEC	627 Amship, Lorain	06 06 84	04 05 68	02 05 69
DURABLE	WMEC	628 Curtis Bay SY	15 11 84	29 04 67	08 12 67
DECISIVE	WMEC	629 Curtis Bay SY	18 03 85	14 12 67	23 08 68
ALERT	WMEC	630 Amship, Lorain	24 07 85	19 10 68	04 08 69
BEAR	WMEC	901 Tacoma Boat	23 08 79	25 09 80	04 02 83
TAMPA	WMEC	902 Tacoma Boat	02 04 80	19 03 81	16 03 84
HARRIET LANE	WMEC	903 Tacoma Boat	15 10 80	06 02 82	20 09 84
NORTHLAND	WMEC	904 Tacoma Boat	09 04 81	07 05 82	17 12 84
SPENCER	WMEC	905 Derecktor	26 06 82	17 04 84	23 12 85
SENECA	WMEC	906 Derecktor	16 09 82	17 04 84	09 05 87
ESCANABA	WMEC	907 Derecktor	01 04 83	06 02 85	03 02 87
TAHOMA	WMEC	908 Derecktor	28 06 83	06 02 85	01 09 87
CAMPBELL	WMEC	909 Derecktor	10 08 84	29 04 86	03 01 88
THETIS	WMEC	910 Derecktor	24 08 84	29 04 86	29 06 88
FORWARD	WMEC	911 Derecktor	11 07 86	22 08 87	01 05 89
LEGARE	WMEC	912 Derecktor	11 07 86	22 08 87	01 12 89
MOHAWK	WMEC	913 Derecktor	15 03 87	18 05 88	04 05 90
FARALLON	WPB	1301 Bollinger		27 08 85	21 02 86
MANITOU	WPB	1302 Bollinger		09 10 85	28 02 86
MATAGORDA	WPB	1303 Bollinger		15 12 85	25 04 86
MAUI	WPB	1304 Bollinger		13 01 86	09 05 86
MONHEGAN	WPB	1305 Bollinger		15 02 86	16 06 86
NUNIVAK	WPB	1306 Bollinger		15 03 86	04 07 86
ORACOKE	WPB	1307 Bollinger		12 04 86	04 08 86
VASHON	WPB	1308 Bollinger		10 05 86	15 08 86
AQUIDNECK	WPB	1309 Bollinger		14 06 86	26 09 86
MUSTANG	WPB	1310 Bollinger		11 07 86	29 08 86
NAUSHON	WPB	1311 Bollinger		22 08 86	03 10 86
SANIBEL	WPB	1312 Bollinger		03 10 86	14 11 86
EDISTO	WPB	1313 Bollinger		21 11 86	07 01 87
SAPELO	WPB	1314 Bollinger		08 01 87	24 02 87
MATINICUS	WPB	1315 Bollinger		26 02 87	16 04 87
NANTUCKET	WPB	1316 Bollinger		17 04 87	04 06 87

COAST GUARD (continued)

SHIP NAME	TYPE	HULL BUILDER	LAID DOWN D M Y	LAUNCHED D M Y	COMPLETED D M Y
ATTU	WPB	1317 Bollinger	04 12 87	04 12 87	09 05 88
BARANOF	WPB	1318 Bollinger	08 06 87	15 01 88	20 05 88
CHANDELEUR	WPB	1319 Bollinger	13 07 87	19 02 88	08 06 88
CHINCOTEAGUE	WPB	1320 Bollinger	17 08 87	25 03 88	08 08 88
CUSHING	WPB	1321 Bollinger	21 09 87	29 04 88	08 08 88
CUTTYHUNK	WPB	1322 Bollinger	26 10 87	03 06 88	15 10 88
DRUMMOND	WPB	1323 Bollinger	23 11 87	08 07 88	19 10 88
KEY LARGO	WPB	1324 Bollinger	01 01 88	12 08 88	24 12 88
METOMKIN	WPB	1325 Bollinger	01 02 88	16 09 88	12 01 89
MONOMOY	WPB	1326 Bollinger	21 03 88	21 10 88	16 12 88
ORCAS	WPB	1327 Bollinger	25 04 88	25 11 88	14 04 89
PADRE	WPB	1328 Bollinger	30 03 88	06 01 89	24 02 89
SITKINAK	WPB	1329 Bollinger	04 07 88	10 02 89	31 03 89
TYBEE	WPB	1330 Bollinger	08 08 88	17 03 89	09 05 89
WASHINGTON	WPB	1331 Bollinger	12 09 88	21 04 89	00 00 89
WRANGELL	WPB	1332 Bollinger	17 10 88	26 05 89	24 06 89
ADAK	WPB	1333 Bollinger	25 11 88	30 06 89	17 11 89
LIBERTY	WPB	1334 Bollinger	26 12 88	04 08 89	22 09 89
ANACAPA	WPB	1335 Bollinger	30 01 89	08 09 89	13 01 90
KISKA	WPB	1336 Bollinger	06 03 89	13 10 89	01 12 89*
ASSATEAGUE	WPB	1337 Bollinger	10 04 89	17 11 89	01 01 90*
GRAND ISLE	WPB	1338 Bollinger	18 06 90		14 12 90*
KEY BISCAYNE	WPB	1339 Bollinger	16 07 90		27 04 91
JEFFERSON ISLAND	WPB	1340 Bollinger	20 08 90		17 04 91
KODIAK ISLAND	WPB	1341 Bollinger	24 09 90	08 02 91	21 06 91
LONG ISLAND	WPB	1342 Bollinger	29 10 90	19 03 91	27 08 91
BAINBRIDGE ISLAND	WPB	1343 Bollinger	03 12 90	19 04 91	14 06 91*
BLOCK ISLAND	WPB	1344 Bollinger	14 01 91		19 07 91*
STATEN ISLAND	WPB	1345 Bollinger	18 02 91		23 08 91*
ROANOKE ISLAND	WPB	1346 Bollinger	25 03 91		27 09 91*
PEA ISLAND	WPB	1347 Bollinger	29 04 91		01 11 91*
KNIGHT ISLAND	WPB	1348 Bollinger	03 10 91		06 12 91*
GALVESTON ISLAND	WPB	1349 Bollinger	08 07 91	15 11 91	17 01 92*

*Delivery date from yard; commissioning date was later.

COMMAND SHIPS

SHIP NAME	TYPE	HULL BUILDER	LAID DOWN D M Y	LAUNCHED D M Y	COMPLETED D M Y
BLUE RIDGE	LCC	19 Phila NY	27 02 67	04 01 69	14 11 70
MOUNT WHITNEY	LCC	20 Newport News	08 01 69	08 01 70	16 01 71
LA SALLE	AGF	3 Brooklyn NY	02 04 62	03 08 63	22 02 64
CORONADO	AGF	11 Lockheed, Seattle	03 05 65	30 07 66	23 05 70

CRUISERS

SHIP NAME	TYPE	HULL BUILDER	LAID DOWN D M Y	LAUNCHED D M Y	COMPLETED D M Y
LEAHY	CG	16 Bath IW	03 12 59	01 07 61	04 08 62
HARRY E. YARNELL	CG	17 Bath IW	31 05 60	09 12 61	02 02 63
WORDEN	CG	18 Bath IW	19 09 60	02 06 62	03 08 63
DALE	CG	19 NYSB, Camden	06 09 60	28 07 62	23 11 63
RICHMOND K. TURNER	CG	20 NYSB, Camden	09 01 61	06 04 63	13 06 64
GRIDLEY	CG	21 Lockheed, Seattle	15 07 60	31 07 61	25 05 63
ENGLAND	CG	22 Todd, San Pedro	04 10 60	06 03 62	07 12 63
HALSEY	CG	23 San Francisco NY	28 08 60	15 01 62	20 07 63
REEVES	CG	24 Puget Sound NY	01 07 60	12 05 62	15 05 64
BELKNAP	CG	26 Bath IW	05 02 62	20 07 63	07 11 64
JOSEPHUS DANIELS	CG	27 Bath IW	23 04 62	02 12 63	08 05 65
WAINWRIGHT	CG	28 Bath IW	02 07 62	25 04 64	08 01 66
JOUETT	CG	29 Puget Sound NY	25 09 62	30 06 64	03 12 66
HORNE	CG	30 San Francisco NY	12 12 62	30 10 64	15 04 67
STERRETT	CG	31 Puget Sound NY	25 09 62	30 06 64	08 04 67
WILLIAM H. STANDLEY	CG	32 Bath IW	29 07 63	19 12 64	09 07 66
FOX	CG	33 Todd, San Pedro	15 01 63	21 11 64	28 05 66
BIDDLE	CG	34 Bath IW	09 12 63	02 07 65	21 01 67
TICONDEROGA	CG	47 Litton/Ingalls	21 01 80	25 04 81	22 01 83
YORKTOWN	CG	48 Litton/Ingalls	19 10 81	17 01 83	04 07 84

CRUISERS (continued)

SHIP NAME	TYPE	HULL BUILDER	LAID DOWN D M Y	LAUNCHED D M Y	COMPLETED D M Y
VINCENNES	CG	49 Litton/Ingalls	20 10 82	14 01 84	06 07 85
VALLEY FORGE	CG	50 Litton/Ingalls	14 04 83	23 06 84	18 01 86
THOMAS G. GATES	CG	51 Bath IW	31 08 84	14 12 85	22 08 87
BUNKER HILL	CG	52 Litton/Ingalls	11 01 84	11 03 85	20 09 86
MOBILE BAY	CG	53 Litton/Ingalls	06 06 84	22 08 85	13 02 87
ANTIETAM	CG	54 Litton/Ingalls	15 11 84	14 02 86	06 06 87
LEYTE GULF	CG	55 Litton/Ingalls	18 03 85	20 06 86	26 09 87
SAN JACINTO	CG	56 Litton/Ingalls	24 07 85	14 11 86	23 01 88
LAKE CHAMPLAIN	CG	57 Litton/Ingalls	03 03 86	03 04 87	08 08 88
PHILIPPINE SEA	CG	58 Bath IW	11 05 86	12 07 87	18 03 89
PRINCETON	CG	59 Litton/Ingalls	15 10 86	02 10 87	11 02 89
NORMANDY	CG	60 Bath IW	07 04 87	19 03 88	09 12 89
MONTEREY	CG	61 Bath IW	19 08 87	23 10 88	16 06 90
CHANCELLORS- VILLE	CG	62 Litton/Ingalls	24 06 87	15 07 88	04 11 89
COWPENS	CG	63 Bath IW	23 12 87	11 03 89	09 03 91
GETTYSBURG	CG	64 Bath IW	17 08 88	22 07 89	22 06 91
CHOSIN	CG	65 Litton/Ingalls	22 07 88	14 10 89	10 05 91
HUE CITY	CG	66 Litton/Ingalls	20 02 89	21 07 90	14 09 91
SHILOH	CG	67 Bath IW	01 08 89	08 09 90	18 07 92
ANZIO	CG	68 Litton/Ingalls	21 08 89	02 11 90	02 05 92
VICKSBURG	CG	69 Litton/Ingalls	30 05 90	12 10 91	14 11 92
LAKE ERIE	CG	70 Bath IW	06 03 90	13 07 91	24 07 93
CAPE ST. GEORGE	CG	71 Litton/Ingalls	19 11 90	11 04 92	12 06 93
VELLA GULF	CG	72 Litton/Ingalls	22 04 91	25 07 92	18 09 93
PORT ROYAL	CG	73 Litton/Ingalls	14 10 91	20 11 92	09 07 94
LONG BEACH	CGN	9 GD/Beth, Quincy	02 12 57	14 07 59	09 09 61
BAINBRIDGE	CGN	25 GD/Beth, Quincy	15 05 59	15 04 61	06 10 62
TRUXTUN	CGN	35 NYSB, Camden	17 06 63	19 12 64	27 05 67
CALIFORNIA	CGN	36 Newport News	23 01 70	22 09 71	16 02 74
SOUTH CAROLINA	CGN	37 Newport News	01 12 70	01 07 72	25 01 75
VIRGINIA	CGN	38 Newport News	19 08 72	14 12 74	11 09 76
TEXAS	CGN	39 Newport News	18 08 73	09 08 75	10 09 77
MISSISSIPPI	CGN	40 Newport News	22 02 75	31 07 76	05 08 78
ARKANSAS	CGN	41 Newport News	17 01 77	21 10 78	13 10 80

DESTROYERS

SHIP NAME	TYPE	HULL BUILDER	LAID DOWN D M Y	LAUNCHED D M Y	COMPLETED D M Y
SPRUANCE	DD	963 Litton/ Ingalls	01 11 72	10 11 73	20 09 75
PAUL F. FOSTER	DD	964 Litton/ Ingalls	06 02 73	23 02 74	21 02 76
KINKAID	DD	965 Litton/ Ingalls	19 04 73	25 05 74	10 07 76
HEWITT	DD	966 Litton/ Ingalls	23 07 73	24 08 74	25 09 76
ELLIOT	DD	967 Litton/ Ingalls	15 10 73	19 12 74	22 01 77
ARTHUR W. RADFORD	DD	968 Litton/ Ingalls	14 01 74	01 03 75	09 04 77
PETERSON	DD	969 Litton/ Ingalls	29 04 74	21 06 75	09 07 77
CARON	DD	970 Litton/ Ingalls	01 07 74	24 06 75	01 10 77
DAVID R. RAY	DD	971 Litton/ Ingalls	23 09 74	23 08 75	19 11 77
OLDENDORF	DD	972 Litton/ Ingalls	27 12 74	21 10 75	04 03 78
JOHN YOUNG	DD	973 Litton/ Ingalls	17 02 75	07 02 76	20 05 78
COMTE DE GRASSE	DD	0974 Litton/ Ingalls	04 04 75	26 03 76	05 08 78
O'BRIEN	DD	975 Litton/ Ingalls	09 05 75	08 07 76	03 12 77
MERRILL	DD	976 Litton/ Ingalls	16 06 75	01 09 76	11 03 78
BRISCOE	DD	977 Litton/ Ingalls	21 07 75	08 01 77	03 06 78
STUMP	DD	978 Litton/ Ingalls	22 08 75	30 04 77	19 08 78
CONOLLY	DD	979 Litton/ Ingalls	29 09 75	25 06 77	14 10 78
MOOSBRUGGER	DD	980 Litton/ Ingalls	03 11 75	20 08 77	16 12 78
JOHN HANCOCK	DD	981 Litton/ Ingalls	16 01 76	29 10 77	10 03 79
NICHOLSON	DD	982 Litton/ Ingalls	20 02 76	28 01 78	12 05 79
JOHN RODGERS	DD	983 Litton/ Ingalls	12 08 76	25 02 78	14 07 79
LEFTWICH	DD	984 Litton/ Ingalls	12 11 76	08 04 78	25 08 79

DESTROYERS (continued)

SHIP NAME	TYPE	HULL BUILDER	LAID DOWN D M Y	LAUNCHED D M Y	COMPLETED D M Y
CUSHING	DD	985 Litton/ Ingalls	02 02 77	17 06 78	20 10 79
HARRY W. HILL	DD	986 Litton/ Ingalls	01 04 77	10 08 78	17 11 79
O'BANNON	DD	987 Litton/ Ingalls	24 06 77	25 09 78	15 12 79
THORN	DD	988 Litton/ Ingalls	29 08 77	14 11 78	16 02 80
DEYO	DD	989 Litton/ Ingalls	14 10 77	20 01 79	22 03 80
INGERSOLL	DD	990 Litton/ Ingalls	16 12 77	10 03 79	12 04 80
FIFE	DD	991 Litton/ Ingalls	06 03 78	01 05 79	31 05 80
FLETCHER	DD	992 Litton/ Ingalls	24 04 78	16 06 79	12 07 80
HAYLER	DD	997 Litton/ Ingalls	20 10 80	27 03 82	05 03 83
ARLEIGH BURKE	DDG	51 85 Bath IW	06 12 88	16 09 89	04 07 91
BARRY	DDG	52 87 Litton/ Ingalls	26 02 90	10 05 91	12 12 92
JOHN PAUL JONES	DDG	53 Bath IW	08 08 90	26 10 91	18 12 93
CURTIS WILBUR	DDG	54 Bath IW	12 03 91	16 06 92	11 02 94
STOUT	DDG	55 Litton/Ingalls	08 08 91	16 10 92	19 08 94
JOHN S. McCAIN	DDG	56 89 Bath IW	03 09 91	26 09 92	02 07 94
MITSCHER	DDG	57 89 Litton/ Ingalls	12 02 92	07 05 93	28 11 94
LABOON	DDG	58 89 Bath IW	23 03 92	20 02 93	14 01 95
RUSSELL	DDG	59 90 Litton/ Ingalls	24 07 92	20 10 93	20 03 95
PAUL HAMILTON	DDG	60 90 Bath IW	24 08 92	24 07 93	14 04 95
RAMAGE	DDG	61 90 Litton/ Ingalls	14 01 93	11 02 94	08 05 95
FITZGERALD	DDG	62 90 Bath IW	09 02 93	29 01 94	16 08 95
STETHEM	DDG	63 90 Litton/ Ingalls	10 05 93	16 07 94	11 09 95
CARNEY	DDG	64 91 Bath IW	03 08 93	23 07 94	29 01 96
BENFOLD	DDG	65 91 Litton/ Ingalls	27 09 93	05 11 94	29 01 96
GONZALEZ	DDG	66 91 Bath IW	03 02 94	17 12 94	03 07 96
COLE	DDG	67 91 Litton/ Ingalls	28 02 94	07 04 95	01 07 96
THE SULLIVANS	DDG	68 92 Bath IW	03 07 94	13 05 95	05 12 96
MILIUS	DDG	69 92 Litton/ Ingalls	08 08 94	16 09 95	09 12 96

SHIP NAME	TYPE	HULL BUILDER	LAID DOWN D M Y	LAUNCHED D M Y	COMPLETED D M Y
HOPPER	DDG	70 Bath IW	25 12 94	18 11 95	02 06 97
ROSS	DDG	71 Litton/Ingalls	09 01 95	17 02 96	19 05 97
MAHAN (ex-BERNARD L. AUSTIN)	DDG	72 92 Bath IW	04 06 95	04 05 96	30 10 97
DECATUR	DDG	73 93 Bath IW	01 10 95	31 08 96	04 03 98
MCFAUL	DDG	74 93 Litton/ Ingalls	04 12 95	25 01 96	07 05 98
DONALD COOK	DDG	75 93 Bath IW	10 03 96	25 01 97	31 07 98
HIGGINS	DDG	76 93 Bath IW	11 08 96	21 06 97	29 11 98
O'KANE	DDG	77 94			
PORTER	DDG	78 94			
OSCAR AUSTIN	DDG	79 95			
——	DDG	80 95			
——	DDG	81 95			
——	DDG	82 95			
KIDD	DDG	993 Litton/ Ingalls	26 06 78	13 10 79	27 07 81
CALLAGHAN	DDG	994 Litton/ Ingalls	23 10 78	19 01 80	29 08 81
SCOTT	DDG	995 Litton/ Ingalls	12 02 79	29 03 80	24 10 81
CHANDLER	DDG	996 Litton/ Ingalls	12 05 79	24 05 80	13 03 82

FRIGATES

SHIP NAME	TYPE	HULL BUILDER	LAID DOWN D M Y	LAUNCHED D M Y	COMPLETED D M Y
KNOX	FF	1052 Todd, Seattle	05 10 65	19 11 66	12 04 69
ROARK	FF	1053 Todd, Seattle	02 02 66	24 04 67	22 11 69
GRAY	FF	1054 Todd, Seattle	19 11 66	03 11 67	04 04 70
HEPBURN	FF	1055 Todd, San Pedro	01 06 66	25 03 67	03 07 69
CONNOLE	FF	1056 Avondale	23 03 67	20 07 68	30 08 69
RATHBURNE	FF	1057 Lockheed, Seattle	08 01 68	02 05 69	16 05 70
MEYERKORD	FF	1058 Todd, San Pedro	01 09 66	15 07 67	28 11 69
W. S. SIMS	FF	1059 Avondale	10 04 67	04 01 69	03 01 70

FRIGATES (continued)

SHIP NAME	TYPE	HULL BUILDER	LAID DOWN D M Y	LAUNCHED D M Y	COMPLETED D M Y
LANG	FF	1060 Todd, San Pedro	25 03 67	17 02 68	28 03 70
PATTERSON	FF	1061 Avondale	12 10 67	03 05 69	14 03 70
WHIPPLE	FF	1062 Todd, San Pedro	24 04 67	12 04 68	22 07 70
REASONER	FF	1063 Lockheed, Seattle	06 01 69	01 08 70	31 07 71
LOCKWOOD	FF	1064 Todd, Seattle	03 11 67	05 09 68	05 12 70
STEIN	FF	1065 Lockheed, Seattle	01 06 70	19 12 70	08 01 72
MARVIN SHIELDS	FF	1066 Todd, Seattle	12 04 68	23 10 69	10 04 71
FRANCIS HAMMOND	FF	1067 Todd, San Pedro	15 07 67	11 05 68	25 07 70
VREELAND	FF	1068 Avondale	20 03 68	14 06 69	13 06 70
BAGLEY	FF	1069 Lockheed, Seattle	22 09 70	24 04 71	09 05 72
DOWNES	FF	1070 Todd, Seattle	05 09 68	13 12 69	28 08 71
BADGER	FF	1071 Todd, San Pedro	17 02 68	07 12 68	01 12 70
BLAKELY	FF	1072 Avondale	03 06 68	23 08 69	18 07 70
ROBERT E. PEARY	FF	1073 Lockheed, Seattle	20 12 70	23 06 71	23 09 72
HAROLD E. HOLT	FF	1074 Todd, San Pedro	11 05 68	03 05 69	26 03 71
TRIPPE	FF	1075 Avondale	29 07 68	01 11 69	19 09 70
FANNING	FF	1076 Todd, San Pedro	07 12 68	24 01 70	23 07 71
OUELLET	FF	1077 Avondale	15 01 69	17 01 70	12 12 70
JOSEPH HEWES	FF	1078 Avondale	15 05 69	07 03 70	27 02 71
BOWEN	FF	1079 Avondale	11 07 69	02 05 70	22 05 71
PAUL	FF	1080 Avondale	12 09 69	20 06 70	14 08 71
AYLWIN	FF	1081 Avondale	13 11 69	29 08 70	18 09 71
ELMER MONTGOMERY	FF	1082 Avondale	23 01 70	21 11 70	30 10 71
COOK	FF	1083 Avondale	20 03 70	23 01 71	18 12 71
McCANDLESS	FF	1084 Avondale	04 06 70	20 03 71	18 03 72
DONALD B. BEARY	FF	1085 Avondale	24 07 70	22 05 71	22 07 72
BREWTON	FF	1086 Avondale	02 10 70	24 07 71	08 07 72
KIRK	FF	1087 Avondale	04 12 70	25 09 71	09 09 72
BARBEY	FF	1088 Avondale	05 02 71	04 12 71	11 11 72
JESSE L. BROWN	FF	1089 Avondale	08 04 71	18 03 72	17 02 73
AINSWORTH	FF	1090 Avondale	11 06 71	15 04 72	31 03 73
MILLER	FF	1091 Avondale	06 08 71	03 06 72	30 06 73

SHIP NAME	TYPE	HULL BUILDER	LAID DOWN D M Y	LAUNCHED D M Y	COMPLETED D M Y
THOMAS C. HART	FF	1092 Avondale	08 10 71	12 08 72	28 07 73
CAPODANNO	FF	1093 Avondale	10 12 71	21 10 72	17 11 73
PHARRIS	FF	1094 Avondale	11 02 72	16 12 72	26 01 74
TRUETT	FF	1095 Avondale	27 04 72	03 02 73	01 06 74
VALDEZ	FF	1096 Avondale	30 06 72	24 03 73	27 07 74
MOINESTER	FF	1097 Avondale	25 08 72	12 05 73	02 11 74
OLIVER HAZARD PERRY	FFG	7 Bath IW	12 06 75	25 09 76	17 12 77
McINERNEY	FFG	8 Bath IW	16 01 78	04 11 78	15 12 79
WADSWORTH	FFG	9 Todd, San Pedro	13 07 77	29 07 78	02 04 80
DUNCAN	FFG	10 Todd, Seattle	29 04 77	01 03 78	24 05 80
CLARK	FFG	11 Bath IW	17 07 78	24 03 79	17 05 80
GEORGE PHILIP	FFG	12 Todd, San Pedro	14 12 77	16 12 78	15 11 80
SAMUEL ELIOT MORISON	FFG	13 Bath IW	04 12 78	14 07 79	11 10 80
SIDES	FFG	14 Todd, San Pedro	07 08 78	19 05 79	30 05 81
ESTOCIN	FFG	15 Bath IW	02 04 79	03 11 79	10 01 81
CLIFTON SPRAGUE	FFG	16 Bath IW	30 07 79	16 02 80	21 03 81
JOHN A. MOORE	FFG	19 Todd, San Pedro	19 12 78	20 10 79	14 11 81
ANTRIM	FFG	20 Todd, Seattle	21 06 78	27 03 79	26 09 81
FLATLEY	FFG	21 Bath IW	13 11 79	15 05 80	20 06 81
FAHRION	FFG	22 Todd, Seattle	01 12 78	24 08 79	16 01 82
LEWIS B. PULLER	FFG	23 Todd, San Pedro	23 05 79	15 03 80	17 04 82
JACK WILLIAMS	FFG	24 Bath IW	25 02 80	30 08 80	19 09 81
COPELAND	FFG	25 Todd, San Pedro	24 10 79	26 07 80	07 08 82
GALLERY	FFG	26 Bath IW	17 05 80	20 12 80	05 12 81
MAHLON S. TISDALE	FFG	27 Todd, San Pedro	19 03 80	07 02 81	13 11 82
BOONE	FFG	28 Todd, Seattle	27 03 79	16 01 80	13 11 82
STEPHEN W. GROVES	FFG	29 Bath IW	16 09 80	04 04 81	17 04 82
REID	FFG	30 Todd, San Pedro	08 10 80	27 06 81	19 02 83
STARK	FFG	31 Todd, Seattle	24 08 79	30 05 80	23 10 82
JOHN L. HALL	FFG	32 Bath IW	05 01 81	24 07 81	26 06 82
JARRETT	FFG	33 Todd, San Pedro	11 02 81	17 10 81	02 07 83
AUBREY FITCH	FFG	34 Bath IW	10 04 81	17 10 81	09 10 82
UNDERWOOD	FFG	36 Bath IW	03 08 81	06 02 82	29 01 83
CROMMELIN	FFG	37 Todd, Seattle	30 05 80	01 07 81	18 06 83

FRIGATES (continued)

SHIP NAME	TYPE	HULL BUILDER	LAID DOWN D M Y	LAUNCHED D M Y	COMPLETED D M Y
CURTS	FFG	38 Todd, San Pedro	01 07 81	06 03 82	08 10 83
DOYLE	FFG	39 Bath IW	23 10 81	22 05 82	21 05 83
HALYBURTON	FFG	40 Todd, Seattle	26 09 80	13 10 81	07 01 84
McCLUSKEY	FFG	41 Todd, San Pedro	21 10 81	18 09 82	12 10 83
KLAKRING	FFG	42 Bath IW	19 02 82	18 09 82	20 08 83
THACH	FFG	43 Todd, San Pedro	06 03 82	18 12 82	17 03 84
DE WERT	FFG	45 Bath IW	14 06 82	18 12 82	19 11 83
RENTZ	FFG	46 Todd, San Pedro	18 09 82	16 07 83	30 06 84
NICHOLS	FFG	47 Bath IW	27 09 82	23 04 83	10 03 84
VANDEGRIFT	FFG	48 Todd, Seattle	13 10 81	15 10 82	24 11 84
ROBERT G. BRADLEY	FFG	49 Bath IW	28 12 82	13 08 83	11 08 84
TAYLOR	FFG	50 Bath IW	05 05 83	05 11 83	01 12 84
GARY	FFG	51 Todd, San Pedro	18 12 82	19 11 83	17 11 84
CARR	FFG	52 Todd, Seattle	26 03 82	26 02 83	27 07 85
HAWES	FFG	53 Bath IW	22 08 83	17 02 84	02 09 85
FORD	FFG	54 Todd, San Pedro	16 07 83	23 06 84	29 06 85
ELROD	FFG	55 Bath IW	14 11 83	12 05 84	06 07 85
SIMPSON	FFG	56 Bath IW	27 02 84	31 08 84	09 11 85
REUBEN JAMES	FFG	57 Todd, San Pedro	19 11 83	08 02 85	22 03 86
SAMUEL B. ROBERTS	FFG	58 Bath IW	21 05 84	08 12 84	12 04 86
KAUFFMAN	FFG	59 Bath IW	08 04 85	29 03 86	28 02 87
RODNEY M. DAVIS	FFG	60 Todd, San Pedro	08 02 85	11 01 86	09 05 87
INGRAHAM	FFG	61 Todd, San Pedro	30 03 87	25 06 88	05 08 89

MINE WARFARE SHIPS

SHIP NAME	TYPE	HULL BUILDER	LAID DOWN D M Y	LAUNCHED D M Y	COMPLETED D M Y
AVENGER	MCM	1 Peterson	03 06 83	15 06 85	12 09 87
DEFENDER	MCM	2 Marinette	01 12 83	04 04 87	30 09 89
SENTRY	MCM	3 Peterson	08 10 84	20 09 86	02 09 89
CHAMPION	MCM	4 Marinette	28 06 84	15 04 89	08 02 91
GUARDIAN	MCM	5 Peterson	08 05 85	20 06 87	16 12 89
DEVASTATOR	MCM	6 Peterson	09 02 87	11 06 88	06 10 90
PATRIOT	MCM	7 Marinette	31 03 87	15 05 90	18 10 91

SHIP NAME	TYPE	HULL BUILDER	LAID DOWN D M Y	LAUNCHED D M Y	COMPLETED D M Y
SCOUT	MCM	8 Peterson	08 06 87	20 05 89	15 11 91
PIONEER	MCM	9 Peterson	05 06 89	25 08 90	07 12 92
WARRIOR	MCM	10 Peterson	25 09 89	08 12 90	30 12 92
GLADIATOR	MCM	11 Peterson	07 05 90	29 06 91	18 09 93
ARDENT	MCM	12 Peterson	22 10 90	16 11 91	18 02 94
DEXTEROUS	MCM	13 Peterson	11 03 91	20 06 92	03 12 93
CHIEF	MCM	14 Peterson	19 08 91	12 06 93	05 11 94
OSPREY	MHC	51 Intermarine	16 05 88	23 03 91	28 08 93
HERON	MHC	52 Intermarine	07 04 89	21 03 92	22 07 94
PELICAN	MHC	53 Avondale		27 02 93	
ROBIN	MHC	54 Avondale		28 04 93	
ORIOLE	MHC	55 Intermarine		22 05 93	
KINGFISHER	MHC	56 Avondale		07 09 93	
CORMORANT	MHC	57 Avondale			
BLACKHAWK	MHC	58 Intermarine			
FALCON	MHC	59 Intermarine			
CARDINAL	MHC	60 Intermarine			01 96
RAVEN	MHC	61 Intermarine			
SHRIKE	MHC	62 Intermarine			01 97

SEALIFT AND PREPOSITIONED SHIPS

SHIP NAME	TYPE	HULL BUILDER	LAID DOWN D M Y	LAUNCHED D M Y	COMPLETED D M Y
2ND LT. JOHN P. BOBO	TAK	3007 GD/Beth, Quincy	16 09 83	19 01 85	14 02 85
PFC DEWAYNE T. WILLIAMS	TAK	3008 GD/Beth, Quincy	16 09 83	18 05 85	06 06 85
1ST LT. BALD LOPEZ	TAK	3009 GD/Beth, Quincy	84	26 10 85	20 11 85
1ST LT. JACK LUMMUS	TAK	3010 GD/Beth, Quincy	84	22 02 86	06 03 86
SGT. WM R. BUTTON	TAK	3011 GD/Beth, Quincy	84	17 05 86	22 05 86
CPL. LOU J. HAGUE, JR.	TAK	3000 Odense/ Bethlehem, Sparrows Point	15 01 83		07 09 84
PFC WM B. BAUGH, JR.	TAK	3001 Odense/ Beth, Beaumont, Texas	15 01 83		12 09 85
PFC JAMES ANDERSON, JR.	TAK	3002 Odense/ Beth, Spar	15 10 83	26 03 85	

SEALIFT AND PREPOSITIONED SHIPS (continued)

SHIP NAME	TYPE	HULL BUILDER	LAID DOWN D M Y	LAUNCHED D M Y	COMPLETED D M Y
1ST LT. ALEX BONNYMAN, JR.	TAK	3003 Odense/ Beth, Beau	15 01 84		30 10 84
PVT. HARRY FISHER	TAK	3004 Odense/ Beth, Spar	15 04 84		24 09 85
SGT. MATEJ KOCAK	TAK	3005 Sun/ National	15 08 83		05 10 84
PFC EUGENE A. OBREGON	TAK	3006 Sun/ National	15 01 83		15 01 85
MAJ. STEPHEN W. PLESS	TAK	3007 Sun/ National	15 05 84		01 05 85
ALGOL	TAKR	287 Rotterdam/ Nat'l	13 10 82		19 06 84
BELLATRIX	TAKR	288 Rheinsthl/ Nat'l	22 10 82		10 09 84
DENEBOLA	TAKR	289 Rotterdam/ Penn	04 05 84		10 09 85
POLLUX	TAKR	290 Weser/ Avondale	21 05 84		31 03 86
ALTAIR	TAKR	291 Rheinsthl/ Avondale	01 02 84		13 11 85
REGULUS	TAKR	292 Weser/ National	29 06 84		28 08 85
CAPELLA	TAKR	293 Rotterdam/ Penn	22 10 82		01 07 84
ANTARES	TAKR	294 Weser/ Avondale	06 10 82		12 07 84
BOB HOPE (sealift)	TAKR	300 Avondale (ordered Sep. 1, 1993)			
—— (option)	TAK	X Avondale			
—— (option)	TAK	X Avondale			
—— (option)	TAK	X Avondale			
—— (option)	TAK	X Avondale			
—— (option)	TAK	X Avondale			
—— (sealift)	TAK	X NASSCO (Ordered Sep. 16, 1993)			
—— (option)	TAK	X NASSCO			
—— (option)	TAK	X NASSCO			
—— (option)	TAK	X NASSCO			
—— (option)	TAK	X NASSCO			
—— (option)	TAK	X NASSCO			

SMALL COMBATANTS

SHIP NAME	TYPE	HULL BUILDER	LAID DOWN D M Y	LAUNCHED D M Y	COMPLETED D M Y
PEGASUS	PHM	1 Boeing, Seattle	10 05 73	09 11 74	09 07 77
HERCULES	PHM	2 Boeing, Seattle	12 09 80	13 04 82	12 03 83
TAURUS	PHM	3 Boeing, Seattle	30 01 79	08 05 81	07 10 81
AQUILA	PHM	4 Boeing, Seattle	10 07 79	16 09 81	16 10 82
ARIES	PHM	5 Boeing, Seattle	07 01 80	05 11 81	18 09 82
GEMINI	PHM	6 Boeing, Seattle	13 05 80	17 02 82	13 11 82
CYCLONE	PC	1 Bollinger	22 06 91	15 02 92	19 12 92
TEMPEST	PC	2 Bollinger	30 09 91	20 06 92	13 01 93
HURRICANE	PC	3 Bollinger	20 11 91	06 03 93	31 07 93
MONSOON	PC	4 Bollinger	15 02 92	06 03 93	26 09 93
TYPHOON	PC	5 Bollinger		20 02 93	12 02 94
SIROCCO	PC	6 Bollinger		18 09 93	05 05 94
SQUALL	PC	7 Bollinger		18 09 93	23 06 94
ZEPHYR	PC	8 Bollinger		12 03 94	15 10 94
CHINOOK	PC	9 Bollinger		12 03 94	
FIREBOLT	PC	10 Bollinger		24 09 94	
WHIRLWIND	PC	11 Bollinger		24 09 94	
THUNDERBOLT	PC	12 Bollinger			
SHAMAL	PC	13 Bollinger			

ATTACK SUBMARINES

SHIP NAME	TYPE	HULL BUILDER	LAID DOWN D M Y	LAUNCHED D M Y	COMPLETED D M Y
STURGEON	SSN	637 GD/EB, Groton	10 08 63	26 02 66	03 03 67
WHALE	SSN	638 GD/Beth, Quincy	27 05 64	14 10 66	12 10 68
TAUTOG	SSN	639 Litton/ Ingalls	27 01 64	15 04 67	17 08 68
GRAYLING	SSN	646 Portsmouth NY	12 05 64	22 06 67	11 10 69
POGY	SSN	647 Litton/ Ingalls	04 05 64	03 06 67	15 05 71
ASPRO	SSN	648 Litton/ Ingalls	23 11 64	29 11 67	20 02 69
SUNFISH	SSN	649 GD/Beth, Quincy	15 01 65	14 10 66	15 03 69
PARGO	SSN	650 GD/EB, Groton	03 06 64	17 09 66	05 01 68
QUEENFISH	SSN	651 Newport News	11 05 64	25 02 66	06 12 66
PUFFER	SSN	652 Litton/ Ingalls	08 02 65	30 03 68	09 08 69

ATTACK SUBMARINES (continued)

SHIP NAME	TYPE	HULL BUILDER	LAID DOWN D M Y	LAUNCHED D M Y	COMPLETED D M Y
RAY	SSN	653 Newport News	01 04 65	21 06 66	12 04 67
SAND LANCE	SSN	660 Portsmouth NY	15 01 65	11 11 69	25 09 71
LAPON	SSN	661 Newport News	26 07 65	16 12 66	14 12 67
GURNARD	SSN	662 Mare Island NY	22 12 64	20 05 67	06 12 68
HAMMERHEAD	SSN	663 Newport News	29 11 65	14 04 67	28 06 68
SEA DEVIL	SSN	664 Newport News	12 04 66	05 10 67	30 01 69
GUITARRO	SSN	665 Mare Island NY	09 12 65	27 07 68	09 09 72
HAWKBILL	SSN	666 Mare Island NY	12 12 66	12 04 69	04 02 71
BERGALL	SSN	667 GD/EB, Groton	16 04 66	17 02 68	13 06 69
SPADEFISH	SSN	668 Newport News	21 12 66	15 05 68	14 08 69
SEAHORSE	SSN	669 GD/EB, Groton	13 08 66	15 06 68	19 09 69
FINBACK	SSN	670 Newport News	26 06 67	07 12 68	04 02 70
NARWHAL	SSN	671 GD/EB, Groton	17 01 66	09 09 67	12 07 69
PINTADO	SSN	672 Mare Island NY	27 10 67	16 08 69	29 04 71
FLYING FISH	SSN	673 GD/EB, Groton	30 06 67	17 05 69	29 04 70
TREPANG	SSN	674 GD/EB, Groton	28 10 67	27 09 69	14 08 70
BLUEFISH	SSN	675 GD/EB, Groton	13 03 68	10 01 70	08 01 71
BILLFISH	SSN	676 GD/EB, Groton	20 09 68	01 05 70	12 03 71
DRUM	SSN	677 Mare Island NY	20 08 68	23 05 70	15 04 72
ARCHERFISH	SSN	678 GD/EB, Groton	19 06 69	16 01 71	17 12 71
SILVERSIDES	SSN	679 GD/EB, Groton	13 10 69	04 06 71	05 05 72
WILLIAM H. BATES	SSN	680 Litton/ Ingalls	04 08 69	11 12 71	05 05 73
BATFISH	SSN	681 GD/EB, Groton	09 02 70	09 10 71	01 09 72

SHIP NAME	TYPE	HULL BUILDER	LAID DOWN D M Y	LAUNCHED D M Y	COMPLETED D M Y
TUNNY	SSN	682 Litton/ Ingalls	22 05 70	10 06 72	26 01 74
PARCHE	SSN	683 Litton/ Ingalls	10 12 70	13 01 73	17 08 74
CAVALLA	SSN	684 GD/EB, Groton	04 06 70	19 02 72	09 02 73
L. MENDEL RIVERS	SSN	686 Newport News	26 06 71	02 06 73	01 02 75
RICHARD B. RUSSELL	SSN	687 Newport News	19 10 71	12 01 74	16 08 75
LOS ANGELES	SSN	688 Newport News	08 01 72	06 04 74	13 11 76
BATON ROUGE	SSN	689 Newport News	18 11 72	26 04 75	25 06 77
PHILADELPHIA	SSN	690 GD/EB, Groton	12 08 72	19 10 74	25 06 77
MEMPHIS	SSN	691 Newport News	23 06 73	03 04 76	17 12 77
OMAHA	SSN	692 GD/EB, Groton	27 01 73	21 02 76	11 03 78
CINCINNATI	SSN	693 Newport News	06 04 74	19 02 77	10 06 78
GROTON	SSN	694 GD/EB, Groton	03 08 73	09 10 76	08 07 78
BIRMINGHAM	SSN	695 Newport News	26 04 75	29 10 77	16 12 78
NEW YORK CITY	SSN	696 GD/EB, Groton	15 12 73	18 06 77	03 03 78
INDIANAPOLIS	SSN	697 GD/EB, Groton	19 10 74	30 07 77	05 01 80
BREMERTON	SSN	698 GD/EB, Groton	06 05 76	22 07 78	28 03 81
JACKSONVILLE	SSN	699 GD/EB, Groton	21 02 76	18 11 78	16 05 81
DALLAS	SSN	700 GD/EB, Groton	09 10 76	28 04 79	18 07 81
LA JOLLA	SSN	701 GD/EB, Groton	16 10 76	11 08 79	24 10 81
PHOENIX	SSN	702 GD/EB, Groton	30 07 77	08 12 79	19 12 81
BOSTON	SSN	703 GD/EB, Groton	11 08 78	19 04 80	30 01 82
BALTIMORE	SSN	704 GD/EB, Groton	21 05 79	13 12 80	24 07 82
CORPUS CHRISTI	SSN	705 GD/EB, Groton	04 09 79	25 04 81	08 01 83

ATTACK SUBMARINES (continued)

SHIP NAME	TYPE	HULL BUILDER	LAID DOWN D M Y	LAUNCHED D M Y	COMPLETED D M Y
ALBUQUERQUE	SSN	706 GD/EB, Groton	27 12 79	13 03 82	21 05 83
PORTSMOUTH	SSN	707 GD/EB, Groton	08 05 80	18 09 82	01 10 83
MINNEAPOLIS-ST. PAUL	SSN	708 GD/EB, Groton	20 01 81	19 03 83	17 03 84
HYMAN G. RICKOVER	SSN	709 GD/EB, Groton	24 07 81	17 08 83	08 09 84
AUGUSTA	SSN	710 GD/EB, Groton	01 04 82	21 01 84	19 01 85
SAN FRANCISCO	SSN	711 Newport News	26 5 77	27 10 79	24 04 81
ATLANTA	SSN	712 Newport News	17 08 78	16 08 80	06 03 82
HOUSTON	SSN	713 Newport News	29 01 79	21 03 81	25 09 82
NORFOLK	SSN	714 Newport News	01 08 79	31 10 81	21 05 83
BUFFALO	SSN	715 Newport News	25 01 80	08 05 82	05 11 83
SALT LAKE CITY	SSN	716 Newport News	26 08 80	16 10 82	12 05 84
OLYMPIA	SSN	717 Newport News	31 03 81	30 04 83	17 11 84
HONOLULU	SSN	718 Newport News	10 11 81	24 09 83	06 07 85
PROVIDENCE	SSN	719 GD/EB, Groton	14 10 82	04 08 84	27 07 85
PITTSBURGH	SSN	720 GD/EB, Groton	15 04 83	08 12 84	23 11 85
CHICAGO	SSN	721 Newport News	05 01 83	13 10 84	27 09 86
KEY WEST	SSN	722 Newport News	06 07 83	20 07 85	12 09 87
OKLAHOMA CITY	SSN	723 Newport News	04 01 84	02 11 85	03 07 88
LOUISVILLE	SSN	724 GD/EB, Groton	16 09 84	14 12 85	08 11 86
HELENA	SSN	725 GD/EB, Groton	28 03 85	28 06 86	11 07 87
NEWPORT NEWS	SSN	750 Newport News	03 03 84	15 03 86	03 06 89
SAN JUAN	SSN	751 GD/EB, Groton	16 08 85	06 12 86	07 08 88
PASADENA	SSN	752 GD/EB, Groton	20 12 85	12 09 87	28 01 89

SHIP NAME	TYPE	HULL BUILDER	LAID DOWN D M Y	LAUNCHED D M Y	COMPLETED D M Y
ALBANY	SSN	753 Newport News	22 04 85	13 06 87	07 04 90
TOPEKA	SSN	754 GD/EB, Groton	13 05 86	23 01 88	21 10 89
MIAMI	SSN	755 GD/EB, Groton	24 10 86	12 11 88	30 06 90
SCRANTON	SSN	756 Newport News	27 06 86	15 04 89	26 01 91
ALEXANDRIA	SSN	757 GD/EB, Groton	19 06 87	25 06 90	29 06 91
ASHEVILLE	SSN	758 Newport News	14 01 87	10 02 90	28 09 91
JEFFERSON CITY	SSN	759 Newport News	19 10 87	15 03 90	29 02 92
ANNAPOLIS	SSN	760 GD/EB, Groton	15 06 88	18 05 91	11 04 92
SPRINGFIELD	SSN	761 GD/EB, Groton	29 01 90	04 01 92	09 01 93
COLUMBUS	SSN	762 GD/EB, Groton	09 01 91	20 06 92	24 07 93
SANTA FE	SSN	763 GD/EB, Groton	25 05 91	12 12 92	11 12 93
BOISE	SSN	764 Newport News	25 08 88	23 03 91	07 11 92
MONTPELIER	SSN	765 Newport News	19 05 89	06 04 91	13 03 93
CHARLOTTE	SSN	766 Newport News	31 07 90	03 10 92	16 09 94
HAMPTON	SSN	767 Newport News	02 03 90	28 09 92	11 06 93
HARTFORD	SSN	768 GD/EB, Groton	22 02 92	04 12 93	15 12 94
TOLEDO	SSN	769 Newport News	08 04 91	28 08 93	28 08 94
TUCSON	SSN	770 Newport News	15 08 91	19 03 94	
COLUMBIA	SSN	771 GD/EB, Groton	15 08 92	24 09 94	
GREENEVILLE	SSN	772 Newport News	31 01 92	17 09 94	
CHEYENNE	SSN	773 Newport News	31 08 92	01 04 94	
SEAWOLF	SSN	21 GD/EB, Groton			
CONNECTICUT	SSN	22 GD/EB, Groton			

STRATEGIC SUBMARINES

SHIP NAME	TYPE	HULL BUILDER	LAID DOWN D M Y	LAUNCHED D M Y	COMPLETED D M Y
LAFAYETTE	SSBN	616 GD/EB, Groton	17 01 61	08 05 62	23 04 63
ALEXANDER HAMILTON	SSBN	617 GD/EB, Groton	26 06 61	18 08 62	27 06 63
THOMAS JEFFERSON	SSBN	618 Newport News	03 02 61	24 02 62	04 01 63
ANDREW JACKSON	SSBN	619 Mare Island NY	26 04 61	15 09 62	03 07 63
JOHN ADAMS	SSBN	620 Portsmouth NY	19 05 61	12 01 63	12 05 64
JAMES MONROE	SSBN	622 Newport News	31 07 61	04 08 62	07 12 63
NATHAN HALE	SSBN	623 GD/EB, Groton	02 10 61	12 01 63	23 11 63
WOODROW WILSON	SSBN	624 Mare Island NY	13 09 61	22 02 63	27 12 63
HENRY CLAY	SSBN	625 Newport News	23 10 61	30 11 62	20 02 64
DANIEL WEBSTER	SSBN	626 GD/EB, Groton	23 12 61	27 04 63	09 04 64
JAMES MADISON	SSBN	627 Newport News	05 03 62	15 03 63	28 07 64
TECUMSEH	SSBN	628 GD/EB, Groton	01 06 62	22 06 63	29 05 64
DANIEL BOONE	SSBN	629 Mare Island NY	06 02 62	22 06 63	23 04 64
JOHN C. CALHOUN	SSBN	630 Newport News	04 06 62	22 06 63	15 09 64
ULYSSES S. GRANT	SSBN	631 GD/EB, Groton	18 08 62	02 11 63	17 07 64
VON STEUBEN	SSBN	632 Newport News	04 09 62	18 10 63	30 09 64
CASIMIR PULASKI	SSBN	633 GD/EB, Groton	12 01 63	01 02 64	14 08 64
STONEWALL JACKSON	SSBN	634 Mare Island NY	04 07 62	30 11 63	26 08 64
SAM RAYBURN	SSBN	635 Newport News	03 12 62	20 12 63	02 12 64
NATHANAEL GREENE	SSBN	636 Portsmouth NY	21 05 62	12 05 64	19 12 64
BENJAMIN FRANKLIN	SSBN	640 GD/EB, Groton	25 05 63	05 12 64	22 10 65
SIMON BOLIVAR	SSBN	641 Newport News	17 04 63	22 08 64	29 10 65
KAMEHAMEHA	SSBN	642 Mare Island NY	02 05 63	16 01 65	10 12 65

SHIP NAME	TYPE	HULL BUILDER	LAID DOWN D M Y	LAUNCHED D M Y	COMPLETED D M Y
GEORGE BANCROFT	SSBN	643 GD/EB, Groton	24 08 63	20 03 65	22 01 66
LEWIS AND CLARK	SSBN	644 Newport News	29 07 63	21 11 64	22 12 65
JAMES K. POLK	SSBN	645 GD/EB, Groton	23 11 63	22 05 65	16 04 66
GEORGE C. MARSHALL	SSBN	654 Newport News	02 03 64	21 05 65	29 04 66
HENRY L. STIMSON	SSBN	655 GD/EB, Groton	04 04 64	13 11 65	20 08 66
GEORGE WASHINGTON CARVER	SSBN	656 Newport News	24 08 64	14 08 65	15 06 66
FRANCIS SCOTT KEY	SSBN	657 GD/EB, Groton	05 12 64	23 04 66	03 12 66
MARIANO G. VALLEJO	SSBN	658 Mare Island NY	07 07 64	23 10 65	16 12 66
WILL ROGERS	SSBN	659 GD/EB, Groton	20 03 65	21 07 66	01 04 67
OHIO	SSBN	726 GD/EB, Groton	10 04 76	07 04 79	11 11 81
MICHIGAN	SSBN	727 GD/EB, Groton	04 04 77	26 04 80	11 09 82
FLORIDA	SSBN	728 GD/EB, Groton	09 06 77	14 11 81	18 06 83
GEORGIA	SSBN	729 GD/EB, Groton	07 04 79	06 11 82	11 02 84
HENRY M. JACKSON	SSBN	730 GD/EB, Groton	19 01 81	15 10 83	06 10 84
ALABAMA	SSBN	731 GD/EB, Groton	27 08 81	19 05 84	25 05 85
ALASKA	SSBN	732 GD/EB, Groton	09 03 83	12 01 85	25 01 86
NEVADA	SSBN	733 GD/EB, Groton	08 08 83	14 09 85	16 08 86
TENNESSEE	SSBN	734 GD/EB, Groton	09 06 86	13 12 86	31 12 88
PENNSYLVANIA	SSBN	735 GD/EB, Groton	02 03 87	23 04 88	09 09 89
WEST VIRGINIA	SSBN	736 GD/EB, Groton	18 12 87	14 10 89	20 10 90
KENTUCKY	SBBN	737 GD/EB, Groton	18 12 87	11 08 90	13 07 91
MARYLAND	SBBN	738 GD/EB, Groton	18 12 87	10 08 91	13 06 92

STRATEGIC SUBMARINES (continued)

SHIP NAME	TYPE	HULL BUILDER	LAID DOWN D M Y	LAUNCHED D M Y	COMPLETED D M Y
NEBRASKA	SBBN	739 GD/EB, Groton	18 12 87	15 08 92	10 07 93
RHODE ISLAND	SSBN	740 GD/EB, Groton	23 04 88	17 07 93	09 07 94
MAINE	SBBN	741 GD/EB, Groton	04 04 89	16 07 94	
WYOMING	SBBN	742 GD/EB, Groton	27 01 90	22 07 95	
LOUISIANA	SSBN	743 GD/EB, Groton	15 05 91	27 07 96	

UNDERWAY-REPLENISHMENT SHIPS

SHIP NAME	TYPE	HULL BUILDER	LAID DOWN D M Y	LAUNCHED D M Y	COMPLETED D M Y
SURIBACHI	AE	21 Beth, Sparrows	16 05 55	03 05 56	20 03 57
MAUNA KEA	AE	22 Beth, Sparrows	31 01 55	02 11 55	17 11 56
NITRO	AE	23 Beth, Sparrows	20 05 57	26 06 58	01 05 59
PYRO	AE	24 Beth, Sparrows	21 10 57	05 11 58	24 07 59
HALEAKALA	AE	25 Beth, Sparrows	10 03 58	17 02 59	03 11 59
KILAUEA	T-AE	26 GD/Beth, Quincy	10 03 66	90 08 67	10 08 68
BUTTE	AE	27 GD/Beth, Quincy	21 07 66	09 08 67	29 11 68
SANTA BARBARA	AE	28 Beth, Sparrows	20 12 66	23 01 68	11 07 70
MOUNT HOOD	AE	29 Beth, Sparrows	08 05 67	17 07 68	01 05 71
FLINT	AE	32 Litton/Ingalls	04 08 69	09 11 70	20 11 71
SHASTA	AE	33 Litton/Ingalls	10 11 69	03 04 71	26 02 72
MOUNT BAKER	AE	34 Litton/Ingalls	10 05 70	23 10 71	22 07 72
KISKA	AE	35 Litton/Ingalls	04 08 71	11 03 72	16 12 72
MARS	AFS	1 National Steel	05 05 62	15 06 63	21 12 63
SYLVANIA	AFS	2 National Steel	18 08 62	15 08 63	11 07 64
NIAGARA FALLS	AFS	3 National Steel	22 05 65	26 03 66	29 04 67
WHITE PLAINS	AFS	4 National Steel	02 10 65	23 07 66	23 11 68
CONCORD	T-AFS	5 National Steel	26 03 66	17 12 66	27 11 68
SAN DIEGO	T-AFS	6 National Steel	11 03 67	13 04 68	24 05 69
SAN JOSE	T-AFS	7 National Steel	08 03 69	12 12 69	23 10 70

SHIP NAME	TYPE	HULL BUILDER	LAID DOWN D M Y	LAUNCHED D M Y	COMPLETED D M Y
CIMARRON	AO	177 Avondale	15 05 78	28 04 79	10 01 81
CIMARRON (Jumbo)	AO	177 Avondale	25 06 90		08 05 92
MONONGAHELA	AO	178 Avondale	15 08 78	04 08 79	08 08 81
MONONGAHELA (Jumbo)	AO	178 Avondale	29 01 90		14 12 91
MERRIMACK	AO	179 Avondale	16 07 79	17 05 80	14 11 81
MERRIMACK (Jumbo)	AO	179 Avondale	06 03 89		11 02 91
WILLAMETTE	AO	180 Avondale	04 08 80	18 07 81	26 09 82
WILLAMETTE (Jumbo)	AO	180 Avondale	30 10 89		07 07 91
PLATTE	AO	186 Avondale	02 02 81	06 02 82	16 04 83
PLATTE (Jumbo)	AO	186 Avondale	26 11 90		16 12 92
SACRAMENTO	AOE	1 Puget Navy	30 06 61	14 09 63	14 03 64
CAMDEN	AOE	2 Puget Navy	17 02 64	29 05 65	01 04 67
SEATTLE	AOE	3 NYSB, Camden	01 10 65	02 03 68	05 04 69
DETROIT	AOE	4 Puget Navy	29 11 66	21 06 69	28 03 70
SUPPLY	AOE	6 National Steel	28 11 88	06 10 90	
RAINIER	AOE	7 National Steel	31 05 90	28 09 91	
ARCTIC	AOE	8 National Steel	02 12 91		
CONECUH	AOE	9 Deferred			
BRIDGE	AOE	10 National Steel			
WICHITA	AOR	1 GD/Beth, Quincy	18 06 66	18 03 68	07 06 69
MILWAUKEE	AOR	2 GD/Beth, Quincy	29 11 66	17 01 69	01 11 69
KANSAS CITY	AOR	3 GD/Beth, Quincy	20 04 68	28 06 69	06 06 70
SAVANNAH	AOR	4 GD/Beth, Quincy	22 01 69	25 04 70	05 12 70
WABASH	AOR	5 GD/Beth, Quincy	21 01 70	06 02 71	20 11 71
KALAMAZOO	AOR	6 GD/Beth, Quincy	28 10 70	11 11 72	11 08 73
ROANOKE	AOR	7 National Steel	19 01 74	07 12 74	30 10 76

Jumbo: Lengthening of ship.

AUXILIARY

SHIP NAME	TYPE	HULLNUM	FY	BUILDER	LAID DOWN D M Y	LAUNCHED D M Y	COMPL] D M
HENRY J. KAISER	T-AO	187	82	Avondale	22 08 84	05 10 85	19 12
JOSHUA HUMPHREYS	T-AO	188	83	Avondale	17 12 84	05 02 86	03 04
JOHN LENTHALL	T-AO	189	84	Avondale	15 07 85	09 08 86	25 06
ANDREW J. HIGGINS	T-AO	190	84	Avondale	21 11 85	12 01 87	22 10
BENJAMIN ISHERWOOD	T-AO	191	85	Penn Ship/ Tampa	12 07 86	15 08 88	Cance
HENRY ECKFORD	T-AO	192	85	Penn Ship/ Tampa	19 01 87	22 07 89	Cance
WALTER S. DIEHL	T-AO	193	85	Avondale	07 08 86	02 10 87	13 09
JOHN ERICSSON	T-AO	194	86	Avondale	13 03 89	25 04 90	18 03
LEROY GRUMMAN	T-AO	195	86	Avondale	06 07 87	03 12 88	02 08
KANAWHA	T-AO	196	87	Avondale	17 07 89	22 09 90	06 12
PECOS	T-AO	197	87	Avondale	15 02 88	23 09 89	06 07
BIG HORN	T-AO	198	88	Avondale	09 10 89	02 02 91	01 07
TIPPECANOE	T-AO	199	88	Avondale	19 11 90	16 05 92	08 02
GUADALUPE	T-AO	200	89	Avondale	09 07 90	15 10 91	26 10
PATUXENT	T-AO (D)	201	89	Avondale	16 10 91	23 07 94	07 06
YUKON	T-AO	202	89	Avondale	13 05 91	06 02 93	25 03
LARAMIE	T-AO (D)	203	89	Avondale	10 01 94	27 05 95	05 04
RAPPAHANNOCK	T-AO (D)	204	89	Avondale	29 06 92	10 12 94	07 11